W9-BTE-752

The Year's Work in English Studies

VOLUME 59

1978

Edited by
JAMES REDMOND

and

LAUREL BRAKE
DAVID DANIELL
ROBIN ROBBINS
A. V. C. SCHMIDT
(associate editors)

Published for

THE ENGLISH ASSOCIATION
by
JOHN MURRAY ALBEMARLE STREET LONDON

British Library Cataloguing in Publication Data

The Year's work in English studies. – Vol. 59 (1978)
1. English Association
820.9

ISBN 0-7195-3821-1

Typeset by Reproduction Drawings Ltd, Sutton, Surrey
Printed in Great Britain by
Redwood Burn Limited
Trowbridge and Esher

Preface

It may help the user of this work to remember that books are sometimes published a year later in the U.S.A. than they are in the U.K. (and vice versa), that the year of publication is not always that which appears on the title-page of the book, and that the inevitable omissions of one year are made good in the next; thus the search for a notice of a book or article may have to extend to the volume after the expected one and sometimes to that which precedes it. Reports of important omissions will earn our gratitude.

Offprints of articles are always welcomed, and editors of journals that are not easily available in the U.K. are urged to join the many who already send us complete sets. These should be addressed to The Editor, *The Year's Work in English Studies*, The English Association, 1, Priory Gardens, Bedford Park, London W4 1TT. We are grateful to the authors and publishers who have made our task easier by supplying books and articles for volume 59. The editors of the *M.L.A. International Bibliography, Anglo-Saxon England, The Chaucer Review, English Language Notes, Philological Quarterly*, and *Restoration and Eighteenth Century Theatre Research* have put us deeply in their debt by providing advance proofs of their bibliographies. In drawing the reader's attention at the beginning of chapters to the main bibliographical aids, we presuppose in each case a reference to the *M.L.A. International Bibliography*, and to the *Annual Bibliography of English Language and Literature* published by the Modern Humanities Research Association.

James Redmond
Westfield College
London University

Abbreviations

ABC	*American Book Collector*
ABELL	*Annual Bibliography of English Language and Literature*
ABR	*American Benedictine Review*
AEB	*Analytical and Enumerative Bibliography*
AHR	*American Historical Review*
AI	*American Imago*
AJES	*Aligarh Journal of English Studies*
AKML	*Abhandlungen zur Kunst-, Musik-, und Literaturwissenschaft*
AL	*American Literature*
ALASH	*Acta Linguistica Academiae Scientiarum Hungaricae*
ALR	*American Literary Realism, 1870–1910*
AN	*Acta Neophilologica*
AMon	*Atlantic Monthly*
AnL	*Anthropological Linguistics*
AnM	*Annuale Medievale*
AN&Q	*American Notes and Queries*
AQ	*American Quarterly*
AR	*Antioch Review*
Archiv	*Archiv für das Studium der Neueren Sprachen und Literaturen*
ArielE	*Ariel: A Review of International English Literature*
ArL	*Archivum Linguisticum*
ArlQ	*Arlington Quarterly*
ArP	*Aryan Path*
ArQ	*Arizona Quarterly*
A.R.S.	Augustan Reprint Society
Arsskrift	*Sydsvenska Ortnamnssällskapets Årsskrift*
AS	*American Speech*
ASch	*American Scholar*
ASE	*Anglo-Saxon England*
ASoc	*Arts in Society*
ASPR	*Anglo-Saxon Poetic Records*
ATQ	*American Transcendental Quarterly: Journal of New England Writers*
AUMLA	*Journal of Australasian U. Language and Literature Ass.*
AUPG	American University Publishers Group Ltd.
AWR	*The Anglo-Welsh Review*
BAASB	*British Association for American Studies Bulletin*
BB	*Bulletin of Bibliography*
BBCS	*Bulletin of the Board of Celtic Studies*
BBSIA	*Bulletin Bibliographique de la Société Internationale Arthurienne*
BC	*Book Collector*

BDEC	*Bulletin of the Department of English* (Calcutta)
BFLS	*Bulletin de la Faculté des Lettres de Strasbourg*
BGDSL	*Beiträge zur Geschichte der deutschen Sprache?*
BHR	*Bibliothèque d'Humanisme et Renaissance*
BI	*Books at Iowa*
BJA	*British Journal of Aesthetics*
BJDC	*British Journal of Disorders of Communication*
BJR	*Bulletin des Jeunes Romanistes*
BJRL	*Bulletin of the John Rylands Library*
B.L.	British Library (formerly British Museum)
BLJ	*British Library Journal*
BLR	*Bodleian Library Record*
B.M.	British Museum (now British Library)
BMQ	*British Museum Quarterly*
BNL	*Blake Newsletter*
BNYPL	*Bulletin of the New York Public Library* (now *Bulletin of Research in the Humanities*)
BP	*Banasthali Patrika*
BRH	*Bulletin of Research in the Humanities*
BRMMLA	*Bulletin of the Rocky Mountain Modern Language Association*
BS	*Blake Studies*
BSE	*Brno Studies in English*
BSLP	*Bulletin de la Société de Linguistique de Paris*
BSNotes	*Browning Society Notes*
BST	*Brontë Society Transactions*
BSUF	*Ball State University Forum*
BuR	*Bucknell Review*
CahiersE	*Cahiers Élisabéthains*
C&L	*Christianity and Literature*
Carrell	*The Carrell: Journal of the Friends of the University of Miami Library*
C.B.E.L.	*Cambridge Bibliography of English Literature*
CE	*College English*
CEA	*CEA Critic*
CEAAN	*Center for Editions of American Authors Newsletter*
CentR	*The Centennial Review*
CERVE	*Cahiers d'Études et de Recherches Victoriennes et Edouardiennes*
ChauR	*The Chaucer Review*
ChiR	*Chicago Review*
ChLB	*Charles Lamb Bulletin*
CHum	*Computers and the Humanities*
CJ	*Classical Journal*
CJIS	*Canadian Journal of Irish Studies*
CJL	*Canadian Journal of Linguistics*
CLAJ	*College Language Association Journal*
CLC	*Columbia Library Columns*
ClioW	*Clio: An Interdisciplinary Journal*
CLJ	*Cornell Library Journal*

CLQ	*Colby Library Quarterly*
CLS	*Comparative Literature Studies*
C&M	*Classica et Medievalia*
ColF	*Columbia Forum*
CollG	*Colloquia Germanica*
CollL	*College Literature*
ColQ	*Colorado Quarterly*
CompD	*Comparative Drama*
CompL	*Comparative Literature*
ConL	*Contemporary Literature*
ConnR	*Connecticut Review*
ContempR	*Contemporary Review*
CP	*Concerning Poetry*
CQ	*The Cambridge Quarterly*
CR	*The Critical Review*
Crit	*Critique: Studies in Modern Fiction*
CritI	*Critical Inquiry*
Critique	*Critique* (Paris)
CritQ	*Critical Quarterly*
CSHVB	*Computer Studies in the Humanities and Verbal Behavior*
CSR	*Christian Scholar's Review*
C.U.P.	Cambridge University Press
CWAAS	*Transactions of the Cumberland and Westmorland Archaeological and Antiquarian Society*
D.A.	*Dictionary of Americanisms*
D.A.E.	*Dictionary of American English*
DAI	*Dissertation Abstracts International*
DHLR	*The D.H. Lawrence Review*
DiS	*Dickens Studies*
DM	*The Dublin Magazine*
D.N.B.	*Dictionary of National Biography*
D.O.E.	*Dictionary of Old English*
DownR	*Downside Review*
DQR	*Dutch Quarterly Review*
DR	*Dalhousie Review*
DramS	*Drama Survey* (Minneapolis)
DSN	*Dickens Studies Newsletter*
DubR	*Dublin Review*
DUJ	*Durham University Journal*
DVLG	*Deutsche Vierteljahrsschrift für Literaturwissenschaft und Geistesgeschichte*
EA	*Études Anglaises*
EAL	*Early American Literature*
E&S	*Essays and Studies*
ECLife	*Eighteenth-Century Life*
ECS	*Eighteenth-Century Studies*
EDH	*Essays by Divers Hands*
E.E.T.S.	Early English Text Society
EHR	*English Historical Review*
EI	*Études Irlandaises (Lille)*

EIC	*Essays in Criticism*
EJ	*English Journal*
ELangT	*English Language Teaching*
ELH	*Journal of English Literary History*
ELN	*English Language Notes*
ELR	*English Literary Renaissance*
ELT	*English Literature in Transition*
ELWIU	*Essays in Literature* (Western Illinois U.)
EM	*English Miscellany*
E.P.N.S.	English Place-Name Society
EPS	*English Philological Studies*
ES	*English Studies*
ESA	*English Studies in Africa*
ESC	*English Studies in Canada*
ESQ	*Emerson Society Quarterly*
ESRS	*Emporia State Research Studies*
ETJ	*Educational Theatre Journal*
EWIP	*Edinburgh University, Department of Linguistics, Work in Progress*
EWN	*Evelyn Waugh Newsletter*
Expl	*Explicator*
FCEMN	*Fourteenth-Century English Mystics Newsletter*
FDP	*Four Decades of Poetry 1890–1930*
FDS	Fountainwell Drama Series
FH	*Frankfurter Hefte*
FLang	*Foundations of Language*
FMLS	*Forum of Modern Language Studies*
ForumH	*Forum* (Houston)
GaR	*Georgia Review*
GL	*General Linguistics*
GR	*Germanic Review*
GRM	*Germanisch-romanische Monatsschrift*
GUP	*Georgetown University Papers on Language and Linguistics*
HAB	*Humanities Association Bulletin*
HAR	*Humanities Association Review*
HC	*The Hollins Critic*
HJ	*Hibbert Journal*
HLB	*Harvard Library Bulletin*
HLQ	*Huntington Library Quarterly*
HOPE	*History of Political Economy*
HQ	*Hopkins Quarterly*
HRB	*Hopkins Research Bulletin*
HSE	*Hungarian Studies in English*
HSL	*Hartford Studies in Literature*
HTR	*Harvard Theological Review*
HudR	*Hudson Review*
IJES	*Indian Journal of English Studies*
IJSL	*International Journal of the Sociology of Language*
IndL	*Indian Literature*
IowaR	*Iowa Review*

IRAL	*International Review of Applied Linguistics*
IShaw	*Independent Shavian*
IUR	*Irish University Review*
JA	*Jahrbuch für Amerikastudien*
JAAC	*Journal of Aesthetics and Art Criticism*
JAF	*Journal of American Folklore*
JAmS	*Journal of American Studies*
JBS	*Journal of British Studies*
JChL	*Journal of Child Language*
JCSA	*Journal of the Catch Society of America*
JEGP	*Journal of English and Germanic Philology*
JEngL	*Journal of English Linguistics*
JFI	*Journal of the Folklore Institute*
JGE	*Journal of General Education*
JHI	*Journal of the History of Ideas*
JIL	*Journal of Irish Literature*
JJQ	*James Joyce Quarterly*
JL	*Journal of Linguistics*
JMH	*Journal of Medieval History*
JML	*Journal of Modern Literature*
JMRS	*Journal of Medieval and Renaissance Studies*
JNT	*Journal of Narrative Technique*
JPC	*Journal of Popular Culture*
JRUL	*Journal of the Rutgers University Library*
JVLB	*Journal of Verbal Learning and Verbal Behavior*
JWCI	*Journal of the Warburg and Courtauld Institutes*
JWMS	*Journal of the William Morris Society*
KanQ	*Kansas Quarterly*
KN	*Kwartalnik Neofilologiczny* (Warsaw)
KR	*Kenyon Review*
KSJ	*Keats–Shelley Journal*
KSMB	*Keats–Shelley Memorial Bulletin*
L&H	*Literature and History*
L&P	*Literature and Psychology*
L&S	*Language and Speech*
Lang&S	*Language and Style*
LanM	*Les Langues Modernes*
LaS	*Louisiana Studies*
LB	*Leuvense Bijdragen*
LC	*Library Chronicle*
LCP	*Library Chronicle* (U. of Pennsylvania)
LCUT	*Library Chronicle of the University of Texas*
LeedsSE	*Leeds Studies in English*
Lg	*Language*
LHR	*Lock Haven Review*
LHY	*Literary Half-Yearly*
Lib	*Library*
LingB	*Linguistiche Berichte*
LingI	*Linguistic Inquiry*
LMag	*London Magazine*

LWU	*Literatur in Wissenschaft und Unterricht*
MÆ	*Medium Ævum*
MCJ News	*Milton Centre of Japan News*
McNR	*McNeese Review*
M&H	*Medievalia et Humanistica*
M&L	*Music and Letters*
MarkhamR	*Markham Review*
MASJ	*Midcontinent American Studies Journal*
MBL	*Modern British Literature*
MD	*Modern Drama*
M.E.D.	*Middle English Dictionary*
MFS	*Modern Fiction Studies*
MHRev	*Malahat Review*
MichA	*Michigan Academician*
MiltonN	*Milton Newsletter*
MiltonQ	*Milton Quarterly*
MiltonS	*Milton Studies*
MinnR	*Minnesota Review*
MissQ	*Mississippi Quarterly*
M.L.A.	Modern Language Association of America
MLJ	*Modern Language Journal*
MLN	*Modern Language Notes*
MLQ	*Modern Language Quarterly*
MLR	*Modern Language Review*
MLS	*Modern Language Studies* (a publication of the Northeast Modern Language Association)
ModA	*Modern Age*
ModSp	*Moderne Sprachen*
MP	*Modern Philology*
MQ	*Midwest Quarterly*
MQR	*Michigan Quarterly Review*
MR	*Massachusetts Review*
MS	*Mediaeval Studies*
MSE	*Massachusetts Studies in English*
MSpr	*Moderna Språk*
MW	*The Muslim World* (Hartford, Conn.)
NA	*Nuova Antologia*
N&Q	*Notes and Queries*
NCF	*Nineteenth-Century Fiction*
NCTR	*Nineteenth Century Theatre Research*
NDQ	*North Dakota Quarterly*
NegroD	*Negro Digest*
NEQ	*New England Quarterly*
NH	*Northern History*
NL	*Nouvelles Littèraires*
NLB	*Newberry Library Bulletin*
NLH	*New Literary History*
NLWJ	*The National Library of Wales Journal*
NM	*Neuphilologische Mitteilungen*
NMAL	*Notes on Modern American Literature*

NMQ — *New Mexico Quarterly*
NMS — *Nottingham Medieval Studies*
Novel — *Novel: A Forum on Fiction*
NRF — *Nouvelle Revue Française*
NS — *Die Neuren Sprachen*
N.T. — New Testament
NTM — *New Theatre Magazine*
NWR — *Northwest Review*
NYH — *New York History*
NYLF — *New York Literary Forum*
N.Y.P.L. — New York Public Library
OB — *Ord och Bild*
OBSP — *Oxford Bibliographical Society Proceedings*
O.E.D. — *Oxford English Dictionary*
OEN — *Old English Newsletter*
O.E.T. — Oxford English Texts
O.H.E.L. — Oxford History of English Literature
OL — *Orbis Litterarum*
OR — *Oxford Review*
O.T. — Old Testament
O.U.P. — Oxford University Press
OUR — *Ohio University Review*
PAAS — *Proceedings of the American Antiquarian Society*
PAPA — *Publications of the Arkansas Philological Association*
PAPS — *Proceedings of the American Philosophical Society*
PBA — *Proceedings of the British Academy*
PBSA — *Papers of the Bibliographical Society of America*
PCLAC — *Proceedings of the California Linguistics Association Conference*
PCP — *Pacific Coast Philology*
P.E.N. — Poets, playwrights, editors, essayists, novelists
PiL — *Papers in Linguistics*
PLL — *Papers on Language and Literature*
PLPLS — *Proceedings of the Leeds Philosophical and Literary Society*
PMLA — *[Publications of the Modern Language Association of America]*
PN — *Poe Newsletter*
POAS — Poems on Affairs of State
PP — *Philologica Pragensia*
PQ — *Philological Quarterly*
PR — *Partisan Review*
PRB — Pre-Raphaelite Brotherhood
PRMCLS — *Papers from the Regional Meeting of the Chicago Linguistics Society*
P.R.O. — Public Record Office
PS — *Prose Studies 1800–1900*
PTL — *PTL: A Journal for Descriptive Poetics and Theory*
PULC — *Princeton University Library Chronicle*
QJS — *Quarterly Journal of Speech*
QQ — *Queen's Quarterly*

QR	*Quarterly Review*
RECTR	*Restoration and Eighteenth-Century Theatre Research*
REEDN	*Records of Early English Drama Newsletter*
RenD	*Renaissance Drama*
RenP	*Renaissance Papers*
RenQ	*Renaissance Quarterly*
Ren&Ref	*Renaissance and Reformation*
RES	*Review of English Studies*
RHL	*Revue d'Histoire Littéraire de la France*
RHT	*Revue d'Histoire du Théâtre*
RLC	*Revue de Littérature Comparée*
RLMC	*Rivista di Letterature Moderne e Comparate*
RLV	*Revue des Langues Vivantes*
RMS	*Renaissance and Modern Studies*
RN	*Renaissance News*
RomN	*Romance Notes*
RORD	*Research Opportunities in Renaissance Drama*
RQ	*Riverside Quarterly*
RRDS	Regents Renaissance Drama Series
RRestDS	Regents Restoration Drama Series
RS	*Research Studies*
RSC	Royal Shakespeare Company
R.S.L.	Royal Society of Literature
R.S.V.P.	Research Society for Victorian Periodicals
RUO	*Revue de l'Université d'Ottawa*
SAB	*South Atlantic Bulletin*
SAQ	*South Atlantic Quarterly*
SatR	*Saturday Review*
SB	*Studies in Bibliography*
SBC	*Studies in Browning and His Circle*
SBHT	*Studies in Burke and His Time*
SBL	*Studies in Black Literature*
SCB	*South Central Bulletin*
SCN	*Seventeenth-Century News*
SCR	*South Carolina Review*
SDR	*South Dakota Review*
SED	*Survey of English Dialects*
SEL	*Studies in English Literature 1500–1900* (Rice University)
SELit	*Studies in English Literature* (Japan)
SF&R	Scholars' Facsimiles and Reprints
SFQ	*Southern Folklore Quarterly*
SH	*Studia Hibernica* (Dublin)
ShakS	*Shakespeare Studies* (Tennessee)
ShawR	*Shaw Review*
ShN	*Shakespeare Newsletter*
SHR	*Southern Humanities Review*
ShS	*Shakespeare Survey*
ShStud	*Shakespeare Studies* (Tokyo)
SIR	*Studies in Romanticism*
SJH	*Shakespeare-Jahrbuch* (Heidelberg)

SJW	*Shakespeare-Jahrbuch* (Weimar)
SL	*Studia Linguistica*
SLitI	*Studies in the Literary Imagination*
SLJ	*Southern Literary Journal*
SM	*Speech Monographs*
SMC	*Studies in Medieval Culture*
SN	*Studia Neophilologica*
SNL	*Satire Newsletter*
SNNTS	*Studies in the Novel* (North Texas State U.)
SoQ	*The Southern Quarterly*
SoR	*Southern Review* (Louisiana)
SoRA	*Southern Review* (Adelaide)
SP	*Studies in Philology*
SQ	*Shakespeare Quarterly*
SR	*Sewanee Review*
SRen	*Studies in the Renaissance*
SRO	*Shakespearean Research Opportunities*
SRS	Salzburg Renaissance Studies
SSELER	Salzburg Studies in English Literature: Elizabethan and Renaissance
SSELRR	Salzburg Studies in English Literature: Romantic Reassessment
SSF	*Studies in Short Fiction*
SSL	*Studies in Scottish Literature*
SSMP	*Stockholm Studies in Modern Philology*
SSPDPT	Salzburg Studies: Poetic Drama and Poetic Theory
S.T.C.	*Short-Title Catalogue*
StHum	*Studies in the Humanities*
SWR	*Southwest Review*
TC	*The Twentieth Century*
TCBS	*Transactions of the Cambridge Bibliographical Society*
TCL	*Twentieth Century Literature*
TDR	*The Drama Review*
TEAS	Twayne's English Authors Series
ThQ	*Theatre Quarterly*
ThRI	*Theatre Research International*
ThS	*Theatre Survey*
THY	*The Thomas Hardy Yearbook*
TkR	*Tamkang Review*
TLS	*Times Literary Supplement*
TN	*Theatre Notebook*
TP	*Terzo Programma*
TPS	*Transactions of the Philological Society*
TQ	*Texas Quarterly*
TRB	*Tennyson Research Bulletin*
TriQ	*Tri-Quarterly*
TSE	*Tulane Studies in English*
TSL	*Tennessee Studies in Literature*
TSLL	*Texas Studies in Literature and Language*
TUSAS	Twayne's United States Authors Series

TWC	*The Wordsworth Circle*
TYDS	*Transactions of the Yorkshire Dialect Society*
UCTSE	*University of Cape Town Studies in English*
UDQ	*University of Denver Quarterly*
UES	*Unisa English Studies*
UMSE	*University of Mississippi Studies in English*
UR	*University Review* (Kansas City)
URev	*University Review* (Dublin)
USSE	*University of Saga Studies in English*
UTQ	*University of Toronto Quarterly*
UWR	*University of Windsor Review*
VN	*Victorian Newsletter*
VP	*Victorian Poetry*
VPN	*Victorian Periodicals Newsletter*
VQR	*Virginia Quarterly Review*
VS	*Victorian Studies*
VSB	*Victorian Studies Bulletin*
VWQ	*Virginia Woolf Quarterly*
WAL	*Western American Literature*
WascanaR	*Wascana Review*
WCR	*West Coast Review*
WF	*Western Folklore*
WHR	*Western Humanities Review*
WLT	*World Literature Today* (Formerly *Books Abroad*)
Wolfen-büttelerB	*Wolfenbütteler Beiträge: Aus den Schätzen der Herzog August Bibliothek*
WSCL	*Wisconsin Studies in Contemporary Literature*
WTW	Writers and their Work
WVUPP	*West Virginia University Bulletin: Philological Papers*
WWR	*Walt Whitman Review*
XUS	*Xavier University Studies*
YER	*Yeats Eliot Review*
YES	*Yearbook of English Studies*
YPL	*York Papers in Linguistics*
YR	*Yale Review*
YULG	*Yale University Library Gazette*
YW	*The Year's Work in English Studies*
ZAA	*Zeitschrift für Anglistik und Amerikanistik*
ZCP	*Zeitschrift für Celtische Philologie*
ZDL	*Zeitschrift für Dialektologie und Linguistik*

Note: Notices of books published in German, identified by the initials H.C.C., have been contributed by H. C. Castein Dr.phil. Lecturer in Modern Languages in the University of London (Goldsmiths' College)

Contents

I

Literary History and Criticism: General Works

T. S. DORSCH

1. Reference Works

The third edition of E. G. Withycombe's *Oxford Dictionary of English Christian Names*[1] adds about forty names to those listed in the second edition of 1950, which had increased by a somewhat larger number those included in the original edition of 1944. Withycombe has also amended or augmented many of his previous entries, often taking note of changes in the usage, frequency, and social standing of names that have taken place over the past quarter century. It may be wondered how far such names as Baruch, Hypatia, Michelle, Sacha, and Senga, among others, may legitimately be regarded as English Christian names, but possibly by now the frequency of their adoption in English families can be said almost to justify their inclusion. Difficult as it is to accept Janice, Marlene, Samantha, and Tracy with pleasure, it is agreeable to find Araminta and Jasmine among the lambs which have returned to the fold. Both in its scholarly historical introduction and its all-important dictionary section, not to mention the appendix on common words derived from Christian names, Withycombe's volume provides much pleasant browsing.

Who Was Who Among English and European Authors, 1931-1949[2], compiled by editors of the Gale Research Company, brings together in a single alphabetically arranged list all the material on English and European writers who were alive between 1931 and 1949 that was recorded in the editions of *The Authors' and Artists' Who's Who* during that period and in *Who's Who among Living Authors of Older Nations* in 1931. It covers minor as well as major poets, playwrights, novelists, essayists, and journalists. These are some 23,000 entries, each providing personal and professional information – education, marriage, religion, works published, contributions to journals, and so forth. The cost of these three stout volumes will probably inhibit their purchase by many individuals, but they are a very useful reference work which ought to be on the shelves of all major libraries.

A much more limited, but also useful, work is *Twentieth Century Children's Writers*[3], edited by D. L. Kirkpatrick with the assistance of nineteen advisers, and with entries provided by about 160 contributors, many of them themselves distinguished writers of children's books or

[1] *The Oxford Dictionary of Christian Names*, by E. G. Withycombe. Third edn. O U.P. pp. xlvii + 310. £4.50.

[2] *Who Was Who Among English and European Authors, 1931-1949*. Detroit, Mich.: Gale Research Company. Three vols. pp. iii + 1564. $96.

[3] *Twentieth Century Children's Writers*, ed. by D. L. Kirkpatrick. Macmillan. pp. xvi + 1507. £17.50.

authorities on the genre. As in the previous work noted, the entries relate only to authors who have been alive in the present century, although they may have been born near the middle of last century, as were J. M. Barrie (1860) and L. F. Baum (1856), the author of the Wizard of Oz books. Again biographical material is included, but this time each entry is followed either by a personal statement by the author concerned, or by a critical assessment which may run to a couple of pages, or at times by both.

2. Collections of Essays

Most of the articles in the 1978 volume of *Essays and Studies*[4] are noticed elsewhere in this volume, and it is therefore not necessary to do much more than list them in order to show the scope of the work. Colin Manlove contributes an interesting essay the title of which gives an indication of its subject-matter – ' "Rooteles moot grene soone deye": The Helplessness of Chaucer's Troilus and Criseyde'. In tracing some of Milton's 'imitations' of Shakespeare, Rachel Trickett suggests that such a study can afford 'a greater awareness of the way in which the creative imagination operates which must provide us with glimpses at least, perhaps an insight, into the art and nature of poetic composition'. Taking arms against those who still see *The Winter's Tale* as a play in which the tragic and the comic portions are 'not articulated', Alastair Fowler argues that, far from being a mere interlude, the pastoral scenes 'present symbols of the repair of nature; of the civilizing effect of art; of the gentling effect of time; of the interplay between nature and grace (as in Perdita's pageant of Flora); and of integration (as in the measurement of time, an emblem of temperance)'. Also writing on *The Winter's Tale*, F. W. Bateson asks, 'How old was Leontes?' Examining the number-words and the reference to time in the play, Bateson concludes that Leontes was twenty-eight years old in Acts I and II, and forty-four in the final acts. K. J. Fielding writes interestingly of the friendship between the Carlyles and Erasmus A. Darwin, demonstrating that, at any rate in his early and middle life, Carlyle was 'much more human, and more truly representative of his age and best work', than is suggested by the account of him given by J. A. Froude, who knew him only in his later years. H. A. Mason discusses the comparative merits of the different prefatory and concluding lines that Tennyson provided for his *Morte D'Arthur* in the first and in subsequent printed versions of the poem. Finally, in 'Hardy's Poetical Metonymy' John Bayley suggests that it is the extensive use that Hardy makes of such devices as personification and metonymy which 'determines our sense of the personal and the original in his poetry'.

Graham Hough has brought together into a volume of *Selected Essays*[5] a number of papers which he has published during the last fifteen years. Most of them have at various times been noticed in *YW*. It is sufficent here to list the contents of the volume, which represent well the range and depth of Hough's criticism. Leaving aside some general papers on critical theory, the most interesting of the essays are 'Narrative and Dialogue in

[4] *Essays and Studies 1978*. Collected by W. W. Robson. N.S. Vol. 31. John Murray, for the English Association. pp. vi + 130. £6.50.

[5] *Selected Essays*, by Graham Hough. C U.P. pp. vii + 274.

Jane Austen', 'The Poetry of Coleridge', 'The Natural Theology of *In Memoriam*', 'W. B. Yeats: A Study in Poetic Integration', 'Vision and Doctrine in *Four Quartets*', 'Dante and Eliot', and 'John Crowe Ransom: The Poet and the Critic'. This is a very worthwhile volume.

Edgell Rickword's early writings, down to 1931, were edited in 1974 by Alan Young, who has now produced a second collection of Rickword's essays down to 1978 entitled *Literature in Society*[6]. They range widely in content over social, political, and literary topics, and in length from two- or three-page reviews to papers of about thirty pages, such as an interesting and welcome study of William Hone. Other writers treated at essay length include Milton, Wordsworth, Hazlitt, Cobbett, Paul Verlaine, and André Malraux. Bunyan, Swift, T. S. Eliot, Auden and Spender are among those who receive less full notice. As a critic Rickword is often stimulating, and at times profound; his essays contain much that will interest readers of *YW*.

Even more versatile than Rickword is C. H. Sisson – poet, novelist, essayist, literary critic, and translator from Latin, French, Italian, and German. *The Avoidance of Literature*[7] is a collection of papers, more than eighty in number, brought together with Sisson's help by Michael Schmidt. Some of the very short pieces, including reviews, are scarcely worth republishing. However, when Sisson develops his ideas, in whatever field, at length, as in the hundred-page study of Walter Bagehot, or in his essay-length reflections on Marvell, or T. S. Eliot, or Yeats, or William Barnes, he emerges as a very worthwhile critic. His literary interests lie to a large degree in the work of modern poets, such as Geoffrey Hill or Martin Seymour-Smith or David Jones; but he writes well also on general topics related to literature, art, religion, or government.

Twenty distinguished French scholars of English literature have contributed to *Hommage à Émile Gasquet*[8], a memorial tribute to Émile Gasquet, who died in 1977. Although Gasquet had published comparatively little at the time of his early death, the ground covered by the papers suggests that he had very wide literary interests – Machiavelli, Elizabethan drama, Metaphysical poetry, Defoe, Jane Austen, and a number of twentieth-century English and American poets. From a number of excellent studies the following may be singled out as possessing special interest 'L'Or sur la scène élisabéthaine', by Marie-Thérèse Jones-Davies, which pays special attention to the anonymous *Impatient Poverty*, Dekker's *Old Fortunatus*, Shakespeare's *Timon of Athens* and *Marlowe's Jew of Malta*; Robert Ellrodt's 'La Fonction de l'image scientifique dans la poésie métaphysique anglaise', which provides fresh insights into the work of most of the metaphysical poets; François Fauré's 'La Religion d'Othello', which claims that Othello is incontestably to be seen as a Christian; and Philippe Séjourné's 'Les Intentions de Jane Austen dans *Sense and Sensibility*: héritage et innovation'.

[6] *Literature in Society: Essays & Opinions (II) 1931–1978*, by Edgell Rickword, ed. by Alan Young. Carcanet. pp. xii + 332. £6.90.

[7] *The Avoidance of Literature: Collected Essays*, by C. H. Sisson, ed. by Michael Schmidt. Carcanet. pp. x + 581. £7.90.

[8] *Hommage à Émile Gasquet (1920–1977)*. Annales de la faculté des lettres et sciences humaines de Nice, No. 34. pp. 228.

3. Forms, genres, themes

One of the leading contentions of Denys Thompson's admirable book *The Uses of Poetry*[9] is that 'poetry is the finest way of using words because it can comprehend the whole of experience'. Thompson aims at describing the part played by poetry in the life of man from the earliest times, in as far as the use of language in primitive periods can be reconstructed, down to the present day. The early records of all peoples demonstrate that rhythmic speech as well as dance formed the staple of all ancient religious observances, and verse was until comparatively late in classical literature the vehicle for history, philosophy, and science. Chapter by chapter, and taking in many ages and many peoples, Thompson brings out the manifold ways in which poetry bound man with his fellows in all the concerns of his life, at any rate until the invention of printing, when it became more sophisticated and ceased to be so essentially a popular possession. He believes, however, that poetry could still be of value in helping people to cope with the strains of modern life and with the implications of vast new fields of knowledge, and also as a humanising influence in an increasingly dehumanising age.

In *Roots of Lyric*[10] Andrew Welsh aims at tracing modern lyrical poetry back to its origins in primitive and folk rhythmical patterns. To this end he studies, under such headings as 'Emblem', 'Image', 'Ideogram', 'Charm', 'Chant', and 'Rhythm', a number of sound patterns, most of them (outwardly at least) comparatively unelaborate, and most of them stemming from periods in the more or less distant past. They include Bantu riddles, American Indian and Eskimo chants and charms (some too from the traditional songs of the Australian aborigines), Chinese verses of various kinds and Japanese Haiku. He shows how the roots of lyric, embodied in such forms as these, were gradually raised to higher dignity, with more striking effect, in poetry from the Renaissance down to the present day, and how some knowledge of these roots may enhance our understanding and enjoyment of the poetry of later periods.

Ernst Häublein's *The Stanza*[11], in the Critical Idiom series, admirably complements G. S. Fraser's *Metre, Rhyme and Free Verse*, an earlier contribution to the same series. While accepting the *O.E.D.* definition of the stanza as generally valid, Häublein examines a number of earlier definitions from the sixteenth century onwards to show how attitudes towards the formal elements of poetry change from age to age. In his second chapter he describes the principal stanzaic patterns of western literature, including some which have been acclimatised from oriental origins, such as the Ghazal and the Haiku. The greater part of his book aims at suggesting 'criteria for relating the stanza to poetic structure', and at 'evaluating the logical relations among stanzas and their place and function as parts within the poetic whole'.

[9] *The Uses of Poetry*, by Denys Thompson. C.U.P. pp. viii + 238. hb £10.50, pb £4.95.

[10] *Roots of Lyric: Primitive Poetry and Modern Poetics*, by Andrew Welsh. Princeton, N.J.: Princeton U.P. pp. xii + 276.

[11] *The Stanza*, by Ernst Häublein. Methuen (The Critical Idiom). pp. viii + 125. hb £4.25, pb £2.

Arthur Heiserman's *The Novel before the Novel*[12], completed just before his early death, was designed as the first of three projected volumes tracing the history of prose fiction in Europe down to the sixteenth century. It deals with the development of prose fiction in classical literature down to about the fourth century AD – largely (after a sensible chapter on the *Argonautica* of Apollonius Rhodius) with the works which are generally known as romances, but which Heiserman prefers, anachronistically, to name novels because of the misleading senses in which the term 'romance' is used nowadays. The works to which he devotes special attention are Chariton's *Chaereas and Callirhoë*, Achilles Tatius's *Clitophon*, Longus's *Daphnis and Chloe*, Apuleius's *The Golden Ass*, and Heliodorus's *Æthiopica* – all of them works with which all students of the European novel ought to be made familiar. He aims at bringing out 'a few of the aesthetic, psychological, and cultural powers that vivify' all these works alike, and thus at establishing certain criteria which may be seen to apply to long fictions of later ages. It is to be hoped that his book will encourage many students of the novel to read the tales that are the subject of his study.

Rhythm in the Novel[13], E. K. Brown's Alexander Lectures, which were first published in 1950, now appear in a welcome reprint. It may be recalled by older readers that this is largely a study of what E. M. Forster called 'repetition with variation' in a number of (chiefly twentieth-century) novels, leading to a full-scale study in the final lecture of Forster's *Passage to India*. Brown's criticism has not dated, and we must be grateful for this reprint.

In *Story and Discourse*[14] Seymour Chatman aims at formulating a general theory of narrative which will apply equally well to the presentation of stories in verbal and in visual media, such as the film. Following the methods of such structuralist critics as Roland Barthes, Tzvetan Todorov, and Gérard Genette, he divides his approach to narrative into a 'what' and a 'way'. 'The what of narrative I call its "story"; the way I call its "discourse".' With wide reference, he analyses the elements of 'story', such as plot, character, and setting; he goes on to 'discourse', the ways in which the story is presented. This is not an easy book to read, but the careful reader will often find it illuminating.

Although much has been written about individual Scottish novelists, in particular Scott, there appears to exist no authoritative and comprehensive history of the Scottish novel. This deficiency is now to some extent made good by Francis Russell Hart's *The Scottish Novel*[15], which covers the field from Smollett to the present day. It is only 'to some extent' made good, for a critical survey of the Scottish novel which

[12] *The Novel before the Novel: Essays and Discussions about the Beginning of Prose Fiction in the West,* by Arthur Heiserman. Chicago, Ill.: Chicago U.P. pp. x + 238. £2.50.

[13] *Rhythm in the Novel,* by E. K. Brown. Lincoln, Neb.: Nebraska U.P. pp. xiv + 118. £6.40.

[14] *Story and Discourse: Narrative Structure in Fiction and Film,* by Seymour Chatman. Ithaca, N.Y.: Cornell U.P. pp. 277. £10.25.

[15] *The Scottish Novel: A Critical Survey,* by Francis Russell Hart. John Murray. pp. xvi + 442. £12.

devotes no more than a chapter of sixteen pages to Smollett, Scott, and James Hogg (though Scott is later given about three further pages and many passing references), while John Galt receives more than twenty pages and Eric Linklater and Robin Jenkins more than forty, can scarcely be said to be well proportioned. However, it is good to find such old friends as Susan Ferrier and Lewis Grassic Gibbon given generous treatment, and there can be very few minor novelists, especially of the present century, who have escaped Hart's net.

A. O. J. Cockshut's *Man and Woman*[16] is an extremely interesting book on the treatment of sexual relations in the English novel from the mid-eighteenth to the mid-twentieth century – roughly from Richardson to D. H. Lawrence and E. M. Forster. Love between the sexes has been a leading pre-occupation of novelists throughout this period, and inevitably Cockshut devotes most of his attention to the major figures; but he has sought out many less well-known works, such as Swinburne's two novels, *Love's Cross-Currents* and *Lesbia Brandon*, J. A. Froude's *Shadows of the Clouds* and *The Lieutenant's Daughter*, and Djuna Barnes's *Nightwood* (1936). In demonstrating how the treatment of love normally reflects the prevalent attitudes of the writer's age, he has shown – what is all too often disregarded – how very deceptive are such blanket terms as 'The Victorian novel' or 'The Victorian temper'. In two valuable chapters at the end of his volume, he has provided a perceptive study of male homosexuality and lesbianism in the novels of the past century or so – those, for example, of Walter Pater, Frederick Rolfe, and E. M. Forster, of Henry James, Radclyffe Hall, and Djuna Barnes.

D. C. R. A. Goonetilleke's *Developing Countries in British Fiction*[17] perhaps shows rather too obviously, in its specialised approach, that is is a Ph.D. thesis adapted for publication. This is not to say that it lacks interest or value, but that, in reading it, one often feels that it could have been enriched by reference, not only to what has been so well written about the developing countries, but also to what has been so well written in English *in* the developing countries which are the subject of Goonetilleke's work. Goonetilleke confines himself almost entirely to the novels of Conrad, Kipling, E. M. Forster, D. H. Lawrence, and Joyce Cary.

In *The Secret of Humor*[18] Leonard Feinberg examines a number of theories of humour that have been formulated from the time of Aristotle onwards – that it depends for its success on the awakening of a sense of incongruity, or of ambivalence, or of superiority, and so forth. He himself concludes that all forms of humour take their rise from what he calls 'playful aggression'. Thus, for example, he sees nonsense humour as aggression against logic and order, scatological humour as aggression against propriety, word-play as aggression against conformity; and in similar fashion he defines sexual humour, cosmic humour, and black humour in terms of some form of aggression. He exemplifies these and other forms of humour copiously, and while some of his illustrations have not much

[16] *Man and Woman: A Study of Love and the Novel 1740–1940*, by A. O. J. Cockshut. Collins, 1977. pp. 221. £4.50.

[17] *Developing Countries in British Fiction*, by D. C. R. A. Goonetilleke. Macmillan, 1977. pp. x + 282. £8.95.

[18] *The Secret of Humor*, by Leonard Feinberg. Amsterdam: Rodopi. pp. vi + 219.

point, some are very funny. His thesis is only partly persuasive; it does not entirely, as he feels, cancel out all those that he rejects.

Comic Drama[19], edited by W. D. Howarth, aims, in a series of papers contributed by former and present colleagues in the University of Bristol, at tracing the development of comic drama in Western Europe from its beginnings in ancient Greece down to the twentieth century. Howarth himself provides an interesting introduction on 'theoretical considerations' relating to comedy, and later a historical account of comedy in France. The salient facts about the comedy of Greece and Rome are presented by Michael Anderson. Glynne Wickham discusses medieval comic traditions and the beginnings of English comedy, and later periods in England are covered by Arnold Hare. Felicity Firth treats comedy in Italy, J. C. J. Metford comedy in Spain and the Spanish *comedia*, and David Thomas comedy in northern Europe. The volume is closed by George Brandt with a paper on twentieth-century European and American comedy in which the influence of such media as cinema, radio, and television is analysed. This book will be of interest to many readers, and will be especially welcome in the drama departments of the universities.

As Robert M. Torrance observes in his lively book *The Comic Hero*[20], the fugitive nature of the comic hero 'will not abide formulation'. Nevertheless, there are many figures in literature whose 'essence lies in being at once heroic and comic'. Such a figure 'can never wholly relinquish the joy in living that is both his innate disposition and his final object, and he perpetually solemnizes existence by wilfully refusing to see it as comic'. Torrance is not persuasive in his argument that Homer's Odysseus, in that he is so entirely the antithesis to Achilles, is the first great comic hero in western literature. He is on much safer ground when he treats some of the 'heroes' of Aristophanes, or the *miles gloriosus* of Plautus, or the medieval Reynard the Fox. Coming down to more recent times, and selecting only a few of the greater 'heroes' of the many of whom he writes, we have admirable chapters on Falstaff and Don Quixote, some telling pages on Abraham Adams and a fuller study of Tom Jones, and an effective discussion of Byron's Don Juan. Leopold Bloom, Gully Jimson, Felix Krull, and the good soldier Schweik are among the twentieth-century figures who conform with Torrance's definition of the comic hero. This is a book which adds much to our understanding, and enjoyment, of a number of fascinating characters in the literature of the world.

In *A Gathered Church*[21] Donald Davie sketches the fortunes of English Dissent, as a significant element in English literature, over the past three centuries or so. No one has questioned the importance of, say, Milton, Bunyan, and Cromwell as 'representative of the dissenting voice in literature, religion, and politics'. Davie's field is much wider than this; he seeks to discover whether the Presbyterians, Baptists, and Independents were the religious bigots and artistic philistines they have so often been represented

[19] *Comic Drama: The European Heritage*, ed. by W. D. Howarth. Methuen. pp. x + 194. £3.95.

[20] *The Comic Hero*, by Robert M. Torrance. Cambridge, Mass.: Harvard U.P. pp. xvi + 346. £10.50.

[21] *A Gathered Church: The Literature of the English Dissenting Interest, 1700–1930* (The Clark Lectures, 1976). O.U.P. pp. 200.

as being. Among the poets Isaac Watts, Charles Wesley, and William Blake, among the novelists Elizabeth Gaskell, George Eliot, Mark Rutherford, and D. H. Lawrence, among prominent figures in other walks of life Michael Faraday, Philip Gosse, Joseph Priestley, and Orde Wingate are the leading representatives of non-conformism whom he discusses and assesses. Not surprisingly, he is able to demonstrate that, though there have been dissenters whose conduct and writings have brought their movements into disrepute, the literature of the English dissenters as a whole has righly earned a high regard, whether on doctrinal or social or aesthetic grounds.

Michael J. C. Echeruo's central thesis in *The Conditioned Imagination from Shakespeare to Conrad*[22] is that, in approaching a work of literature which involves what he terms an 'exo-cultural' character or theme, we must take into account the influence of the 'culturally-conditioned imagination' on both the creation and the realisation of a work of art. As he sees it, a work of literature combines the conventions of the 'language of literature' with those of the 'language of culture'. Turning from the theoretical to the practical, he examines two 'exo-cultural' figures in the plays of Shakespeare, Shylock and Othello, as he believes they would have been seen by an Elizabethan audience. With special reference to Aphra Behn's hero in *Oroonoko* and Defoe's Man Friday, he goes on to discuss 'exo-cultural' heroes of the Enlightenment, again aiming at showing how these characters from alien backgrounds might have been received by those who read about them. Finally, with parallels drawn from Melville's Queequeg in *Moby Dick*, he makes a close study of some of Conrad's characters, especially in *The Nigger of the Narcissus*.

John Colmer's *Coleridge to Catch-22* is a work of considerable interest. Some decades ago C. S. Lewis demonstrated that the 'great divide' in European ways of thought came not, as was traditionally held, as a discernible split between medieval and Renaissance, but rather as an upheaval in man's consciousness brought about by the French Revolution, and still more by the Industrial Revolution – even as at present we are crossing another great divide into the nuclear age. Like Lewis, Colmer argues that significantly new attitudes towards society developed towards the end of the eighteenth century, manifested in a variety of methods of analysis – 'realistic rendering, persuasion, utopian fantasy, and protest'. Taking us through the nineteenth century, Colmer notes the reflection of the thought of the advancing decades in the writings of, among others, Coleridge, John Stuart Mill, Thomas Love Peacock, Disraeli, Dickens, Mrs Gaskell, George Eliot and Charles Kingsley, as each of these writers offers a criticism of society in his or her novels. Henry James, Mark Rutherford, George Gissing and Ford Madox Ford are others whom Colmer takes into account. Turning to the present century, he considers the analysis of society offered by such writers as C. F. G. Masterman, H. G. Wells, E. M. Forster and D. H. Lawrence. Colmer ends with a penetrating study of some recent writers whose criticism of society is presented in 'an unusual blend of

[22] *The Conditioned Imagination from Shakespeare to Conrad*, by Michael J. C. Echeruo. New York: Holmes & Meier and London: The Macmillan Press. pp. viii + 135. £6.95.

[23] *Coleridge to Catch-22: Images of Society*, by John Colmer. New York: St. Martin's Press. pp. viii + 240.

farce, black comedy, and tragedy' – George Orwell, Joseph Heller, and Kurt Vonnegut. This book has much to offer to readers of *YW*.

In *Language and Style*[24] E. L. Epstein draws a distinction between two types of style (which he defines as 'the regard that *what* pays to *how*') – public style and private style. In what he calls 'the public literature game', the facts of language are utilised to represent anything in the universe except 'the private depths of the speaker'. In 'the private game' the facts of language are utilised to represent nothing in the universe except, ultimately, those private depths. With some detailed illustration, Epstein considers such things as the psychological bases of style, certain genre and period styles, and the choice of diction. In playing these two games, he says, 'human beings are constantly reforming and transforming the world. . .The results of this process are literature and society'.

George Watson's *The Discipline of English*[25] is a very sensible book. Watson aims at counteracting some of the pernicious doctrines that were propagated in the 1960s to 'The Generation That Was Lied To': for example, 'that you can command your native language, and even write it, with little or no systematic training; that literature is less a body of knowledge than a free-play area for personal judgement; and that there is a formula called the New Something which is about to solve the riddle of everything'. Watson remains unrepentantly convinced – alas that so many do not share his conviction! – 'that no one can know a subject if he knows nothing of its history, or misunderstands that history'. He has therefore written a book for those who accept, or can be persuaded to accept, that English is a 'discipline', in the fullest academic sense of the work, and not a leisure activity. The first, and longer, section of the book is a lucid account of recent trends in literary criticism, leading to what Watson believes to be the true functions of criticism. The second section, 'How to Read', offers guidance on how to read, work, and write, together with much practical advice on the facilities that are available to advance these activities. This is a wise book, and it could be read with pleasure and profit by any student of literature.

We may readily agree with Evan Watkins when he argues, in *The Critical Act*[26], that 'the sophistication of terminology and method in current criticism' often leaves us remote from actual works of literature. It is questionable whether his own methods bring us any nearer to such works. The greater part of his book is devoted to analysis of the techniques, in Part I of such structuralist critics as Northrop Frye, E. D. Hirsch, Roland Barthes, and Jacques Derrida, in Part II of the Marxists such as Raymond Williams and Fredric Jameson. Rejecting their methods, Watkins develops a theory of criticism in terms of what he describes as 'dialectical encounter with literature'. Like some of those from whose views he dissents, he employs a good deal of abstract critical jargon, and he does not always think clearly. He is rather more satisfactory when he ties himself down to dissection of specific writings, such as the poems of Charles Tomlinson and

[24] *Language and Style*, by E. L. Epstein. Methuen (New Accents). pp. xii + 92. £5.

[25] *The Discipline of English: A Guide to Critical Theory and Practice*, by George Watson. Macmillan. pp. 125. hb £6.50, pb £2.25.

[26] *The Critical Act: Criticism and Community*, by Evan Watkins. New Haven, Conn.: Yale U.P. pp. xii + 251. £10.80.

W. S. Merwin, or William Faulkner's *Absalom, Absalom!*

Katharine M. Briggs continues her valuable work in folklore with *The Vanishing People*[27], which, as her subtitle informs us, is 'A Study of Traditional Fairy Beliefs'. Confining herself in the main to the tradition of Great Britain, Dr Briggs deals, chapter by chapter, with almost every aspect of fairy lore: among others, common beliefs about fairy origins, house fairies, nature fairies, fairy dwellings, fairy changelings, the powers exercised by fairies, fairies in their dealings with mortals, fairy mortality, and fairy sports. Her accounts of all these matters are profusely illustrated with tales and anecdotes from many sources, and her book is pleasantly embellished with drawings by Mary I. French. Her glossary of fairies, in which she lists about 150 fairy names, her very full book list and her three indexes add considerably to the interest and value of her volume.

4. Bibliographical Studies

Volume XXXI of *Studies in Bibliography*[28], edited like its thirty predecessors by Fredson Bowers, contains the usual interesting mixture. G. Thomas Tanselle opens the volume with a long paper, 'The Editing of Historical Documents', in which he describes the editorial policy of some American learned societies which exist to promote publication, discusses the merits of certain editions for which they have been responsible, and urges closer communication between editors in all fields. In an article entitled 'Wynkyn de Worde's "Sir Thopas" and Other Tales', Thomas J. Garbáty concludes that, far from merely having followed Caxton's second edition of Chaucer, as has hitherto been accepted, de Worde 'ranks as a textual authority *independent* of Caxton'. Rollo G. Silver gives an account of the career of Samuel Nelson Dickinson, a notable American printer, type-founder, and publisher in the first half of the nineteenth century. In 'Greg's "Rationale of Copy-Text" Revisited', Fredson Bowers demonstrates that 'Greg's rationale distinguishing the authority of substantives and accidentals is a sound one. However, a modern editor must always be aware that when he follows Greg he is not necessarily dealing with the same conditions and that the frame of reference may therefore alter in subtle ways that end with important differences.' Stephen Spector, noting textual disruptions that have been brought about in early printed books by unusual folding of sheets, proposes a method of analysing watermark sequences 'which can not only discover the ways in which gatherings were orginally formed, but can also identify and locate textual disruptions where this might otherwise be impossible'.

Among shorter contributions, B. J. McMullin provides a helpful study of 'The Direction Line as Bibliographical Evidence', with reference to the 1683 edition of John Crowne's *City Politiques*. Early editions of Chaucer figure again in Bradford Y. Fletcher's 'Printer's Copy for Stow's *Chaucer*'. Fletcher shows that, of the twenty-four poems that John Stow added in

[27] *The Vanishing People: A Study of Traditional Fairy Beliefs*, by Katharine M. Briggs. Batsford. pp. 218. £5.95.

[28] *Studies in Bibliography: Papers of the Bibliographical Society of the University of Virginia*, Vol. XXXI, ed. by Fredson Bowers. Charlottesville, Va.: U.P. of Virginia. pp. vi + 277. $20.

his 1561 *Chaucer* to those published in previous editions of Chaucer (of his additions only three are now accepted as genuinely Chaucerian), fourteen were taken from what is now Trinity College, Cambridge, MS R. 3.19, and the rest from other early sources; he decides that in some cases Stow's print is 'certainly itself an authority', and requires further investigation. Sir Philip Sidney's sonnet sequence was first printed in a quarto of 1591: MacD. P. Jackson brings forward evidence that the printer of this quarto was John Charlewood, whose printing-house was fairly productive in the period 1558–1595. In '"wife" or "wise" – *The Tempest* I. 1786' Jeanne Addison Roberts, having examined many copies of the Folio, including some not collated by Charlton Hinman, argues, not altogether convincingly, that 'wise' is an incorrect reading due to the progressive deterioration of the letter f in the printing, so that it soon began to look like the long s. Continuing his study of George Steevens's 1785 Variorum *Shakespeare*, William C. Woodson notes that it was a considerable revision of the 1778 Variorum, with contributions from half a dozen scholars, including Edmond Malone.

The volume continues with an article by Ernest W. Sullivan II, who provides information about 'Manuscript Materials in the First Edition of Donne's *Biathanatos*'. A. S. G. Edwards describes some hitherto unexamined manuscripts of Marvell's satires in the Portland Collection in the Nottingham University library. Harold Love's article, 'Preacher and Publisher: Oliver Heywood and Thomas Parkhurst', throws new light on publishing practices in the seventeenth century. Richard Wendorf provides evidence that Robert Dodsley, the famous publisher, was much given to 'editing' poems entrusted to him by such poets as Gray, Collins, Dyer, and Shenstone – not always to their satisfaction. Two papers are devoted to Sherwood Anderson: William S. Pfeiffer argues that *Mary Cochran* was not, as is usually asserted, exclusively a product of Anderson's apprentice years, but was begun between 1909 and 1912, and laid aside only in about 1921. Ray Lewis White lists, with bibliographical details, Anderson's fugitive pamphlets and broadsides from 1918 to 1940. Philip Stratford draws attention to the fact that there are many variant readings in different editions of Graham Greene's novels, especially the five editions of *The Heart of the Matter*, some of them attributable, not to Greene himself, but to his American publishers. Finally Timothy Crist and Clinton Sisson offer 'Additions and Corrections to the Second Edition of Donald Wing's *Short-Title Catalogue*'.

The collection of essays assembled by Colin Steele under the title *Steady-State, Zero Growth, and the Academic Library*[29] is an important attempt to resolve some of the dilemmas confronting the administrators of academic libraries throughout the English-speaking world. In technology the term 'steady-state' signifies a system in which input and output can be adjusted to preserve a state of equilibrium. In librarianship the concept means in effect inefficiency and stagnation, for the progressive restriction of finances, coupled with rocketing inflation and union demands, is resulting in a state of affairs in which academic libraries can no longer supply

[29] *Steady-State, Zero Growth, and the Academic Library*. A collection of essays ed. by Colin Steele. London: Clive Bingley and Hamden, Conn.: Linnet Books. pp. 148.

the services which it is their special function to supply. The contributors, representing libraries in England, Australia, New Zealand, and America, discuss the problem from many points of view. Perhaps the most positive general conclusion that emerges is that, in a period of economic retrenchment, 'smaller, more flexible and less costly collections may well constitute an alternative path of development for libraries'.

It is probable that the book trade has produced a greater number of fascinating personalities than almost any other commercial enterprise. In *Antiquarian Books*[30] Roy Harley Lewis has given a delightful account of this trade in almost all its facets, and particularly of the people who run it or have run it. In his first chapter Lewis introduces us to many booksellers who for one reason or another have been worthy of notice, among them Dr Johnson's father, and Bernard Lintot, and the famous spies of a few years ago, Mr and Mrs Peter Kroger. Then come some of the great collectors, such as J. P. Morgan and Sir Thomas Phillipps. Lewis goes on to retail anecdotes about the more enterprising booksellers of whom he has special knowledge – Gustave David of Cambridge and his son; Bernard Quaritch, Charles W. Traylen, Charles P. Everitt and Colin Franklin; and he talks, too, about the compilation of *S.T.C.* by A. W. Pollard and G. R. Redgrave. One of his most astonishing stories, in the chapter on book thieves, tells of the theft in one night in 1977 of no fewer than 26,000 volumes from the famous bookshop of Messrs Thomas Thorp in Shoe Lane. There are further chapters on celebrated forgers, such as Thomas Wise, and on book auctions. It all makes very good reading, but it is a pity that a book about, among other things, good printing should contain a large number of misprints.

David Higham's *Literary Gent*[31] is both extremely entertaining and extremely enlightening. Higham has been for more than half a century a literary agent, and the many authors for whom he has acted include the Sitwells, Leonard and Virginia Woolf, Vita Sackville-West, Harold Macmillan, Dorothy Sayers, and T. S. Eliot. Through these and other authors he has been brought into close relationship with their publishers, Michael Joseph, Victor Gollancz, Jonathan Cape, Max Schuster, Blanche and Alfred Knopf and others. His book takes us, with many amusing anecdotes, into the heart of the twentieth-century writing and publishing world, and will be of great interest to all who are interested in the literary scene of recent decades.

The second supplement to Robert B. Slocum's *Biographical Dictionaries and Related Works*[32] brings up to more than 12,000 the number of entries in the original volume and its supplements. The nature of the volume is adequately indicated by the long subtitle provided in the footnote below.

[30] *Antiquarian Books: An Insider's Account*, by Roy Harley Lewis. Newton Abbot, Devon: David & Charles. pp. 200. £4.95.

[31] *Literary Gent*, by David Higham. New York: Coward, McCann & Geoghegan Inc. pp. x + 334. $12.50.

[32] *Biographical Dictionaries and Related Works: An International Bibliography of Collective Biographies, Bio-bibliographies, Collections of Epitaphs, Selected Genealogical Works, Dictionaries of Anonyms and Pseudonyms, Historical and Specialized Dictionaries, Biographical Materials in Government Manuals, Bibliographies of Biography, Biographical Indexes, and Selected Portrait Catalogs*. Second Supplement, ed. by Robert B. Slocum. Detroit: Gale Research Co. pp. xviii + 922. $35.

It is good that such a work as this should be made as full and accurate as possible when research reveals new or up-to-date information.

The Gale Research Company continues its useful series of literary information guides with *English Fiction 1660-1800*[33], compiled by Jerry C. Beasley. This provides nearly 1,500 entries noting valuable sources for research into the fictional literature of the period covered. The first part lists general and comprehensive sources of background information. The second part is devoted to twenty-nine individual authors of the stature of Bunyan, Defoe, Fielding, Goldsmith, Johnson, Sterne and Swift. Listed for each author are principal works, editions, collections of letters and diaries, biographies, bibliographies and critical studies. Students of the first great period of the English novel will find this a very helpful volume.

Another useful bibliographical series is *English and American Studies in German*[34], which has appeared annually for the past ten years under the editorship of Werner Habicht. Like its predecessors, the present issue offers summaries in English of books and dissertations which appeared during the year preceding its publication. Averaging rather more than two pages in length, these summaries give a very clear indication of the nature of the works treated, almost invariably sufficient to enable the reader to determine whether it will be worth his while to seek out the originals.

Two further volumes of *Bookman's Price Index*[35] have been issued, containing between them about 100,000 entries for books listed in recent catalogues prepared by fifty-odd English and American dealers in rare books. The entries, arranged alphabetically, supply, among other bibliographical information, the authors' names, the titles, descriptions of the books and their condition, and the prices at which the books were offered. These large tomes will be of special value to dealers and librarians, but they are not without interest for amateur collectors and other people interested in books.

5. Miscellaneous

Laurence J. Peter's *Quotations for Our Time*[36] is a very large collection of what the blurb calls 'gems of brevity, wit and originality relevant to the problems of today', arranged alphabetically under several hundred headings, presumably to facilitate the discovery of an apposite quotation or two for an after-dinner speech or a political oration. Although the quotations are drawn from many nations and periods, the great majority come from the present century, and betoken very wide reading (and very diligent copying) on the part of the compiler. However, the brevity is rather more in evidence than the wit, or indeed the originality, and it is difficult to

[33] *English Fiction 1660-1800: A Guide to Information Sources*, by Jerry C. Beasley. Detroit: Gale Research Co. pp. xvi + 313. $18.

[34] *English and American Studies in German: Summaries of Theses and Monographs*, ed. by Werner Habicht. Tübingen: Niemeyer. pp. xiv + 218.

[35] *Bookman's Price Index: A Guide to the Values of Rare and Other Out-of-Print Works*, ed. by Daniel F. McGrath. Vol. 13, pp. x + 734; Vol. 14, pp. x + 756. Detroit: Gale Research Co. Each vol. $64.

[36] *Quotations for Our Time*, compiled by Laurence J. Peter. Souvenir Press. pp. 540. £5.95.

feel that the volume will provide the agreeable bed-time browsing that one expects from a dictionary of quotations.

With the help of a research team of seventeen co-adjutors, Justin Wintle and Richard Kenin have compiled *The Dictionary of Biographical Quotation of British and American Subjects*[37]. Their aim is 'to give an impression of the rich diversity of the things people have written and said about one another'. The qualities they have looked for are 'critical or psychological acuity, lively satire, ingenious wit or good humour, articulate calumny or delicious malice, . . . fine reflection and original perspective'. As a rule the quotations manifest one or other of these qualities, though many appear pretty pointless. Some thousands of subjects, none of them living, are included, and the quotations run in number from one or two for such figures as Henry Knox or Dolly Payne Madison (was either worth mentioning?) to more than a hundred for Shakespeare (could even so many do him justice?), in length from two or three words (son énorme fumier' – Voltaire on Shakespeare) to half a column, and in time-span from the Venerable Bede to Malcolm X. Every reader will note both many felicities and many surprising omissions. About forty quotations are taken from Thomas Fuller, but he himself is not given an entry – and what a fascinating one there could have been! On Piers Gaveston, where is the epitaph on the monument which stands on the spot near Kenilworth where he was slain 'by barons lawless as himself'? And so the list might go on. But of course there is much to be enjoyed in this substantial volume. The editors, however, deserve a black mark for their slipshod proof-reading.

Himself a poet and the Oxford Professor of Poetry, John Wain might be expected to put together an especially interesting anthology of poetry. This he has done in *Personal Choice*[38]. Obviously from the breadth of his reading he could have compiled a fascinating anthology of many thousands of pages; but, limited to about two hundred pages, he has managed, without going much beyond poets whom we all love, to select not only many of the 'obvious' passages, but also many of which we at once say, 'Of course, but why hasn't this been in the anthologies before?'.

Denis Wood's *Poets in the Garden*[39] is another of the more satisfying anthologies of the year. As its title suggests, it is made up of (mainly verse) passages about gardens, particularly garden flowers, and more particularly flowers as they are seen by lovers to reflect the beauty or the virtues of their loved ones. Wood has spread his net widely, and has culled his flowers from all periods of English poetry, varied by an occasional passage of prose (usually from the Bible) or of verse in a European langauge; and he has gone beyond the obvious 'anthology-pieces' to include passages from such less well-known, but nevertheless attractive, poets as James Hurdis, R. S. Hawker, H. D. Rawnsley, and Agnes Mary Frances Robinson. His volume is embellished with beautiful reproductions of old prints.

How does one assess the quality of 'light verse', or its success in achieving

[37] *The Dictionary of Biographical Quotation of British and American Subjects*, ed. by Justin Wintle and Richard Kenin. Routledge & Kegan Paul. pp. xviii + 860. £10.50.

[38] *Personal Choice: A Poetry Anthology*, ed. by John Wain. Newton Abbot, Devon: David & Charles. pp. 224. £4.95.

[39] *Poets in the Garden: An Anthology of Garden Verse*, compiled by Denis Wood. John Murray. pp. 127. £2.95.

what it sets out to do? 'To raise a good-natured smile was the major part of this work written', said Charles Dibdin in his *Comic Tales and Lyrical Fancies* of 1825. Kingsley Amis has had no easy task in producing a successor[40] to W. H. Auden's *Oxford Book of Light Verse* published in 1938, but it is difficult not to feel that he has done a better job than Auden in putting together a collection of verses that 'raise a good-natured smile'. He goes back no earlier than Shakespeare, and probably two-thirds of his passages date from the present century; and perhaps he has shown too great a fondness for indecorous limericks. Never mind. He has discovered some gems from such unlikely sources as Samuel Wesley ('A Pindaric on the Grunting of a Hog'), Benjamin Franklin, Hartley Coleridge, Lord Tennyson and Thomas Hardy, and in the twentieth century he must have had to reject dozens of worthy candidates; but he has found room for generous selections from such masters of the genre as Robert Graves, T. S. Eliot, John Betjeman, W. H. Auden and Philip Larkin. Every reader will miss favourites (for example, a number of poems in *The Oxford Book of English Verse* which are serious in intention but ludicrously 'light' in effect), but every one will discover with delight a number of poems he would have been glad to have thought of had he been invited to compile a new book of English light verse.

Published at the beginning of 1930 by D. B. Wyndham Lewis, enlarged later in the same year with the help of Charles Lee, and further enlarged in 1948, *The Stuffed Owl*[41], one of the great classics among English anthologies, has at long last been given certainty of immortal renown by its inclusion in Everyman's Libary. It is not necessary to do much more than remind readers that this is an anthology of 'good Bad Verse', a term which is illuminatingly defined by Lewis in a long preface. The collection includes gems from the writings of almost all the acknowledged great English poets since the mid-seventeenth century, as well as of such largely neglected 'masters' as Martin Farquhar Tupper, Cornelius Whur, and Thomas Haynes Bayly. Some readers will probably be surprised at the omission of bad poems which are favourites of their own, such, perhaps, as those of the Homer of the North, William McGonagall, or, from *The Oxford Book of English Verse*, Frederick Locker-Lampson's 'At Her Window'. But we can't have everything. Among the delights of the volume are the biographical notes ('Of Chatterton it is said that after the composition, at the age of ten, of an Ode on the Last Judgment he became more cheerful than he had formerly been'). The only regrettable thing about this edition is that the eight cartoons by Max Beerbohm with which the original edition was embellished have not been included.

It might be felt that Oxford has over the centuries been adequately pictured in English literature. But can Oxford in all its multifarious aspects be adequately pictured – in how many pages of writing? In *The Oxford Book of Oxford*[42] Jan Morris offers us four hundred pages of tributes, old

[40] *The New Oxford Book of English Light Verse*, chosen by Kingsley Amis. O.U.P. pp. xxxvi + 347.

[41] *The Stuffed Owl: An anthology of bad verse*, selected and arranged by D. B. Wyndham Lewis and Charles Lee. Dent (Everyman's Library). pp. xxxi + 264. £3.95.

[42] *The Oxford Book of Oxford*, chosen and ed. by Jan Morris. O.U.P. pp. xii + 402.

and new, to the Oxford that so many of us carry in our hearts' cores. Her delightful anthology is roughly chronological. It begins with the founding fathers in the thirteenth century, with their faith that the university, or at any rate the city, was probably established in Biblical times, and brings us forward to (and beyond) the famous Oxford Union debate of 1933, 'That this House will in no circumstances fight for its King and Country' – that momentous debate that so grievously misled Ambassador Joseph Kennedy and his compatriots, and Hitler and his compatriots, into interpreting a decision based on academic debating skills as a declaration of intent of the British nation. Between these early and late outlooks Jan Morris has fitted many hundreds of observations on Oxford as it has appeared to writers of many centuries. This is an anthology that Oxonians in particular, but not only Oxonians, will greatly enjoy.

Not many years ago the hope was expressed in this chapter that the flood of translations of Catullus by which we were at that time being overwhelmed would soon be stemmed. There has, indeed, been a lull, but it is difficult not to be troubled by the appearance of a new version by Frederic Raphael and Kenneth McLeish[43]. Catullus is a poet of many moods and many nuances of feeling. These translators have captured very little of him. Where he is virulent or obscene they seldom rise above vulgarity. Where he is delicate, graceful, tender (any of the things suggested by his favourite word *venustus*), they are seldom better than awkward and pedestrian. Could there be anything much more ham-fisted than this rendering of the famous *Odi et amo* epigram:

> I hate and I love. Why do that? Good question.
> No answer, save 'I do'. Nailed through either hand?

In the nine lines of his 'Row us out from Desenzano' Tennyson conveys more of the 'feel' of Catullus – or at any rate one half of him – than the whole of this volume, or, for that matter, all the post-war translations put together.

[43] *The Poems of Catullus*, translated by Frederic Raphael and Kenneth McLeish. Jonathan Cape. pp. 120. £3.50.

II

English Language

RICHARD M. HOGG and MARY BRENNAN

This chapter is divided into two sections. The first, by Richard Hogg, deals with historical studies, including the history of linguistics, and all dialectological and lexicographical material, whether historical or not, as well as linguistic studies bearing on the literary use of English. In the second section Mary Brennan deals with descriptive studies, all general bibliographical material, and all publications in cognate fields of enquiry relevant to the English scholar.

Section I

(a) Introductory

In comparison with 1977, the current year appears to have produced a much more even spread of work across the subject areas. Thus the concern expressed in *YW* 58 over the lack of work, especially in syntax, but also in all aspects of the Middle English period, must be at least temporarily abated by both the quantity and the quality of the relevant work which I have encountered this year. It is clear, however, that work on aspects of vocabulary far outweighs that on any other part of the field. Without wishing to deny the value of much of that work, whether or not such an imbalance is altogether desirable must be considered. Might it not, distressingly, be a sign of a retreat by many historical linguists and philologists from the areas which have been invaded by current theoretical linguistics into an area which is thought to be 'safe'? This cannot be helpful to anyone.

If the community of scholars can be viewed as an army, then there is no doubt that the bibliographers in it form its catering corps. And this year we have been fed on rather thin gruel. The only work which I have seen is Russell Becker's 'Materials for English Historical Linguistics: an Annotated Bibliography of Concordances' (*JEngL*, Vol. 12, pp. 1–11), which lists 61 concordances from one for *Beowulf* up to one for Stephen Crane. A bare minimum of information is given about each. I have seen no more than a reference to a bibliography of histories of linguistic thought by E. F. K. Koerner[1], which must be one of the series of rather variable bibliographies coming from the Dutch publisher John Benjamins.

For a general indication of the amount of work being done in the fields of Old and Middle English, we may turn as usual to the annual research in progress lists in *NM*. It is good to see that all three lists show an increase

[1] *Western Histories of Linguistic Thought, 1822–1976: an Annotated Chronological Bibliography*, ed. by E. F. K. Koerner. Amsterdam: John Benjamins.

in language work. Thus Carl T. Berkhout, in 'Old English Research in Progress 1977–1978' (Vol. 79, pp. 291–300) lists two items under *Language Studies* (one of which is a dissertation), one under *Prosody* and no fewer than ten items under *Word Studies*. 'Middle English Research in Progress' (Vol. 79, pp. 403–410), the care of which has been transferred from R. H. Robbins to P. J. Horner, L. C. Gruber and B. J. Harvood, (which has been consequently rearranged so that most studies appear under the headings of individual Middle English works) has one item under the heading *Philological*, two under *Middle Scots* and two under *General Studies*, a total of five, and hence an improvement of five over last year. In 'Chaucer Research in Progress 1977–1978' (Vol. 79, pp. 301–306) Thomas A. Kirby reports six items under *Prosody and Language*, thus tripling last year's return. All in all, this is a highly encouraging contrast with what I had to report in *YW* 58. Carl T. Berkhout, of course, also compiles the annual bibliography of materials published on Old English language in *ASE* ('Bibliography for 1977, §2: Old English Language', Vol. 7, pp. 271–276), where there are about 110 entries, roughly in line with last year, although it should be pointed out that many of the entries refer to publications of an earlier date.

In what follows the material is divided under the following heads (which differ slightly from last year): (b) general; (c) history of linguistics; (d) dialectology; (e) phonology/orthography; (f) syntax/morphology; (g) vocabulary; (h) onomastics; (i) stylistics. Within each division general works come first, followed by chronologically restricted works in historical sequence.

(b) General

Three extremely well-known general introductions to linguistics and aspects of English language have appeared this year in new editions. We discuss them below not merely in the order general to particular, but also in the order 'virtually unchanged' to 'greatly changed'. Thus the most important feature of the new edition of Leonard R. Palmer's *Descriptive and Comparative Linguistics*[2] is that it is a paperback edition at a price which the average undergraduate will be able to afford. The text of the book, however, is fundamentally unchanged from the 1972 edition. Despite the addition of a second author, Thomas Cable, the third edition of Albert C. Baugh's *History of the English Language*[3] will be all too familiar to many readers. The major changes, such as they are, are to be found in Chapter Two on the Indo-European family and in the final chapter on English in America, where recent trends are reflected by the considerable discussion of Black English. But other areas have been left as they were, including such topics as Middle English dialects, where the work of McIntosh and Samuels is represented by no more than a single footnote. This is only one of the many pieces of evidence which demonstrates that the anti-linguistic bias of the earlier editions remains as strong as ever (despite ritualistic obeisance to Chomsky from time to time). It

[2] *Descriptive and Comparative Linguistics: a Critical Introduction*, by Leonard R. Palmer. Faber & Faber. pp. 430. pb £3.95.

[3] *A History of the English Language*. Third Edition, by Albert C. Baugh and Thomas Cable. Routledge & Kegan Paul. pp. xvi + 438. hb £7, pb £3.95.

must also be pointed out that since the authors have replaced the old map of the counties of England with a new map showing the post-1974 administrative regions, they should therefore have changed references such as 'Westmorland' to 'Cumbria'. Since they have not, the American reader, and possibly many British ones too, will be hopelessly confused. Finally here we should note a third, posthumous, edition of Sidney J. Baker's *The Australian Language*[4]. A comparison with the original 1945 edition shows many changes and additions. I do not have access to the second (1966) edition, but the internal evidence suggests that not a great many changes have been made in the past twelve years. The Australian publishers indicate that they wish to keep revising this standard work in the light of new information which is sent to them.

Two dauntingly massive collections of papers appeared this year. Mohammed Ali Jazayery, Edgar C. Polomé and Werner Winter have edited a four-volume *Festschrift* for Archibald Hill[5], and papers by Bammesberger, Dyen, Hall, Hamp, King, Kuryłowicz, Ruth Lehmann, Lepschy, Levin, Olmsted, Szemerenyi and Vennemann contained therein will be referred to (via the running title *Hill-Festschrift*[5]) under the appropriate headings below. The other collection also stretches over four volumes, and this is *Universals of Human Language*, edited by Joseph H. Greenberg[6]. This collection is the result of the Stanford University Project on Linguistic Universals, but despite Greenberg's interest in typology, these four volumes contain far more material of interest to the synchronic linguist than to the diachronic linguist, and therefore will be discussed in section two of this chapter. Another *Festschrift*, this time of rather more normal size, is that presented to the Swedish Anglicist Alarik Rynell and edited by Mats Ryden and Lennart Björk[7]. Articles of interest in this collection include those by Jacobson, Lindkvist, Löfvenberg, Melchers, Ryden and Wijk, and these will be noted (via the running title *Rynell-Festschrift*[7]) under the appropriate headings below.

Three other works do not fall into any convenient category. In 'What Are We Going to Do about It Now That We're Number One?' (*AS*, Vol. 53, pp. 169–198), James Sledd characteristically throws some well-aimed tomahawks at current linguistic totem-poles, not only in the field of dialectology but also in general linguistic theory. Isidore Dyen ('Subgrouping and Reconstruction', *Hill-Festschrift*[5], Vol. 3, pp. 33–52), argues cogently that it is necessary to subgroup language families in order to reconstruct the parent language, and that subgrouping is not an activity to be undertaken only after the parent language has been reconstructed. Finally, since the book will primarily be used by those studying Old English language, we ought to mention a second edition of Henry Sweet's

[4] *The Australian Language*, Third Edition, by Sidney J. Baker. Milson's Point, N.S.W.: Currawong Press; London: Hutchinson. pp. xiv + 517. £12.

[5] *Linguistic and Literary Studies in Honor of Archibald A. Hill*, 4 Vols., ed. by Mohammed Ali Jazayery, Edgar C. Polome and Werner Winter. The Hague: Mouton. pp. 412, 363, 374, 392.

[6] *Universals of Human Language*, 4 Vols., ed. by Joseph H. Greenberg. Stanford, Calif.: Stanford U.P.

[7] *Studies in English Philology, Linguistics and Literature Presented to Alarik Rynell*, ed. by Mats Ryden and Lennart A. Björk. Stockholm Studies in English, 46. Stockholm: Almqvist & Wiksell. pp. 187.

A Second Anglo-Saxon Reader, revised by T. F. Hoad[8]. Despite the fact that all the texts have been rechecked and amended in the light of this century's scholarship and that some texts have been replaced by others, the new edition has some unfortunate deficiencies from a purely practical point of view. Firstly, there is far too much overlap with the Whitelock edition of Sweet's *Reader*, especially in the case of both early and late Northumbrian texts. Could not, for example, some other extract from *The Lindisfarne Gospels* have been chosen? Secondly, not only is there no glossary, which is arguably unnecessary in such a book, there is not even an *index verborum*, which would have been of immense help to the linguistic student. This looks like a most unfortunate case of penny-pinching.

(c) History of Linguistics

Clearly the most important work in this area during 1978 is to be found in *TPS* 1978, which takes the form of a commemorative volume to celebrate the centenary of the Neogrammarian movement. The papers which will probably be of most interest to the historical linguist are: R. H. Robbins, 'The Neogrammarians and Their Nineteenth-Century Predecessors' (pp. 1–16), Henry M. Hoenigswald, 'The *Annus Mirabilis* 1876 and Posterity' (pp. 17–35), and Anna Morpurgo Davies, 'Analogy, Segmentation and the Early Neogrammarians' (pp. 36–60). It may be only a matter of personal interest that I found Morpurgo Davies' paper especially valuable, since all three papers display an enviably high level of scholarship and intellect. Furthermore, the other papers, by W. S. Allen, T. Bynon and N. E. Collinge, must also be required reading.

Turning back now almost to the beginnings of linguistics in the West, in 'Apollonius Dyscolus: a Pioneer of Western Grammar' (*EWIP*, Vol. 11, pp. 107–119) Alan Kemp offers an introduction to and brief summary of one of the most important of Greek grammarians. Kemp relates Apollonius' work to that of Thrax and points out where he has interesting insights of his own into the structure of language, although, according to Kemp, at best these are cloaked in a somewhat obscure style.

A considerable amount of work has been published this year on the grammarians of the Renaissance and the seventeenth century. In chronological order we have first Viljo Kohanen's 'On the Development of an Awareness of English Syntax in Early (1550–1660) Descriptions of Word Order by English Grammarians, Logicians and Rhetoricians' (*NM*, Vol. 79, pp. 44–58). Kohanen seems rather too eager to ascribe intelligent awareness of problems of word-order to the early writers whom he discusses, and hence the article is not fully convincing. In 'Linguistic Speculations of Edward Brerewood (1566–1613)' (*Hill-Festschrift*[5], Vol. 1, pp. 257–262) John A. Rea claims that Brerewood shows considerable refinement for his time in his discussion of the evolution of the Romance languages. Joseph L. Subbiodo ('William Holder's *Elements of Speech* (1669)', *Lingua*, Vol. 46, pp. 169–184) provides an enthusiastic but somewhat thin study of Holder's work as a phonetician and teacher of the deaf.

Moving forward to the eighteenth century, Ulrich Ricken's *Grammaire*

[8] *A Second Anglo-Saxon Reader*, Second Edition, by Henry Sweet, revd. by T. F. Hoad. Oxford: Clarendon Press. pp. xii + 237. £7.50.

et Philosophie au Siècle des Lumières[9] is a survey of the debate amongst French linguists and philosophers of the time on the relationship between the 'natural' order of thoughts and the order of words in natural languages, especially as they were reflected in French as opposed to Latin word order. Ricken concentrates on the debates between empiricists such as Condillac and rationalists such as Du Marsais. He also provides a useful and extensive bibliography. In 'Sir William Jones: a New Perspective on the Origin and Background of His *Common Source*' (*GUP*, Vol. 14, pp. 1–68), Robert J. Kispert demonstrates at length that the so-called 'discoverer of Sanskrit' was by no means as original in his thinking as has often been supposed and that, indeed, he had no great interest in philology as such.

Aside from the *TPS* volume mentioned above, we should note that Claudine Normand has edited an issue of the periodical *Langages* entitled *Saussure et la Linguistique Pré-Saussurienne*[10]. The editor supplies an introduction, P. Caussat writes on Saussure and the Neogrammarians. C. Puech and A. Radzynski consider language as a social phenomenon, J.-L. Chiss considers the nature of the dichotomy between synchrony and diachrony, and I. Hombert looks at Saussure's American contemporary William D. Whitney. 'Some Aspects of Baudouin de Courtenay as Book-Reviewer' (*Hill-Festschrift*, Vol. 1, pp. 227–232), by D. L. Omsted, is a rather slight account of de Courtenay's reviewing activities. When we reach the present century, two papers stand out as especially interesting. Giulio C. Lepschy ('Changes of Emphasis in Modern Linguistics', *Hill-Festschrift*[5], Vol. 1, pp. 189–199) highlights the point that many alleged 'histories of linguistics' are in fact quests for one's intellectual ancestors and that the problem of how best to study the phenomenon of language historically remains unsolved. Finally, William Haas, in 'Linguistics 1930–1980' (*JL*, Vol. 14, pp. 293–308), gives a highly critical, but typically Haasian and by no means unsympathetic, view of the impact of generative grammar on linguistics and the recent confusion, as he sees it, between pragmatics and semantics.

(d) Dialectology

Firstly we may give at least a qualified welcome to a new edition of G. L. Brook's well-known introductory work, *English Dialects*[11]. Unfortunately, like so many other 'new' editions, this represents little more than a reprinting of earlier editions, for, apart from some updating of the bibliography, there are no obvious changes. On a more theoretical level, Raven I. McDavid Jr, in 'The Gathering and Presentation of Data' (*JEngL*, Vol. 12, pp. 29–37), is especially interesting on the different approaches made towards presentation and publication of the several U.S. regional dialect atlases. More on the theory of dialectology from an American point of view seems to be promised by Ann Louise Sen's 'Reconstructing Early American Dialects' (*JEngL*, Vol. 12, pp. 50–62), but regrettably the paper

[9] *Grammaire et Philosophie au Siècle des Lumières*, by Ulrich Ricken. Villeneuve d'Ascq: Publications de l'Université de Lille III. pp. 241.

[10] *Saussure et la Linguistique Pré-Saussurienne*, ed. by Claudine Normand. *Langages*, Vol. 49.

[11] *English Dialects*, Third Edition, by G. L. Brook. The Language Library. André Deutsch. pp. 232.

represents little more than a fairly elementary first-year undergraduate lecture.

For the dialects of the Old English period it is natural to turn first to further work by Alan S. C. Ross on the late Northumbrian dialects. On this occasion ('A Point of Comparison between Aldred's Two Glosses', *N&Q*, Vol. 223, pp. 197–199) Ross compares the only passage which is glossed in both *The Durham Ritual* and *The Lindisfarne Gospels* and he concludes that the major difference between the two glosses lies in the vocabulary used. This leads conveniently to two papers by German authors. Much the more weighty of the two is 'Kritische Bemerkungen zu Angaben über die Verbreitung einiger angeblich westsächsischer Dialektwörter' (*Anglia*, Vol. 96, pp. 5–44) by Franz Wenisch. Wenisch considers nine words which have previously been considered to be West Saxon in origin and he shows, with both considerable documentary evidence and considerable repetition, that they were all of common Old English origin. It is worth noting that tucked into this article is an expanded version of the Mitchell, Ball and Cameron list of short titles for Old English texts, which the editors of *Anglia* say will be used from now on in that periodical. Why, then, were they not extracted from the article and placed in a more prominent position? Bernhard Diensberg, in 'Westsächsischer Lehnwörter in Merzischen AB-Dialekt?' (*Anglia*, Vol. 96, pp. 447–450) reject the possibility of a West Saxon origin for a number of verbal forms with 'unexpected' *u* in their roots and suggests instead that such *u*'s are the result of various morphological reformations.

As we move further into the Middle English period we still remain with vocabulary, for in 'The Middle English Poem *The Four Foes of Mankind*' (*NM*, Vol. 79, pp. 137–144) Angus McIntosh analyses the lexis of the originally Northern poem and shows it to have been remarkably faithfully copied by its London scribe, who even preserved words which had little or no currency in the South. Elizabeth S. Sklar's 'The Dialect of Arthour and Merlin' (*ELN*, Vol. 15, pp. 88–94) contains a somewhat unlikely ascription of a Sussex origin to this romance.

The major publication this year concerning present-day dialects is undoubtedly *The Linguistic Atlas of England*, edited by Harold Orton, Stewart Sanderson and John Widdowson[12]. The atlas contains 249 phonological maps, sixty-five lexical maps, eighty-three morphological maps and nine syntactic maps. All the maps are commendably clear, with the one general exception that areas separate from the principal isoglosses are far from clearly marked: compare here Barbara Strang's remarks on *A Word Geography of England* (*YW* 55.49–50). A comparison with the *Linguistic Atlas of Scotland* where the two atlases overlap once again emphasises the greater range of responses that the Scottish team were able to elicit with their different research techniques, and this, together with the clarity of presentation mentioned above makes one wonder whether the English atlas does not give an impression of a non-existent uniformity. In the end I think one's doubts are allayed, but it is interesting to compare the seven lexical maps which this new atlas and the *Word Geography* have in common. There is much more detail here, and the consequent difference in

[12] *The Linguistic Atlas of England*, by Harold Orton, Stewart Sanderson and John Widdowson. Croom Helm.

isogloss patterning is quite startling. This and other points can be usefully followed up in W. Nelson Francis' review of *Word Geography* (*AS*, Vol. 53, pp. 221–231). Finally, we may note two U.S. dialect studies. In 'Perspectives for a Linguistic Atlas of Kansas' (*AS*, Vol. 53, pp. 199–209) Albert B. Cook III outlines the history of past and present surveys of an area largely neglected by American dialectologists, whilst Timothy C. Frazer ('South Midland Pronunciation in the North Central States', *AS*, Vol. 53, pp. 40–48) examines the isoglosses of various diphthongal forms in the North Central States of the U.S.A. as part of a dialect boundary between the Northern and Midland dialect areas.

(e) Phonology/orthography

In what has been a very satisfactory year for phonological studies, we should first mention the collection of papers given at the International Conference on Historical Phonology held in Poland in 1976, which has been published under the editorship of Jacek Fisiak as *Recent Developments in Historical Phonology*[13]. Almost all the papers are of very high quality, but perhaps special note should be taken of Roger Lass' 'Mapping Constraints in Phonological Reconstruction: on Climbing down Trees without Falling out of Them' (pp. 245–286). Here Lass concentrates on the problem of how, given a reconstructed form and its reflexes in a set of cognate languages, one can determine 'appropriate pathways' between the reconstruction and the reflexes. Lass provides a stimulating analysis of many crucial problems in historical linguistics. Other papers here of major interest to the Anglicist and historical linguist include those by DeKeyser, Harris, Hoenigswald, Tops, Valentin and Vincent. For the specialist undergraduate Philip Baldi and Ronald N. Werth have edited *Readings in Historical Phonology: Chapters in the Theory of Sound Change*[14], an anthology of sixteen reprinted papers or extracts from larger works. The collection is divided into three sections, covering the neogrammarians, the structuralists and the generativists, and each section is preceded by a brief and scarcely adequate introduction. However the choice of papers, from Paul and Verner up to Kiparsky and Labov, is very good. Where necessary, papers have been translated into English, although not always very happily. English translations of three major works (partly condensed) in Nordic linguistics are to be found in *On Dating Phonological Change*, edited by Thomas L. Markey[15]. The papers are by Axel Kock, Lennart Moberg and Ernst Wigforss, and many readers will be glad to see them in an easily accessible form, even if one has to put up with some purple passages in an otherwise useful introduction.

There are a number of single articles of general interest. Bh. Khrishnamurti ('Areal and Lexical Diffusion of Sound Change', *Lg*, Vol. 54, pp. 1–20) examines a major case of lexical diffusion in a subgroup of the

[13] *Recent Developments in Historical Phonology*, ed. by Jacek Fisiak. Trends in Linguistics, Studies and Monographs, 4. The Hague: Mouton. pp. xi + 455.

[14] *Readings in Historical Phonology: Chapters in the Theory of Sound Change*, ed. by Philip Baldi and Ronald N. Werth. University Park, Penn.: Pennsylvania State U.P. pp. 376. £10.15.

[15] *On Dating Phonological Change*, ed. by Thomas L. Markey. Linguistica Extranea, 1. Ann Arbor, Mich.: Karome Publishers. pp. xxviii + 85.

Dravidian family, and his discussion of such key questions as what we mean by the concept of 'shared innovation' will interest all historical phonologists. In 'Putting the Dynamic into Sound Change' (*LingB*, Vol. 56, pp. 44–52) Charles V. J. Russ takes another look at Early Modern and Modern English sound changes in the light of work by Samuels and Lass. Theo Vennemann's 'Vowel Alternations in English, German and Gothic: Remarks on Realism in Phonology' (*Hill-Festschrift*[5], Vol. 1, pp. 337–359) is most interesting for being a very early (1971) advocacy of Natural Generative Phonology. Robert D. King ('Rule Replication', *Hill-Festschrift*[5], Vol. 1, pp. 175–182) suggests that where similar or identical 'rules' reappear in a language at different stages of its evolution, this may be due to surface-phonetic constraints, but the discussion is most remarkable for containing no data.

Turning now specifically to English, Alan S. C. Ross gives, in 'The Variation of Initial [k] and [g] in English' (*N&Q*, Vol. 223, pp. 339–343), what is primarily a listing of words in English where there is variation between these two sounds. I failed to understand why there was no mention of forms such as *can/gan*. With regard to Old English phonology readers of last year's *YW* may recall a promise to discuss here Suk-San Kim's *A History of the Vowels of Early (West Saxon) Old English*[16]. Despite its Korean publishers, this work is basically a Michigan dissertation dating from 1967. This, of course, correctly implies that it is an extremely detailed and thorough study, in this case of the graphemes and phonemes of the manuscripts of the *Pastoral Care*, especially the Hatton manuscript. Dr Kim concentrates on the vocalic and diphthongal phonemes of this manuscript and the result is what will become, if used in conjuction with Cosijn's grammar, an essential reference work. In 'Rounding and Fronting in Old English Phonology' (*Lingua*, Vol. 46, pp. 157–168) Charles Jones argues that several Old English sound changes, from Breaking and *i*-Umlaut through to Anglian Smoothing should be viewed as phonetically homogeneous, and in 'The Duke of York Gambit: a Variation' (*Lingua*, Vol. 44, pp. 255–266) there are some further remarks by Richard M. Hogg which still leave the problems surrounding this sound change no nearer to a solution.

There is very little to note for the Middle English period, but Gillis Kristensson ('A Note on OE /e:ow/ and OFr /y/ in Middle English', *SN*, Vol. 50, pp. 25–27) must surely be right when he argues, following Luick and against Jordan, for an early date for the merger of ME /eu/ and /iu/. Judith Grant, C. Peterson and Alan S. C. Ross, in 'Notes on the Rhymes of *Pearl*' (*SN*, Vol. 50, pp. 175–178) give details of various important rhyme-types in that poem, especially concerning open and closed *e* and *o* and between long and short vowels. The data are largely uninterpreted.

For the Early Modern period there are two useful book-length works, both (almost inevitably?) from Sweden. Bror Danielsson gives us the second part of his *Sir Thomas Smith, Literary and Linguistic Works*[17],

[16] *A History of the Vowels of Early (West Saxon) Old English*, by Suk-San Kim. Seoul: Pan-Korea Book Corp. pp. 272. . US $4.58.

[17] *Sir Thomas Smith, Literary and Linguistic Works, II: De Recta et Emendata Linguae Graecae Pronuntiatione*, ed. and trans. by Bror Danielsson. Stockholm Studies in English, 50. Stockholm: Almqvist & Wiksell. pp. 218.

which contains a translation of Smith's important treatise on the pronunciation of Greek. The relevance of this for the history of English phonology is clearly brought out by a useful, if brief, index. Then, in *Richard Hodges's "The English Primrose" (1644)*[18], Torkel Nöjd presents an exhaustive study of Hodges's treatment of the stressed vowels and diphthongs. This book is, in fact, a doctoral dissertation, and it is not easy to consult, but Nöjd is especially interesting in his discussion of the evolution of /ai/ in Hodges's speech. Two more theoretical articles are worth mentioning. In 'Phonological Constraints and Sound Changes' (*Glossa*, Vol. 12, pp. 125–136) Marianne Cooley interestingly relates loss of initial /kn/ and /gn/ sequences in Early Modern English to surface phonetic constraints operating in the language at the time and thence to the contemporaneous rise of the sequence /juw/. Harald Tzeutschler ('Towards Concreteness in the Description of Early Modern English Vowel Alternations', *JL*, Vol. 14, pp. 207–225) attacks the abstractness of the Chomsky–Halle account of Hart and Wallis, but he does so in such a mechanical fashion that even if one wishes to sympathise with him, it is difficult to follow him all the way.

Turning now to orthographical studies, I have not had the opportunity to see what may very well be a most interesting study, namely *L'orthographie de l'Anglais* by Georges Bourcier[19]. Michael A. Howard's *The Runes and Other Magical Alphabets*[20] is so naive and credulous, and displays so unhealthy an interest in the occult, that it can safely be recommended to no one. (I must admit, however, to having particularly enjoyed reading about the Old English rune 'Porn' and also the Old English poem 'The Husband's Wife'.) On a rather more prosaic level we may mention a rather slight discussion of Milton's prose pronunciation by Thomas N. Corns ('Punctuation in Milton's Vernacular Prose', *N&Q*, Vol. 223, pp. 18–19) and Mark Aronoff's suggestion that *–or*, *–our* and *–er* in British English possibly distinguish various morphosyntactic features ('An English Spelling Convention', *LingI*, Vol. 9, pp. 299–303) Finally, Axel Wijk enters another plea for the teaching of a reformed spelling system in 'Regularized English: A Proposal for an Effective Solution of the English Reading Problem' (*Rynell-Festschrift*[7], pp. 170–178).

(f) Syntax/Morphology

The current fashion for typological studies could not hope to find a more archetypical expression than that in *Syntactic Typology*, edited by Winfred P. Lehmann[21]. No doubt the articles of most interest to readers of *YW* will be the editor's own article on English as a 'characteristic SVO language', together with the introduction and the conclusion, both again by Lehmann. The title of the introduction – 'The Great Underlying Ground-Plans' – serves as an accurate warning that Lehmann appears to

[18] *Richard Hodges's 'The English Primrose' (1644)*, by Torkel Nöjd. Stockholm Studies in English, 45. Stockholm: Almqvist & Wiksell. pp. xxiv + 194.

[19] *L'orthographe de l'Anglais*, by Georges Bourcier. Paris: Presses Universitaires de France. pp. 253.

[20] *The Runes and Other Magical Alphabets*, by Michael A. Howard. Wellingborough, Northants: Thorsons.

[21] *Syntactic Typology*, ed. by Winfred P. Lehmann. Studies in the Phenomenology of Language. Hassocks, Sussex: Harvester Press. pp. xiv + 463. £12.50.

have been carried away by his alleged typological discoveries, many of which, to say the least, are vague and uncertain, and a feeling of scepticism soon overcomes the reader. There are fine papers in this volume, notably by Kuno and Comrie, but they, unfortunately, will be of less interest to the Anglicist.

There are three articles to note concerning particular points in the general history of English syntax. In 'A Diachronic Treatment of English Quantifiers' (*Lingua*, Vol. 46, pp. 295–328) Anita M. Carlson presents an account of quantifiers which is firmly within the type of theory recently presented by David Lightfoot. Carlson here argues that a quantifier category is not needed in the syntactic description of English until the Early Modern period. On the other hand, George B. Jack, in '*Rome's Destruction* and the History of English' (*JL*, Vol. 14, pp. 311–312), corrects a howler in Lightfoot's 1977 paper, see *YW* 58.17). Sven Jacobson uses evidence from adverbs and an unconvincingly abstract analysis to suggest that Old English had SOV word order in 'Adverb Generation in a Historical Perspective' (*Rynell-Festschrift*[7], pp. 64–73).

As usual, Bruce Mitchell has something sensible to say with regard to Old English syntax. In 'Old English *oð þæt* Adverb?' (*N&Q*, Vol. 223, pp. 390–394) he not only supports Eric Stanley's suggestion that *oð þæt* could function as an adverb, but he suggests that the adverbial usage may be original. It is instructive to compare a further paper by Mitchell ('Prepositions, Adverbs, Prepositional Adverbs, Postpositions or Inseparable Prefixes, in Old English', *NM*, Vol. 79, pp. 240–257) with the pseudonymous Jan Vat's 'On Footnote 2: Evidence for the Pronominal Status of *þær* in Old English Relatives' (*LingI*, Vol. 9, pp. 695–716), for the papers are on almost the identical topic, but whereas Mitchell is both extremely cautious and exclusively data-orientated, Vat has the unbounded certaintly only possible in a highly theoretical approach. It would be an interesting exercise to give an extremely good student both papers and see what his reaction was to such diametrically-opposed studies.

Some of the most interesting work for years on Middle English syntax is to be found in three articles by George B. Jack ('Negative Concord in Early Middle English', *SN*, Vol. 50, pp. 29–39); 'Negative Adverbs in Early Middle English', *ES*, Vol. 59, pp. 295–309); 'Negation in Later Middle English Prose', *ArL*, Vol. 9, pp. 58–72). It would be pointless to summarise them here, but it must be said that Jack's combination of an extremely careful approach to the data and a wide knowledge of linguistic theory will revolutionise our knowledge of Middle English negation, and these three articles are essential reading for all. Of much less importance is Joan M. Maling's 'The Complementizer in Middle English Appositives' (*LingI*, Vol. 9, pp. 719–725), although she is quite correct to refute some rather silly claims made by N. Chomsky and H. Lasnik in a 1977 paper in the same periodical. Finally we may note that Dieter Stein ('Counterderivational Constraints on Variable Rules', *LingB*, Vol. 53, pp. 29–37) hides, in somewhat opaque language and theory, evidence to show that *do*-periphrasis in Shakespeare is at least partially controlled by the degree of phonotactic grammaticality of the predicted affix form.

As usual, there is only a thin scattering of work on morphology. In 'On Reconstruction in Morphology' (*Hill-Festschrift*[5], Vol. 3, pp. 267–283)

Oswald Szemerenyi stresses the importance of paradigmatic and systemic relations in morphology, together with interesting insights into the Indo-European personal pronoun system. Perhaps the most interesting work, however, will be Konrad Sprengel's *A Study in Word Formation*[22]. In what was originally a doctoral thesis, Sprengel has taken up the fascinating idea of comparing the history of the prefixes *fore-* and *pre-* in English. The book will be most useful for its empirical observations, but it should also be pointed out that Sprengel has a chapter on the German equivalents of these prefixes and a chapter, rather less useful, on the generative description of such prefixation. Another largely empirical study, this time using the Brown Corpus of present-day American English, is *Semantic Patterns of Noun-Noun Compounds* by Beatrice Warren[23]. This book is most immediately notable for the richness of the data and the statistical analyses of that data, but perhaps of more general interest is Dr Warren's claim that a semantic classification of compounds is possible on a far more extensive scale than has been suggested by, for example, Marchand. Whilst she may be right to argue against great pessimism here, it seems to me that optimism must necessarily be accompanied by brute force. Lastly on the topic of morphology, we may mention the unabashedly feminist approach to language of Julia P. Stanley and Susan W. Robbins in 'Going Through the Changes: the Prounoun *She* in Middle English' *PiL*, Vol. 11, pp. 71–88).

(g) Vocabulary

No one interested in matters lexical could fail to be satisfied with the amount of interesting work which has appeared this year. For example, if we consider the major dictionaries which are currently being published, it is noteworthy that in most cases, even if a part of the dictionary has not been published, there has appeared something relevant to that project. Thus, for Old English, Angus Cameron and Ashley Crandell Amos ('The Dictionary of Old English: a Turning Point', *ES*, Vol. 59, pp. 289–294) have produced an interim report on the progress of the new *D.O.E.* An unlemmatised concordance of all Old English texts in microfiche is promised for 1979 or 1980 and it is hoped that the dictionary itself may appear in the late 1980s. Paralleling this, Jane Roberts, in 'Towards an Old English Thesaurus' (*Poetica*, Vol. 9, pp. 56–72), gives an account of an Old English Thesaurus which is arising out of the work at Glasgow University on a Historical Thesaurus of English. Her reflections on topics such as *hapax legomena* serve only to whet the appetite. For the Middle English period we may note the appearance of another fascicle of the (still erratically distributed) *Middle English Dictionary*[24], which now takes us as far as *muche*.

Richard W. Bailey fills in the next chronological period with *Early Modern English*[25], a provisional collection of 4,400 citations following on

[22] *A Study in Word-Formation*, by Konrad Sprengel. Tübingen: Gunter Narr. 1977. pp. 310. DM 38.

[23] *Semantic Patterns of Noun-Noun Compounds*, by Beatrice Warren. Gothenburg Studies in English, 41. Gothenburg: Acta Universitatis Gothoburgensis. pp. 226. SwCr 60.

[24] *Middle English Dictionary, Part M6 (Moleine – Muche)*, ed. by Sherman M. Kuhn. Ann Arbor, Mich.: U. of Michigan P. 1977. pp. 641–768.

[25] *Early Modern English: Additions and Antedatings to the Record of English Vocabulary, 1475–1700*, ed. by Richard W. Bailey. Hildesheim & New York: Georg Olms. pp. xvii + 367.

from and adding to the *Michigan Early Modern English Materials* published in 1975. This collection is only, of course, a temporary stop-gap, presumably, however, of considerable duration, until a dictionary for the period is possible. Economy and the computer are no doubt jointly responsible for a rather unclear typography. The usefulness of the *Longman Dictionary of Contemporary English,* edited by Paul Procter[26], undoubtedly lies in its sophisticated linguistic approach together with the fact that it uses much of the material collected in *The Survey of English Usage* at University College London. One point which worried me, however, is its heavy emphasis on idioms, not all of which seem correctly labelled. Is it right, for example, to label *have a care* as 'informal' rather than 'archaic'?

Howard G. Zetler has edited a strange creature called *Ologies and Isms: a Thematic Dictionary*[27], which is a dictionary of abstract terms ending not only in *–ology* and *–ism* but also in, for example, *–graphy, –mancy* and *–phobia*. The items are arranged alphabetically within themes. There are many omissions, such as *morphophonology* and *transformationalist* and the definitions are variable. Thus members of the Conservative Party will be as distressed at the definition of *Toryism* as radicals will be at the omission of *sexism*.

Even the 'colonies' assert their lexical independence with two dictionaries. Grahame K. W. Johnston has edited *The Australian Pocket Oxford Dictionary*[28] in a most welcome fashion and Jean Branford's *A Dictionary of South African English*[29], although not designed primarily for the specialist, has such useful features as brief discussions of various syntactic points. In both cases, however, one can detect a slightly excessive zeal for independence, and in the case of the South African Dictionary there are a number of words where Anglicisation seems doubtful, at least to one who has never visited that country.

With so many dictionaries being published it is perhaps as well that there is also a sufficiency of work on lexicography. In *The Theory of English Lexicography 1530–1791* Tetsuro Hayashi[30] gives us a survey from the earliest polyglot and hard word dictionaries through Johnson and concluding with Walker's *Pronouncing Dictionary*. There is some reasonable documentation here, but Hayashi is rather uncritical and unperceptive and he is especially weak on questions of prescriptivism. Rather more interesting on a quite similar topic is Harold B. Allen's 'Samuel Johnson: Originator of Usage Labels' (*Hill-Festschrift*[5], Vol. 4, pp. 193–200).

There are two extremely important works in this year's issue of *American Speech*. In 'American Lexicography, 1945–1973' (*AS*, Vol. 53, pp. 83–140) Clarence L. Barnhart presents a critical review and summary of American dictionaries since the last war, and his judicious comments on

[26] *Longman Dictionary of Contemporary English,* ed. by Paul Procter. Harlow, Essex: Longman. pp. xxxix + 1303.

[27] *–Ologies and –Isms: a Thematic Dictionary*, ed. by Howard G. Zetler. Detroit, Mich.: Gale Research Co. pp. 277.

[28] *The Australian Pocket Oxford Dictionary*, ed. by Grahame K. W. Johnston. Melbourne: Oxford U.P. pp. xxiv + 975. £6.50.

[29] *A Dictionary of South African English*, ed. by Jean Branford. Cape Town: O.U.P. pp. xxvii + 308.

[30] *The Theory of English Lexicography 1530–1791*, by Tetsuro Hayashi. Studies in the History of Linguistics, 18. Amsterdam: John Benjamins. pp. xii + 168. Hfl. 45.

Webster's Third are especially useful. Meanwhile James B. McMillan ('American Lexicology, 1942–1973', *AS*, Vol. 53, pp. 141–163) provides a theoretical companion study to Barnhart, paying special attention to the specific problems of American lexis. One interesting point which arises from Garland Cannon's descriptive survey of the words listed in Merriam-Webster's *6,000 Words* ('Statistical Etymologies of New Words in American English', *JEngL*, Vol. 12, pp. 12–18) is that affixation and compounding account for over half the items, whereas borrowing accounts for only five per cent of the items.

Turning now to etymological studies proper, in 'Indo-European *6*' (*Hill-Festschrift*[5], Vol. 3, pp. 81–90) Eric P. Hamp promisingly reconstructs a single shape for that numeral in Indo-European, namely **ksu̯eks*. Then W. B. Lockwood continues his lexico-ornithological studies with 'The Philology of Auk and Related Matters' (*NM*, Vol. 79, 391–397), where he considers the relation of *auk* to *hawk* and also the proverb 'as drunk as an auk'. There is more on Old English etymology from Alfred Bammesberger: in 'On the Gloss to Matthew 28.8 in *The Lindisfarne Gospels*' (*Hill-Festschrift*, Vol. 3, pp. 9–12) he points out once more that *abloncgne* is most probably an error and that it can hardly be the past participle of some verb **ablangan*, a view still put forward in Campbell's *Grammar*, despite the scepticism expressed a long time ago by Toller. Still on Old English, R. D. Fulk ('Old English *icge* and *incge*', *ES*, Vol. 59, pp. 225–256) argues for the view of Klaeber that these two words in *Beowulf* are etymologically connected.

For Early Modern English, Alan S. C. Ross ('*Morse*', *N&Q*, Vol. 223, p. 533) points out that this word in Caxton meaning 'walrus' is unlikely to have come into English from Lappish via Basque, as suggested by V. Kiparsky. Alan J. Bliss invites us to consider the remarkable complexities of Anglo-Irish etymology in '*Bother* and *Pother*' (*N&Q*, Vol. 223, pp. 536–540). Two examples of folk etymology are discussed in W. Terence Gordon's '*Piggy Bank*: the Name and the Object' (*AS*, Vol. 53, pp. 232–233) and F. G. Cassidy's 'Another Look at *Buckaroo*' (*AS*, Vol. 53, pp. 49–51).

In a reasonable crop of interpretive studies we may mention first Karl-Gunnar Lindkvist's *'At' versus 'On', 'In', 'By'*[31]. The most interesting part of this unfortunately bad-tempered book will be the author's argument that the usage of *at* in Middle English is first and foremost a continuation of Old English usage and that we should not go in search of a source in Old French usage. The other part of this book is concerned with present-day usage of *at*, and further remarks on this topic by the same writer are to be found in 'Some Notes on *At* as a Preposition of Place in English' (*Rynell-Festschrift*, pp. 102–107). In 'Old English Words and Patristic Exegesis – *hwyrftum scriþað*: a Caveat' (*MP*, Vol. 75, pp. 44–48) Stanley B. Greenfield argues cogently against an over-sophisticated use of patristic exegesis when the data at hand clearly contradict the consequent interpretation; a further work of interest for Old English semantics is Anatoly Liberman's 'Germanic *sendan* and "to make a sacrifice"' (*JEGP*, Vol. 77,

[31] *'At' versus 'On', 'In', 'By': on the Early History of Spatial 'At' and Certain Primary Ideas Distinguishing 'At' from 'On', 'In', 'By'*, by Karl-Gunnar Lindkvist. Stockholm Studies in English, 49. Stockholm: Almqvist & Wiksell. pp. 90.

pp. 473–488). There are four papers concerning interpretive problems in Middle English. Simonne T. R. O. d'Ardenne ('Additional Note to SW *iseh towart*, EMEVP, 286', *ES*, Vol. 59, pp. 114–115) argues that the prefix *i-* still has a perfective sense in the AB dialect; Roger Dahood ('A Lexical Puzzle in *Ancrene Wisse*', *N&Q*, Vol. 223, pp. 1-2) suggests that *locunges-efter* is a nonce compound to translate *obseruantias*; W. G. East ('*The Owl and the Nightingale*, 11. 427–428', *ES*, Vol. 59, pp. 442–443) suggests that *flockes* here may mean '(snow-)flakes', which the phonology might just allow; and Thorlac Turville-Petre ('two Notes on Words in Alliterative Poems', *N&Q*, Vol. 223, pp. 294–296 suggests that *tried* in 1.4 of *Gawain* may mean 'exposed' and argues against Nicholas Jacobs' interpretation of *porte* as 'Ottoman government', cf. *YW* 58.20.

There are a number of useful discussions of particular lexical sets, the most extensive of which is Mats Ryden's *Shakespearian Plant Names*[32]. This work, however, will probably be of more interest to the student of literature than of language, and a rather more linguistic approach to the same lexical set is to be found in the same author's 'The English Plant Names in Gerard's *Herball* (1597)' (*Rynell-Festschrift*[7], pp. 142–150), which is of clear importance to the student of this area. In 'Late 15th Century "Terms of Association" in Ms. Pepys 1047' (*N&Q*, Vol. 223, pp. 7–12) Tom L. Burton provides a list of collective nouns in this manuscript, several of which are new or in new collocations. Eric G. Stanley ('*Peytral* and the Like for the *OED Supplement*', *N&Q*, Vol. 223, pp. 533–536) looks at various connected nouns for 'horse-armour', itself not in the O.E.D. As someone who was not in Britain at the time, I found Sarah Lawson's 'To Coin a Phrase: the Vocabulary of Decimalization' (*NM*, Vol. 79, pp. 398–402) a rather disappointing paper.

As always there is a fair crop of antedatings and additions to the O.E.D. and other dictionaries. Collections of such data are to be found in Roland Hall's 'Words Not in the Dictionaries: A–N' (*N&Q*, Vol. 223, pp. 342–347); 'The New Supplement to the O.E.D.: Some Antedatings' (*ES*, Vol. 59, pp. 521–522) by the same author; and Philip Hines Jr 'Antedatings, Postdatings and Additions to O.E.D. in Theobald 1728–1744' (*N&Q*, Vol. 223, pp. 12–14). Individual words are noted in: George R. Keiser, '*Epworth*: a ghost word in the M.E.D.' (*ELN*, Vol. 15, pp. 163–164); Lister M. Matheson, 'A Middle English Antedating of *Protocol*' (*N&Q*, Vol. 223, pp. 204–205); Wayne H. Siek, '*Pause*: an Antedating of O.E.D.' (*N&Q*, Vol. 223, p. 445); Wayne H. Siek, '*Skirmisher*: a new sense and an antedating of O.E.D.' (*N&Q*, Vol. 223, p. 160); S. J. Sillars, 'Avison's *Subject*: an O.E.D. antedating' (*N&Q*, Vol. 223, p. 14); Elizabeth A. Swaim, '*Circulating Library*: Antedatings of O.E.D.' (*N&Q*, Vol. 223, pp. 14–15); James Turner, 'The Verb *Landscape*: an O.E.D. Antedating' (*N&Q*, Vol. 223, p. 160).

(h) Onomastics

The work published in this year is undoubtedly less in quantity than last year, and it does not in general have the long-lasting importance of

[32] *Shakespearean Plant Names*, by Mats Ryden. Stockholm Studies in English, 43. Stockholm: Almqvist & Wiksell. pp. 117.

some of the previous year's material, but nevertheless there is definitely some work of interest. Sir William Addison's *Understanding English Place-Names*[33] is a work written by an amateur for amateurs, and the author makes no pretence to great originality; rather, he offers a brief account, heavily relying on the *EPNS* surveys, to highlight what might fascinate the newcomer to place-name studies. Although the book seems a trifle heavy-going in places, the overwhelming impression is that the author will be a successful awakener of interest. I would have liked to compare here Margaret Gelling's *Signposts to the Past*[34], but regrettably I have not been able to see a copy.

There seem to have been only two articles of general interest published this year, of which the more important must be 'Place-Names and Settlement in the North Riding of Yorkshire' (*NH*, Vol. 14, pp. 19–46), in which Gillian Fellows Jensen brings up to date A. H. Smith's *EPNS* study and points out how cautious we must be in citing place-name evidence as an indicator of settlement patterns. Then Ralph W. V. Elliott continues his studies of the *Gawain*-poet in 'Hills and Valleys in the *Gawain* Country' (*LeedsSE*, Vol. 10, pp. 18–41). Here Elliott considers the range and distribution of topographical terms in Middle English alliterative verse, especially of the North and North-West Midlands.

The other place-name studies concentrate on a single element or name. Thus Gillis Kristensson has two articles on such topics. In '*Konga* and English Place-Names in *Cong-*' (*Årsskrift* 1978, pp. 24–31) he compares Swedish *Konga* with English *Congham, Conghurst* and *Congleton*, and suggests that all are derived from an element which was in Old English **cung*, Old Danish **kungr*, meaning 'protuberance'. Then in 'A Textual Note on *The Owl and the Nightingale*' (*N&Q*, Vol. 223, pp. 199–200) he plausibly emends line 304 so that support is given to Old English **mǣrs*, Middle English *mers* 'boundary'. In 'The Place-Name *Helford*' (*Neophilologus*, Vol. 62, pp. 294–296) Martyn F. Wakelin very interestingly suggests that the second element here is Middle English *ford* < Old English *ford* with semantic, but *not* phonological, influence from Middle Cornish *forth* 'way, passage'. P. A. Wilson ('*Eaglesfield*: the place, the name, the burials', *CWAAS*, Vol. 78, pp. 48–54) brings primarily archaeological evidence to bear on the possibility that this may be another instance of an *Eccles*-name. Two other studies of individual names are M. T. Löfvenberg's 'The Place-Name *Latchingdon*' (*Rynell-Festschrift*[7], pp. 108–111) and B. Lindström's '*Sevehod Lane*, London' (*N&Q*, Vol. 223, p. 292).

There are only three short notes on personal names this year. In 'The *Este*' (*N&Q*, Vol. 223, pp. 100–104) Alan S. C. Ross gives a survey of the name and of the ethnic origins of this tribe mentioned in the Anglo-Saxon *Orosius*. F. I. Dunn and (appropriately) Diana Deterding predate Miss Withycombe's first citation of the name *Diana* by about 300 years in '*Diana*, an Early Occurrence of the Name' (*N&Q*, Vol. 223, pp. 532–533). Finally, Nicholas Jacobs, in '*Clanvowe*' (*N&Q*, Vol. 223, pp. 292–295) suggests a Welsh etymology for this surname.

[33] *Understanding English Place-Names*, by Sir William Addison. Batsford. pp. 159. £5.50.

[34] *Signposts to the Past*, by Margaret Gelling. J. M. Dent.

(i) Stylistics

The study of the language of literature can often be these days a pursuit of enormous technical complexity, which sometimes appears to obfuscate rather than clarify. Newcomers to the subject, therefore, will be pleased to see *Language and Style*, a brief and simple introduction by E. L. Epstein[35]. Useful as this book will be, one must object to Epstein's discussion of sound patterns in poetry, where he discusses lines from Donne and Milton without even mentioning that the pronunciation of early seventeenth-century English was rather different from that of today. More advanced students of the subject will want to read Samuel R. Levin's *The Semantics of Metaphor*[36]. Using basically a Katzian model of semantics, Levin suggests that metaphor in non-poetic language is construed in various ways to make the expression conform to a truth-value in this world. In poetic language, however, the process is, Levin claims, the reverse. Poetry creates an imaginary world, in which the metaphors of the poem are phenomenalistic, thus they are literal and linguistically non-deviant in the poem. Important as any work by Levin must be, I find his arguments rather less than compelling. I do not believe that I read poetry in the way he suggests. Levin also offers a brief defence of the linguistic analysis of poetry in 'The Position and Function of Linguistics in a Theory of Poetry' (*Hill-Festschrift*[5], Vol. 4, pp. 127–135).

Even those sceptical about highly formalistic approaches to literary language may well be impressed by the collection of papers edited by Wolfgang U. Dressler in *Current Trends in Textlinguistics*[37]. Here there are new papers by such leading workers in the field as Petöfi, van Dijk, Longacre, Grimes, Enkvist, Ellen Prince, Hasan, Harweg and Kuno, altogether an exceptionally wide-ranging and formidable collection which will be indispensable for those who wish to keep up with recent activity in stylistics. Another highly theoretical work is the English translation of Maria Corti's *An Introduction to Literary Semiotics*[38]. Although Professor Corti is a leading figure in Italian linguistics, I found this monograph advocating a semiotic approach to literature rather too general and consequently heavy-going for my taste. There is too much form and not enough content.

Under the title *Poétique Générative*, Jean-Jacques Thomas and Daniel Delas[39] have edited an issue of the periodical *Langages* which contains two critical surveys of generative stylistics together with an annotated bibliography of some 210 items. Also partly periodical and partly book is *Essays in Literary Semantics*, edited by Trevor Eaton[40]. Here are reprinted six articles from the *Journal of Literary Semantics*, the authors being Dolezel, Eaton, Foulkes, Fowler, Hirsch and Werth. I fail to see the purpose of such a reprinting exercise.

[35] *Language and Style*, by E. L. Epstein. New Accents. Methuen. pp. xii + 92.

[36] *The Semantics of Metaphor*, by Samuel R. Levin. Baltimore, Md. and London: The Johns Hopkins U.P.

[37] *Current Trends in Textlinguistics*, ed. by Wolfgang U. Dressler. Research in Text Theory, 2. Berlin: Walter de Gruyter. pp. vi + 308. DM 72.

[38] *An Introduction to Literary Semiotics*, by Maria Corti. Bloomington, Ind. and London: Indiana U.P. pp. xi + 176. £8.75.

[39] *Poétique Générative*, ed. by Jean-Jacques Thomas and Daniel Delas. *Langages*, Vol. 51.

[40] *Essays in Literary Semantics*, ed. by Trevor Eaton. Heidelberg: Julius Groos. pp. 120. DM 20.

In turning to Winfried Nöth's 'Systems Analysis of Old English Literature' (*PTL*, Vol. 3, pp. 117–137) we move only half-way from the general to the particular. For here we have the highest of high theory, the speciality of this periodical, and I find myself feeling rather less shame-faced than perhaps I ought to be in saying I found this paper quite incomprehensible. It is with some relief, therefore, that I turn to Susan Wittig's *Stylistic and Narrative Structures in the Middle English Romances*[41], for here we have, despite some formalism, an extremely detailed and sympathetic study of twenty-seven Middle English romances. Wittig uses the techniques of tagmemic grammar and Levi-Strauss' analysis of traditional patterns of myth to establish her argument, but does so in a germane and clear fashion. She concludes that these romances are intensely formulaic both in terms of form and content, and whilst she may be unable to convince us of their literary merit she does increase our understanding of these works in their context. Another important work in the field of medieval literary language is *Medieval Eloquence*, edited by James J. Murphy[42]. Here we have a collection of fourteen original papers on both the theory and practice of medieval rhetoric. The papers on theory cover writers from Cicero and Boethius up to Ranulph Higden, and papers on practice include Jackson J. Campbell on Old English, the editor himself on *The Owl and the Nightingale*, and Robert O. Payne on Chaucer. This is an extremely learned and valuable collection which the specialist will undoubtedly use with profit.

Two shorter works on medieval language are worthy of mention. In '*Wið Scharpe Sneateres*: Some Aspects of Colloquialism in *Ancrene Wisse*' (*NM*, Vol. 79, pp. 341–353), Cecily Clark gives a stimulating introduction to the problems of colloquialism in Middle English, and she has some interesting remarks on the presence of Romance loans in apparently colloquial passages. Matsuji Tajima, in 'Additional Syntactic Evidence against the Common Authorship of Ms. Cotton Nero A.x' (*Es*, Vol. 59, pp. 193–198) seems to me to take a rather optimistic view of some very marginal statistics.

There are two papers on the language of Shakespeare. Josephine Roberts ('*King Lear* and the Prefixes of Inversion', *NM*, Vol. 79, pp. 384–390) analyses the distribution of *un-* in *King Lear* as a contribution to the pattern of imagery in the play, whilst Kathleen Wales ('An Aspect of Dynamic Language: a Note on the Interpretation of *King Lear* III. vii. 113: "He childed as I father'd" ' (*ES*, Vol. 59, pp. 305–404) rather laboriously suggests a plausible meaning for the line.

Those who tire of the technical approaches to literary language may welcome Kenneth C. Phillipps' *The Language of Thackeray*[43]. Following his earlier study of Jane Austen and similar works by G. L. Brook and others, Phillipps here presents a quite a-linguistic analysis with so heavy a concentration on vocabulary that lexical indigestion in the reader is a major probability. The chapter on the language of *Henry Esmond* is perhaps the

[41] *Stylistic and Narrative Structures in the Middle English Romances*, by Susan Wittig. Austin, Tex. and London: U. of Texas P. pp. ix + 233.

[42] *Medieval Eloquence: Studies in the Theory and Practice of Medieval Rhetoric*, ed. by James J. Murphy. Berkeley, Los Angeles and London: U. of California P. pp. xii + 354. £11.25.

[43] *The Language of Thackeray*, by Kenneth C. Phillipps. The Language Library. André Deutsch. pp. 205. £6.50.

most interesting, but Phillipps surely loses the struggle to convince us of Thackeray's stylistic abilities and the whole work suffers from its lack of any clear linguistic focus. Systems analysis of literary language (see above) is surely going too far, but here Phillipps does not go far enough. In 'Mrs. Gaskell and Dialect' (*Rynell-Festschrift*[7], pp. 112–124) Gunnel Melchers offers a brief survey of some of the more obvious dialectal features as they are represented in *Mary Barton* and *Sylvia's Lovers.* Finally, Robert A. Hall Jr looks at the beginnings of a well-known style in two very early works in 'Primicias Estilisticas de P. G. Wodehouse' (*Hill-Festschrift*[5], Vol. 4, pp. 55–61).

Of the rather few items dealing with prosody and metrics which have appeared this year, perhaps the one of most general interest will be Mervin Barnes and Helmut Esau's clear refutation of some recent generative work which emphasises syllable-counting procedures ('English Prosody Reconsidered', *Lang&S*, Vol. 11, pp. 212–222). Unfortunately the notes to the article do not correspond with the text. The remainder of the items concentrate on Old English metrics. F. H. Whitman's 'Rules Governing the Meter of *þa–*, *þær–* and *siððan–* verses in *Beowulf*' (*ES*, Vol. 59, pp. 385–389) is a detailed study which helps to show the extent to which the meter of *Beowulf* is determined by syntax. Jerzy Kuryłowicz ('Linguistic Fundamentals of the Meter of *Beowulf*' (*Hill-Festschrift*[5], Vol. 4, pp. 111–119) deals interestingly with the relation between morphophonemics and metrics, and Ruth P. M. Lehmann ('Contrasting Rhythms of Old English and New English', *Hill-Festschrift*[5], Vol. 4, pp. 121–126) makes a rather curious attempt to demonstrate by way of translation how linguistic change must lead to the loss of Old English verse forms.

Section II

The range of publications relating to areas covered in this section continues to grow, although accessibility to such items is becoming more and more limited. It is, therefore, impossible to give an adequate account of all relevant publications. As in *Vol. 58*, no separate heading is given for works dealing solely with English. Many of these works can be placed under the *Linguistic Theory* section which deals with syntactic, semantic and phonological theory, in that order. Theory is here interpreted in its widest sense. The English Language is the focus of interest in many of these works, and I have largely ignored items which focus exclusively on languages other than English. One notable feature of this year's collection is the speed with which conference papers can now be assembled into book form. The delay between presentation and publication has often meant that works are partially outdated before they are readily available. Of course, there is a price to pay in the minimising of editorial control and involvement. In some cases, at least, the price is too high in that works of unequal merit are assembled without thought for the coherence of the book as a unit.

Again, as in previous years, a major source of difficulty to the reviewer is the vast number of publications relating to English Language teaching, especially TESL and TEFL. This material is largely excluded from this survey except where individual items include original theoretical or descriptive contributions. For those whose interests lie within this area, *Language*

Teaching and Linguistics: Abstracts[44] contains useful material, while *Language and Language Behavior: Abstracts*[45] covers the wide field of theoretical and applied linguistics.

Adequate and up to date linguistic bibliographies are badly needed, although one can fully appreciate the efforts and resources required to produce such volumes. The UNESCO publication[46] prepared by the Permanent International Committee of Linguistics was last issued in 1976 for the year 1975. Two non-English publications are worth mentioning here. *Bulletin Signalètique: Sciences du Language*[47], which is oriented primarily to French publications, and *Bibliographie Linguistischer Literatur*[48]. The latter is a particularly thorough and wide-ranging series which covers General Linguistics, English, German and the Romance Languages. Students unfamiliar with German should not be put off by the title as many English works and major linguistic periodicals are cited. *Lingua*[49] contains its extremely useful and regular 'Survey of Books' in the January and September issues. Over seventy titles are arranged, with short descriptions, under topic headings. Given the manner in which doctoral dissertations in linguistics can sometimes influence theory and description, it is useful to keep a check on items in *Dissertation Abstracts International*[50] and *American Doctoral Dissertations*[51]. Because the number of dissertations is so large, finding those which are truly worthy of close perusal can be problematic, but those interested in specific specialist areas should find these volumes worth consulting.

I turn now to single volume bibliographical sources. Perhaps the most important contribution this year is *A Bibliography of Contemporary Linguistic Research*[52] edited by G. Gazdar, E. Klein and G. K. Pullum. The editors have not attempted to be completely consistent and comprehensive in their listings, but have included items which they regard as essential to the working linguist. Rather surprisingly, books as such are generally excluded from the listings, although exceptions include conference proceedings, specialised anthologies and rapid-publication, litho-printed books. The rationale for the focus on articles as opposed to books

[44] *Language Teaching and Linguistic: Abstracts*. Cambridge: C.U.P. Vol. 12.

[45] *Language and Language Behavior: Abstracts*. Ann Arbor; Mich.: Sociological Abstracts Inc. Vol. 12.

[46] *Linguistic Bibliography for the Year 1974 and Supplement for Previous Years*, ed. by J. J. Beylsmit. Permanent International Committee of Linguists UNESCO. Antwerp: Spectrum. pp. xlvi + 546.

[47] *Bulletin Signalètique: Sciences du Language*. Paris: Centre de Documentation Sciences Humaines. Vol. xxxii.

[48] *Bibliographie Linguistischer Literatur: Bibliographie zur allgemeinen Linguistik und zur anglistischen, germanistischen und romanistischen Linguistik*. Band 4: 1978 und Nachträge früherer Jahre. Bearbeitet von Elke Suchan. Unter Mitarbeit von Paul Georg Meyer. Frankfurt am Main: Vittorio Klostermann. pp. xxxix + 464 (large).

[49] *Lingua*. Vol. 46. Amsterdam and New York: North Holland Publishing Company.

[50] *Dissertation Abstracts International (A) The Humanities and Social Sciences*. Ann Arbor; Mich.: U. Microfilms International Limited. Vol. 39.

[51] *American Doctoral Dissertations*. Ann Arbor; Mich.: U. Microfilms International Limited.

[52] *A Bibliography of Contemporary Linguistic Research*, ed. by G. Gazdar, E. Klein and G. K. Pullum. New York and London: Garland Publishing, Inc. pp. xix + 425.

is that the former are seen as the primary means of disseminating information and ideas within the profession of linguistics. The entries are alphabetical, by author, and the items are numbered. Subjects fall into four main categories: general constraints on grammars; grammatical rules; problem areas in linguistic description and particular schools of thought. Certain journals have been excluded because of the variable standard of their articles: thus *Linguistics* is omitted entirely, although it is difficult to see why the worthy articles should have to suffer the same fate as their weaker counterparts. A major query about the volume concerns the ease of access to many of the items they cite, especially the newly termed 'parajournals'. These include publications of individual linguistics societies or universities, such as the Chicago Linguistics Society, the Berkeley Linguistics Society and the Indiana University Linguistics Club. My own experience suggests that while these are easily available in North America, they are often difficult to obtain in British university libraries. In many cases, books, especially collections of articles, may be more accessible to the European audience. Moreover, in some subject areas, (e.g. Sign Language Studies), the editors include parajournal items which have been clearly superceded by more recent articles in books. It is also questionable whether this editorial policy allows adequate attention to be given to individual authors: M. A. K. Halliday is represented by one entry which hardly does justice to his work and influence. For these reasons, this bibliography is, at times, a frustrating collection, yet it is undoubtedly an essential source book. The topic lists are organised clearly and simply and the editors are obviously closely in touch with current trends in linguistics.

A much less theoretically oriented work is the second edition of *Linguistics and English Linguistics*[53] compiled by Harold B. Allen. This is a useful collection aimed more at the student rather than the active linguist. As the cut-off date for entries is early 1975, some subject areas, such as Language Acquisition and Sociolinguistics, seem considerably under-represented given the upsurge of research during the last five years.

Two rather more specialised volumes have also appeared this year. The first, which has not been available to the reviewer, is a bibliography on *Logic and Language* by Barbara Hall Partee[54]. This is a new and revised edition of a 1971 publication and given Partee's expertise in this field, this is likely to be a helpful guide. The second specialist work is on *Pragmatics*[55]. Publications on speech act theory, presuppositions, implicature and frame analysis are among the 1500 entries. Annual supplements will appear in the *Journal of Pragmatics*. This volume is an indispensable guide to this fast growing area of linguistics activity.

Those who find biographical data an aid to understanding will be interested in *A Biographical Dictionary of the Phonetic Sciences*[56] which

[53] *Linguistics and English Linguistics* (2nd Edition), comp. by Harold B. Allen. Goldentree Bibliographies in Language and Literature. Arlington Heights, Ill.: A.H.M. Publishing Corporation. pp. xv + 183.

[54] *Bibliography of Logic and Language*. Barbara Hall Partee

[55] *Pragmatics: An Annotated Bibliography*, ed. by Jef Verschueren. Amsterdam Studies in the Theory and History of Linguistic Science 5. Information Sources in Linguistics. Vol. 4. Amsterdam: John Benjamins B.V.

[56] *A Biographical Dictionary of the Phonetic Sciences*, ed. by Arthur J. Bornstein, Lawrence J. Raphael and C. J. Steven. New York: The Press of Lehman College.

includes details of the lives and work of important figures in phonetics and phonology. A *Glossary of Transformational Grammar*[57] is noted but unseen.

Linguistic Theory

This section begins with some relatively lightweight, general introductions to language and linguistics. *A New Invitation to Linguistics*[58] by Joseph H. Greenberg is a short enjoyable introduction for the complete beginners: this small book contrasts sharply with the four volume presentation, also by Greenberg, discussed in later paragraphs. Julia Falk[59] has produced a revised version of her 1973 survey of basic concepts in linguistics. The major change is the addition of a section on 'Further Explanation' at the end of each chapter containing supplementary material. The book is aimed directly at an undergraduate audience as is Fromkin and Rodman's *An Introduction to Language*[60]. In the latter case, the authors maintain a refreshingly sane and often humorous approach to the subject, while leading the student to a deeper understanding of linguistic issues.

Carol Eastman[61] covers much of the same ground in a more traditional format, concentrating on possible conflicts between theory and description. Yet another revised edition of an introductory work is that edited by William Orr Dingwall[62], which contains articles on various aspects of language study including 'Generative Phonology' (Theodore Lightner), 'Linguistic Metatheory' (Barbara Hall Partee), 'Neurolinguistics' (W. O. Dingwall and Harry A. Whitaker) and 'Sociolinguistics' (W. Labov).

An introductory text of a rather different kind is produced by Barbara Hall Partee in *Fundamentals of Mathematics for Linguistics*[63]. It may seem strange to mention such a book so early in this review, yet it is important in making relevant mathematical concepts available to the serious student of linguistics. Given the fact that many basic mathematical techniques and concepts underlie formal linguistic theory, from Chomsky to Montague, it is essential that such information be presented in a clear and understandable way. Partee, in recognising the fears of many linguistics students in the face of axiomatic systems and mathematical notations, gears her text to making this whole subject area less formidable and as she hopes, even pleasurable.

As indicated by Richard Hogg in section one of this chapter, Joseph Greenberg has edited a four volume work on *Universals of Human Lan-*

[57] *Glossary of Transformational Grammar*, by Jeanne Ambrose Grillet. Rowley, Mass.: Newbury House. pp. vii + 166.

[58] *A New Invitation to Linguistics*, by Joseph H. Greenberg. Anchor Press. 1977.

[59] *Linguistics and Language: A Survey of Basic Concepts and Implications*, by Julia S. Falk. 2nd Edition. New York: John Wiley & Sons. pp. xv + 448.

[60] *An Introduction to Language*, by Victoria Fromkin and Robert Rodman. New York and Montreal: Holt, Rinehart & Winston. pp. 386.

[61] *Linguistic Theory and Language Description*, by Carol M. Eastman. Philadelphia: J. B. Lippincott Company.

[62] *A Survey of Linguistic Sciences*, ed. by William Orr Dingwall. Stamford, Conn.: Greylock Publishers. pp. xv + 399.

[63] *Fundamentals of Mathematics for Linguistics*, by Barbara Hall Partee. Stamford, Conn.: Greylock Publishers. pp. xiii + 242.

guage[64]. Each volume has an editorial and an introduction and all articles are preceded by abstracts. Volume 1, which is combined with methodology and theory, has an introduction by Charles Ferguson. In one short article of a few pages, Ferguson draws together evidence on adult talk to young children from twenty-seven different languages. One suspects that this 'density' of information may often obscure rather than reveal. Volume 2 deals with topics in phonology and has an introduction by J. H. Greenberg; Volume 3 on word structure covers a variety of topics including gender, tense and numeral systems. The final volume, introduced by E. A. Moravcsik, deals with syntactic topics such as interrogative systems, definiteness and referentiality. It is impossible to do justice to this type of work in a few short comments. However, one wonders whether the impact of multi-volume works is ultimately counter-productive. Specialist anthologies in particular topic areas are probably more helpful to both expert and student. Language universals are also considered in a collection of conference papers edited by Hansjacob Seiler. Contributors include E. Keenan, H. Parret, K. L. Pike and P. L. Garvin[65].

Current Issues in Linguistic Theory[66] was unintentionally omitted from *YW* 58. The volume includes original contributions from Noam Chomsky ('Conditions on Rules of Grammar'), Joshua A. Fishman ('The Sociology of Language: Yesterday, Today and Tomorrow'), Charles Fillmore ('Topics on Lexical Semantics') and Wallace Chafe ('The Recall and Verbalization of Past Experience'). Kenneth and Evelyn Pike[67] have produced a new introduction to grammatical analysis which reflects their own concerns with tagmemic analysis. Their account includes several important new developments within this theory, particularly in relation to discourse structure. While the work is impressive and thorough, it does appear rather daunting to those unfamiliar with or unenthusiastic about tagmemic grammar. Nevertheless, they do aim to take the new student through the stages of practical grammatical analysis so that the individual is armed with sound techniques to approach as yet undescribed human languages.

Morris Halle, Joan Bresnan and George A. Miller have edited an important collection of papers[68] on the interactions between theories in linguistics and psychology. The editors suggest that developments in these two areas have been leading to similar conclusions but by different paths. Recent theoretical accounts have limited the role of transformations within generative grammar and Bresnan's contribution examines the function and nature of the lexicon to see whether it can account for facts previously accounted for by transformations. George Miller's chapter on language and perception

[64] *Universals of Human Language*. 4 volumes, ed. by Joseph H. Greenberg. Stanford, Calif.: Stanford U.P.

[65] *Language Universals: Papers from the Conference held at Gummersbach/Cologne, Germany 1976*, ed. by Hansjacob Seiler. Tübingen Beitrage zur Linguistik III. Tübingen: Gunter Narr Verlag. pp. 328. DM. 68.

[66] *Current Issues in Linguistic Theory*, ed. by Roger W. Cole, Bloomington, Ind.: Indiana U.P. pp. viii + 303.

[67] *Grammatical Analysis*, by Kenneth L. Pike and Evelyn B. Pike. Arlington, Tex.: The Summer Institute of Linguistics and the University of Texas at Arlington. pp. xxx + 505.

[68] *Linguistic Theory and Psychological Reality*, ed. by Morris Halle, John Bresnan and George A. Miller. M.I.T. Bicentennial Studies. Cambridge, Mass.: The M.I.T. Press. pp. xvii + 329.

develops the discussion of the form and function of lexical entries. Among other intriguing discussions, Susan Casey examines the processes which underlie the incredibly speedy acquisition of lexical items by young children. She estimates that the average six year old has an active vocabulary of 14,000 words and computes a steady rate of vocabulary acquisition of nine words per day. The nature and role of the lexican is discussed further in *Papers from the Parasession on the Lexicon*[69]. Contributions include 'Discovering What Words Can Do' (Eve V. Clark); 'Applying Montague's Views on Linguistic Metatheory to the structure of the Lexicon' (David Dowty); 'On the Organisation of Semantic Information' (Charles Fillmore) and 'Logic and the Lexicon' (James D. McCawley).

Turning now to more specific theories of grammar, Simon C. Dik[70] develops an account of functional grammar which incorporates two types of rules: those which govern verbal interaction as a form of co-operative activity (pragmatic) and those which govern the structured linguistic expressions used in this activity. Dik provides a contrastive account of formal and functional grammars: within formal grammar, language is seen as an abstract object while in functional grammar language is an instrument of social interaction. However, it is doubtful whether all those who adopt a formal approach would necessarily accept the major differences between the two types of grammar as presented in the schema (pp. 3–5). Do all formal linguistics accept that the primary function of language is the expression of thought? Despite the temptation to simplify such contrasts, Dik's work is worthy of careful study.

Thomas Ballmer's *Logical Grammar*[71] approaches the theory of grammar in a rather novel way. He tries to avoid what he considers to be deficiency in other theories of grammar, including those of Chomsky and Montague, by regarding punctuation signs as 'fully fledged linguistic entities with a phono-graphemic, a morpho-syntactic and a semantico-pragmatic aspect'. More specifically, punctuation signs are seen as special kinds of morphemes or words which combine preceding words in order to form sentences and combine preceding sentences in order to set up texts. This attempt to make punctuation signs part of the internal structure rather than markers of that structure is a unique but doubtful strategy. Michael Kac's co-representational theory[72] recognises two distinct levels of representation, a categorial level and a relational representation. The author uses English to provide a helpful illustrative account of the major principles within his theory.

I turn now to a set of items in which English grammar is the main focus of concern. Carle Bache[73] aims to discover and illustrate the principles

[69] *Papers from the Parasession on the Lexicon.* Chicago, Ill.: Chicago Linguistics Society. pp. 364.

[70] *Functional Grammar*, by Simon C. Dik. North Holland Linguistics Series 37. Amsterdam and New York: North Holland Publishing Company. pp. xi + 230.

[71] *Logical Grammar: With Special Consideration of Topics in Context Change* by Thomas Ballmer. North Holland Linguistics Series 39. New York and Amsterdam: North Holland Publishing Company. pp. xi + 375.

[72] *Co-representation of Grammatical Structure*, by Michael B. Kac. Minneapolis, Minn.: U. of Minnesota P. pp. 168. $15.

[73] *The Order of Pre-Modifying Adjectives in Present Day English*, by Carle Bache. Odense: Odense U.P. pp. 99.

governing the sequential ordering of two or more pre-modifying adjectives in the English noun phrase. The focus is primarily descriptive rather than theoretical. The author uses a corpus of 4,500 written examples from both fiction and non-fiction to examine reversibility, distinctiveness and preference in these sequences. Thus, in some instances, the order can be reversed, in others reversibility is unallowable, while in yet others acceptable grammatical reversal brings about a change of meaning. The detailed examples and discussion could well provide the basis for a more theoretical account of this area.

In an item unforgivably missed last year, my colleage in this chapter, Richard Hogg, provides a detailed discussion of the *English Quantifier Systems*[74]. In a thorough account using plenty of illustrative material, the quantifiers 'all', 'every', 'each', 'both', 'any', 'some', and 'many' are analysed. Given the importance of quantifiers within a whole range of current theories, it is refreshing to see here an equal attention to descriptive detail.

Another volume which pays proper attention to descriptive detail without losing its theoretical perspective is Judith N. Levi's volume on complex nominals. This term is used to cover three related and partially overlapping sets of expressions: nominal compounds ('apple cake', 'colour television', 'daisy chain'); nominalisation ('constitutional amendment', 'film producer', 'metal detection') and noun phrases with non-predicating adjectives ('electric shock', 'electrical engineering', 'musical comedy'). All of these expressions have in common a headword, preceded by a modifying element, typically a noun or adjective. Probably the least explored type is the third. The main feature of such adjectives is that they cannot appear in the predicate position ('an electrical engineer' – 'an engineer who is electrical'). Some of the examples cited by Levi do seem at least doubtful cases ('solar generator', 'musical comedy'); however, such examples do not bring into question the detailed argumentation. Bauer's work on nominal compounding[76] is also worth attention. This is a revised edition of a doctoral thesis and while the author admits that her own thinking on important aspects of her theory has changed, she leaves discussion of her changes to as yet unpublished papers. Nevertheless, Bauer is probably right that there is enough original material within the volume to make it worthy of publication. D. S. N. Bhat[77] deals with pronominalisation in many languages, including Hindi, Japanese and English while N. R. Norrick[78] aims to describe factive complementation in contemporary American English within a generative semantic framework. Definite and indefinite

[74] *English Quantifier Systems*, by Richard Hogg. North Holland Linguistics Series 34. Amsterdam and New York: North Holland Publishing Company. 1977. pp. viii + 179.

[75] *The Syntax and Semantics of Complex Nominals*, by Judith N. Levi. New York and London: Academic Press. 1978. pp. xxiv + 301.

[76] *The Grammar of Nominal Compounding with Special Reference to Danish, English and French*, by Laurie Bauer. Odense: Odense U.P. pp. 250.

[77] *Pronominillization: A Cross-Linguistic Study*, by D. S. N. Bhat. Poona, India: Deccan College Postgraduate and Research Institute. pp. xi + 98. Rs 20.

[78] *Factive Adjectives and the Theory of Factivity*, by Neal R. Norrick. Linguistische Arbeiten 64. Tübingen: Max Niemeyer Verlag. pp. xi + 131. DM 32.

reference is discussed by John A. Hawkins[79] using a pragmatic-semantic approach.

Tense and aspect receive attention by several authors this year. Michael Bennett and Barbara Partee[80] provide a review and criticism of Montague's work on tense and aspect. They suggest a new notion – that of 'a true sentence at an interval of time' – is necessary for a fully adequate theory. Christian Rohrer's[81] collection of papers aims to show how the temporal structure of verbs can be represented in a formal system and how the meaning of a verb interacts with the meaning of tense forms and temporal adverbs. Robert W. McCoard[82] applies pragmatic analysis to the verb system while Lars Hermerén[83] analyses the meanings of the English modal auxiliaries with reference to a corpus of written English.

An attempt to specify the kinds of linguistic contexts in which temporal connectives such as 'when', 'before', 'until', and 'since' can occur is provided in the reproduction of Heinämäki's 1974 discussion produced by the Indiana University Linguistics Club[84]. David Townsend and Thomas Bever[85] cite experiments to show that differences in the form of main and subordinate clauses may be due to differences in the internal representation of different parts of a stimulus.

A detailed examination of various aspects of English phrase structure can be found in R. Jackendoff's Monograph *X Syntax*[86]. The book provides motivation for a richer account of base structure. A central chapter elaborates Chomsky's *Remarks on Nominilization*[87] into a highly constrained and explicit theory of constituent structure.

A fascinating collection of articles on *Questions*[88] has been edited by Henry Hiz. The editor focuses on one peculiar feature of questions, that they cannot be true or false. Contributors take different approaches to the problem: linguistic, logical and philosophical. Among many impressive contributions there are papers by authors such as Zellig Harris, D. H. Kahn and J. Hintikka. The discussions of 'yes–no' questions by Dwight Bolinger will be welcomed by many practitioners. Bolinger points out that an

[79] *Definiteness and Indefiniteness: A Study in Reference and Grammatically Prediction*, by John A. Hawkins. Croom Helm Linguistics Series. Croom Helm. pp. 316.

[80] *Toward the Logic of Tense and Aspect in English*, by Michael Bennett and Barbara Partee. Bloomington, Ind.: Indiana U. Linguistics Club.

[81] *Papers on Tense, Aspect and Verb Classification*, ed. by Christian Rohrer. Tübingen Beitrage zur Linguistik 110. Tübingen: Gunter Narr Verlag. pp. 161.

[82] *The English Perfect: Tense Choice and Pragmatic Inferences*, by Robert W. McCoard. North Holland Linguistics Series, 38. Amsterdam and New York: North Holland Publishing Company. pp. viii + 279.

[83] *On Modality in English: A Study of the Semantics of the Modals*, by Lars Hemerén. Lund Studies in English, 53. Lund: C.W.K. Gleerup. pp. 195.

[84] *Semantics of English Temporal Connectives*, by Orvokki Heinämäki. Bloomington, Ind.: Indiana U. Linguistics Club. pp. 132.

[85] *Main and Subordinate Clauses: A Study in Figure and Ground*, by David G. Townsend and Thomas G. Bever. Town & State of publication, Columbia U.

[86] *X Syntax: A Study of Phrase Structure*, by Ray Jackendoff. Linguistic Inquiry Monographs. Cambridge, Mass.: M.I.T. Press. pp. xii + 249.

[87] *Remarks on Nominilization*, by Noam Chomsky in 'Studies on Semantics in Generative Grammar'. The Hague: Mouton.

[88] *Questions*, ed. by Henry Hiz. Synthese Language Library, Vol. 1. Dordrecht, Holland, Boston, Mass. and London: D. Reidel Publishing Co. pp. xvii + 366.

answer to a so-called yes–no question can have any shade of confirmation that lies across the spectrum from absolute plus to absolute minus.

A further volume on questions[89] takes us a cross the flexible boundary between syntax and semantics. The contributors have a background in both anthropology and linguistics and this is reflected in the papers. Each article 'focuses on the interface between individual use of language and the force conveyed by particular linguistic forms'. An attempt to formulate a theory of questions is made by E. Goody while other contributors examine topics such as questions in care-taker-child dialogue and politeness forms and strategies across divergent cultures.

C. L. Ebeling[90] develops a theory of semiotactics which combines the study of linguistic invariants, the hypothesis that all elements in a language system are inter-related and the requirement that all concepts of the theory must be rigorously defined and discovery procedures employed to locate exemplifications of the theory. Footnotes are given page by page but this large book would have benefited from reference lists and detailed bibliography. *Practical Semantics*[91] explores semantics in terms of a 'theory of action'. Heringer suggests that there are two requirements for such a theory: descriptive techniques which allow a systematic description of the make-up of a linguistic action and an account of how the acts of speaking are embedded within the rest of action.

A collection of papers on formal semantics edited by Franz Guenthner and Christian Rohrer[92] has as its main focus the problems of defining the concept of truth for a language, with respect to interpretation. Two of the articles are by Lennart Aquist who also contributes to *Meaning and Translation*[93]. This volume aims to clarify the basic features of the two major approaches to translation. According to the editors, Quine's work suggests that translation is essentially an object of analysis, while Montague's approach regards it as a method of analysis. In the latter approach, translations from natural languages to languages of predicate logic or modal and intensional logic are used to represent the logical structure of ordinary language. Important contributions are made by H. Putnam, E. Keenan, J. Katz and R. Cooper. *Logic, Pragmatics and Grammar*[94] omitted from *YW* 58 is also relevant to this area. Other items noted but unavailable for review are *Foundations of Logico-Linguistics*[95] by William

[89] *Questions and Politeness: Strategies in Social Interaction*, ed. by Esther N. Goody. Cambridge: C.U.P. pp. viii + 324.

[90] *Syntax and Semantics: A Taxonomic Approach*, by C. L. Ebeling. Leiden: E. J. Brill. pp. xi + 519.

[91] *Practical Semantics: A Study in the Rules of Speech and Action*, by Hans Jürgen Heringer. Trends in Linguistics, Studies and Monographs, 3. The Hague: Mouton. pp. viii + 224. DM 56.

[92] *Studies in Formal Semantics: Intentionality, Temporality, Negation*, ed. by Franz Guenthner and Christian Rohrer. North Holland Linguistics Series 35. Amsterdam and New York: North Holland Publishing Company. pp. vii + 265.

[93] *Meaning and Translation*. Philosophical and Linguistic Approaches, ed. by F. Guenthner and M. Guenthner. Duckworth. pp. 364.

[94] *Logic, Pragmatics and Grammar*, ed. by Östen Dahl. Lund: Studientlitteratur. 1977. pp. 295.

[95] *Foundations of Logico-Linguistics, A Unified Theory of Information, Language and Logic*, by William S. Cooper. Dordrecht, Holland: D. Reidel Publishing Co. pp. xvi + 249. $34.25.

S. Cooper; *Game Theoretical Semantics*[96] edited by Esa Saarinen and *Inferential Semantics*[97] by Frederick Parker Rhodes.

A further volume[98] in the consistently useful Syntax and Semantic series, examines the flourishing area of pragmatics. Grice's seminal article 'Logic and Conversation' has been updated by his contribution 'Further Notes on Logic and Conversation'. The volume also includes discussion of negation, conversational implicature and negative raising. Speech acts are examined by Richard Lanigan[99] in a critical discussion which uses Merleau Ponty's 'Phenomenology of Communication' as a basis for his own theoretical framework. Text linguistics and discourse analysis also remain popular areas of study. Joseph Grimes[100] has edited a selection of papers on discourse which includes discussions of theme oriented referential strategies. Wolfgang Dressler's collection of articles[101] provides a brief historical introduction to text linguistics as well as actual examples of textural analysis.

The boundary between pragmatics, functional and semiotic approaches to language on the one hand, and sociolinguistics on the other is not always easy to draw. Several items which straddle this boundary are included here because of their relevance to theoretical issues. Michael Halliday's *Language as Social Semiotic*[102] has a sound basis in his own theory of grammar combined with his concern to examine language in the process and experience of education. The only disappointment with this book is that most of the articles have appeared elsewhere: two chapters out of thirteen consist of previously unpublished material. Those who feel a little uneasy about Halliday's enthusiasm for Bernstein's work may find some solace in the clear exposition of the relationships between language and education. Many readers will be all too familiar with the progress of linguistic development in Halliday's son Nigel: let us hope that before too long we will be given an updated account which examines in detail the complex intricacies of function and structure in later language acquisition. One of the most enjoyable chapters in the book is Herman Parret's interview with Halliday. Parret voices many of the queries which must be familiar to many readers of Halliday: How exactly can we characterise the difference between 'use' and 'function'? What is the difference between 'function' and 'meaning'? This is a useful collection for both student and linguist, theorist and practitioner.

A project partially inspired by Halliday's functional-systemic grammar, is described by Anthony Davey in *Discourse Production*[103]. Davey ex-

[96] *Game-Theoretical Semantics*, ed. by Esa Saarinen. Dordrecht, Holland: D. Reidel Publishing Co. pp. xiv + 385. $47.40.

[97] *Inferential Semantics*, by Frederick Parker Rhodes. Harvester Studies in Cognitive Sciences. Hassocks. Sussex: The Harvester Press. pp. xv + 347.

[98] *Pragmatics*, ed. by Peter Cole. Syntax and Semantics 9. New York and London: Academic Press. pp. xii + 340. $21.50.

[99] *Speech Act Phenomonology*, by Richard L. Lanigan. The Hague: Martinus Nijhoff. 1977. pp. 137.

[100] *Papers on Discourse*, ed. by Joseph E. Grimes. Texas: The Summer Institute of Linguistics Inc. pp. viii + 389.

[101] *Textlinguistik*, ed. by Wolfgang Dressler. Wege der Forschung, 427. Darmstadt: Wissenschaftliche Buchgesellschaft. pp. vi + 427.

[102] *Language as Social Semiotic – The Social Interpretation of Language and Meaning*, by Michael Halliday. Edward Arnold. pp. 256.

[103] *Discourse Production: A Computer Model of Some Aspects of a Speaker*, by Anthony Davey. Edinburgh: Edinburgh: U.P. pp. vii + 168.

amines how the speaker gets from what he wants to be said to the words to say it with the aid of a computer programme modelling the speaker. *The Social Context of Language*[104] edited by Ivana Marková examines the notion of context and its various roles in relation to language. Bruner's contribution stresses the importance of four precursors to language: the expression of intentions and the mother's interpretation of such expressions; aspects of early reference; joint action and pre-requisites for predication. Walkerdine and Sinha show how the neglect of context can bring into question experimental work including that of Piaget. This volume includes contributions from John Dore, David MacNeill and R. Rommetveit. The range of contributors reflects the spread of topics brought together in the study of language and context.

I turn now to the final major section under *Linguistic Theory*, that of Phonology. This year has seen the publication of several important works in this area. One of the most impressive is Victoria Fromkin's linguistic survey of tone[105]. As Fromkin points out the majority of the world's languages are tone languages, therefore a comprehensive and viable theory of language must be capable of answering the following questions: What are the physiological and perceptual correlates of tone? How do tonal and non-tonal features interact? What are the necessary and sufficient tone universals? Should tone be represented segmentally or suprasegmentally in the lexicon? How do children acquire tone systems? The articles in this volume illustrate what is known at the present time about these and other tone-related issues. James McCawley's chapter, 'What is a tone language' faces the fundamental definitional problem head-on. One answer presented is that 'What is basic to the role of pitch in a tone language is not its contrastiveness but its lexicalness'. The volume is thorough and informative: a particularly helpful feature is the index of tone languages which cites the language, the language family and the country in which it is used.

Elements of Tone Stress and Intonation[106] brings together papers on individual languages as well theoretical models of these areas. Jean-Marie Hombart presents a model of tone systems; Ellen Schauber looks at the interaction of tone and semantics in Navajo while George Clements examines the ways in which tone and syntax are interrelated in Ewe. The contributors discuss the more general issues within the context of specific descriptive material. Mark Lieberman[107] examines three aspects of how a sentence is said, its stress, its tune and its phrasing, and develops a metrical grid to account for these phenomena.

Alan Bell and Jean Hooper[108] have edited a volume which brings together studies illustrating the range of phenomena that a theory of syllables or segment organisation must account for. As well as specific

[104] *The Social Context of Language*, ed. by Irana Marková. Chichester and New York: John Wiley. pp. ix + 241.

[105] *Tone: A Linguistic Survey*, ed. by Victoria Fromkin. New York and London: Academic Press. pp. xi + 292.

[106] *Elements of Tone Stress and Intonation*, ed. by Donna Jo Napoli. Washington, D.C. Georgetown U.P. pp. v + 173.

[107] *The Intonational System of English*, by M. Y. Lieberman. Bloomington, Ind.: University Linguistics Club. pp. 211.

[108] *Syllables and Segments*, ed. by Alan Bell and John B. Hooper. Amsterdam and New York: North Holland Publishing Company. pp. viii + 247.

language analyses, the volume includes discussion of the role of the syllable in early language development and the development of phonological rhythm. Two shorter publications from the Indiana University Linguistics Club also deal with syllables: C. J. N. Bailey[109] examines the syllable using data from twenty-eight different rules to support several principles of English syllabisation, while Blair A. Rudes takes *Another Look at Syllable Structure*[110].

Several items are concerned with more theoretical issues. Christiane Baltaxe[111] attempts to provide an examination of distinctive feature theory by providing a comparative analysis of the work of Trubetzkoy and Jacobson. Didier Goyvaerts[112] looks at the development of phonological theory in the years since the publication of *Sound Patterns of English*. He argues that generative phonologists have focused on the elegance and economy of linguistic description at the expense of learnability. A different way of writing phonological descriptions is proposed using what Goyvaerts terms concrete phonology. *A Formal Theory of Exceptions in Generative Phonology*[113] uses an analysis of inter-vocalic -d in Modern Dutch in order to provide a coherent account of phonological irregularities. Niels Davidsen-Nielsen[114] provides an account of the history and development of the notions of neutralisation and archiphoneme together with his own version of neutralisation. A practical workbook in generative phonology, providing exercises and phonological problems in specific languages has been prepared by Stanley M. Whitney[115].

Finally pride of place in this section must be given to an undoubted classic in phonological literature, *Six Lectures On Sound and Meaning*[116] by Roman Jacobson. This small book contains lectures given at L'École Libre des hautes études New York during the year 1942–3. The contents are of course familiar from Jacobson's other writings but as Levi-Strauss comments in his preface, the text allows the reader some hint of the power of Jacobson's oral presentation and the impact of his ideas. Where the large works may remain formidable and imposing, even to the enthusiastic student, this small book can challenge and inspire.

Psycholinguistics

Psycholinguistics as a whole remains a flourishing area of activity but

[109] *Gradience in English Syllabization and a Revised Concept of Unmarked Syllabization*, by C. J. N. Bailey. Bloomington, Ind.: I.U.L.C. pp. 49.

[110] *Another Look at Syllable Structure*, by Blair A. Rudes. Bloomington, Ind.: I.U.L.C. pp. 22.

[111] *Foundations of Distinctive Feature Theory*, by Christiane Baltaxe. Baltimore: University Park Press. pp. xx + 219. $17.50.

[112] *Aspects of Post-SPE Phonology*, by Didier L. Goyvaerts. Antwerp: E. Story-Scientia P.V.B.A. pp. 234.

[113] *A Formal Theory of Exceptions in Generative Phonology*, The Netherlands: The Peter De Ridder Press. pp. ii + 313.

[114] *Neutralization and Archiphoneme: Two Phonological Concepts and Their History*, by Niels Davidsen-Nielsen. Publication of the Department of English, U. of Copenhagen. Vol. 7. Copenhagen: Wilhelm Fink Verlag.

[115] *Generative Phonology Workbook*, by Stanlay M. Whitney. Madison, Wisc.: U. of Wisconsin P. pp. 125.

[116] *Six Lectures on Sound and Meaning by Roman Jacobson*. Trans. from the French by John Mepham. Cambridge, Mass.: M.I.T. Press. pp. xxvi + 116. $13.95.

the majority of titles presented here relate to language development. Only two introductory texts have been available: a very thorough and well organised book by D. J. Foss and D. T. Hakes[117] and a shorter yet stimulating offering by David Palermo[118]. James V. Wertsch[119] has edited a collection of articles representing recent trends in Soviet psycholinguistics. He suggests that trying to understand the assumptions behind Soviet work may help Western researchers to develop and reassess their own theories. Ann Cutler and David Fay[120] have produced a new edition of the classic work on speech errors by Rudolph Meringer and Carl Mayer. The editors produce a very clear introductory article which is likely to encourage those unfamiliar with the Gothic script to make the effort to read the original. Astin Heen Wold[121] tries to interpret individual cognitive strategies in the light of social psychological aspects of message transmission. She is concerned primarily with the temporal sequence of information.

The bulk of material in this section is concerned with language development. One of the best known researchers in the field of language acquisition is Lois Bloom and she is eminently suited to edit a volume of *Readings in Language Development*[122]. This volume has been prepared with the specific intention of supplementing *Language Development and Language Disorders*[123] although it can be used quite independently of this. The work provides a core of readings in language development, language disorders, psycholinguistics and special education. The first section provides a historical perspective and introduces the reader to various methodologies within child language research. Classic articles by W. E. Leopold, Jean Berko Gleason and Martin D. S. Braine are reproduced here. Section 2 examines the work on infant behaviours and the links between infant behaviour and later linguistic development. Section three concentrates on vocabulary, section four on grammar and section five on language in use. Comprehension is well served in section seven and in the final section linguistic and non-linguistic processes underlying language acquistion are examined. Dan Slobin's 'Cognitive Prerequisites for the Development of Grammar' and Eve V. Clark's 'Non-Linguistic Strategies and the Acquisition of Word-Meanings' stand out here as essential reading for all child language students. The volume as a whole is well organised and should provide a stable resource in acquisition studies. The Bloom and Lahey volume aims to examine language disorders within the context of normal language acquisition. The authors make a positive step towards linking

[117] *Psycholinguistics: An Introduction to the Psychology of Language*, by Donald J. Foss and David T. Hakes. Englewood Cliffs, N.J.: Prentice Hall. pp. xiv + 434.

[118] *Psychology of Language*, by David S. Palermo. Glenview, Ill.: Scott Foreman & Co. pp. 261.

[119] *Recent Trends in Soviet Psycholinguistics*, ed. by James V. Wertsch. White Plains, N.Y.: M.E. Sharpe Inc. 1977.

[120] *Versprechen and Verlesen*, by Rudolph Meringer and Carl Mayer. New Edition, with intro. article, by Anne Cutler and David Fay. Classics in Linguistics. Vol. 2. Amsterdam: John Benjamin, B.V. pp. xl + 207.

[121] *Decoding Oral Language*, by A. Heen Wold. European Monographs in Social Psychology 12. New York and London: Academic Press. pp. xi + 214.

[122] *Readings in Language Development*, ed. by Lois Bloom. Chichester and New York: John Wiley. pp. xii + 506.

[123] *Language Development and Language Disorder*, by Lois Bloom and Margaret Lahey. Chichester and New York: John Wiley.

theory and practice, providing goals and methods in clinical practice as well as theoretical and descriptive information.

Action Gesture and Symbol[124] examines whether there is a link between preverbal and verbal levels of language. After a clear introductory chapter by Andrew Lock, the book provides chapters on theoretical perspectives, the evolutionary background, communicative actions and the establishment of gesture, a core section dealing with the movement from gesture to symbol and a final section on symbols and society. The range of articles and the way in which they are organised and integrated into a single volume is most impressive. Contributors include Jerome Bruner, Colin Trevarthen, Patricia Greenfield, Linda Ferier and many others actively involved in acquisition research. Specific topics include the language-like behaviour of free-living chimpanzees and the creation of language by linguistically deprived deaf children.

The careful planning and integration of Lock's book is sadly lacking in Nickel's *Psycholinguistics*[125] which deals primarily with topics in first and second language acquisition. The editor, explaining the 'editorial parsimony' of the volume suggests that this is not entirely out of place in the practically oriented field of applied linguistics 'where generous toleration of errors that do not seriously distort meaning seems to be the norm'. If this is the case, then surely it is to be regretted. One can admire the desire to facilitate the fast production of conference proceedings but not at the expense of good editorial practice. Those with the patience to explore will find the good with the bad in the present volume.

Paula Menyuk's introduction to language acquisition[126] is useful as an overview but rather disappointing in detail. Jill and Peter de Villiers[127] have also produced an introductory textbook which moves steadily through the stages from pre-language to later grammar and includes chapters on processes and constraints and language in developmentally disabled children. The issues are clearly explained for the beginning student. Moerk[128] aims to bring together theoretical positions usually considered as in conflict in his discussion of early language development. Not unexpectedly such integration seems rather forced at times, but Moerk's individual approach to the issues can be stimulating and helpful.

A large and impressive volume of articles edited by Robin W. Campbell and Philip T. Smith[129] is based on the Psychology of Language Conference held at Stirling University, Scotland in June 1976. Indeed the volume shows that it is possible to combine relatively fast publication of conference papers together with high standards of presentation. The present volume explores how in recent years work on acquisition has shifted from

[124] *Action Gesture and Symbol: The Emergence of Language*, ed. by Andrew Lock. New York and London: Academic Press. pp. xiv + 588. £22.

[125] *Psycholinguistics*, ed. by Gerhard Nickel. Stuttgart: Hochschulverlag. pp. 383.

[126] *Language and Maturation*, by Paula Menyuk. Cambridge, Mass.: M.I.T. Press. pp. x + 180.

[127] *Language Acquisition*, by Jill G. de Villiers and Peter A. de Villiers. Cambridge, Mass.: Harvard U.P. pp. viii + 312.

[128] *Pragmatic and Semantic Aspects of Early Language Development*, by Ernst L. Moerk. Baltimore: University Park P. pp. x + 330.

[129] *Language Development and Mother-Child Interaction*, ed. by Robin W. Campbell and Philip T. Smith. Recent Advances in the Psychology of Language. New York and London: Plenum Press.

syntactic and phonological description to the 'amorphous' domains of semantics and pragmatics. This shift is reflected in the two large sections devoted to those aspects. Contributors include John Dore, Catherine Snow, Jerome Bruner and many others actively involved in acquisition research. In a particularly interesting contribution, Gordon Wells examines 'what matters for successful language development?' and claims that work on the Bristol data shows that it was the range of pragmatic functions addressed to the child that proved to be the best predictor of the child's language development.

N. Waterson and C. Snow[130] have edited a collection of articles derived from the Third International Child Language Symposium held at the School of African and Oriental Studies, University of London in September 1975. The editors note five far-reaching changes which have taken place in acquisition research since 1960: 1) growing interest in semantic and pragmatic aspects; 2) interdependence of linguistic and communicative context; 3) the recognition of the links between linguistic and cognitive development; 4) the importance of perceptual processes and 5) the re-interpretation of the nature of the 'innateness' hypothesis. All of these changes are reflected in the present volume and again many of the familiar names in acquisition research can be found here. To some extent, the dictates of the conference organisation has affected the nature of the articles: they are generally rather short due to the time limitation of the conference and this brevity often leaves the reader eager for more detailed information.

Naomi Baron[131] examines the links between the types of linguistic change noted in historical linguistics and the learning strategies adopted by the child. Stephen A. Blache[132] is primarily interested in the acquisition of distinctive features in child phonology. In order to explore this area more adequately, Blache provides a comparative analysis of the Jacobson/Halle theories, a detailed discussion of the acquisition model developed by Jacobson, a review of the research in this area and a way of applying the theoretical model to actual data. This is a well organised and well argued account of one topic in language development.

T. S. Cazacu[133] suggests that children's language has a social function from a very early stage. She bases her generalisation on her analysis of the content and form of dialogues among Romanian children in natural situations. Barbara Eneskar[134] provides discussion of and data from the longitudinal and multi-variable study of 250 Swedish children. The relationship between perceptual and productive strategies in learning the phonology

[130] *The Development of Communication*, ed. by Natalie Waterson and Catherine Snow. Chichester and New York: John Wiley. pp. xxv + 498.

[131] *Language Acquisition and Historical Change*, by Naomi S. Baron. North Holland Linguistic Series, 36. New York and Amsterdam: North Holland Publishing Company. pp. xiv + 320.

[132] *The Acquisition of Distinctive Features*, by Stephen A. Blache. Baltimore: University Park P. pp. xiv + 337.

[133] *Dialogue in Children*, by Tatiana Slama Cazacu. Janua Linguarum Series Mina, 149. The Hague: Mouton. 1977. pp. 157. DM 43.

[134] *Children's Language at Four and Six – A Longitudinal and Multivariable Study of Language Abilities among Children*, by Barbara Eneskar. Malmo, Sweden: C.W.K. Gleerup. pp. 69.

of early lexical items is explored by Harriet Klein[135]. Lise Menn[136] looks at the development in communcative competence of one child and Brian MacWhinney[137] develops a model of morphophonological structure showing the integration of the processes of rote, combination and analogy with reference to acquisition in sixteen languages. A further collection of articles on language acquisition is *The Child's Conception of Language*[138] which includes contributions from E. Clark, A. Sinclair, D. Slobin and others. This item has not been available for examination.

Finally in this section we move away from Language Development to other general psycholinguistic concerns. *Language Interpretation and Communication*[139] edited by David Gerver and H. Wallace Sinaiko is the record of a NATO Symposium on this topic held in Venice in 1977. As the editors comment, given the unique and important role of interpretation within international affairs, it is rather surprising that the linguistic and cognitive processes involved have received so little attention. The conference papers reflect the interdisciplinary approach. One unique feature of the conference was the involvement of sign language interpreters: their task is particularly interesting to the psycholinguist in that it involves not merely translation from one language to another, but a change of language medium. Again the editors and publishers are to be congratulated for the speed of publication.

W. J. M. Levelt and G. B. Flores D' Arcais have edited a series of papers[140] deriving from a symposium on language perception. This volume includes an extremely useful review article by Levelt on 'A Survey of Studies on Sentence Perception, 1970–1976' which has a reference list of 274 items. Other contributions deal with the prosody of speech perception, sentence processing and the clause boundary and the perception of complex sentences.

Sociolingustics

No attempt is made here to cover the vast range of materials on specific language areas and language communities. General overviews and theoretically important contributions are given priority. *Linguistic Variation: Models and Methods*[141] is significant both theoretically and descriptively.

[135] *The Relationship Between Perceptual Strategies and Productive Strategies in Learning the Phonology of Early Lexical Items*, by Harriet Klein. Bloomington, Ind.: I.U.L.C. pp. 155.

[136] *Pattern, Control and Contrast in Beginning Speech: A Case Study in the Development of Word Form and Word Function*, by Lise Menn. Bloomington, Ind.: I.U.L.C. pp. 291.

[137] *The Acquisition of Morphophonology*, by Brian MacWhinney. Monographs of the Society for Research in Child Development, Serial No. 174, Vol. 43. Chicago, Ill.: U. of Chicago P.

[138] *The Child's Concept of Language*, ed. by A. Sinclair, R. J. Jarvella and W. J. M. Levelt. Berlin and New York: Springer Verlag. DM 38, $20.90.

[139] *Language Interpretation and Communication*, ed. by David Gerver and H. Wallace Sinaiko. NATO Conference Series: Series III Human Factors, Vol. 6. New York: Plenum Publishing Corporation. pp. 438. $35.

[140] *Studies in the Perception of Language*, ed. by W. J. M. Levelt and G. B. Flores d' Arcais. Chichester and New York: John Wiley, pp. xviii + 335.

[141] *Linguistic Variation Models and Methods*, ed. by David Sankoff. New York and London: Academic Press. pp. 304. $17.50, £11.35.

While specific language communities receive close attention, the main impact comes from the discussion of theoretical issues, such as the nature of variable rules, the structure of the lexicon and quantitative occurrence restrictions. Other topics discussed include semantic field variability, language variation and linguistic competence, cross-language analyses of phonological phenomena and variation in the acquisition process. There is much here to interest the theoretical linguist, the psycholinguist, the sociolinguist and the language practitioner.

The collection of articles relating to *Sociolinguistic Patterns in British English*[142] again brings together empirical studies which have implications for theoretical models. Topics covered include: the sociolinguistic and geographical diffusion of vocalic mergers in East Anglia; post vocalic /r/ in Scottish English; consistency and variability in Glaswegian English; prosodic and paralinguistic features in Tyneside English; patterns of linguistic variation in three inner-city Belfast communities and linguistic code switching in a Northern Ireland village.

Sociolinguistics[143] edited by Gerhard Nickel is produced in the same series as the Psycholinguistics volume mentioned in the previous section. This collection is smaller than its companion but suffers from the same lack of organisation. Perhaps the copy I located was faulty, but not only was there no index or reference list, there was no contents list. The reader thus has absolutely no idea how to approach the volume and I would predict that many will reject the overall contents because of this. Of course, this would be a pity as there are interesting items which provide a clue to the different approaches Nickel recognises are at work in European and American sociolinguistics.

Joshua Fishman has produced yet another formidable volume on the sociology of language[144]. This time his concern is with 'Societal Multilinguism'. Topics discussed in detail include language contact, language maintenance and shift, the spread of languages of wider communication and the re-establishment of functional allocation. Further editorial commentary in the way of introductions to each section would have helped relative newcomers to find their way around this huge text. There is little doubt that this book will become another of the foundation texts of work in Sociolinguistics. Fishman has also co-edited a related volume on *The Spread of English*[145] which examines the way in which English is used as an additional language in many parts of the world.

John Schumann[146] examines the pidginisation process in second language acquisition by presenting a case study of a thirty-three year old Costa Rican. The author attempts to account for the slow progress made and proposes a 'pidginization hypothesis' which predicts that where social and psychological distance prevails, we will find pidginisation persisting in

[142] *Sociolinguistic Patterns in British English*, ed. by Peter Trudgill. Edward Arnold. pp. 192. £11.95.

[143] *Sociolinguistics*, ed. by Gerhard Nickel. Stuttgart: Hochschulverlag. pp. 165.

[144] *Advances in the Study of Societal Multilinguism*, ed. by Joshua A. Fishman. Contributions to the Sociology of Language, 9. The Hague: Mouton. pp. xiii + 842.

[145] *The Spread of English*, ed. by Joshua A. Fishman, Robert L. Cooper and Andrew W. Conrad. Rowley, Mass.: Newbury House Publishers. pp. 336.

[146] *The Pidginization Process: A Model for Second Language Acquisition*, by John H. Schumann. Rowley, Mass.: Newbury House Publishers. pp. ix + 190.

the speech of second language learners. The structure, status and origin of Creole languages is discussed by Valdman[147] with particular reference to Creole French.

The 1978 Georgetown University Round Table on Language and Linguistics[148], brought together people from ten different countries on linguistic and educational issues relating to bilingualism. This is a thorough and useful volume with sections on bilingual education policy; bilingual education and dialects; strategies for the implementation of bilingual education. More general sociolinguistic issues are discussed in McCormack and Wurm[149]. This volume contrasts sharply with the Nickel volume on Sociolinguistics above, in that several years have elapsed since the conference it derives from was in session. However, the topics discussed are still in the forefront of sociolinguistic activity.

One of the most traditional techniques in sociolinguistics is that of the interview. Lindsey Churchill[150] takes this as her starting point and attempts to analyse the question-answer process scientifically.

General

A series of source volumes containing valuable materials not easily available elsewhere have been produced in the last few years by Plenum Publishing. This year's volumes deal with the Aboriginal Sign Languages of the Americas and Australia. Volume 1 *North America*[151] contains an introduction to the study of sign language among North American Indians. Three classic works by Garrick Mallery are reproduced. In the second volume, *The Americans and Australia*[152], eighteen short articles on the Plains Sign Language of North America are reproduced; there is one article on the Urubu Sign Language of Brazil and nineteen articles on the Australian Aboriginal Sign Language. The dates of publication range from 1880 to the present day.

Sebeok in his introduction suggests that only a semiotic approach can provide an adequate account of the whole sign system, with its high degree of iconic and indexical signs. Certainly by examining these systems we may gain insights into present day sign language systems used within deaf communities, gesture systems within communicative interaction and human language and communication in general. The earlier volumes on

[147] *La Créole: Structure, statut et origine*, by Albert Valdman. Paris: Klincksiech. pp. xvi + 403. F. 170.

[148] *Internal Dimensions of Bilingual Education*, ed. by James Alatis. Georgetown University Round Table on Language and Linguistics, 1978. Washington, D.C.: Georgetown U.P. pp. x + 688.

[149] *Approaches to Language: Anthropological Issues*, ed. by W. C. McCormack and Stephen A. Wurm. World Anthropology Series. The Hague: Mouton. pp. xiii + 672.

[150] *Questioning Strategies in Sociolinguistics*, by Lindsey Churchill. Rowley, Mass.: Newbury House Publishers. pp. xi + 161.

[151] *Aboriginal Sign Languages of the Americas and Australias*, ed. by D. Jean Umiker-Sebeok and Thomas A. Sebeok. Vol. 1. North America. Classic Comparative Perspectives. New York: Plenum Publishing Corporation. pp. 474.

[152] *Aboriginal Sign Languages of the Americas and Australias*, ed. by D. Jean Umiker-Sebeok and Thomas A. Sebeok. Vol. 2. New York: Plenum Publishing Corporation. pp. 384.

Native Languages of the Americas, Vol. 1[153] and Vol. 2[154] include classic articles on the North American Indian Languages and Methodological and theoretical articles by linguists such as Suarez, Barthel and Longacre.

Two collections on sign languages have also appeared this year. *Sign Language of the Deaf*[155] edited by I. M. Schlesinger and L. Namir is a rather mixed collection from contributors who have very mixed ideas on the nature and structure of sign language systems. W. C. Stokoe writes with sensitivity and long experience on problems in sign language research, Gordon Hewes discusses the phylogeny of sign language and Hilde Schlesinger examines the acquisition of a bimodal language. The linguistic section of the book is rather disappointing in that it barely touches upon the major areas of sign linguistic research. Crystal and Craig take a particularly conservative view of the nature of human sign language, although their focus of attention here is a contrived sign system. *Understanding Language Through Sign Language Research*[156] lives up to its title by bringing together a series of papers which show both the similarities between sign language and spoken language and the different patterns of organisation which seem unique to the manual-gestural modality. The articles provide closely detailed accounts of specific areas in sign language analysis as well as sections on neurolinguistic and psycholinguistic research. This is a welcome addition to linguistic research and understanding. The first published linguistic study of British Sign Language[157] examines the notion of diglossia in the sign system used by the British deaf community.

I turn now to several items which may be of use to the student, teacher or clinician. T. F. Wallwork[158] provides an examination of language in its social context. This is relatively non-technical but clearly written and could well form part of an initial introduction to language studies. H. G. Widdowson[159] also directs his account of communication and communicative competence to the practising teacher.

Two somewhat more clinical contributions are Ruth Lesser's investigation of aphasia[160] and Developmental Dysphasia[161] by Maria A. Wykke. Lesser brings together valuable information which is not easily accessible. Her approach is more 'linguistic' than other writers' in that she uses the levels of phonology, syntax and semantics as a framework of reference.

[153] *Native Languages of the Americas*, ed. by Thomas A. Sebeok. Vol. 1. North America. New York: Plenum Publishing Corporation. 1976. pp. 648.

[154] *Native Languages of the Americas*, ed. by Thomas A. Sebeok. Vol. 2. Central and South America. New York: Plenum Publishing Corporation. 1977. pp. 550.

[155] *Sign Language of the Deaf: Psychological Linguistic and Sociological Perspectives*, ed. by I. M. Schlesinger and Lila Namir. Perspectives in Neurolinguistics and Psycholinguistics. New York and London: Academic Press. pp. 480. $22, £15.

[156] *Understanding Language Through Sign Language Research*, ed. by Patricia Siple. Perspectives in Neurolinguistics and Psycholinguistics. New York and London: Academic Press. pp. xiv + 378.

[157] *Diglossia and British Sign Language*, by Margaret Deuchar. Austin, Tex.: Southwest Educational Laboratory: Sociolinguistics Working Paper, 46.

[158] *Language and People*, by J. F. Wallwork. Heinemann. pp. ix + 178. £2.25.

[159] *Teaching Language as Communication*, by H. G. Widdowson. Oxford: O.U.P. pp. xi + 168.

[160] *Linguistic Investigations of Aphasia*, by Ruth Lesser. Language Disability and Remediation Series. Edward Arnold. pp. 236. £9.95.

[161] *Developmental Dysphasia*, ed. by Maria A. Wyke. New York and London: Academic Press. pp. xii + 180. £7.80, $16.65.

Developmental Dysphasia is a collection of articles on a multi-disciplinary approach.

Finally, those who find reading some of the volumes mentioned in this year's crop of linguistic books rather difficult, might like to comfort themselves with George Steiner's Volume, *On Difficulty and Other Essays*[162].

[162] *On Difficulty and Other Essays*, by George Steiner. Oxford: O.U.P. pp. xi + 209.

III

Old English Literature

T. A. SHIPPEY

Comprehensive bibliographies of Anglo-Saxon studies appear annually in *ASE* and *OEN*, the former prepared by a team of scholars (Carl T. Berkhout, Martin Biddle, T. J. Brown, Peter A. Clayton and Simon Keynes), the latter by Carl Berkhout alone. *OEN* also publishes an annual account of 'The Year's Work in O. E. Studies', again a co-operative effort co-ordinated by Rowland L. Collins; and abstracts of as yet unpublished papers delivered at some American conferences. The list of 'OE Research in Progress' published annually in *NM* is also at present compiled by Carl T. Berkhout.

1. Social, Cultural and Intellectual Background

Several important and impressive volumes have appeared in this area this year. Of these the weightiest and handsomest is, as might be expected, Volume 2 of *The Sutton Hoo Ship-Burial: Arms, Armour and Regalia*, by Rupert Bruce-Mitford[1]. This comes to some notably firm conclusions. Though the spears in the mound were all of native manufacture, the dies for the long strips on the shield appear to be the work of 'the same man' who made those for the shield from the Vendel 12 burial. If the shield was made in England, its maker brought his dies and punches from Eastern Scandinavia. The helmet is like Vendel examples too, only better and perhaps older: 'a date as early as c. A.D. 500. . .cannot be excluded'. Admiration is expressed not only for the 'technical skill' evident in the jewellery, but also for its creator's 'abnormal boldness and independence'. Modern gem-cutters felt they could do no better even with much more sophisticated equipment. The whetstone/sceptre, however, continues to arouse a certain disquiet. Mr Bruce-Mitford is now sure that the stag-image must have been mounted on one end of the stone bar, with a cup on the other end to support the object's weight while its holder was sitting. But while the bar 'has certainly never been used to sharpen anything', a utilitarian threat lurks behind its ritual function; the heads on it look 'grim', even 'murderous', hint at 'sacral power', denote 'an object in its essence thoroughly pagan'.

Possibly not less important, though very much at the other end of the economic scale, is *The Graveney Boat* described by Valerie Fenwick[2] – a tenth-century coaster, about forty-five feet long and capable of carrying

[1] *The Sutton Hoo Ship-Burial, Vol. 2: Arms, Armour and Regalia*, by Rupert Bruce-Mitford. British Museum Publications. pp. xvi + 651. 24 colour plates. £50.

[2] *The Graveney Boat: a Tenth Century Find from Kent* (British Archaeological Records British Series 53), by Valerie Fenwick. Oxford: BAR. pp. xx + 348. £9.

a cargo of seven tons, beached a thousand years ago for repair and then abandoned. Its fortunate preservation gives life to many of the Old and Middle English seafaring terms recorded in the glossary, while its cargo, startlingly, included lava quern-stones and hops, 'the first concrete evidence for the early use of hops in British brewery'. Perhaps we need not rethink *beor* after all; the traditional rhyme quoted in *YW* 56.66 turns out to be no truer than most such.

Further accounts of Anglo-Saxon *materialia* are to be found in *Viking Age York and the North*, a collection edited by R. A. Hall[3], and in two volumes of 'British Archaeological Reports', *Anglo-Saxon and Viking Age Sculpture and its Context*[4], and *Bede and Anglo-Saxon England*[5]. Among several interesting articles in the first of these three are Arthur MacGregor's account of 'Industry and Commerce in Anglo-Scandinavian York' (varied and thriving), J. T. Lang's 'Anglo-Scandinavian Sculpture in Yorkshire' (which confirms the area's independence and sense of continuity), and P. H. Sawyer's 'Some Sources for the History of Viking Northumbria', which include manuscript evidence from St Peter's, York, and St Cuthbert's, Durham, later chronicles, additions to the Durham *Liber Vitae*, Aldredian collects, and much else. From these Professor Sawyer concludes on the whole that the Scandinavians were tolerated, or better, by the Northumbrian English and even on occasion by the Church. There is considerable support for this view in the volume on *Sculpture*, especially in James Lang's 'Continuity and Innovation in Anglo-Scandinavian Sculpture', which uses new carvings found in the cemetery under York Minster to show that 'many of the features hitherto regarded as Scandinavian can be traced to English, insular origins'. A certain insular self-confidence begins to appear also in the *Bede and Anglo-Saxon England* volume. David M. Wilson's 'The Art and Archaeology of Bedan Northumbria' considers the treasures found on St Ninian's Isle in the Shetlands to argue that while these are Pictish themselves, they drew their inspiration from elsewhere, perhaps from Northumbria; the cultural areas of Pictland and Northumbria were in fact allied, and 'the old adage that all things beautiful come from Ireland is no longer true'. For similar conclusions from different evidence see, incidentally, Molly Miller, 'Eanfrith's Pictish Son' (*Northern History*).

Several of the articles in the last-mentioned volume concentrate however on the Ruthwell Cross. R. T. Farrell's 'The Archer and Associated Figures on the Ruthwell Cross – A Reconsideration', explains them as deriving from patristic comment on such texts as Psalm 90; the eagle is Christ, whose wings protect us from the archer-*feond*. Rosemary Cramp also sees a stress on 'Christ in majesty' in 'The Evangelist Symbols and their Parallels in Anglo-Saxon Sculpture'. Éamonn Ó Carragáin, however, goes a good deal further in 'Liturgical Innovations Associated with Pope Sergius and the Iconography of the Ruthwell and Bewcastle Crosses', to

[3] *Viking Age York and the North* (Council for British Archaeology Research Report 27). CBA. pp. iv + 73. £6.

[4] *Anglo-Saxon and Viking Age Sculpture and its Context: papers from the Collingwood Symposium on Insular Sculpture from 800 to 1066* (BAR British Series 49), ed. by James Lang. Oxford: BAR. pp. x + 223. £4.50.

[5] *Bede and Anglo-Saxon England: Papers on the 1300th anniversary of the birth of Bede* (BAR British Series 46), ed. by J. T. Farrell. Oxford: BAR. pp. x + 172. £3.50.

saying, for example, that the reason the South face has panels depicting Annunciation and Crucifixion is that both were thought to have taken place on the same *date*, a fact emphasised by the new ceremonial introduced by Pope Sergius (686–701). The same Pope also ordered that the *Agnus Dei* should be sung at the moment of breaking of bread, two elements also present in the Cross's iconography. Perhaps the link he established between Crucifixion and Annunication accounts also for the link between Cross and Mary in *The Dream of the Rood*, lines 90–94.

In the same volume Winthrop Wetherbee's 'Some Implications of Bede's Latin Style' praises Bede's 'clearsighted, unembarrassed indifference to superficial graces of style', seen as a 'domestication of Virgil'; one has to say, though, that it is not 'safe enough to take for granted a first-hand knowledge of Virgil', see Meyvaert, *YW* 57.44. In *Medieval Eloquence*[6], Calvin B. Kendall's 'Bede's *Historia ecclesiastica*: The Rhetoric of Faith' illustrates Bede's use of figures and tropes. Much of interest can be found meanwhile in the Jarrow Lectures for successive years (which should have been mentioned before): in 1975 R. A. Markus discussed 'Bede and the Tradition of Ecclesiastical Hagiography'[7], in 1977 Per Jonas Nordhagen spoke on 'The Codex Amiatinus and the Byzantine Element in the Northumbrian Renaissance'[8], with special reference to the 'Ezra page', the work of 'a Byzantine painter come from Italy'; in 1978 Richard N. Bailey's 'The Durham Cassiodorus'[9] discussed the iconography of and the artistic use of templates in illustrations to the Durham commentary on the Psalms. The most interesting Bede studies of recent years, however, are the 1976 Jarrow lecture, Henry Mayr-Harting's 'The Venerable Bede, the Rule of St Benedict and Social Class'[10], and another contribution to *Bede and Anglo-Saxon England*, Patrick Wormald's 'Bede, *Beowulf* and the Conversion of the Anglo-Saxon Aristocracy'. The former makes clear Bede's lack of interest in aristocratic society. He valued St Benedict's insistence on obedience to seniority *within the monastery*; he said nothing about his own genealogy and liked priests from nowhere, such as Aidan and Fursey; he believed in 'clericalism', in an *élite* of learned monks raised to the priesthood. What then would have been his attitude to 'founder's kin' and the cosy corruption of many Northumbrian monasteries? One can guess. Patrick Wormald argues accordingly, if iconoclastically, that 'if a modern historian wishes to understand the conversion of the Anglo-Saxon aristocracy, he has less to learn from Bede, than from other sources' – especially from *Beowulf*. Though the author of this poem was probably a cleric, he was not a cleric like Bede ('a fundamentalist', 'a rather isolated figure'); that is why the 'ethical tone' of his poem contains 'a profound ambiguity

[6] *Medieval Eloquence: Studies in the Theory and Practice of Medieval Rhetoric*, ed. by James J. Murphy. Berkeley, Los Angeles and London: U. of California P. pp. xii + 354. $17.75.

[7] *Bede and the Tradition of Ecclesiastical Hagiography* (Jarrow Lecture 1975), by R. A. Markus. Published by the Rector of Jarrow. pp. 19.

[8] *The Codex Amiatinus and the Byzantine Element in the Northumbrian Renaissance* (Jarrow Lecture 1977), by Per Jonas Nordhagen. Published by the Rector of Jarrow. pp. 18, 10 ill.

[9] *The Durham Cassiodorus* (Jarrow Lecture 1978), by Richard N. Bailey. Published by the Parish of Jarrow. pp. 28, 2 plates.

[10] *The Venerable Bede, The Rule of St. Benedict and Social Class* (Jarrow Lecture 1976), by Henry Mayr-Harting. Published by the Rector of Jarrow. pp. 28.

...both unquestionably "secular" and almost idealistic'. Mr Wormald notes that Bede's grammar does not use illustrations, not even respectable Virgilian ones, from secular literature; his attitude to graceless pagans was that of Alcuin; but their attitude was not the only one, certainly not that of the many aristocratic foundations mentioned by severer historians only to be condemned. If we are to understand the composition of *Beowulf*, Mr Wormald suggests, 'the ideological heritage of Western Christianity in the early Middle Ages is the wrong place to look'. Literary scholars need very much to read both these pieces, before persevering in disagreement.

An interesting sidelight on the Easter controversy is recorded by Kenneth Harrison, 'Easter cycles and the equinox in the British Isles' (*ASE*): maybe Bede had *seen* the British were wrong about their dates. Another scientific (if gruesome) piece is Stanley Rubin's 'St. Cuthbert of Lindisfarne: a Medical Reconstruction' (*Transactions of the Architectural and Archaeological Society of Durham*); and Cecil A. Hewett's 'Anglo-Saxon carpentry' (*ASE*) gives accounts of the many pre-Conquest tusked tenons, splayed rebates, barefaced lap-dovetails and scribed shoulders astonishingly surviving to the present day, like Cuthbert's bones.

There is a useful introduction to such subjects, and many others, in G. A. Lester's *The Anglo-Saxons: How they Lived and Worked* (1975)[11]; and the collection of essays on *The South Saxons*[12], edited by Peter Brandon, also shows a proper variation of literary evidence by that of archaeology, ecology and place-names. In the editor's own consideration of 'The South Saxon *Andredesweald*', even the swineherd who avenged alderman Cumbra finds a context; the forest was pig-pastureland. The new and sceptical approach to history is however summed up in many ways by P. H. Sawyer's *From Roman Britain to Norman England*[13], which (among much else) tries to break away from over-dependence on Bede and the *Anglo-Saxon Chronicle* by the use on the one hand of tangibles like coins, landscapes, technologies, but on the other of the subtle structures of modern anthropology. Some of the research which has influenced Professor Sawyer is summed up in Margaret Gelling's *Signposts to the Past: Place-Names and the History of England*[14]; another cross-reference of similar type may be found in Gillian Fellows Jensen's 'Place-Names and Settlement in the North Riding of Yorkshire' (*Northern History*). The 'continuity' seen by students of sculpture shows itself also in the English vills which accepted Viking settlers without changing their names, in the man buried in pagan style in Wensley churchyard. One can image what Alcuin would have thought of tolerant gestures like that!

Further corroboration of this new historical consensus can be found in *Ethelred the Unready*[15]. Several of the papers in this express doubt

[11] *The Anglo-Saxons: How they Lived and Worked*, by G. A. Lester. Newton Abbot, London and Vancouver: David & Charles. 1976. pp. 168. £3.95.

[12] *The South Saxons*, edited by Peter Brandon. London and Chichester: Phillimore. pp. viii + 248. £8.75.

[13] *From Roman Britain to Norman England*, by P. H. Sawyer. Methuen. pp. x + 294. hb £9.50, pb £4.95.

[14] *Signposts to the Past: Place-Names and the History of England*, by Margaret Gelling. J. M. Dent. pp. 256. £6.50.

[15] *Ethelred the Unready: Papers from the Millenary Conference* (BAR British Series 59), ed. by David Hill. Oxford: BAR. pp. vi + 273. £6.

about the authority of the *Chronicle*, as indeed of Ælfric and Wulfstan. In 'The Reign of Æthelred II, a Study in the Limitations of Royal Policy and Action', P. A. Stafford argues that the king's incompetence was not the true reason for failure, which was caused by 'the strength of the nobility', 'the difficulties of effecting change without affecting loyalties' and the competition of power-groups including the Church. N. P. Brooks's 'Arms, Status and Warfare in Late-Saxon England' also asserts the power of the military nobility; heriots were not commuted for cash, the transfer of weapons remained a practical reality. In another brilliant paper, 'Æthelred the Lawmaker', Patrick Wormald revalues the much-despised codes of Æthelred, weighs the influence in them of Wulfstan, redates them, shows their relationship to 'Carolingian pastoral imperialism', and notes the existence in them of the attitude summed up in the preacher's marginal note: 'Argument weak: shout like mad!' But maybe the shouting was Wulfstan's, not Æthelred's. Christine E. Fell meanwhile re-interprets 'Edward King and Martyr and the Anglo-Saxon Hagiographical Tradition', again expressing doubt over traditional history and the tale of Ælfthryth, that archetypal wicked stepmother; and Simon Keynes once more points to the Chronicler as largely responsible, unfairly, for 'The Declining Reputation of King Æthelred the Unready'. There were some still praying for the king's soul in the reign of Canute.

To judge from the more general articles in *The OE Homily and its Backgrounds*[16], literary scholars have not yet been much affected by these radical historical rethinkings. Milton McC. Gatch's 'The Achievement of Ælfric and his Colleagues in European Perspective' praises Ælfric for the original idea of providing 'a cycle of exegetical homiletical texts in the vernacular', something which has no known Continental precursors, though some successors. Cyril L. Smetana discusses the influence from the Continent of 'Paul the Deacon's Patristic Anthology'. P. A. Stafford, though a contributor to *Ethelred the Unready* above, here seems constrained by a more orthodox literary context to explain 'Church and Society in the Age of Ælfric' as largely united; the Æthelred codes are an indication of an age that 'totally confused the religious and the secular' – or was it, see Wormald above, an *archbishop* who totally confused the religious and the secular, at least when he was writing up the minutes? One solid piece of evidence on the Benedictine Reform comes from Helmut Gneuss, 'Dunstan and Hrabanus Maurus. Zur Hs. Bodleian Auctarium F.4.32' (*Anglia*). This shows that the 'Dunstan drawing' in that manuscript is, like the two-line verse attached to it, the work of St. Dunstan himself. The first line and the drawing are imitated from Hrabanus Maurus's *Figurengedichte* no. 28, and the second line is a memory of Statius.

On manuscripts, J. J. G. Alexander's *Insular Manuscripts: Sixth to the Ninth Century*[17] complements Elzbieta Temple's succeeding volume (see *YW* 57.44). It includes items from seventy-eight MSS, among them the Book of Lindisfarne and the Book of Kells, but also many others 'only

[16] *The OE Homily and its Backgrounds*, ed. by Paul E. Szarmach and Bernard F. Huppé. Albany, N.Y.: State U. of New York P. pp. viii + 267. $35.

[17] *Insular Manuscripts: Sixth to the Ninth Century*, by J. J. G. Alexander (Vol. 1 of the 'Survey of Manuscripts Illuminated in the British Isles', gen. ed. J. J. G. Alexander). Harvey Miller. pp. 219. 380 illustrations. £38.

slightly less splendid', the Codex Amiatinus, the Leningrad Bede, the Book of St Chad, and the prayer-book that once belonged to Alfred's wife. D. W. Rollason's 'Lists of saints' resting-places in Anglo-Saxon England' (*ASE*) looks at two MSS of a short O.E. document apparently once two separate halves, the first pre-Viking in saints and locations, the second post-1013. P. R. Robinson shows how to identify 'Self-contained units in composite manuscripts of the Anglo-Saxon period' (*ASE*), with instances from such homily collections as Hatton MS 115 or the Vercelli Book. In *Medieval Eloquence* (see above), M. B. Parkes's 'Punctuation, or Pause and Effect', shows how 'concern. . .to elucidate the text' carried more weight with scribes than pronunciation or intonation patterns. Ann Knock's 'The *Liber Monstrorum*: an unpublished manuscript and some reconsiderations' (*Scriptorim*) concludes that the fifth MS of this work 'gives no further encouragement to the theory of Anglo-Saxon origin'.

Feminism continues to make forays into this field. Jane Tibbetts Schulenburg's 'Sexism and the celestial gynaeceum – from 500 to 1200' (*JMH*) tells us that female saints, donors and institutions shrank in number from 700 onwards; and three studies from *Medieval Women*[18], ponder Anglo-Saxon ladies in history. Joan Nicholson's '*Feminae gloriosae*: women in the Age of Bede' leaves us wondering what those 'communities of high-spirited girls' were like. Janet E. Nelson's 'Queens as Jezebels: the Careers of Brunhild and Balthild in Merovingian History' at least proves one English slave-girl became a queen of France. Pauline Stafford's 'Sons and Mothers: Family Politics in the Early Middle Ages' *inter alia* puts the blame for Edward's murder squarely on his stepmother Ælfthryth (but see Christine Fell above). The *mentalités* approach is taken further by Charles M. Rodding, 'Evolution of Medieval Mentalities: a Cognitive-Structural Approach' (*AHR*); he believes that the period was characterised by modes of thought now, according to Piaget, most commonly found in under-tens – 'moral realism', 'mechanical observation', less *contritio* than *satisfactio*. Alexander Murray, 'Money and robbers, 900–1100' (*JMH*) more pragmatically argues that trade, coins and theft are all linked. A twelfth-century illustration of the hanging of the robbers of St Edmund's tomb shows less remorse than technical efficiency, a case of early capitalist 'backlash'.

Continuities of various kinds are illustrated in Thomas H. Bestul's, 'The Collection of Anselm's Prayers in British Library MS Cotton Vespasian D. xxxvi' (*MÆ*); Daniel Huws's 'A Welsh Manuscript of Bede's *De natura rerum*' (*BBCS*); Judith Grant's 'A New *Passio Beati Edmundi Regis [et] Martyris*' (*MS*); and in the 406 phonological, lexical and other maps of *The Linguistic Atlas of England*[19]. R. H. C. Davis's 'The *Carmen de Hastingae Proelio*' (*EHR*) however removes that work from authority, 'as a source for the history of the Norman Conquest it is simply ridiculous'. At the other end of the period, indeed strictly speaking beyond it, no-

[18] *Medieval Women: presented to Professor Rosalind M. T. Hill on her seventieth birthday* (Studies in Church History Subsidia 1), ed. by Derek Baker. Oxford: Blackwell. pp. xii + 399. £12.50.

[19] *The Linguistic Atlas of England*, ed. by Harold Orton, Stewart Sanderson and John Widdowson. London: Croom Helm; Atlantic Highlands, N. J.: Humanities Press. No pagination. £42.50.

one would wish to be without two companion volumes, the well-edited and introduced texts and translations of *Gildas: The Ruin of Britain and other works*[20], and *St. Patrick: his Writings and Muirchu's Life*[21].

2. Vocabulary

Three German studies consider the question of dialects in O.E. Franz Wenisch, 'Sächsische Dialektwörter in *The Battle of Maldon*' (*Indogermanische Forschungen*, 1977 for 1976) argues against the thesis that O.E. poets wrote 'common poetic language'; *gehende* is found in only three poems, including *Maldon*, and has no clear Anglian examples in prose, while *ætforan*, though more complex, is also a southern word. *Ofermod* too may be dialect. The same author however, in 'Kritische Bemerkungen zu Angaben über die Verbreitung einiger angeblich westsächsische Dialektwörter' (*Anglia*), reclassifies nine words once thought to be West-Saxon as 'common O.E.'; his scepticism here makes the *Maldon* evidence look stronger. Bernhard Diensberg denies that there are 'Westsächsische Lehnwörter im merzischen AB-Dialekt?' (*Anglia*); the ones he considers turn out also to be common.

On single words, Alfred Bammesberger writes a footnote to Grinda (*YW* 58.51) in *BBCS*, 'O.E. *broc* and Middle Irish *broc(c)*'. The Irish word is borrowed from the English, itself probably a back-formation from *brocian*, 'hurt, afflict, molest'. R. D. Fulk, 'O.E. *Icge* and *Inge*' (*ES*), sees the two words as indeed connected and meaning probably 'fiery' or 'shining'. Anatoly Liberman has *Beowulf* 600, *swefeð ond sendeþ*, in mind in 'Germanic *sendan* "to make a sacrifice"' (*JEGP*); the phrase might be a verbal relic, with Hondscio as a vestige of sacrifice. The Old Norse parallels are more convincing. Ida Masters Hollowell, '*Scop* and *Woðbora* in O.E. Poetry' (*JEGP*), also goes back to pagan times to argue that these two words were once clearly demarcated, the former a praise-singer and entertainer, the latter a seer linked with 'Wodenesque ecstasy', singer of the *gied*, also a relic of cult ceremony. *The Order of the World* is seen as one such vatic composition adjusted to Christianity. Patrizia Lendinara's 'Ags. *wlanc*: alcune annotazioni' (*Annali*, Naples, sez. germ., Fil. germ., 1976), shows authors of the *Riddles* exploiting the ambiguities of the word, between 'brave', 'proud', 'vain-glorious', 'sensual', 'zealous' and so on. I regret that I have not been able to see M. von Rüden's study, '*Wlanc*' *und Derivate im Alt- und Mittelenglischen: eine wortgeschichtliche Studie*[22]: it might have cleared the picture.

Even more obscure cases are considered by Bruce Mitchell, 'O.E. *Oð þæt* Adverb?' (*N&Q*); one should beware of drawing 'precise grammatical boundaries' between main and subordinate clauses, and reflect that the word could sometimes mean 'at length'. As for the same author's 'Prepo-

[20] *Gildas: The Ruin of Britain and other works* (Arthurian Period Sources Vol. 7), ed. and trans. by Michael Winterbottom. London and Chichester: Phillimore. pp. vi + 162. hb £4.50, pb £2.25.

[21] *St. Patrick: his writings and Muirchu's Life* (Arthurian Period Sources Vol. 9), ed. and trans. by A. B. E. Hood. London and Chichester: Phillimore. pp. viii + 101. hb £3, pb £1.50.

[22] '*Wlanc*' *und Derivate im Alt- und Mittelenglischen: eine wortgeschichtliche Studie*, by M. von Rüden.

sitions, Adverbs, Prepositional Adverbs, Postpositions, Separable Prefixes, or Inseparable Prefixes, in O.E.', (*NM*) its title indicates the problem. Translators – and even more lexicographers – of O.E. will have to read this article carefully. Lotte Motz, 'Burg–berg, burrow–barrow' (*Indogermanische Forschungen* 1977 for 1976), wishes to see the words as indicating natural/manmade habitations, not heights, while W. Kienast, 'Germanische Treue und "Königsheil"' (*Historische Zeitschrift*), believes that **trewwo* had from Tacitus's time some ethical connotation relatable to the *comitatus* spirit.

The Dictionary of Old English meanwhile continues. A. Crandell Amos gives the '1977 Progress Report' in *OEN*, and he and Angus Cameron record 'The Dictionary of O.E.: a Turning Point' in *ESts*. The entire corpus is now in computer-readable form, and editorial work has begun.

3. Old English Literature: General

Two authors grapple this year with the problem of influence-detection within a rhetorical tradition. In *Medieval Eloquence*, Jackson J. Campbell's 'Adaptation of Classical Rhetoric in O.E. Literature' recognises a pervasive problem: 'a completely untutored person competent in his own language has the resources for producing practically all the *figurae verborum* and *figurae sententiarum*'. One can however see, in Ælfric, in Wulfstan, in *The Phoenix* and elsewhere, Anglo-Saxon authors recognising and imitating the rhetorical structures of their sources. Where there is no source the problem is greater; but Professor Campbell is sure the *Beowulf*-poet was trained in Latin rhetoric too, though this 'has its profound effect without ostentatiously calling attention to itself'. Hildegard L. C. Tristam's 'Stock Descriptions of Heaven and Hell in O.E. Prose and Poetry' (*NM*) demonstrates some unquestionably repeated patterns, such as the 'noun *butan* noun', '*a butan ende*' phrases, or the *Unsagbarkeitstopos*, and comments also on the influence of the apocryphal *Visio Pauli*; when the mere in *Beowulf* and Blickling Homily 17 are compared, though, they appear parallel only in 'rhetorical properties', not subject or theme. One should 'concentrate on the individual treatment of patterns available'.

Morton W. Bloomfield's 'The Wisdom Tradition', given as one of the Sixtieth Anniversary Memorial Lectures Seijo Gakuen, at Seijo University, notes the growing interest in the Western world in material once considered irretrievably dull. What has made the change, he notes, is the awareness of how much information on world-views is locked up in proverbs, laws, and Polonius' speeches; one of the functions of scholarship is to 'raise us out of our own civilization or our own immediate concerns'.

An attempt is made to provide more material for students in the revision of Henry Sweet's *A Second Anglo-Saxon Reader (Archaic and Dialectal)*, by T. F. Hoad[23]. This follows the 1887 first edition closely, and consists largely of some hundred pages of Epinal-Erfurt and Corpus Glossaries, plus inscriptions, fragments, the name-list of the Durham *Liber Vitae*, charters etc. The texts are presented with scrupulous accuracy, but there are no notes or even explanations, so that the student who is sup-

[23] *A Second Anglo-Saxon Reader (Archaic and Dialectal)*, ed. by Henry Sweet, 2nd revised ed. by T. F. Hoad. Oxford: Clarendon Press. pp. xii + 237. £7.50.

posed to be becoming familiar with 'the leading features of the non-West-Saxon dialects' will have to be a freakishly hardy and dedicated soul. It is sad to see that the highest ambition of 1978 philology is 1887 philology with every i dotted.

Finally, Margaret Martin offers 'A Note on Marginalia in *The Vercelli Book*' (*N&Q*). The words *Cum pervenisse[t]* at the foot of fol. 136v. are not from Luke 22.40, as Celia Sisam suggests (*YW* 57.53–4), but from an antiphon for the feast of St Andrew, found for example in the Worcester Antiphonal, in Ælfric's 'Homily on the Nativity of St. Andrew', perhaps in *Dream of the Rood* 33–41. This may support a Kentish origin for the book; Rochester's patron saint was Andrew.

4. Old English Poetry: General

Pride of place here must certainly go, for its evident utility, to the *Concordance to the ASPR*[24]. Its uses are innumerable: for the student of syntax, the student of poetic diction, the lexicographer, the person suddenly asked (like this reviewer) to say something about images of wealth in O.E. poetry and able instantly to look up – with curious results – all poetic uses of *penig* and *pund, sceatt* and *scilling* and dozens more. There are traps in the volume, apparently inevitable in anything at any point computer-derived. Hononyms are not separated, so that all those scholars unable to tell *god* from *gód* by themselves will be left unenlightened; as the editor says ruefully, 'context is all'. It is the Krapp-Dobbie edition of *ASPR* which has been concorded, furthermore, not the MSS, so once again the responsibility is on users to check. However, so it should be. The 'thoroughly analyzed concordance' of which Professor Bessinger dreams might well stifle all further initiative. In any case 'second best straight away' has on occasion proved a good motto.

In general considerations of the poetry, 'orality' is still much in dispute. Edward R. Haymes's *Das mündliche Epos*[25] does not contribute a great deal, since its author has not budged an inch from Parry-Lord-Magoun. The existence of checks to their theory in O.E. is recognised, but brushed away: 'no-one could any longer dispute the existence of a highly-developed oral epic in the O.E. period. . .Present investigation recognises the poetic language as an oral one'. But it doesn't; and some people can; and they do, too. A very much more balanced approach underlies Barbara Raw's *The Art and Background of O.E. Poetry*[26]. Miss Raw begins as if nothing were known for sure about the poems at all, as if they were completely mysterious artefacts from nowhere. What then can be concluded about them? The state of the MSS leads her to suggest they 'did not belong to a written but an oral tradition'. The nature of the words used about poems in poems leads on to new definitions of the *leoð*, the *spell*, the *gied*, the *gleo*, what is said and what is sung, what is sad and what is joyful. The general character-

[24] *A Concordance to the Anglo-Saxon Poetic Records*, ed. by J. B. Bessinger Jr, programmed by Philip H. Smith Jr, with an index of compounds compiled by Michael H. Twomey. Ithaca and London: Cornell U.P. pp. xl + 1510. $45.

[25] *Das mündliche Epos*, by Edward R. Haymes. Stuttgart: Metzler. 1977. pp. viii + 49.

[26] *The Art and Background of OE Poetry*, by Barbara C. Raw. Edward Arnold. pp. vi + 148. £7.95.

istics of the tradition are described: the use of 'authenticators', the role of the poet, the lack of movement, the delight in the generic. Single observations are however continually generated by this process, like recognised items in an inventory of strange goods: there is only one specific tree in the O.E. poetic corpus, *yðlaf*; 'flotsam', is used in *Beowulf* with rare imagination; and in O.E. poetry even emotions are made by smiths. This book gives a subtle view of many poems, in which generalisation is never too powerful to admit exceptions, nor indeed vice versa. Also highly to be recommended are two articles by Geoffrey R. Russom, 'Artful Avoidance of the Useful Phrase in *Beowulf, The Battle of Maldon*, and *Fates of the Apostles*' (*SP*), and 'A Germanic Concept of Nobility in *The Gifts of Men* and *Beowulf*' (*Speculum*). The first of these rejects the now-traditional dichotomy between the free variation of literate poets and the formulaic rigidity, or 'thrift', of oral ones by showing how O.E. poets rang deliberate changes on phrases they must have known, without in the process abandoning the traditional nature of their diction; there must have been, then, either 'oral poets with skills not foreseen by Parry, Lord and Magoun', or else literate ones with a highly respectful attitude to their past. In similar style, but with entirely different content, the second article shows that the 'gifts of men' theme has much more to do with lists of artistocratic qualities in Old Norse, with 'a well-defined picture of the literary nobleman', than with the parable of the talents (as claimed by Cross, *YW* 43.60). Professor Russom maintains a proper distance between himself and. on the one hand, the excesses of Edward Haymes above; on the other, the views condemned in David S. Berkeley's 'Some Misapprehensions of Christian Typology in Recent Literary Scholarship' (*Studies in English Literature 1500–1900*). This last piece differentiates between types, antitypes and archetypes; explains some standard confusions; and cites Lewis E. Nicholson's account of Scyld's burial as a *figura* of baptism (*YW* 44.71) among them. Scholars need more than a perusal of Auerbach's 'Figura' to understand types.

There have been several interesting comparative pieces recently. Karl Hauck's *Wielands Hort*[27] relates smiths to shamans, with much German and Scandinavian as well as O.E. material, but proceeding to an interpretation of the Franks Casket. On it we should see three master-craftsmen, their three *Schicksalsfrauen*, their three magic objects of ring, arrows and goblet. These relate to the Three Magi, the legends of Solomon, of Romulus and Remus; the casket is *ein einheitliches Gesamtprogramm*; its centre is the hoard of divinely-descended objects. Using Celtic material, Patrick Sims-Williams writes one piece on the *Finnsburg Fragment* (see section 9 below), but puts his conclusions there into a wider context in 'Riddling Treatment of the "Watchman Device" in *Branwen* and *Togail Bruidne Da Derga*' (*Studia Celtica*); the watchman who looks out and cannot understand what he is seeing is related as a narrative device to the poetic devices of kenning, riddle, gnome. All four are 'self-conscious experiments in manipulating analogies'. Nick Jacobs's piece in Welsh, 'Y Traddodiad

[27] *Wielands Hort: Die sozialgeschichtliche Stellung des Schmiedes in frühen Bildprogrammen nach und vor dem Religionswechsel* (Kungl. Vitterhets Historie och Antikvitets Akademien, antikvariskt archiv 64). Stockholm: Almkvist and Wiksell. 1977. pp. 31. 15 illustrations.

Arwrd hen Sæsneg o'i gymharu â'r dystiolaeth gymraeg', in *Astudiethau ar yr Hengerdd*[28], suggests that Welsh poetry is in a sense more heroic, if less sympathetic and more inveterate, than O.E. Though the role of poets in the two societies seems comparable, it may be that wandering poets (like 'Widsith') were obliged to make stories of the traditions even of their own recent enemies. *Deor* is compared with the Welsh *dadolwch*, poems which plead for reconciliation. There is an English summary of the article. In what is now old-fashioned style, E. J. Sharpe's 'The O.E. Runic Paternoster' in *Symbols of Power*[29], leaps from runes to incantations to sungods. It does however mention a modern superstition, 'Old Nick's Latin', the SATOR-AREPO formula; this was known to Anglo-Saxons too, see Tate, section 7 below.

On metre, William G. Moulton proves the existence of 'Secondary Stress in Germanic Alliterative Verse' (*Amsterdam Studies in the Theory and History of Linguistic Science*, Series IV, 1977), by relating 'heightening' to 'shortening' under Sievers's rules. In more complex style F. H. Whitman gives 'Evidence for the Metrical Interdependence of O.E. A- and B-Lines' (*Neophilologus*), by looking at lines containing *hwilum*; the rules derived work only if whole lines are taken as units.

I have not been able to see either of Patrizia Lendinara's pieces, 'L'eroe sulla spiaggia' or 'I cosidetti "Versi Gnomici" del Codice Exoniense e del MS. Cotton Tiberius B. i, una ricerca bibliografica', both in *Annali*, Naples, sez. germ. Fil. germ. (1977).

5. Beowulf

The radical uncertainties about the nature of Anglo-Saxon culture which have shown themselves in sections 1 and 4 above are displayed here in near-total disagreement between two books, Whitney F. Bolton's *Alcuin and Beowulf: an Eighth Century View*[30], and this reviewer's *Beowulf*, in the Arnold's 'Studies in English Literature' series[31]. Naturally one's objectivity cannot be trusted at this point; readers of this account will have to draw their own conclusions. However it seems that both parties in this dispute believe their own approach is historical, complex and supported by facts. The doubt must therefore be over what is a 'fact'. Professor Bolton takes the opinions of Alcuin as data about how an eighth-century intellectual would have seen the poem; he claims this may not give a 'definitive' view, but does give a 'representative' one. Two chapters on Alcuin's literary theory and practice are accordingly balanced against two on *Beowulf*, the former pair asserting the importance of 'moral grammar', verbal exactness, interpretation via presentation (see Parkes, section 1 above), and rhetorical complexity, the latter pair arguing for the Babylonian folly of the Danes, the penitential progress of Beowulf himself.

[28] *Astudiaethau ar yr Hengerdd (Studies in Old Welsh Poetry)*, ed. by Rachel Bromwich and R. Brinley Jones. Cardiff: U. of Wales P. pp. xii + 390. £12.95.

[29] *Symbols of Power*, ed. by H. R. Ellis Davidson. Cambridge: D. S. Brewer, and Totowa N.J.: Rowman & Littlefield. pp. x + 182. £4.50.

[30] *Alcuin and Beowulf: an Eighth Century View*, by Whitney F. Bolton. New Brunswick, N.J.: Rutgers U.P. pp. xii + 200. $13.

[31] *Beowulf* (Studies in English Literature 70), by T. A. Shippey. London: Edward Arnold. pp. 64. hb £3.95, pb £1.95.

The poem asks *quanto magis*? – if a pagan was virtuous, how much more so should Christians strive to be. This reviewer by contrast believes with Professor Bloomfield (see section 3 above) that there is more information inside texts than is often realised, and that *Beowulf* has through its modern history been too much oppressed by (widely variant) historical 'backgrounds'. The problem is to understand an ethic at many points alien and even embarrassing to our own, e.g. over drink, boasting and violence. The main clues are maxims, repeated words and scenes, the poet's own strongly expressed opinions; the main misleader is the word 'irony', a concept socially determined and therefore prone to change. It is true that the image of the poet thus generated does not look much like Alcuin or Bede. But were they 'representative' Anglo-Saxons (see Wormald, Mayr-Harting in section 1 above)?

Similar irresolvable oppositions manifest themselves in several articles. Peter A. Jorgensen, 'Beowulf's Swimming Contest with Breca: Old Norse Parallels' (*Folklore*) cites many swimming matches in *fornaldarsǫgur*, to indicate a Scandinavian archetype and reject Celtic influences. Sylvia Huntley Horowitz, however, thinks little of 'Bear's Sons' and more of parallels between 'Beowulf, Samson, David and Christ' (*Studies in Medieval Culture*). The Anglo-Saxon hero, we are told rather dangerously (see Berkeley, section 4 above) is a 'type'. Clarence Steinberg opts 'For a Servian Reading of *Beowulf*: Further Studies in O.E. Onomastics' (*NM*), but does no more than repeat earlier name-studies while offering 'a critical mode that could have been applied to the poem in its time', and suggesting half-heartedly that sophistication in coinage for example *might* prove sophistication in *litterae humaniores*. Martin Stevens, 'The Structure of *Beowulf*: from Gold-hoard to Word-hoard' (*MLQ*), sees feast giving way to rest, song to silence, dialogue to monologue as the poem progresses. Jerome Oetgen lists oscillations of 'Order and Chaos in the World of *Beowulf*' (*ABR*). Brian A. Shaw, 'The Speeches in *Beowulf*: a Structural Study (*ChauR*) arranges the hero's fifteen speeches in a pattern of correspondences; it is asserted that Beowulf's '*Ne sorga, snotor guma*' to Hrothgar is the mid-point of this pattern, and that the speeches after that (one of them before Grendel's mother has even been seen by Beowulf) 'build up to the dragon fight'.

On more definable issues, Norman E. Eliason's 'Beowulf, Wiglaf and Wægmundings' (*ASE*) declares that Wiglaf must be the hero's sister's son; his father was a Swede, so he cannot inherit; it was important for the poet to keep up a sense of gloom. Raymond P. Tripp Jr offers another unexpected new view in 'The Restoration of *Beowulf* 2769b and 2771a, and Wiglaf's Entrance into the Barrow' (*ELN*). If the MS readings *leoma* and *wræce* are kept, one has a scene in which Wiglaf is almost overcome by the 'fascination of the hoard. . .the cursed and forbidden values of the un-Christian past'. Considering the poet's involvement with the poem once more, Marijane Osborn's reading of 'The Great Feud: Scriptural History and Strife in *Beowulf*' (*PMLA*) shows how the Cain references, and others, introduce 'a perspective inaccessible to [the poet's] protagonists', but of course easily understood by his audience. The effect is one of sadness, but also of enhancing 'the native grandeur of the human soul'; perceptive analyses are given of several turning-points and instances of *synchysis*, 'liquid syntax'. John C. MacGalliard, 'The Poet's Comment in *Beowulf*' (*SP*), also distinguishes what the characters say from what the poet says, seeing in the latter a pervasive enthusiasm. In a thoughtful discussion of the hoard and the spells it is noted that Wiglaf's opinion, '*Oft sceall eorl monig*', is an 'expression of intense grief', not ratified by the poet; these variant opinions are what creates the poem's complexity. Nicholas Jacobs evaluates 'Anglo-Danish Relations, Poetic Archaism and the Date of *Beowulf*' in *Poetica*, Tokyo (1977), arguing against Professor Whitelock's influential reluctance to date the poem in a post-Viking period by indicating there *were* areas of England where Danes were assimilated, even popular. The Offa 'digression' might or might not indicate a Mercian connection. At the end any date between 700 and 1000 seems open.

On metre, F. H. Whitman continues a series of connected articles, see section 4 above. '*Beowulf* 1404b' (*ELN*) argues that Dobbie's *þær heo* is a better emendation than Klaeber's *swa*. His 'Rules Governing the Meter of *þa-*, *þær-*, and *Siððan-* Verses in *Beowulf*' (*ESts*) are in essence that when beginning a verse with those words the poet normally allowed one more unstressed syllable to precede the main stress in 'standard' verses, two more in 'light' ones; most variations on this are readily classifiable and grammatically forced. 'Light' verses do not however form part of the theory of Jane-Marie Luecke, O.S.B., whose *Measuring O.E. Rhythm: An Application of the Principles of Gregorian Chant-Rhythm to the Meter of Beowulf*[32] expands the article commented on in *YW* 56.69.The Solesmes school of Gregorian chant does appear to offer an analogue to O.E. poetry, and has a method of dealing with irregular rhythms, which is clearly a *desideratum*. However for a full understanding of its nature one suspects one would have to hear it sung. One point about the thesis presented is that it would explain the many short, irregular or non-alliterating lines in the *Beowulf* MS normally emended *metri causa* by editors. Marijane Osborn suggests another illusion to lost technique in '*Reote* and *Ridend* as Muscial Terms in *Beowulf*: Another kind of Harp?' (*Neophilologus*); the words in line 2457 do not mean 'joy' and 'riders', but respectively 'a rota' and 'strumming', so that harp-music is contrasted once more with death.

Classroom practicalities, meanwhile, are brought to light by several accounts in *OEN* of how *Beowulf* is taught, with much brewing of mead and playing at funerals; times have changed since this reviewer was taught (briefly) by the librarian of Corpus Christi, Cambridge. Alain Renoir thinks accordingly that translators deserve 'more scholarly credit'; his 'The Ugly and the Unfaithful: *Beowulf* through the Translator's Eye' (*Allegorica*) compares translations to mistresses, either ugly and faithful or fair and fickle. A compromise emerges in the text-and-translation of *Beowulf* prepared by Michael Swanton[33]. This is plainer, bolder, less intimidated by scholarship than that of Howell D. Chickering (see *YW* 58.56) – though Mr Swanton does note that the poem has generated nearly three thousand learned papers, more than any other single work! Notes and translating-

[32] *Measuring OE Rhythm: An Application of the Principles of Gregorian Chant-Rhythm to the Meter of Beowulf* (Literary Monographs 9), by Jane-Marie Luecke, O.S.B. Madison, Wisc.: U. of Wisconsin P. pp. x + 158. $15.

[33] *Beowulf*, ed. with notes and transl. by Michael Swanton. Manchester: Manchester U.P., and New York: Barnes & Noble. pp. vi + 212. hb £7.50, pb £2.50.

style derive on the whole from what might be called the 1950s' Chambers-Wrenn-Whitelock-Klaeber consensus.

6. The Junius Manuscript

One of the few remaining gaps in the corpus of editions of longer O.E. poems is plugged by A. N. Doane's *Genesis A: A New Edition*[34]. A distinctive feature of this is the presentation of the sections of the Vulgate actually being translated on the pages facing the poem itself; one can see at a glance what the poet was working from. There is also extensive commentary on the Bible and its glosses, pursuing the argument that the poet knew what he was doing, how and where to omit, expand, intercalate etc. Once again it is possible to see very quickly what the poet might have been expected to say, even if doubt remains as to how far he actually did so. He did not, the introduction admits, 'impose a discursive spiritual interpretation', but allowed for 'the fact that there inevitably is one in the mind of the reader'. He left 'suggestive interstices of meaning'. Like the rest of the edition, the glossary is thorough, including all words and forms except 'a few high-frequency words where no ambiguity seems likely'.

The same critic offers a solution to '*Genesis B* 317a: *sum heard gewrinc*' (*PQ*, 1977): either from *wrencan*, so 'twisting, torture', or *gewring*, 'what is wrung out, potion, drink', so the bitter drink of death – or of Circean transformation. E. G. Stanley, '*Sum heard gewrinc* (*Genesis B* 317)' (*N&Q*), agrees that the emendation to *geþwing* is questionable, but derives the MS reading from *gewringan*, 'press, wring out'. Kathleen E. Dubs, '*Niobedd*: Bed of Death and Rebirth' (*AN&Q*, 1976) uses *Phoenix* 553 to explain *Genesis B* 343: just as the Phoenix will be reborn, so will Lucifer, as Satan. Hell might also be a symbolic deathbed, for human souls. I regret that I have been able to see only one section of Ute Schwab's series of four articles, 'Ansätze zu einer Interpretation der altsächsischen Genesisdichtung' (*Annali*, Naples, sez. germ. Fil. germ., 1974–7); it seems a major piece of work containing much of interest for Anglo-Saxonists.

Paul F. Ferguson explains '*Exodus*: 107–111a' (*ELN*) by taking *Heofonbeacen. . .oðer wundor* as the subject of *beheold*, and emending *setlrad* to *seglrad*, 'sea'. Or should it be *seglrod*? That would make it possible to say 'that the way across the sailroad is the way of the sailrod', or even sail-rood. On *Daniel*, David A. Jost gives some 'Biblical Sources of O.E. *Daniel* 1–78', (*ELN*) in Chronicles, Kings and Jeremiah; the poet may have known a synthesised account of the sack of Jerusalem. G. D. Caie, 'The O.E. *Daniel*: A Warning against Pride' (*ESts*), argues that 'the poet's aim is to warn his audience in times of prosperity of the dangers of *wlenco* and *oferhygd*'; three interlinked narratives show Nebuchadnezzar and Belshuzzar repeating the sins of the Israelites at the start, stealthy complacency and then intellectual presumption.

7. The Poems of the Vercelli Book

There are six articles this year on *The Dream of the Rood*. D. R. Howlett, 'Two Notes on *The Dream of the Rood*' (*SN*), feels that his

[34] *Genesis A: A New Edition*, ed. by A. N. Doane. Madison, Wisc.: U. of Wisconsin P. pp. xiv + 416. £24.50.

earlier pieces on that poem (*YW* 57.54) were 'understated' and attempts to rectify this. The opinion of R. I. Page that the runes were not part of the original design of the Ruthwell Cross is rejected in favour of a symmetrical reconstruction of lines, half-lines and hypermetric lines. As for the Vercelli text, some addition and compression of lines would make 'Fitt 1', lines 1–38, correspond to the 'Golden Section', and further give (almost) the right ratio of lines between Cross and dreamer. George S. Tate, 'Chiasmus as Metaphor: the *Figura Crucis* tradition and *The Dream of the Rood*' (*NM*), sees the device of chiasmus as hinting at the letter chi, a cross; it is 'an embedded icon of the mystery the poem seeks to mediate', like the *Figurengedichte* of Hrabanus Maurus and the SATOR-AREPO box (see Gneuss and Sharpe respectively, sections 1 and 4 above). Bruce Karl Braswell, '*The Dream of the Rood* and Aldhelm on Sacred Prosopopoeia' (*MS*), remarks that Aldhelm noted several cases in the Bible of trees speaking, rivers clapping their hands etc., and sent his work to Aldfrith of Northumbria. Adamnan did the same with his *De locis sanctis*. Since Aldfrith's court was probably responsible for the Ruthwell Cross, it is possible that a Northumbrian poet could have put the two learned works together. Annemarie E. Mahler would rather ascribe the poem to King Alfred's circle. In '*Lignum Domini* and the Opening Vision of *The Dream of the Rood*: a viable hypothesis?' (*Speculum*), she suggests the poem's opening vision is of 'a reliquary cross', lines 7b–9a indicating a cross mounted on a globe, as in a drawing from the Winchester New Minster *Liber vitae*; perhaps this had been made to house Alfred's fragment of the True Cross, one of only four known in England before 1000. In this article *earmra ærgewin* is explained as 'a reference to animal-interlace patterns on the golden surface'. John P. Hermann, '*The Dream of the Rood*, 19a: *Earmra Ærgewin*' (*ELN*) sees the phrase as referring not to a specific act of violence but to an ancient conflict, a *fyrngeflit*, in the cosmos as in the soul of man. That is why the Dreamer is *synnum fah* – his stains and wounds were received in the enduring struggle. A. D. Horgan's '*The Dream of the Rood* and Christian *Tradition*' (*NM*) argues that the poem derives from the account of the Resurrection in the apocryphal *Gospel of Peter*, where a heavenly voice asks 'Hast thou preached unto them that sleep?' and the Cross answers 'Yea'. Archbishop Theodore of Canterbury could have brought the book to England. But the poet seems to have rejected the conventional idea that the 'sleepers' were the patriarchs and prophets in the underworld; he turns such historical ideas into 'mythic categories'.

In 'Geometrical Design of the O.E. *Andreas*' (*Poetica*, Tokyo), Robert D. Stevick also amplifies earlier understatement, for which see *YW* 56.74. He now proposes a geometrical rather than arithmetical model for the poem. In essence what has been done is to write down the number of lines in each Fitt, then in successive rows to add up 1 and 2, 2 and 3, 1 and 2 and 3, and so on, producing 135 separate numbers. These are then sieved for patterns, sums, 'golden sections'. An attractive feature is that Professor Stevick does confront the problem of how 'a tenth century writer' (?) could construct such a design without Arabic numerals; he could have done it with a straight edge, compass, and a few other tools. A point left uncertain is whether the scheme means anything. The 'golden section' of the whole poem is at line 1038 (1112 if one adds Professor Stevick's allowance of lost lines). This is indeed 'framed' by short lines, and by the mention of numbers. It is however in the middle of a sentence, a scene, a fitt. Did the poet think that a significant point? Or just mark it *en passant*?

8. The Exeter Book

The most important piece this year is by John Pope, on the actual make-up of the Exeter Book; but since it goes on to offer new readings and a new interpretation of *The Husband's Message* it is considered with the articles on shorter poems, below. On the longer poems, Sarah Larratt Keefer demonstrates 'The "Techne" of the *Christ I* Poet' (*Neophilologus*), with close analyses of lines 1–15, on architecture, 35–49, on Mary, and 301–25, on locked doors. The mention of Isaiah in line 303 is not a mistake, since the sources for the Latin antiphon it draws on included Isaiah 22.22 as well as Ezekiel 44.1–2. It seems a little harsh to declare that earlier scholars have 'undermined' the poem, that it is 'worthy of deeper scholarship than it has hitherto received'. Karl P. Wentersdorf explains '*Guthlac A*: the Battle for the Beorg' (*Neophilologus*) as a claiming of a 'secret heathen spot', a 'sacroneme', for the Church. Guthlac's purpose was to 'uproot. . .superstitious awe' of barrows. Edward M. Palumbo's *The Literary Use of Formulas in Guthlac II*[35] seems a rather similar exercise in spoiling the Egyptians, since it uses all the 'repeated phrases/supporting evidence/underlining' paraphernalia of the 'formulaic' school to prove yet again that literate poetry can contain formulas. The specific exercise carried out is to show that 'the clearly literate *Guthlac II* poet had a stronger preference for formulas than the possibly unlettered *Guthlac I* poet', and that most formulas are literary devices, not line-fillers. But what seem to this reviewer evident line-fillers are claimed for literature; of the six words for 'sad' or 'sadness' in *Guthlac* 1051–61, e.g., it is said 'Each adds a different note to the mental anguish'. Claude Schneider also engages with poetic diction in 'Cynewulf's devaluation of heroic tradition in *Juliana*' (*ASE*). His view is that words like *eorl, æþeling, cempa* in the poem either have no surviving connotations of heroic activity, or else are used so that we may perceive a discrepancy between 'traditional heroic values' and 'a Christian standard of behaviour'. The devil says a Christian man may be a *Metodes cempa*, but he is mistaken; that is his 'low view of spiritual conflict'. In one metaphor the Germanic mead-hall is likened to Hell (though actually what the poet says is that in Hell the sinners need *not* expect to receive rings in the wine-hall, which could be, of course, no more than a statement of truth). In 'Cynewulf's *Juliana*: A Case at Law' (*Allegorica*), Lenore MacGaffey Abraham dates the poem to the late tenth century on legal grounds. The story of the source has been rewritten to conform to actual practice which could have existed only in that period. To believe this one has to accept the scourging as a case of *anefang*, a formal attempt at repossession of the thing in dispute (Juliana), along with other equivalencies. Even so there seems to be considerable 'extra-judiciary persecution' left over.

Study of the shorter poems in this collection is considerably furthered

[35] *The Literary Use of Formulas in Guthlac II and their Relation to Felix's Vita Sancti Guthlaci*, by Edward M. Palumbo. The Hague and Paris: Mouton. 1977. pp. 87. $15.50.

by John C. Pope's 'Palaeography and poetry: some solved and unsolved problems of the *Exeter Book*', in the *festschrift* for N. R. Ker, *Medieval Scribes, Manuscripts and Libraries*[36]. Part I of this considers losses to the text. Ten leaves are missing, which shows clearly enough that both *Riddle 70* and *Resignation* really consist of two unrelated fragments each. More surprisingly, a whole quire appears to have gone astray between *Guthlac II* and *Azarias*, a strip having been cut from the top of the start of quire vii, fol. 53, to disguise the fact that the poem was already in full flow. But Professor Pope kindly accepts that the *Seafarer*, though overlapping quires x and xi, is probably a whole. Part II turns to '*The Husband's Message*: A crucial reading, an attempted restoration and some related problems'. The reading is *iw* for *in*, line 3. The speaker is a piece of wood cut from a yew-tree, in fact a runic stick. *Riddle 60* should be taken as part of the same poem, an account of the yew tree (which was only by accident or prolepsis *be sonde. . .æt merefaroþe*). If one accepts Professor Pope's view it would ruin the opinion of D. R. Howlett, '*The Wife's Lament* and *The Husband's Message*' (*NM*), that the two poems form a diptych, with a unifying symmetry in the line-numberings. The same author propounds a similar symmetry in 'The Structure of *The Rhyming Poem*' (*NM*) using evidence from capitals, punctuation, rhyme schemes, hypermetric lines and general sense. As often, though, 'structural' divisions seem to run against the grain of syntax. Can lines 43–4 really be an independent central unit? Kelvin S. Kiernan adds to Boethian theory with '*Deor*: the Consolations of an Anglo-Saxon Boethius' (*NM*), seeing three allusions: the Geat-Mæthhild stanza derives from Orpheus and Eurydice, Wayland is in Alfred's Boethius too, and the pairing of Theodric and Eormenric parallels Alfred's pairing of Theodric and Nero. There may then be a direct link between the poem and the Alfredian work: but is it acceptable to translate *hi seo sorglufu slæp ealle binom* as 'that grieving love (of his) took her from death entirely'?

James B. Spamer, 'The Marriage Concept in *Wulf and Eadwacer*' (*Neophilologus*) catches an echo of Matthew 19.6 in the last lines of that poem, concluding that the female speaker is denying any 'claim of marriage which Eadwacer might have upon her'; and Marijane Osborn finds a similarly plausible parallel in 'Venturing upon Deep Waters in *The Seafarer*' (*NM*). From the shallow waters of mere *fuga saeculi*, she suggests, the 'seafarer' is turning to the deep waters, the *hean streamas*, of the contemplative life. That is why he can say *sylf* at line 35 without contradicting the fact that he has been to sea before; the same image is found in Horace, Cassian and elsewhere. Less convincingly, Arnold V. Talentino sees 'Moral Irony in *The Ruin*' (*PLL*). It looks more like moral disapprobation, as one decay after another is seen as the builders' fault; but even good people are mortal. The *Rune Poem*'s lines quoted in this article do not say that men fail each other and *so* God kills them, but men are *bound* to fail each other because God has laid His doom upon us! John M. Fanagan surveys the 'elegiac' group and others in 'An Examination of Tense-Usage in some of the Shorter Poems of *The Exeter Book*' (*Neophilologus*). More personal poems have more past tenses, present-tense poems have in common 'their

[36] *Medieval Scribes, Manuscripts and Libraries: Essays Presented to N. R. Ker*, ed. by M. B. Parkes and Andrew G. Watson. Scolar Press. pp. xvi + 395, 84 plates.

very overtly religious or moralising themes': this last group has as its acme *The Gifts of Men!* (See Russom, section 4 above).

On non-elegiac poems, Thomas P. Campbell, 'Thematic Unity in the O.E. *Physiologus*' (*Archiv*), repeats the discovery of Lothar Frank (1971) that panther, whale and partridge form a connected unit signifiying Christ, devil and mankind, from a theme in Ephesians; and there are several pieces on riddles. Kevin Crossley-Holland offers engaging modernistic versions of all but the obscurest cases in *The Exeter Riddle Book*[37]. Marie Nelson notes 'The Paradox of Silent Speech in the Exeter Book Riddles' (*Neophilologus*), an interesting piece, especially if read in conjunction with Professor Pope's account of *The Husband's Message* immediately above. Perhaps ox, river, fish, chalice and reed-pen are not the only silent speakers in O.E. It will be seen that Matthew Marino is well out of date in insisting on 'The Literariness of the *Exeter Book Riddles*' (*NM*), and declaring they 'have too rarely been viewed as literature'. It is refreshing, though, to see them as 'deceits', to have *Riddle 66* preferred to *Riddle 40* on the grounds of brevity, and to have it admitted that there may be such a thing as 'lack of aesthetic preparation' (in *Order of the World*). Heidi and Rüdiger Göbel give 'The Solution of an O.E. Riddle' (*SN*); 28 is not 'John Barleycorn' but 'pattern-welded sword'. Patrizia Lendinara counts 351 items in 'Gli Enigmi del Codice Exoniense: una Ricerca Bibliografica' (*Annali*, Naples, sez. germ. Fil. germ., 1976), with 41 more in appendixes.

9. Other Poems

The most interesting item here is Patrick Sims-Williams's splendidly titled '"Is it fog or smoke or warriors fighting?": Irish and Welsh parallels to the *Finnsburg* fragment' (*BBCS*). With copious citation from Irish, Welsh, Norse and other material, the author proves that the traditional view of *[hor]nas byrnað* etc. is right. It is a watchman speaking. The Celtic parallels are not 'more subtle and delicate', but more exuberant and fanciful. The O.E. version of the common 'watchman's false explanation' device concentrates attention uniquely on Hnæf's psychology, as he comes to the true answer perhaps against his will. Invention along traditional lines is also given a dominant role in Norman Blake's 'The genesis of *The Battle of Maldon*' (*ASE*), which suggests that the poet may not have known anything except what is in the *Vita Oswaldi*, adding details to it under the constraints of O.E. convention – a need for displays of loyalty, exchange of speeches, barriers to speak across, and not least for a grand heroic gesture. It is in the nature of heroes to be trapped though not deceived by guile, says Professor Blake; *landes to fela* and *ofermod* express 'despairing admiration'. That the poet *did* know something after all is suggested by Margaret A. L. Locherbie-Cameron, 'Ælfwine's Kinsmen and *The Battle of Maldon*' (*N & Q*). It seems that Ælfwine son of Ælfric son of Ealhelm must have been sister's son to men who opposed Byrhtnoth, Dunstan and the Edward faction; yet he supported Byrhtnoth (as Byrhtnoth indeed loyally defended Æthelred).

[37] *The Exeter Riddle Book*, translated by Kevin Crossley-Holland, drawings by Virgil Burnett. The Folio Society. pp. 139. No price.

There is a translation of '*The Battle of Brunanburh*' by Louise Wright in *OEN*. Stanley R. Hauer sees 'Structure and Unity in the O.E. Charm *Wið Færstice*' (*ELN*), in terms of two triplets of wild riders/gods, mighty women/witches, smiths/elves; evil is fought with evil, (or to offer another folk-saying, 'one nail drives out another'). T. D. Hill has a much more learned root in Ephesians 3.18–19 for 'The Theme of the Cosmological Cross in Two O.E. Cattle Theft Charms' (*N&Q*). Though transmitted by Sedulius, Alcuin, Ælfric etc., this use of the Cross as a definer of space and imposer of order shows allegory need not always have been 'recondite and learned'.

10. Prose

Questions of syntax appear, in several pieces, to be filtering into discussions of style – a welcome development, but also one likely to intimidate. Many will be pleased to hear David Carkeet confessing, 'Aspects of O.E. Style' (*L&S*, 1977), that 'much can be made out of rather modest syntactic principles', and proving it too by his study of ways in which Anglo-Saxons tried normally to avoid saying things like *sio hiord þe unwærne biþ gehrist*; different strategies are apparent in different MSS, e.g. of Gregory's *Dialogues*. The O.E. Bede is similarly distinguished from the *Pastoral Care* in Richard Wolcott Clement's 'An Analysis of Non-Finite Verb Forms as an Indication of the Style of Translation in Bede's *Ecclesiastical History*' (*Journal of English Linguistics*); while the O.E. *Apollonius* is used comparatively to show the effects of Latin syntax in Alfred R. Wedel, 'Participal Construction in the High German and West Saxon of the 11th and 12th Centuries: Latin and Germanic Differences' (*JEGP*). Less convincing is W. Rybarkiewicz, 'The word order in O.E. prose and the functional sentence perspective' (*Studia Anglica Posnaniensia*, 1977). Maybe 'given' elements do tend to precede 'new' ones even in O.E., but a larger sample than *Chronicle* 755 is needed to prove it. Alan S. C. Ross thinks 'The *Este*' (*N&Q*) of Wulfstan ought to be **Æste*; he notes 'A Point of Comparison between Aldred's Two Glosses' (*N&Q*), and shows that Aldred could not have referred to his Lindisfarne glosses when he turned to the *Durham Ritual*.

Ingvar Carlson's edition of *The Pastoral Care* from MS Cotton Otho B. ii is completed posthumously in a second volume, with notes and glossary[38]. David Yerkes explains 'The Medieval Provenance of Corpus Christi College, Cambridge MS 322' (*Trans. Cambridge Bibliographical Society*) as being Worcester; and notes 'A Neglected Transcript of the Cotton MS of Wærferth's O.E. Translation of Gregory's *Dialogues*' (*NM*). Ronald E. Buckalew also shows that 'Leland's Transcript of Ælfric's *Glossary*' (*ASE*) must have been based on a MS not otherwise attested, perhaps from Glastonbury.

Most literary emphasis continues to fall, however, on Ælfric. The editors' 'introduction' to *The O.E. Homily and Its Backgrounds* (see note

[38] *The Pastoral Care, edited from British Library MS Cotton Otho B. ii, Part II (f. 25v. a/4 to end)*, by Ingvar Carlson, completed by Lars-G. Hollander *et al.* (Acta Universitatis Stockholmiensis, Stockholm Studies in English 48). pp. 198, 2 plates. £5.90.

16 above) stresses that in the 'major reconsideration of this long-neglected body of writing', Ælfric is going to be 'the measure of excellence', since he is 'the major author of the period by virtue of every possible criterion'. 'Originality?', mutters the sceptic. He was methodical, reports Ann Eljenholm Nichols, 'Methodical Abbreviation: a Study in Ælfric's Friday Homilies for Lent' (*O.E. Homily*); he knew how to cut, to embed, to turn question into statement. He could point up distinctions between good and evil, asserts Keith A. Tandy, 'Verbal Aspect as a Narrative Structure in Ælfric's *Lives of Saints*' (*O.E. Homily*); the 'meaningful nuances' of his verbs show how beasts and pagans are limited to the punctual, but God and good men extend to the durative. The adjectives etc. in his alliterative style were not mere line-fillers, claims Ruth Waterhouse, in 'Affective language, especially alliterating qualifiers, in Ælfric's Life of St. Alban' (*ASE*) – though the heavy use of such qualifiers in b-half lines looks a little suspicious. Ælfric translated the same saint's life as Chaucer, the same author notes in '"A Rose by any other Name": Two Versions of the Legend of Saint Cecilia' (*NM*). Who did it better? Ælfric is less sensuous, more symbolic, more 'implicit and restrained'.

He was of course a monk, a fact rather lost sight of in Bernard F. Huppé's 'Alfred and Ælfric: A Study of Two Prefaces' (*O.E. Homily*). Or, to be more accurate, Professor Huppé assumes tacitly that when King Alfred wrote *ciricean, stowa, Godes ðiowa*, he meant 'monks, monsteries'. This questionable belief makes it difficult to give proper weight to the monastic partisanship which is one of the most obvious elements of the *Preface to Genesis* (as opposed to the *Preface to the Pastoral Care*), along with high valuation of Latin and overt dedication to spirit rather than letter. Both Prefaces can be split up into rhetorical units, or 'clausules'. What cannot? Raachel Jurovics also gives considerable space to 'Augustinian-inspired rhetoric' in '*Sermo Lupi* and the Moral Purpose of Rhetoric' (*O.E. Homily*), but also betrays a loose grip on real conditions in Ethelred's day. D. R. Letson's 'The Poetic Content of the Revival Homily' (*O.E. Homily*) relies heavily on alliteration, 'thematic unity' ('widespread. . . in the Christian Middle Ages'), and even 'thematic interlace'. Ælfric was a poet, Cynewulf a homilist, Alcuin admired 'vernacular poetics', the Blickling and Vercelli collections were products of the Benedictine Reform.

The motive behind that piece seems to be to have all the nice people on the same side, a thesis, alas, betrayed by Malcolm Godden in 'Ælfric and the Vernacular Prose Tradition' (*O.E. Homily*). This suggests that Ælfric would have regarded the Blickling and Vercelli collections as *gedwyld*, and points to their use of sensational apocrypha and heretical belief; Ælfric may have seen and disapproved of books very like them. He seems also to have known, even been trained on, Alfredian translations – the Bede, Boethius, *Pastoral Care* and *Dialogues*, which last is incidentally not ascribed by Dr Godden to Alfred rather than Wærferth, though the volume's editors foist that opinion on him in their 'Introduction'. At least the Alfredian works were free of unreliable influences like Caesarius. Yet Ælfric in his turn became a quarry for lesser men, his purisms ignored.

Robin Ann Aronstam may therefore be right to see theological primitiveness in 'The Blickling Homilies: a Reflection of Popular Anglo-Saxon

Belief', part of a collection called *Law, Church and Society*[39]. Little evidence is offered, however, and why such homilies should be 'oriented more towards conversion than education' one cannot imagine. Were they for the Danes? Marcia A. Dalbey more convincingly traces 'Themes and Techniques in the Blickling Lenten Homilies' (*O.E. Homily*); they are moral, varied, not particularly unified thematically, more interested in social obligations than asceticism, in man and man rather than man and God. Paul E. Szarmach rejects the similarly modest view of C. L. Wrenn, that 'there is not much literary interest in these sermons'. In 'The Vercelli Homilies: Style and Structure' (*O.E. Homily*) he searches for literary skill and power; many time-worn lecturers' devices are applauded. 'The Influence of Caesarius of Arles on Two O.E. Homilies' is meanwhile demonstrated in *N&Q* by Harry Jay Solo, following the well-known article by J. E. Cross (*YW*, 38.78). Professor Cross continues his current investigations with 'Mary Magdalen in the *O.E. Martyrology*: The Earliest Extant "Narrat Josephus" variant of her Legend' (*Speculum*); three unpublished Latin texts are given and are compared with the O.E.

By far the most useful contribution this year to studies of the Benedictine Reform is Hans Sauer's edition of *Theodulfi Capitula in England*[40]. This considers in the most thorough fashion the forty-one Latin MSS of the work, five of them English, traces the relationships of these latter to the two O.E. versions, and edits both of those, plus the O.E. 'Macarius Homily' inserted in one MS, plus the two associated Latin texts. It is interesting to note that Theodulf's *Capitula* were valued mostly by bishops, that they may have had an effect on Vercelli Homily 3, that one of the O.E. versions, a relatively free rendering, may descend from an original from Worcester or Lichfield. But this is a vital work for any student of the period to read. I much regret that I have not been able to see the preceding volume in this series, Roland Torkar's *Eine altenglische Übersetzung von Alcuins 'De virtutibus et vitiis*[41]

Several minor pieces are brought to notice this year. In the Ker *festschrift* (see note 36 above) Pierre Chaplais looks at 'The Letter from Bishop Wealdhere of London to Archbishop Brihtwold of Canterbury: the earliest original "letter close" extant in the West', and concludes it is certainly a genuine (Latin) autograph of 704–5, written at a date when Brentford was a border-town, and Essex and Wessex at odds. In 'Lapidary Traditions in Anglo-Saxon England: part I, the background; the O.E. lapidary' (*ASE*), Peter Kitson edits a short O.E. text from Christ Church, Canterbury. Its origin, he believes, was a set of Latin glosses compiled in England in the 680s to explain the gems of the Apocalypse. Two items were lost, two others acquired, and someone in the tenth century with a

[39] *Law, Church and Society: Essays in Honor of Stephan Kuttner*, ed. by K. Pennington and R. Somerville. Philadelphia: U. of Pennsylvania P. 1977. pp. xii + 340. $22.50.

[40] *Theodulfi Capitula in England*, ed. by Hans Sauer (Münchener Universitäts-Schriften, Texte und Untersuchungen zur Englischen Philologie 8). Munich: Wilhelm Fink. pp. xvi + 521. DM 68.

[41] *Eine altenglische Übersetzung von Alcuins 'De virtutibus et vitiis', Kapitel 20 (Liebermanns Judex)*, ed. by Roland Torkar (series as above, 7). Munich: Wilhelm Fink. 1977. pp. 375. DM 48.

rather imperfect grasp of Latin translated them into O.E., expanding them with material from Augustine and Solinus. Another short new 'text' of O.E. is the 'OE Liturgical Rubrics in Corpus Christi College, Cambridge, MS422' (*Anglia*). These had defeated B. Fehr and N. R. Ker, but R. I. Page has managed to read some previously illegible bits. They are rubrics for charms, baptism, baptism of the sick etc. The scribe manages to call fallen angels *apostolicis* (for *apostaticis*), but *crisma* is used 'in two distinct technical senses'. Dr Page wonders, indeed, what 'the OE reader would have made' of these pieces. In three minor articles Pier Giorgio Negro, 'Contributo al Miglioramente dell' Edizione di Cambridge (*Annali*, Naples, sez. germ. Fil. germ. 1976), corrects errors in K. Wildhagen's 1910 edition of *Der Cambridger Psalter*; Linda E. Voigts comments on a page of 'British Library, Cotton Vitellius C. iii, f. 82' (*OEN*), with a drawing influenced by a Carolingian MS at St Augustine's, Canterbury; and Nigel Barley reproves 'the notorious lack of anthropological perspective among Anglo-Saxonists' and threatens 'a fuller semiotic treatment' of 'The Letter to Brother Edward' (*NM*). Revulsion at simultaneous eating and excreting stirs thoughts of ritual pollution, 'added to all [which], of course, we find the symbolism of the Christian mass'. Dr Barley's opinion may be summed up quite fairly as '*Pensée sauvage* rules, OK?'.

The degenerate descendants of O.E. works perhaps deserve the final tribute of a sigh. Michael Lapidge indeed shows a steep rise in culture and ability after the Conquest in 'Dominic of Evesham: "Vita S. Ecgwini Episcopi et Confessoris"' (*Analecta Bollandiana*). Dominic's revision of the *Life* by Byrhtferth is presented for comparison with its original, edited by J. A. Giles in 1854; the Anglo-Saxon's 'perverse penchant for numerology' shows up badly against his successor's grace and skill. For less favoured people and institutions, though, things went worse. In 'MS Cotton Vespasian A. xxiii: the Vespasian Homilies' (*Manuscripta*), Mary P. Richards shows us four sub-Ælfrician pieces modernised by someone not sure of his O.E., for an audience also unfamiliar with such simple words as French *curt* and Latin *angeli*. They may have been 'unlettered clergy' round Rochester. Matters were probably worse elsewhere. The poor, insignificant nunnery of Wintney in Hampshire has bequeathed us one book only, 'Die Winteney – Version der *Regula Sancti Benedicti*: Eine frühmittelenglische Bearbeitung der altenglischen Prosaübersetzung der Benediktinerregel', considered by Mechthild Gretsch in *Anglia*. The author seems to have worked from Æthelwold's O.E. text and a Latin one, modernising, and altering the former towards the latter, perhaps with a certain lack of confidence in the vernacular. The Wintney nuns may have got their book from a bishop in Winchester, like his predecessor 250 years before concerned for *þa ungelæredan inlendisce*, but unlike him able to do very little for them.

IV

Middle English: Excluding Chaucer

T. P. DOLAN, A. J. FLETCHER and L. E. MITCHELL

1. General and Miscellaneous Items

With due reference to Frances Yates (*YW* 47.147) Beryl Rowland succinctly deals with 'Bishop Bradwardine on the Artificial Memory' in her lively selection of quotations from Fitzwilliam Museum Cambridge MS Egerton 613, which contains twenty-one verse and prose items in English, but his suggestions for *imagines* are strikingly *agentes*. Betty Hill for the first time provides a full and illuminating description of British Library MS Egerton 613, which contains twenty-one verse and prose items in English. Anglo-Norman, Continental French, and Latin (*N&Q*). In an appendix she introduces and edits from this MS a macaronic address to a nun which contains such interesting phrases as 'do wel and aue wel', and other items comparable with the tradition of *Ancrene Wisse* and allied texts. P. Theiner[1] discusses 'The Literary Uses of the Peasants' Revolt of 1381' in Gower's *Vox Clamantis*, Book I, and in Froissart's *Chroniques*, neither of which is sympathetic to the rebel cause, but which treat the events differently. Gower elevates it to a major cosmic disorder, with apocalyptic overtones, whereas Froissart sees it as a humdrum squabble among the lower classes, with Wat Tyler as a sort of vice figure. With reference to earlier critics of *A Preface to Chaucer* Paul Theiner presents an interesting discussion of 'Robertsonianism and the Idea of Literary History', which Robertson viewed as an intellectual construct (*SMC*, 1976). His adherence to such a construct has led him to replace historical process by allegorical exposition, and so his arbitrary division of the outline of the literature of Europe into two epochs, medieval and modern, compromises his claim to be 'historical'.

Drawing on his very wide reading, C. H. Talbot[2] describes the lives of 'Children in the Middle Ages' from *infantia* to *pueritia*. He corrects a number of popular misconceptions (for example, that child mortality was mainly due to disease, malnutrition, etc.): many died as the result of accidents, and evidence shows that parents were far from being indifferent to the loss of their children.

Animals in Folklore[3], edited by J. R. Porter and W. M. S. Russell,

[1] *Actes du VIe Congres de l'Association Internationale de Littèrature Comparèe/ Proceedings of the 6th Congress of the International Comparative Literature Association*, ed. by Michel Cadot, Milan V. Dimić, David Malone, and Miklós Szabolsci. Stuttgart: Bieber, 1975, pp. 303–6.

[2] *Children's Literature: Annual of the Modern Language Association on Children's Literature and the Children's Literature Association*, VI, 1977, 17–33.

[3] *Animals in Folklore*, ed. by J. R. Porter and W. M. S. Russell. The Folklore Society Mistletoe Series. Cambridge, England: D. S. Brewer Ltd., and Totowa, N.J.: Rowman & Littlefield, for the Folklore Society. pp. x + 292. Frontispiece, 2 plates, 24 figures. £9.

contains a set of papers, most of which were read at a conference at the University of Reading in 1976 on Witchcraft, Magic and the Animal World. The main preoccupations included Animal Motifs, Regional Studies, Shape-Changing, and Animal Images. Medievalists will be attracted to J. R. Porter's essay on 'Witchcraft and Magic in the Old Testament and their Relation to Animals', and H. R. Ellis Davidson's on 'Shape-Changing in the Old Norse Sagas'. E. R. Cawte's study of *Ritual Animal Disguise*[4], sub-titled 'A Historical Study of Animal Disguises in the British Isles', will be of interest to later medievalists: 'dressing as an animal. . .has been recorded in Britain since the fourteenth century, when a man carved a frame, made to represent a horse'. Indeed, the hobby-horse is the major interest of this book. Its manifestations in pageants and plays are traced from the oldest record, in a poem by the fourteenth-century Anglesey poet Gruffudd Gryg. There is much information about costs, performances, players, etc. The book contains twenty-four illustrations and thirteen maps showing geographical distribution. The first of the three Appendices provides a geographical index of animal disguise custom in the British Isles; the second carries notes for the body of the text; and the third gives a full list of references to published works on the phenomenon (e.g. E. D. Mackerness on 'The Yardley Gobion Morris').

2. Alliterative Poetry

Alliterative poetry in the early Middle English period is dealt with only in two rather peripheral articles on Laȝamon. Shirley Kossick's 'The *Brut* and English Literary Tradition' (*UES*) somewhat sweepingly asserts that 'Laȝamon's poetic manner. . .is dependent on Old English verse, and at the same time represents a forward link with the "alliterative revival" of the fourteenth century', but in fact concentrates almost exclusively on the poet's links with the Old English tradition. Carolynn Van Dyke provides a text and translation of 'The First English Story of King Lear: Laȝamon's *Brut*, ll. 1448–1887' (*Allegorica*), together with an introductory note dealing mainly with the ways in which Laȝamon's version can be seen to anticipate Shakespeare's handling of the Lear story.

The metre of the poetry of the Alliterative Revival is discussed in very different ways by Robert William Sapora Jr and Elizabeth Salter. Sapora propounds *A Theory of Middle English Alliterative Meter with Critical Applications*[5], constructed uncompromisingly on a foundation of theoretical linguistics, that claims to describe all but a handful of Middle English alliterative lines. His approach enables him to make a number of suggestive comments on the handling of metre in the various poems analysed (which include the *Gawain*-group, *St. Erkenwald*, the A-version of *Piers Plowman*, and large portions of the alliterative *Morte Arthure* and *The Destruction of Troy*). It is, however, so rigidly theoretical that it inevitably

[4] *Ritual Animal Disguises*, A Historical and Geographical Study of Animal Disguise in the British Isles, by E. C. Cawte. The Folklore Society Mistletoe Series. Cambridge, England: D. S. Brewer Ltd., and Totowa, N.J.: Rowman & Littlefield, for the Folklore Society. pp. xvi + 293. 24 illustrations; 13 maps. £7.

[5] *A Theory of Middle English Alliterative Meter with Critical Applications*, by Robert William Sapora Jr. Speculum Anniversary Monographs, I. Cambridge, Mass.: Medieval Academy of America. 1977. pp. xii + 118. hb $11, pb $5.

becomes over-schematic, as in the underlying assumption that there was a steady evolution from Old English to Middle English alliterative verse. Elizabeth Salter's 'Alliterative Modes and Affiliations in the Fourteenth Century' (*NM*) seems refreshingly pragmatic by contrast. She stresses the need to re-examine the nature of the relationship between English homiletic prose and English poetry during the fourteenth and fifteenth centuries, and to look particularly at the way in which such prose may provide both some of the staple materials of the great poems of the age and some of their basic metrical forms. Langland, for example, may well have refined his alliterative verse out of rougher hybrid writings of a semi-accentual nature such as Gaytryge's *Treatise*, which shares so many similarities of verbal groupings with *Piers Plowman* as to suggest that Langland may well have known some version of it.

In 'Hills and Valleys in the *Gawain* Country' (*Leeds SE*), Ralph W. V. Elliott analyses the words used to denote these geographical features in a number of alliterative poems, assessing their place in the vocabularies of literary and geographical landscapes. He suggests that the local topographical terms used in some poems (notably *The Wars of Alexander*, the alliterative *Morte Arthure*, and *GGK*) may provide extra evidence for their places of composition.

Thorlac Turville-Petre provides 'Two Notes on Words in Alliterative Poems' (*N&Q*), arguing that 'tried' in *GGK* 4 could mean 'exposed' and that 'porte' in the alliterative *Morte Arthure* 2609 surely simply means 'port' and not 'Ottoman government' as recently suggested by Jacobs (*N&Q*, 1977: see *YW* 58.80). Turville-Petre also writes on 'Nicholas Grimald and *Alexander A*' (*ELR*, 1976), giving an account of the sixteenth-century manuscript which contains the only known text of this romance, and commenting on the informed interest shown by the scribe in his copying of it.

Elizabeth Salter also investigates 'The Timeliness of *Wynnere and Wastoure*' (*MÆ*), arguing strongly for a reconsideration of the assumptions about the dating of the poem that have put it in its accepted place as a formative work in the development of fourteenth-century alliterative poetry. A careful re-examination of the evidence leads her to conclude that its supposed references to the events of 1352 are not nearly as clear-cut as has generally been thought, and that the verbal portrait usually assigned to the Black Prince may not apply to him at all: the heraldic description which is often taken as alluding to his escutcheon in fact corresponds much more closely to the arms of the Wingfields, a family who were prominent among the English nobility throughout the latter fourteenth century. Similar ground is covered by David Lawton's article on 'Literary History and Scholarly Fancy: the Date of two Middle English Alliterative Poems' (*Parergon*, 1977), in which he attacks Gollancz's datings of both *St. Erkenwald* and *Wynnere and Wastoure*. He is less radical in his revision of Gollancz's theories about the latter poem than Salter, but he too argues vigorously that its dating and consequent placing in literary history are much more uncertain than is generally assumed.

In 'Typology and Justice in *St. Erkenwald*' (*ABR*), Lester L. Faigley claims that the poem's blurring and fusing of legendary and historical materials can best be understood when the text is examined from a typological point of view. The specific 'historical' foreground must be seen in the context of the timeless background of providential design.

James L. Boren discusses 'Narrative Design in the alliterative *Morte Arthure*' (*PQ*, 1977). He finds that the poem is divided into six major segments framed by a Prologue and Epilogue and linked by a variety of sophisticated 'articulating techniques': this careful structuring of the narrative is 'the poet's own contribution to the traditional story and a key to the meaning with which he has invested the account of Arthur's fall'. In 'The Date of the alliterative *Morte Arthure*'[6], Larry D. Benson argues that some details of the poet's accounts of the geography and politics of Northern Italy, together with some of his references to current English affairs, point to a date of around 1400 for the poem. James D. Johnson sets out to prove the existence of 'Formulaic Thrift in the alliterative *Morte Arthure*' (*MÆ*), and supports his thesis by an analysis and tabulation of the 'formulaic systems' consisting of the combination of an adjective plus the noun *knight* to be found in the text.

3. The Gawain-Poet

As Malcolm Andrew and Ronald Waldron's edition of *The Poems of the Pearl Manuscript*[7] is the third 'collected edition' of the texts to appear in three years, comparisons with its predecessors (Cawley and Anderson, 1976, and Moorman, 1977: see *YW* 76.64 and 77.80–1) cannot be avoided. Whereas both of the latter are aimed primarily at the general reader rather than the specialist, the former seems to fall somewhere between this approach and that of the scholarly editions of the individual poems. While it cannot, within the limits of a one-volume edition, fully equal the completeness of the critical apparatus of the individually-edited texts, it does gather together a great deal of up-to-date information, and includes a lively introductory discussion of the poems, a fairly full commentary (printed below the text for ease of reference) and glossary and a very comprehensive bibliography, plus a useful appendix reproducing the most significant passages from the Vulgate used as source-material in the poems. Altogether this is a book that should prove very handy for students.

Writing on *The Art of the Gawain-Poet*[8], W. A. Davenport takes as his starting-point the assumption that by now it may be taken for granted that there is such an entity as 'the *Gawain*-Poet'. He sets out to discuss the poet's work primarily in terms of its 'effectiveness as poetry and as fiction': the tools of historical scholarship are rather eschewed, though by no means left out of account. A separate chapter is devoted to each poem of the manuscript. The approach is generally lively and thoughtful, especially perhaps in the section on *GGK*, where Davenport writes particularly well on the combination of romance and realism in the poem, and also in the final chapter on 'The Poet and his Art', which discusses such pervading charac-

[6] In *Medieval Studies in Honor of Lillian Herlands Hornstein*, ed. by Jess B. Bessinger Jr and Robert R. Raymo. New York: New York U.P. 1976. pp. x + 225. Frontispiece; 9 figures. $25.

[7] *The Poems of the Pearl Manuscript*, ed. by Malcolm Andrew and Ronald Waldron. York Medieval Texts, second series. Edward Arnold. pp. 376. £15.95.

[8] *The Art of the Gawain-Poet*, by W. A. Davenport. University of London, the Athlone Press. pp. xiii + 233. £8.95.

teristics as the poet's interest in combining different levels of meaning (especially in the points at which the various levels conflict with and even contradict one another).

S. L. Clark and Julian N. Wasserman make a rather general survey of 'The *Pearl*-Poet's City Imagery' (*SQ*). They point out the importance of images of inclusion in and exclusion from enclosed spaces of all kinds in the poems: in particular, God's final judgement is constantly conceived of in terms of inclusion in or exclusion from the Heavenly City.

A lonely swimmer against the prevailing tide, M. Tajima brings 'Additional Syntactical Evidence against the Common Authorship of MS Cotton Nero A.x' (*ES*). He finds 'important differences' between *GGK* and the other three poems in their use of the neuter personal pronoun *hit/hyt*.

Analysing 'The Introduction to the Dream in *Pearl*' (*MÆ*), Claude Luttrell suggests that it presents us with 'a eulogy, later seen as epitaph'. He emphasises the debt of the opening stanzas to the courtly love tradition, and argues that they form part of 'the balance of opposing forces, in the earthly and heavenly evaluations of the "pearl"', arrived at in the poem as a whole. M. J. Wright rather arbitrarily yokes together *Pearl* and Chaucer's Knight's Tale in a discussion of 'Comic Perspective in Two Middle English Poems' (*Parergon*, 1977): *Pearl*'s principal perspective is grandly said to be that of 'divine comedy'. Louise Dunlap finds a highly elaborate network of 'Vegetation Puns in *Pearl*' (*Mediævalia*, 1977) which serves the purpose of establishing 'both the importance and the limits of vegetational growth as an analogy for spiritual growth' – an analogy which she sees as being of the deepest significance within the poem.

There are also three briefer notes on points of interest in *Pearl.* Firstly, in 'Imagery of Roundness in William Woodford's *De Sacramento Altaris* (c. 1382/3) and its Possible Relevance to the Middle English *Pearl*' (*N&Q*), Laurence Eldredge points out the striking similarity between the clusters of images relating to roundness in the two texts. Writing on 'Pearl's Head Dress' (*Archiv*), Peter J. Lucas suggests a new interpretation for the difficult textual crux 'Her lere leke' in 1.210, according to which the whole line could be made to read 'She had enclosed her face (i.e. with a wimple); [and it was] encompassed all around'. Finally, J. Grant, C. Peterson, and A. S. C. Ross provide a number of linguistic 'Notes on the Rhymes of *Pearl*' (*SN*).

Charlotte C. Morse's study of *The Pattern of Judgment in the "Queste" and "Cleanness"*[9] begins by describing the 'paradigm of the vessel' as an image (or complex of images) of human life and how it is to be judged, as reflected in the Bible and medieval commentaries upon it. She then proceeds to apply this 'paradigm' to two texts that do not at first sight appear very closely related, the Old French *Queste del Saint Graal* (Malory's version of the story is also taken into account) and the Middle English *Cleanness*: in fact, she does not attempt to establish any direct connection between the two, but divides the main body of her book into two separate studies, one of each text. In her discussion of *Cleanness*, she makes a valiant attempt to find ordered patterns of structure and theological theme running through the poem: insisting, for example, that each of the stories it con-

[9] *The Pattern of Judgment in the "Queste" and "Cleanness"*, by Charlotte C. Morse, Columbia and London: U. of Missouri P. pp. x + 238. $16.50.

tains should be read as a type of the wedding-feast parable in the opening section, with its emphasis on clean and unclean vessels and related images. It must be said, however, that her analysis of *Cleanness* (as of the various versions of the *Queste*) suffers from the manner in which both texts have been made to fit into her preconceived theory.

'*Purity*: the Cities of the Dove and the Raven', by S. L. Clark and Julian N. Wasserman (*ABR*), pursues in rather more detail some of the ideas raised in their more general article on the *Gawain*-Poet's city imagery discussed above. They, too, argue that *Cleanness* is essentially a poem about judgement, conceived of primarily in spatial terms of inclusion in and exclusion from cities.

Only one article deals specifically with *Patience*: Morton W. Bloomfield discusses the relationship between '*Patience* and the *Mashal*'[10], suggesting that the Middle English poem may be seen as belonging to the genre of the *mashal*, a type of wisdom-literature originally found in Hebrew writings, whose general form is discernible in a number of medieval narratives with a moral bias.

Among the various avenues of research followed up in this year's crop of studies of *GGK*, the favourite topic of Gawain's fault gets its usual share of detailed scrutiny. In a very densely-argued article on 'The Three Hunts and Sir Gawain's Triple Fault' (*ABR*), Louis Blenkner argues that the account of the three blows in Fitt IV, 'pointedly recalling the three hunted animals' of Fitt III, suggests principles relating the deer, the boar, and the fox to the bedroom temptations undergone by Gawain. The three animals are made to figure not only the irascible, concupiscible and rational powers respectively, but also their associated chivalric sins of *couardyse, couetyse* and *vntrawþe*. 'Gawain's Fault: "Angardez Pryde"', by A. Francis Soucy (*ChauR*), suggests that Gawain's failing, at least in his own eyes, consists in excessive pride in his reputation as a knight and as a 'fader of nurture'. On a more positive note, Victoria L. Weiss's 'The Medieval Knighting Ceremony in *GGK*' (*ChauR*) finds a number of significant parallels between the events of Gawain's final encounter with the Green Knight and the details of medieval dubbing ceremonies, and suggests that in a certain sense Bertilak is giving Gawain the accolade of a 'real man', and a true even though flawed knight.

Two articles focus on the element of drama in the poem. In 'Decapitating Drama in *GGK*' (*DQR*), Judith Perryman makes the suggestion that the Green Knight's head could have been a false 'property' one surmounting his real head. Her speculations on the 'dramatic' elements in the text as a whole, leading to the theory that the poet may have envisaged 'some type of dramatic reading' for his text, are rather more vague, as is the argument of 'The Drama of *GGK*' by Wendy M. Reid (*Parergon*), which bases the claim that 'drama was a shaping force in the poem's composition' on the part-parallels the writer finds between certain features of *GGK* and almost every kind of late-medieval dramatic or semi-dramatic entertainment from folk-ritual to joust.

[10] In *Medieval Studies in Honor of Lillian Herlands Hornstein*, ed. by Jess B. Bessinger Jr and Robert R. Raymo. New York: New York U.P. 1976. pp x + 225. Frontispiece; 9 figures. $25.

In 'Bertilak's Lady: The French Background of *GGK*'[11], Richard R. Griffith argues that the poem uses as background material the thirteenth-century French Vulgate *Merlin* and its later anonymous 'continuation', particularly the sections dealing with the aggressive knight Bertolais (rendered as 'Bertelak' in a fifteenth-century English redaction of the story) and his wife, the pseudo-Guenevere. Margaret Charlotte Ward ransacks the Old French versions of Ovid's *Ars Amatoria* and *Remedia Amoris*, together with the Old French 'bestiaries of love', in an attempt to trace further connections between the hunt and bedroom scenes in Fitt III: 'French Ovidian Beasts in *GGK*' (*NM*). Juxtaposing 'Two Transfigurations: Gawain and Æneas' (*ChauR*), George Sanderlin spectulates that, if 'ver' in the difficult passage *GGK* 864–68 can be translated as 'Spring', the lines may contain a reference to a similar passage in Virgil's *Æneid*.

Patricia A. Moody's 'The "childgered" Arthur of *GGK*' (*SMC*, 1976) emphasises the delicate irony and ambiguity of the opening description of Arthur and his court. Victor Yelverton Haines' avowedly conjectural article on 'Allusions to the *felix culpa* in the Prologue of *GGK*' (*RUO*, 1974) concentrates on the possible references to the idea that he finds in the first stanza of the romance.

In 'Staffordshire and Cheshire Landscapes in *GGK*' (*North Staffordshire Field Studies*, 1977), Ralph W. V. Elliott argues ingeniously and at length that specific locations may be found for such physical features in the poem as the Green Chapel and the park surrounding Bertilak's castle.

Finally, Kathleen Basford's study of *The Green Man*[12], while not directly concerned with literary texts (concentrating almost entirely on the Green Man as portrayed in church sculpture), is an enjoyable and copiously-illustrated book that illuminates one part of the 'traditional' background of *GGK*.

4. Piers Plowman

A major desideratum has been satisfied by A. V. C. Schmidt's edition of *William Langland: The Vision of Piers Plowman, A Complete Edition of the B-Text*[13], which provides, for the first time at manageable cost, an extremely well-glossed and annotated version of the whole text, based on Trinity College Cambridge MS B.15.17, the same as that used by Kane and Donaldson (*YW* 56.88–9). He comes to different conclusions from them, and thus his text may be 'nearer to that of Skeat' than theirs. One quibble may be that he has perhaps tried to do too much on the side of textual criticism (see parts VII and VIII of the Introduction, the apparatus on

[11] In *Machaut's World: Science and Art in the Fourteenth Century*, ed. by Madeleine Pelner Cosman and Bruce Chandler. Annals of the New York Academy of Sciences, 314. New York: New York Academy of Sciences. pp. xiii, 348. $30.

[12] *The Green Man*, by Kathleen Basford. Ipswich, Suffolk: Derek Brewer. pp. 128. frontispiece; 95 plates. £8.50.

[13] *William Langland The Vision of Piers Plowman A Complete Edition of the B-Text*, A Critical Edition of the B-Text based on Trinity College Cambridge MS B.15.17 with selected variant readings, an Introduction, Glosses, and a Textual and Literary Commentary, by A. V. C. Schmidt. London, Melbourne and Toronto: J. M. Dent & Sons Ltd. New York: E. P. Dutton & Co. Inc. pp. xlviii + 364. £6.95.

each page, and the textual and lexical parts of the Commentary), using space that could have been given over, more profitably from the students' and teachers' point of view, to interpretation and explanation. Contrast the amplitude of Bennett's notes (*YW* 53.89). That said, we find very many illuminating suggestions (e.g. for *lymeyerd*, IX 181), richly informative annotations (e.g. Felice the Fair, XII 46), and convincing interpretations (e.g. XIII 150–171). The main perplexing moments in the poem (the Pardon, the Dowel-Dobet-Dobest triad, etc.) are all clearly dealt with. Sometimes the editor simply refers in the notes, quite rightly, to full discussions elsewhere (e.g. for Haukyn, the Tree of Charity, etc.); sometimes he provides full explanations of his own, which he either presents here (e.g. for usury, *pure tene*, etc.) or has published elsewhere (e.g. for *Anima*). The volume opens with a concise and sensitive introduction covering The Versions of *Piers Plowman*; Authorship, Audience, and Date; The Literary Tradition of *Piers Plowman*; The Structure of *Piers Plowman*; The Poem's Themes; Langland's Poetic Art; The Textual Problems of the B-Version; Editorial Procedure. At the end there is a short, perhaps too short, appendix on Langland's alliterative verse, and an index of proper names. All in all a most welcome production.

Derek Pearsall's edition of the C-text of *Piers Plowman by William Langland*[14] puts this version before us in its entirety for the first time since Skeat, whose notes are used as the basis for the commentary at the foot of each page and the glossary at the back. At the front is a short, readable, and sympathetic literary and textual introduction, followed by a select bibliography which, very surprisingly, omits Willi Erzgräber, *William Langlands "Piers Plowman" (eine Interpretation des C-Textes)* (*YW* 38. 83–4). Bennett and Donaldson are adduced as important aids for the content of the notes. There is, for instance, a reference to Donaldson in Pearsall's view of Langland's learning (p. 19) which, in the light of recent work (for example, Schmidt, *YW* 50.97; Lindemann, *YW* 58.83), may no longer be tenable. The base text, Huntington Library MS HM 143, is the same as that which forms the basis of George Russell's forthcoming edition of the C-text in the Athlone series. Three other MSS are also consulted: British Museum MS Add. 35157, Trinity College Cambridge MS R. 3.14, the 'Ilchester' MS (now University of London MS [S.L.] V. 88), as well as Skeat's MS. Items for annotation are chosen with severe discrimination and presented with great clarity (e.g. on *mede* and *mercede*, III 332–405; on the Pardon, IX 3 and 291; on *lymzerd*, X 283, where he is perhaps less adventurous than Schmidt: see above); on *Rechelesnesse*, XI 196, etc.). Cross-references back and forth in the text are very helpful, as are the notes calling attention to C's deletions from B (for example, at IX 293 and XVI 157). According to the editor, 'C may be less exciting, but it makes better sense' than B, a claim which, thanks to him, can now be assessed. We are all much in his debt.

Daniel Maher Murtaugh considers four passages in relation to *Piers Plowman and the Image of God in Man*[15]: the speech of Lady Holy

[14] *Piers Plowman by William Langland*, An Edition of the C-text by Derek Pearsall. (York Medieval Texts: Second Series. General Editors: Elizabeth Salter and Derek Pearsall) Edward Arnold Ltd. pp. vi + 416. £15.95.

[15] *Piers Plowman and the Image of God in Man*, by Daniel Maher Murtaugh. Gainesville, Fla.: The University Presses of Florida. pp. viii + 129. $8.50.

Church, Piers's directions for finding Truth, Wit's account of the 'Castle of Caro', and the Tree of Charity 'amyddes mannes body'. Chapter 2 contains a most enlightening essay on 'The Dialectic of Truth', dealing with the way in which this word is used in selected passages, with cross-references to the C-text. Chapter 3 concerns 'The Social Dimension' of man's life in this world, and the relationship between King, Conscience, and Mede. Chapter 4 presents a straightforward exposition of the 'Learning and Grace' controversy in the Vita de Dowel, with references to contemporary teachers such as Ockham, to show how man's free will and God's foreknowledge can be accommodated in certain aspects. Chapter 5 proceeds from R. W. Frank's reading of this passage (*YW* 38.83), and also from Meroney's view (*YW* 31.78), to claim that 'the pardon scene presents to us the Old Testament "figure" and its fulfillment, the decalogue of Moses and the Redemption, superimposed one upon the other'. The chapter ends with an illuminating account of the significance of the 'Piers-Christ' figure, which includes the image of God and man. Chapter 6 has little relevance to the rest of the book and is quite redundant. Its title, 'The Essential Poem at the Centre of Things', is taken from a poem by Wallace Stevens, and it introduces a mercifully short, rather uneasy set of forced correspondences between the two poets. There is no bibliography, and the index is limited, but nevertheless the book as a whole is fresh, and makes its point.

A. J. Colaianne presents *Piers Plowman: An Annotated Bibliography of Editions and Criticism, 1550–1977*[16] (quite comprehensive, but 'selective, with special emphasis on critical studies published from 1875–1977') with two purposes in mind: 'first, to provide a comprehensive review of scholarship and criticism concerning William Langland and the three versions of his alliterative masterpiece *Piers Plowman* and, second, to suggest some directions for future studies of this mysterious and problematic work'. The latter aim is summarily executed in a brief epilogue which could, perhaps, have been omitted. The main section is divided into four parts: I. Biographical Studies and the Problems of Authorship; II. Editions and Textual Studies: Selections and Translations; III. Critical Interpretation; Style, Metre, and Language. This bibliography takes its place with those of Bloomfield (*YW* 20.61), Proppe (1972), and Fowler (*YW* 52.80). English, French, Italian, Czech, Polish, and Japanese studies are listed, as well as 'a substantial number of important English, American and German dissertations', which could also have been omitted because, as it is arbitrary, it does not remove the necessity of searching through *Dissertation Abstracts*, etc. Each of the four sections commences with a short introductory essay, and the total number of entries, most of which are followed by summaries of their contents, is 672, with an additional eighteen studies listed in an Appendix under the heading 'Studies not listed in Chapter I which comment on the question of authorship'. The book will prove decidedly useful for both students and teachers of *Piers Plowman*.

Susan H. McLeod unnecessarily reduces the importance of 'The Tearing of the Pardon in *Piers Plowman*' (*PQ*), and proposes that '[Truth] sent a

[16] *Piers Plowman An Annotated Bibliography of Editions and Criticism, 1550–1977*, by A. J. Colaianne. New York & London: Garland Publishing Inc. pp. xii + 195. $18.

message to Piers' which, in B VII 9–104, explains what is to come in the Pardon: neither Piers nor the Priest recognises the point that doing well is superior to getting pardons. This article explains the Pardon, but not the tearing. In a very well-argued note, using MS readings from the A-, B-, and C-versions, Lister M. Matheson regards Skeat's Vernon reading of 'mis-happes' at Passus VIII 79 as 'An Example of Ambiguity and Scribal Confusion in *Piers Plowman*' (*ELN*). Kane reads 'mysshapen' (from MS T.C.C. R. 3.14) which, in its various spellings, could be graphemically identical (and would give better sense) to the plural of the rare noun 'mis-shape', 'a cripple'. In a singularly inconsequential note, Charles Lionel Regan associates 'John Gower, John Barleycorn, and William Langland' (*AN&Q*). *Confessio Amantis* VI 11 60 ('. . .the cuppe') may be an echo of the A-text V 213 ('. . .cuppe').

Referring to B Passus XVIII 424–31, Raymond St.-Jacques very convincingly associates 'Langland's Bells of the Resurrection and the Easter Liturgy', probably that part involving the *Elevatio Crucis* (*ESC*, 1977). Earlier commentators (e.g. Skeat, Goodridge, Salter and Pearsall) had explained it as an allusion to the Good Friday 'creeping to the cross' ceremony. John N. King deals with his author's quarto edition of *The Vision of Pierce Plowman* (1550) (*YW* 57.67–8) in his fascinating study of the millenarian 'Robert Crowley: A Tudor Gospelling Poet' (see *YW* 57.67), whose techniques are here shown to derive ultimately from the tradition of the medieval sermon, by way of medieval homiletic satire, including estates literature (*YES*). Now we can put Crowley's edition of *Piers Plowman* in the context of his other pre-occupations and achievements, thanks to this article which is excellent (except for a curious throw-away remark on p. 227, fn 2). In an important note, which helps to corroborate the view that Langland was neither superficial nor a magpie in his learning, Thomas D. Hill identifies 'Christ's "Three Clothes": "Piers Plowman" C. XI. 193' with the white, red, and purple garments worn by Christ before he was stripped and crucified (*N&Q*). Ambrose, in his *Expositio Evangelii Secundum Lucam*, and Ludolf of Saxony, in his *Vita Christi*, supply the explanation.

Robert Adams presents a major study of 'The Nature of Need in *Piers Plowman* XX' [6–50] where, he convincingly claims, Langland is 'dramatizing' Job 41.13 ('faciem eius præcedit egestas') (*Traditio*). He cites both Gregory's commentary on this verse, in the *Moralia*, and also the author of the *Liber de Antichristo*, who uses what Gregory says about Need, 'to imply that the new mendicant orders are acting as the false heralds of a false messiah'. Referring to an article by John Burrow (*EIC*, XV), Maureen Quilligan discusses 'Langland's Literal Allegory' with particular reference to the Pardon scene and, in a most enlightening final section, to the 'just'/'joust' punning (*EIC*). Reading allegory spiritually is 'paradoxically the most literal kind of reading'.

Piers Plowman: La Genèse Littéraire des Trois Versions, by Guy Bourquin (Paris, 1978), was not seen.

5. Romances

Susan Wittig's book on *Stylistic and Narrative Structures in the Middle*

English Romances[17] aims at providing a 'linguistic model of analysis' of the genre, based essentially on a study of the large group of non-cyclical metrical romances (twenty-seven main texts are listed as the basis for her study). The proposed model views each narrative as a 'system of relations' stretching from the surface structure of the formulaic style common to these texts to the underlying deep structure of Middle English romance. This approach leads to an interesting discussion of the ways in which the romances tend not only to use standard formulae and motifs in their telling of a story, but also to use them according to a pre-set pattern or 'grammar', though it is a pity that Miss Wittig's analysis is to some extent weakened by her failure (perhaps inevitable in view of the wide stylistic variety of the texts studied) to define quite closely enough exactly what constitutes a 'formula'. In her discussion of the larger-scale narrative structures of the romances, too, there is a certain tendency to fall into generalisations that once again seems due to the very large and varied field covered.

'The origin and meaning of Middle English *romaunce*' (*Genre*, 1977), by Paul Strohm, painstakingly traces the developments in the usage of Old French *romans* in the twelfth century and of Middle English *romaunce* in the thirteenth, fourteenth and fifteenth centuries, together with that of the related terms *storie, geste* and *lay*, and arrives at the conclusion that 'a concept of *romaunce* was generally shared and the term was used to classify and describe actual narratives'.

In a lively article, W. R. J. Barron writes 'A propos de quelques cas d'écorchement dans les romans anglais et français du Moyen Age'[18], charting the appearances of the motif of skinning alive as a punishment for feudal treason both in English and French romance and in contemporary actuality.

Carol Falvo Heffernan's edition of *Le Bone Florence of Rome*[19] falls disappointingly below the general standard of the Manchester series of Old and Middle English texts. Its main weaknesses lie in the rather erratic textual notes and glossary. The introduction does provide an extended discussion of the background of the story and of the romance's own literary qualities, though here again the discussion shows a certain superficiality at times, as in the discussion of the 'archetypal' theme of the persecuted woman from the Middle Ages to D. H. Lawrence. The same author also contributes '*Raptus*: A Note on Crime and Punishment in *Le Bone Florence of Rome*'[20], in which she suggests that the poet's treatment of the abduction of Florence by Egravayne reflects a growing respect in

[17] *Stylistic and Narrative Structures in the Middle English Romances*, by Susan Wittig. Austin Tex: and London: U. of Texas P. pp. x + 224. £11.20.

[18] In *Mélanges de littérature du moyen age au xxe siècle offerts à Mademoiselle Jeanne Lods, professeur honoraire de littérature médiévale a l'Ecole Normale Supérieure de Jeunes Filles, par ses collègues, ses élèves et ses amis*. Collection de l'Ecole Normale Supérieure de Jeunes Filles, 10. 2 vols. Paris: Ecole Normale Supérieure. pp. xxi, 603; 604–902. frontispiece portrait. 120 fr.

[19] *Le Bone Florence of Rome*, ed. by Carol Falvo Heffernan. Old and Middle English Texts Series. Manchester: Manchester U.P. 1976. pp. x + 225. £8.50.

[20] In *Medieval Studies in Honor of Lillian Herlands Hornstein*, ed. by Jess B. Bessinger Jr and Robert R. Raymo. New York: New York U.P. 1976. pp. x + 225. Frontispiece; 9 figures. $25.

the eyes of contemporary society for the woman's right to free consent in marriage and for the sanctity of her marriage-bond.

One of the most stimulating of the other studies of individual non-cycle romances is Dean R. Baldwin's 'Fairy Lore and the Meaning of *Sir Orfeo*' (*SFQ*, 1977). He argues that the fact that all Orfeo's actions and those of the fairy king conform to the requirements of traditional fairy lore implies that the hero's actions may best be understood in the light of those traditions: 'In the pattern itself is meaning enough'.

E. M. Bradstock traces 'The Penitential Pattern in *Sir Gowther*' (*Parergon*), concentrating on the Northern version of the romance. He finds that the poem is clearly structured to show Gowther going through the various stages of repentance and reparation for sin, and also to throw into relief the link between moral and knightly perfection: the stages of Gowther's penitence and of his movement towards ideal knighthood are inseparably linked together.

In a note on 'An Unremarked Fictional Version of the Legend of Guy of Warwick' (*AN&Q*), J. L. Gaunt draws attention to the earliest surviving 'fictional' version of the story, a hybrid text cast partly in verse and partly in prose dating from the mid-seventeenth century.

Writing on 'The Glastonbury Legends and the English Arthurian Grail Romances' (*NM*), Valerie M. Lagorio examines the influence of Glastonbury Abbey's claims to Arthurian and Arimathean connections on the English Grail romances from *Arthour and Merlin* to Malory's *Morte Darthur*. Robert W. Ackerman takes a fresh look at 'Madden's Gawain Anthology'[21], enquiring into Madden's motives and procedures in assembling his collection and assessing the scale of his achievement. David L. Hoffman's 'Cult and Culture: "Courtly Love" in the Cave and the Forest' (*Tristania*) rather ploddingly surveys the treatment of the forest and cave episodes in almost the entire range of Tristan romances, but has very little to say specifically about courtly love.

Discussions of individual romances include Gail K. Hamilton's careful study of 'The breaking of the Troth in *Ywain and Gawain*' (*Mediævalia*, 1976). She emphasises the concern of the Middle English redactor with truth in all human relationships, and pays particular attention to his exploration of both the positive and the negative qualities inherent in insistence upon truth to one's word. It is through the process of experience that 'a proper definition of *trowth* is worked out in *Ywain and Gawain*'. Hamilton's main point has already been effectively made by Penelope Doob in *Nebuchadnezzar's Children*, pp 141ff (*YW* 55.93). In a note on '*Sir Perceval of Galles, Le Conte du Graal* and *La Continuation-Gauvain*: The Methods of an English Adaptor' (*EA*), Keith Busby finds sufficient similarities of narrative, phraseology and spirit between the three texts to justify the supposition that both French romances were drawn upon by the English author. Discussing 'Artistic Design in the Stanzaic *Morte Arthur*' (*ELH*), Sherron E. Knapp defends the poem's 'harmony of design and execution', and argues that the structure of the romance is governed by its author's fascination with the abiding consequences of quickly-passing events.

[2] See Note 12, p. 83.

6. Gower, Lydgate, Hoccleve

L. B. Burke argues that there is a distinct lack of negative stereotypes for 'Women in John Gower's Confessio Amantis' (*Mediævalia*) and that their absence accounts for some of the mellowness of tone which has been ascribed to the work. She illustrates her point by a selective investigation of Gower's treatment of his sources, and concludes that the mitigation of traditional misogyny owes something to Gower's intention to celebrate rather than denigrate the married state. L. Ebin claims that 'Lydgate's Views On Poetry' (*AnM*) have been neglected, yet they provide important insights into his aims as a poet, into his views upon poetry's function and also into the poetic practices of the fifteenth century in general. She deduces Lydgate's views partly by an investigation of certain key words in his usage (though sometimes the context in which her key word appears fails to convince us of the meaning which she ascribes to it), and she concludes that these views find a more explicit treatment in his fifteenth-century successors.

A. S. G. Edwards traces 'The Influence of Lydgate's *Fall of Princes* c. 1440–1559: A Survey' (*MS*), presenting evidence to suggest that the poem's ultimate Latin source, the *De casibus virorum illustrium* of Boccaccio, was little known in England, and that any demand for it may have been obviated by the accessibility of Lydgate's work. Lydgate's *Fall* appears to have had little competition, and Edwards gives illuminating examples of how it was used by later medieval and Renaissance writers. R. F. Green offers two pieces. In 'Lydgate and Deguileville Once More' (*N&Q*), she challenges a hypothesis that John Stow's ascription of the verse translation of the *Pèlerinage de la Vie Humaine* to Lydgate was a misunderstanding. She argues that the external evidence favours Lydgate's authorship of the verse translation. 'Notes on Some Manuscripts of Hoccleve's *Regiment of Princes*' (*BLJ*) identifies an unnoticed fragment of Hoccleve's *Regiment* in fragment 90 of BL MS Harley 5977, which she proceeds to connect with a fragment of the same work and manuscript contained in Bodleian Library MS Rawlinson D. 913, f. 63. She discusses the textual affiliations between these fragments and other *Regiment* manuscripts, and concludes by pointing out that the scribes of the *Regiment* poems contained in BL MSS Arundel 59 and Harley 372 are one and the same.

In 'Poet and Patron in Early Fifteenth-Century England: John Lydgate's *Temple of Glas*' (*Parergon*), J. Wilson attempts to show that when Lydgate revised this poem in at least two different versions, he was trying to cater for the tastes of those for whom the poem was intended. She concludes that in trying to do so, he has produced a dislocation between the form and content of the poem. R. F. Yeager has provided 'A Bibliography of John Gower Materials Through 1975' (*Mediævalia*) which lists additions and translations of Gower's works and works of uncertain authorship. The bibliography also includes publications on Gower which appeared during 1975.

7. Middle Scots Poetry

C. R. Bradley, in 'The Phoenix in *The Kingis Quair*: Some Confusion'

(*AN&Q*) points out that there is no reference anywhere in *The Kingis Quair* to a phoenix, contrary to J. A. W. Bennett's claim in his book *The Parlement of Foules: An Interpretation* (Oxford, 1957), p. 110 (v. *YW* 38.101–2). R. D. Drexler examines 'Dunbar's "Lament for the Makaris" and the Dance of Death Tradition' (*SSL*), and suggests some of the forms in which Dunbar may have met the tradition. The article proceeds to assess the literary merit of the poem. In 'Dunbar's Giant: "On the Resurrection of Christ", Lines 17–24' (*Anglia*), T. D. Hill suggests that the imagery of the central, third stanza of Dunbar's Resurrection Ode has been carefully conceived, and that it reflects the movement of the whole poem. He finds that the word 'gyane' unites within itself the dual aspects of Christ as man and God, aspects which are found uncombined at the beginning and end of this stanza, and that the integration of these aspects in this word mirrors an integration of the themes of the opening and concluding stanzas.

R. D. S. Jack argues in 'Caxton's *Mirrour of the World* and Henryson's "Taill of the Cok and the Jasp"' (*ChauR*) that the principal source for Henryson's poem is to be found in Chapter 5 of Caxton's *Mirrour of the World* rather than in the versification of the *Romulus* by Gualterus Anglicus and in the *Isopet de Lyon*, as is generally maintained. His case rests upon verbal parallels between Caxton and Henryson, and upon shared similarities of theme and treatment. I. W. A. Jamieson attempts to determine whether a coherent and consistent theory of the function of poetry is to be found in Henryson's poems in '"To preue thare preching be a poesye": Some Thoughts on Henryson's Poetics' (*Parergon*) and concludes that there is.

B. W. Kliman argues in 'John Barbour and Rhetorical Tradition' (*AnM*) that Barbour knew the teaching of the rhetorical manuals of his day and that he not only applied it skilfully, but that he also went beyond its formulations. She compares Barbour's poem with the precepts of Geoffrey de Vinsauf, and gives a somewhat pedestrian account of points of comparison and of divergence; her account of Barbour's style would have benefited from ampler proofs for its corroboration. In 'Dunbar and the Franciscans' (*MÆ*), R. J. Lyall provides an interesting analysis of Dunbar's poem 'How dumbar wes desyrd to be ane freir', and seeks to elucidate the ironies in it by reference to Franciscan spiritual literature. He concludes that the poem ought to be viewed as an anti-mendicant satire. He also offers 'Some Observations on *The Dregy of Dunbar*' (*Parergon*), and suggests that the poem is fundamentally serious, that it contains ironic praise of the materialistic life of Edinburgh and a genuine wish that King James IV will successfully complete his period of penance at Stirling. The author also suggests that Dunbar may have been taking a sidelong glance at John Ireland, a counsellor and member of the court.

A. A. MacDonald reviews three 'Recent Editions of the *Kingis Quair*' (*Neophilologus*), those of J. R. Simon (1967), J. Norton-Smith (1971) and M. P. McDiarmid (1973) (*YW* 48.81, 52.94–5, and 54.96–7 respectively). The review is balanced, pointing out blemishes and felicities, and concludes that Simon's text provides the most careful linguistic analysis, that Norton-Smith's is the text most suitable for an undergraduate market, and that McDiarmid's is the most attractive to use. J. MacQueen provides many illustrations of the social and intellectual context of 'The Literature of Fifteenth-Century Scotland' (in *Scottish Society in the Fifteenth Century* edited by J. M. Brown). His article is primarily a survey, but he finds time to expatiate on certain selected matters, as for example the provision of a numerological analysis of the *Kingis Quair*.

W. S. Ramson offers 'A Reading of Henryson's *Testament*, or "Quha falsit Cresseid?"' (*Parergon*) which examines selected aspects of Henryson's poem in a somewhat wordy manner. The author's anecdotal opening is comic and largely redundant; comedy vanishes, if not redundancy, as the piece progresses. In 'Henryson and Nominalism' (*JMRS*), R. J. Schrader seeks to illustrate the philosophical climate surrounding Henryson, and surveys aspects of medieval nominalism. He concludes that Henryson reveals himself to have been especially in accord with the later Ockhamists, notably with the philosophical position taken in the work of the fifteenth-century Nicholas of Cusa. L. M. Sklute, in 'Phoebus Descending: Rhetoric and Moral Vision in Henryson's *Testament of Cresseid*' (*ELH*), discusses the rhetorical techniques by which Henryson gives a semblance of charity and humanity to what is in fact his stringent and rigid moral judgement on Cresseid, and how the ostensibly sympathetic presentation of Cresseid is undercut by irony. He finds that the poem's two descriptions of the sun as setting, and never as rising, are diagnostic of the dark judgemental morality of the poet.

8. Lyrics and Miscellaneous Verse

Professor Siegfried Wenzel has made a welcome contribution to a largely unexamined area of Middle English studies with his book *Verses in Sermons: Fasciculus Morum and its Middle English Poems*[22]. The book is organised into four chapters. The first considers such matters as the date and authorship of the *Fasciculus Morum*, its contents and structure, its influence and uses, and provides a list of all manuscripts known to Wenzel with brief descriptive notes on each. The second chapter is very well documented, and is the most comprehensive survey so far of the function of English verse in the medieval sermon. The third chapter offers a fascinating study of the vagaries of the textual transmission of the English verses in the *Fasciculus*. The final chapter edits all these verses with a commentary on each.

'*The Boke of Cupide* Reopened' (*NM*) by C. S. Rutherford presents a case for regarding Clanvowe's poem not as a covert moral allegory on the effects of lust and its remedy but as a lighthearted treatment of the traditional courtly theme of the bitter-sweetness of love. The author finds that the nature of the poem's dependence upon Chaucer and the use which it makes of the conventions of the debate genre justify his conclusion.

In '*Miles*: A Crux in MS. Harley 2253' (*NM*), H. Bergner proposes that a crux in the Harley lyric *Lenten ys come wiþ loue to toune*, the word *miles*, be emended to *males* (modern English 'males'). He discusses and rejects previous emendations. In his note 'The Companions of St. Bruno in Middle English Verses on the Foundation of the Carthusian Order'

[22] *Verses in Sermons: Fasciculus Morum and Its Middle English Poems*, by Siegfried Wenzel. Cambridge, Mass.: The Medieval Academy of America. pp. x + 234. $20.

(*Speculum*), R. Boyer identifies the names of St Bruno's companions listed in verse 24 of a Middle English poem on the foundation of the Carthusian order. He demonstrates that they are not the traditional companions of St Bruno but are rather the names of some famous Carthusians. W. L. Braekman prints 'A Middle English Didactic Poem on the Works of Mercy' (*NM*) for the first time, providing brief notes on its subject matter and including substantive variants of the text from another manuscript copy. His description of the written dialect of the poem, which he prints as 'an irregular or "mixed" Midland dialect', does no justice to certain of its orthographies, which are in fact strongly East Anglian.

In his note '"I sing of a Maiden": A Fifteenth-Century Sermon Reminiscence' (*N&Q*), A. J. Fletcher draws attention to the appearance of the final couplet of this lyric in a Latin sermon manuscript of the fifteenth century. From evidence provided by the sermon in which the lyric appears, he demonstrates that it must on occasions have been sung, and that it must have been far commoner than its solitary appearance in the Sloane manuscript might suggest. H. Hargreaves prints for the first time '*De Spermate Hominis*: A Middle English Poem on Human Embryology' (*MS*) preserved in the National Library of Scotland, MS 23.7.11, ff. 89v–90r. He goes on to discuss how the content relates to particular traditions in medieval embryological theory.

T. D. Hill, in '"Half-Waking, Half-Sleeping": A Tropological Motif in a Middle English Lyric and its European Context' (*RES*), attempts to explain the opening two lines of the M.E. lyric 'Sodenly afraide' and particularly the expression 'half wakyng, half slepyng', by a search for analogues elsewhere in medieval literature. He derives from his interesting documentation a perhaps too stringent explanation of the significance of the expression in the lyric, that it denotes 'the time *between* sin and repentance when a man must choose to awaken or to fall back into the sleep of sin'. Using internal evidence provided by the poem, D. R. Howlett determines 'The Date and Authorship of the Middle English Verse Translation of Palladius' *De Re Rustica*' (*MÆ*). He dates it to 1442 or 1443, and goes on to make a case for its ascription to one Thomas Norton, chaplain to Humfrey, Duke of Gloucester. J. Johnston, in 'The Points of Thomas Becket' (*N&Q*), examines the variation in the number of points given by vernacular lyrics and carols for the reasons why Thomas Becket was martyred. She concludes that fifteen points may be the number mentioned in the earliest stages of this tradition surrounding Becket, and that this number may also have some historical foundation in the list of points given by William of Canterbury.

In 'The Middle English Poem *The Four Foes of Mankind*: Some Notes on the Language and the Text' (*NM*), A. McIntosh illustrates the northernisms in the language of *The Four Foes* poem and comments on how unusually conservative is the preservation of its northern forms by its south-east Midland scribe. He concludes with a list of explanatory notes on the poem's difficult words and phrases. W. I. Miller, in 'The Middle English Ballad "Robyn and Gandeleyn" (line 57)' (*N&Q*), proposes a new reading of the word 'sāchloþis' in line 57 of the ballad. He plausibly suggests that it is a misspelled earlier appearance of O.E.D.'s *Samcloth*. V. Nelson studies the badly burned 'Cot. Tiberius E. VII: A Manuscript of the *Speculum*

Vitae' (*ES*) in order to determine how its scribe has treated the *Speculum* text that he was copying. By a careful comparison with a text of the *Speculum* reproduced and edited from BL MS Additional 33995, she demonstrates that the Tiberius scribe sometimes compresses the text, sometimes expands it, and generaly indulges in 'Change for its own sake'.

In his article 'A Middle English Poem on the Eucharist and Other Poems by the Same Author' (*Archiv*), D. S. Pickering edits a poem from Bodleian Library MS Add. C. 280 and discusses it comprehensively from textual, linguistic and literary points of view. He makes a strong case for a common authorship which he claims that it shares with three other M.E. poems, and suggests that the author of all four poems was possibly a cleric who worked in Norfolk about the middle of the fourteenth century. In '"Annot and John" and the Ploys of Parody' (*SP*), D. J. Ransom's attempted vindication of the excessive description of the woman in Harley lyric *Annot and John*, though occasionally unconvincing, nevertheless offers the view that the poem is purposely factitious, and is a burlesque on the convention of the idealisation of the mistress. He uncovers innuendoes and ambiguities which undermine the ostensible meaning of certain lines, producing a 'conflict between sensuality and sublimity' upon which the humour of the poem depends.

In his note '"Sulch sorw I walke with": Line 4 of "Foweles in the Frith"' (*N&Q*), C. Revard corrects the generally current misreading of line 4 of *Foweles in the Frith*. The word 'Mulch' is to be read rather as 'Sulch'. A. G. Rigg compares three recent editions of 'The Red Book of Ossory: Editions by Edmund Colledge, O.S.A., Richard Leighton Green and Theo Stemmler' (*MÆ*) in a review article, and uses his own editorial acumen to suggest many improvements, including the detection of mis-transcriptions and the proposal of emendations. He also considers how the authorship of poems XLVIII–LX, not in fact by Ledrede, but by Walter of Wimbourne, disturbs the notes of the three editors. In her piece 'Alliterative Modes and Affiliations in the Fourteenth Century' (*NM*), E. Salter suggests that materials lying on the border of prose and accentual verse deserve greater consideration as possible stimuli for the 'alliterative revival' than they have received. She draws heavily upon John Gaytryge's sermon and upon the unpublished sermons of BL MS Additional 41321 for illustrations.

From a brief survey of the function of the metaphors of bondage in medieval literature, S. S. Smith, in '"Adam lay i-bowndyn" and the Vinculum Amoris' (*ELN*), suggests that the bonds of Adam in this lyric may be viewed not only as those which chained him in hell, but also as those which chained him in love to God. In this way the opening line may be seen as an immediate ratification of the poem's celebration of the theme of the *Felix Culpa*. T. Stemmler offers 'Observations on Some Difficult Passages in the Harley Lyrics' (*N&Q*) and proposes various emendations to the texts of three of the lyrics. These are *Lystneþ, Lordynges, a newe songe ichulle bigynne, Alle þat beoþ of huerte trewe* and *Ichot a burde in a bour ase beryl so bryht*. In his note 'A Contemporary Reference in a Fourteenth-Century Carol' (*N&Q*), D. W. Whitfield demonstrates a similarity existing between an incident referred to in a fourteenth-century carol and one referred to under the year 1363 in a minor fourteenth-century chronicle contained in BL MS Additional 47214, on fol. 19v. He proceeds to offer further evidence in support of the conjectured Franciscan authorship of the carol.

E. Wilson prints 'An Unpublished Passion Poem in British Library MS Harley 4012' (*N&Q*) for the first time. He provides notes on the manuscript and on the text of the poem. In a somewhat diffuse article 'The Canticle of Canticles, Two Latin Poems, and "In a Valley of þis Restles Mynde"' (*MP*), J. I. Wimsatt attempts to persuade us that the M.E. lyric, like two Latin poems 'Quis est hic qui pulsat ad ostium' and 'Dulcis Iesu memoria', embodies a contemplative experience of the soul in which the soul briefly encounters God and is then drawn back to active life in the world. His reading depends upon the poem's treatment of the text of *Canticum Canticorum* and upon medieval exegesis of that book, notably as found in St Bernard's sermons on the Song of Songs.

In the first of three volumes which will form 'a new edition of the poem with thorough analysis of the poet's sources, ideas, and techniques', Sarah M. Horrall edits 'approximately one third' (9228 lines) of *The Southern Version of Cursor Mundi*[23], a work of which the only modern edition is Morris's text of the Northern version (reprinted 1961–6). In an appendix she provides a massively informed and useful set of explanatory notes and also a list of errors in Morris's text, both of which items will be continued in future volumes. Her base text is MS Arundel LVII^5, College of Arms, London, with missing lines supplied from MS Trinity College Cambridge, R. 3. 8., and additional variants from Bodleian Laud Misc. 416, and B.L. Additional MS 36983. She 'can accept none of the previously published MSS stemma[ta], for reasons which will be fully discussed and justified in Volume III'. The present volume has a bibliography of primary and secondary sources. The book is a model of editorial excellence, and presents this major exegetical text in a most accessible and attractive way. It is to be hoped that there will be a glossary.

9. Malory and Caxton

E. M. Bradstock argues that 'The Juxtaposition of "The Knight of the Cart" and "The Healing of Sir Urry"' (*AUMLA*) was intentional, and serves to illustrate more clearly two conflicting loyalties within Lancelot. It is suggested that the Lancelot of the 'Cart' episode, the lover of Guinevere, undergoes in the 'Urry' episode a development towards the spiritual stature of a 'Grail winner', a role which becomes increasingly important as the *Morte Darthur* draws to a close. T. Grove, in 'Sexual Intemperance and the Fall of the Round Table' (*Silliman Journal*) makes an obvious point when he connects the fall of the Round Table with the sexual intemperance of Uther, Arthur and Lancelot. The article is concerned mainly with establishing the close linking of the emerging pattern of downfall with the acts of intemperance, and concludes that Malory shows the destructive nature of uncontrolled sexual desire.

L. Helling and H. Kelliher put forward evidence to suggest that 'The

[23] *The Southern Version of Cursor Mundi*, Volume I, ed. by Sarah M. Horrall. General Editor Sarah M. Horrall. Ottawa: U. of Ottawa P. pp. 431. $18.

Malory Manuscript' (*BLJ*) and the only complete edition of Caxton's *Morte Darthur* were orginally together in Caxton's Westminster office at some stage between 1480 and 1483. They conclude that the manuscript may have provided one of the exemplars which Caxton used for his edition. S. E. Holbrook provides a careful and well written examination of 'Nymue, the Chief Lady of the Lake, in Malory's *Le Morte Darthur*' (*Speculum*). He distinguishes two distinct ladies of the Lake in the *Morte*, and examines the role and function of the one named Nymue, deciding that Malory presents her favourably, and not as the cunning temptress which she is in some of the other Arthurian material. S. Knight aims to assess the 'Style and the Effects of Style in Malory's Arthuriad' (*Parergon*), and distinguishes what he calls a basic style, which is characterised by a balance and co-ordination stressed by the frequent repetition of conjunctions, and the variations upon it.

In their piece 'Tristram in the *Morte Darthur*' (*Tristania*), N. H. and L. J. Owen outline and endorse the arguments of Malory critics for a unified design in the *Morte*, and they commend particularly the division of the work into three major sections. They argue that the second and central section, the Tristram, is itself in three parts (as are the first and third of the major sections) and that this triadic structure, conditioned by a medieval aesthetic principle of proportion, is in fact to be perceived in a portion of the *Morte* which has generally been considered disorganised. In 'Chivalry and Malory's Quest of the Holy Grail' (*Parergon*), G. R. Simes examines some of the ways in which Malory's treatment of chivalry differs from that found in the *Queste del Saint Graal*. The author's contention that the pre-eminence of ascetic, spiritual values in the French did not suit Malory's views seems obvious enough. In 'Lancelot and the Concept of Honour in the *Morte Darthur*, Parts VII and VIII' (*Parergon*), J. Wilson suggests that the downfall of the Round Table may have been caused by the high value attributed to honour. She sees in Lancelot's behaviour a casuistic adherence to the letter and not the spirit of honour, and generally examines the role of honour throughout Books VII and VIII.

10. Other Prose

All Wyclif textual studies must be seen in a new light with the publication of Anne Hudson's *Selections from English Wycliffite Writings*[24]: 'none of the English texts can certainly be ascribed to Wyclif himself'. Hence, for example, Knapp's book on Wyclif's prose style (*YW* 58.98–9) is seriously undermined as also, to a much lesser extent, are Hargreaves's article (*YW* 47.88) and, of course, Krapp (1915). Following on from, and expanding, her earlier work, the Introduction is a model of reasoned and informed research covering what is known of the facts of Wyclif's life, his writings, his heretical views, and the achievements of his followers, the Lollards (a term whose 'first official use so far known is in bishop Wakefield of Worcester's register in 1387'). Two main considerations governed her selection of texts: 'first, to show the range of Lollard interests and the

[24] *Selections from English Wycliffite Writings*, edited with an Introduction, Notes and Glossary by Anne Hudson. Cambridge: C.U.P. pp. xii + 234. £10.50.

balance of their preoccupations; second, to illustrate the various types of Lollard tract, sermon and satire.' The texts are listed under four headings: I. The Nature of Wycliffite Belief; II. The Lollards and the Bible; III. Lollard Polemic; IV. Lollard Doctrine. At the end a short introduction is provided for each of the twenty-seven texts and also a brief set of notes explaining points of difficulty in the text. For instance, No 14, Prologue to Wycliffite Bible: Chapter 15 (which includes an absorbing discussion of the problems faced by one of the translators of the Wycliffite Bible), requires a note to explain the difficulty over rendering the Latin 'ablatif case absolute' in English. These end-notes also carry very comprehensive bibliographical references, and the volume concludes with a glossary, an index of proper names, and a select bibliography. This book will make the job of teaching Wyclif or, if we accept the editor's claim, Wycliffite writings, both easier and more satisfying than heretofore.

Vincent DiMarco and Leslie Perelman edit *The Middle English Letter of Alexander to Aristotle*[25] from the sole MS, Worcester Cathedral f. 172 (paper, third quarter of the fifteenth century) which contains another seventeen items in all. See their earlier article (*YW* 58.103). The introduction includes sections on 'The Scribe of the MS' – his other productions, his hand, his language; the Latin *Epistola Alexandri ad Aristotelem*, sources and influence of the *Epistola*, the *Epistola* in Old English, the *Epistola* in Middle English literature; the Latin Source of the Middle English Letter, possibly the same version as is preserved in Cambridge University Library MS Mm. 5.29 (2434), which is published alongside the M.E. text; Notes on the Texts. They conclude this very welcome edition with a Table of Variants, Notes and Selected Glossary (far too skimped) and a Bibliography. Teachers of the Nowell Codex will also be pleased (see *YW* 1.36–7).

Mary Felicitas Madigan's study of *The Passio Domini Theme in the Works of Richard Rolle: His Personal Contribution in its Religious, Cultural, and Literary Context*[26] will serve as a useful elementary introduction to the subject, because she sets out to be as comprehensive as possible, as will be seen from the list of contents. Chapter I treats of *Traditional Elements Reflecting the Milieu* (covering the Bible and the Liturgy, Iconography, Medieval Spirituality, the Rhetorical Tradition, and Natural English Attitudes); Chapter II turns to Rolle's Contribution to Medieval Devotional Literature; Chapter III introduces Rolle's *Meditations on the Passion* (Manuscripts, Editions, Purpose, Sources, Analogues, Influence); Chapter IV presents A Stylistic Analysis of the *Meditations on the Passion*; and, finally, Chapter V looks at the *Passio Domini* theme in the other works of Rolle, which 'prove that the passion was a core theme of his concept of the spiritual life'. This chapter ends with a discussion of The Prose of the *Commandment*, in which she tackles the difficult problem of demonstrating the extent to which Rolle's prose and rhythm conform to that of the classical *cursus*. After the succinct conclusion the appendix

[25] *The Middle English Letter of Alexander to Aristotle*, ed. by Vincent DiMarco and Leslie Perelman. *Costerus* (Essays in English and American Language and Literature) New Series Volume XIII. Amsterdam: Editions Rodopi. pp. iv + 194.

[26] *The Passio Domini Theme in the Works of Richard Rolle: His Personal Contribution in its Religious, Cultural, and Literary Context*, by Mary Felicitas Madigan. SSELER. Salzburg: Institut für Englische Sprache und Literatur, Universität Salzburg. pp. iv + 347. £19.75.

contains firstly, Textual References: the shorter version of the *meditation* survives in only one MS which has been edited by Ullmann (1884), Horstmann (1895), and H. E. Allen (1931, selections only); the longer version survives in four MSS, Bodley MS e Musaeo 232, Uppsala University MS C. 494, Cambridge University MS Add. 304, British Museum MS Cotton Titus C. XIX. The last MS. has never been printed, and a transcript of it, folios 92b–117b, is printed here. The final section of the appendix presents the evidence for crediting Rolle with the authorship of the *Meditations*. This handy volume ends with a select bibliography (primary sources, editions, secondary sources), but unfortunately there is no index.

Helen M. Moon presents an edition, with commentary and notes, of a dialogue entitled *þe Lyfe of Soule*[27], which has never before been edited or printed and which survives in three MSS – MS Bodley Laud Misc. 210 (mid-fourteenth century), Huntington Library MS Huntington 502 (fourteenth century), and British Library MS. Arundel 286 (slightly later), all three of which probably 'derive from the same or very similar parent manuscripts' and are written in a 'South Midland dialect with very nearly the same Southern or West Midland variations'. The Laud MS is chosen as the basic text, with variants of the Huntington MS 'recorded as completely as possible in the footnotes' and only significant variants listed from Arundel 286. This edition deals firstly with the MSS, and includes an interesting section on its language with sections on inflections, phonology, vowels, consonants and diphthongs (consistently misspelt 'dipthongs'), which provides evidence to date the MSS 'somewhere between 1370–1450'. The edition considers the relationship of the text to the Wycliffite canon, demonstrating the similarity between *þe Lyfe's* biblical quotations and 'those from the so-called Wyclif Bible'. Similarities, too, are evident in A. C. Paues's edition of *Fourteenth Century Biblical Verses* (1904), part of which the author excerpts and helpfully prints in an Appendix for the sake of comparison. The volume ends with a bibliography, which surprisingly omits Hudson (*YW* 54.103).

Michael E. Sawyer provides *A Bibliographical Index of Five English Mystics: Richard Rolle, Julian of Norwich, The Author of the Cloud of Unknowing, Walter Hilton, Margery Kempe*[28], which covers monographs, articles, reviews, masters' theses, and doctoral dissertations written up to 31 December 1976. 'Whenever possible' Sawyer provides annotations. For instance, he indicates where information is to be found on Rolle in a 1929 dissertation by M. E. Rasin and records that 'it is well written and well worth reading'. Elsewhere he lists a play called 'The Saintl[in]ess of Margery Kempe', by J. E. Wulp, notes when it was first written ('it was later a Broadway show'), and states that a copy of it is available at the Center for Performing Arts in New York. Rolle has 307 entries, Julian 125, the Cloud author 55, Hilton 91, Kempe 52. There are five appendixes: Early Studies of Richard Rolle, starting with a work by Louis Dupin (Paris 1693–1715); Rolle's Works in Collective Editions: Tables of Contents; Essays on Julian

[27] *þe Lyfe of Soule: An Edition with Commentary*, by Helen M. Moon. SSELER. Salzburg: Institut für Englische Sprache und Literatur, Universität Salzburg. pp. xcii + 122.

[28] *A Bibliographical Index of Five English Mystics*, compiled and annotated by Michael E. Sawyer. Pittsburgh, Penn: The Clifford E. Barbour Library, Pittsburgh Theological Seminary. pp. xii + 126. $8.

of Norwich; *Cloud of Unknowing*-Works in Collective Editions: Tables of Contents; A Collective Edition of Hilton's Works: Table of Contents. The Index is decidedly useful and apparently trustworthy.

George B. Jack uses an excellent representative selection of early Middle English prose texts to furnish firm evidence for his discussion of 'Negative Adverbs in Early Middle English' (i.e. *ne*, and the combination *ne. . .nawt*) (*ES*). These two are used in different types of clauses: *ne*, 'invariably in negative interrogative clauses, usually in negative clauses containing some further negative element (with the exception of the conjunction *ne*), and usually in negative clauses with *bute(n)* giving the sense "only" '; *ne. . .nawt*, 'generally preferred in negative declarative and optative clauses with the verb preceding the subject and in negative imperative clauses'. In another paper, George B. Jack uses the same texts, with the *Kentish Sermons* in addition, for his consideration of 'Negative Concord in Early Middle English' which, following Labov's terminology (*YW* 53.64), he defines as 'a rule of syntax. . .by virtue of which certain words acquire a negative form when they occur within a negative clause' (*ani* becoming *nan, euer neuer,* etc.) (*SN*). The point of this paper is to show and explain cases where a 'positive' form is found in negative clauses. Basing his analysis on prose texts dating from the early fourteenth century to the first half of the fifteenth, and deriving from a variety of dialect areas, George B. Jack deals with 'Negation in later Middle English Prose' (*ArL*) under two aspects: 1. 'the various methods of marking negation within a clause'; 2. the rule of 'negative concord' (see above). His conclusion includes a new suggestion for the supplementation and eventual loss of *ne*.

Roger Dahood presents and convincingly solves 'A Lexical Puzzle in "Ancrene Wisse" ' (*N&Q*). In the Corpus MS (f. 2a 4), the preposition *efter* should be taken with *locunges*, making *locunges-efter*, a 'nonce compound . . .translating *obseruantias*'. In an important and very illuminating study, C. Clark considers ' "Wiþ Scharpe Sneateres": Some Aspects of Colloquialism in "Ancrene Wisse" ', a work which, like other homiletic material, includes many instances of simulated dialogue (*NM*). By contrast with the frequently complicated syntax of expository passages, the colloquial sections have the simplicity and, at times, elliptical features of speech, and the vocabulary is similarly distinctive (e.g. exclamations such as *A, Lo, Me*, etc., and colloquialisms, like *gab, babble*, etc.).

Robert W. Ackerman draws our attention to Part I in his revealing study of 'The Liturgical Day in *Ancrene Riwle*' (*Speculum*). The anchoress's *horarium* began at 3.30 a.m. and ended at 7 p.m., a taxing day full of prayers and devotions 'more in accord with monastic custom than has usually been recognized'. By contrast with B. Kliman (*YW* 58.97), Cheryl Frost does not regard her author as a misogynist, in her article with the curiously wrong-headed title: 'The Attitude to Women and the Adaptation to a Feminine Audience in the *Ancrene Wisse*' (*AUMLA*) (why 'adaptation'?: she writes as if there were an *Ur-Ancrene Wisse* aimed at men). The author's 'imagery, *exempla*, and stylistic habit' [?] seldom imply women's inferiority and show a distinct attempt to appeal to a female audience.

J. P. H. Clark examines the problem of 'Walter Hilton and "Liberty of Spirit" ', a phenomenon which Hilton refers to in *Scale* 2.26, in the light of the corrective glosses written in a copy of Margaret Porete's *Mirror of Simple Souls* by 'M.N.' (*DownR*). A person in a state of perfect contemplation should not consider himself to be so free that he can escape from being sorry for past sins: what matters is 'forgetfulness of one's own merits or demerits through confidence in God'. Mary P. Richards presents a succinct, perhaps too succinct, discussion of 'MS Cotton Vespasian A.XXII: The Vespasian Homilies', the four vernacular homiletic pieces which occur on ff. 54r.–57v. (*Manuscripta*). She describes their linguistic significance, briefly analyses each of the four, noting how they differ from each other in length and form, compares them with other homilies (e.g. the *Kentish Sermons*), and suggests the kind of audiences for whom they would have been used.

A. S. G. Edwards provides bibliographical 'Notes on the Polychronicon' as additions to the lists of Latin and English MSS in Taylor's edition (1966) (*N&Q*). He makes the important point that there are three other versions of the work (in whole or in part) in Middle English. According to Kathleen H. Power, the history and original formation of Winchester MS 33 are difficult to establish, and she introduces part of it as 'A Newly Identified Prose Version of the Trevisa Version of the *Gospel of Nicodemus*', of which chapters 1–8 are close to Trevisa's version (*N&Q*). Reference is made to other versions – Salisbury MS 39, BM Add MS 16, 165, and MS Harley 149 (ed. B. Lindström: see *YW* 55.137). With wide-ranging phonological cross-references, Nicolas Jacobs proposes that 'Clanvowe' should be derived from Llanfocha, the Welsh name of St Maughans, a church and parish on the Herefordshire border (*N&Q*).

Joan Young Gregg traces 'The Exempla of "Jacob's Well": A Study in the Transmission of Medieval Sermon Stories' in two parts. The first section presents 'The Source Study', finding what the exempla may be attributed to – the main source is the *Alphabetum Narrationum*; the second section compares the stories in 'Jacob's Well' with those in the *Alphabetum* to show how the author has selected and reshaped his material (*Traditio*, 1977).

Morphologische Untersuchungen zur Ancrene Riwle, by Bernhard Diensberg (Bonn: Rheinische Friedrich-Wilhelms-Univ., 1975), was not seen.

11. Drama

General Studies

William Tydeman's carefully-organised book on *The Theatre in the Middle Ages: Western European Stage Conditions, c. 800–1576*[29] provides a synthesis of the available information about medieval stage conditions in Britain, France, Germany and Spain. His material is divided into a series of chapters each dealing with a different kind of medieval theatre production, running from what is known of pagan rituals and folkplays via the staging of Latin and liturgical drama to the 'street theatre' of the processional

[29] *The Theatre in the Middle Ages: Western European Stage Conditions, c. 800–1576*, by William Tydeman. Cambridge: C.U.P. pp. xii + 298. 16 ill. hb £14.50, pb £4.95.

mystery cycles and the 'open air theatre' of the morality plays and others indended for large public settings. There are also sections on 'Resources and Effects', 'Performers', and 'Financing the plays', and an epilogue on the rise of the professional theatre. He concentrates mainly on the large-scale productions of church and civic authorities: very little is said about the lesser medieval theatre of the streets and elsewhere (the smaller-scale English moralities are scarcely touched upon, for example). But, as Tydeman points out, the evidence for medieval stage locations except for the largest and most spectacular productions is extremely fragmentary, and this is a book that expressly avoids the speculative and controversial, sticking firmly to the task of gathering together such information as is available. Altogether this is a most useful survey of the subject.

Francis Edwards' *Ritual and Drama: the Medieval Theatre*[30] in fact deals mainly with the medieval English stage. Edwards is a producer of and actor in medieval and other plays rather than an academic researcher in the field, and his rather simplistic (though lively and engaging) study deserves a brief mention alongside Tydeman's book primarily because it is filled with a very vivid sense of the possibilities of medieval drama as theatre.

Drama and Art: An Introduction to the Use of Evidence from the Visual Arts for the Study of Early Drama[31], by Clifford Davidson, is really a textbook setting out the elements of a 'systematic approach to collecting and classifying information about relevant art from centres of dramatic activity in England' (and to some extent on the Continent as well). After an introductory chapter defending the value of this kind of study for the furthering of our knowledge of the details of medieval drama productions, Davidson discusses how to set about gathering evidence from the visual arts; standardisation of subject headings and abbreviations; the use of card files and of the computer; the proper establishment of dating and such matters; and the use of evidence of costumes. The final chapter gives practical examples of ways in which medieval art can be used to extend our understanding of individual plays. This book may seem very elementary, but should prove of value, relating as it does to an area of research where a very great deal of new ground still remains to be broken. Following very much along the path recommended by Davidson, Gail McMurray Gibson writes on 'Long Melford Church, Suffolk: Some Suggestions for the Study of Visual Artifacts and Medieval Drama' (*RORD*). She describes the features of the church relevant to the drama, such as a tomb designed for use as an Easter Sepulchre, an alabaster relief of the Adoration of the Magi, and the details of the fifteenth-century stained-glass windows. 'Demonic Imagery in the English Mystery Cycles', by Rhoda-Gale Pollack (*TN*), rapidly surveys the iconography of medieval devils from which artists and producers of plays could draw a great variety of grotesque images, and lists some of the specific references to the materials of demonic costumes to be found in medieval records relating to staging.

[30] *Ritual and Drama: The Medieval Theatre*, by Francis Edwards. Guildford and London: Lutterworth Press. 1976. pp. 127. 8 figs; 8 plates. pb £2.95.

[31] *Drama and Art: An Introduction to the Use of Evidence from the Visual Arts for the Study of Early Drama*, by Clifford Davidson. Early Drama, Art, and Music Monograph Series, I. 1977. Kalamazoo, Michigan: The Medieval Institute. pp. iv + 169. 14 plates. hb $10.95, pb $4.95.

Peter Meredith briefly describes the projected 'Leeds Descriptive Catalogue of Medieval Drama' (*RORD*), together with a sample entry for the Chester plays.

Ian Lancashire writes on 'Records of Early English Drama and the Computer' (*CHum*), describing the use made of computers by the contributors to the Records of Early English Drama project, and outlining the data structure for its planned computerised key to the records' evidence about performers and performance activities. He also supplies a 'Bibliography of printed records of early British drama and minstrelsy for 1976–7' (*REED*). Ann Lancashire adds a note on 'Research in progress: London craft guild records' (*REED*), reporting on her work on this very large source of material.

On a far more theoretical plane than any of the foregoing, Carol Wightman's 'The Genesis and Function of the English Mystery Plays' (*SMC*, 1977) grandly ascribes the 'sudden' appearance of the mystery cycles in the late fourteenth and early fifteenth centuries to the economic and social climate of Europe after the Black Death. Paula Požar discusses 'Time in the Corpus Christi Cycles: "Aesthetic" and "Realistic" Modes' (*PLL*). Beginning with a highly technical definition of these two modes of 'time-perception', she proceeds to a comparison between the handling of time in the Passion sequences of the York and N-town cycles respectively, and concludes that 'the two cycles demand their audiences use radically different modes of perception' to grasp what is happening in the plays.

In the search for an answer to his question, 'Why do the Shepherds Prophesy?' (*CompD*), Thomas P. Campbell examines the history of the relationship between the shepherds and prophecy in the liturgical drama and in the Advent liturgy itself. He avoids assuming a direct link between the liturgical and secular shepherd drama, but finds that the themes of prophetic fulfilment and spiritual community are fundamental to both. The shepherds of the English mystery cycles prophesy because they are the traditional intermediaries between expectation and fulfilment at the moment of the Messiah's birth.

John R. Elliott Jr compiles a 'Census of Medieval Drama Productions' put on in 1976–8 (*RORD*).

York

Poetry and Drama in the York Corpus Christi Play[32], by Richard J. Collier, is written in the hope of altering prevailing critical attitudes to the poetry of the Corpus Christi plays. Poetry is here seen as the crucial element of the drama's effectiveness as theatre. Collier begins by analysing the various verse forms and kinds of poetic language (homiletic, lyric, and narrative) to be found in the York cycle, and goes on to study the use of each kind of poetic language in turn. His thesis that the fusion of formality and naturalness in the poetry of the York playwrights is a mark of the cycle as a whole is interesting and well-argued, and he does succeed in showing how the poetry in the plays deliberately supplements and comments on the action. Even if we do not go as far as Collier in assuming

[32] *Poetry and Drama in the York Corpus Christi Play*, by Richard J. Collier. Hamden, Conn: Archon Books. pp. 303. $17.50.

that the medieval playwright would have thought of himself primarily as a poet rather than as a dramatist, this is a thoughtful book that will add a new dimension to our appreciation of the plays.

In '"Places to hear the play": pageant stations at York, 1398–1572' (*REED*), Meg Twycross charts the locations of the stations of the York cycle with the help of information gained from a study of the surviving leases and records of payments for playing places.

There is a whole crop of reviews of the Poculi Ludique Societas' performance of the York cycle at Toronto in 1977, all of which cannot be noted here: but two in particular, Alexandra F. Johnston's 'The York Cycle: 1977' (*UTQ*) and John W. Velz's 'The York Cycle of Mystery Plays' (*CahiersE*) are of particular interest in that they comment on the lessons the production held for scholars of medieval drama as well as on its purely theatrical qualities.

Towneley

The *Second Shepherds' Play* attracts by far the most attention here. Maynard Mack Jr's discursive article 'The *Second Shepherds' Play*: A Reconsideration' (*PMLA*) points out a number of dramatic parallels between Mak and the announcing Angel, and suggests that the former, with his aura as a precursor of events and challenger to the accepted order of things, functions dramatically as a bridge to the birth of Jesus. On the subject of 'Grace Enacted: The *Secunda Pastorum*' (*Parergon*, 1976), Jennifer Strauss focuses on the role of the Shepherds as the embodiment (to some extent at least) of divine grace in both halves of the play. Thomas J. Jambeck's note on 'The Canvas-tossing Allusion in the *Secunda Pastorum*' (*MP*) remarks that the action of 'canvassing' carried connotations of sieving and winnowing (and hence may possibly symbolise the Last Judgement winnowing), and also came to mean punishing in a ridiculous way, so that the tossing of Mak may well hold more connotations than the obstetric one usually assigned to it. Cherrell Guilfoyle writes on '"The Riddle Song" and the Shepherds' Gifts in the *Secunda Pastorum*: with a Note on the "Tre callyd Persidis"' (*YES*), and backs up her highly conjectural but decidedly attractive theory that the Edinburgh Riddle 'My Love gave me a Cherry a Cherry without a stone. . .' was already in circulation when the play was being written, and could therefore have influenced the symbolism of the Shepherds' gifts to the Christ-child, with a wealth of information about other versions of the riddle and the folklore it contains. She also notes that *Ludus Coventriae*'s substitution of a cherry tree for the 'persea' tree of earlier legend may reflect a preference for native folklore symbolising divine and virgin birth. In 'Comic Mockery of the Sacred: *The Frogs* and the *Second Shepherds' Play*' (*ETJ*), Rose A. Zimbardo yokes this most unlikely pair of plays together with the assertion that they both share comedy's perpetual concern with the contradiction between false conceptions and true understanding.

George A. West makes 'An Analysis of the Towneley Play of *Lazarus*' (*PQ*, 1977), claiming that the unique placing of the Towneley *Lazarus* after the *Judicium* is quite deliberate and stems from the play's exceptionally full development of the meaning of the story so that Lazarus becomes not only an example of God's love (as in the other cycles) but also a figure eliciting the fear of death and God's judgement of sin.

Arieh Sachs' 'Ikonographia shel Tziporim be-Mister-'yat *Ha-Mabbul*' (*Bamah*, 1976) was accessible to this reviewer only in an English synopsis according to which the article relates the Towneley Play of *Noah* to the depiction of the Flood in the Holkham Bible Picture Book.

N-Town

Writing on 'Law and Disorder in *Ludus Coventriae*' (*CompD*), Lynn Squires focuses mainly on the handling of the theme in the Passion I segment of the cycle, where she finds that the general concern with obedience to God's law is narrowed down to a more specific concern for reforming fifteenth-century English legal practice. Gail Murray Gibson's '"Porta haec clausa erit": comedy, conception, and Ezekiel's closed door in the Ludus Coventriae play of "Joseph's Return"' (*JMRS*) argues cogently that the 'locked door' episode in the play is not just a bit of fabliau-type by-play, but also presents a 'comic parody of the Virgin's Divine Conception of Christ, a parody in which Joseph unwittingly re-enacts the very mystery of Incarnation he will soon be doubting'. In 'A Note on the Attribution of 1.746 of the Coventry *Weavers' Pageant*' (*Archiv*), Laurence Eldredge contends that this marginal addition to the text should be ascribed to Joseph and not (as is usual) to Jesus.

Chester

In his study of 'The History and Development of the Chester Cycle' (*MP*), Lawrence M. Clopper makes a very thorough investigation of the documents relating to the cycle which enables him to arrive at a fairly detailed account of its history, and leads him to the conclusion that the content, shape, and techniques associated with the Chester cycle are early sixteenth century rather than medieval in date.

Discussing 'Divine Power in the Chester Cycle and Late Medieval Thought' (*JHI*), Kathleen M. Ashley holds that Chester's apparent simplicity and singlemindedness by comparison with the other cycles may be accounted for by the idea that Chester is the most strongly influenced by the philosophical pre-occupations of the fourteenth and fifteenth centuries, and reflects thematically the late medieval obsession with God's omnipotence.

In '"And sheepe will I keepe no more": Birth and Rebirth in the Chester *Adoration of the Shepherds*' (*ABR*), Kevin J. Harty argues that the Shepherds' religious vocations 'are simply the logical final step in the deepening of their understanding of the Incarnation', but adds that as what is known of the Chester Cycle indicates a strong link between the plays and the Benedictine Abbey of St Werburgh's in Chester, it is also possible that the play's advocacy of religious vocations may stem in part from the abbey's influence. Harty also contributes 'The Identity of "Freere Bartholomewe" (Chester Play VI 565): A Suggestion' (*AN&Q*, 1977), quoting from Eusebius and the *Legenda Aurea* to support his hypothesis that there was a tradition according to which the authorship of the apocryphal gospel of the pseudo-Matthew was assigned to Matthew's fellow apostle Bartholomew.

Moralities and Non-Cycle Plays

The Theatre of Man: Dramatic Technique and Stagecraft in the English Medieval Morality Plays[33], by Sumiko Miyajima, takes as the focus of its study the plays of *The Pride of Life, The Castle of Perseverance, Wisdom, Mankind*, and *Everyman*. The heart of the book lies in the long third chapter on dramatic technique and stagecraft in each play: *Perseverance* is dealt with at the greatest length (Miyajima is very hostile to the 'theatre in the round' school of thought on the staging of the play), but there are also useful discussions of the unusually detailed stage directions of *Wisdom* and the evidence they yield on the staging of the moral plays, and on *Everyman* seen in the context of the stagings of sixteenth-century Dutch morality plays. The remainder of the book, dealing on the whole with more general topics, is more sketchily worked out: no real attempt is made to put the plays in an ordered relationship either with one another or with the development of the morality genre as a whole.

Natalie Crohn Schmitt's rather general article on 'The Idea of a Person in the Medieval Morality Plays' (*CompD*) claims that 'these plays which we call allegories are to a far greater extent than we have realised representations of a phenomenological reality' for a medieval audience.

In 'The *Mary Magdalene* of Bishop's Lynn' (*SP*), Jacob Bennett claims that the language and local colouring of the Digby play belong to Bishop's Lynn. Mary Loubris Jones' 'Sunlight and Sleight-of-hand in medieval drama' (*TN*) discusses the particular staging problems inherent in the fact that medieval plays had to achieve their special effects in the broad light of day, with particular reference to the solutions arrived at in the course of a recent university production of *Mary Magdalen*. Jones also provides a more detailed discussion of 'How the Seven Deadly Sins "Dewoyde from þe woman" in the Digby *Mary Magdalen*' (*AN&Q*) drawing on stage directions from Tudor interludes to support her suggestion that Mary must have stood before some concealing object from which the Sins could leap out as though emerging from her body.

Nancy Cotton gives an account of 'Katherine of Sutton: The First English Woman Playwright' (*ETJ*), who refurbished the Easter dramatic offices for her Barking nunnery during her term as abbess there in the later fourteenth century.

Diana Wyatt transcribes and discusses 'Two Yorkshire fragments: perhaps dramatic?' (*REED*), two manuscript fragments that may once have formed part of a dramatic text. In 'Plays and Playing at Thetford and nearby, 1498–1540' (*TN*), Richard Beadle prints and comments upon the entries relating to early dramatic activities in one of the surviving registers of the Cluniac Priory of St Mary at Thetford: there are numerous records of payments to troupes visiting the priory, to parishes in Thetford in connection with plays and to various neighbouring villages for the same purpose. He also writes on 'The East Anglian "Game-place": a possibility for further research' (*REED*), noting a fifteenth-century reference to the existence of circular playing-places in England and raising the possibility that the East Anglian 'game-place' was just such a permanent structure.

[33] *The Theatre of Man: Dramatic Technique and Stagecraft in the English Medieval Morality Plays*, by Sumiko Miyajima. 1977. Clevedon, Avon: Clevedon Printing Co. pp. vi + 193. £6.

V

Middle English: Chaucer

JOYCE BAZIRE and DAVID MILLS

1. General

A bibliography for the current year will be found in 'Chaucer Research, 1978. Report No. 39' by Thomas Kirby (*ChauR*).

Derek Brewer's *Chaucer: The Critical Heritage*[1] is an anthology of Chaucer criticism with 'a more specifically critical orientation' than Caroline Spurgeon's anthology. This means that mere allusions and duplications are excluded and that some contributions are quoted at greater length to give them critical autonomy. The two volumes together contain 155 'Comments', from Deschamps to Rosemond Tuve, in chronological sequence and under author. Each item has a brief headnote giving source, information about the author, and pointing its central concern; these items are placed by reference to the evolving patterns of Chaucer criticism set out in introductory essays to the two volumes, which are intended to be read consecutively. Each volume also contains a repeated bibliographical note and summary of the principal editions of Chaucer's work up to 1933. Brewer discerns three stages of Chaucer criticism – the fourteenth- and fifteenth-century view of his work as a manifestation of the rhetorically-centred poetic of the English Gothic tradition; the humanist tradition, manifested in the Neoclassical and Romantic approaches which dominate the remainder of the anthology and were produced by 'the generally cultivated amateur critic and reader'; and the most recent criticism, after 1933, 'by salaried academics, not gentlemen', in which the earlier sense of innocent pleasure in literature, the elegance of style and the appeal to the educated 'common reader' have receded. The anthology ends as the last movement begins to emerge. Because Chaucer has been continually read and admired during and after his lifetime, comments and criticisms of his work provide a touchstone of general trends in English taste over that period. Brewer documents this taste succinctly and, while indicating continuities and developments in the themes and concerns of Chaucer criticism, also realises its frequently idiosyncratic and diverse nature. (Reviewed by A. G. Rigg, *RES*, 1979, pp. 336–8; R. T. Davies, *N&Q*, 1979, pp. 62–3.)

Brewer's second book, *Chaucer and his World*[2], gives newcomers to Chaucer a social and historical context for the poet's career and, with its 212 illustrations, is appropriately entertaining and informative, despite a

[1] *Chaucer: The Critical Heritage*, Vol. I, *1385–1837*, Vol. II, *1837–1933*, ed. by Derek Brewer. London, Henley and Boston, Mass.: Routledge & Kegan Paul. Vol I, pp. xii + 342, Vol. II, pp. viii + 510. £17.50.

[2] *Chaucer and his World*, by Derek Brewer. New York: Dodd, Mead & Co. Inc.; London: Eyre Methuen Ltd. pp. 224. $20.

tendency to worldly-wise generalisation and to biographical speculation. (Reviewed by John H. Fisher, *Studies in the Age of Chaucer*, 1979, pp. 170–77.) William Woods's *England in the Age of Chaucer*[3] provides a readable background history of the period; and, though references are made to the poet and his work (with the *Roman* definitely ascribed to him), a putative life-story of the poet is not intended.

Discussing 'Chaucer's Patristic Knowledge' (*Proceedings of the P.M.R. Conference*, 1976), Francis X. Murphy considers that the poet reflects 'an Augustinian pre-occupation with the beauty, and the Boethian brooding over the caducity of mortal things, shot through with what might be termed an Ovidian affectation for the ridiculous in the foibles of human behavior'. In 'Chaucer and the Nominalist Questions' (*Speculum*), Russell A. Peck uses Ockham's observations on epistemology to explore 'Chaucer's attitudes toward language, intellective processes, fantasy, and trust'. He stresses their shared empiricism, the sense (for example in the *Book of the Duchess*) that willing and knowing are the same process with cognition at its end, but in addition he examines their awareness of barriers to cognition, partly through weakness of will (for example in the *House of Fame*) and also through problems of language itself. In a sense both Ockham and Chaucer may be called 'nominalists'. But 'Chaucer, not a poet given to hiding his intellectual influences, never once formulates a nominalist thought directly or even refers, so far as I can tell, to a single nominalist thinker', states Victoria Rothschild. Her review-article of books by David and Gardner (*YW* 57.89; 58.107–8), 'A Choice of Two Chaucers' (*TLS*), regrets the polarisation of the medievalists' concern with Chaucer's Gothic structure and his modernist critics' obsession with the elusive fictions of an artistic persona.

Stephen Knight sets out to discover, in 'Politics and Chaucer's Poetry'[4] how far Chaucer 'revealed and evaluated the patterns of conflict in human life'; after an analysis of the poet's works under several headings, he concludes that 'Chaucer's art does have interest for the modern radical', 'that we may even learn from it', and that 'Chaucer's art seethes with political life'. In the same book David Lawton comments in 'English Poetry and Society': 'There seems to me to be no reason why Chaucer's limited range, socially, should not be indicated, and even indicted'. In 'Chaucer's Beards' (*Archiv*) Margaret Jennings C.S.J. presents a collection of references to beards in Chaucer's works, particularly the *Tales*, and indicates traits of the owners which interpretation of the differing kinds provides. In his comments on 'Chaucer and Lists of Trees' (*Reading Medieval Studies,* 1976) with accompanying tables, Piero Boitani shows how both Boccaccio and Chaucer used their sources, and how change is revealed in the latter's usage, from his hesitancy in the *Romaunt* to the *parlement* and the *Knight's Tale*, where his contact with Boccaccio and the classics led to new possibilities. In a somewhat rambling article, James S. Whitlark considers 'Chaucer and the Pagan Gods' (*AnM*, 1977) and the light in which his age

[3] *England in the Age of Chaucer,* by William Woods. New York: Stein & Day. 1976. pp. viii + 230.

[4] In *The Radical Reader,* ed. by Stephen Knight and Michael Wilding. Sydney: Wild & Woolley. 1977. pp. 239.

regarded them. In examples provided by the Old Testament, Ruth M. Ames finds material for 'Prototype and Parody in Chaucerian Exegesis' (*Acta*), particularly in the several uses of the *Song of Songs*. She argues that most of them were part of the common culture and that Chaucer's parody was meant to be as sincere in its own way as his piety was in its way, so that he 'could safely laugh at both popular vulgarization and learned allegorization'. Rossell Hope Robbins, speculating on 'Geoffroi Chaucier, Poète Français, Father of English Poetry' (*ChauR*), suggests both that Chaucer's poetry – now unknown – previous to the *Book of the Duchess* had brought him a reputation as a poet, and also that he composed in French.

Eiko Ito uses the framework of case-grammar in his attempt to specify and trace the interconnection of the semantic functions and syntactic structures of 'Reflexive Verbs in Chaucer' (*SELit*). He distinguishes reflexive verbs as being 'semantically characterized by internal self-directedness' and finds examples clustering particularly round verbs of motion, psychological verbs, and verbs of social behaviour. Morton Donner discusses the purpose and variety of 'Derived Words in Chaucer's Language' (*ChauR*) as evidence of Chaucer's consciousness of and feeling for language. In 'Chaucer's Decasyllabic Line: the Myth of the Hundred-year Hibernation' (*ChauR*) Karen Lynn describes the results of a computer application of the Halle-Keyser thesis to a limited corpus of lines from Chaucer, Hoccleve, Lydgate, Dunbar, and Skelton. She notes that the later poets expand possibilities found in Chaucer and also add new ones, but, most interestingly, that they achieve greater line-complexity, a fact for which she offers some explanations.

Starting from a comparison of the rhetorical skills of the Pardoner – a 'bad man' who produced good results in his audience – and the Parson – the 'good man', unwilling to falsify himself by any art – Robert O. Payne proceeds to examine 'Chaucer's Realization of Himself as Rhetor'[5], one aspect of a rhetorical issue which receded into the background of most medieval discussion. Through his understanding of the old Augustinian paradox, Chaucer creates the first-person narrator as a poetic concretion of his perception. The change of model from text/reader to speaker/hearer produced perils for speaker and hearer, and it is these that Chaucer explores in the *House of Fame*; in *Troilus* we see the *persona*-guide in action, with its ironic device of Chaucer's impersonating himself.

Although Beryl Rowland's *Birds with Human Souls*[6] is a general alphabetical dictionary of birds and their symbolic meanings, whose reference is wider than Chaucer or the Middle Ages, Chaucerians will find their poet well represented in its index. Jackson Campbell Boswell adds 'Chaucer and Spenser Allusions Not in Spurgeon and Wells' (*Analytical & Enumerative Bibliography*, 1977). 'Two Additional Allusions to Chaucer in the Work of Stephen Hawes' (*AN&Q*) are provided by Donald W. Rude. Beverly Boyd asks 'Whatever Happened to Chaucer's Renaissance?' (*Fifteenth Century*

[5] In *Medieval Eloquence: Studies in the Theory and Practice of Medieval Rhetoric*, ed. by James J. Murphy. Berkeley, Los Angeles, Ca. London: U. of California P. pp. xii + 354.

[6] *Birds with Human Souls: A Guide to Bird Symbolism*, by Beryl Rowland. Knoxville, Tenn.: U. of Tennessee P. pp. xviii + 214.

Studies), arguing that Chaucer's Italian period is only one manifestation of contemporary knowledge in England of the Italian Renaissance, and that the absence of humanist successors to Chaucer is a result of conservative and repressive reactions to the rapid changes in fourteenth-century England. Paolo Cherchi reproduces, with translation, the chapter on Chaucer in Karl Friedrich Flögel's *Geschichte der komischen literatur* of 1784–7 which is, so far as we know, 'The First German Essay on Chaucer' (*ChauR*).

Ann C. Haskell's chapter, 'The Portrayal of Women by Chaucer and His Age'[7] in the main covers the topos generally, but pays some particular attention to the *Wife of Bath's Tale*. The major part of M. J. Wright's 'Comic Perspective in Two Middle English Poems' (*Parergon*, 1977), concerned with *Pearl* and the *Knight's Tale*, is a study of 'aspects of comic perspective, divine comedy and *contemptus mundi*'; but first a distinction is drawn between the two latter, in which the ending of *Troilus* is involved. Wright regards the *Knight's Tale* as a secular analogue to divine comedy, where the viewpoint of the poem remains a worldly one. George Kane enumerates 'Outstanding Problems of Middle English Scholarship' (*Acta*) and pays considerable attention to the works of Chaucer. He supports his arguments by a survey of deficiencies in past editions and studies. Using examples from the works of Chaucer among others, S. T. Knight discusses 'Some Aspects of Structure in Medieval Literature' (*Parergon*, 1976), and points also to Chaucer's movement towards a naturalistic art, more developed than in other medieval writers.

As its title suggests, Ann Thompson's *Shakespeare's Chaucer*[8] deals with Shakespeare's considerable knowledge of his predecessor. Chaucer's influence on six extant and seven lost non-Shakespeare plays from 1558–1625 is used as background evidence and numerous examples of Chaucer's influence on Shakespeare are cited; but at the centre of the study are extended comparisons of *Troilus and Cressida* with *Troilus and Criseyde* and of *The Two Noble Kinsmen* with the *Knight's Tale*, each in its different way attesting Shakespeare's selective and imaginative use of Chaucer for his own artistic ends.

William Calin writes in 'The Poet at the Fountain: Machaut as Narrative Poet'[9] about the 'naïve, blundering, comic Narrator' as developed by Machaut, who is thus shown to have preceded Chaucer in the use of such a character. The title of Calin's 'Defense and Illustration of *fin' amor*: Polemical comments on the Robertsonian approach' (*Stanford French Review*) summarises the contents of a book useful for Chaucer studies although no examples from that poet are cited. There is a brief section on Chaucer in Douglas Kelly's chapter, 'Verisimilitude and Imagination: The Crisis in Late Courtly Poetry'[10].

[7] In *What Manner of Woman: Essays on English and American Life and Literature*, ed. by Marlene Springer. New York U.P. 1977. pp. xx + 357.

[8] *Shakespeare's Chaucer: A Study in Literary Origins*, by Ann Thompson. Liverpool, Lancs.: Liverpool U.P. pp. xi + 239. £8.75.

[9] In *Machaut's World: Science and Art in the Fourteenth Century* (*Annals of the New York Academy of Science*), ed. by Madeleine Pelner Cosman and Bruce Chandler. New York: New York Academy of Science. pp. xiv + 348.

[10] In *Medieval Imagination: Rhetoric and the Poetry of Courtly Love*, by Douglas Kelly. Madison, Wisc. and London: U. of Wisconsin P. pp. xvi + 330.

2. Canterbury Tales

In their important discussion of 'The Production of Copies of the *Canterbury Tales* and the *Confessio Amantis* in the Early Fifteenth Century'[11] A. I. Doyle and M. B. Parkes argue against the existence of centralised scriptoria before Caxton and for the existence of 'a bespoke trade consisting of independent craftsmen working to specific commissions'. Their example is the five scribes of Trinity College Cambridge MS R.3.2 (581) – datable as *circa* 1408–26 – three of whom were responsible for other manuscripts, though they never again appear together in the same manuscript. Scribe B wrote, *inter alia*, the Hengwrt and Ellesmere manuscripts, Scribe D the Oxford Corpus Christi College MS 198 and London BL MS Harley 7334, the four earliest manuscripts of the *Tales*, each one distinctive. Stressing the word 'compiled' in the Ellesmere colophon, the authors argue that the four manuscripts 'reflect different attempts to impose a necessary external organization upon Chaucer's unfinished work. No one attempt has any special authority, but that found in the Ellesmere copy has had more influence upon modern editors' since Ellesmere has had imposed upon it a more sophisticated *ordinatio*, attested by the layout of the manuscript, than the other 'editions'. William F. Hutmacher's *Wynkyn de Worde and Chaucer's 'Canterbury Tales': A Transcription and Collation of the 1498 Edition with Caxton² from the 'General Prologue' through 'The Knight's Tale'*[12] is intended as a study leading to an edition of the 1498 printing. (Reviewed by N. F. Blake, *N&Q*, 1979, pp. 160–1.)

A morpheme dictionary based on the verse tales (though excluding links and the unfinished *Cook's Tale*) is the most recent result of Walter S. Phelan's 'The Study of Chaucer's Vocabulary' (*Computers and the Humanities*) by computer, but tables of word-frequency distribution and of semantic density are in preparation – the latter supporting 'the quadrilateral dimensions of Chaucer's couplets' – and the author looks further ahead to semantic collation and *thesaurus proprius*. Judith A. Johnson discusses the social nuances implied by the use of '*Ye* and *Thou* among the Canterbury Pilgrims' (*MichA*, 1977), looking particularly at the Host as addresser and addressee. 'A four-stress pausing line or non-pentameter that occasionally expands to five stresses in the second unit' with final *–e* 'pronounced to focus on key words that most often appear either before the virgule or in rhyme' is Allan B. Fox's view of metrical type in the *Tales*. Primarily concerned with Heywood's prosody in 'Chaucer's Prosody and the Non-Pentameter Line in John Heywood's Comic Debates' (*Lang&S*, 1977), he sees it as a development of Chaucer's non-pentameter form. Fox argues strongly that the focus of prosodic rules should be the verse-sentence, not the individual line.

Writing 'In Defense of the Bradshaw Shift' (*ChauR*), George R. Keiser attempts to counter the recent arguments in favour of the Ellesmere order and suggests ways in which the adoption of the Bradshaw Shift would

[11] In *Medieval Scribes, Manuscripts & Libraries: Essays presented to N. R. Ker*, ed. by M. B. Parkes and Andrew G. Watson. Scolar P. pp. xvi + 395.

[12] *Wynkyn de Worde and Chaucer's 'Canterbury Tales': A Transcription and Collation of the 1498 Edition with Caxton² from the 'General Prologue' through 'The Knight's Tale'* by William F. Hutmacher. Amsterdam: Editions Rodopi N.V. pp. vii + 223. pb 40 Dutch glds.

enhance the artistry of the *Tales*. In 'Other Voices in the "Canterbury Tales"' (*Criticism*, 1977), Jerome Mandel first examines voices other than Chaucer's own in the *General Prologue*, emphasising that, in the portraits of the Monk, Friar, and Parson, the pilgrim's very words are produced in indirect discourse (for example ll. 184–8, really the Monk's own words). Apart from the tales of the Pardoner and Wife and the first part at least of that of the Canon's Yeoman, Mandel maintains that all the tales may have been written originally for Chaucer's voice, before the conception of the whole work. Mandel discusses finally the *Merchant's Tale*, the influence of the prologue on its tone, and the ambiguous voice at its beginning in praise of marriage. Wolfgang E. H. Rudat finds a combination of 'Heresy and Springtime Ritual: Biblical and Classical Allusions in the *Canterbury Tales*' (*Revue Belge de Philologie et d'Histoire*, 1976) and seeks an explanation of the Retraction in the 'heretical' implications. The essay finds compatibility between the opening of the Prologue and Vergil's second *Georgic* 323–31; and this compatibility implies a sexual motivation for the religious pilgrimage. Rudat then considers the extension of such interplay in the tales, notably the pear-tree episode of the *Merchant's Tale* which 'combines the folkloristic motif of the Phallic Ritual with the Biblical Tree-of-Knowledge motif'.

Only one chapter of Thomas D. Cooke's *The Old French and Chaucerian Fabliaux: A Study of Their Comic Climax*[13] is devoted to three of the six examples he would classify in this genre in Chaucer. Cooke's analysis of the tales depends on his belief that it is the comic climax 'which forms and shapes all else to its purpose'. To demonstrate Chaucer's handling of this kind of tale, Cooke takes the *Shipman's Tale*, which in economy and symmetry closely resembles the French fabliaux, and the Miller's, which develops the potential of the fabliau. In the *Merchant's Tale*, although the central section is that of a fabliau, Chaucer makes so many additions and alterations to the type (e.g. the comic climax does not end the tale) that the shape can barely be distinguished. (Reviewed by Glending Olson, *Studies in the Age of Chaucer*, 1979, pp. 151–5; Enrico Giaccherini, *MÆ*, 1979, pp. 300–2). Among the papers on Reynard and on the fabliaux (in *Epopée animale, Fable et Fabliaux*), which may serve as background information to Chaucerians, Beryl Rowland contributes a useful article on 'Distance and Authentication in Chaucer's comic tales' (*Marche Romane*) in which she first comments on the salient features of the fabliaux, and then describes how Chaucer uses, develops, and enriches this kind of tale.

Joseph L. Baird is struck by the ironies of Dryden's phrase 'God's Plenty' (*Maledicta*) in connection with Chaucer in view of the double meaning of its Chaucerian counterpart, *Goddes foyson* (I. 3165). In 'Chaucer and the English Reformation' (*Neophilologus*) Felix Swart describes the circumstances under which the spurious tales of the Pilgrim and the Plowman came to be included in sixteenth-century editions of the *Tales*, concluding that they were intended to establish Chaucer as a supporter of the English Reformation. In 'Interpreting Blake's *Canterbury Pilgrims*' (*CLQ*, 1977) Warren Stevenson explores 'Blake's antithetical method, employing ironic juxtaposition and counterpoint' in his depiction

[13] *The Old French and Chaucerian Falbiaux: A Study of Their Comic Climax*, by Thomas D. Cooke. Columbia and London: U. of Missouri P. pp. 220. £8.40 and $15.

of *The Canterbury Pilgrims*. The relevant sections of Howard Loxton's *Pilgrimage to Canterbury*[14] provide a guide to the activities of pilgrims, the Pilgrim Ways to Canterbury, and the city itself. (Reviewed by M. N. Boyer, *Speculum*, 1979, pp. 597–8.)

In 'History and Form in the General Prologue to the *Canterbury Tales*' (*ELH*), Loy D. Martin finds the literary origins of the *Prologue* in the rhetorical catalogue, already developed by Chaucer in his vision-poems such as the *Parlement of Fowles* to define 'an extraordinary mode of human experience or knowledge'. The pilgrimage, like the dream, involves the displacement of men from their everyday backgrounds and a corresponding suspension of the antithesis of time and timelessness. This new literary extension may originate in the interactions and anxieties attendant upon social restructuring in the fourteenth century. Gerald Morgan seeks 'The Design of the *General Prologue* to the *Canterbury Tales*' (*ES*) in the conformity of its portrait-sequence to 'the ranks of English society as it was constituted in the late fourteenth century'. In sustaining this view, he investigates more closely Brewer's binary social distinction of noble and ignoble in order to indicate the complex hierarchy within each group. In 'Creation in Genesis and Nature in Chaucer's *General Prologue* 1–18' (*PLL*), J. C. Nitzsche argues for a 'specific thematic and structural indebtedness of [the *Prologue* opening] to the hexameral creation of the cosmos and its inhabitants in the Book of Genesis'. Five of L. Whitbread's 'Six Chaucer Notes' (*NM*) refer to the *General Prologue*, one to the *Monk's Tale*. Hugh T. Keenan notes 'A Curious Correspondence: Canterbury Tales A 24–25, Mirk's *Festial*, and Becket's Martyrdom' (*AN&Q*), which refers to the probable number of pilgrims. In 'The *General Prologue* to the *Canterbury Tales*, Lines 345–346: The Franklin's Feast and Eucharistic Shadows' (*NM*) he also suggests that through a connection with manna, the fact that *it snewed. . .of mete and drynke* in the Franklin's house may imply Eucharistic foreshadowings.

Piero Boitani's work on *Chaucer and Boccaccio*[15] is, despite the title, the result of a close study of the *Teseida* and the *Knight's Tale* only, with a third of it devoted to an essay on the *Teseida*. Although a more compact structure would have improved the monograph, it contains much useful information. To illustrate Chaucer's methods of adaptation, a detailed comparison is provided between *Teseida* Book VII and the corresponding part of the *Knight's Tale*. Boitani shows how, in his use of the *Teseida*, Chaucer translated, adapted, invented, and conflated, and, by certain associations of the text, was led on to use the work of other authors, such as Boethius. In the remainder of his detailed comparison, Boitani considers plot and structure, characterisation, iconography and decoration, and style, all of which illuminate Chaucer's manner of working and his skill as a poet. Writing on 'The Education of Chaucer's Duke Theseus'[16], John Reidy

[14] *Pilgrimage to Canterbury*, by Howard Loxton. Newton Abbot, Devon, London and Vancouver: David & Charles; Totowa, N.J.: Rowman & Littlefield. pp. 208. £6.50 and $13.50.

[15] *Chaucer and Boccaccio*, by Piero Boitani. Medium Ævum Monographs, New Series VII. Oxford: Society for the Study of Mediæval Languages and Literature. 1977. pp. v + 210. £5.

[16] In *The Epic in Medieval Society: Aesthetic and Moral Values*, ed. by Harold Scholler. Tübingen: Max Niemeyer Verlag. 1977. pp. xi + 410.

concentrates on criticism of Theseus not in accord with the view of him 'as a noble philosophical representative of the divine order'. Using Maurice H. Keen's *The Laws of War in the Late Middle Ages*[17] he shows that Theseus was a consistent character; following an accepted honourable military code in the earlier part of the tale. But, after these events and the failure of his plan to resolve the conflict between Palamon and Arcite, he reached a Boethian understanding of life.

Commenting on 'Chaucer's Nicholas and Saint Nicholas' (*NM*), Michael Harry Blechner provides examples of the several ways in which the activities of the former contrast with and even parody those of the latter.

In identifying 'The Narrative Style of The Man of Law's Tale' (*M & H*), Paul M. Clogan discusses the nature of the tale's genre, connecting it with saints' lives and romances. Important in this connection are the narrator-*persona* and the fact that, while hagiography 'serves an "external truth", and romance is turned inward upon itself', the two do also share certain features. One is the clerkly narrator-figure (established in his mediating role between tale and audience in the often-puzzling prologue and early part of the tale), who continually comments on the actions and characters in the tale with a stylistic technique reminiscent of hagiographical practices. Clogan examines closely the structural components of the tale – Chaucer's additions – and the paratactic construction. While the presence of the narrator is intended to stylise emotions and actions, the biblical parallels 'stress the presence of some kind of ritual which balances and checks the presence of cruelty and horror in the Tale'; the rime royal stanza serves to emphasise the paratactic structure as well as to exemplify its use as a 'pathetic medium'. S. L. Clark and Julian N. Wasserman discuss with considerable illustrative material 'Echoes of Leviathan and the Harrowing of Hell in Chaucer's *Man of Law's Tale*' (*The South Central Bulletin*).

Although he admits that there are parts that do not 'fit', Eric D. Brown, in 'Symbols of Transfiguration: A Specific Archetypal Examination of the *Wife of Bath's Tale*' (*ChauR*), explains at some length Jungian theories on the dual nature of the mother archetype which parallels the dual nature of the Wife's tale, and he also considers the motif of Demeter-Kore. Then Brown explains the tale in these terms, pointing out the significance of the fact that most of the knight's relationships and experiences are connected with women, and that he himself 'goes full cycle through a symbolic year before he. . .recognizes his own anima'. Brown does concede that contemporary values as well as creative necessity may have distorted the degree to which the tale can be viewed in the way he proposes. Donald B. Sands's 'The Non-Comic, Non-Tragic Wife: Chaucer's Dame Alys as Sociopath' (*ChauR*) constitutes a commentary on several varied past discussions of the Wife's character in the light of his belief that she is 'labouring under a character disorder which makes her acceptable to herself, but productive of conflict with others'. Discussion of 'The Wife of Bath's Fourth and Fifth Husbands and Her Ideal Sixth: The Growth of a Marital Philosophy' (*ChauR*) leads T. L. Burton to conclude that the Wife tries to make more of her past experience than is warranted, and that she cared greatly for her fourth husband and was deeply wounded by him. With her fifth she wished

[17] *The Laws of War in the Late Middle Ages*, by Maurice H. Keen. London and Toronto: U. of Toronto P. 1965.

to be mastered sexually, but otherwise to go her own way; and her tale shows how a sexually masterful man can yet be made to allow his wife independence in other spheres. In '"That she was out of alle charitee": Point-Counterpoint in the *Wife of Bath's Prologue* and *Tale*' (*ChauR*), James W. Cook is concerned with the theology of grace and of the sacraments, together with the views of certain influential churchmen on these matters. The tale is important for Cook's interpretation of the Wife's character, since she can by no means be equated with the Hag. The first part of Rodney Delasanta's 'Alisoun and the Saved Harlots: A Cozening of our Expectations' (*ChauR*) emphasises the Wife's taking precedence at the Offertory, and also her scarlet hose, through the stories of Rahab and other harlots, while the greater part discusses the *upsid-doun* relationship between the Wife and Mary Magdalene. Only 1.534 of the Wife's prologue recalls the story of Abigail, first the wife of Nabal and then of David. But Robert Cook, in querying 'Another Biblical Echo in the Wife of Bath's Prologue?' (*ES*) suggests that Abigail's story in text and gloss, while reflecting the Wife's experience, also offers her an authoritative rebuke.

Robert A. Pratt notes Chaucer's use of an aspect of medieval science in 'Albertus Magnus and the Problem of Sound and Odor in the Summoner's Tale' (*PQ*).

Whereas Petrarch used the tale as a religious exemplum, Chaucer combines religious and secular details, as Warren Ginsberg notes in 'The Clerk's Tale and its Teller' (*Criticism*). In Chaucer's tale there is a two-directional pull, caused by the Clerk's additions, which reveals that he has not understood that Walter's actions are put beyond objection by the very nature of Griselda's forbearance. In Petrarch no sympathy was required for Griselda, but the Clerk produces the latter both by his comments on Walter's behaviour and by a few lines of reproach from Griselda. And yet the Clerk has also strengthened the religious impact of the story. Only in his Epilogue does he speak plainly, and here apparently supports the Wife. Ginsberg concludes that the contradictions shown in the Clerk's character make him almost a 'walking litotes'. Maintaining that 'Clothing Makes a Queen in *The Clerk's Tale*' (*JNT*, 1977), Roger Ramsey looks to the imagery of the tale to provide the key to distinguishing what is the poet's interpretation of his story rather than the Clerk's. As he considers the chief pattern of the imagery to be clothing, Ramsey examines passages that deal with clothing and its connection with Griselda's *degre*, the way in which it is bound up with her behaviour during her vicissitudes of fortune. John Wall reads 'The *Clerk's Tale* as Parable' (*Parergon*, 1974) with detailed illustrations to support his argument. In the course of prefatory remarks to 'Petrarch's *Griselda*: An English Translation' (*Mediaevalia*, 1977), Emilie P. Kadish, having emphasised Petrarch's effective alterations from Boccaccio's version, then provides a useful translation for comparison with Chaucer's tale.

Morton W. Bloomfield suggests in '*The Merchant's Tale*: A Tragicomedy of the Neglect of Counsel – The Limits of Art' (*Medieval and Renaissance Studies*) that we have a 'tale of limits and their transgressions', one in which parody and irony play a great part. He provides a detailed catalogue of the former, but for the latter refers mainly to Germaine Dempster's work. He tries to establish January as a somewhat sympathetic character, but he does not agree that the tale is a tragedy, although it carries tragic implications – as well as romantic and comic – and lays emphasis on January's mental as well as physical blindness. Emerson Brown Jr discusses 'Chaucer, the Merchant, and Their Tale: Getting Beyond Old Controversies. Part I' (*ChauR*). He examines the criticism of, but himself supports, the traditional view that there is a consistent narrative voice – distinct from the poet's – to be found in the tale, which is thus firmly linked to the prologue; by this means the rather lighthearted bawdy story, indicated by the analogues, has been darkened. In addition to noting the effects of the 'extracts' from the *Song of Songs* in the tale, Douglas Wurtele comments on 'The Figure of Solomon in Chaucer's *Merchant's Tale*' (*Revue de l'Université d'Ottawa*, 1977). Solomon, who is equated with the *Sponsus*, also stands in relation to Christ. It is by well-placed references to Solomon that the Merchant associates Christ with January's 'profane garden'. This sacrilegious parody Wurtele regards as an angry reaction to the Clerk's exemplum. Wurtele also shows the 'Ironical Resonances in the *Merchant's Tale*' (*ChauR*) to be both overt in the parody of *Canticum Canticorum* and covert 'in the chain of allusive insinuations'. By means of these the Merchant deliberately establishes May as an 'anti-Virgin counterpart to Griselda'. Having examined 'The Reputation of Queen Esther in the Middle Ages: *The Merchant's Tale*, IV [E] 1742–45' (*BSUF*), Kevin J. Harty – exceptionally, but apparently justifiably – sees the irony of the comparison as deriving from her reputation for wifely virtue. L. L. Besserman looks at 'Chaucer and the Bible: The Case of the *Merchant's Tale*' (*Hebrew University Studies in Literature*) and decides that, though references are purely arbitrary, there are nevertheless patterns of reference that have stylistic and thematic implications. The study of 'Tree Paradigms in the *Merchant's Tale*' (*Acta*) by Anthony Annunziata pursues further the use of the word *tree* and *true* (which he links etymologically); the allegorical significance of the tree-imagery throughout the tale; and the tree as a structural device, which involves both the Tree of Jesse and the Trees of Virtues and Vices. George R. Keiser believes that 'Chaucer's Merchant's Tale, E 2412–16' (*SSF*) reflects the Merchant's attitude to his own wife. William B. Ewald III makes 'A Correction to the Robinson Edition of Chaucer' (*ELN*), arguing that *right* (IV. 1662) should be glossed as 'funeral' and not as 'wedding'.

Charles Larson argues in '*The Squire's Tale*: Chaucer's Evolution from the Dream Vision' (*RLV*, 1977) that the tale was an early creation only later assigned to the Squire – and one ill-suited to him. He propounds reasons for linking it with the *House of Fame* and *Anelida*, suggesting that in all three Chaucer was experimenting with theme and form, trying to turn his poetic talents in a new direction, but not completely succeeding. Arguing that in the other tales of the Marriage Group the subject of marriage fits in smoothly, J. Terry Frazier in 'The Digression on Marriage in the *Franklin's Tale*' (*SAB*) proposes that in that tale the ideal marriage contract is merely prefatory. Since the terms of the agreement never really affect the story, the real themes are *trouthe* and *gentillesse*, the first providing the problem, the second the solution. The Franklin, having been commanded to tell a tale, is trying to fit it into the framework of the Marriage Group, but his digressions from the supposed subject prevent a 'coherent, thematically consistent tale'. Anthony E. Luengo's concern with 'Magic and Illusion in *The Franklin's Tale*' (*JEGP*) is directed not only to the actual illusions worked by the clerk, but also to the moral implications of the tale since the characters fail to distinguish between appearance and reality. Parallels with the Fall are indicated in 'Deception and Self-Deception in "The Franklin's Tale"' (*Proceedings of the P.M.R. Conference*, 1976) by Susan Mitchell, but she shows that it is Dorigen's own inadequate knowledge of herself that almost causes her fall. Dorigen not only lacked the self-knowledge required of Medievals, but in addition was torn with conflicting emotions. She gives the illusion that she is the courtly lady, when really she is the bourgeois wife, but, once she has realised that, first Aurelius and then the Clerk too experience self-knowledge. Thus the tale concludes with redemption after the fall. Gordon N. Ross has a note on '"The Franklin's Tale" and "The Tempest"' (*N&Q*).

Concerned at the continuing appeal of Chaucer's story despite its clearly flawed structure, and prompted by the emotional intensity and complexity with which this simple tale is invested, Thomas L. Kinney seeks 'The Popular Meaning of Chaucer's "Physician's Tale"' (*Literature and Psychology*) at the level of the unconscious. Regarded as a dream, the tale balances sexuality and eroticism against parental warmth and love and 'presents the hesitation, perhaps refusal, of a young woman to accept her sexual maturation'. In 'Spiritual Sickness in the Physician's and Pardoner's Tales: Thematic Unity in Fragment VI of the *Canterbury Tales*' (*ABR*) Katherine B. Trower stresses the linking idea of healing in the Fragment, here allied both to the motive of personal profit from sickness and also to a concern with the terminal rather than the transcendental act of dying. The corruption of justice in both stories is particularly exemplified from the Pardoner's misapplied biblical allusions which, with the knight's intervention, also imply positive values against which both tales can be set. Bruce Moore, in '"I wol no lenger pleye with thee": Chaucer's Rejection of the Pardoner' (*Parergon*, 1976), shows that pilgrim as a curious mixture of power and sterility. Although he flaunts himself, he is none the less detached from himself and his performance is a form of defence from self and the world. In his joking attempts to sell his relics, he singles out for his buffoonery his opposite, and not only are the Host's words a reply, but they also get rid of the Pardoner. An explanation for the kiss between the Host and the Pardoner is offered in Elise K. Parsigian's 'A Note on the Conclusion of *The Pardoner's Tale*' (*Rackham Literary Studies*, 1975). In his performance the Pardoner has in fact captivated the pilgrim-audience too, and although the Host's outburst relieves their tension, it also challenges a link in the religious chain, albeit a lowly one. So the Host personally as well as vicariously 'makes it up'. Discussing 'The Pardoner's Quarrel with the Host' (*PQ*, 1976), Robert E. Jungman holds that the dispute fully illustrates Timothy 6, that teaching based on *cupiditas* is bound to lead to a quarrel. In 'Chaucer's Numismatic Pardoner and the Personification of Avarice' (*Acta*) Walter Scheps looks at the combination of numismatic and iconographic allusions in the Pardoner's presentation.

In his analysis of 'Language and Meaning in Chaucer's *Shipman's Tale*' (*ChauR*), George R. Keiser begins with the significance of the oaths used by the various characters as part of the larger pattern of imprecise use of language. By this the characters conceal from themselves, as well as from each other, their real motives and the transient nature of their life. Keiser maintains that the narrator concurs in their attitudes and argues for making him undoubtedly the speaker in the Man of Law's endlink, thus joining the two tales. The relationship between 'The "Shipman's Tale" and the Fabliaux' (*ELH*) is problematic, since the tale departs from the genre in many respects. As Peter Nicholson points out, the usual bawdiness is lacking, and the major point seems to be the commercialisation of sexual dealings, not the triumph of one character over another; Chaucer's interest lay in the values of the characters and in the verbal irony, all of which depend on the bourgeois setting. In 'The Meeting at the Gate: Comic Hagiography and Symbol in *The Shipman's Tale*' (*Studies in Iconography*, 1977), Theresa Coletti seeks to develop a comparison between the stories of two couples – the meeting of the wife in the tale with her husband at the gate on his return from his business and the meeting of Anne and Joachim at the Golden Gate of Jerusalem. Michael Yots discusses Chaucer's usual use of the proverb of the happy bird at sunrise and its specific appropriateness in 'Chaucer's *Shipman's Tale*' (*Expl*).

From his interpretation of details of the Prioress's portrait in the *Prologue*, Charles Moorman proceeds in 'The Prioress as Pearly Queen' (*ChauR*) to consider her speech in particular, concluding that she is a Cockney who tells a highly appropriate tale. Discussing 'Wynkyn de Worde's "Sir Thopas" and Other Tales' (*SB*), Thomas J. Garbaty demonstrates that for his 1498 edition de Worde used as base text for *Thopas* not Caxton, but another manuscript with superior readings, 'a "Hengwrt manqué", a slightly corrupt descendant of this fine manuscript'. He concludes that de Worde was led by a deficiency in his Caxton exemplar (from near the end of the *Prioress's Tale* to the end of the *Monk's Tale*) to the careful selection and scrupulous presentation of a very good manuscript. In 'Chaucer's *Tale of Melibee* as an Example of the *Style Clergial*' (*ChauR*) Diane Bornstein argues that Chaucer deliberately cultivated this style by expanding, omitting, elaborating the structure, and employing doublets and introductory phrases as he translated the *Livre de Mellibee*. The claims are supported by parallel columns of words and phrases comparing the two versions.

In 'Grammar, Manhood, and Tears: the Curiosity of Chaucer's Monk' (*MP*) Kurt Olsson sees the Monk appropriately presented as *grammaticus*, but discerns *curiositas* in his hunting-pursuits and in the sequence of examples which 'works backwards, implicitly answering each of Philosophy's questions [in Boethius] with an error of a "foryetynge"'. From a secular concept of tragedy, *curiositas* leads him to locate the end of things in a worldly Fortune and to conclude that Man should guard his pleasure. Tragedy is divorced from its appropriate function and style and the tale becomes a philosophical and psychological justification for concealing one's inner self. Tracing parallels between the tale and Books II–IV of Boethius, Douglas L. Lepley suggests that 'The Monk's Boethian Tale' (*ChauR*) uses its tragedies aptly 'to teach Philosophy's lessons on the nature of false and true felicity'. Martha S. Waller's 'The Monk's Tale: Nero's Nets and Caesar's Father – an Inquiry into the Transformations of Classical Roman History in Medieval Tradition' (*Indiana Social Studies*

Quarterly) examines as two aspects of the transmission of classical material to the Middle Ages the classically-derived tradition of Nero's golden nets and the English medieval tradition of Julius Caesar's lowly origins which are found in the tale.

Despite the title, 'Chauntecleer and the Eagle' (*ESA*), in her article Heather Boyd is concerned mainly with the former, who demonstrates what the other only spoke of. But she acknowledges that the display of rhetoric is only one strand in the web of the tale, a tale in which, she maintains, the real and apparent narrators come very close together. Norman Simms, in 'Nero and Jack Straw in Chaucer's *Nun's Priest's Tale*' (*Parergon*, 1974), examines the background to Chaucer's allusion in the tale to the 1381 uprising, concentrating on Jack Straw and the noise his *meyne* made in their murderous pursuit of the Flemings. He then relates it to its context, and to the allusion in the *Monk's Tale* to Nero, whose story he also describes. As part of 'Reynard the Fox in England'[18] N. F. Blake discusses the connection of the *Nun's Priest's Tale* with the *Roman de Renart*, noting finally that in 'England all animal stories were religious and not secular'.

In an important discussion of 'The Sources of Chaucer's "Second Nun's Tale"' (*MP*), Sherry L. Reames, drawing on suggested Latin sources and the closest Middle English analogues, concludes that Chaucer followed *Legenda Aurea*'s version of the legend closely to 1.344, but thereafter employed a text of the longer *Passio* (best approximated by Antonio Bosco's 1600 edition), and this he treated more freely. An appendix of detailed comparisons explains why Kölbing's proposed source – the Latin legend translated from the Greek version for the menology of Symeon Metaphrastes (best approximated by Aloysius Lipomanus's 1571 edition) – is unacceptable. Denying the suggestion that 'Marriage and the *Second Nun's Tale*' (*TSL*) are connected with the 'Marriage Group', Marc D. Glasser asserts that the tale's purpose is to illustrate the 'balancing of the purpose of an earthly calling, marriage, against the goals of a higher calling, martyrdom'. The three sections of the poem are linked by Cecilia's growth as a saint, from her initial concern with her own perfection and salvation to her marriage, which proves an experience that then sets her on her career of conversion and martyrdom. These changes are reflected in her mode of speech, and, as the tale progresses, her marriage recedes into the background and is finally lost sight of. Since the versions by Ælfric and Chaucer of the legend of St Cecilia are so similar, both generally and in detail, they may have relied on a common Latin source. But there are also divergences, which produce distinctive modes of presentation. Both similarities and divergences are detailed by Ruth Waterhouse in '"A Rose by Any Other Name": Two Versions of the Legend of Saint Cecilia' (*NM*).

Lee W. Patterson characterises the *Parson's Tale* as 'an instance of a clearly defined and recognizable genre, the manual intended exclusively for penitential use' in 'The Parson's Tale" and the Quitting of the "Canterbury Tales"' (*Traditio*). The tale's clear and logical overall structure

[18] In *Aspects of the Medieval Animal Epic* (Proceedings of the International Conference: Louvain May 15–17, 1972), ed. by E. Rombauts and A. Welkenhuysen. 1975. Louvain: Louvain U.P.: The Hague: Martinus Nijhoff. pp. xvi + 268 + 4 plates + 24 figures.

expresses an essentially metaphysical and theoretical approach to its subject, a statement of general truth distinct from the individual views of truth which the individualised tales and tellers convey and after which this tale can be shown to have been written. After the Manciple's praise of silence – a corrective to the story-telling game – the Parson presents a sober and prosaic alternative, 'a rejection of all personal speaking that does not confront, in the sacramental language of penance, the sinfulness of the human condition'. The subsequent Retraction represents Chaucer's response to this revaluation of poetic language and compels us to see the tale also as an example of literary penance. In 'Penance and Poetry in the *Canterbury Tales*' (*PMLA*) Rodney Delasanta likewise regards the tale as an appropriate preparation for confession at Canterbury after the descent from Harbledown and sees the Retraction as the result of Chaucer's own examination of conscience. But he discerns a parodic employment of eschatological elements in the earlier tales which points to the Parson's final call to repentance, and notes that his abjuration of fables recalls Jesus's words in John 16:25 before entering Old Jerusalem.

3. Troilus and Criseyde

The appearance of the facsimile of the Corpus Christi College, Cambridge MS 61 of *Troilus and Criseyde*[19] is a major event in *Troilus* studies. This clear reproduction of the text, with a colour reproduction of the famous frontispiece portrait, will be an indispensable tool for students and researchers. M. B. Parkes contributes an informed and scholarly account of the manuscript and its history, arguing that the uncompleted illustrative programme 'may serve as a salutary reminder of the limits of English taste or extravagance, or both, in the early fifteenth century, by contrast with what had become acceptable on the continent'. Elizabeth Salter seeks analogues to the iconography of the frontispiece, supported by numerous illustrations, and urges that the ultimate stylistic influences lie in 'Parisian work of the late fourteenth and early fifteenth centuries', and also that its potential ownership should be sought among families with French connections and a taste for French book-painting. Though the frontispiece may not represent a historical scene, its creation is historically significant. (Reviewed by Donald C. Baker, *Studies in the Age of Chaucer*, 1979, pp. 187–93.)

To describe *The Genre of 'Troilus and Criseyde'*[20] as tragedy is misleading unless one recognises that Boccaccio's *de casibus* tragedy is based upon a reading of Boethius which misses its emphasis upon human freedom and the inner state of Man, argues Monica E. McAlpine. In his narrator Chaucer has set the contradictory potential of his narrative, a *de casibus* tragedian and also a love-poet who, in exploring the mutability of love, is led from detachment to the recognition of a universal love which comprehends him. Troilus thus is seen to progress from a stereotype of courtly

[19] *Troilus and Criseyde: Geoffrey Chaucer: A Facsimile of Corpus Christi College Cambridge MS 61*, with introductions by M. B. Parkes and Elizabeth Salter. Cambridge: D. S. Brewer Ltd. pp. 23 + plates of fols. 1–151 and front papers. £65.

[20] *The Genre of 'Troilus and Criseyde'*, by Monica E. McAlpine. Ithaca, N.Y. and London: Cornell U.P. pp. 252. £8.75.

love to recognition of a deeper love, one undiminished by the physical loss of its object, which can lead him to choose inactivity when Criseyde is exchanged, to reject jealousy, and finally to continue to love the unfaithful Criseyde. Then, in a significant study of Criseyde, the heroine is seen striving to preserve her integrity against the constraining forces of original sin, inherited psychology, and circumstance, and in some measure succeeding; she is not a representative of worldly mutability in the *de casibus* tradition but conforms to Boethian tragedy just as Troilus conforms to Boethian comedy. For Chaucer the false certainties of the *de casibus* tradition are one aspect of the selective and simplifying nature of literature which he emphasises, most notably in his epilogue, 'a long litany of the limitations of the artist and his work of art'. (Reviewed by R. T. Davies, (*N&Q*), 1979, pp. 61–2; S. A. Barney, *Speculum*, 1979, pp. 588–600.)

H. L. Rogers discusses 'The Beginning (and Ending) of Chaucer's *Troilus and Criseyde*'[21], stressing Chaucer's debt to the epic tradition, particularly in encompassing the whole subject and its themes in the opening lines and also in realising the poet in that passage. Rogers explores this opening adumbration, stressing its complex connections with, and implications for, the ending of the poem. J. Keith Hardie examines 'Structure and Irony in Chaucer's *Troilus and Criseyde*' (*Publications of the Arkansas Philosophical Association*, 1977), discerning a 'nest' of structures in which the 'omniscient: vision of the contemporary Christian finally replaces the courtly love viewpoint of the narrator which has hitherto dominated the poem. Allusions to Statius's *Thebaid* and the failures of vision manifested in 'the upside-down values of Troilus, Criseyde and the narrator' contribute to the ironic structure and generate images of blindness. In '"Rooteles moot grene soone deye": The Helplessness of Chaucer's Troilus and Criseyde' (*E&S*) Colin Manlove locates the poem's moral in the separation of the private world of love from the public world of national affairs, noting that for Troilus the warrior-role is abandoned, while for Diomede love is merely an extension of it. The two approaches are vested in opponents in the national struggle which engulfs the love affair, but the tragedy was avoidable and the *contemptus mundi* conclusion, though unquestionable, represents only a secondary solution. In 'The Nature of Nature: Criseyde's "Slydyng Corage"' (*ChauR*), Peggy A. Knapp sees Criseyde as verisimilar woman and image of the morally neutral self-protective patterns of Nature and finds, in attitudes of the other characters towards her, images of the varying attitudes of Man to Nature.

Heiner Gillmeister discusses 'Chaucer's *Kan Ke Dort* (*Troilus*, II, 1752), and the "Sleeping Dogs" of the Trouvères' (*ES*). He regards Chaucer's phrase as a possible Anglo-Norman form of the final phrase in the proverb 'Il fait mal esveillier le chien qui dort', and goes on to propose a consciousness of the conventions of the *descort* in Chaucer's usage. *Troilus and Criseyde* is one of four medieval English works from which David G. Byrd illustrates the symptoms of the lover's illness, 'Blanche Fever: the Grene Sekeness' (*BSUF*). Comparing 'Boccaccio and Chaucer on Cassandra' (*PQ*, 1977), Peggy Ann Knapp describes how Chaucer adds philosophical insight to Boccaccio's psychological insight. Ann M. Taylor regards the dense

[21] In *Festschrift for Ralph Farrell*, ed. by Anthony Stephens, H. L. Rogers and Brian Coghlan. Berne, Frankfurt am Main, Las Vegas: Peter Lang. 1977. pp. 234.

cluster of appearances of 'Criseyde's "Thought" in *Troilus and Criseyde*, (II, 598–812)' (*AN&Q*, 1977) as significant in estimating the deliberation of her actions, and then compares that passage with one concerned with Troilus's thoughts, which are directed to his feelings rather than his actions. In a poem ascribed by the copyist to 'Stewart' in the sixteenth-century Bannatyne MS, Pandarus answers a young man's questions about women's loyalty ambiguously, and Susan Schibanoff suggests, in 'Chaucer and "Stewart's" Pandarus and the Critics' (*SSL*), that some of our seemingly 'new' views of Pandarus existed some centuries ago.

4. Other works

Linda Ann Loschiavo considers the evidence for 'The Birth of "Blanche the Duchesse": 1340 versus 1347' (*ChauR*). Stephanie Hollis, who discusses 'The Ceyx and Alceone Story in The Book of the Duchess' (*Parergon*, 1977), argues that the parallels between the tale of Alceone and the ensuing dream show how the images of the tale 'are confusedly refracted by the dream in various guises and disguises'. The darker side of the Garden of Love is explored in 'The other side of the garden; an interpretive comparison of Chaucer's *Book of the Duchess* and Spenser's *Daphnaida*' (*JMRS*) by Duncan Harris and Nancy L. Steffen, to show the extent of the difference in method and effect in the telling of stories which use similar conventions. Both poets tried to show that life and death qualify, but do not cancel out, each other, and both tried to suggest a sense of proportion in grief. By a detailed examination, the authors show that to this end, instead of Chaucer's variety of tone and incident, Spenser concentrates on the single emotion.

Although 'The Endings of Chaucer's *House of Fame*' (*ES*), proposed by various scholars over the years, are usefully summarised and evaluated by Kay Stevenson, the thesis of the article is that a satisfactory climax would not have been possible, and that there has been established in the poem 'a carefully constructed pattern of repetition and contrast', the one reflecting on the other in the manner of the portraits of the *General Prologue*. The clue to the meaning of the poem seems to emerge when the significance of the House of Rumour is afforded a more prominent place, and when the two houses of Fame are related to earlier scenes in both Books I and II.

In 'Reading Nature: The Phenomenology of Reading in the *Parliament of Fowls*' (*Mediævalia*, 1977), Judith Ferster aims to show how in this work Chaucer 'responds to the moral concerns of medieval aesthetic theory by describing the dangers of self-interested interpretation and suggesting a solution'. 'Will' is important in the poem since it implies choice and therefore causes problems. The whole poem concerns choice – choice in many circumstances, beginning with that between this world and the next. The allegorical *Wille* also needs to be interpreted since this implies several meanings, which can and do cause confusion for the reader. In the first part of the poem the 'I' of the narrator controls the poem, but, in the parliament, the presentation is more formal. Having posed the problem, Judith Ferster makes her way carefully through the poem, pointing out the problems of interpretation, and concludes that 'the real subject of discussion between Chaucer and the audience of the *Parliament* is writing and reading'. A. J. Gilbert illustrates 'The Influence of Boethius on the *Parlement of Foulys*' (*MÆ*), arguing that Boethius provides the basis for the thematic unity between the epitome of the *Somnium* and the love-vision. Kathleen E. Dubs and Stoddard Malarkey, who discuss 'The Frame of Chaucer's *Parlement*' (*ChauR*), suggest that Chaucer was concerned, not with the 'role of the secular poet of human love', but with achieving 'the successful fusion of form and content'. In a detailed study, Emil A. Mucchetti assesses 'The Structural Importance of the Proem and the *Somnium Scipionis* to the Unity of *The Parliament of Fowls*' (*Publications of the Arkansas Philological Association*, 1978).

Reviewing various themes in 'The Revision of the Prologue to the *Legend of Good Women*: an Occasional Explanation' (*SAB*), John H. Fisher argues that the marriage of Richard II to the seven-year-old Princess Isabel of France in 1396 provides the probable occasion for the revision and accounts for the excision of passages of personal devotion and sexual innuendo. 'Machaut provides the nearest precedents, the most probable chief sources, for all of Chaucer's independent love lyrics printed in Robinson except *The Complaint of Venus*. . .and *A Balade of Complaint*' argues James I. Wimsatt, with numerous examples, in 'Guillaume de Machaut and Chaucer's Love Lyrics' (*MÆ*). The influence may indicate Chaucer's participation in a literary coteric at the court of the 1360's. In 'Chaucer's *Nembrot*: A Note on *The Former Age*' (*MÆ*) A. V. C. Schmidt reviews the developing interpretation of the biblical Nimrod, finding Chaucer's source in the *Glossa Ordinaria*, and demonstrates his significant adaptation of this personage as 'an almost purely symbolic figure'. Imagery of bridling and subjection, a self-conscious 'literariness', an inappropriateness of subject to speaker, astrological inevitability, all suggest to Melvin Storm in 'The Mythological Tradition in Chaucer's *Complaint of Mars*' (*PQ*) that the poem's theme is that the martial man should avoid love because it corrupts and weakens manly strength. The allusion to the Brooch of Thebes suggests an awareness of a positive alternative interpretation.

Helge Nordahl's study, 'Ars Fidi Interpretis (un aspect rhétorique de l'art de Chaucer dans sa traduction du Roman de la Rose)' (*ArL*, 1978), treats in detailed categorisation Chaucer's methods of translation of *la haute fréquence des combinaisons tautologiques*, a marked feature of the *Roman*.

VI

The Earlier Sixteenth Century

R. E. PRITCHARD

Prose

During the year the ninth volume of the Yale edition of Thomas More, *The Apology*[1], appeared. The introduction, by J. B. Trapp, discusses More's activities as a controversialist, opposing and putting down heretical works and men, and defending the activities of the church. There is a discussion of Christopher St German, (whose *Treatise concerning the Division* – iteself included here – provoked More's apology), a summary of More's argument, and a discussion of his methods. More's response to dissent was sternly authoritarian and repressive; in this work, his technique is that of full quotation and lengthy and careful refutation. Although More's characteristic wit and colloquial vigour appear occasionally, in general, as the editor admits, the extended process of argument and counter-argument is wearisome. The editor's own writing, however, is clear, vigorous and scholarly; there are good illustrations and appendixes, an extensive bibliography and full glossary.

Good illustrations are the main feature of the excellent catalogue to the National Portrait Gallery's exhibition of Moreana, *'The King's Good Servant': Sir Thomas More*[2], together with extensive annotation of the illustrated MSS., editions and pictures. Arthur F. Kinney, in *Rhetoric and Poetic in Thomas More's Utopia*[3], sets the *Utopia* in the context of Renaissance rhetorical exercises as carried out in the Henrician Inns of Court and by contemporary tutors: the composition of persuasive speeches by opposed imaginary characters in order to prove legal points. Thus, in Book Two, Raphael, arrogant and prejudiced, delivers a faulty encomium on improper principles, demonstrating false judgement. Plato's *Sophist* indicates the difference between the two books – the first is icastic (representational, truthful art), the second fantastic (distorting and illusory). In each book Raphael proceeds from the reasonable to deformation. *Utopia* was intended for a limited audience, and makes great demands on the subtlety and skill of the reader.

Saad El-Gabalawy discusses the tradition of 'Christian Communism in *Utopia, King Lear* and *Comus*' (*UTQ*, Vol. XLVII, No. 3) that can also be found in John Ball and the later Anabaptists and Hutterites. In *Utopia*

[1] *The Apology of Sir Thomas More*, The Complete Works of St Thomas More, Vol. 9, ed. J. B. Trapp. New Haven, Conn. and London: Yale U.P. (1979) pp. xciii + 461.

[2] *'The King's Good Servant': Sir Thomas More*, J. B. Trapp and H. Schulte Herbrüggen. Ipswich, Suff.: Boydell Press (1977). pp. 147.

[3] *Rhetoric and Poetic in Thomas More's Utopia*, (Humana Civilitas 5), by Arthur F. Kinney. Malibu: (1979). pp. ii + 36.

and his early writing, More is critical of private property, which is associated with the sin of *superbia*, and favours the ideals of community and common ownership; King Lear and Gloucester advocate 'redistributive justice'; and Milton's Lady argues for *sobrietas*. In all three writers, the purpose of Christian communism is the preparation of men on earth for the city of God.

In *Moreana* (Vol. XV, Nos. 59–60) Nancy R. Sodeman analyses the 'Rhetoric in More's English Dialogues', comparing *Concerning Heresies* with *Of Comfort*, with respect to the devices of amplification – use of fallacies, topics of argument, and figures of thought – as they are employed within three modes of persuasion, i.e. appeals to reason, to emotion, and from the speaker's personality, and notes the progress to a more exploratory, meditative and personal effect. Carole Weinberg, in 'Thomas More and the Use of English in Early Tudor Education', notes More's regard for and fluency in the English language, and suggests the influence of the teachers at Magdalen College School. Anne Lake Prescott, in 'Thomas Nash (1588–1648) and Thomas More', discusses Nash's *Quaternio* (1633), a dialogue on ways of pursuing a happy and useful life: Nash defends his use of dialogue, joke and merry tale by reference to More, from whom he quotes, though the extent of the influence does not seem to be great. In 'Rousseau, *L'Utopie* et Thomas More', Jean Roussel notes that in his earlier years Rousseau dismissed *Utopia* as merely impracticable in this world, but in his later years saw man's need to prepare for another world. C. C. Doyle, in 'Ambassadors in Chains', suggests a pun in *Utopia* on *legatus/ligatus*, making the ambassadors' chains signs of servitude. Warren Wooden, in 'An Unnoticed Sixteenth Century Reference to More's *Utopia*', notes John Foxe suggesting in a sermon of 1570 that gossips and 'such stoicall stomackes' should be sent to Utopia as a Noplace suitable for social misfits.

In *Moreana* (Vol. XVI, No. 62) Louis L. Martz provides an account – and defence – of More's *Confutation of Tyndale's Answer*. The work's enormous length is the result of More's concern that each chapter, while countering one of Tyndale's arguments, should be representative of, or epitomise, the whole: repetition is intended to have a cumulative and unitive effect. Tyndale's logical and eloquent progress is countered not only by argument but by repetition, digression, and emotionalism and innuendo, often of a rather deplorable kind.

Poetry

Nan C. Carpenter, in 'St Thomas More and Music: The Epigrams' (*Renaissance Quarterly*, Vol. XXX, No. 1), discusses various of More's epigrams connected with music; in *Moreana* (Vol. XVI, No. 62), she repeats much of this material, adding Richard Stanyhurst's translation, in leonine hexameters, of More's jocose epitaph on Henry Abyngdon.

Robert S. Kinsman has produced a useful annotated bibliography of John Skelton[4], that records both primary materials and secondary scholarship in books, articles and theses, with the various printings of his work and records of his life. The bibliography is divided into eight periods from

[4] *John Skelton, Early Tudor Laureate* by Robert S. Kinsman. Boston, Mass.: G. K. Hall. pp. liii + 179.

1530 onwards; the last two deal with 1916–33, 'Skelton and the Modern Poets' – particularly Graves and Auden – and 1935–77, 'Skelton and the Academic Critics'. The boom in Skelton studies in recent years is remarkable: twenty-eight items are listed for the 1940s, fifty for the 1950s, eighty-three for the 1960s. Paul McLane, in 'Religious Orders in Skelton's *Colyn Cloute*' (*ELN*, Vol. XVI), notes that while Wolsey is not the only religious attacked there, Skelton, perhaps because of his associations with the Benedictines at Westminster Abbey, treats monks and nuns more sympathetically than friars, whom he satirises in traditional manner. In the same volume Richard F. Green, in 'The Verses Presented to King Henry VII', traces and prints the MS. of the poem eulogising Henry VII included in 'Poems attributed to Skelton' in Dyce's edition, and argues that there is only Ashmole's assertion to connect this piece with Skelton.

Jonathan Z. Kamholtz, in 'Thomas Wyatt's Poetry: The Politics of Love' (*Criticism*, Vol. XX, No. 4), extends discussions in Thomson, Southall, Mason and Hannen, to consider the relationship between politics and love in Wyatt's lyrics, where the political and amatory could become metaphors for each other (as Tottel's editor partly realised). Wyatt sees himself as helpless before political and sexual authority, which themselves cannot create stability in their world; he seeks such stability, attempting to create at least a poetic order in a world that prevents any other. Stanley J. Koziskowski notes (*N&Q*, Vol. 25. No. 5) some interesting verbal analogies between Churchyard's complaint of Jane Shore in *Mirror for Magistrates* and Wyatt's 'They flee from me', but goes further: Jane is implicitly linked with Dame Fortune, which encourages an identification of Wyatt's wayward mistress in her loose gown with Fortune, who elsewhere (*Coll. Poems* 47) also kissed Wyatt flatteringly. Wayne H. Siek (*N&Q*, Vol. 25, No. 2 and No. 5) notes uses by Wyatt of 'skirmisher' and of 'paused' that predate the O.E.D.'s earliest citations of 1565 and 1908 respectively. Edgar F. Daniels corrects earlier misinterpretations of Surrey's 'In the Rude Age' (*Expl* Vol. 36, No. 4).

General

One of the most interesting books on the period for some time is Gordon Kipling's *The Triumph of Honour*[5]. This assesses the impact of Burgundian culture on earlier Tudor England, with particular emphasis on pageants, chivalry, the book trade, painting and poetry, and argues that much that has been labelled Italianate in Tudor art and culture may be traced to Netherlandish and Burgundian culture. Henry VII's new Richmond palace and the early Tudor courtiers' literary tastes and combination of learning and chivalry are in the Burgundian tradition. *Speke Parrot* is compared with Lemaire de Belges's *Epistres de l'Amant Vert*, and *Magnyfycence* with Fillastre's *Toison d'Or* which, in Burgundian fashion, presents magnificence as the chief of princely virtues. Wyatt's poetic techniques and literary models are those of the rhetoricians of Burgundy and northern France, such as de Belges and Molinet, and Kipling draws some suggestive and persuasive parallels. He also discusses extensively the Burgundian-style allegorical festival ('the triumph of honour') planned for Prince Arthur's

[5] *The Triumph of Honour: Burgundian Origins of the Elizabethan Renaissance*, by Gordon Kipling. The Hague: Leiden U.P., (1977). pp. xiv + 188.

wedding, relating its technique and meaning to *The Faerie Queene*. Further chapters on Tudor 'disguisings' and pageants show how the English masque derives from Burgundy. Kipling emphasises the importance for Spenser of the Flemish connection, and links *The Faerie Queene* with Burgundian pageants, Guileville's allegorical romance *Pèlerinage*, and Gheeraert's engraving of William of Orange as St George; in Book V Spenser sees the salvation of the Netherlands as the one truly magnificent duty of modern chivalry. The book is handsome, well illustrated, readable and stimulating.

VII

Shakespeare

DAVID DANIELL and ANGUS EASSON

1. Editions

Macbeth[1] is another title in the series edited by Maynard Mack, noted last year. There is a general introduction; a note on the Elizabethan theatre; a textual note (which is certain that the Hecate scenes are interpolated, though less definite on possible cuts and revisions); an imagined performance ('In the Theater of the Mind'); study questions; and a list of books, films and records. The introduction makes useful points about Shakespeare's use of and departures from his sources, raises possible links with King James, emphasises the 'fateful' nature of the Weird Sisters, then considers the mythic quality of the story and the nature of the protagonists. A good deal is included, without being dogmatic or distorted. The notes are adequate. It is a reasonable schools' edition.

2. Textual Matters

In 'The First Quarto of *Pericles* Reconsidered' (*SQ*), S. Musgrove seeks to bring forward new evidence relevant to the Quarto's textual history, arguing that much of the earlier portion derives from foul papers and the later from a reported version. Musgrove argues that a pre-Shakespearean *Pericles* by more than one author existed in some form; that Shakespeare saw the working draft of its first two acts, touched them up but left them very imperfect; that Shakespeare completed the play by writing his own acts III – V; that a clean promptbook was made for theatrical use; that the Quarto printing was unauthorised, from a rough draft down to the end of III.i, the gaps in the manuscript being filled in by reported work or rough cobbling, and from a reasonably good report of III.ii to the end, the work being divided between two shops and at least three compositors. Jeanne Addison Roberts, claiming that the history of the evolution of Shakespeare's text can sometimes reveal in vivid and interesting ways the pressures of literary judgements and bibliographical study, proceeds in '"Wife" or "Wise" – *The Tempest* 1. 1768' (*SB*) to demonstrate that the 'f' of 'wife' was damaged early in printing: bibliography proves the reading that was an 'emendment' in Rowe's edition and has vexed the literary judgement of editors ever since. The problems of the editor are entertainingly considered by G. Blakemore Evans ('Shakespeare Restored – ONCE AGAIN!') in a collection not previously noticed in this chapter[2]. Evans

[1] *Macbeth*, ed. by Maynard Mack and Robert W. Boynton (Hayden Shakespeare). New York: Hayden (1973) pp. vii + 141.

[2] *Editing Renaissance Dramatic Texts*, ed. by Anne Lancashire. New York and London: Garland (1976). pp. vi + 130. £7.

relates this to his work on the Riverside Shakespeare and particularly stresses the danger of excessive veneration for tradition. In the same collection, though not directly on Shakespeare, G. R. Proudfoot considers editorial alertness and responsibility in 'Dramatic Manuscripts and the Editor' and Arthur Freeman what happens between copy-text and publication in 'Inaccuracy and Castigation: The Lessons of Error'; while the papers of Beatrice Corrigan and A. G. Reichenberger on editing Italian and Spanish Renaissance drama make clear how, without necessary cause for complacency, English drama has profited by a long tradition of editing. On eighteenth-century editors, John Hazel Smith considers Styan Thirlby's contribution to Theobald's 1733 edition, adding to the article of Christopher Spencer and John W. Velz (1970; misdated in *YW* 53.149; in 'Styan Thirlby's Shakespearean Commentaries: A Corrective Anaylsis' (*ShakS*) he reports on the discovery of a copy of Pope's edition with Thirlby's annotations, used by Theobald, which suggests also the possibility that Thirlby contemplated his own edition. Dr Thirlby, of Jesus College Cambridge, who so influenced Theobald both as editor and commentator, turns out to note marginally such gems as 'Did you not forget yourself here a little, Willy?' and 'Fie Shakespear this is clumsy'. William C. Woodson reports in 'The Printer's Copy for the 1785 Variorum Shakespeare' (*SB*) that since his 1975 article he has discovered the printer's copy, catalogued in the British Library as simply another copy of the 1778 Variorum. It is now possible to reach more precise conclusions regarding the scope and genesis of 1785.

3. Biography and Background

In 'Finding Shakespeare's "Lost Years"' (*SQ*), Robert E. Burkhart challenges the idea that 1584/5 – 1592 is any darker than other periods of Shakespeare's life and suggests Shakespeare joined an acting company, probably Leicester's, shortly after 1585. Andrew Gurr reverts to 'Shakespeare's Marriage' (*Listener*), developing his earlier speculation that one of the sonnets was to Anne Hathaway before her marriage. Wayne H. Phelps speculates usefully in 'Edmund Shakespeare at St. Leonard's, Shoreditch' (*SQ*) as to whether a baptismal entry of 1607 refers to a son of Edmund, whose burial is already known, while Allan Pritchard's 'Elizabeth Walker and Shakespeare's Stratford' (*N&Q*) offers information about first Stratford personalities connected with Stratford and apparently overlooked in Anthony Walker's *The Holy Life of Mrs Elizabeth Walker* (1690). In ' "The Paths I Meant unto Thy Praise": Jonson's Poem for Shakespeare' (*ShakS*), Sara van den Berg suggests the need to look at the First Folio poem as a whole, finding that its success 'ultimately depends on the presence of both men in the poem'. The 'Folger 1560 View of London' is shown by Kent Cartwright (*SQ*) to have no independent authority, being a copy of a copy from the 1560 original.

Nan Cooke Carpenter attempts to open up possibilities in 'Shakespeare and Music: Unexplored Areas' (*RenD* 1976) but provides no answers to, or real lines of investigation from, her own questions. An interesting and entertaining paper by G. R. Hibbard, 'Love, Marriage and Money in Shakespeare's Theatre and Shakespeare's England'[3], considers the differ-

[3] *The Elizabethan Theatre: VI*, ed. by G. R. Hibbard. London and Basingstoke: Macmillan. pp. xiii + 160.

ences between love depicted in romantic comedy and love in the society of the time. A range of historical examples is given and Middleton's *A Chaste Maid in Cheapside* considered as well *Midsummer Night's Dream, The Taming of the Shrew, Much Ado* and *Othello*, Hibbard concluding that Shakespeare touches us more in what he says about love and marriage, though Middleton and others give us more factual detail about the way matters were viewed and dealt with in Shakespeare's England.

The reproduction of *A Folio of Shakespeare Engravings*[4], taken from drawings by Henry William Bunbury and originally published by Thomas Macklin between 1792 and 1796, makes a handsome volume. The collection is prefaced by a brief life of Bunbury (1750–1811) and, since the pictures reflect the staging and costumes of Bunbury's time, an account of the Georgian Theatre (not always accurate in detail: e.g. 'Davencourt' for 'Davenant'). Falstaff is the most popular subject (six out of the twenty plates) and comedy predominates amongst the rest. It must be confessed that the pictures themselves are not exciting: they may provide information about the theatre, but they scarcely illuminate or comment upon or take inspiration from the plays.

4. General Criticism

David Bevington's bibliography[5] attempts to list those books and articles that cannot safely be ignored; he is properly selective, his single criterion being: What critical studies should be familiar to student or scholar who undertakes an essay or dissertation on any particular Shakespearean topic? The items are presented without comment beyond the occasional factual clarification, though asterisks indicate what Bevington considers indispensable. Except for the history of Shakespeare criticism, few items before 1930 are included, since Bevington largely wishes to represent the present state of studies. German and French items are included, but not those in other languages, though English-language items by foreign critics are. It is possible to argue that, highly selective though Bevington has been (and only drudges like the authors of this chapter know the full weight of the annual output on Shakespeare), there is still a little too much. Under 'The Histories, General Studies' does one really *need* the books by Moody E. Prior and Robert B. Pierce? They appear in most American critics' bibliographies on the Histories, it is true: but they are not very good books. And some of us have found Robert F. Willson Jr much less than helpful, though entries under his name duly appear. The sections are usefully and clearly divided, and there is good cross-referencing. There are a few mistakes (D. Nicol Smith's *Shakespear in the Eighteenth Century* has no mention under Shakespeare's editors, though included elsewhere, and it is long since *YW* was published by O.U.P.) but by and large this is an excellent work of reference.

The same cannot be said of Gareth and Barbara Lloyd Evans' *Everyman's Companion to Shakespeare*[6]. They set out to provide material that a

[4] *A Folio of Shakespeare Engravings taken from the Drawings by Henry William Bunbury and Presented to H.R.H. the Duchess of York with a foreword by Sir William Napier Bunbury, Bart.*, ed. by John Bailey. London: Ariel Press. pp. [9] + 20 engravings.

[5] *Shakespeare*, by David Bevington (Goldentree Bibliographies in Language and Literature). Illinois: AHM Publishing Corporation. pp. xxii + 259. £5.75.

[6] *Everyman's Companion to Shakespeare*, by Gareth and Barbara Lloyd Evans. J.M. Dent. pp. xiv + 368. £7.50.

multiplicity of readers of Shakespeare will find useful and engaging. The book is divided into four main sections: The Man and his Times; Shakespeare in Performance; The Works; Stratford upon Avon and Shakespeare. The contents of the first of these shows how they have tried to be original and the resulting confusion how they have failed. After a useful Calendar of Events, Shakespeare's Appearance refers to the images (including apparent acceptance of Hotson's identification of Hilliard's Unknown Man; see *YW* 58.130), but instead of an outline of Shakespeare's life the Evanses go through the myths and legends, properly rebutting most of the apocrypha but giving an odd angle to the biography. The lists of Eminent Men and Women, Places and so on, scarcely offer anything to the beginner in Shakespeare. The second section is much better, though some of the comments on the illustrations are eccentric, but even here the section on films is only adequate, radio and television are not included, and the item on Shakespeare and Music is ludicrous: of the pieces randomly listed, at least seven have no meaningful connection with Shakespeare at all – Tchaikovsky's *Tempest*, for instance, is based on Ostrovsky's *Storm*, while Bellini's *Romeo and Juliet* (as the title is incorrectly given) went back to the Italian original. In section three, the plot outlines are skilful enough, but to read that on *Measure for Measure*, for instance, is to see how summary must distort, while a mini-anthology of famous pieces adds very little to a reader's understanding. Worse, though, is Murray J. Levith's *What's in Shakespeare's Names*[7], which is ill-written and badly thought-out. An examination of names would be interesting; Levith however shows little sensitivity either to sound or sense. Is Seaton in *Macbeth* homonymous with Satan? Does Anne Bullen's first name link her with the mother of the Virgin Mary? Does a reader of the dramatis personae of *Othello* know 'from the sound of the names that this will not be a comedy'? Levith is often simplistic (of Owen Glendower, 'the name drew forth the character') and takes little account of historical linguistics or likelihood: free association is constantly brought into play, apparently on the principle that, with Shakespeare, anything goes.

To move from that to Stanley Wells' *Shakespeare: An Illustrated Dictionary*[8], is to arrive at a haven of sanity, great learning lightly presented, and much helpfulness. Here in well under two hundred pages of pleasingly large type, with admirable pictures, is all an intelligent general reader needs, from 'Act-and-scene divisions' to 'Zeffirelli'. It scores over, for example, F. E. Halliday's *Penguin Shakespeare Companion* (1964), also a one-man work, by focusing so much more on the present, with fine pictures of recent events (good to have Henry VI illustrated by Alan Howard). Though one-third the length, it really does convey a lot, giving under 'Vocabulary', in a total of thirteen words, two kinds of basic information, where Halliday refers out to a much older 21-page article, even then hard to come by. A page on 'Authorship' concludes by saying that attempts to displace Shakespeare 'have been based usually on snobbery (the idea that a humble man from the country would not have been

[7] *What's in Shakespeare's Names*, by Murray J. Levith. George Allen & Unwin. pp. 147. £8.50.

[8] *Shakespeare: an Illustrated Dictionary*, by Stanley Wells. Kaye & Ward. pp. vii + 216. £4.25.

equipped to write the plays), the desire for self-advertisement, or mere folly'. The pictures earn their places, one of the strangest being that from Max Reinhardt's *Midsummer Night's Dream* film, 1935. And yet, the faintest shadow of doubt sometimes crosses the mind. Does Haydn deserve three lines on the basis of one song-setting? Polanski a reference, then only cross-referred to *Macbeth*? Who will look up Frank Martin for his opera *Der Sturm* (1956) based on *The Tempest*? And what on earth is Emilia Lanier doing here? The virtues of Stanley Wells include a marvellous lucidity, and in his *Shakespeare: The Writer and His Work*[9], a Special in that series, he accomplishes in eighty-odd pages a beautifully balanced, clear and comprehensive account of the man, his work, his state in print, and attitudes to him on stage and in the study since his death. Again, there are splendid, unusual pictures, which manage to be both mainstream and unexpected at the same time. A most therapeutic booklet.

S. C. Sen Gupta writes from Calcutta, and for an Indian market, *A Shakespeare Manual*[10], covering roughly the same ground as the familiar Cambridge *Companion* of Muir and Schoenbaum, though without the technical details. He begins with a general but lucid account of Shakespeare criticism 'Through the Ages', and then writes well on 'Shakespeare the Man'. In 'Shakespeare and His Sources' he shows a slightly less firm grip on anything outside the well-known core of the canon (the young Margaret's marriage with the young Henry VI is precisely *not* 'a diplomatic move'). Further chapters are 'Pastoral Romance and Romantic Comedy: *Rosalynde* and *As You Like It*'; 'Tragedy and Comedy: Barabas and Shylock'; and 'The Textual Problem: An Unorthodox Approach', which tackles the apparent confusion from the serene position of observing, quite correctly, a 'comprehensive unity of impression'. The booklet ends with the text of a lecture 'The Substance of Shakespearean Comedy' given by Sir Mark Hunter in India in 1912.

John W. Draper's *Orientalia and Shakespeareana*[11] is a most extraordinary, and scholarly, book. The first two chapters, called Study I and Study II, are about Omar Khayyam and Fitzgerald, including pictures of ancient artefacts 'owned by the author'. Study III is on 'The Origin of Rhyme', and cleverly argues oriental sources for the device, concluding that 'sometime before 1500 B.C. rhyme seems to have originated with the Indo-Iranians north of the Caspian, and from there spread south into India and later to Iran, east to China, and still later to the Mediterranean world, where the cult of Mithra gave it to Christian hymnology and so to all Europe'. Study IV extends this research to the Pacific, with astounding conclusions. Study V links Zoroastrian Chant and Early Christian Plainsong. Then, suddenly, Study VI is 'Shakespeare's Play That Was Not Played', arguing that *Troilus and Cressida* was written apparently on government order for a political situation that never arose and, since its pacifist theme lends itself poorly to drama, it was printed but not performed'. Study VII analyses, most usefully, Shakespeare and Barbary, and

[9] *Shakespeare: The Writer and His Work*, by Stanley Wells. Longman Group for The British Council. pp. 104. £1.50.

[10] *A Shakespeare Manual*, by S. C. Sen Gupta. Calcutta: O.U.P. pp. 157. £2.25.

[11] *Orientalia and Shakespeareana*, by John W. Draper, Ph.D. New York: Vantage Press. pp. 203. $6.95.

then further Studies relate Shakespeare to his experience of Muscovy, the Turk, Abbas Akbar ('Shakespeare has but five clear references to Iran'), India, Indians and the Indies. Professor Draper's first volume appeared in 1913, and this last book carries the sense of a view of Shakespeare almost from the elevation of Eternity, as if Prospero were expressing some of his wisdom. A book, most certainly, for every Shakespeare library.

John Erskine Hankins' *Backgrounds of Shakespeare's Thought*[12] looks at first like the kind of American Liberal-Arts College book which majors in Shakespeare and minors in everything else. It is in fact a good book from a serious and important critic, 'an attempt to bridge the gap between what Shakespeare read and what he wrote and trace the connections between the two'. It is more than a catalogue of references: when an illustration from Shakespeare appears, it is explained and put in the context of contemporary thought very usefully indeed. The first five chapters alone present, unpretentiously, fully up-to-date material on 'The Universal World', 'Numbers', 'The Psychology of Perception' and 'The Unsettled Humours' before focusing on the particular condition of man in 'The Human Condition', 'The Ascent of Man' and 'The Conduct of Life'. The pages on Numbers are stimulating and illuminating and take the modern mystique out of the subject – it is a relief *not* to find that you should have had twenty years with Frances Yates before you can begin to understand Shakespeare. And ten pages on the Hamlet–Ophelia relationship in II.ii of that play, discussing kissing-carrion and conception, are worth a host of recent pontifical articles from the Mid-West. Maynard Mack, no less, is quoted as saying it is 'the most thorough account of the background of Shakespeare's thought that has ever come my way'; he might have added 'and the most readable'.

Robert Weimann's book[13], originally published in German in 1967, appears now in a revised English version: Robert Schwartz acts as both translator and editor, material published subsequently by Weimann being incorporated, with his active co-operation, into this edition. Weimann argues for a dynamic relationship between Shakespeare and his audience in which the living traditions of folk ritual and dramatic imitation interact and so produce the characteristic mingling of dramatic illusion with an interchange between character/actor and audience that is part of the power of Shakespeare. Weimann traces the folk tradition from the earliest evidences of ritual and mimes in the classical world through their survival into the Middle Ages as the folk forms of mumming and the like, feeding importantly into the Corpus Christi cycles. The discussion of the playing areas – divided between the 'place' (*locus*) above and the 'arena' (*platea*) where the audience also stood, the characters of illusionistic drama remaining in the *locus* while those of the folk tradition move freely over the *platea* between them and the audience – is particularly illuminating, for instance, on the grotesqueries of Towneley's Second Shepherds play. When Weimann extends this argument into Shakespeare, the Fool in comedy as

[12] *Backgrounds of Shakespeare's Thought*, by John Erskine Hankins. Hassocks, Sussex: The Harvester Press. pp. 296. £10.50.

[13] *Shakespeare and the Popular Tradition in the Theater: Studies in the Social Dimension of Dramatic Form and Function*, by Robert Weimann. Baltimore and London: Johns Hopkins U.P. pp. xxii + 325. £12.

well as in *King Lear*, and also features of Hamlet, become newly explicable, since Shakespeare had available and extended features of both the folk and the humanist traditions. This is well developed in the section on '*Figurenposition*', the physical placing of characters upon the stage and their shifting roles as they shift their positions, while the earlier discussion of the folk figure's 'impertinent' remarks (both cheeky and beside the point) leads to an illumination of Hamlet's 'impertinency'. Weimann argues with subtlety and an awareness of difficulties: if words like 'folk' and 'the people' and 'plebs' are never quite satisfactorily defined, Weimann is not unaware of the difficulties they present. He writes persuasively and shows a flexibility and largeness not common amongst Marxist critics. His approach and his ability to synthesise quantities of material are akin to those of Mikhail Bakhtin in *Rabelais and His World*, a book and author never mentioned by Weimann. It is an approach that relies upon evidence that is often fragmentary or overlaid with later accretions, the materials of which are often structural rather than verbal, and where it can be tempting to build upon very little evidence: a fragment of a play from Oxyrhynchos hardly seems to justify the link made with Feste's catechism of Olivia, while the interpretation of the moment in *Twelfth Night* hardly catches the delicate complexities of character and situation. Yet this is an uncommon example and Weimann proceeds over difficult territory, able to make it clear that he is not talking about source studies and direct influences, since Shakespeare often could not have been conscious of the originals which fed into his theatre. As well as throwing light on the grotesque and on the physical conditioning effect of Shakespeare's platform stage, Weimann also persuasively integrates the comic interludes and subplots. Perhaps in claiming the common view of these is as light relief, diversions from the serious matter in hand, he is too much arguing against old-fashioned views of Shakespeare, yet he shows well that when they are 'viewed as constituent parts of the play's form and pressure. . .they can be seen as *structurally* very like the uncomic interlude'. Now that this translation exists, Weimann's work will be more readily integrated into Shakespeare studies: the translation reads well, though the printing of certain commonly repeated words (e.g. 'postritual') without hyphens is a minor irritation.

Mats Rydén in *Shakespearean Plant Names*[14], which takes its impulse from an article (1964) by Rolf Nordhagen, seeks to discuss not every floral context in Shakespeare, but those plant names which offer problems of identification and interpretation, reference being made throughout to the Swedish translations of Shakespeare. Rydén's goal is to determine 'Shakespearean meaning' in the dramatic context, not to examine Shakespeare's plant knowledge as such. Plants such as hebona, samphire, and dian's bud, fruits, and epithets such as 'daisied' and 'pioned' receive particular attention. There is a bibliography and indexes of English, Swedish and Modern Latin plant names in this attractively produced and illustrated work. It is good, too, to have a finely-produced and moderately-priced re-

[14] *Shakespearean Plant Names: Identifications and Interpretations*, by Mats Rydén (Stockholm Studies in English XLIII). Stockholm: Almqvist & Wiksell. pp. 117. Sw. Kr. 61.

print of J. E. Harting's *The Ornithology of Shakespeare*[15]. Genuinely informative, Harting in 1864 was author of *The Birds of Middlesex*, and he generates great interest, not least in his incidental pictures of Elizabethan rural life. Shakespeare's accurate eye and ear for so many creatures is continually striking; though, in the modern introduction, the Editor of 'Birds and Country' Magazine feels he has to apologise for the inadequacies of 'writers years ago' who 'indulged in "poetic licence". Such blemishes, deliberate or otherwise, were overlooked. Thus', he goes on, 'Shakespeare, and other poets, referred to the singing nightingale as *she* whereas it is the male that sings'.

Joan Rees, in an excellent study[16], aims 'to observe Shakespeare's handling of his stories for the light this may throw on the creative imagination engaged in his plays'. By approaching through story, Rees can suggest how certain plays were shaped and the ways in which Shakespeare became involved with his materials or dramatic problems during writing. After an opening which looks at non-dramatic development in the two narrative poems, the book considers plays in groups, with separate chapters on *Hamlet* and *Lear*. Rees finds evidence of 'creative excitement' in *The Merchant of Venice*, for instance, with its rapid using of the 'casket' material, while the shape of *Much Ado* is determined by too little creative excitement over Hero and Claudio with the consequent expansion of the story of Beatrice and Benedick. Rees is particularly interesting on the 'problem' plays and how in *Measure for Measure* the incapacitating of most of the major characters from action means that Shakespeare sustains the play's vitality by the lowlife characters. Other chapters look at a variety of plays as they use conversation rather than action (*Twelfth Night* and *The Tempest*); are restricted by historical materials (*Henry IV* and the Roman plays): or represent a new phase of narrative concern, as with the pattern of reconciliation in the last plays. On *Hamlet*, Rees is perceptive, often exciting, while she links *Lear* to other explorations in satire, finding that here 'fool and satirist are united and then transcended'. This is a book which can be recommended to students for new ways of experiencing the plays, yet which also will repay frequent rereading. Michael J. C. Echeruo's *The Conditioned Imagination from Shakespeare to Conrad*[17] argues that in approaching literature that involves 'exo-cultural' characters or themes, we need to take account of the 'culturally-conditioned imagination' of the audience on both the creation and the realisation of the work of art. He looks at *The Merchant of Venice* and *Othello* in terms of the Jew and the Moor. These surveys of Elizabethan expectation are quite useful, but they seem almost to insist that we cannot read beyond the historical circumstances of the plays' creation. Shylock 'is introduced in the play specifically as a Jew stereotype', while if Iago is a 'devil' as a 'matter of personal guilt, Othello is one as a matter of fact'. The chapters are suggestive, but leave the reader uncertain about his further course. J. M. Nosworthy's inaugural

[15] *The Ornithology of Shakespeare*, by James Edmund Harting. Old Woking, Surrey: Gresham Books. pp. xii + 321. £5.25.

[16] *Shakespeare and the Story: Aspects of Creation*, by Joan Rees. Athlone Press. pp. 239. £8.95.

[17] *The Conditioned Imagination from Shakespeare to Conrad*, by Michael J. C. Echeruo. New York: Holms & Meier, and London: Macmillan. pp. 135. £6.95.

lecture, *Shakespeare Puts the Clock Back*[18], considers Shakespeare's pre-occupation with the passing and ravages of time. Commenting that Shakespeare was a very nostalgic person, Nosworthy goes on to argue that the acute personal responses were put to dramatic account. He considers the 'ubi sunt' theme, which culminates in Justice Shallow and Hamlet, and the interplay of 'ancient', 'old' and 'antique', concluding with *Coriolanus* as Shakespeare's last sad verdict on history. Allan Brissenden, in a volume not previously noticed[19], has edited a collection to celebrate the centenary of English teaching at Adelaide University. The opening piece, J. I. M. Stewart's 'Who Was Shakespeare?' is not unentertaining, but has nothing new to say about the authorship controversy. R. S. White's 'Oaths and the Anti-Comic Spirit in *Love's Labour's Lost*' begins interestingly with a general statement about the comedies' anticomic impulses or attitudes, finding these give endings that are more qualified, bracing and open-ended than the surface festivity suggests, and goes on effectively to ask how in this play Shakespeare manages to keep the anti-comic mechanism going and how he develops it without allowing it to become a stale, trivial redundancy. Allan Brissenden himself writes sensibly but without sparkle on 'Shakespeare's Use of Dance: *Love's Labour's Lost, Much Ado about Nothing* and *The Merry Wives of Windsor*'. Better, once past the snigger-ing euphemism of the title, is Kevin Magarey's 'The Touch-Stone and the Toilet: Nature as Shakespeare's Irreducible in *As You Like It*', which argues that the play has a theme and that it is 'nature', finding that the fortune of the three main characters 'cancels out art for them', so they are left only with nature. The final Shakespearean essay in the collection is by F. H. Mares, who in exploring the sources of the play suggests 'The Equivo-cations of *Hamlet*', and who in showing how Hamlet and the audience are denied simple information and straightforward moral choices, leads us to interesting considerations.

Three pieces by John Berryman appeared in a posthumous volume[20], not previously noticed. 'Shakespeare at Thirty' is a consideration of the dramatist's career to 1594, concentrating in particular upon *Love's Labour's Lost*; 'Notes on *Macbeth*' relates the play to its supposed occasion as a royal play; and 'Shakespeare's Last Word' celebrates, with exuberance and pleasure, *The Tempest*. Eugene M. Waith touches on this last in '"Give Me Your Hands": Reflections on the Author's Agents in Comedy'[21], as well as *Midsummer Night's Dream* and *As You Like It*, while in the same volume Alvin Kernan considers 'Shakespeare's Essays on Dramatic Poetry: The Nature and Function of Theater within the Sonnets and the Plays', looking at artistic self-consciousness as an expression of fundamental values and concerns that began to emerge in the Renaissance.

John P. Sisk takes up 'Ceremony and Civilization in Shakespeare' (*SR*),

[18] *Shakespeare Puts the Clock Back*, by J. M. Nosworthy. Cardiff: Wales U.P. pp. 25. £0.50.

[19] *Shakespeare and Some Others: Essays on Shakespeare and Some of his Con-temporaries*, ed. by Alan Brissenden. Adelaide: English Department, U. of Adelaide (1976).

[20] *The Freedom of the Poet*, by John Berryman. New York: Farrar, Straus & Giroux (1976). pp. x + 390. £10.45.

[21] *The Author in His Work: Essays on a Problem in Criticism*, ed. by Louis L. Martz and Aubrey Williams. New Haven, Conn. and London: Yale U.P. pp. xix + 407.

urging that we should avoid a temptation, because Shakespeare does on occasion enforce the conviction that ceremony and honesty are incompatible, to search for a Shakespeare who will serve the transgressive spirit of modernism that might see Iago as tragic hero. In the same journal, L. C. Knights considers 'Shakespeare and History' and in particular chaos and its confrontation, finding in 'all these envisagings of a general doom, not supernaturally determined but brought on by man himself. . .a peculiar urgency'. Knights interestingly suggests that in the handling of material there is an awareness by Shakespeare of the abyss underlying the forms of civilisation and (what Knights finds harder to define, though it is suggestively explored) a development in Shakespeare's dramatic relationship to language, manifesting itself not only as a concern with the language of truth but also as an increasing mastery of the language of deception, including self-deception. Other articles cover aspects of Shakespeare's language; Martin Lehnert's 'Shakespeare in der Sprache unserer Zeit' (*SJW*) in relation to the language of his age and Karl P. Wentersdorf's 'Shakespearian Shards' (*SN* 1977) on the meaning of 'shard' when not a fragment of earthenware or brick, showing convincingly that for the sixteenth century it would be 'dung', not 'wing-case' or 'wing' as modern editors give. In a more general discussion, Margreta De Grazia's 'Shakespeare's View of Language: An Historical Perspective' (*SQ*) challenges the application to Shakespeare of modern views of language with regard to the difficulty of expressing meaning and of its slipperiness as a medium. She links her argument to usage in *Lear, Coriolanus* and some of the sonnets.

Anselm Schlösser considers strangers, natives and barbarians in 'Von Freunden, Eingeborenen und Barbaren bei Shakespeare' (*SJW*), while Alan C. Dessen in 'The Logic of Elizabethan Stage Violence: Some Alarms and Excursions for Modern Critics, Editors, and Directors' (*RenD*) finds it related to playhouse practice and that it tends against realism. Two articles that touch incidentally on Shakespeare are Nancy M. Goslee's 'From Marble to Living Form: Sculpture as Art and Analogue from the Renaissance to Blake' (*JEGP*), which refers briefly to *Timon* and *Winter's Tale* in a consideration of attempts to define sculpture as a separate art, and Quentin M. Hope's 'Winter Pastoral and Winter Reverie' (*CLS*), which touches on 'When icicles hang by the wall' as an example of winter pastoral. John Dean says little that's new in 'Shakespeare's Influence on *Moby Dick*, or Where There's a Will, There's a Whale' (*CahiersE*), pointing to links between Ishmael and Hamlet, the diabolical and *Macbeth*, and Ahab's final development and Lear.

Vastly more interesting is Philip Edwards in 'Shakespeare and the Healing Power of Deceit' (*ShS*), a suggestive if deliberately inconclusive discussion. Deceit is the mark of the Shakespearean villain, yet others also practice seeming: Duke Vincentio, Prince Hal, Portia. So if not only villains are its practitioners, why does Shakespeare seem to get so worked up about deceit? Comedy requires deceit, but beyond plot complication, many of the traditional deceptions in Shakespeare's comedies are morally interesting. In a consideration of various kinds of deceit, Edwards moves towards the proposition that Shakespeare was deeply interested in the moral implications of well-intentioned deceit and the possibility that there was a real puritanism in Shakespeare. Andrew S. Cairncross in 'Shakespeare and Ariosto: *Much Ado About Nothing, King Lear*, and *Othello*' (*RenQ* 1976) looks at the relationship and argues for Shakespeare's ability to read Italian.

Not previously noticed is Richard Levin's 'Third Thoughts on Thematics' (*MLR* 1975), which picks up from his 1972 article: this further instalment of his investigations is prompted by his earlier reflections having produced no decline in the trend. Levin adopts his familiar tactics of giving extracts from anonymously-presented critics and concludes that the thematic approach is so popular because it is the easiest form of criticism. Not unrelated is Armin-Gerd Kuckhoff's piece, in German, on the conclusion of plays and the resultant perspective (*SJW*). In the same journal, also in German, Thomas Metscher considers the relationship of Shakespeare's drama to reality.

Supposedly specialist studies produce some of the year's most extraordinary offerings. Buckner B. Trawick's *Shakespeare and Alcohol*[22] is the sort of book that gets Shakespeare studies a bad name. 'No commentator', he says 'has called attention to the frequency and the significance of Shakespeare's references to alcoholic beverages' of which he finds 360 'references' and 196 'figures of speech'. We might well hope not. He finds that there are (1) numerous scenes 'in which drinking is a sign of hospitality or friendhsip' (*sic* – or should we say *hic*?) (2) '*Excessive* drinking often leads to unhappiness' (3) 'Alcohol is associated with murder in a significant number of instances' including – why had we not seen this before? – the murder of Duncan which 'follows hard upon the drinking at Macbeth's castle'. The book, written, if you please, on grants from the University of Alabama, has forty pages of unintentionally comic statistics, including an enormous pull-out table (not, sadly, of the kind one can drink at). The taped-on free sample had disappeared, one assumes, before the copy reached these offices.

From there it is an easy leap to *The Poems of Shakespeare's Dark Lady* introduced by A. L. Rowse[23]. Even the title of this book is a double lie. The volume prints from a 1611 edition one long religious poem, 'Salve Deus Rex Judaeorum, Written by Mistris Aemilia Lanyer. . .' a woman who has no connection with Shakespeare whatever. It is Mr Rowse's most profitable delusion, foisted with braggart intolerance on to the public year by year, that this woman 'is' the 'Dark Lady of the Sonnets'. Rowse's desperate fantasies about Shakespeare's sexual relations with this woman and with Southampton are again trotted out, though he has silently dropped the misreading of Forman's handwriting on which the entire structure is based. The poem, attended by dedicatory verses, and mildly feminist, is not of any great merit.

We may note here Martha Andresen-Thom who in *ShakS* answers Juliet Dusinberre (*YW* 56.145), producing another feminish piece, more reasonable than Dusinberre's, but still not pointing out that Dusinberre's

[22] *Shakespeare and Alcohol*, by Buckner B. Trawick. Amsterdam: Rodopi. pp. 100. Hfl. 40, –, 25, –.

[23] *The Poems of Shakespeare's Dark Lady, Introduction by A. L. Rowse*. Jonathan Cape. pp. xiii + 144. £4.95.

title is seriously misleading, as there are in it only two or three pages on Shakespeare, at the very end.

Ernest B. Gilman writes *The Curious Perspective: Literary and Pictorial Wit in the Seventeenth Century*[24]. Though he discusses Donne, Herbert, Greville and Marvell, Shakespeare is central, and *Richard II, Twelfth Night* and *A Midsummer Night's Dream* are most helpfully illuminated in the light of the remarkable tricks of optical perspectives current in Shakespeare's time. His chapter on *Richard II* appeared in a previous form (*RenD*) (*YW* 57.141); his conclusion is important, that shifting patterning and perspective in the play lead to no unequivocal point of view. One must see 'both the "controlling majesty" of kingship and the vanity of the "hollow crown"'. His demonstration of Orsino's 'natural perspective that is and is not' illuminates the whole play, and his exposition of beast-head images is valuable for *A Midsummer Night's Dream*.

In *Critical Dimensions: English, German and Comparative Literature: Essays in Honour of Aurelio Zanco*[25], G. Wilson Knight writes on 'Shakespeare and Society', concluding 'We must beware of studying Shakespeare's sociology without attending to the imponderables'. C. Haines patronises *The Comedy of Errors* in a general essay of little value. C. W. Watts writes on 'Shakespearean Themes: The Dying God and the Universal Wolf', A. Lombardo on *Troilus and Cressida*, and F. Ferrara on *Timon of Athens*. Also of little value are the essays by John W. Crawford reprinted in *Discourse: Essay [sic] on English and American Literature*[26], where there are slight sermonettes on *Julius Caesar*, Falstaff, *Cymbeline*, and 'A Lesson in Communications' which characteristically says nothing in four pages. We have also received *Aspects of Literature*[27] by Vasvanath Chatterjee which contains 'Shakespeare and Astrology', 'Tagore as a Shakespearean Critic' and 'T. S. Eliot and the Problems of *Hamlet*'.

Several pieces discuss the history of criticism. John Crawford (not, surely, the one we have just noted?) analyses *Romantic Criticism of Shakespearian Drama*[28]. After a chapter intelligently surveying the relevant history of Shakespeare criticism well into the twentieth century, with some speculation about why it should be so, he analyses *Hamlet, Antony and Cleopatra, Henry V* and *The Merchant of Venice*, each chapter presenting a useful account of Romantic critics and their comments, quite often producing unexpected insights. More valuably, in fact, Joan Coldwell edits *Charles Lamb on Shakespeare*[29] which gathers together for the first time in one volume all of Lamb's commentary on Shakespeare,

[24] *The Curious Perspective: Literary and Pictorial Wit in the Seventeenth Century*, by Ernest B. Gilman. New Haven, Conn. and London: Yale U.P. pp. xii + 267. £11.50.

[25] *Critical Dimensions: English, German and Comparative Literature Essays in Honiur of Aurelio Zanco*, ed. by Mario Curreli and Alberto Martino. Cuneo: Saste. pp. xiv + 555. Lire 30,000, 15,000.

[26] *Discourse: Essay on English and American Literature*, by John W. Crawford. Amsterdam: Rodopi. pp. vi + 100. Hfl. 40, –.

[27] *Aspects of Literature*, by Vasvanath Chatterjee. Calcutta: Progressive Publishers. pp. 189. Rs. 15.

[28] *Romantic Criticism of Shakespearian Drama*, by John Crawford. SSEL. Salzburg: Institut für Englische Sprache und Literatur. pp. 202.

[29] *Charles Lamb on Shakespeare*, ed. by Joan Coldwell. Gerrards Cross, Bucks.: Colin Smythe. pp. 175. £6.95.

making accessible Lamb's fragments and single paragraphs as well as the longer, more formally argued pieces, and those of the *Tales* from Lamb's own hand (basically the major tragedies). A well-illustrated book, with a helpful introduction.

Little real weight can be given to *Shakespeare's Magnanimity: Four Tragic Heroes, Their Friends and Families*[30], of which alternate chapters are written by Wilbur Sanders and Howard Jacobson. The book opens with a – wisely unattributed – 'Induction' with Dramatis Personae including 'Mulligrub' and 'Sir Affable Ponder', fourteen deeply embarrassing pages of 'witty' discussion which reminds us of those hearty American Elizabethan Banquets in which everything is supposed to be 'authentique' and part of the English 'heritage'. The ensuing relaxed chapters read like self-congratulatory seminars in which everyone sparkles. A case is made, certainly, for Elsinore's domesticity, for Macbeth as purifier, for an unmanned Antony, a thinking Coriolanus, but it could all have been in a few pages without clutter: one nine-line paragraph in the *Macbeth* chapter brings in Western films, Clytemnestra, Norse sagas, *Woyzeck* and Dostoevsky.

Ralph Berry, by contrast, also covering a number of plays, actually has something to say. The book *The Shakespearean Metaphor*[31], is a study of some of the ways in which Shakespeare exploits the possibilities of metaphor. Berry's prime interest is in metaphor as controlling structure, to detect the extent to which a certain metaphoric idea informs and organises the drama. Thus, 'the first half of *Richard III* describes an actor immersed in role-playing, the second half shows him confronting the realities from which his playing had excluded him'. Bastardy controls *King John*, and the language of the sonnet *Romeo and Juliet*. The double effect of the relations between Chorus and play inform *Henry V*, and the final scene of *Hamlet* permits the hero in a special sense to say 'one'. *Tempus edax rerum* controls *Troilus and Cressida*, and Berry finds, stimulatingly, that the interrelation of war and sex is the underlying statement of *Coriolanus*. Finally, *The Tempest* is metaphor itself.

Translation occupies a good deal of this year's relevant output. J. M. Ellis D'Allesandro in 'Guazzo and Shakespeare: 'Perspectives of a Problem' (*RLMC*) suggests that Shakespeare used Guazzo's *Civile Conversatione* translated by Pettie in 1581, completed in 1586. Anna Kay France's book, *Boris Pasternak's Translations of Shakespeare*[32], though it is as much about Pasternak as it is about Shakespeare, is extraordinarily helpful even to non-Russian readers. What happens to Shakespearean locutions when moved through Pasternak's mind sets up all sorts of unexpected reverberations, finely caught by Professor France. From Tokyo comes a major new series, of which we here notice the first five annual volumes, called *Shakespeare Translation*[33].

[30] *Shakespeare's Magnanimity: Four Tragic Heroes, Their Friends and Families*, by Wilbur Sanders and Howard Jacobson. Chatto & Windus. pp. 187. £4.95.

[31] *The Shakespearean Metaphor: Studies in Language and Form*, by Ralph Berry. Macmillan. pp. 128. £7.95.

[32] *Boris Pasternak's Translation of Shakespeare*, by Anna Kay France. Berkeley, Los Angeles and London: U. of California P. pp. x + 277. £10.50.

[33] *Shakespeare Translation*: Vol. 1 (1974). pp. 97; Vol. 2 (1975). pp. 123; Vol. 3 (1976). pp. 93; Vol. 4 (1977). pp. 119; Vol. 5 (1978). pp. 99; Vol. 6 (1979). pp. 130; Vol. 7 (1980). Tokyo: Yushodo Shoten/London: Eurospan (distributors). £13.50 each vol.

The enterprise warrants close attention. Vol. 1 (1974) contains in particular H. W. Donner on 'Some problems of Shakespearean Translation', a valuable general essay, though directed specifically towards Swedish. A brief note from Balz Engler announces the new bilingual German prose translation, and Jürgen Wertheimer's theoretical/linguistic essay of some technical complexity tackles 'Text Type and Strategy of Translation'. Wolfgang Riehle comments on Erich Fried's *Othello*, showing in detail how the lavish praise of the *Times Literary Supplement* was misplaced. Other articles deal with translations of scenes or plays into Japanese, Hindi, and Bengali and the present state of translation in Norway, Korea, and Japan. Vol. 2 (1975) discusses the state of translation of Shakespeare into Spanish, Russian, Danish and Japanese, and includes essays on the first Greek translation (1818) and comparisons, of *Hamlet* soliloquies into Spanish, and of the *Sonnets* into Germany. Jagannath Chakravorty tackles well the problems of getting *Lear*'s storm-scene into Bengali, Hindi and Marathi. Vol. 3 (1976) continues the surveys with Scandinavian problems arising in the *Sonnets*, personification as a problem in German, accounts of early Arabic work, and Shakespeare in Poland. Jürgen Wertheimer analyses communication and its consequences, focusing on comparisons of German versions of the opening of *Macbeth*, and Avraham Oz looks at the problem of puns. Jagannath Chakravorty gives an Indian view of Verse *versus* Prose. Vol. 4 (1977) surveys Portuguese and Greek translations, and *Hamlet* problems in Chinese and Japanese, as well as getting the *Sonnets* into Romanian. A new German translator, Wolfgang Swaczynna, is discussed. Olga Akhmanova and Velta Zadornova write on 'The Philology of Translation', and Toshiko Oyama expounds 'A Translator's Dilemma'. Finally Vol. 5 (1978) is a memorial both to Toshiko Oyama and T. J. B. Spencer. Here Rudolf Stamm compares six German versions of *Hamlet* 111.iv.1–32; Giorgio Melchiori gives an Italian view of translating Shakespeare; the *Sonnets* into Hungarian, and the state in Hindi, and recently in Japan, are surveyed. A charming essay by Olga Akhmanova and Velta Zadornova from Moscow deals with the problem of getting quotations across in another language. This entire series is already very distinguished, and handsomely produced; it is of great importance.

To conclude this section, we note three items of increasing significance. Richard David's *Shakespeare in the Theatre*[34] has been widely noticed. Mr David contributed annual theatre-notes to six volumes of *Shakespeare Survey* in the 1950s, and has addressed the Stratford Summer Schools. He likens his work here to Lichtenberg on Garrick and Hazlitt on Kean. Yet the book is deeply dismaying. Four chapters purporting to give the elementary material necessary for a full appreciation of Shakespeare today are so eccentric and uneven that it is a book to be kept out of the hands of students. The remaining chapters discuss recent performances of nineteen plays, all but one at the RSC. He is good at conveying space and activity in words: but on every page factual notes are served up with opinion-sauce, and a lot of unattributed Summer School gossip. His scholarship is laughable, as when he says that 'the only possible defence' of the unity of the two *Henry IV* plays 'comes from a Japanese scholar, Keiji Aoki' published

[34] *Shakespeare in the Theatre*, by Richard David. Cambridge: C.U.P. pp. xv + 263. £7.50.

in Kyoto in 1973, or that the first to notice the presence of the Christian 'last things' in *Macbeth* was 'Professor Guy Butler' in a 'lecture delivered at Grahamstown in July 1976'. His theatre-history is lamentable – all theatrical excellences go back to Cambridge, if you please, in the 1930s, and the final chapter gives large space to Terence Gray (Cambridge again) in January 1929. What are we to think of a book which under this title, and with those intentions, mentions no recent literature, not even Peter Brook's famous book? The book is dedicated to Glen Byam Shaw, and in the preface expresses effusive thanks to Harley Granville-Barker 'who, in the autumn of 1934, generously allowed me to share his walks in the Bois de Boulogne'.

Next, a surprise. A casette tape in a series *History Makers* called *William Shakespeare 1564–1616*[35] 'a dramatised biography in stereo by Kenneth Allen' (who writes books about the sea), with a foolishly out-of-date and inaccurate bibliography, fills one with dread. Out-of-tune 'Tudor' music, wincingly stilted acting, a B-picture script. . .one fears it all, from blush-making experience. But not a bit of it. This is an excellent piece of work, beautifully made, compelling to listen to, and both accurate and tactful. A picture of Shakespeare really does come across as of a man with a convincingly larger dimension to his imaginative abilities. The history is modestly pressed, and the music actually in tune. This is to be recommended.

Finally, a fine, scholarly and indispensable book from Ann Thompson, *Shakespeare's Chaucer*[36]. Her primary aim 'is to establish beyond doubt that Shakespeare not only read Chaucer but knew his work unusally well and was influenced by it in several different ways'. This she does. The result is a very important book indeed, and a rare example of the gracious development of post-graduate research into a marvellous book. She establishes once and for all what had never been precise before, that Shakespeare *did* read Chaucer, extensively. She explains that Chaucer was for the Elizabethans both ' "father" of a tradition which did not exist, and perfector of a vernacular which was remote and archaic, while his reputation as a learned and moral writer rested on very shaky ground and was already subject to scepticism and challenge. Yet it is apparent from all the references to him that despite everything he was widely read and enjoyed'. Ann Thompson puts a lot of recent source-commentary into perspective, and reveals the curious ignorance and prejudice of many modern critics. She is well aware that 'one can very rarely prove his influence beyond any doubt, but must frequently be satisfied with no more than a high degree of probability'. A splendid chapter follows the use of Chaucer by other dramatists 1558–1625, and then in Shakespeare outside *Troilus and Cressida* and *Two Noble Kinsmen*, tricky ground, well traversed, making use of proverbial sayings, 'mere names', non-proverbial ideas, images, verbal borrowings, and general influence. She finds the *Knight's Tale* behind *A Midsummer Night's Dream*, of course, but also the *Troilus* behind Brooke and behind *Romeo and Juliet*. The long *Troilus and Cressida* chapter,

[35] *William Shakespeare 1564–1616: a Dramatised Biography in Stereo*, by Kenneth Allen. History Makers Cassettes. London: Ivan Berg Associates (Audio Publishing) Limited. 60 mins.

[36] *Shakespeare's Chaucer: a Study in Literary Origins*, by Ann Thompson. Liverpool: Liverpool U.P. pp. x + 239. £8.75.

including an analysis of the play, shows 'not very close reference and. . . very few places where a verbal parallel can be claimed' but Chaucer's ideas presented structural and thematic methods to Shakespeare, and his explicitness about a story 'at once both tragic and sordid' inspired the peculiar tone and attitude which Shakespeare adopted in this particular play. The same method, of dramatic analysis (occasionally, it must be said, lacking in subtlety) shows that Shakespeare and Fletcher had quite different ways with the source in *Two Noble Kinsmen*. The book concludes with a table showing comparatively Shakespeare's Chaucerian references, play by play. Such an important book deserved wider marketing, and certainly better editing.

In general criticism of the comedies, we note Karlheinz Hoffmann's *Verliebtheit und Rollenspiel in Shakespeares Verkleidungskomödien*[37]. This is an important study of the problem of how girls dressed as boys can successfully act out amorousness.

R. S. White interestingly draws attention in 'Dawn in Some of Shakespeare's Comedies' (*SoRA*) to a shift from the use of evening to end the earlier comedies (the day's span of *Comedy of Errors*, for instance) to a use of dawn and the time of struggle betwixt night and morning, with its suggestion of new beginnings beyond the action as in *The Merchant of Venice* and *Much Ado*. In 'The Loss of Men and the Getting of Children: "All's Well That Ends Well" and "Measure for Measure"' (*MLR*), Alexander Welsh looks at the way these plays dramatise the reluctance to marry and suggests that their reasoning 'is fundamentally biological rather than cultural, and biology admits only two possible ends of human existence: the continuation of the species and individual death'. Shakespeare, Welsh claims, wishes to strip away 'culture' in order 'to make sense of birth and sex and death in their nakedness'. Whereas the earlier comedies embraced marriage wholeheartedly, now marriage and generation are seen as problematical.

There are two general studies of the Histories. Paul Bacquet, in *Les Pièces Historiques de Shakespeare*[38], analyses themes, structure and characters in this first volume on the first Tetralogy and *King John*. He gives a sensible, thorough and very readable account. Though not Tillyard-bound, mercifully, he is still a touch old-fashioned, and breaks no new ground. He concludes with the customary genealogical tables, but then sensibly adds five pages of significant dates. John Wilders' *The Lost Garden: a View of Shakespeare's English and Roman History Plays*[39] is quiet, low-key and unpretentious, and a great relief after the last half-dozen general books on the Histories in recent years, all American, and all showing signs of a desperate quest after Shakespeare as political sage, the Bard as philosopher in sympathy with national traumas not unlike those in American history in the years between the assassination of Kennedy and the election of Carter. A lot of fresh energy came into History Play studies

[37] *Verliebtheit und Rollenspiel in Shakespeares Verkleidungskomödien*, von Karlheinz Hoffman. SSEL. Salzburg: Institut für Englische Sprache und Literatur. pp. 134.

[38] *Les pièces historiques de Shakespeare: 1. La première tetralogie et "Le Roi Jean"*, by Paul Bacquet. Paris: Presses Universitaires de France. pp. 235.

[39] *The Lost Garden: A View of Shakespeare's English and Roman History Plays*, by John Wilders. Macmillan. pp. xi + 154. hb £6.50, pb £2.95.

with the American gift for seeing everything in the world as America writ slightly different, and that was all to the good. Ridding the subject of the Tudor Myth from Tillyard has made matters much more open. John Wilders takes the fresh opportunities very well, and understands the new freedoms. The plays are not vehicles for star parts, nor fictions with 'characters', nor exemplary moral tracts, nor academic studies of some fashionable abstract noun or other, but dramas full of people. He could have done with a better title – it is going to be assumed that he is presenting the loss of Eden as a controlling metaphor, and the book is richer than that. Occasionally he lapses in his commentary-method. Unsubtle about the *Henry VI* plays, narrow about *Henry V*, out-of-date on *Richard II*, he rises to excellence in the chapter 'Prayer, Prophecy and Providence'. He is fine whenever he touches Falstaff.

A major book on the tragedies is Howard Felperin's *Shakespearean Representation: Mimesis and Modernity in Elizabethan Tragedy*[40]. Felperin wrote the best book on the Romances for some time (*YW* 53.154). Here he asks how Shakespeare can be both our contemporary and an Elizabethan. 'Does it really matter to our effort at understanding *Macbeth* that the culture within which Shakespeare wrote held different views of religion, government, psychology – of virtually any aspect of social and individual existence we may care to name – and that these different views are everywhere reflected in the play?' He asks how Elizabethan drama came to be described as understandable only within a medieval tradition, but at the same time demonstrating the presence of that tradition only in fossil form. He develops a theory of the relation between literary history and mimesis, whereby a given work 'openly uses or abuses a great deal of previous art only to create the illusion that it uses no art at all, that it presents the thing itself'. There follows a good chapter on the complexities of form of *Hamlet* (which complexities are then carried further into *Othello*, *King Lear* and *Macbeth* with increasing profundity) before going on in a final chapter to look at Tourneur, Middleton, Webster and Ford. Alan Dessen's *Elizabethan Drama and the Viewer's Eye*[41] covers, pretentiously, some of the same ground as Felperin, but here the author is so talkative and self-absorbed as to get between the reader and Shakespeare, which is unforgiveable. It is basically a book offering (with, in the end, unbearable self-importance) a brief survey of a few stage-effects, grown out of the observations of some moments in Moralities which make up his long-winded essay in *ShakS*, 'Homilies and Anomalies: the Legacy of the Morality Play to the Age of Shakespeare'. Felperin's book, which denies the major thesis of Dessen's, is altogether more desirable company.

In 'Apuleius and the Bradleian Tragedies' (*ShS*), John J. M. Tobin suggests that *The Golden Ass* was a favourite text of Shakespeare's: he finds plot parallels between it and *Hamlet* as well as details of wording and likeness. When he claims that *Othello* represents the transformation of a man into an ass, we might wonder about the difference between the literal and the figurative, and if there is arguably a link between the sisters of

[40] *Shakespearean Representation: Mimesis and Modernity in Elizabethan Tragedy*. Princeton, N.J.: Princeton U.P. pp. viii + 199. £8.60.

[41] *Elizabethan Drama and the Viewer's Eye*, by Alan C. Dessen. Chapel Hill, N.C.: U. of North Carolina P. pp. xl + 176. £11.95.

King Lear and those of the Psyche episode: Thrasileon's disguise as a bear seems a remote link to Macbeth's image of himself as the baited bear. The claim gains weight from a well-written piece, even if not every example is equally convincing. Margaret Garber in '"Vassal Actors": The Role of the Audience in Shakespearean Tragedy' (*RenD*) considers the way in which an audience is simultaneously active and passive, her concern being with an audience both within the play and within the theatre. Eliot Slater continues his investigations with 'Word Links between "Timon of Athens" and "King Lear"' (*N&Q*), suggesting on the basis of links with earlier and later plays that *Timon* is earlier than *Lear*. Henryk Zbierski approaches the tragedies in terms of genre in 'Some Aspects of Development and Decline of Shakespearean Tragedy' (*Studia Anglica Posnaniensia*), which seeks to revive the idea that the final tragi-comedies are somehow inferior, love being the root of the failure: 'Shakespeare's return to the subject matter of love as the main theme' in *Antony and Cleopatra* was 'as fatal to him as Cleopatra was to Antony'. This reviewer murmurs that there is more than one way of seeing the outcome of *that* play.

Three pieces in *ShS* consider the Roman plays in varied ways. John W. Velz takes the two views, that Shakespeare was profoundly Roman or profoundly Elizabethan, in 'The Ancient World in Shakespeare: Authenticity or Anachronism'. Along with a survey of the varying opinions, Velz suggests Shakespeare may have equated *Romanitas* with *eloquentia* and that he made a deliberate effort to forge answerable styles for his Roman plays. He pursues other features of possible Roman identity and suggests the need for more study of Shakespeare's reading and use of Virgil (see Jan Kott's essay, discussed last year). It is difficult to know quite what to make of Bruce Erlich's 'Marxian-structuralist' viewpoint in 'Structure, Inversion, and Game in Shakespeare's Classical World': quite apart from a number of minor errors and some highly dubious claims in passing, a lot of the piece could be seen as mere wordplay. Certainly in *Troilus and Cressida* we may agree that the drama's singular effect lies in the clash of literary conventions with their ironic reversals and further that 'parody' is not really the right term for this, but is it then helpful to talk of the play setting forth the 'loss' of texts? The idea that the work is a supreme example of literary self-nullification is useful (and compare G. K. Hunter on this play, below), but Erlich then turns to 'plot' and to dubious procedures again. His main discussion, on *Antony and Cleopatra* and its organisation in terms of two value-systems, each representing an *already*-formed civilisation and each an inversion of the other, is interesting and valuable: the article should be read for this, but not for the way it comes to it. Ann Thompson links two essentially 'Roman' plays in 'Philomel in "Titus Andronicus" and "Cymbeline"', beginning from a link of 'impossible' moments in the two: Imogen's lament over Cloten's headless trunk and Marcus' lament over Lavinia's mutilations. Thompson explores the uses of the Philomel myth and the concepts of cutting and lopping over against the tree which flourishes and then examines the two scenes in some detail. The use of classical allusion seems narrative rather than dramatic, the consequent slowing-down emphasising in one case the inaction of Marcus in the face of horrors, in the other an inner collapse and loss of identity that Imogen and Posthumus both suffer.

Only one general work on the late Romances is to hand, a collection edited by Carol McGinnis Kay and Henry E. Jacobs[42]. A number of the contributors turn their attention to masque elements, and *Pericles* is notably neglected in a collection not so varied as one might hope. The editors open by stating what seems a widespread critical belief in the United States, that until recently only *The Tempest* of the Romances 'had received any great measure of critical or dramatic attention': if this were so, what is a reasonable volume might appear a remarkable one. Norman Sanders opens with 'An Overview of Critical Approaches to the Romances', which is useful, and is followed by Northrop Frye on 'Romance as Masque', previously published in substance in *Spiritus Mundi* (1976). Frye argues that New Comedy was running down, hampering as a dramatic form, yet the Old Comedy was not available to Shakespeare (Frye suggests a relationship between Old Comedy and *Troilus and Cressida*): romance and masque both represent 'two directions of dramatic experiment away from the established form'. In the discussion that follows he includes both *The Two Noble Kinsmen* and *Henry VIII*. Clifford Leech in 'Masking and Unmasking in the Last Plays' pursues the masque (and anti-masque) as well as the mask. He looks at the use of anti-masque elements in Jacobean drama and finds Shakespeare beginning to use them in *Timon*. Leech finds something uncomfortable in what Shakespeare is doing in the father–daughter relations of the last plays and the unmasking at the end of the plays leads him to speculate on what follows the dawn they promise Howard Felperin's 'Romance and Romanticism: Some Reflections on *The Tempest* and *Heart of Darkness*, or When is Romance No Longer Romance?' includes a challenge to Frye's historical process: for him the serenity and completeness of the Renaissance is a myth, *The Tempest* raising questions about Prospero and his behaviour. In 'Fathers and Daughters in Shakespeare's Romances', Cyrus Hoy sees Lear and Cordelia standing behind all the father–daughter relationships of the Romances. This is hardly original, but he goes on more interestingly to survey the plays up to *King Lear* and beyond, suggesting that Shakespeare 'is engaged in a quest to free the imagination from all the shrill mistress–wife–mother figures who have inhabited the late tragedies'. He then focuses on Prospero and Miranda. Quite usefully suggestive is Joan Hartwig in 'Cloten, Autolycus and Caliban: Bearers of Parodic Burdens', who rightly says that parody emphasises similarity as well as contrast and explores the structural relationship between these characters and their plays. She is perceptive on the likenesses in character and development between Posthumus and Cloten: it relates usefully to Harry Zuger's article on Posthumus (*YW* 57. 131). Joan Warchol Rossi argues for the primacy of Holinshed as the source of Shakespeare's inspiration in '*Cymbeline*'s Debt to Holinshed: The Richness of III.i'. Charles Frey suggests in 'Tragic Structure in *The Winter's Tale*: The Affective Dimension' that we need to explore more fully 'how the romances portray man's mistrust and mistreatment of women and with what dramatic impact', and shows this usefully, but David M. Bergeron in 'The Restoration of Hermione in *The Winter's Tale*' goes for a version of

[42] *Shakespeare's Romances Reconsidered*, ed. by Carol McGinnis Kay and Henry E. Jacobs. Lincoln, Neb. and London: Nebraska U.P. pp. ix + 224. £9.10.

the play that had no revived Hermione and finds the spur to revision in a 1611 Lord Mayor's show by Anthony Munday. The link has some interest, but the evidence cited from Forman hardly stands up and the relation between Munday's scene and (say) Greene's *James IV* would seem as likely as any. Charles R. Forker compares Shakespeare near the beginning and end of his career in 'Immediacy and Remoteness in *The Taming of the Shrew* and *The Tempest*', seeing both works as experimental, concluding that 'as Shakespeare approached the end of his highly experimental and successful career as an illusionist, he came finally to prefer simplicity before Heaven to virtuosity before man'. In a suggestive essay, worth pursuing even where it doesn't quite hold together, 'Where the Bee Sucks: A Triangular Study of *Dr Faustus, The Alchemist*, and *The Tempest*', David Young looks at their relationship as plays of stage magic particularly in the areas of language, dramatic decorum, and illusion. The volume concludes with a lengthy though select bibliography as an aid to study of the plays.

5. Shakespeare in the Theatre

Very little polemic or obsession with particular theatrical ideas or ideologies emerges in the surveys of performance, either from the writers or the productions. Roger Warren saw 'Comedies and Histories at Two Stratfords, 1977' (*ShS*), and is able to compare directly *A Midsummer Night's Dream* at Ontario (celebrating its twenty-fifth season) and on the Avon. In the latter John Barton captured an Elizabethan combination of courtly and rural, while in Canada Robin Phillips placed the Queen herself at the centre. Warren expresses relief that both productions took place in designs which bore demonstrable relationship to the style, tone and events of the play. In Barton's production, Patrick Stewart's Oberon was 'virtually naked, muscular and dark-skinned, with long curling black hair', able to range from benevolence to fury to exceptional sensuous tenderness. The presence of the fairies counteracted Theseus' scepticism and at the end the court lay down to sleep for the fairies' blessing. At Ontario, the force of Maggie Smith's Titania was felt, the part doubled with Hippolyta, her costume as Elizabeth making the whole play, as it were, a dream of the Queen's. This interpretation involved some forcing and much elaborate contrivance, while the 'something of great constancy' speech, which might have enforced the director's concept, was gabbled. Ontario's *Richard III*, dominated by Margaret Tyzack's Queen Margaret, was otherwise unremarkable, but *All's Well that Ends Well* was played as wry humour rather than for cheap laughs: Warren notes that the problems Helena faced were complicated by Ontario's stage – the present reviewer would observe that we shall go down as an age that persisted in creating theatres of designs for which no plays had ever been written and in which performance is forced to overcome obstacles: Ontario, Chichester, Sheffield, Manchester's Royal Exchange, the National's Lyttelton, and the Mermaid to name a few. In England, Warren found Trevor Nunn's *As You Like It* bizarre, a baroque scheme, with an added opening prologue and much of the dialogue sung, which backfired in the audience's derision of Hymen. Terry Hands's direction of the first unadapted *Henry VI* at Stratford on Avon worked especially well for Part 1, but there was a problem in the lack of clarification of the central characters. Some rearrangements were made: when Joan was dragged off, Margaret was brought on, but this anticipation of Margaret's diabolical dominance was not fulfilled, Warren declares, though it could be said that he is unfair to Helen Mirren. Both Julian Glover's Warwick and Alan Howard's Henry were praised. In *SQ*, Homer D. Swander gives an account of these plays in this production, and the preparations by Terry Hands and the actors. This same production is considered by G. K. Hunter in 'The Royal Shakespeare Company Plays *Henry VI*' (*RenD*), who particularly compares it with the Hall/Barton 1963–4 version. Where the latter went for plot, the former goes for character. Hunter considers the effect of performing the plays in sequence, but concludes on the production that only the most unselfish ensemble playing can succeed and 'it is hard to see how the demand can be satisfied under the conditions of the modern professional style'.

In 'Shakespeare in Britain' (*SQ*), J. C. Trewin covers more ground for 1977 than in the past, but necessarily in less detail. He found *Henry VI* at Stratford moved splendidly in performance and liked details such as Emrys James's neurotic York, 'undeniably a father for *Richard III*'. *Coriolanus* was praised but *As You Like It* not cared for. Trewin does not share much of the enthusiasm for Trevor Nunn's *Comedy of Errors*, transferred to London: 'this frenzy in modern dress disturbed only those who find more seriousness in the play than is generally acknowledged'.

At Chichester *Julius Caesar* offered actors as Portia and Calpurnia, while at the St George's the acoustic problem had been overcome. The Prospect Company had Derek Jacobi, who restored the princeliness to Hamlet, and a highly praised *Antony and Cleopatra*. D. J. Palmer reviews '*Macbeth* at the National Theatre, 1978' and '*The Tempest* at Stratford, 1978' (both *CQ*), finding the Hecate episodes the heart of the former and a use of spectacle based on the text; the latter, on an island that was test and trial rather than paradise, stressed Propsero's limitations. The BBC's Shakespeare cycle produced two brief introductions: Germaine Greer on 'Juliet's Wedding' and Brigid Brophy on 'As You Like Shakespeare' (both *Listener*).

The reviews in *SQ* are extended in number. A useful survey by Berners A. W. Jackson considers 'The Shakespeare Festival: Stratford, Ontario, 1953–1977', from forty-two performances of two plays to ten plays, six by Shakespeare, over twenty-two weeks in 1977. He includes a long survey of directors, changes and so on. The 1977 Ontario season is reviewed by Ralph Berry: *A Midsummer Night's Dream* was 'visually stunning, intellectually null, and theatrically superb', while Brian Bedford was praised for finding ways other than Olivier's to play Richard III. Herbert S. Weil at Monmouth was stimulated by audiences, many of whom did not know the plays and so experienced them freshly: *Measure for Measure* included dumbshows and a rejection of Mariana by Angelo. Elsewhere Jack Jorgens and Jan Levic found *I Henry IV* with Richard II's funeral as dramatic prologue; while a revival of Orson Welles' 1936 voodoo *Macbeth* disappointed Roger Hapgood.

Reports of Boston, New Jersey, Washington (where in *As You Like It* the celebration of the killing of the deer was produced as an intensely erotic dream of Rosalind) and so around and across America in eleven more accounts. Dennis Bartholomeusz and Alan Brissenden report from Australia and there are reports from Tokyo, Tel Aviv, Hungary, Belgium, Basel, West Germany and Oslo. Also in *SQ*, J. R. Mulryne in '*Coriolanus* at Stratford-Upon-Avon: Three Actors' Remarks' interviews Coriolanus, Aufidius, and a Tribune. S. Schoenbaum gives a survey of the Royal Shakespeare Company in 'Seeing Shakespeare Plain' (*TLS*).

An Italian 1972 production is the concern of Stephen de Lannoy's '*Le Roi Lear* de Shakespeare dans une mise en scène de Giorgio Strehler' (*Voies de la création théâtrale*), illustrated by many photographs and complemented in the same journal by Jean Jacquot's '*Le Roi Lear*: Lecture d'une mise en scène et relecture de l'œuvre'. The highly acclaimed *Macbeth* at Stratford's Other Place in 1976 is considered in detail by Hersh Zeifman (*ThRI*), while the Cyprus *Measure for Measure* is looked at by Nicos Shiafkalis and by Heinz-Uwe Haus (both *SJW*).

East German productions are surveyed by Armin-Gerd Kuckhoff (*SJW*, 1976) who surveys eight different plays, the photographs including one from a puppet film of *The Winter's Tale*. From West Germany Christian Jauslin (*SJH*, 1977) reports on twenty different plays, of which *A Midsummer Night's Dream* was the most popular, while under *Romeo and Juliet* are listed not only a musical by Kishon and Prokofiev's ballet, but also (*pace* the Lloyd Evanses) Bellini's unconnected *I Capuletti ed i Montecchi*.

Shakespeare on the Soviet stage in the 1970s is surveyed by Alexej V. Bartoschewitsch (*SJW*), while Werner Habicht has a wide ranging consideration of specific literary and theatrical approaches to Shakespeare (*Anglia*). A welcome extension of the Folger Library's resources, reported in *SQ*, is the archive of Shakespeare on Film established in 1975.

J. C. Trewin's *Going to Shakespeare*[43] is presented as a spectator's discursive notebook and is intended to suggest to relative newcomers to the plays some of the things to watch and listen for: from a lifetime of watching Shakespeare, Trewin seeks to illuminate the shape of a play, particular lines or speeches, to draw attention to cuts and recent or traditional business. The plays are taken in the Riverside edition's chronological order: each has something of its stage history, variously emphasised, details of the plot and some commentary upon characters. The Duke in *Measure for Measure* is declared an equivocal person (probably more useful to a newcomer than the 'grace divine' concept) and Trewin mentions Tyrone Guthrie's production, where the Duke revealed his identity to the Provost by his stigmata, while the dramatic highlight of Isabella's plea for mercy is supported by Peter Brook's asking Barbara Jefford to remain silent as long as the audience would stand it: she varied between 35 and 120 seconds. Trewin also notes the shifts in the handling of the Duke's marriage proposal. These are quite useful, perhaps all the stimulus the intelligent play-goer will need to read over before setting out. There are no pictures.

Charles Marowitz has gone to Shakespeare and variously come back with spoils. His book, *The Act of Being*[44], is not primarily about his

[43] *Going to Shakespeare*, by J. C. Trewin. George Allen & Unwin. pp. 288. £6.95.
[44] *The Act of Being*, by Charles Marowitz. Secker & Warburg. pp. x + 196. £6.50.

Shakespeare versions, but about his method, its development ('No one ever taught me how to act or direct. Everything in this book is the result of an eclecticism') and its application. But many examples are taken from his Shakespeare experience (*Hamlet* when talking about subtext; Iago as puritan; rehearsing *Measure for Measure*), and Appendix 4 is 'An *Othello* Casebook'. Another kind of method is E. S. Brubaker's concern in *Shakespeare Aloud*[45]. The polemical tone of the opening should not conceal the basically sound (if elementary) discussion of stress patterns in Shakespeare's verse and the approach to its realisation on stage. Disagreement would arise over some of Brubaker's examples, but much more limiting is a failure to go on to any consideration of larger units of speech or of the rhetoric of Shakespeare's drama, while surely it is strange to find the assumption that stress in modern speech is standard, especially within American English. Still, the book will do no harm and might even prompt a proper study of Shakespeare's prosody.

Two theatrical autobiographies deserve some attention. It is perhaps unfair to John Fraser to call *The Bard in the Bush*[46] 'autobiography': it is meant to be an entertaining account of touring two-handed Shakespeare extracts (*The Merchant of Venice* and *Macbeth*) for the British Council in Africa. It would be better than it is if Fraser had eschewed his facetious tone, but he obviously enjoyed himself and the responses are interesting: no giggles from the schoolchildren at 'unsex me here' or at references to breasts even when manipulated by Lady Macbeth, but great shrieks at Macbeth and his lady embracing, a 'public display of affection between the sexes' being 'both weak and highly indecorous'. Shylock was laughed at, there being no sympathy for the underdog. A much better book and infinitely more important in terms of this chapter is Ben Iden Payne's *A Life in a Wooden O*[47]. First, this is splendidly entertaining. It is made up of Payne's recollections, of part of his account of his Elizabeth productions, and of excerpts from a series of radio talks, though apart from truncations and omissions (very little about his private life) the book does not show signs of editorial cobbling. Second, it is full of fascinating information about touring at the turn of the century, about Benson's company (Payne admired Benson highly), about the Abbey Theatre, where Payne was at the *Playboy* première and was director, the Horniman Theatre in Manchester, and the development of Shakespeare production at the Carnegie Tech under the initial impulse of William Poel. It is the work of an intelligent and lively mind, who took *his* farewell of the stage with a production of *The Tempest* in 1968 at the age of 87 – Payne died in 1976. It is deeply human, constantly amusing, and intriguingly informative. Yeats appears backstage looking like a priest; Edward VII's guttural speech is tinged with a German accent; Miss Horniman gives Payne free rein; Payne has Poel produce *Measure for Measure*, is never convinced by the 'tones', and is surprised by Poel's puritanism in cutting. Deserves to be bought and read.

[45] *Shakespeare Aloud: A Guide to his Verse on Stage*, by E. S. Brubaker. Lancaster, Penn.: E. S. Brubaker (1976). pp. 65. $2.25.

[46] *The Bard in the Bush*, by John Fraser. Hart-Davis, Macgibbon. pp. 176. £5.95.

[47] *A Life in a Wooden O: Memoirs of the Theatre*, by Ben Iden Payne. New Haven, Conn. and London: Yale U.P. (1977). pp. xvii + 205. £10.80.

Three papers in *The Elizabethan Theatre: VI*[48] consider aspects of theatres. Richard Hosley offers the first part of 'A Reconstruction of the Fortune Playhouse' (Part II will appear in Vol. VII) in which he notes previous reconstructions, adduces new details and takes issue with other reconstructions. In 'The Presentation of Plays at Second Paul's: The Early Phase (1599–1602)', Reavley Gair considers the staging of Marston's plays, the consequent nature of the stage, and suggests the playhouse's exact site. M. C. Bradbrook's aim is an understanding of the plays by relating the archaeological and the thematic literary approaches by considering the audience structure. 'Shakespeare and the Multiple Theatres of Jacobean London' interestingly finds perverted masque elements in *Macbeth* and *King Lear*, and takes a vigorous swipe at both Glynne Wickham and Frances Yates on the Romances, but doesn't seem to achieve what Bradbrook hoped. Graham Parry has found 'A New View of Bankside' (*ShS*), a sketch by Hollar for the Long View, which emphasises the circular shape of the Globe and its double gable. David George's 'Another Elizabethan Stage' (*TN*) interprets a diagram in a Quarto of *II Henry IV* as a stage outline and grouping: he suggests its orientation and meaning, then not entirely convincingly suggests that it possibly represents the Globe.

Arthur H. Scouten's '*Julius Caesar* and Restoration Shakespeare' (*SQ*) looks at the evidence for the play's popularity and performance in the period, while in 'More Restoration Manuscript Casts and Dates and a New Restoration Promptbook' (*TN*), Edward A. Langhams includes a cast list, probably of 1691, for *The Merry Wives*. An interesting piece, 'The Popularity of Shakespeare's Plays, 1720–21 through 1732–33' (*SQ*), by Paul Sawyer, uses not only the number of performances but also receipts and suggests some evidence of a preference for adapted Shakespeare, while Thomas Bauman considers another kind of popularity in 'Opera Versus Drama: *Romeo and Juliet* in Eighteenth-Century Germany' (*ECS*). The play was probably known through Garrick's version, and Weisse's version, which preserved the unities, influenced the librettist of Benda's opera. Julia Curtis has an amusing sidelight in 'Tate Wilkinson's Costume Notebook' (*TN*), for the Theatre Royal, York 1789–94, which includes Hamlet's 'Black Velvet sute' (Osric was to wear 'his own Close') and a Shylock Dress. 'Canadian Evaluations of Edmund Kean' (*TN*) by Yashdip Singh Bains and Norma Jenckes includes comments on his playing in five Shakespeare plays. A nineteenth-century provincial manager is the subject of Russell Jackson's 'Shakespeare in Liverpool: Edward Saker's Revivals 1876–81' (*TN*). Saker presented Shakespeare spectaculars, including *The Winter's Tale*, apparently an elaboration of Charles Kean's 1856 version, in which when Leontes defied the oracle, the stage darkened and a thunderbolt glanced across towards the dais.

Stanley Wells's talk on 'The Other Shakespeare' (*Listener*) considers burlesque; it is an adjunct to his presentation of the burlesques themselves, two more volumes of which have appeared[49]. As Wells points out, contem-

[48] *The Elizabethan Theatre: VI*, ed. by G. R. Hibbard. London and Basingstoke: Macmillan. pp. xiii + 160.

[49] *Nineteenth-Century Shakespeare Burlesque*, ed. by Stanley Wells. Diploma Press. Vol. IV *The Fourth Phase: F. C. Burnand, W. S. Gilbert and others (1860–1882)*. pp. xxv + 321; Vol. V *American Shakespeare Travesties (1852–1888)*. pp. xiv + 303.

porary allusion abounds (to Fechter, for instance) and there is a still greater slackening in these later examples between the burlesques and their original: the meanness of so much burlesque is occasionally avoided therefore and a passage Wells points to, F. C. Burnand's parody of 'The barge she sat in', is indeed pleasing, partaking more of imitation than burlesque proper.

Three non-English approaches are considered by Michel Grivelet in 'Copeau, Shakespeare, et le Spectateur' (*EA*); by Christa Neubert-Herwig and Lily Leder on Benno Besson's experiments with Shakespeare (*SJW*); and by A. James Arnold in 'Césaire and Shakespeare: Two Tempests' (*CompL*), an adaptation for a negro theatre, after Shakespeare, by a Martinican playwright: comparison of the two plays 'leads necessarily to considerations of theater as a critical reflection on the value system of western humanism'

Clive Barker is not a Marxist and has produced only two Shakespeare plays, so one feels his limitations in 'Marxist Interpretations of Shakespeare: A Director's Comment' (*SJW*), but on his experience with *Much Ado about Nothing* he has interesting points to make. Useful to round off this section is Bernard Beckerman's 'Explorations in Shakespeare's Drama' (*SQ*), a survey that begins from the evidence of an important change in Shakespeare studies, with the centrality of analysis through performance, and sees the need to take stock. He considers what has emerged by way of writers and directors and how the non-verbal side of Shakespeare has come to be emphasised. This kind of assessment is useful even if only as an interim report and the chance to take stock of the kind of activities with which this section (itself a comparatively new feature of this chapter) is concerned.

6. Individual Plays

All's Well That Ends Well

In 'Painter's "Ermino Grimaldi" and Shakespeare's "All's Well That Ends Well"' (*N&Q*), John Edward Price argues that Shakespeare's use of 'Ermino Grimaldi' enforces his use of Painter's version: Painter's use of the word 'courtier', not in the Italian and only once in the French, enforced Shakespeare's stress on courtiership.

Antony and Cleopatra

Robert P. Kalmey explores interestingly the implied value of the characters in 'Shakespeare's Octavius and Elizabethan Roman History' (*SEL*), starting from the persistent commonplace in modern criticism that sees Octavius in the role of ideal prince, the moral superior of the dissolute Antony, despite Cleopatra's final scathing comment on him as 'ass,/ Unpolicied'. Octavius, Kalmey suggests, had two aspects for the Elizabethans: as crowned Emperor he was example of the ideal prince, but before this the very same Elizabethan histories of Rome characterise him as a vicious tyrant who foments civil war. It may not follow that Cleopatra holds 'his bloody civil war victories in abhorrent contempt', but the piece is useful claim for Egypt and the lovers. Although the theme has been explored before, John Coates in '"The Choice of Hercules" in *Antony and*

Cleopatra' (*ShS*) claims there is a richer and more complex meaning than earlier critics (he cites Kermode in *Renaissance Essays*) have seen. Hercules in some accounts has eloquence and has the role of the complete man: the music under the stage may suggest Hercules' descent into his own nature to bridle his impulses. Coates sees Antony beginning a progress towards self-purification and self-control, so allowing the poetry of Acts IV and V to be accepted as 'the real expression of something real'. If not fully convincing, attempts to release this play from the moralists are welcome. Jean Fuzier writes on the play's rejection of the expected pattern of tragedy in '*Antony and Cleopatra's* Three-Stage Tragic Structure: A Study in Development' (*CahiersE*): although he seems unaware of Anne Barton's richly suggestive piece (*YW* 55.214), he interestingly explores how the play stands as the rewarding outcome of a series of less conclusive if interesting experiments in tragic structure. He considers *Pyramus and Thisbe* and *Romeo and Juliet* and points to experiments in *Hamlet, Othello,* and *Macbeth* (though one may feel these very examples also point to the uniqueness of this play). The short-time data are looked at by J. M. Maguin's 'A Note on Shakespeare's Handling of Time and Space Data in *Antony and Cleopatra*' (*CahiersE*) to see how the substitution of a short-time dramatic narrative for an impossible and undramatic long-time one is effected. Not seen was an issue of *Signal* devoted to a series of essays on the play.

As You Like It

Judy Z. Kronenfeld, following up her piece on 'The Pastoral Cult of Solitude' two years ago (*YW* 57.130), with which this somewhat overlaps, writes in *SQ* on 'Social Rank and the Pastoral Ideals of *As You Like It*'; Ms Kronenfeld, apparently a social anthropologist (she has published on Claude Lévi-Strauss), has a manner which is dense, long-winded, and heavily footnoted. *As You Like It*, she concludes, 'is unusual in the context of those pastoral works that involve an actual confrontation between the high and the low'.

Coriolanus

A perceptive and well-written piece by Gail Kern Paster, 'To Starve with Feeding: The City in *Coriolanus*' (*ShakS*), looks at Rome and the Forum in relationship to the play's central character. The framing of the action with images of the community, 'first hungry, then sated and spent', suggests that the tragic outcome has as much to do with the nature of the Forum as that of Coriolanus. Paster goes on to consider what Rome is: for Volumnia and Rome the end of the play is comic, but even if we would not have the community die for Coriolanus the images established mean that 'it survives diminished, starved by such feeding'. Victor Skretkowicz, in '*Coriolanus* (I.iii.44): An Alternative Emendation' takes up the vexed issue of 'Contenning', arguing that it is a stage direction which has become incorporated into the speech. But the evidence he can produce for the practice referred to is nil and his 'parallels' are of no such kind of stage direction.

Hamlet

To deal first with a piece of little significance: in *Hamlet, Prufrock and Language*[50], Zulfikar Ghose writes a mercifully brief monograph described

[50] *Hamlet, Prufrock and Language*, by Zulfikar Ghose. Macmillan. pp. 106. £6.95.

as 'unorthodox. . .it will delight and perplex, amuse and annoy, enlighten and enrage the scholars'. The verbs here are altogether too strong. 'It gives no footnotes, is not influenced by past learning, neglects all the accepted theories about *Hamlet*. And yet it creates a new approach to the play which no future criticism could afford to ignore'. Mr Ghose's achievement is to have written 105 pages of drivel about a few plays he's read and to have persuaded Macmillan's to publish it at £7. Mr. Ghose is the former hockey correspondent of *The Observer*.

The ground of yet another psychoanalytical approach to the play would appear to be quicksand: yet Avi Erlich's *Hamlet's Absent Father*[51] is an important book, successfully challenging Freud and Jones, demonstrating not repressed patricidal impulses but a complex search, partly unconscious, for a strong father. This book really is an advance, and a much needed one, on Ernest Jones' now seriously out-of-date tribute to his master's 'misleading hunch' about Hamlet, as Erlich calls it. A sensible opening chapter defends psychonanlysis as a critical method for this play. Occasionally the reader of later chapters feels he is being called on to swallow perhaps a little too hard, but nothing like as much as in other work in this field. The book is constantly revealing, and is in steady touch with all kinds of recent *Hamlet* criticism as well as the texts themselves, so that one is always in the position of being close to a living play rather than either a case-history or a theoretical construction. This is a book from a younger academic which gives one confidence that this particular discipline has an honourable future.

A helpful article in *SEL*, Joseph Westlund's 'Ambivalence in The Player's Speech in *Hamlet*' shows clearly how the strategem of the Player's speech, the recital of which seems so perfectly suited for stirring Hamlet to vengeful action, works instead to reinforce his passion. In *SQ*, Jason P. Rosenblatt writes on 'Aspects of the Incest problem in *Hamlet*', a long analysis of levirate marriage based on Leviticus 18.16. 'If Claudius can "smile and smile", it is partly because blurred distinctions between two superficially similar institutions afford him, if not a true refuge, at least a role to play. . . Conflicting Scriptural passages, together with their commentaries, help to identify Claudius' role as a travesty of the *levir*'s role. They also help to explain the intensity of Hamlet's antipathy toward his "uncle-father and aunt-mother" '. To the old argument about whether the world of *Hamlet* is Catholic or Protestant must now be added the assertion that it is really Jewish; one must record 'not proven'. Also in *SQ*, Karl P. Wentersdorf tackles the problem of identifying 'Ophelia's Long Purples', deciding it was probably the wild arum or cuckoo-pint, noting 'the consistency with which – from the thirteenth to the nineteenth centuries – it has been known, in England and elsewhere, by 'grosser' phallic names': and David Haley examines, brilliantly, the evidence and shows that the elder Hamlet carried a poleaxe, so that Horatio's words can be paraphrased, 'That was the same armour he wore in the judicial combat with Norway; that was just his frown at the instant he struck his studded poleaxe on the ice, in their angry exchange before the fight'.

[51] *Hamlet's Absent Father*, by Avi Erlich. Princeton, N.J.: Princeton U.P. pp. xi + 308. £11.

Henry IV

In 'The old Honour and the New Courtesy: *I Henry IV*', (*ShS*), G. M. Pinciss sets out to analyse the relation of the actions of Hotspur and honour, and Hal and courtesy, 'according to the two most influential Elizabethan handbooks on courtly manners', i.e. Castiglione and Elyot. He neatly underlines what most readers of the play understand, that Hotspur is graceless and deficient, his medieval values already obsolete. Hal, by contrast, embodies the new Renaissance virtues summed up in the word 'courtesy'. R. B. Bennett in *CahiersE* suggests that in 'the tavern scene' (i.e. *I Henry IV* II.iv) a genuine crisis occurs for Hal 'not in immoral inclination but rather in irresponsible timing' at the rejection of Bracy, with potentially disastrous consequences. This excellent essay casts light on many parts of this play. In *SQ* Warren J. Macisaac looks very briefly at names in the *Henry IV* plays.

Henry V

G. P. Jones, in '*Henry V*: The Chorus and the Audience' (*ShS*) starts from an account of the supposed standard interpretation of the Chorus' role which is surprisingly crude. Jones, one feels, has seen too few good performances (Emrys James' Chorus for a recent RSC production by Terry Hands gave the lie to everything that underlies Jones' points of difficulty). Similarly, he is provincial and old-fashioned in his authorities, quoting only two more recently than 1956, both making distinctly obvious points. Jones argues that the Chorus, occurring only in the Folio text, is 'the mechanism for adapting the material to a court performance'. This is ingenious, but fails to tackle all the incidental problems: postulating adaptation for 'more cramped conditions than usual', should he not raise the problem of the lack of adaptation of the huge cast-list? Does not evidence from elsewhere in Shakespeare suggest that 'a more sophisticated and cultured audience' would be *less* tolerant, in fact? His unconvincing speculations about dating do little to help the main argument about the poetry. Jones says that his hypothesis that the 1605 performance was in the Royal Cockpit is 'plausible, fits all the known facts, and explains those facts better than alternative theories'. His self-congratulation is sadly vitiated by the fact that modern performers do not find those problems from which he begins.

Gareth Lloyd Evans has adapted an interesting performance available on 60 minutes of cassette tape[52].

Henry VIII

John D. Cox on '*Henry VIII* and the Masque' (*ELH*) declares that we lack an explanation for Shakespeare's artistic choice of royal spectacle and pageantry in his last play and after interesting discussion concludes that its singular dramaturgy 'can be seen as an experiment in adapting the principles of the court masque to the dramatic tradition of the public theaters'.

Julius Caesar

From the United States Military Academy, West Point, comes 'Patrick

[52] *Henry V*, adapted by Gareth Lloyd Evans (*The Times Shakespeare*) London: Authortapes and Tercrest Ltd. 1976.

Henry's "Liberty or Death" Speech and Cassius's Speech in Shakespeare's *Julius Caesar*' (*The Virginia Magazine of History and Biography*), a short but elaborate claim that the final few words of Patrick Henry's speech in Second Virginia Convention, 23 March 1775, echoed Cassius at *Julius Caesar* I.ii.93–7.

King John

Eugene M. Waith, in 'King John and the Drama of History' (*SQ*) explores accounts of former productions, and criticism, and concludes 'it may be that the tendency to look first for a pattern of ideas has kept us from understanding the power that critics once found in scene after scene' because, going for historical settings and costumes, they allowed history to be 'instrumental in Shakespeare's creation of drama'. In *ShakS*, Eamon Grennan writes 'Shakespeare's Satirical History: A Reading of *King John*', a ponderous commentary on the play seeing it as 'a caustic epilogue to his early histories. . .' leading him 'away from the idea of history as *historia* to a larger, more humanly various, and undestructible concept of history as, in Tolstoy's phrase, "the life of peoples and of humanity" '.

King Lear

A pleasingly subtle and well-written essay by John J. McLaughlin, 'The Dynamics of Power in *King Lear*: An Adlerian Interpretation' (*SQ*), approaches the play in psychological terms, without making them a strait-jacket or losing sight of the drama: it shows, as Alan Sinfield did (*YW* 56.185), that a psychological approach can be fruitful, especially if it is not Freudian. Adler, McLaughlin points out, sees a striving for superiority as the single motivating force behind all human behaviour; people create life-plans based on their goals and then pattern their lives on those plans as though they were objectively true. Cordelia's response is that of the youngest child who, not bearing to be frustrated, not only refuses to compete but chooses to be obstinate, while her sisters are explicable in terms of 'masculine protest'. Lear, like his 'kind' daughters, has a distorted life-plan, but Goneril, Regan, and Edmund die victims of their neuroses, whereas Lear dies cured. One does not have to accept every point to find this a rewarding piece.

Rewarding in a different kind of way is Kathleen Wales's 'An Aspect of Shakespeare's Dynamic Language: A Note on the Interpretation of *King Lear* III.vii.113: "He Childed as I Fathered!" ' (*ES*), which focuses on a detail of language to consider the dynamic nature of Shakespeare's language and to suggest that this in turn reflects his worldview, as well as reminding us that much exploration remains to be done in this field. Wales looks at the possible meanings of the group and suggests that reference to the theme of reversal of kinship supports a linguistically dynamic interpretation. Peter Milward takes up again ' "Nature" in Hooker and *King Lear*' (*ShStud*), though he says it is not just repetition of Danby and Whitaker, since neither 'cared to develop a precise correlation between Hooker's idea of nature and that of Shakespeare in *King Lear*'. He argues that in rewriting *King Leir*, Shakespeare rewrote a Puritan play, 'with an emphasis on human nature in its fallen condition prior to its resurrection in Christ', as a 'Catholic' play. Saad El-Gabalawy suggests in 'Christian Communism in

Utopia, King Lear, and *Comus*' (*UTQ*) that the theme of social justice through distribution is not a chance impulse of Shakespeare's, linking it to More's and Milton's work. More about Hazlitt than Shakespeare is W. P. Albrecht's 'Hazlitt, Passion, and *King Lear*' (*SEL*), which is concerned to see how Hazlitt defines the role of passion in tragedy and especially in *King Lear*: the reader or viewer acquires both knowledge and power by confronting a painful world which may 'bring the whole mind to bear on a process of moral re-ordering'.

The suggestion of Katherine Duncan-Jones in 'Kent, Caius, and Lear's Swordmanship' (*N&Q*) that Caius was not Kent's alias but rather a servant of Lear's former days by whom Kent seeks to prompt his master to remember the past, is far-fetched, especially in the dramatic context (some of Weimann's suggestions about the folk tradition of non-pertinent remarks in his book reviewed above may be more apropos). Two notes pick up from notes mentioned last year: George Walton Williams's 'Second Thoughts on Lear's "Good Block" ' (*SQ*) challenges 'block' = 'scheme or stratagem' and would make it Lear's crown of flowers; while K. J. Wilson's 'Shakespeare's "Tameness of a Wolf" ' (*N&Q*) adds another possibility by seeing 'a boy's love' linked to the depiction of the young man of the Sonnets. In the same journal, Michael Cameron Andrews finds sexual innuendo in the Fool's phrase ' "And I'll Go to Bed at Noon" ', backing it up from contemporary examples and from the play. Gordon N. Ross strains after an olfactory pun in Gloucester's 'Do you smell a fault' (*Expl*), hearing 'fault' as 'fart'.

Seeking to recover the play's power to make us suffer, Edward Pechter 'On the Blinding of Gloucester' (*ELH*) mainly poses a series of questions. Horst Oppel in 'The Phenomenon of Acceleration in *King Lear*' (*AJES*), suggests that the play's structure of time is of a special nature: he begins with earlier observations on the speed of events within the play and relates this to the acceleration of Christian views of history, which from earliest time saw the world hastening towards the Apocalypse; these ideas were revived in Protestant thinking. *King Lear* takes up the theme of acceleration and thereby touches upon concepts within Protestant theological history, but the play radically reverses all Christian concepts related to the 'promised end'. Oppel goes on to interpret this parallelism as evidence of the play's anti-Christian meaning: and concludes suggestively that in *King Lear* 'neither world history nor the individual existence of man is propelled toward the salvation which Christ announced'.

Horst Oppel, in *Die Vorgeschichte zu King Lear im Lichte moderner Adaptationen*[53], hopes to show what illumination is afforded to the play by looking at the earlier versions of the story before studying modern adaptations, including those by W. T. Moncrieff, Gordon Bottomley, and Edward Bond, as well as Eugene O'Neill's *Desire Under the Elms*. He considers Lear from political and familial aspects, before discussing children and fools, and the Gloucester-plot.

Love's Labour's Lost

John Kerrigan, in *EIC*, suggests in 'Love's Labour's Lost and the Circling Seasons' that 'it is Shakespeare's implication of each season in its opposite

[53] *Die Vorgeschichte zu King Lear im Lichte moderner Adaptationen*, von Horst Oppel. Wiesbaden: Franz Steiner Verlag. pp. 64.

that makes one question John Wilders's claim that the play ends with "unresolved and irreconcilable opposites" ' – a conclusion that goes back, of course, far beyond Wilders. Kerrigan builds a somewhat fantastic commentary on the circling of the seasons, placing great and trendy-donnish importance on Jaquenetta's baby, 'the result of the fun at the lodge', which 'will be there, under the owls and cuckoos, when a twelvemonth and a day. . .has passed'.

Macbeth

Marvin Rosenberg has made the major contribution on the play this year[54], not least in terms of length: the book might be yet more effective if it were a third or a half shorter, not least by controlling the metaphorical convolutions of the style. Rosenberg's earlier books on *Othello* and *King Lear* are well-known: one on *Hamlet* is now in active preparation. The method adopted is similar to that of the earlier works: Rosenberg moves through the play, examining it closely in dramatic terms, drawing upon evidence from performances in the past and performances especially related to this study, where the use of 'innocent' audiences was invaluable to get reactions from those who did not know what was coming next. On the appearance of Banquo's ghost, for example, Rosenberg considers the dramatic meaning and effect (should the audience see the ghost first and observe Macbeth's reactions, as the Folio stage-direction indicates: or be equally astonished as Macbeth?) before considering the way the appearance is achieved and the reaction of various actors (Garrick, Salvini, Irving). Rosenberg's industry and achievement are admirable, and though it is perhaps more useful as a stimulus on particular scenes or moments than as an overview, the account is full of matter.

Richard Horwich's 'Integrity in *Macbeth*: The Search for the "Single State of Man" ' (*SQ*) begins from the apparent oddity of Macbeth having two antagonists, in Malcolm and Macduff, and finds a dramatic explanation in integrity, a central pre-occupation of the play, tracing this quality through. In 'Macbeth as Player King: The Banquet Scene as Frustrated Play within the Play' (*SJW*), Robert F. Willson suggests, building from Emrys Jones's *Scenic Form in Shakespeare*, that though not a play within a play as 'The Mousetrap' is in *Hamlet*, the supper scene deserves closer study as a self-contained unit, related to but distinct in tone from what precedes and follows it. He relates it to illusion and the destruction of Macbeth. Ann Pasternak Slater swells a note into an essay in 'Macbeth and the Terrors of the Night' (*EIC*), offering two hitherto unnoticed sources in Nashe and Lavater, which are matters of tone rather than just particular parallels. A note which is content to be a note, Joan Heiges Blythe's ' "Men Must Not Walk Too Late" ' (*N&Q*) finds that in a world of necessary verbal ambiguities, Lennox hints at the need for men to be vigilant and armed. The accepted glosses upon 'gallowglasses' are challenged by Joseph E. Egan's ' "Of Kernes and Gallowglasses": An Error in *Macbeth*' (*MLN*), which also points out they are an anachronism. A cassette[55] offers an introduction and dramatic excerpts from the play. Gareth Lloyd Evans

[54] *The Mask of Macbeth*, by Marvin Rosenberg. Berkeley, Calif. and London: California U.P. pp. xiv + 802. £17.50.

[55] *Macbeth*, adapted by Gareth Lloyd Evans (*The Times Shakespeare*). London: Authortapes and Tercrest Ltd. 1976.

presents it as a Jacobean thriller and within the compass of the form this is a vivid introduction to the play, whether for newcomers to Shakespeare or for schools. Z. A. Usmani's 'The Drama of Value in *Macbeth*' (*AJES*) looks at the play's polarities and the final restoration in Malcolm of the 'regenerative, wholesome and fair value-life'.

Measure for Measure

A sprightly argument for the dramatic experience and integrity of the play, which can be usefully associated with Richard Levin's essays over the past decade, is Harriett Hawkins's '"The Devil's Party": Virtues and Vices in *Measure for Measure*' (*ShS*), which takes issue with Arthur C. Kirsch's 1975 essay in the same journal. Hawkins argues that despite Kirsch's arguments, the fact remains that any number of (quite rightly) unanswered questions and unsolved problems seem to have been built into the text by Shakespeare himself; and furthermore that these problems and questions are immeasurably more interesting than solutions propounded by modern scholars. After mentioning several problems not soluble by scholarly appeals to contemporary orthodoxies, Hawkins concentrates upon Isabella's erotic imagery and Angelo's sadism. Her conclusions about approaches to the play seem shapely, flexible and capable of recognising complexity.

Another investigation of the play's problems, also very worthwhile, is Christopher Palmer's 'Selfishness in *Measure for Measure*' (*EIC*), which takes issue over the assumption that the play is 'moral' (he uses Nosworthy's New Penguin edition as a convenient representative of the view) and asks whether there is an increase in self-knowledge and a moral transformation involving subjection or transcendence of the individual and its false values and whether the play will soothe or improve us if this is true? He finds that the leading characters are reluctant to learn what experience offers to teach them, while the minor ones, each demanding a different response and comprehension from us, cannot be harmonised and it is futile to attempt to do so. It is not necessary to agree with or to find outstandingly original everything Palmer says for this to be a pertinent piece.

The proceedings of a conference on the play are given, mostly in German, in *SJH*: Raimund Borgmeier spoke on the necessity, possibility and limits of historical interpretation; Herbert Grabes on the nature of the characters and the changing sense of history; Hermann Fischer on comparative dramatic structure between the play and the adaptations of Davenant and Gildon; Jan Kott on the structure of interchangeability; while in an English-language contribution T. S. Dorsch considered '*Measure for Measure* and its Contemporary Audience'. Dorsch asks whether the original audience would have been puzzled by the things that perplex us. He finds it more straightforward, more clearly a comedy for the first audience, than modern reactions allow, challenging the idea of the Duke's lack of control and questioning that Isabella has yet reached the formal state of 'novice'.

Ralph Berry finds, in 'Language and Structure in *Measure for Measure*' (*UTQ*), an opposition between the underworld and overworld, between which is interposed the iron grid of the law. He pursues this in terms of language, finding that it tends to crystallise into a lower (essentially, a sexual) implication, as well as into a higher sense in which it is overtly employed. Gary Taylor, in '*Measure for Measure*, IV.ii.41–46' (*SQ*) challenges the editorial removal of 'Clown' (i.e. Pompey) from the expansion of Abhorson's proof that his profession is a mystery.

The Merchant of Venice

Joan Ozark Holmer writes in *ShakS* 'Loving Wisely and the Casket Test: Symbolic and Structural Unity in *The Merchant of Venice*', a heavy commentary on the play concluding 'Through Shakespeare's masterful juxtaposition of unwise calculations for gain with more wise hazards for love the casket and flesh-bond plots are more symbolically and structurally interrelated than is generally suggested'. Monica J. Hamill, in *SEL*, suggests in 'Poetry, Law and the Pursuit of Perfection: Portia's Role in *The Merchant of Venice*' that Portia has a special place as 'The Renaissance assumed an intimate relationship between poetry and law: the ancient poets, the founders of civilised society, were praised as the first legislators among men. . .'. This is a valuable piece, slightly over-positive about Antonio.

A good up-to-date, full-length, study of this play has been needed for a long time. Lawrence Danson, in *The Harmonies of The Merchant of Venice*[56], provides it, though the result is thorough and comprehensive rather than original. It is a sound, sensible book, a little plodding in places, held together, appropriately, by the idea of harmony, with the circle seen as the most varied figure. Danson follows the well-known dualities, seeing all of them resolved in 'a ring of harmony'.

The Merry Wives of Windsor

Robert F. Fleissner, in a *ShakS* piece called 'The Malleable Knight and the Unfettered Friar: The Merry Wives of Windsor and Boccaccio' says 'so far no-one has taken Boccaccio, specifically his marvellous Story of Friar Alberto and the Angel Gabriel, as a principal source' for this play. One's initial retort is that there could be very good reason for this strange neglect, and one's final judgement confirms the first reaction. This is a ludicrous piece with five pages of notes in small print: Fleissner has been too busy reading and writing to stop to think.

A Midsummer Night's Dream

Something is going very wrong with the criticism of this play. The best piece this year is in fact mainly about *The Tempest*. G. R. Hibbard, in *ShS*, contributes 'Adumbrations of *The Tempest* in *A Midsummer Night's Dream*', and is especially acute on the similarities of the magic, which 'effects transformation' between dream and waking consciousness, seeing the connection in Shakespearean imagination between 'play (tale), player (shadow) and life (dream)'. Then, scarcely original in its main idea, A. A. Ansari's 'Shakespeare's Allegory of Love' (*AJES*) considers the play as an exploration of the various manifestations of the irrationality of love; and in *ShakS* David Ormerod is all too original, for in his 'The Monster in the Labyrinth' he once again goes over the business of the world of Theseus, with massive bibliographical reference, yet apparently in ignorance of a

[56] *The Harmonies of The Merchant of Venice*, by Lawrence Danson. New Haven, Conn. and London: Yale U.P. pp. ix + 202. £10.80.

good deal of recent work, including the seminal essay by Stephen Fender, and instead unnecessarily calling on the quite out-dated Jan Kott. Theseus' 'gravity, dignity and rationality. . .an image of correct sexual hierarchy' is once again linked with the labyrinth and the Minotaur, as if it had not been done before.

Whatever are we to make of *Oberon's Mazed World*[57], described on the title-page as 'A Judicious Young Elizabethan Contemplates *A Midsummer Night's Dream* with a Mind Shaped by the Learning of Christendom Modified by the New Naturalist Philosophy and Excited by the Vision of a Rich, Powerful England', and by T. Walter Herbert, who has been a member of the faculty at the University of Florida for many years? 'This book, he begins, 'offers to endow with a certain thoughtfulness the laughter of people' who look at the play. The thoughtfulness is, very sadly, all about how such a beautifully produced book was ever thought to be a contribution to serious Shakespearean studies. 'We learned a new and merry inflection for our voices' Herbert says on one page, 'when we recognised homely accidents as Robin's pranks, the sparkle of spring flowers as fairies' handiwork'. One of the many marginal sub-headings (in a quaintly authentic imitation of the Heritage of Printing, no doubt) says 'The Babylonian World as a Bugaboo Within the Athenian Dream'. In fact, some chapters are not un-useful, for example that on 'The Animist Frame of Mind', but the whole thing is expressed with such a determined whimsicality, such a phoney ye-olde manner, that it is as embarrassing as the prospectus for some Elizabethanne Heritage Experience in a small mid-West town. That is quite apart from the sort of lunatic inversion of matter suggested by such random sentences as '*The Double Helix* describes a twentieth-century variant on the kind of intellectual profit we in 1595 sought from community in operation. . .Formulations worked with and against one another in his and their busy heads. . .'.

Othello

An excellent piece by Arthur Kirsch, 'The Polarization of Erotic Love in *Othello*' (*MLR*), shows none of the strait-jacketing that Harriet Hawkins objects to in his earlier piece on *Measure for Measure* (see above). Beginning from the dramatic contrast, so marked in the play, and the particular difficulty *Othello* poses for the critics 'because its preoccupations are so unremittingly sexual', Kirsch finds a noble, loving, sexual Othello, of whom both Iago and Desdemona are part, who believes Desdemona cannot be true because he becomes convinced that he himself is unlovable: and so that Desdemona's attraction to him is in itself perverse. The play's first half celebrates his erotic love for her; while in the second, his torment and psychological disintegration can be measured by his loss of her. Brian F. Tyson's parallelism, argued in 'Ben Jonson's Black Comedy: A Connection between *Othello* and *Volpone*' (*SQ*), scarcely adds up to a convincing conclusion. The Venetian settings, the use of intrigue and accident, of jealousy, of a handkerchief even, may link the plays but hardly of themselves suggest a close rapport between Shakespeare and Jonson at the time, *circa* 1605.

[57] *Oberon's Mazed World*, by T. Walter Herbert. Baton Rouge, La. and London: Louisiana State U.P. pp. xix + 200. £8.25.

Allan Shickman raises an interesting possibility in 'A Turning Picture in Shakespeare's *Othello*?' (*N&Q*): he suggest that beside the well-known two-way pictures, which change as they are viewed obliquely from left to right, there were also triple pictures, offering a third scene when viewed head-on; and that Desdemona weeping, obedient, and a devil may, to Othello's mind, be such a show. Three notes on names in the play offer various possibilities: Samuel L. Macey's 'The Naming of the Protagonist in Shakespeare's *Othello*' (*N&Q*) sees Iago's aberrantly Spanish name as linked to popular associations between the Devil and Spain, while St James was the 'moorkiller'.

William C. Woodson's 'Iago's Name and Holinshed and the Lost English Source of *Othello*' (*N&Q*) calls in question Ridley's theory of a lost *Othello* source in English, by pointing to a king Iago or Lago in Holinshed, whose twenty-eight years reign matches Iago's age; Robert F. Fleissner's 'The Moor's Nomenclature' in the same journal links Othello to the Emperor Otho, who stabbed himself, while the same writer considers 'Othello as the Indigent Indian: Old World, New World, or Third World?' (*SJW*) and finds the Moor was a base 'Indian' of India, not the New World.

Pericles

'The Design Wonder in *Pericles*' (*AJES*) is the concern of Maqbool H. Khan and particularly its structural patterning through a relaxed, leisurely drift of the narrative. Like the other Romances, it is a departure from the world of the tragedies and, despite affinities with the earlier comedies, adds wonder to the joy of previous happy resolutions.

The Phoenix and the Turtle

Hermann Anders and Heinz-Uwe Haus investigate the setting to music of the poem in 'Zur Vertonung Von Shakespeares Poem *The Phoenix and the Turtle*' (*SJW*).

The Rape of Lucrece

'"A piece of Skilful Painting" in Shakespeare's *Lucrece*' by S. Clark Hulse (*ShS*) examines the more than two hundred lines of description of tapestry or painting of Troy in the poem, seeing such passages as iconic. This essay analyses the achievement of various arts present here, at first unable to help Lucrece to 'read' her own character, then, working verbally rather than visually, enabling her to move 'from *ecphrasis to prosopopoeia* to *icon*'. A slightly muddled second section does not clarify the difficult question of why she kills herself.

Richard II

In *SEL*, Allan Shickman writes on the 'Perspective Glass' as a gloss on II.ii.14–27 and elsewhere, with intriguing illustrations. (See also *General Criticism*.)

Romeo and Juliet

Gareth Lloyd Evans has adapted an interesting performance on cassette tape, running for sixty minutes[58].

[58] *Romeo and Juliet*, adapted by Gareth Lloyd Evans (*The Times Shakespeare*). London: Authortapes and Tercrest Ltd. 1976.

Sir Thomas More

In considering 'Linguistic Evidence for the Date of Shakespeare's Addition to Sir Thomas More' (*N&Q*), MacD. P. Jackson finds on the evidence of colloquial forms that everything points to composition no earlier than 1600.

The Sonnets

Michael J. B. Allen's 'Shakespeare's Man Descending a Staircase: Sonnets 126–154' is disappointing, being built on Philip Edwards's comment on Patrick Cruttwell's comment on Thorpe's ordering of Shakespeare's poems. He gives a long, detailed analysis, with more than a touch of *ipse dixit* about it, which is sometimes barely comprehensible.

A good deal is happening in *Sonnet* studies. S. C. Campbell's two books demand close attention[59]. The basis of her work is yet another suggested rearrangement of Thorpe's order to produce a double series, each containing seventy-seven sonnets. It is highly ingenious, and does involve much less tinkering than one would expect. It is dismaying to find the intention to 'make clearer the unfolding story which they hold' as if this were a *sine qua non* of all Sonnet work. But the development of the idea that the Dark Lady is seen to be a negative image of the fair youth is at once challenging, and lifts the whole argument clear of autobiographical, Rowse-like territory. The edition prints a conservatively modernised text and a lively introduction, written in what we can thankfully describe as English. Parallel to the edition is an expository volume explaining the thought in detail. The major change is of course moving the Dark Lady sonnets to an earlier point, allowing the poet to return from that misadventure to health and the original friendship. There is not the space here to explain all the fulness of the argument, which is continually impressive. A great virtue of the work is that, though it comprehends a great deal, it does not try to find an answer to everything.

The text of the *Sonnets* by Ingram and Redpath, first published in 1964, now appears in a corrected edition[60]. It holds up well, even against more modern competition.

The Taming of the Shrew

Karl P. Wentersdorf writes in *SEL* 'The Original Ending of *The Taming of the Shrew*: A Reconsideration', which is interesting and scholarly speculation about dislocation prior to the Folio text, including the loss of linking Sly scenes.

The Tempest

A usefully suggestive essay by Ronald B. Bond, 'Labour, Ease, and *The Tempest* as Pastoral Romance' (*JEGP*), questions what the pastoral elements are in the play, linked though it often is to pastoral. He finds only

[59] *Shakespeare's Sonnets: edited as a continuous sequence* by S. C. Campbell. Bell & Hyman. pp. xxxvi + 177. pb £1.95. *Only Begotten Sonnets: A Reconstruction of Shakespeare's Sonnet Sequence*, by S. C. Campbell. Bell & Hyman. pp. x + 241. £8.85.

[60] *Shakespeare's Sonnets*, ed. by W. G. Ingram and Theodore Redpath. Hodder & Stoughton. pp. xxxiv + 382. hb £7.95, pb £3.95.

two pastoral moments, Gonzalo's description and the Masque: yet the first is in the imagination and the second a vision. The play's airy edifice, he concludes, after looking at Caliban, Ferdinand, and Prospero, 'rests on the foundation of civic duty and social responsibility'.

Strongly Christian in tendency, yet also explanatory in ways that are suggestive even when not entirely successful, George Slover's 'Magic, Mystery, and Make-believe: An Analogical Reading of *The Tempest*' (*ShakS*) considers anew the question: 'on what grounds – by what standards of interpretation – can we infer anything from *The Tempest* about Shakespeare's own understanding of his art?'. He looks at the treatment of the Bermuda pamphlets; at the analogy between Prospero the magician and Shakespeare the showman; and at the play's theology. From this threefold structure he finds (in ways not so unlike Weimann's in his book reviewed above) that performers and the audiences constitute 'a community not only in the common action of making believe, but also in the common action of believing'. Gordon N. Ross links the ending of the masque to the magician's breaking of illusion in '*The Franklin's Tale* and *The Tempest*' (*N&Q*), while Georg Seehase writes in German on Prospero's entry into the community – or, the wonderful adventures of commonsense (*SJW*).

Timon of Athens

Ruth Levitsky disputes the *Everyman* pattern of the play in '*Timon*: Shakespeare's *Magnyfycence* and an embryonic *Lear*' (*ShakS*), finding it more related to Moralities which embody the conflict and debate themes. She considers the common theme of 'magnificence' in *Timon* and *Lear*, and how the great-souled man will bear up under the burden of either prosperity or of adversity, a primary interest being in how Timon's reaction to his new status fails to manifest 'magnificence', especially when compared to Skelton's Prince or to King Lear. But if this is reasonable enough, Levitsky then begins to juggle with 'fortitude' and 'stoic indifference' (themselves disparate) as equivalents to 'magnificence', suggesting that Timon and Lear and Gloucester strive for a kind of Stoic indifference with which Apemantus was born. Here thematic search seems to negate what might be briefly illuminating. The value of the talent is Lewis Walker's concern in 'Money in *Timon of Athens*' (*PQ*). He seeks to explain its increase in value through a passage in Cicero on the testing of friends. The appropriateness of 'lukewarm' water at Timon's banquet is shown by Henry D. Janzen (*Expl*).

Troilus and Cressida

There is a large (and mainly interesting) crop of essays on the play. G. K. Hunter's admirable '*Troilus and Cressida*: A Tragic Satire' (*ShStud* 1974–5) begins from the observation that despite its medieval rather than Homeric origins, the play is quite unmedieval, even anti-medieval. He explores with subtlety how far the availability of medieval versions and Homer's work (in Chapman's translation) might produce a clash and a distinctive effect. With great tact Hunter considers how Shakespeare might be acquainted with Homer, suggesting that if the modern reader 'is likely to be appalled if he catches an unimpeded view of the bleak ferocity of the

Iliad', then for Shakespeare, totally unfamiliar with it, it might be 'a profoundly unliberating shock', and '*Troilus and Cressida* is, I take it, the record of that shock'. From this, without forcing his case, Hunter suggests how Shakespeare politicised the world of Homer, the result being to render Homeric heroes as inadequate human beings. The problematic nature of the play (Hunter places it in a genre of tragic satire) is naturally the concern of other writers. Carolyn Asp, in 'Transcendence Denied: The Failure of Role Assumption in *Troilus and Cressida*' (*SEL*), finds that love and order in breakdown mock any striving for immutability: she looks to see whether art and above all the theatre offers the transcendence that the characters continually seek. Characters have traditional roles, assume roles, or are thrust into them. Asp finds this helps us to understand such puzzles as Hector's apparently absurd reversal over the returning of Helen and sees the play self-consciously examining the chasm between the immutability of art and the transcience and degradation of life. This same sense of degradation is fundamental to Rolf P. Lessenich's view in 'Shakespeare's *Troilus and Cressida*: The Vision of Decadence' (*SN* 1977). Whether or not he is right to suggest that Troy is at its nadir of decay in 'The Matter of Troy' (destruction in war is not necessarily decadence), he finds effeminacy and homosexuality the grotesque results of lust as a perversion of courtly love. The play is a tragedy with a perverted catastrophe where whatever is 'richly expected, hyperbolically announced, or ostentatiously begun, ends in blank nothingness'. The materials at Shakespeare's command, again, engage David M. Jago in 'The Uniqueness of *Troilus and Cressida*' (*SQ*). He locates the play's dissimilarity from Shakespeare's other work in the author's treatment rather than in the materials themselves. Sexual emotion is thrown aside by men as soon as it threatens to hinder society's preoccupation with honour. In 'The Problem of Identity in *Troilus and Cressida*' (*AJES*), A. A. Ansari finds that in Troilus's shift from pure love to blind and animal hatred, we have the orbits in which he moves and the reason for his instability. Interesting is Robert E. Wood's 'The Dignity of Morality: Marlowe's *Dido* and Shakespeare's *Troilus*' (*ShakS*), which looks at the two plays' similar applications of style and dramatic technique. He finds structural links, too, that suggest Shakespeare learnt from as well as surpassed Marlowe. Shakespeare's use of satire in tragedy 'was clearly not unprecedented'.

Twelfth Night

Alan Brissenden in *CahiersE* compares 'The Dance in *As You Like It* and *Twelfth Night*', also with reference to *A Midsummer Night's Dream* and *Much Ado*. He suggests a pavan at the end of *As You Like It* rather than a hay, as Long has maintained: and notes that though no dance ends *Twelfth Night*, dance references within the play support the notion of decayed courtliness. He especially points to the irony of Toby's reference to the unified dance, the passing measures pavan.

Gareth Lloyd Evans has adapted an interesting performance, available on sixty minutes of cassette tape[61].

[61] *Twelfth Night*, adapted by Gareth Lloyd Evans (*The Times Shakespeare*). London: Authortapes and Tercrest Ltd. 1976.

The Winter's Tale

Peter Berek explores the ideas of 'imitation' and 'mock' in the Statue scene and their implication for the play in ' "As We Are Mock'd with Art": From Scorn to Transfiguration' (*SEL*), relating them to a general conflation of 'art' and 'nature'. The derisory sense of 'mock' is teased out and Berek concludes that Shakespeare 'wittily acknowledges the two meanings' the word can have. Carol Thomas Neely overstates her case in 'Women and Issue in *The Winter's Tale*' (*PQ*), but usefully picks up from earlier discussion by Patricia Southard Gourlay (*ELR* 1975) and two articles by Murray M. Schwartz in *AI* (1973, 1975). It is a 'feminist' reading, in that it stresses the way in which the final reconciliation is brought about through the women, who are in league with time, nature and the play's pagan gods by virtue of their acceptance of sexuality and childbirth, separation and change, growth and decay. Instead of a bilaterial structure, Charles W. Hiett's 'The Function of Structure in *The Winter's Tale*' (*YES*) argues for a triple one and against the unifying function of parallel action. Perdita's two sea voyages are structural interruptions that precede and initiate the second and third movements. For A. F. Bellette in 'Truth and Utterance in *The Winter's Tale*' (*ShS*) the play is at odds with romance, for it most insists on what romance resists: 'fidelity of words to the observable truth of human experience'. What is essentially a note by Carolyn Asp, 'Shakespeare's Paulina and the *Consolatio* Tradition' (*ShakS*) looks at the apparent uniqueness in Renaissance drama of Paulina's role as female counsellor, linking her to the female *consolatio*-figure found in Boethius and Dante. Charles Frey's 'Interpreting *The Winter's Tale*' (*SEL*) is a general discussion of the problems of interpretation and our relationship to the play and the performance, attached to the particular of a play that presents problems in a genre approach. A new aesthetic is suggested by 'A Glimpse of the Sublime in Warburton's Edition of *The Winter's Tale*' (*ShakS*), by Irene G. Dash who finds that Warburton's emphasis on the pastoral scenes endowed the play with a new life in the eighteenth century.

VIII

English Drama 1550 – 1660: Excluding Shakespeare

BRIAN GIBBONS and BERNARD HARRIS

1. Editions

The Malone Society's offering for this year is John Heywood's *A Play of Love*[1]. Since this was printed in 1534 the work is outside the period of this review, but the later history of the play requires that it be recorded. An edition of Middleton and Rowley's *A Fair Quarrel* has been added to an established series[2]. There will be interest in a new series, which has commenced with volumes devoted to Middleton, Tourneur and Massinger[3]. David Frost selects *A Mad World, My Masters, A Chaste Maid in Cheapside, Women Beware Women*, and *The Changeling*. Apart from the last two plays mentioned the choice is obviously wide open with such a prolific and collaborative dramatist as Middleton. However, the selection is justified, even if the editor casts a side-long glance at *The Revenger's Tragedy* with the parenthetical comment 'sometimes erroneously assigned to Tourneur'. George Parfitt's inclusion of that play in the canon of Tourneur is predictably cautious. Colin Gibson's choice of Massinger consists of *The Duke of Milan, The Roman Actor, A New Way to Pay Old Debts*, and *The City Madam*. The balance of two tragedies and two comedies is obviously sensible, but it would have been good to have a tragi-comedy, such as *The Renegado*. However, there will be a general welcome for a publishing policy which restores to us selections or collections of plays rather than single texts. The volumes are rather expensive, but well printed, strongly bound, and attractive to read. The introductory material is brief, but does not weary us with recapitulations of critical opinion. The plays have been edited with clear, purposive aims, admirably realised. The series is to be welcomed unconditionally.

2. Books and articles

Philip Dust's study of the criticism of *Gorboduc* and *Ralph Roister Doister*, and William D. Wolf's related articles on *Gammer Gurton's Needle* and *Cambises* (*ELR*), are useful accounts of the fortunes of those early

[1] *A Play of Love* by John Heywood. The Malone Society reprints. O.U.P. pp. x, thereafter unpaginated. For subscribers.

[2] *A Fair Quarrel* by Thomas Middleton and William Rowley, ed. by George R. Price RRDS. Edward Arnold. pp. xxvi + 138. hb £8, pb £3.95.

[3] Plays by Renaissance and Restoration dramatists: gen. ed. Graham Storey. Cambridge: C.U.P. Thomas Middleton, *Selected Plays*, ed. by David L. Frost. pp. xxiii + 415. £12. Cyril Tourneur, *The Plays*, ed. by George Parfitt. pp. xvii + 197. £7.50. Philip Massinger, *Selected Plays*, ed. by Colin Gibson. pp. xiv + 385. £11.

plays. David M. Bergeron's 'Elizabeth's Coronation Entry (1559): new manuscript evidence' (*ELR*) adds to our knowledge of what should have been an auspicious event. William Baillie has written on 'The date and authorship of *Grim the Collier of Croydon*' (*MP*). F. Kiefer has published an annotated bibliography of studies on 'Seneca's influence on Elizabethan tragedy' (*RORD*). Sandra Billington considers evidence of sixteenth-century drama at St John's College, Cambridge (*RES*): a rediscovered account book and loose folio leaf contain lists of costumes and properties, with clues to plays performed and dates of their performance. D. S. Bland has added further entries to his checklist of drama at the Inns of Court (*RORD*). Reavley Gair (*N&Q*) provides names and details of some chorister-actors at Paul's in both successive acting companies there. M. Smith (*N&Q*) gives biographical notes on personnel at the Second Blackfriars: Edward Kirkham, Thomas Kendall and Henry Evans.

William Ingram's biography of Langley[4] is a thorough and interesting life of the theatrical entrepreneur, notorious bully and litigant, known usually only for having built the Swan theatre. The book provides a fresh perspective from which to view the Swan and the Boar's Head, the question of play censorship (Langley was involved in *The Isle of Dogs* affair), and the intricate maze of financial and legal deals that underpinned Elizabethan theatrical management and dramatic companies. The book is based on original research into documents in the Public Record Office and other libraries in London, and is a valuable addition to knowledge in this subject.

Joel B. Altman's book[5] is an extremely long account of the intellectual tradition centred on Erasmus and More which sought to teach by question, by debate, by the exploration of topics through rhetorical development of thesis and counter-thesis: an activity that required participants to make up their own minds through an educative process of serious play. Altman's line of argument is parallel to that of Duncan (see the review later). Duncan and Altman both discuss Heywood and Marlowe as key instances of the More tradition expressed in dramatic form. Altman has a chapter on Castiglione's *Courtier*, More's *Utopia* and Sidney's *Arcadia*, as well as chapters on Terence as studied in Tudor grammar schools, and detailed accounts of Lyly, 'Senecan' tragedy, and Marlowe. The book is sensitive to the increasing complexity of form and technique in Elizabethan drama but its claim to provide 'a new theory of Elizabethan drama' to account for the major plays, in terms more appropriate than the 'still widely held assumption that by and large Elizabethan drama lies in a homiletic tradition', is scarcely vindicated in practice, and indeed the account of specific plays in the second half of the book is very orthodox. The familiarity of his interpretation of Lyly and Marlowe (acknowledged by the many footnotes) indicates that the originality of the book is in the first part, which deals with the rhetorical tradition in non-dramatic literature and education in the sixteenth century. Here Altman has valuable things to say and is well worth consulting; his tendency to dismiss the importance of popular traditions of theatre, including the Morality tradition, may itself be dismissed as, at best, play of mind.

[4] *A London Life in the Brazen Age: Francis Langley 1548–1602*, by William Ingram. Cambridge, Mass., and London: Harvard U.P. pp. ix + 335. £12.25.

[5] *The Tudor Play of Mind*, by Joel B. Altman. Berkeley, Los Angeles and London: California U.P. pp. ix + 406. £13.

Elizabeth Storey Donno (*NM*) argues that *Edward II* should be seen in terms of a double rising and falling action; the play is in two matched halves, producing, in Sidney's terms, the emotions of admiration and commiseration in the spectators as Mortimer and Edward are counterpointed. It has two catastrophes close together, and we should see this as carefully organised, not as evidence of structural and generic uncertainty. Michael J. Warren (*N&Q*) discusses that stage-direction in *Edward II* 'Enter with Welch hookes, Rice ap Howell, a Mower, and the Earle of Leicester'. He notes that a welsh hook was the name for an agricultural tool used for mowing (something like a scythe), as well as a long-handled weapon like a partisan. He argues that it is thematically appropriate for all three characters, rather than the mower alone, to carry agricultural implements.

Richard A. Martin writes at length on 'Marlowe's *Tamburlaine* and the language of romance' (*PMLA*), proposing the term 'romance' as a mode which offers simplified moral facts, a self-referential system of metaphors, and an artificial dream-world relieved from the anxieties of reality. Admiration of Tamburlaine involves a challenge to our ethical sensibilities. John Norton-Smith (*N&Q*) considers *Dr Faustus* I.iii.1–4, and argues for the 1604 text against the usually preferred 1616 version, on the grounds that the 1604 text follows orthodox astronomy of the time (as seen in Macrobius). He wonders whether this instance of 1604's correctness suggests a more general superiority of the 1604 version.

A number of important articles by G. K. Hunter, reviewed in past years in this chapter, have now been gathered into book form[6]. The essays deal with specific writers – Marlowe, Seneca, Kyd – , with the traditions of tragi-comedy, Senecan tragedy and Elizabethan tragedy, and varieties of English Renaissance comedy. W. David Kay, in 'Ben Jonson and Elizabethan dramatic convention' (*MP*) considers a range of plays by other dramatists in which themes, conventions and motifs familiar to readers of Jonson recur, sometimes indicating his readiness to utilise the stage tradition of his own time.

A. Richard Dutton writes ably on 'The sources, text and readers of *Sejanus*: Jonson's "integrity in the story"' (*SP*). He notes that Jonson's version presents a much clearer confrontation between the forces of evil and those of virtue than occurs in his sources, Tacitus and others. Moreover, the confrontation is hardly shaded at all – as it is in the sources – by the unpredictability of human affairs or the vagaries of human nature. He considers that Jonson's play can be understood as it stands, independent of any knowledge of the sources, and as it stands it presents a dynamic examination of vice in action and of the failure of virtuous men to construct a viable alternative. It is a play about the fall of a royal favourite (two years after the fall of Essex), and the dense marginal references to classical sources in the printed text may well be a bluff, a disguise, to protect Jonson from censors who rightly detect the play's drive towards the presentation of problems and questions of immediate Jacobean relevance. Dutton grants that the play has an additional significance when read in conjunction with its sources. The essay perhaps over-estimates the degree to which *Sejanus* still needs defence in these terms, but it remains a clear

[6] ***Dramatic Identities and Cultural Tradition*, by G. K. Hunter. Liverpool, Lancs: Liverpool U.P. pp. xiv + 362. £12.50.**

and interesting account. R. P. Corballis has considered 'the second pen' in the stage version of *Sejanus* (*MP*). He argues from the evidence of Chapman's commendatory poem in the quarto of *Sejanus* and certain letters of Jonson and Chapman in 1605 that Chapman was 'the second pen' in the stage version, and that his original contributions often lie just beneath a thin Jonsonian veneer. Corballis has also written on Chapman and Machiavelli (*Parergon*), and on '*The Widow's Tears*: two plots or two parts?' (*Parergon*). In the same journal William Dean writes on Chapman's *May Day* as 'A comedy of social reformation'. Dean (*N&Q*) cites an allusion to Chapman's *The Widow's Tears* in 1668, earlier than the often quoted allusion in 1691. He finds an analogue of the play's plot in Puteanus, *Comus* (1608).

Ralph Alan Cohen has written on 'The importance of setting in the revision of *Every Man in his Humour*' (*ELR*). His account of the change of setting is full of suggestive comments, detailed and not simply generalised. His essay includes a map, and justifies his conclusion that Jonson's 'systematic approach in transporting his first successful play from Florence to London suggests that he had become aware of the importance of a carefully drawn setting'. Joan Carr's 'Jonson and the classics: the Ovid-plot in *Poetaster*' (*ELR*) contains an interesting defence of Jonson's impartiality in his projection of poetic authorities. Her essay is notable for its clever, sympathetic understanding of Jonson's interests, and her response to the potency of the material. 'If Horace and Virgil are a projection of Jonson's ideals, Ovid is a projection of his fears. . .Ovid's plight is Jonson's personal appeal to his audience not to misunderstand poet-satirists like himself as they undertake their morally arduous and even politically dangerous vocation'. Leah S. Marcus's '"Present occasions" and the shaping of Ben Jonson's masques' (*ELH*), is an equally attractive and persuasive statement. She argues that Jonson's 'middle masques are at least as carefully grounded in "present occasions" as his earlier and later productions'. *Christmas His Masque* and *The Vision of Delight* are given full attention, and they repay it. Her judgement is decisive and eloquent: 'Taken together, Jonson's 1616–7 masques make a significant statement about England, both in its present malaise and in an idealised state of health. In their portrayal of the nation's imbalances and in their suggestions for a remedy, both works follow closely James's own pronouncements and policies'.

Karl F. Zender's 'The unveiling of the goddesses in *Cynthia's Revels*' (*JEGP*) is a detailed and learned argument that the unveiling is foreshadowed from the outset of the play, is integrated into the play's imagery, and performs a central function in the resolution of the play's action. Ronald Huebert sees the extreme polarised ethical terms of *The Revenger's Tragedy* as offering an instance of the excluded middle (*UTQ*). The play world is divided into knaves and fools, with no intermediate characters, and this exclusive design is repeated in the language of the play. This is a short straightforward discussion which unfortunately does not develop its propositions in much detail. Paul Lewis opens an interesting line of enquiry about Jacobean tragedy in general when noticing connections between *The Atheist's Tragedy* and the Gothic novel, *The Castle of Otranto*.

Jane Sherman offers to solve the problem of 'The Pawns' allegory in Middleton's *A Game at Chesse*' (*RES*). She notes that 'the high tension of the pawns' plots has continued to seem so unwarranted that *A Game at Chesse* has always attracted more praise than good reason for praise'. She refers to Estates Morality convention to explain the dramatic mode of the pawns' plots, and works out the action in detail in these terms. Though the argument is too complex and lengthy to summarise, it is very persuasive in terms of the play, and also in terms of the allegory of the Spanish match, which, it is argued, constitutes its occasion. We are to see *A Game at Chesse* as a 'tight hard caricature of current affairs, dealing at its centre with the single outstanding constitutional issue of the day'. The essay is an excellent example of how to discuss a play in relation to its historical background: its reading of the allegory is sensitive to Jacobean habits of allusion, and it adds evidence of Middleton's political affiliations at this period.

Paula Johnson discusses *The Changeling* in terms of 'Dissimulation Anatomised' (*PQ*). R. V. Holdsworth defends the octavo reading of *Women Beware Women*, III.i.77, 'pewterer' (*N&Q*). David M. Bergeron writes about 'The Wax Figures in *The Duchess of Malfi*' (*SEL*). He reviews the sources for wax figures proposed by editors of the play (Lucas and Russell Brown), noticing the fact that in the Lord Mayor's Show in 1624 a wax effigy of Prince Henry, full size, was presented, and that there was a tradition of funeral effigies. Webster's concerns in the play include an interest in how death is commemorated: figures cut in alabaster kneeling at tombs being only the simplest way. William Babula contributes to a rich volume of *The Elizabethan Theatre VI*[7] an article on 'The avenger and the satirist: Marston's Malevole', and proposes that Malevole is able to combine the roles of avenger and satirist because the world of the play, though corrupt, is not irredeemably so. In contrast, R. A. Foakes 'On Marston, *The Malcontent*, and *The Revenger's Tragedy*' finds *The Malcontent* unconvincing except as entertainment when performed, and argues that the seriousness of Marston is most apparent to critics who study the play as readers not as spectators or directors; serious speeches tend to be dissipated in their effect by the play's action; by contrast, in *The Revenger's Tragedy* farce and comic effects are subordinated to and support a serious main action; *The Malcontent* is seen by comparison as 'almost frivolous'. The critical terms of Foakes's discussion are perhaps more sensitively adjusted to the discussion of Tourneur than of Marston in this essay, particularly in relation to the vexed questions of parody, self-conscious theatricality and what might be generally termed 'comic effects'. His appeal to recent performances of both plays indicates the debt owed by modern scholars to the subsidised theatre companies of Britain today – The Nottingham Playhouse presented Marston's *Antonio* plays in 1979, having presented *The Malcontent* in 1973.

Michael Scott has written a short but effective book on Marston[8]. He pays welcome attention to the plays in performance, but although his book-jacket is derived from Jonathan Miller's production of *The Malcontent*, and due interest is taken in the modern revivals of Marston, this

[7] *The Elizabethan Theatre VI*, ed. by G. R. Hibbard. London: Macmillan, and Ontario, Canada: Waterloo U.P.

[8] *John Marston's Plays: theme, structure and performance*, by Michael Scott. Macmillan. pp. 129. £8.95.

is a sharp, useful critique of a much misread dramatist, and follows through the thematic and theatrical images of the plays with ingenuity, subtlety and the necessary understanding of wit. The book is perceptive, not least in paying more than token interest to *Sophonisba*. It is also acute. Scott remarks in a chapter on 'Dreams, Innovation and Technique' that 'Marston was a major figure in moving towards the creation of the total dramatic image: the language not only of words but also of sounds, actions and dreams'. The book explores the complexities of Marston's insights in sympathetic and intelligent detail. Donald K. Hedrick's 'The masquing principle in Marston's *The Malcontent*' (*ELR*), notes that the play 'arrives at a curious moment in literary history: at the culmination of Elizabethan tragedy in Shakespeare and at the pivotal time in the development of the court masque, when Jonson begins to introduce a high literary seriousness into the genre'. The 'moment' is eloquently identified, and the conclusion that the play discloses a 'shrewd and subtle demonstration of the mutually supportive tension of satiric agent and hero, of satiric elements and heroic, and perhaps even of the structures of satire and epic' is satisfying evidence that this difficult play has been appreciated.

G. R. Hibbard has written a lively, informative and useful article on 'Love, Marriage and Money in Shakespeare's Theatre and Shakespeare's England' (*Elizabethan Theatre VI*). He inspects Elizabethan attitudes to these topics, and the laws, and relates them to plays by Middleton and Shakespeare. Brownell Salomon offers a guide to *Critical Analyses in English Renaissance Drama*[9], which contains 511 entries, and surely ought to have contained many more, and been more useful, but his criterion excludes books and articles which do not treat a play in its entirety. Thus, for instance, the name of M. C. Bradbrook appears only once, with reference to a play by Peele! The absurdity of Salomon's project would have appealed to Ben Jonson.

A conveniently assembled set of essays on *Every Man in his Humour* and *The Alchemist*[10] has been edited by R. V. Holdsworth, who not only makes a judicious selection of the material available but writes a cogent introduction which is in itself a notable addition to the sensitive consideration of Jonson's purpose. There have been several theatre studies. Michael Neill considers 'Wits most accomplished Senate: the audience of the Caroline Private Theatres' (*SEL*). This is a discursive essay which does not adduce new material from archives or other historical sources, but, rather, reviews occasional material, such as prologues and epilogues, printed with texts of the plays, and evidence from within the plays themselves. He considers the presence of women in the audiences as a significant influence on changing tastes, and this large-scale survey is interesting as stimulus to further investigation.

In *The Elizabethan Theatre VI* volume Reavley Gair writes in detail on 'The presentation of plays at Second Paul's (1599–1602)'. He draws on detailed research to argue that the site of the playhouse was the garth of the chapter-house precinct and extended up to the buttresses of the

[9] *Critical Analyses in English Renaissance Drama*, by Brownell Salomon. Bowling Green, Ohio: Bowling Green U. Popular P.

[10] *Ben Jonson, Everyman in his Humour and The Alchemist*, cricital essays ed. by R. V. Holdsworth. Casebook series, gen. ed. A. E. Dyson. Macmillan. pp. 244. £6.25.

chapter house. He includes a map. His account of Marston's Antonio plays, as being deliberately designed to be played in a small indoor theatre, is interesting, as are his speculations deduced from Paul's Boys' plays about the size of the stage. Gair promises a book on Second Paul's which may help to add fact to this interesting area of the drama of the period. Richard Hosley's 'A reconstruction of the Fortune Playhouse: Pt I' discusses the depth of the stage, the height of tiring-house storeys, the number and size of the bays of the playhouse frame, and the location of yard entrances and staircases. The article has exemplary clarity and is highly detailed. Neil Carson's 'John Webster, the apprentice years' believes that Webster's beginning in the uneasy experimental atmosphere of the Second Paul's, with its tension between the naive illusionism of the popular style of Dekker and Heywood and the self-conscious critical awareness of Marston, helped shape his mature dramaturgy, with its power to fuse these seemingly contrasting kinds of writing.

M. C. Bradbrook's 'Shakespeare and the multiple theatres of Jacobean London' surveys the very various occasions and places for play-performances in the period, and argues that Shakespeare's last romances are written in an open form which makes an appeal to every kind of audience, by no means concentrating on the limited exclusive Court-masque taste and its spectators. This is a typically fresh and informative contribution from a major authority on the subject and period. Stanley Wells writes entertainingly on the circumstances of the RSC's revival of *The Revenger's Tragedy* in 1966, citing prompt books (including all John Barton's additions, which he reproduces), newspaper reviews, and his own memory. This is a salutary discussion of the play in performance and of the particular period in the English theatre, and the quotations from reviews make amusing, if not improving, reading.

Bruce R. Smith has written on 'Productions of Seneca's plays on the English Renaissance stage' (*RenD*). Felix Bosonnet offers a methodical analysis of *The function of stage properties in Christopher Marlow's plays* (The Cooper monographs, Basel). This is a worthwhile study, but it is not always attentive to accretions of meanings in properties as they are repeatedly used in a play. Bosonnet's strictly applied method, if set in a more supple relationship to Marlowe's full dramatic art, might yield an even richer harvest of illumination of this supremely theatrical writer. Francis Teague carefully analyses 'Ben Jonson's stagecraft in *Epicoene*' (*RenD*), Patrick R. Williams discusses 'Ben Jonson's satiric choreography' (*RenD*), and R. B. Parker chronicles '*Volpone* in performance 1921–72' (*RenD*).

Douglas Duncan's *Ben Jonson and the Lucianic Tradition*[11] is an interesting and speculative argument (which may be felt to be stronger in its general considerations and orientation than its particulars). Duncan puts a case for the importance of Lucian's 'art of teasing', of teaching by devious processes of moral and intellectual testing, as an informing element in sixteenth-century English drama, in Marlowe, and in Jonson. Duncan acknowledges the presence of diverse traditions of thought and representation in English Renaissance drama, but his stress is placed on the intellectual satiric traditions of *The Praise of Folly*, the *Colloquies*, and *Utopia*, in

[11] *Ben Jonson and the Lucianic Tradition*, by Douglas Duncan. Cambridge: C.U.P. pp. viii + 252. £12.50.

which he supposes Jonson found a learned authority to accompany the popular dramatic traditions of the Morality and Roman comedy. Duncan acknowledges that More, Erasmus and Lucian did not dominate Jonson's mind and imagination, though the nature of his enquiry leads him to concentrate on their line. The first part of the book, on the tradition of Lucianism in the sixteenth century, is perhaps the more valuable, though the second part, dealing with the major comedies, is worth consulting. The book is agreeably written and commendably proportioned.

Ronald F. Miller's analysis of 'Dramatic form and dramatic imagination in Beaumont's *The Knight of the Burning Pestle*' (*ELR*) posits a change of emphasis during the course of the play. William C. Woodson's 'The casuistry of innocence in *A King and No King* and its implications for tragi-comedy' (*ELR*) studies a mode of argument, and demonstrates its dramtic possibilities. This is a welcome essay, in that it follows the convention of literary criticism, and breaks with it, as the play does. The latter is seen, perceptively, as both 'a successful exploitation of and a fey triumph over an alien sentimental audience'. Thus the play 'demonstrates a serious recognition of the danger of laxity' and 'indicates that Beaumont and Fletcher were themselves disturbed by the sentimental tragi-comedy which their audience seemed to demand'.

Katherine Duncan-Jones notes a literary allusion to Charles Blount, Earl of Devonshire (formerly Lord Mountjoy), in Ford's poems, *Fames Memoriall* and *Honor Triumphant* (*RES*), as a starting-point from which to recognise that Ford's interest in the story of Blount's love for Penelope Rich is reflected in *The Broken Heart* and perhaps also in *'Tis Pity*. The suggestion is very interesting. Michael Neill's 'The moral artifice of *The Lovers Melancholy*' (*ELR*) is a work in progress, full of allusive reference, and close reading. There is some hope that this play may be attentively edited in due course. William S. Milne's 'Milton's masque, occasion, form and meaning' (*CQ*), finds that *Comus* 'is not a failed drama or an arcane allegory' but 'exquisitely adapted to the occasion'. The article makes good use of the extent to which the unity of the masque may be said to consist of 'marrying the two related forms – the masque and the academic disputation'.

M. Drandt has written on 'Comic, tragic, or absurd? On some parallels between the farces of Joe Orton and seventeenth-century tragedy' (*ES*). The major parallels are between *Loot* and *Hamlet*, obviously, and *What the Butler saw* with *The Revenger's Tragedy*, from which it takes its epigraph. The notes are detailed, effectively deployed, and some distinctions maintained.

IX

The Later Sixteenth Century: Excluding Drama

R. C. HOOD

This chapter is arranged as follows: 1. General; 2. Sidney; 3. Spenser; 4. Poetry; 5. Prose. A selective review of books may be found in *SEL*.

1. General

Richard J. Schoeck finds the present state of scholarship in the period disappointing[1]. Basic research tools are still less than adequate, too much attention is concentrated on familiar writers like Sidney and Spenser, and there is a lack of imaginative critical enterprise generally. His selective bibliography pays tribute to a lost golden age of criticism, and he feels that hope for the future depends on the production of more and better texts, more widely dispersed critical enquiry, the promotion of interdisciplinary studies and the co-ordination of particular research interests to produce a larger comprehension of the Renaissance. With some exceptions, the following pages tend to confirm rather than mitigate his sense of unease.

As if in response to one of Schoeck's complaints, Richard W. Bailey introduces as a by-product of continuing work towards the *Dictionary of Early Modern English* a provisional collection of *Additions and Antedatings to the Record of English Vocabulary, 1475-1700*[2]. The value of such a work is obvious. Some 4,400 citations have been gathered from contributions to *N&Q*, glossaries to individual texts and scholarly monographs on the language of particular authors. Each word is given the appropriate *O.E.D.* cue-reference and the citations are helpfully full and precisely located.

Terry Comito's variation on a fashionable theme, *The Idea of the Garden in the Renaissance*[3], treats the garden as 'organized space' with numinous properties – both a place and an occasion for that fulfilment of self in relation to an ordered cosmos which is paradise regained. The material on which he draws is sometimes vertiginously diverse, and his exposition can be convoluted, but his chapter on the garden of love is excellent and he describes convincingly the changed sense of cosmic order which led the Renaissance to turn inside-out the medieval enclosed garden,

[1] *English Literature*, by Richard J. Schoeck, in *The Present State of Scholarship in Sixteenth Century Literature*, ed. W. M. Jones. Columbia and London: U. of Missouri P. pp. xi + 257.

[2] *Early Modern English: Additions and Antedatings to the Record of English Vocabulary, 1475-1700*, ed. R. W. Bailey. Hildesheim and New York: Georg Olms Verlag. pp. xvi + 367. DM. 58.

[3] *The Idea of the Garden in the Renaissance*, by Terry Comito. New Brunswick: Rutgers U.P.; Hassocks, Sussex: Harvester. pp. xiii + 278, 20 plates. £12.50.

discovering an exciting prospect for self-realisation in the phenomenal world of nature.

Of the year's several studies and epitomes of Renaissance attitudes and thinking, Agnes Heller's *Renaissance Man* (now available in translation[4]) is the most comprehensive. Looking forward from the classical *polis* to the Italian city-state and beyond, she provides a sympathetic account of the evolution of a dynamic concept of man and a pluralistic system of values. Her treatment of literature as evidence is generally trite, but her discussion of large issues like the process of secularisation in thought, the growth of individualism, changing concepts of time and history and the emergence of a distinctive 'stoic-epicurean' ideal is supported by a careful survey of many leading thinkers, notably Machiavelli and Bacon.

Stevie Davies bases her *Renaissance Views of Man*[5] on seven extracts from the work of notable writers through two centuries, including Ficino, Pico, Erasmus, Luther and Milton. Her pieces catch some of the major spiritual, social and political stances of the period, but there is something singularly unhappy in her strenuous effort to establish through introductions and notes a context sufficiently full and precise for the appreciation of her selections. Often the material itself offers sharper insights than her somewhat unadventurous commentary, as when the exuberance of Pico modulates into the urbane humanism of Erasmus which Luther acidly dismisses as trivialising and evasive. There is perhaps an argument here for the technique used by Ross and McLaughlin in their *Portable Renaissance Reader* (at last available in England[6]) of exposing the reader to a mass of lightly structured contemporary material and allowing it to ferment suggestively in the mind.

Allen G. Debus in *Man and Nature in the Renaissance*[7] traces the development of the exact sciences between the mid-fifteenth and mid-seventeenth centuries with attention to religious and philosophical principles as opportunity permits. He is nicely alert to the paradoxes exposed by his study, emphasising the devotion of natural philosophers in the sixteenth century to that ancient authority their work inevitably undermined, and showing how intimately the movement towards a mechanistic philosophy became involved with a vigorous interest in all aspects of natural magic following the rediscovery of the Hermetic corpus. There could be no more telling illustration of the general principle that Renaissance thought refuses to travel in straight and perspicuous lines.

Increasing feminist interest in the Renaissance must be one reason for the re-issue of Ruth Kelso's monumental digest of two centuries of English and European treatises on women, *Doctrine for the Lady of the Renaissance*[8]. Not surprisingly she fails in her quest to discover a sense of women

[4] *Renaissance Man*, by Agnes Heller, tr. R. E. Allen (Originally published as *A Reneszánsz Ember*, Akademiai Kiadó, Budapest, 1967.) Routledge & Kegan Paul. pp. xii + 481.

[5] *Renaissance Views of Man*, by Stevie Davies. Manchester, Lancs.: Manchester U. P. pp. xi + 203. hb £6.50, pb £1.95.

[6] *The Portable Renaissance Reader*, ed. James Bruce Ross and Mary Martin McLaughlin. Hardmondsworth, Middx.: Penguin. pp. xii + 756. £2.25. (First published in U.S.A. by The Viking Press Ltd., 1953.)

[7] *Man and Nature in the Renaissance*, by Allen G. Debus. Cambridge: C.U.P. pp. x + 159. hb £7.95, pb £2.50.

[8] *Doctrine for the Lady of the Renaissance*, by Ruth Kelso. Chicago, Ill. and London: U. of Illinois P., 1956, re-issued 1978. pp. xiii + 475. £15.85.

as women in a male-orientated society, though her chapter on Women at Court suggests that something approaching a recognition of a distinctively feminine sensibility might be possible for a privileged few. Kelso's habit of conflating original material in re-structured paraphrase makes her book less than ideal for scholarly plundering, but her vast bibliography of primary sources on 'The Lady' (if read in conjunction with its Preface) is an invaluable research tool.

T. Hahn describes the decline of the American Indian in the ranks of Renaissance Man in his article 'Indians East and West: Primitivism and Savagery in English Discovery Narratives of the Sixteenth Century' (*JMRS*). At first the fortuitous inheritor of the persisting medieval image of the virtuous Indian, he was increasingly degraded in the Western mind by antagonistic pressures, religious, economic, and political. Hahn's point that the idealised and brutish images co-existed for a time (as Montaigne's essay on Cannibals attests) lends extra weight to the debate between Carol Elaine Dooley and Alice Fox about the provenance, status, and function of the Salvage Man in Book VI of *The Faerie Queene* (see[19] p. 182). In her 'Divina Virago: Queen Elizabeth as an Amazon' (*SP*) W. Schleiner reminds us that the Amazon was another figure of equivocal reputation in the Renaissance, making it an impossible courtesy-title for Elizabeth except in the Armada context where emphasis on her martial prowess might sanction complimentary allusions to Penthesilea especially, the heroic defender of Troy.

Finally, Arthur Freeman presents a kind of anti-masque of Renaissance Man in *Elizabeth's Misfits*[9]. His pathetic, shabby, unscrupulous or merely roguish non-heroes seem unconsciously to expose the grand ideals of the time or parody its heroic achievements, and it seems appropriate that Freeman should include a life of Vennard, whose notorious non-spectacle, *England's Joy*, made such a splendid if unintentional comment on nationalistic pride. The book is designed primarily to entertain, though Freeman's chapter-notes offer some clues for those interested in Renaissance sub-literature; and without pretending to be a serious critique it confirms that there is ample scope and material for a properly subversive revisionist account of the Renaissance.

2. Sidney

The annotated checklist of 'Recent Studies in Sidney, 1970–77' by A. J. Colaianne and W. L. Godshalk (*ELR*) brings almost up to date Godshalk's earlier review of work published between 1945–69 (*ELR*). Books and articles listed in the general sections of *ABELL*, *YW* and the M.L.A. bibliography are usefully distinguished under several headings, and the brief summaries of their contents are scrupulous and fair. Colaianne adds that 'although specialized work in specific areas will always be useful, studies which broaden the context in which to place Sidney's art are badly needed. Though signs of revitalization may be seen, the criticism on Sidney is in need of new perspectives'.

If there is little evidence of 'revitalisation' in this year's work on Sidney,

[9] *Elizabeth's Misfits: Brief Lives of English Eccentrics, Exploiters, Rogues, and Failures, 1580–1660*, by Arthur Freeman. New York and London: Garland. pp. xii + 239, 8 illustrations. £15.

Josephine A. Roberts' *Architectonic Knowledge in the 'New Arcadia' 1590* is at least worth serious attention[10]. Arguing that Sidney's purpose in the revised *Arcadia* was to expose the old idea of the self-centred, self-sufficient hero whose adventuring involved personal glory rather than moral self-knowledge and public service, she describes Arcadia as a centre where the lessons of the Princes' Asian journey can be assimilated through retrospective narrative and re-applied in testing circumstances. She discusses classical precedents for the idea of the educative journey, analyses the decorum of the narrative modes and placing of the tales, and offers an interesting if finally insufficient account of Amphialus as the discarded type of the inadequate hero.

Starting from the premise that Sidney's Protestantism committed him to promoting conviction of sin and the necessity for faith, Andrew D. Weiner's *Sir Philip Sidney and the Poetics of Protestantism* offers an implausible account of the *Old Arcadia* as a dogmatic Christian tract[11]. There is little exceptional in Weiner's review of the moral and spiritual collapse of Arcadia, but his determination to enforce a narrow religious perspective unfortunately distracts the reader from the better parts of his book – the consideration of the Eclogues as a sharp comment from the harmonious world of the shepherds on the grotesqueries of princely conduct, and the role of the narrator in the *Arcadia* seen as a five-act comedy.

Lower down the scale of critical achievement comes Roswitha Mayr's *The Concept of Love in Sidney and Spenser*[12]. A simplistic account of the conventions of courtly love, Petrarchism and neo-Platonism provides the basis of her comparative study, mainly in terms of their sonnet sequences. If her conclusions are embarrassingly trite, her commentary is so banal as to make its brevity welcome. Her almost total reliance on received critical judgements confirms the impression that her observations are to be found more interestingly elaborated elsewhere.

In 'Distance and Astonishment in the Old *Arcadia*: A Study of Sidney's Psychology' (*TSLL*) Myron Turner observes the Arcadians struggling to recover the sense of ideal self from which they are estranged by 'astonishment' in the face of experience. He finds an unexpectedly positive emphasis on risky improvisation as an antidote to that psychic paralysis or attitude of rational stoicism which impedes the necessary operation of grace to re-integrate the self. Also unexpected is the degree of sympathy which Gary L. Litt finds given to Klaius in his 'Characterization and Rhetoric in Sidney's "Ye Goatherd Gods"' (*SLitI*). Differentiating precisely between the 'characters' of Strephon and Klaius, he puts interesting emphasis on 'the chaotic disintegration and reversals of character' in stanzas nine and ten, describing the consequences within the art of the poem and its characters of the failure to ritualise grief adequately.

In 'Celebration and Insinuation: Sir Philip Sidney and the Motives of Elizabethan Courtship' (*RenD*) Louis Adrian Montrose argues plausibly

[10] *Architectonic Knowledge in the 'New Arcadia' 1590: Sidney's use of the Heroic Journey,* by Josephine A. Roberts. SRS no. 69. Salzburg: Institut für Englische Sprache und Literatur. pp. 329.

[11] *Sir Philip Sidney and the Poetics of Protestantism: A Study of Contexts,* by Andrew D. Weiner. Minneapolis, Minn.: U. of Minnesota P. pp. xiii + 227.

[12] *The Concept of Love in Sidney and Spenser,* by Roswitha Mayr. SRS no. 70. Salzburg: Institut für Englische Sprache und Literatur. pp. 110.

that through the simplified pastoral mode of *The Lady of May* Sidney gave challenging expression to the complex political dilemma of the Elizabethan courtier. Inevitably, however, his critique was ignored and his frustrations had to be sublimated or exorcised (as in the heroic *Triumph of the Fortress of Perfect Beauty*) since Elizabeth's system was incapable of resolving them.

There is little new in the argument of Alan Sinfield's 'Astrophil's Self-Deception' (*EIC*) that Sidney intends us both to appreciate and see through Astrophil's compulsively hopeful casuistry as he encounters opposition from abstract Virtue and the more substantial Stella, but his view of Sidney's insistent moral purpose unfortunately underestimates the more complex processes of the later poems in the sequence.

3. Spenser

Once again virtually no Spenserian stone is left unturned. Helena Shire's *A Preface to Spenser* attempts too much and fails to maintain a consistent and satisfying level of critical address[13]. She does succeed in establishing a sense of Spenser as a learned poet responsive to the pressures of his historical moment, and briefly discusses many of the concepts necessary to a full appreciation of his work, including astrology and numerology. Her selections from his poetry are rather scrappy and (with the notable exception of *The Shepheardes Calender*) her demonstration of critical method is less than felicitous. Her regard for Spenser is clear, but her pedagogic manner, cultivation of elaborate diagrams, and false attempt to stress his modern 'relevance' are unfortunate irritants.

In *Spenser's Pastorals: The Shepheardes Calender and 'Colin Clout'*[14] Nancy Jo Hoffman argues that the pastoral mode of the earlier poem is specifically contrived to dramatise a variety of (sometimes conflicting) attitudes to life, moods and states of being rather than to mediate immutable particular truths. Spenser's use of the same mode in 'Colin Clout' to record irreconcilable contradictions of personal response to contemporary affairs upsets the original design, making inevitable his retreat into pastoral monody and the esoteric role of poet-priest. Hoffman's book feels rather long for its basically straight-forward thesis, and her attempt to define the peculiar status of Spenser's images of nature involves unnecessary mystification.

M. O'Connell shows in *Mirror and Veil: The Historical Dimension of* Spenser's 'Faerie Queene'[15] that Spenser found authority in the *Æneid* for giving his epic a serious historical dimension. Book I is a virtuoso presentation of history as the fulfilment of sacred myth and is flexible enough to accommodate successfully a variety of historical allusions. Book V however shows the collapse of such expertise under the pressure of personal and national anxieties. Spenser's discomfort as the apologist of history results in a withdrawal into the private vision of Book VI where the con-

[13] *A Preface to Spenser,* by Helena Shire. London and New York: Longman. pp. xii + 196. Illustrated. pb £2.75.

[14] *Spenser's Pastorals: 'The Shepheardes Calender' and 'Colin Clout'*, by Nancy Jo Hoffman. Baltimore and London: Johns Hopkins U.P., 1977. pp. xi + 152. £7.

[15] *Mirror and Veil: The Historical Dimension of Spenser's Faerie Queene',* by M. O'Connell. Chapel Hill, N.C.: U. of North Carolina P., 1977. pp. xiii + 220. £17.10.

cern with history is abandoned. O'Connell's approach involves a well-balanced application of historical knowledge.

The common concern with Spenser's loss of poetic assurance also appears in T. H. Cain's *Praise in 'The Faerie Queene'*[16]. Cain's thesis is that since praising inevitably involves an act of self-demonstration, Spenser's celebration of Elizabeth can provide a reliable index to the rhythm of his poetic aspiration and confidence. Predictably, the *Mutabilitie Cantos* are seen to complete the loss of that faith in Elizabeth and the Orphic power of verse which were characteristic of Book I. Cain's discussion of the increasingly imperfect 'images' of Elizabeth in the poem exposes the inability of his programme to do justice to the complex poetic activity of the evolving narrative but provides many insights valuable in their own right.

Several critics are interested in Spenser's treatment of grief. In 'The other side of the garden: an interpretative comparison of Chaucer's *Book of the Duchess* and Spenser's *Daphnaida* (*JMRS*) Duncan Harris and Nancy L. Steffen conclude that Spenser 'creates in the grieving shepherd Alcyon an instructional example, a personification of excessive, blasphemous grief whose very extremity forces the poet's audience to recall the tenets of proportion'. W. A. Oram (see[19] p.182) concurs in seeing the poem as a warning and an encouragement to respond more adequately to the challenge of Mutability. Moving to different territory, G. R. Crampton in 'Spenser's Lyric Theodicy: The Complaints of *The Faerie Queene* III, iv' (*ELH*) shows how the complaints of Britomart, Cymoent and Arthur are technically and thematically related 'to convey a growingly severe sense of disquiet about, criticism of, life's postlapsarian conditions – emotion unrequited or random, death, and evil'. Hugh Maclean's '"Restlesse anguish and unquiet paine": Spenser and the Complaint, 1579–1590'[17] takes a wider view, tracing Spenser's 'awakening recognition of the functionally sophisticated role that complaint might play in larger poetic structures'. He presents the five major complaints of Book III as the culmination of this process and describes the 'organizing principle' to which they collectively relate.

Spenser's artistic control is the subject of several articles. Kent T. van den Berg defends the integrity of *Mother Hubbard's Tale*[18]. Using Puttenham's definition of prosopopoeia as 'counterfeit in personation' he argues that the narrator's controlled presence establishes a contrast between that responsible counterfeiting which is the true process of art and the expedient counterfeiting which characterises the morally unstable real world. In 'Spenser's *Amoretti and Epithalamion* of 1595: Structure, Genre and Numerology' (*ELR*) Carol V. Kaske suggests that 'the three flaws alleged against the middle part of the volume. . .dramatize the discomforts of the lover as fiancé; all of them are expressions of sexual frustration which are portrayed as resolved in *Epithalamion*'. She supports her argu-

[16] *Praise in 'The Faerie Queene'*, by Thomas H. Cain. Lincoln, Neb. and London: U. of Nebraska P. pp. 229, 8 illustrations. $13.95.

[17] In *The Practical Vision: Essays in English Literature in Honour of Flora Roy*, ed. J. Campbell and J. Doyle. Waterloo, Ontario: Wilfrid Laurier U.P.

[18] K. T. van den Berg, *'The Counterfeit in Personation', Spenser's Mother Hubbard's Tale*, in *The Author in His Work*, ed. L. L. Martz and A. Williams. New Haven, Conn.: Yale U.P. £16.20.

ment with some comparatively leaden numerological speculation.

In more general terms, R. Helgerson suggests in 'The New Poet Presents Himself: Spenser and the idea of a Literary Career' (*PMLA*) that in successfully combining as subjects amorous contemplation with heroic action Spenser realised his ambition to achieve a literary career out of what was usually considered a diversion. The separation of these elements in the later verse indicates not a retraction of poetic conviction but a considered devaluation of the claims of the active world. Paul Alpers' 'Narration in *The Faerie Queene*' (*ELH*) denies that the poem is controlled through an omniscient narrative voice. In the early books, 'authority' is provided by an address to suprapersonal truths, and interpretative generalisations have a merely provisional status. But Spenser later finds difficulty in sustaining this narrative method and resorts increasingly to the lyric mode for the expression of complex ideas. In 'Allegory: The Renaissance Mode' (*ELH*) M. L. Caldwell distinguishes two extremes of allegory – that in which meanings are clearly signalled by its creator, and that which puts responsibility on the reader to supply them. Spenserian allegory occupies an intermediate position, infusing the *litera* with unexpected meanings which ultimately satisfy by their sense of 'rightness'.

For M. S. Gohlke in 'Embattled Allegory: Book II of *The Faerie Queene*' (*ELR*) the keynote of the book is repression not temperance, and she relates the irreconcilable disparity between Guyon's moral vision and his more quixotic responses to experience to Spenser's overall failure in the poem to achieve 'a vision of permanent moral order in which the anguished divisions of human experience are alleviated and integrated into the perspective of eternity'. D. W. Burchmore in 'The Unfolding of Britomart' (*RenP* 1977) adduces evidence from emblems to suggest that the figure of Venus is 'unfolded' in the triad of Belphoebe, Amoret and Florimell. The combination of their qualities in Britomart gives her peculiar mythographic status, giving even greater significance to her projected union with Arthegall. In 'Duality in Spenser's Archaisms' (*SLitI*) David A. Richardson sees the archaisms as an imaginative experiment in vernacular resources. They can be rustic, homely and pejorative or they can confer grace and authority, depending on the controlled decorum of their context. M. J. Allen in 'The Harlot and the Mourning Bride'[17] wastes her suggestion that Spenser's readers would recognise in Una and Duessa the familiar romance archetypes of the mourning virginal bride whose virtue is finally rewarded and her faithless harlot counterpart by failing to pursue its implications in a reading of the narrative.

On a lighter note, F. A. Hughes in 'Psychological Allegory in *The Faerie Queene* III, xi and xii' (*RES*) greatly enjoys herself interpreting the Busirane episode in terms of humoral psychology with the House as the brain and Britomart, investigating a psyche in distress, 'confronted by a set of symptoms to interpret without benefit of medical tuition'. The idea of Amoret as a drunken nymphomaniac is striking indeed. In '*Semper Eadem*: Spenser's "Legend of Constancie"' (*MLR*) R. H. Wells abandons himself to the claim that 'Book VII was intended, without doubt, to elaborate the mystery of the Queen's dual nature: her notorious flexibility as a politician on the one hand, and her steadfast devotion. . .to her divinely appointed mission on the other'.

The annual tournament of Spenserian tennis at Kalamazoo[19] has produced some more and less interesting rallies mostly from comparative newcomers to the professional circuit. John Webster and Michael L. Donnelly anatomise Gabriel Harvey in a learned and largely incomprehensible debate about the rationale of Spenser's poetics. J. M. Walker argues with ingenious implausibility that the Maleger episode is 'about' the poet's responsibility for preserving the failing cultural memory. Jay Farness rescues Spenser from the Blatant Beast by arguing that the unsatisfactoriness of Book V is deliberate as Spenser's richer poetic impulses expose the inadequacy of the 'official' narrative voice. Michael P. Mahoney somehow manages to relate Busirane and Meliboe in a piece about the false perspectives of art removed from experienced awareness achieved through vigorous action, and appals Brenda Thaon by his parallel between the House of Busirane and Colin's vision on Mt Acidale. Hugh MacLauchlan suggests that Book II progresses just in time from a pagan perspective of blood revenge to a Christian affirmation of grace mediated through Arthur – an interpretation which Elizabeth Bieman thinks reflects too severely on Guyon who, as a fairy knight, can hardly be expected to show expertise in Christian theology. Stephen A. Nimiss resurrects Alan Charity to discuss with Cherie Anne Haeger what kind of typological method might appropriately be applied to Spenser's epic. Jerome S. Dees concedes that a sense of tripartite structural principle can elucidate parts of Book II but warns the over-ingenious Robert Lanier Reid against the modern critical rage for discovering structures of symmetry in the poem. Louis Adrian Montrose reveals himself a master of symmetry in the conclusion of his paper on *The Shepheardes Calender*: 'Colin enacts an amorous courtship of Rosalind, a social courtship of Eliza, a spiritual courtship of Dido. Each of these wooings is also the exploration of a particular mode of poetic power and form; each is a manifestation of the arduous courtship of the Muse'. Both Alexander Dunlop and Carol Barthel are variously interested in *Amoretti* as a record of the process of courtship; and Anne Shaver and Humphrey Tonkin mull over the mythographic provenance and significance of Spenser's Diana-figures.

Lastly, Penguin Books have added to their already distinguished list of poetic texts *The Faerie Queene* edited (conservatively and sympathetically) by Thomas P. Roche Jr and C. Patrick O'Donnell Jr[20]. The notes should satisfy those who want a simple access to basic meaning whilst the frequent citation of more specialist studies should be useful to the more demanding reader. As a comparatively cheap scholarly, annotated edition of the complete poem this will no doubt become a popular and standard volume.

4. Poetry

Gordon Braden's *The Classics and English Renaissance Poetry: Three Case Studies* is the most stimulating book of the year[21]. Two of his studies

[19] *Spenser at Kalamazoo: Proceedings from a Special Session at the Thirteenth Conference on Medieval Studies in Kalamazoo*. Cleveland, Ohio: Cleveland State U. Microfiche only.

[20] *Edmund Spenser: The Faerie Queene*, ed. Thomas P. Roche Jr and C. Patrick O'Donnell Jr. Harmondsworth: Penguin. pp. 1247. £4.95.

[21] *The Classics and English Renaissance Poetry: Three Case Studies*, by Gordon Braden. New Haven, Conn. and London: Yale U.P. pp. xv + 303. £12.60.

are pertinent here – Golding's Ovid and the Hero and Leander story. Moving with admirable agility from the particular to the general and consistently refusing to dissociate linguistic decision from historical moment, Braden argues that Golding was specially placed to create a distinctive voice of 'supple shyness' which helped to form the typical Elizabethan mixture of awe and familiarity towards the exotic. His close analysis of Musæus' dark, obsessive, and finally destructive poem leads to a placing of Marlowe's work, though Chapman (who seems unnervingly close to Musæus in spirit and technique) is given disappointingly brief attention.

In *Poetry and Courtliness in Renaissance England*[22] Daniel Javitch establishes a close connection between the arts of courtly behaviour and the traditional strategies of poetry by comparing Castiglione's *Courtier* with Puttenham's *Arte of English Poesie*. If this made the poet a welcome mediator of courtly values, the decay of the courtly myth gave him a new independent role as moral legislator to society – a position Javitch finds epitomised in Book VI of *The Faerie Queene*. The simplicity of Javitch's patterns makes them too easily challengeable, but his cogently argued thesis should provide an interesting base for further critical enquiry.

Although Helen Cooper offers a comprehensive history of the mode from its beginnings in her enviably learned *Pastoral: Medieval into Renaissance*[23], her real concern is with the continuing influence of vernacular *bergerie* literature. If artistic self-consciousness and an obsession with love-melancholy are distinctive Renaissance contributions to the mode, she argues that detailed descriptions of shepherd life, the theme of happy love and the sceptical moral perspective on sophisticated life derives essentially from the *bergerie* tradition. In a work of this scope and disposition there is little opportunity for exhaustive literary criticism, though Cooper gives brief consideration to the work of Sidney, Spenser, Shakespeare and Drayton.

In *French Poets and the English Renaissance*[24] Anne Lake Prescott tackles the question of what literate Englishmen of the sixteenth and seventeenth centuries 'made of' French Renaissance poetry – that is, how they appreciated and re-worked it. Separate chapters on Marot, Du Bellay, Ronsard, Desportes and Du Bartas briefly describe the work of each, establish its distinctive features, discuss translations and 'quotations' by English poets, and assess direct 'critical' comments in prose and verse. Prescott's method allows her to recover a helpfully authentic contemporary picture, displacing later critical judgements and uninformed assumptions about how the work of her poets was received.

Many would support William J. Kennedy's argument that the study of strategies of voice and address is a good way to appreciate the norms – and therefore the developing life – of genre, mode and style. Fewer will admire his demonstration of the principle in the wide-ranging *Rhetorical*

[22] *Poetry and Courtliness in Renaissance England*, by Daniel Javitch. Princeton, N.J.: Princeton U.P. pp. 165. £8.60.

[23] *Pastoral: Mediaeval into Renaissance*, by Helen Cooper. Cambridge: D. S. Brewer; Totowa, N.J.: Rowman & Littlefield, 1977, reprinted 1978. pp. 257. £10.

[24] *French Poets and the English Renaissance: Studies in Fame and Transformation*, by Anne Lake Prescott. New Haven, Conn. and London: Yale U.P. pp. xiv + 290. £11.90.

Norms in Renaissance Literature[25]. His commentary is too often tedious and commonplace, and his manner sometimes approaches the absurd, as when he discusses with unalleviated gravity rivers, rooms, beds, ears and feet as the 'fictive audience' of Petrarch's verse. His unshakable conviction that rhetoric serves an inflexibly moral purpose naturally tends to a devaluation of Sidney's *Astrophil and Stella* by comparison with Petrarch's *Rime*.

SLitI is a prolific source of articles on verse. In 'The Petrarchan Tradition as a Dialectic of Limits' Richard Waswo presents Petrarch as the mediator of a tradition in which the stance of the adoring, idealising lover is put under increasing pressure by changing social exigencies and the moral demands of true religion. He suggests that Greville's *Caelica* appropriates this tradition although usually considered anti-Petrarchan. Ronald A. Rebholz in 'Love's Newfangleness: A Comparison of Greville and Wyatt' argues that both poets see infidelity as the inevitable consequence of the fallen state, though in Wyatt's verse this recognition is usually hidden behind the surprised, bewildered and offended tone of his speakers whilst Greville's more open scepticism shows itself in a voice which is knowing, cynical or contemptuously cavalier. In 'Aesthetic and Mimetic Rhythms in the Versification of Gascoigne, Sidney and Spenser' Susanne Woods coins new terms in an effort to undermine further a sense of simple distinction between plain and ornate styles. Her instincts may well be right but her method involves too subjective an application of judgement to command authority for her conclusions.

M-K. G. Orlandi in 'Ovid True and False in Renaissance Poetry' (*PCP*) finds that true 'Ovidian' poetry is more than just erotic mythological narrative. Its characteristic shifts of diction, tone and levels of discourse create a challenging variety of perspectives as it enacts the very idea of metamorphosis and focuses attention on the unstable but crucial moment in the narrative flow. C. T. Neely's comparative study 'The Structure of English Renaissance Sonnet Sequences' (*ELH*) invites us to be less suspicious about their design. Apparent awkwardness in structure, especially in their conclusions, should be seen as the natural consequence of changed social circumstances and psychological imperatives rather than a failure to achieve the complete artistry of their Italian models. Finally, in 'Moral History and Daniel's *The Civil Wars*' (*JEGP*) R. B. Gill argues that Daniel's belief in individual responsibility and the working of moral law in a cyclical pattern of recurring event is not incompatible with a Providential sense of history, though in seeming to transpose God into metaphor it shows the result of conflicting secular and religious demands, and 'the trend of Renaissance historiography towards clear, immediate forms of explanation'.

Amongst new editions, R. D. S. Jack's *A Choice of Scottish Verse, 1560–1660* is a welcome reminder of the fact of the Scottish literary Renaissance[26]. Jack prints Montgomerie's *The Cherrie and the Slae* and Hume's *Of the Day Estivall* in full, along with an extended extract from

[25] *Rhetorical Norms in Renaissance Literature*, by William J. Kennedy. New Haven, Conn. and London: Yale U.P. pp. vii + 229. £9.70.

[26] *A Choice of Scottish Verse, 1560–1660*, ed. R. D. S. Jack. Sevenoaks, Kent: Hodder & Stoughton. pp. 183. pb £3.50.

Stewart's *Roland Furious* and a generous selection of lyrics and sonnets. His useful introduction gives a well-balanced account of the strengths and weaknesses of the tradition and a helpful discussion of the major poems. Footnote glosses and brief textual/explanatory notes make the verse reasonably accessible to the non-initiate. By contrast, Eirian Wain's *George Chapman: Selected Poems* is a disappointing addition to the Carcanet series[27]. She acknowledges that Chapman is at his best in the long poem but the severity of her selection gives him no chance to show it. *Ovid's Banquet of Sense* at least might have been printed in full. Wain's introduction is of little critical help, except for a few comments on *Hero and Leander*. Curiously, she describes this as completed by Chapman 'in his own vein but with no lowering of its high level of moral intensity', and she appears to see Chapman's didactic *tours de force* as merely unfortunate aberrations.

Tetsumaro Hayashi has produced a modernised edition of *The Poetry of Robert Greene*, a collection of 106 poems including *A Maiden's Dream* and other poems from the prose works and plays[28]. He provides a select bibliography of primary and secondary works, anthologies in which Greene has been represented, and general studies of Elizabethan verse. There is however no critical apparatus or commentary, and the marginal glosses are far from adequate. This is a welcome, serviceable replacement for the outdated and inadequate works of Dyce, Bell and Collins, but it is a less than ideal basis for the scholarly work Hayashi hopes to stimulate.

R. M. Schuler has edited *Three Renaissance Scientific Poems* for the *SP* Texts and Studies series (vol. 75, no. 5). His general introduction discusses the English Renaissance tradition of 'scientific poetry', whose most popular subjects were alchemy and medicine, and which shows some literary ambition although primarily concerned to transmit material in a form pleasant and easily assimilated. The poems are: William Blomfield's *The Compendiary of the Noble Science of Alchemy, or Blomfield's Blossoms, 1557*; Christophorus Ballista's *The Overthrow of the Gout*, translated by B.G., 1577; and an early seventeenth-century translation of Book 1 of Buchanan's *De Sphaera* (see p. 191). Each is provided with a helpful introduction identifying its specific context, a critical apparatus, and full explanatory notes.

5. Prose

Pride of place must go to James L. Harner's scrupulously compiled and usefully annotated bibliography of criticism, *English Renaissance Prose Fiction, 1500-1660*[29]. The scope of the book is ample, including 'all individual works generally regarded as Renaissance prose fiction'. It lists early editions and studies between 1800 and 1976 including doctoral theses. Harner's efficient arrangement of his various checklists makes the

[27] *George Chapman: Selected Poems*, ed. Eirian Wain. Manchester, Lancs.: Carcanet. pp. 90. pb £1.25.

[28] *The Poetry of Robert Greene*, ed. Tetsumaro Hayashi. (Ball State Monograph no. 27, Publications in English no. 19). Muncie: Ball State U.P., 1977. pp. xiv + 168. Not for sale.

[29] *English Renaissance Prose Fiction, 1500-1660: an annotated bibliography of criticism*, ed. James L. Harner. Boston, Mass.: G. K. Hall. pp. xxiv + 556. £23.50.

book pleasurable to use: entries are divided into four main sections (Bibliographies, Anthologies, General Studies and Authors/Translators/Titles) and each entry in the last section contains up to three sub-divisions (Bibliographies, Editions, and Studies). This is an invaluable reference work for those engaged in research at any level.

Castiglione's *Courtier* has inspired two full-length studies different in approach but equally appreciative of the book's artistry and coherence. In *Baldesar Castiglione: a reassessment of the Courtier*[30] J. R. Woodhouse offers an essentially practical interpretation, arguing that the early books supply a blueprint for survival in an uncertain world and for the achievement of that acceptability which allows the courtier to perform his basic role as advisor. The emphasis on service in Book 4 is therefore the natural conclusion of the work rather than an embarrassed afterthought. Woodhouse leaves unresolved the vexed question of how dissimulation becomes the creditable servant of truth and is not quite convincing in his claim that Bembo's speech perfects the design of the whole; but his closely-argued interpretation is strongly reinforced by his knowledge of the political, cultural and philosophical circumstances which affected Castiglione.

The liveliness of Wayne A. Rebhorn's *Courtly Performances* derives from his variety of perspectives on *The Courtier*[31]. He broods over key words, describes the composition of the book in terms of Renaissance group portraiture, discusses its relation to the form of the symposium and draws on behavioural theory for an account of its social mechanisms, stressing the potential aggressiveness beneath the civilised surface. Like Woodhouse he finds a satisfactory placing for Book 4 in the overall structure. He can be repetitive and obvious, and his methods will irritate some readers; but in general his book is lucid, well-written and stimulating.

The *Centre de Recherches sur la Renaissance* has published contributions to two colloquies on the subject of gold in the Renaissance[32]. Essays deal with painting, economics, and the literature of several languages. Eliane Cuvelier's contribution is on Thomas Lodge and Usury, 'Thomas Lodge, Censeur de l'Usure'. Analysing his *Alarum Against Usurers* and *A Looking-Glass for London and England* she comments on their sympathetic appeal to those ruined by others' malpractice; but in the slightly later *Wits Miserie*, with its medieval rhetoric, she finds a more interesting Counter-Reformation Catholic unwillingness to divorce economics from morality (as Bacon advocated in his essay on usury).

In *The Rhetoric of Love in Lyly's 'Euphues and his England' and Sidney's 'Arcadia' 1590*, James Eugene O'Hara Jr uses a statistical analysis of selected passages in order to distinguish more authoritatively between the style and rhetorical practices of the two writers[33]. Some of his con-

[30] *Baldesar Castiglione: a reassessment of The Courtier*, by J. R. Woodhouse. (Writers of Italy Series no. 7). Edinburgh: Edinburgh U.P. pp. xi + 217. £5.50.

[31] *Courtly Performances: Masking and Festivity in Castiglione's 'Book of the Courtier'*, by Wayne A. Rebhorn. Detroit, Mich.: Wayne State U.P. pp. 238, 8 illustrations. $16.95.

[32] *L'Or au Temps de la Renaissance: du Mythe à l'économie*, ed. M. T. Jones-Davies. Paris: Université de Paris – Sorbonne. pp. 126.

[33] *The Rhetoric of Love in Lyly's 'Euphues and his England' and Sidney's 'Arcadia', 1590*, by James Eugene O'Hara Jr. SRS no. 76. Salzburg: Institut für Englische Sprache und Literatur. pp. v. + 169.

clusions are predictable, others more unexpected: Sidney has no absolute resistance to the devices of 'euphuism' though he was supposed to find it distasteful, and the length of their periods (properly understood) shows no significant difference although Sidney's are usually claimed to be longer. Finally O'Hara claims that Euphuism is characterised by 'isocolon-parison', Arcadianism by 'polyptoton'.

Richard S. M. Hirsch has produced the first critical edition of *R. I., The Most Pleasant History of Tom a Lincolne* for the Renaissance English Text Society[34]. Written probably in 1599 and 1607 this popular and spirited two-part novella, a grim romantic fantasy with a semi-Arthurian framework involving adultery, illegitimacy, fornication, suicide, murder and matricide, is not a moralising tale although its second part dramatises the fearsomely ubiquitous consequences of the original 'sins'. Hirsch provides a full critical apparatus and his introduction includes a short biography of its author Richard Johnson, a discussion of its prose style, and references to its more important analogues in drama and verse.

Two articles involve the grotesque in Elizabethan literature. In 'Physical Deformity and Chivalric Laughter in Renaissance England' (*NYLF*) J. J. O'Connor collects examples largely from chivalric romances showing how grotesque figures of various kinds were commonly treated with sadistic humour. He suggests that the same phenomenon in more 'respectable' literature may serve a more complex purpose than the alleviation of anxiety about the 'unnatural'. B. C. Millard's 'Thomas Nashe and the Functional Grotesque in Elizabethan Prose Fiction' (*SSF*) concentrates on *The Unfortunate Traveller* as a peculiarly vigorous attempt to create an equal tension between the terrible and the ridiculous and an early experiment in the use of the grotesque as a structural device in picaresque narrative.

A number of articles involve religious prose of various sorts. It seems doubtful whether the checklist provided by Ronald B. Bond in 'The 1559 Revisions in *Certayne Sermons or Homilies*: "For the Better Understandyng of the Simple People"' (*ELR*) will contribute in any large way to an appreciation of the plain style, though it does offer some limited insight into what words and phrases might in this context be considered 'difficult'. J. D. Moss in 'Variations on a Theme: The Family of Love in Renaissance England' (*RenQ*) prints the formal confession of a Familist convert giving useful information about the recruiting methods and beliefs of the strange and elusive Messianic sect whose following in England had grown large enough by 1580 for Elizabeth to proclaim it heretical. In 'Joseph Hall and Protestant Meditation' (*TSLL*) Ronald J. Corthell is in more orthodox territory, arguing that *The Arte of Divine Meditation* can be seen as a formative Protestant manual of meditation, anticipating in the nature of its exercise the Augustinian principle of illumination as developed later in the seventeenth century.

Two minor works of fiction receive disappointed and disappointing critical attention respectively. S. Knapp's explication of 'Love Allegory in John Grange's *The Golden Aphroditis*' (*ELR*) concludes bleakly that

[34] *R.I., The Most Pleasant History of Tom a Lincolne*. ed. R. S. M. Hirsch. Columbia, S.C.: U. of South Carolina P. pp. xxxii + 122. $14.95.

Grange understood neither the implications of his mode nor 'the limits on human ability to find immanence and transcendence in the same place and person'. Perhaps the tale is best appreciated at the level of its bizarre surface? H. Bonheim's desultory study of 'Robert Greene's *Gwydonius: The Carde of Fancie*' (*Anglia*) requires a more purposeful sense of distinction between the merely derivative and conventional and the distinctive and innovatory to justify its argument that the 'pamphlet' made a 'not insignificant' contribution to the development of prose fiction in the following quarter century.

Finally, D. C. Peck prints a splendid anti-Leicester pamphlet (B.L. Sloane MS 1926, fols 35–43 verso) under the title 'News from Heaven and Hell: A Defamatory Narrative of the Earl of Leicester' (*ELR*). Written shortly after Leicester's death, this inventive, irreverent, satirical account of his futile attempt to enter heaven, and his subsequent reception in hell, is more outrageous than bitter. It shows familiarity with the notorious *Leicester's Commonwealth*, but completes the scurrilous offensive with charges of later date.

X

The Earlier Seventeenth Century: Excluding Drama

BRIAN NELLIST and NICK SHRIMPTON

This chapter is arranged as follows: 1. General, by Brian Nellist; 2. Poetry by Nick Shrimpton, with sections on Jonson and Marvell by Brian Nellist; 3. Prose, by Brian Nellist.

A selective review of books may be found in *SEL*.

1. General

If we tend incautiously to take sight as the natural metaphor for knowledge, Ernest B. Gilman in *The Curious Perspective*[1] offers a scholarly corrective. With lucid detail, he shows how the Renaissance discovery of perspective quickly developed into anxiety about the dependence of the world of appearance upon point-of-view. He analyses the theory supporting the various witty devices of optical illusionism and uses it as an analogy for the criticism of the fallible reason in the poetry of Donne, Herbert, Greville and Marvell. William A. McClung in *The Country House in English Renaissance Poetry*[2] also compares styles in visual and verbal artefacts. In a well-illustrated book, he provides a pictorial commentary on the criticisms of contemporary architecture in the poems of Jonson, Carew and Herrick. More pertinently, maybe, he demonstrates their purely literary antecedents in Latin and native sources. The study of the poetry would have benefited from attention to more recent criticism.

C. N. Manlove in *Literature and Reality, 1600–1800*[3] maintains that the loss in this period of a containing image of the *summum totalis* leaves the relation between experience and generalisation in critical plight. Through a study of selected writers from Donne to Cowper, he shows the variety of compromises achieved. Donne, for example, subdues awkward fact to argument, whereas Jonson honours particulars at the expense of intellectual exploration. The book is a sequence of lively, polemical readings of individual texts, where the relation between detailed study and general thesis is too uncertain to constitute evidence for the argument.

[1] *The Curious Perspective: Literary and Pictorial Wit in the Seventeenth Century*, by Ernest B. Gilman. New Haven, Conn. and London: Yale U.P. pp. xii + 267. $16, £11.50.

[2] *The Country House in English Renaissance Poetry*, by William A. McClung. Berkeley, Los Angeles, Calif. and London: U. of California P. 1977. pp. [viii] + 192. £7.50, $11.95.

[3] *Literature and Reality, 1600–1800*, by C. N. Manlove. Macmillan. pp. x + 238. £8.95.

Luigi Sampietro in *La Scuola del Cuore*[4] presents Walton, Christopher Harvey and Bunyan as devisers of 'Anatomies'. The general category proves less interesting than the detailed study; Harvey's possible relationship with Thomas Hooker's analysis of the stages of conversion, for instance, or the ways in which *Mr Badman* differs from a novel. Gillian Evans has produced in *The Age of the Metaphysicals*[5] an introduction to biographical, historical, intellectual and critical contexts for the benefit of the proverbial 'Sixth Form Student'. It will supply to first readers a reliable sense of the insights offered by informed study.

In 'Richard Haydocke: Translator, Engraver, Physician' (*Library*), Karl-Josef Höltgen unravels with exemplary scholarship the biography of an exemplary virtuoso, and interprets the emblems he devised on brass, panel and printed page. Frederick O. Waage in 'Touching the Compass: Empiricism in Popular Scientific Writing of Bacon's Time' (*HLQ*) identifies Bacon as less the prophet of science than of invention, concerned with the social uses of enquiry, and shows how this programme corresponded with the work of a number of contemporary minor investigators who presented their researches within an ethic of progress and human improvement.

2. Poetry

This has been a particularly good year for studies of Jacobean poets better known for their plays. No less than four articles examine the verse of George Chapman. One of these (discussed below) uses *Ovids Banquet of Sense* to illuminate Donne's 'The Ecstasy'. Gerald Snare (*SP*), however, concentrates directly upon Chapman's poem. Provoked, like so much recent criticism, by Frank Kermode's argument that this is an ironic work, displaying the misuse of reason, the essay attempts to re-establish its moral respectability by interpreting it instead as a literary manifesto. Two other articles consider the only slightly less controversial topic of the continuation of *Hero and Leander*. John Huntington (*SLitI*) argues persuasively that Chapman's poem, though undoubtedly 'graver' than Marlowe's, is more playful and ambiguous than its author's reputation as a solemn Stoic might suggest. Albert C. Labriola (*ELN*) claims that the relationship between the lovers is presented as one based on an over-simplified view of the tri-partite character of Venus. For those new to his work, two brief but stimulating chapters on Chapman as poet and translator, and a select bibliography, are to be found in M. C. Bradbrook's monograph *George Chapman*[6].

Francis Beaumont's *Poems* were published nearly a quarter of a century after his death. None the less, as J. P. Hammersmith (*PBSA*) demonstrates, his printer used manuscript copy even for the second edition of 1653. It cannot therefore be assumed that the texts in this volume (which includes stray poems by Donne, Jonson, Cleveland and Herrick) are mere reprints. A third distinguished man of the theatre, Philip Massinger, makes a rare

[4] *La Scuola del Cuore e altre Anatomie del Seicento Inglese*, by Luigi Sampietro. Saggi di Letterature Moderne, Sezione di letteratura inglese.3. Bologna: Pàtron. pp. 193. L. 4800.

[5] *The Age of the Metaphysicals*, by Gillian Evans. Blackie. pp. [iv] + 140. £2.75.

[6] *George Chapman*, by M. C. Bradbrook. Harlow, Essex: Longman for The British Council, 1977. pp. 60.

appearance as a poet in an article by J. H. P. Pafford (*N&Q*). To the eight previously known poems by Massinger we may now add a ninth, an 'Elegy on Sir Warham St. Leger' found in the manuscript commonplace-book of John Clavell.

James Cobbes has hitherto been obscure even as a dramatist: now two independent pieces of research have begun to coax him from the shadows. Robert M. Schuler (*PBSA*) has found documents in the British Library which not only confirm his authorship of at least two plays but also show him to have been the first English translator of some important contemporary works. Elsewhere (*SP*) Schuler prints one of these translations, a verse rendering of the first book of George Buchanan's *De Sphaera*, together with a note on scientific poetry in the English Renaissance. Ted-Larry Pebworth (*PBSA*, 1977) mentions Cobbes while discussing the status of Walton's *Reliquiae Wottonianae* (1651) as a copy text for Sir Henry Wotton's poetry. A study of the poem 'Dazel'd Thus, with Height of Place' confirms the superiority of Walton's volume and illustrates the practice of 'appropriation' to which manuscript poems were subject. One such appropriation, by 'Alphonso Mervall', applied Wotton's poem (originally about the Earl of Somerset) to the Duke of Buckingham. This exotic gentleman, whose original 'Elegy on the Duke of Buckingham' Pebworth prints in an appendix, proves to be none other than James Cobbes, operating under a pseudonym.

Steven L. Bates and Sidney D. Orr base *A Concordance to the Poems of Ben Jonson*[7] on the Herford and Simpson old-spelling text, and their computer has recorded the variant spellings as separate entries. Cross-reference sorts the problem out. Statistics are supplied for the absolute and relative frequency with which each word is used in the corpus, and the book is completed by a list of the total vocabulary ranked according to usage. This is obviously an essential tool for research not only into Jonson but into the lexical uses of seventeenth-century poetry in general.

Two articles attend to general strategies in Jonson's poetry. Ira Clark (*Criticism*) claims that imitation involved the calculated transcending of his models. The epigram is rescued from the licence and scurrility of Martial and directed to moral ends. John Lemly (*ELH*, 1977) sees the poet as increasingly obtruding upon the reader in the later poems the self-portrait of a flawed presence. Like an anti-masque, this prefaces the prophetic voice honouring the realm of true values. Sara van den Berg (*ShakS*) argues with substance that the lines to Shakespeare present an image of the other dramatist close to Jonson's view of his own achievement: Shakespeare validates yet transcends ancient usage and so demonstrates the true relation of art to nature. J. Z. Kronenfeld (*SP*) rather forensically acquits Jonson of the charge of insulting paternal love in the elegy for his son and attributes the error to over-eager expectations of life. The attempted re-interpretation of life as loan from God appeals to a traditional topic of consolation. Susanne Woods (*SEL*) indicates in great detail how the formal structure of the Cary-Morison ode itself embodies the poem's argument. In shorter notices, Peter Beal (*RES*) points out that 'A Rodomontade' in the Vieth edition of Rochester is in fact by Jonson; D. Heyward Brock (*PBSA*)

[7] *A Concordance to the Poems of Ben Jonson*, compiled by Steven L. Bates and Sidney D. Orr. Athens, Ohio: Ohio U.P. pp. xiv + 878. $40.

uses the method of clause-analysis to attribute three of the four disputed elegies in the canon to Jonson; and Edgar F. Daniels (*Expl*) deftly clears up the difficulty of l.14 of 'To Heaven' when he argues that a modifier is misplaced.

The Spenserians have had a more than usually thin time. One of the three articles on Drayton, by Paula Johnson (*SLitI*), argues that he is not in his mature work a Spenserian at all, before going on to draw elaborate (and peculiar) political conclusions from the fact that *Poly-Olbion* is not dedicated to King James. Barbara C. Ewell (*SP*) discusses the way in which Drayton shapes *Poly-Olbion*, pointing to various 'modes of unification'. William A. Oram (*SP*) addresses himself to the problem of why Drayton speaks of *The Muses Elizium* as 'a new way over Parnassus'. His answer is that the pastoral world is here a symbol of imaginative play and that Drayton is unusually honest about its limitations. The article is distinguished by the historical scope of its conclusion, which argues that Drayton's late works demonstrate the two distinct traditions which derive from the 'serious fiction' of Spenser. Cedric C. Brown and Margherita Pira (*RES*) supply some further evidence for the claim, made in 1976 by Joan Ozark Holmer (*PBSA*, 1976), that the third book of William Browne's *Britannia's Pastorals* was written in 1624.

The great event in the world of Donne has been the completion, after twenty-six years, of the Oxford edition of his poetry. W. Milgate's *The Epithalamions, Anniversaries and Epicedes of John Donne*[8] provides a suitably distinguished conclusion to this endeavour. Milgate differs from Grierson in his choice of the third edition of Sylvester's *Lachrymae Lachrymarum* for the 'Elegy on Prince Henry', and of the 1611 and 1612 editions of the *Anniversaries* for the first and second of those poems respectively. Elsewhere the copy text remains that of the 1633 *Poems*. None the less it has been possible to make some improvements on the text in all cases. The volume also contains a collection of Donne's Latin epigraphs and inscriptions, the group of 'Elegies upon the Author' printed in the early editions, and a characteristically helpful and expert commentary. Whether or not it is true, in the words of Professor Milgate's introduction, that 'few modern readers would deny' that the *Anniversaries* 'have claims to be considered the finest long poems written in English between *The Faerie Queene* and *Paradise Lost*' few modern readers would wish to be without this admirable edition of them. A second edition of Helen Gardner's *The Divine Poems*[9], with which the series commenced in 1952, appears as the project reaches its end. Her revisions, especially in the Textual Introduction, take account of new material discovered in the intervening quarter of a century.

A. C. Partridge's *John Donne: Language and Style*[10] is a curiously disorganised book, in which chapters are not necessarily about the topics mentioned in their titles, and where the Preface and 'Conclusions' fail to

[8] *The Epithalamions, Anniversaries and Epicedes of John Donne*, ed. by W. Milgate. Oxford: The Clarendon Press. pp. lxviii + 240. £12.50.

[9] *The Divine Poems of John Donne*, ed. by Helen Gardner. Second edition. Oxford: The Clarendon Press. pp. xcviii + 158. £9.

[10] *John Donne: Language and Style*, by A. C. Partridge. Andre Deutsch. pp. 260. £7.50.

make clear the purpose of the study. In practice we are offered a commentary (primarily but by no means exclusively linguistic) on a series of verse and prose extracts. The criticism, unfortunately, begs more questions than it answers. Ronald E. MacFarland's 'Figures of Repetition in John Donne's Poetry' (*Style*, 1977), though far briefer, is in many ways a more satisfactory example of stylistic analysis. MacFarland examines the deployment and effect of six rhetorical figures. The technical analysis is expert without being arid, and there is a refreshing willingness to recognise that Donne's rhetoric is sometimes overdone.

Alan Armstrong (*ELH*, 1977) brings an equal, though different, expertise to the debate over whether or not Donne is an Ovidian. He traces the way in which Elizabethan writers defined the elegy by its matter rather than its metre, before discovering, in the 1590s, that classical precedent allowed the form to be erotic as well as funereal. Once Marlowe had established the iambic pentameter couplet as an accentual equivalent of the elegiac distich, the new mode flourished. Donne's 'Elegies' are not translations. But their witty sensuality, urban settings and use of a self-conscious persona are sufficient to mark them out as Ovidian.

John Huntington (*ELH*, 1977) makes a contribution to another long-running debate, best known, in Helen Gardner's phrase, as the 'argument about "The Ecstasy"'. Is this a philosophical poem about the interdependence of body and soul or a witty seduction poem merely clothed in Platonism? Huntington draws parallels with *Ovids Banquet of Sence* and Davies's *Orchestra* before suggesting a solution in the ambiguity about sensual experience found in the work of the Florentine Neoplatonist Marsilio Ficino. Marvin Morillo (*N&Q*) discusses 'The Canonization', criticising the numismatic evidence on which Susan Burchmore (*N&Q*, 1977) based her late dating, and argues for composition around 1603.

Elsewhere the 'Songs and Sonnets' have been poorly served. Roger A. Cognard (*Expl*), discovering that the word 'damp' can mean a stifling gas found underground, offers a wild conflation of images of dampness and mining from different poems. Presented in these terms Donne sounds like a writer-in-residence at the National Coal Board. Noam Flinder (*Expl*) claims implausibly that 'The Undertaking' sets up a sententious persona resembling Polonious (sic) as a target for laughter. Steven H. Gale's 'Analysis of "Love's Growth"' (*Horizontes*) is actually an elementary paraphrase, and Michael V. Fox (*Expl*) makes some scarcely less obvious points about 'A Nocturnal upon S. Lucy's Day'.

Edgar F. Daniels (*Expl*) claims that the words 'cruel friends' in the epigram 'Pyramus and Thisbe' refer to the lovers themselves rather than to other people. M. Thomas Hester (*SEL*), discussing 'Satire 3', attempts to find in it the structure of a religious meditation. Donne's explicitly religious poetry is examined in Jean Fuzier's contribution to *De Shakespeare à T. S. Eliot*[11], which discovers some fresh parallels to his combination of the sacred and the erotic in the work of Lazare de Selve and Jean de la Ceppède. The most interesting of the individual studies of Donne's religious verse is an article by John Nania and P. J. Klemp (*Ren&Ref*) which continues the

[11] *De Shakespeare à T. S. Eliot: Mélanges offerts à Henri Fluchère*, ed. by Marie-Jeanne Durry, Robert Ellrodt and Marie-Thérèse Jones-Davis. Études anglaises 63. Paris: Didier, 1976. pp. 290. 158 fr.

recent interest in the formal structure of 'La Corona'. Though the sequence 'weaves a crown', they argue, it is not circular. Instead, three pairs of poems arrange themselves around a central sonnet. This, 'Temple', describes Christ in the middle year of his life. A Latin pun on 'corona' (also meaning a crowd, here of doctors) confirms the centrality of the episode. John J. Pollock (*ES*) argues unconvincingly with Helen Gardner's statement that 'an Everlasting night' in Donne's 'A Hymn to Christ' means death, suggesting instead a state of religious awe. David J. Leigh, S.J. (*SP*) draws elaborate theological conclusions from a possible pun on Donne's wife's maiden name in the final line of each stanza of 'A Hymn to God the Father', without pausing to consider whether the quibble is present in the first place. Susan Linville (*Expl*) quarrels intelligently with previous interpretations of the final couplet of the Holy Sonnet 'If poisonous minerals'. Unfortunately, though she does point towards a more coherent reading, her particular alternative is so obscurely expressed that it is hard to be sure exactly what it is.

In a long review of Helen Vendler's *The Poetry of George Herbert* Richard Strier (*MP*, 1977) spoke of 'a renaissance in Herbert criticism within the past decade'. The rebirth has continued. Indeed Herbert might even be thought to have had, without benefit of a centenary, a richer year than Marvell. Much of this is due to Amy M. Charles who has followed her facsimile of *The Williams Manuscript*[12] with the first scholarly biography of the poet, *A Life of George Herbert*[13]. The crucial problem for any biography of Herbert is whether or not Walton was right in his claim that the poet entered the church reluctantly, after the death of his 'Court-hopes'. Professor Charles treats the matter with lucidity and decision. Walton's explanation is 'both inaccurate and untimely'. The poet's service in Parliament 'represented nothing more than filling the family seat when no other male Herbert was available'. Some months before the death of King James he had decided to fulfil his long-standing enthusiasm for divinity by taking orders. This thickly documented biography will not win any new readers for the poetry, but for those who are already enthusiasts it will be an invaluable tool. Much the same might be said of the computer-derived *Concordance to the Complete Writings of George Herbert*[14], edited by Mario A. Di Cesare and Rigo Mignani. All of Herbert's known prose and verse, in English, Latin and Greek, is included, a generous attitude to variants excludes only those which were modifications of spelling, and both alphabetical and numerical frequency lists are supplied.

One of the midwives of this recent rebirth of Herbert criticism, Stanley Fish, has at last published a full-length study of the poet. His book, *The Living Temple: George Herbert and Catechizing*[15] is a brief but brilliant exploration of the critical paradox whereby Herbert's poetry is felt to be simultaneously restless and secure. Formalist critics, trapped by their

[12] *The Williams Manuscript of George Herbert's Poems*, facsimile with intro. by Amy M. Charles. Scholar's Facsimiles: New York, 1977. pp. xxxvi + 222.

[13] *A Life of George Herbert*, by Amy M. Charles. Ithaca, N.Y. and London: Cornell U.P., 1977. pp. 244.

[14] *A Concordance to the Complete Writings of George Herbert*, ed. by Mario A. Di Cesare and Rigo Mignani. Ithaca, N.Y. and London: Cornell U.P. pp. 1344. £22.50.

[15] *The Living Temple: George Herbert and Catechizing*, by Stanley Fish. Berkeley, Calif. and London: U. of California P. pp. x + 202. £8.

tendency to see poems as objects rather than experiences, are, he suggests, obliged to adopt one or other of these analyses. Fish's alternative solution is to see *The Temple* as a 'Socratean catechism' in which the reader is instructed by being set problems. The implied distinction between the 'Socratean' and the Socratic makes the point that the end of such specifically Christian catechising is a sense, not of self-sufficiency, but of dependence on a supervening God. Success and disappointment, assurance and uncertainty are therefore all perpetually implicit in the process. Subsequent chapters demonstrate the extent to which temple-building was an established metaphor for catechism, and trace its conventional stages. Eventually a strange, but scrupulous, conclusion preserves the argument from any taint of the prescriptive fallacy which it originally set out to avoid. This is a work of genuine intellectual distinction, as subtle as it is learned, and the one indispensable publication of the year.

Beside it much of the other criticism seems out-dated or out-classed. Barbara Leah Harman has written a trio of articles on topics close to those of Fish. 'George Herbert's "Affliction (I)": The Limits of Representation' (*ELH*, 1977) attempts to explain the characteristic collapse at the end of the poem in terms of a struggle between an autobiographical impulse and a sense that such activity is not divinely sanctioned. More convincingly, she examines 'The Collar' (*PMLA*) in the light of recent theoretical accounts of the grammar of narrative. The poem, she suggests, first constructs and then destroys a fiction of personal autonomy and coherence. A similar approach prompts her comparison (*MLN*) between the narrative procedures of Herbert and Coleridge: for the Romantic poet discourse generates the world; for Herbert human speech is always displaced by the utterance of God. Philip Gallagher (*ELN*, 1977) quarrels with Stanley Fish over a point of detail in 'The Forerunners'. The chalk, he suggests, is an allusion not to Exodus but to the classical convention whereby a white stone marks a happy day. This dubious claim supposedly enhances the poem's ambiguity. Clifford Davidson (*EM*) argues that the temple is an image of creation as perfected by grace and art.

Ina Schabert (*Anglia*) asks whether metrical and rhetorical structures carry implicit meaning, taking examples from the verse of Herbert and Byron. The stylistic irregularities in *Don Juan*, it is suggested, reflect what the poet sees as a godless and chaotic universe. Herbert's harmonious technique, by contrast, is the manifestation of a sense of cosmic order. If this article might perhaps be thought to protest too much, Greg Crossan's (*Expl*) is modest to the point of insignificance. An ambiguously sexual metaphor may, he suggests, be perceived in the opening stanza of 'Love (III)'. David L. Simpson (*Expl*), working in similar terms, suggests an allusion to the Song of Solomon in the 'season'd timber' of 'Vertue'.

Some distinguished bibliographical work completes the roll-call of Herbert studies. Kenneth Alan Hovey (*RenQ*) offers stylistic and biographical evidence for the attribution of the English poem 'To the Queen of Bohemia' to George Herbert. His surmises are confirmed by Ted-Larry Pebworth and Claude J. Summers in 'Recovering An Important Seventeenth Century Poetical Miscellany: Cambridge Add. Ms. 4138' (*TCBS*). This collection, compiled in Cambridge between 1610 and 1631, and mislaid since the 1880s, contains early texts of poems by Carew, Randolph,

Corbett, Strode and Henry King. The general conservatism of its attributions makes it of value in determining the authorship of several previously doubtful poems, including 'To the Queen of Bohemia'. This now takes its place as Herbert's longest English poem not included in *The Temple*. George Herbert's elder brother Edward, Lord Herbert of Chirbury (as Amy M. Charles insists we should spell it) receives equally expert attention from J. M. Shuttleworth (*NLWJ*) who provides an annotated checklist of printed works by and about him, as the first step towards a complete bibliography.

The Cavalier poets have been well served, in a different but no less vital way, by the provision of what will surely become the standard student text of their work. Thomas Clayton's *Cavalier Poets*[16] prints more than three hundred poems by Herrick, Carew, Lovelace and Suckling in a modernised text based on the old-spelling O.E.T. editions. Excellent notes are supplied, together with a chronological table, a glossary, a 'Note On Renaissance Cosmology' and a select bibliography. One possible weakness, at a time when Herrick's critics tend increasingly to refer to poems from *Hesperides* as 'H23' or 'H205', is that no indication is given of the place of poems in a complete edition. But this modestly priced volume will, especially as a paperback, receive wide and pleasurable use.

'Trust to Good Verses': Herrick Tercentenary Essays[17] is a book in which H-numbers cluster as thickly as K-numbers on a record sleeve. The articles are papers from the 1974 Robert Herrick Memorial Conference, held at the University of Michigan-Dearborn to commemorate the three-hundredth anniversary of the poet's death. Ted-Larry Pebworth and four assistants provide a useful selected and annotated bibliography and Roger B. Rollin supplies a general introduction. The latter explains the tenor of the conference, in a slightly chilling phrase, as a 'revisionist' views of Herrick (meaning that he is held to be a serious and significant artist rather than a charming craftsman) before drifting off into an unhelpfully psychological account of the poems. Not all the essays, fortunately, are obsessed with seriousness and significance. Gordon Braden demonstrates the casual way in which Herrick borrows verbal detail from the classics, appropriating attractive phraseology without regard to its original context. William Oram makes similar points about the sacred allusions. Herrick, he suggests, invokes the Bible 'in a spirit of fun' and makes purely playful use of religious ceremonies. The claim that this is true of the *Noble Numbers* as well as the *Hesperides* is a dubious one, but his account of Herrick as a sociable and sensuous anticipation of the later seventeenth century is intriguing. Virginia Ramey Mollenkott will have none of it. For her, Herrick is a predecessor of Blake, possessed of a 'transcendental integrative vision' which makes all his poems religious.

After this extravagance the humbler insights of conventional literary scholarship come as a relief. James S. Tillman identifies Herrick's poems to his brother Thomas and to Endymion Porter as georgic rather than pastoral encomia. John T. Shawcross investigates the names of Herrick's mistresses

[16] *Cavalier Poets: Selected Poems*, ed. by Thomas Clayton. O.U.P. pp. xxiv + 364. hb £7.95, pb £2.95.

[17] *'Trust to Good Verses': Herrick Tercentenary Essays*, ed. by Roger B. Rollin and J. Max Patrick. Pittsburgh, Pa: U. of Pittsburgh P. pp. vi + 292.

in *Hesperides*, reaching the cautious conclusion that Herrick 'sometimes' used the names with etymological significance. Helen Marlborough reminds us that the epigram could traditionally be used for praise as well as satire, and compares Herrick's performance in this field with that of Ben Jonson. T. G. S. Cain discusses Herrick's poems on transience as a mode of non-religious meditation. Herrick's popularity in Japan is explained by Shonosuke Ishii in terms of his similarity to classical Japanese verse. A. E. Elmore argues that the two hundred 'prosodically varied' poems in *Hesperides* were written in anticipation of a musical setting. J. Max Patrick re-examines the history of Herrick's reputation, suggesting that L. C. Martin's picture of a peak of fame before 1630 is based on a misunderstanding.

The remaining essays are less convincing. Avon Jack Murphy claims that Herrick consciously distributed those poems in *Hesperides* which make some statement about poetry in order to display the persona's developing literary self-consiousness. Achsah Guibbory confuses aesthetics with fetishism in her suggestion that the concentration upon Julia's clothes involves a transformation of the woman into an art object, and her further claim that Herrick prefers art to nature is based on a very selective reading of his work. (Has she read 'To Dianeme', or 'Upon Julia's Breasts', or 'Clothes Do But Cheat and Cozen Us'?) Norman K. Farmer has some interesting things to say about William Marshall's frontispiece for the 1648 edition of *Hesperides*, but unfortunately accompanies them with a good deal of less cogent material. Claude J. Summers's essay is a painful exercise in which an earnest attempt to make a case for Herrick as a major political poet struggles with an irrepressible loathing of his royalist views.

Herrick has received further attention elsewhere. A. B. Chambers (*SP*, 1977) argues that 'Corinna's Going a Maying' celebrates pagan and Christian rites at the same time, but fails to make his case conclusive. Gene Montague (*Expl*) re-examines the angling image in 'Upon Julia's Clothes'. Robert W. Halli Jr (*Expl*) somehow manages to make both too much and too little of the word 'protestant' in 'To Anthea, Who May Command Him Anything'.

Carew is the subject of a single article, in which Ada Long and Hugh Maclean (*SEL*) suggest that his wit is more searching than is generally acknowledged and attempt to distinguish a third, distinctive style from his Jonsonian and Donne-like manners. Warren W. Wooden (*WVUPP*) discusses the contribution made to Suckling's literary reputation by his love letters, 'complex, sophisticated and unconventional works' which share many themes with his poetry. Richard Fanshawe's translation of Guarini's *Il pastor fido*[18] is the latest volume in the Edinburgh Bilingual Library. The two texts, Italian and English, appear side by side and, though J. H. Whitfield's introduction has little to say about Fanshawe, it does draw attention to the way in which he frequently substitutes 'a graphic particular word' for the elegant generalities of his original.

Sister Veronica Delany's *The Poems of Patrick Cary*[19] is an admirable edition of a neglected minor Caroline poet. The old-spelling text, taken

[18] *Il pastor fido/The Faithfull Shepherd*, ed. by J. H. Whitfield. Edinburgh Bilingual Library (11). Edinburgh: Edinburgh U.P. 1976. pp. x + 414. £2.50.

[19] *The Poems of Patrick Cary*, ed. by Sister Veronica Delany. Oxford: The Clarendon Press. pp. xcvi + 128. £8.

from the unique holograph manuscript in Abbotsford Library, supersedes that given in Saintsbury's *Minor Poets of the Caroline Period*. Excellent appendixes discuss the poet's use of emblems and his musical settings, the commentary is painstaking (the degree of individual identification achieved for the Annes, Betties, Lucies, Maries, Katherines, Pegs and Ruths of 'Surely now I'me out of danger' is astonishing), and the introduction provides the first adequate biography of Cary. As Douglas Bush (*TLS*) points out in his long review of the volume, Lord Falkland's younger brother now emerges as a figure in his own right for the first time. Waller's 'Verses to Dr George Rogers' are said, by Gary P. Storhoff (*Expl*), to demonstrate the poet's ability to develop political ideas within a conventional format.

Ruth Berman (*N&Q*) corrects Morris and Withington's gloss on 11.23–26 of Cleveland's 'Upon Sir Thomas Martin', making clear in the process the point of the heraldic joke. Another of Cleveland's references is elucidated by Ralph Leavis (*N&Q*). 'Leero' and 'Alphonso' in ll.27–28 of 'A young man to an old woman courting him' refer, respectively, to a species of bass viol and to a way of tuning it. On a larger scale, a shrewd awareness of contemporary events on the continent is discovered by W. D. McGaw (*SN*) in the unlikely setting of William Habington's devotional poem 'Nox nocti indicat Scientiam'.

The tercentenary year of Marvell's death has produced seven volumes devoted to his life and work. In the two volumes which collect essays and lectures there are some overlapping material and some omissions (little on the prose, nothing on the Mower poems). *Tercentenary Essays*[20] opens with a survey of Marvell's critical reputation by Elizabeth Story Donno, the fluctuations in which she attributes to the incalculable nature of the poet himself as much as to changes of taste. Thomas Clayton argues that Marvell's conscious play with perspective is the source of the coruscations of the poetry. On the other hand, Joseph Pequigney claims that the two dialogues of the Soul and the 'Drop of Dew' shift their vocabulary at the close from Platonic-ethical to Christian terms to achieve stable resolutions. Harold Toliver presents a poet consciously seeking to transcend his medium and using the analogies of music and picture to demonstrate their limitations. French Fogle indicates the open-endedness of the debate about the 'Coy Mistress', and John Hackett, who surveys the same criticism, tries to rescue the poem from the apparently factitious logic of the speaker by claiming the collusion of the lady herself. Kenneth Friedenreich shows, interestingly, how atypical of contemporary poetry is Marvell's refusal to countenance either guilt or anxiety in the face of death. The poetry's this-worldly view-point guarantees its civilised poise. Joseph H. Summers also enlarges the discussion by his study of a recurrent theme: a transforming moment which offers release from the fluctuations of process. The vocabulary of masque, Muriel Bradbrook argues, with typical economy, is transformed by Marvell into a private ritual, in which mind triumphs over dark circumstance and advances out of the distant spaces of retreat. Isobel G. MacCaffrey, in an important essay, sees 'Appleton House' as a criticism of the excessive hopes and sudden panics of the imagination, which has to be

[20] *Tercentenary Essays in Honour of Andrew Marvell*, ed. by Kenneth Friedenreich. Hamden, Conn.: Shoestring P. pp. 314. $20.

forced into a proper relation with the facts of history. Maren-Sofie Røstvig demonstrates elements of circular design in 'The Unfortunate Lover' and 'Appleton House'. Warren L. Chernaik reads in the late satires a dialectic between political dismay, which threatens speech itself, and confidence in irony, as truthful voice. Joseph Messina valiantly defends the unity of 'Last Instructions' as mock heroic containing an episode of authentic heroic.

The York volume, *Approaches to Marvell*[21], opens with an essay by Christopher Hill detailing the religious and political assumptions shared with Milton. To C. A. Patrides, Marvell's acknowledged elusiveness is a considered response to man's fallen condition. A. J. Smith traces a shared metaphysical pre-occupation, that the fruition of pleasure seals its death, and sees in Marvell's concern for innocence, garden-paradises and reserved tone, strategies to evade that destiny. S. K. Heninger finds in the occasional poetry contrasted Aristotelian and Platonic conceptions of time. Christopher Ricks, in a fresh and spacious essay, identifies the presence of reflexive imagery, where an object is compared with itself, as a search for coherence but a confession of disharmony, in the failure to find true analogy. The cultural implications of this phenomenon are extended to later literature, including contemporary Ulster poets. John Carey studies Marvell's characteristic fear of restriction, which transforms experience into a recurrent trap. Balachandra Rajan elegantly derives Marvell's strength as a poet from the balancing of possible stances and, uniquely, raises the critical issue of whether this also constitutes a limitation. Philip Brockbank allows the contemporary troubled history of Bermuda to exercise ironical commentary on the poem. Louis Martz attributes to the aftermath of war a mannerist aesthetic shared by Marvell and Herrick. Robert Ellrodt sharply distinguishes between introspection and mental image and shows how Marvell's poetry is self-conscious without being confessional. Frank Warnke compares the fusion of fertility and allowed disorder in 'Appleton House' to the 'green world' of Shakespeare's comedies. Barbara Lewalski reads the religious poems as an attempt to heal the divisions of nature and grace. J. A. Wittreich Jr finds in the lines to *Paradise Lost* a double defence, of Milton against contemporary attack, and of Marvell's own poetry against Milton's example. Donald M. Friedman shows that the contemporary physiology of the eye transformed perception from a physical to a mental operation, and that the distance between visual impression and interpretation was of characteristic interest to Marvell. John Dixon Hunt, in the field he has made his own, shows how the diversity, especially of Italian gardens, provides analogies for the poetry, with its interest in hieroglyphic codes, illusionism and the cultivation of the sensibility.

Mr Hunt's more extended contribution, *Andrew Marvell, His Life and Writings*[22], is an original modification of biography. It attributes the various interests apparent in Marvell's writings to the points in his life experience when they might be supposed to have their origins. The dangers of speculation are, of course, apparent to so sophisticated a writer and the

[21] *Approaches to Marvell: the York Tercentenary Lectures*, ed. by C. A. Patrides. London, Henley, and Boston, Mass.: Routledge & Kegan Paul. pp. xvii + 354. £9.95.

[22] *Andrew Marvell: His Life and Writings*, by John Dixon Hunt. Paul Elek. pp. 206. £8.95.

guesses usually convince; for example the location of the religious poems in the period at Eton. More than in most critical lives, a recognisable personality is elicited by the author, albeit contradictory. The British Library catalogue for its exhibition on the occasion, *Andrew Marvell Poet and Politician*[23], compiled by Hilton Kelliher, is a comprehensive and faultless survey of what *is* known about the poet. The descriptions of printed books and MSS make the work an invaluable contribution to the scholarship of its subject.

R. I. V. Hodges's *Foreshortened Time*[24] is a provoking, digressive, dazzlingly stylish attempt to see in Marvell a figure who consciously reacts to a shift in the collective intellectual assumptions of his age. Ramist logic, the alteration of pictorial modes, and Hobbesian psychology appear as agencies and evidence, and excellent and fresh things get said along the way, about Gilbert, Bacon and Hobbes, for instance. The central argument is justified by too few references to the poetry earlier, and the later study of Marvell's political poems is not entirely convincing. But the sheer energy of mind is never less than stimulating. Annabel M. Patterson in *Marvell and the Civic Crown*[25] argues with patient detail for the consistency of viewpoint and literary practice in the political poems. Marvell compels the traditional forms of public rhetoric into greater obedience to the needs of truth. The idealism of the claim *ut pictura poesis* is checked by calculated indecorum in the 'Painter' poems, to display the grotesqueness of political fact. In prose, the aggressions of polemic give way to the sobriety of history. Despite the wildness of occasional detail (Maria Fairfax as Cromwellian activist) a coherent argument is validated.

Elizabeth Story Donno edits the Critical Heritage volume on Marvell[26], which ends with Eliot's 1921 essay. The introduction traces the transformation of patriot into poet and surveys criticism subsequent to the end-date. The essays of John Ormsby, H. C. Beeching and F. C. Bickley have more than purely historical interest.

Among articles, Judith Scherer Herz (*MLQ*) argues for a general debt to Milton's 1645 *Poems* and provides evidence of co-incidence of vocabulary, image and idea. M. Gregory (*Poetics*) offers a familiar account of 'To his Coy Mistress', applying the unfamiliar terminology of linguistic description. Mario L. D'Avanzo (*Expl*) replaces the 'Iron gates' by the 'strait gate' of Matthew 7. Marvell's Nymph has lost her virtue as well as her fawn according to John J. Teunissen and Evelyn J. Hinz (*ELH*). The shared etymology of *foetus* and fawn leads them to read the poem as a sublimated account of the gestation and premature birth – and death – of Sylvio's child. T. Katherine Thomason's nymph (*SEL*) is by contrast blamed for indulging 'petting', in every sense, at the expense of emotional maturity. Sandra

[23] *Andrew Marvell: Poet and Politician 1621–78*, compiled by Hilton Kelliher. British Museum Publications. pp. 128. £7.

[24] *Foreshortened Time: Andrew Marvell and Seventeenth Century Revolutions*, by R. I. V. Hodge. Cambridge: D. S. Brewer; Totowa, N.J.: Rowman & Littlefield. pp. [vi] + 170. pb £3.

[25] *Marvell and the Civic Crown*, by Annabel M. Patterson. Princeton, N.J.: Princeton U.P. pp. x + 264. $16, £10.70.

[26] *Andrew Marvell: The Critical Heritage*, ed. by Elizabeth Story Donno. London, Henley, and Boston, Mass.: Routledge & Kegan Paul. pp. xvii + 385. £8.95.

Billington (*N&Q*) usefully indicates a contemporary use of theatrical image for the king's plight, as in the 'Horatian Ode'. James Turner (*EC*) shows the extent of Marvell's acquaintance with the technicalia of military handbooks in 'Appleton House', and goes on to argue that this recurrent language of violence is transformed to the peaceful ends of life, garden, harvest, food, in the poem. A. S. G. Edwards (*SB*) describes versions of the Restoration satires among the Portland MSS at Nottingham.

Kenneth Friedenreich's *Henry Vaughan*[27] is a useful introductory account of the Silurist as both poet and prose writer. The brief biography dismisses the idea of a dramatic religious conversion, there are clear summaries of recent thought about his debts to Welsh literature, the Bible and his brother's Hermetic philosophy, and individual chapters are devoted to all his major publications except *Thalia Rediviva*. The most original section of the book is that concerned with 'Vaughan and Nature'. Both nineteenth-century accounts of Vaughan as a prototype Romantic, and the more recent tendency to subordinate his landscapes to Hermetic or Augustinian themes, are rejected. Instead he is placed in the context of the landscape poetry of his age. In connection with this it is perhaps appropriate to mention here J. G. Turner's checklist of English topographical poetry 1600–1660 (*N&Q*). More than two hundred examples are recorded and a lively introduction outlines the subdivisions of the genre. John J. Pollock (*Expl*) finds in Vaughan's 'The Dawning' an identification of Christ and nature drawn from the Hermetic tradition.

Karl Josef Höltgen's *Francis Quarles, 1592–1644*[28] is a lengthy and learned study of the most popular English poet of the seventeenth century, combining original biographical research with some careful literary analysis. The history and theory of emblem technique are extensively explored, and readers without German are provided with an excellent English summary of the arguments. Catherine Cole Mambretti (*PBSA*, 1977) describes a new Orinda poem (an epithalamium found in a manuscript in the National Library of Wales) and discusses the status of the other manuscript poems recently attributed to Katherine Philips. Anna E. C. Simoni (*Neophilologus*) describes the Dutch poetry of William Fennor. Previously known as a minor English writer, Fennor is now firmly established as both soldier and literary polyglot. R. Coogan (*N&Q*) notes that Robert Tofte translated twelve poems by Petrarch in the course of his version of Varchi's *The Blazon of Jealousie*, developing an eccentric version of sonnet-form in which to do so. James J. Yoch (*SP*) traces the image of the glowing palace in sixteenth- and seventeenth-century English writing. The glow, predictably, wore off somewhat after the fall of Charles I. James Turner (*N&Q*) corrects August Imholz's suggestion (*N&Q*, 1977) that the ambiguous religious poem 'I hold for faith' first appeared in 1679. It was, in fact, already widely known in 1640. Nicholas Temperley (*SB*, 1977) settles a puzzling bibliographical point by establishing that 'Middleburg Psalms' were editions of the metrical psalms with prose versions in the margin.

[27] *Henry Vaughan*, by Kenneth Friedenreich. Boston, Mass.: Twayne. pp. 180. $9.50.

[28] *Francis Quarles, 1592–1644*, by Karl Josef Höltgen. Tübingen: Niemeyer. pp. xviii + 376. DM 98.

3. Prose

Regrettably little attention has been devoted to prose writing of the period this year. Reinhard H. Friederich in the first of two articles on Donne's *Devotions* (*ArielE*) uses a post-Kierkegaardian vocabulary with tact to analyse the varieties of fear and its gradual transformation from a negative to a positive use. In *ELH* he identifies a double dread in the book, claustrophobia of the body and agoraphobia of space; the discovery of God's presence relates the two and releases from both. Ernest W. Sullivan II (*SB*) shows the extent of John Donne Jr's interference with his father's text of *Biathanatos* in the presentation copies. P. G. Stanwood (*RES*) examines a MS in Dublin, containing contemporary notes for two of the sermons of 1625, and shows the nature of their revision during preparation for publication.

John Feather (*Library*, 1977) shows that Harington's *Oceana* was transferred to a politically neutral printer to secure publication. Florence Sandler (*HLQ*) argues that under cover of discussing the Holy Land in his *Pisgah-Sight*, Fuller comments extensively on English politics from his Erastian and moderate position. William McCarthy (*Criticism*) shows that Davenant's preface to *Gondibert* uses revolutionary claims to disguise its actual conservatism, a defensive posture against the past which has more to do with modernity than its ostensible claims to novelty. John Stachniewski (*Neophilologus*) offers further information about Burton's debt to John Abernathy and indicates his mitigation of the Puritan's analysis of despair. Günther Wiese, *Untersuchungen zu den Prosaschriften Henry Vaughans*[29] offers systematic description of the material and surveys earlier research. Reformation books of private prayer and earlier *artes moriendi* are used to supply analogues and sources for Vaughan's two original prose works, which occupy most of the study. Dr Wiese identifies recurrent patterns of image, again with analogues, and this is likely to be of great use to students of the poetry. The notice taken of the translations is slighter and more derivative.

Walton's *Compleat Angler*[30] has been honoured with a facsimile of the first edition, printed clearly, on good paper and bound in calf at reasonable price. Scholars as well as readers will be glad to have the first version of a work, subsequently much revised and expanded, made so agreeably available. G. d'Hangest in the *festschrift* for Henri Fluchère[11] claims that angling is for Walton the pastime of the Christian epicurean, marked by austerity, the quiet contemplation of nature, and a patient self-knowledge. The 1658 revision of the life of Donne conflates references to God and the King to offer Royalist propaganda, according to Herbert Rothschild Jr (*N&Q*). Walton's politics figure in two further articles. F. G. P. Kellendonk (*Neophilologus*, 1977), by comparing two versions of the translation of Wotton's panegyric on Charles I, attributes both to Walton, partly on the basis of acknowledged faults of Latinity, partly for their well-timed political effect. Jonquil Bevan (*Library*, 1977) shows Walton as the loyal and practical friend of his publisher, Richard Marriot, and decisive influence on the high-church and Royalist bias of Marriot's list.

[29] *Untersuchungen zu den Prosaschriften Henry Vaughans*, by Günther Wiese. Salzburg: Institut für Englische Sprache und Literatur. pp. 156. pb, no price given.

[30] *The Compleat Angler or the Contemplative Man's Recreation*, by Izaac Walton. Adam & Charles Black. pp. [xvi] + 246. £7.50.

XI

Milton

C. A. PATRIDES

1. General

1978 has yielded a work towering not only over the year's studies but commanding the prospect over decades past and to come. Noticed below more extensively, Roland Mushat Frye's *Milton's Imagery and the Visual Arts*[1] deserves a place of honour at the outset in that it weds authority in argument and lucidity in style to provide a patently important contribution to our understanding of Milton's mind in poetry. Selected by the Milton Society as one of the year's two recipients of the James Holly Hanford Award, the work was also the recipient of the American Philosophical Society's John Frederick Lewis Prize.

Another unmistakably prominent contribution is the long-awaited *Milton Encyclopedia*, now being published by Bucknell University Press under the general editorship of William B. Hunter Jr. Four volumes of this mighty endeavour have now appeared[2]; the publication of the remaining four is imminent. 'This compilation', we are told, 'attempts to bring together all the important information and opinion concerning the life and works of John Milton'; yet 'in some ways [it] has grown to be a study of English civilisation of Milton's time and a history of literary and political matters since then'. The lengthier essays draw one's attention first, and one's impression after reading some of the more substantial contributions – especially on Milton's response to the 'Arts of Design' (by Amy L. Turner), to the Bible (James H. Sims), to Dante (Albert R. Cirillo) and Italian literature generally (F. T. Prince), to the classical epic (George deF. Lord), to Hebraism (Harold Fisch), and to historiography (French Fogle) – is distinctly favourable. One responds no less favourably to the attempted surveys on 'Diction' (by Katherine D. Carter) and, especially, on 'Influence' (by John T. Shawcross, James G. Nelson, and Harry Blamires); to the extremely useful roll-calls, whether under 'Illustrators' (by Joseph A. Wittreich), or under 'Editions' both of the poetry and of the prose (by Shawcross), or under 'Attributions' of a variety of poems, tracts, and other items to Milton (also by the omnipresent and omniscient Shawcross); and to the numerous original essays, in particular those on 'Decrees, Divine' (by John M. Steadman), 'Ecclesiology' (Michael Fixler), 'Ethics' (Albert

[1] *Milton's Imagery and the Visual Arts: Iconographic Tradition in the Epic Poems*, by Roland Mushat Frye. Princeton, N. J.: Princeton U.P. pp. xv + 408; with 8 plates in colour. and 261 in black and white. $37.50.

[2] *A Milton Encyclopedia*, gen. ed. William B. Hunter Jr; co-editors: John T. Shawcross and John M. Steadman; assoc. eds. Puvis E. Boyette and Leonard Nathanson. Canbury, N.J.: Bucknell U.P.; London: Associated University Presses. Vol. I, pp. 208; Vol. II, pp. 206; Vol. III, pp. 200; Vol. IV, pp. 218. Each volume $25; £13.50.

W. Fields), 'Humanism' (Albert R. Cirillo), and 'Imagery, Visual and Auditory' (Wayne Shumaker). Some flaws there are, notably the several inadequate entries here and there; but all in all the enterprise is a testimony to the vision and the industry of the editors in the first instance, and of the contributors in the second. A co-operative endeavour worthy of emulation hereafter, *A Milton Encyclopedia* is sufficiently imaginative in conception, prodigal in range, and authoritative in execution, to merit our approbation as a major contribution to our understanding of Milton and his age.

David M. Miller's general account of Milton's poetry[3] is a useful attempt to provide prefatory guidance for two kinds of readers, specified as 'the student reading Milton seriously for the first time, and the nonspecialist who wishes a companion voice as he renews acquaintance with Milton's genius'. The student in question, it should be understood, is likely to be the inexperienced undergraduate about to enter the world of Milton's poetry at an elementary level. He will certainly find here the basic 'facts' and, equally, surveys of the poems – sometimes mere surveys of 'what happens', but more often useful preliminary considerations of the interlocked movements within the given poem: the Nativity Ode, *L'Allegro* and *Il Penseroso, Comus, Lycidas, Paradise Lost, Paradise Regained*, and *Samson Agonistes*. Miller is not concerned to provide a critical biography of the poet after the fashion of, say, David Daiches's *Milton* (1957); and he is even less interested in delineating the poetry in relation to the scholarship that has gathered about it, perhaps in distant emulation of James H. Hanford's once useful *Milton Handbook*. The former approach would in any case be unlikely since Miller eschews sophisticated readings for suggestive ones; and the latter would be impossible since the book would necessarily have been much more impressive than it is. In the event, Miller's effort may be recommended as one that looks beyond itself in both its immediate perceptions and its mode of articulation. Miller certainly writes very lucidly, his nicely turned phrases extending from the comment on the Nativity Ode's ever-moving images that 'collapse linear evolution into timeless art' to Samson's 'visceral exchanges with Dalila and Harapha'. One of the happiest of his utterances occurs in the preface, where it is said that Milton always 'strove to subdue the pride of art to the glory of God, and it is remarkable that, in pursuing the second, he so often achieved the first'.

A book entitled *Milton and Sex* does not, on the face of it, appear to be very promising. But its author, Edward Le Comte[4], possesses credentials which remove him far from the merely sensational. 'The subject', he tells us in the preface, 'is of some importance'; and he adds with well-advised caution that his readers should not be surprised if they find themselves in 'the realm of the speculative'. He then starts rousingly – or, lest I be accused of punning, promisingly – with a glance at the 'gumms of glutenous heat' in *Comus* (l. 917). In short, this is a study which attends to details through a microscope. But the telescopic view is not eschewed since

[3] *John Milton: Poetry*, by David M. Miller. TEAS, 242. Boston, Mass.: Twayne. pp. 199. $8.95.

[4] *Milton and Sex*, by Edward Le Comte. London: Macmillan; New York: Columbia U.P. pp. x + 154. £6.95; $12.50.

Le Comte examines the probable implications of 'the shattering impact' of Milton's first marriage, revisits 'the vulgar charge of misogyny', surveys the satiric barbs centred on sex in the polemical prose, and – in what is the book's major contribution – studies the 'perfect marriage' before the Fall in a chapter flanked on the one hand by the demonic strain in Milton's Hell and on the other by the dramatic situation in *Samson Agonistes*. Le Comte's *Milton and Sex* is certainly about the one but not solely about the other.

The *Milton Quarterly* continues its sage policy of reproducing visual interpretations of the Fall of Man. The range of the illustrations provided may be gathered from the third of its four issues this year, which reproduces on its covers the frontispiece to the Book of Genesis in the Geneva Bible of 1583 and the expulsion scene in the Flemish Medici Tapestries of *circa* 1550. But other subjects are not bypassed, witness the reproduction in the year's first issue of Andrea Mantegna's 'Samson and Delilah'.

Milton's relations with Marvell are delineated in two of the contributions to this year's tercentenary celebrations of Marvell[5]. The first, Christopher Hill's 'Milton and Marvell', details the political orientation of the two men and posits affinities beyond the commonly accepted ones; while the second, Joseph A. Wittreich's 'Perplexing the Explanation: Marvell's "On Mr. Milton's Paradise Lost"', focuses on Marvell's tribute to his friend's epic poem in order to comprehend its implications for the literary careers of both. In a third essay published elsewhere, Judith S. Herz's 'Milton and Marvell: The Poet as Fit Reader' (*MLQ*), the two poets are juxtaposed yet again, this time through useful speculations on the influence that each may be said to have exerted on the other.

Some of the year's other essays are necessarily wide-ranging. George Miller, Kenneth J. Ames and John Huntley in 'Milton in the Classroom: Some Experiences and Perspectives' (*MiltonQ*) indulge in several speculations – some intriguing, nearly all subjective – as well as one ringing declaration of rather alarming implications ('Milton. . .strikes me more and more as a poet of defeat'). Sandra M. Gilbert in 'Patriarchal Poetry and Women Readers: Reflections on Milton's Bogey' (*PMLA*) marshals the views of novelists like Virginia Woolf to assert their diverse responses to 'the first of the masculinists'. Rachel Trickett in 'Shakespeare and Milton' (*E&S*) revisits a much-laboured field and fascinatingly calls attention to the Shakespearean echoes in passages such as Christ's speech in *Paradise Regained*, II, 457–65. Edward Le Comte in 'Sly Milton: The Meaning Lurking in the Contexts of his Quotations' (*Greyfriar*) revises a zestful study already noticed in these pages (*YW* 57.178). Clifford Davidson in 'The Young Milton, Orpheus and Poetry' (*ES*) studies the associations of the Orphic paradigm in relation to Milton's vocation, and responds to his subject with a noteworthy stylistic felicity. Thomas W. Hayes in 'Natural Law and Milton's Attack on Corruption' (*BuR* 1977) provides one of the most sustained examinations of Milton's intricate attitude to natural law. Leonard R. Mendelsohn in 'Milton and the Rabbis: A Later Inquiry' (*SEL*) argues that Milton's knowledge of rabbinic literature was limited and his borrowings were 'sporadic'.

[5] *Approaches to Marvell: The York Tercentenary Lectures*, ed. by C. A. Patrides. London and Boston, Mass.: Routledge & Kegan Paul. pp. xvii + 354. £9.95; $23.50.

Elijah Fenton's life of Milton – the most popular work of its kind in the eighteenth century – has been deemed worthy of a reprint; but since its total of eight pages costs $6.50, one can be permitted to wonder how many readers will find the expense warranted[6].

Milton Studies appeared this year in two volumes: the eleventh in the series, with B. Rajan as guest editor[7]; and the twelfth, edited as usual by James B. Simmonds[8]. The Rajan volume, subtitled *The Presence of Milton*, aspires through its six essays to provide as many considerations of Milton's influence – or, better still, 'the many forms of relationship that arise from and declare the Miltonic continuity'. The essays constitute, we are informed, an exploratory 'beginning'; yet their effect is far more substantial, responsibly argued and well written as they all are. Earl Miner in 'Dryden's Admired Acquaintance, Mr. Milton' would have profited much from a study of the most important relevant essay, Bernard Harris's '"That soft seducer, love": Dryden's *The State of Innocence and Fall of Man*' in *Approaches to 'Paradise Lost'* (ed. C. A. Patrides, 1968); even so, Milton's general impact on Dryden is expertly set forth, the limits of their convergence clearly affirmed and the lines of demarcation never blurred. Barbara K. Lewalski in 'On Looking into Pope's Milton' demonstrates Pope's 'intelligent but never idolatrous admiration for many facets of Milton's genius and works' and rightly discriminates between the stylistic debt to Milton in the translations of the *Iliad* and the *Odyssey* ('most extensive and significant') and that in the *Dunciad* ('most extensive, most significant, and most creative').

Joseph A. Wittreich in 'Blake's Milton: "To Immortals. . .a Mighty Angel"' extends the connections between the two poets he had so admirably detailed in his full-length study *Angel of Apocalypse: Blake's Idea of Milton* (*YW* 56.211–2). Edna Newmeyer in 'Wordsworth on Milton and the Devil's Party' examines the extent to which both Wordsworth and Coleridge recognised in Satan not the hero of *Paradise Lost* but mankind's arch-enemy. Douglas Bush in 'The Milton of Keats and Arnold' generalises with characteristic grace and acumen on Keats's 'intense and finely perceptive admiration for Miltonic art' and on Arnold's 'classic formulations of general attitudes and ideas which existed before him and which he did much to establish as orthodoxy'. B. Rajan, finally, in 'Milton and Eliot: A Twentieth-Century Acknowledgment' discriminates subtly between imitation and influence, annexing Eliot's opposition to Milton to the former, and his actual response to him to the latter. Rajan's wide-ranging remarks in his introduction to this entire volume, incidentally, should be regarded with care in that they are so many signposts to the further exploration of the vital subject of Milton's influence.

The 'presence of Milton' in a particular period is the exclusive province

[6] *The Life of John Milton*, by Elijah Fenton. Intro. by Edward Le Comte. Norwood, Pa.: Norwood Editions, 1977. pp. iii + 8. $6.50.

[7] *Milton Studies XI: The Presence of Milton*, ed. by B. Rajan. Pittsburgh: U. of Pittsburgh P. pp. xiv + 129. $9.95.

[8] *Milton Studies XII*, ed. by James B. Simmonds. Pittsburgh: U. of Pittsburgh P. pp. xi + 266. $14.95.

[9] *Milton and the Romantics*, ed. by Luther L. Scales Jr. pp. 27. $2. To be edited hereafter by Stuart Peterfreund and Arthur Weitzman; subscriptions from The Department of English, Northwestern University, 360 Huntington Avenue, Boston, Mass. 02115, USA.

of the most specialised new journal yet, *Milton and the Romantics*[9]. Appearing but once a year, its third 'volume', published in 1977, encompasses within its twenty-five pages several reviews and three illuminating essays: Jerome A. Kramer's '"Virtue, Religion, and Patriotism": Some Biographies of Milton in the Romantic Era'; Stephen C. Behrendt's '*Comus* and *Paradise Regained*: Blake's View of Trial in the Wilderness'; and Stuart Peterfreund's 'Wordsworth, Milton, and the End of Adam's Dream'. The fourth volume is promised for 1980.

Four other studies of Milton and the Romantics may also be mentioned: Stephen C. Behrendt's 'The Mental Conquest' (*BS*), which provides a perceptive study of Blake's designs for *Comus*; Karen Mulhallen's 'William Blake's Milton Portraiture and Eighteenth Century Milton Iconography' (*CLQ*), which reproduces and annotates fourteen visual interpretations of the poet to confirm the thesis that Blake adapted traditional modes of apprehension to his particular purposes; Paul Sherwin's 'Dying into Life: Keats's Struggle with Milton in *Hyperion*' (*PMLA*), which attends to the response to Milton by Keats; and Stuart Peterfreund's 'In Free Homage and Generous Subjection' (*TWC*), which examines Milton's impact on *The Excursion*.

So far as the eighteenth century is concerned, Lillian D. Bloom in 'Addison's Popular Aesthetic: The Rhetoric of the *Paradise Lost* Papers' – part of a composite volume cited below[14] – provides the most sustained reading to date of Addison's much-misunderstood essays on the epic, while Michael J. Marcuse investigates 'The Pre-Publication History of William Lauder's *Essay on Milton's Use and Imitation of the Moderns in his Paradise Lost* [1749]' (*PBSA*) and relieves Samuel Johnson of any complicity in the deception of the public perpetrated by Lauder. But 'the presence of Milton' is also detected in still further studies, notably Phyllis Cole's 'The Purity of Puritanism: Transcendentalist Readings of Milton' (*SIR*), which collects the responses of Emerson, Margaret Fuller, and others. Finally, Miltonic allusions in Melville, Emily Dickinson, and Faulkner, are noted by Leslie E. Sheldon (*Melville Society Extracts*), Wolfgang Rudat (*AN&Q*), and Beth Burch (*Notes on Contemporary Literature*).

Arthur E. Barker, who in 1976 was honoured with one collection of essays (*YW* 57.178), is now honoured with another[10]. This second enterprise is equally disappointing: as noted below, three of the four essays appertaining to Milton are of uncertain merit, although one (by Douglas Chambers) displays a promise that may well be realised in a more sustained study.

The year's bibliographical surveys and sustained reviews include those by G. K. Hunter (*SR*), Virginia R. Mollenkott (*MiltonQ*), and Claes Schaar (*ES*). It should also be recorded that the second volume of the annual publication of the Milton Centre of Japan, *MCJ News*, includes a bibliography of Japanese studies of Milton in 1976.

2. The Shorter Poems

Mason Tung proposes the influence on *In quintum Novembris* of Virgil's conception of *Fama* or Rumour (*MiltonQ*). George W. Smith Jr in 'Milton's

[10] ***Familiar Colloquy: Essays presented to Arthur Edward Barker***, **ed. by Patricia Bruckmann. Toronto: Oberon P. pp. 230.**

Method of Mistakes in the Nativity Ode' (*SEL*) attends to the structural implications of the errors followed by their correction throughout the poem. Hugh MacCallum in 'The Narrator of Milton's "On the Morning of Christ's Nativity"' (in the Barker volume)[10] comments on the poem impressionistically and, surprising for such a perceptive reader of Milton, derivatively. Michael O'Connell and John Powell in 'Music and Sense in Handel's Setting of Milton's *L'Allegro* and *Il Penseroso*' (*ECS*) argue in sustained fashion that Handel's decisive interpretation of the twin lyrics encompasses playful elements and retains to the end an impressive tentativeness about the claims of Mirth and Melancholy respectively. Mary Ann McGuire in 'Milton's *Arcades* and the Entertainment Tradition' (*SP*) maintains that the poem is 'a superb adaptation of received generic conventions', particularly in that it is a version of the entry episode in an estate entertainment. George Falle deploys the phrases 'a solemn measure . . .a iust proportion' (in the Barker volume)[10] superficially to argue their application to 'At a Solemn Music' on the one hand and Dryden's 'Song for St Cecilia's Day' on the other. Mary Christopher Pecheux in '"At a Solemn Musick": Structure and Meaning' (*SP*) discerns in the poem a significant attention to the musical octave – widely credited as symbolic of the ultimate harmony – that successfully weds external form and internal argument.

Comus is crucially regarded as 'pure Spenserian epithalamium' in the wide-ranging discourse by Richard Neuse, 'Milton and Spenser: The Virgilian Triad Revisited' (*ELH*), which argues with an optimum of suggestiveness the case for the decisive impact of Virgil on Spenser and Milton. Karl P. Wentersdorf in 'The "Rout of Monsters" in *Comus*' (*MiltonQ*) usefully examines various transformations of the Circe legend and the import of Milton's symbolic beasts. Daniel L. Colvin in 'Milton's *Comus* and the Pattern of Human Temptation' (*Christianity and Literature*) argues that the masque is concerned with action dependent on 'the proper knowledge of the self and the world and a concentrated exercise of the proper faculties'. Saad El-Gabalawy in 'Christian Communism in *Utopia, King Lear*, and *Comus*' (*UTQ*) speculates without substantial evidence on whether More, Shakespeare and Milton partook of a 'movement' aimed at 'the amelioration of material conditions of all men through the sharing of goods'.

Lycidas has a precise context in the memorial volume of 1638 within which it first appeared; and that context is now available in the facsimile of *Justa Edovardo King*[11], published by Norwood Editions with an introduction, translation of all the Latin poems, and notes – all the work of the indefatigable Edward Le Comte. The edition is indispensable and should be readily accessible not only in libraries but within reach of all serious readers of the pastoral elegy.

A symposium on *Lycidas*, held at the Milton Centre of Japan, encompassed three papers – Hiroichiro Doke's 'The Theme and Structure of *Lycidas*', June Harada's 'A Monodic Approach to *Lycidas*', and Haruhiko Fujii's 'The Three Patterns of Movement in *Lycidas*' – now abstracted by their authors with an introductory note by Akira Arai (*MCJNews*).

[11] *Justa Edovardo King*, with introduction, annotation and notes by Edward Le Comte. Norwood, Pa.: Norwood Editions. $20.

William E. Cain in '*Lycidas* and the Reader's Response' (*DR*) emphasises the importance of the transcendence of the literal, phenomenal world by 'a higher truth'. Edward W. Tayler in '*Lycidas* Yet Once More' (*HLQ*) discourses with characteristic suggestiveness on 'the fugitive ways' the poem attends to the life of historical personages even as it engages in a dialogue with its predecessors within the tradition of the pastoral elegy. Michael Lieb in ' "Yet Once More": The Formulaic Opening of *Lycidas*' (*MiltonQ*) discourses on the poem's pagan, biblical, and political dimensions, especially in relation to their eschatological burden. J. Martin Evans annotates the dolphins that waft Lycidas (l. 164) by citing the death of another poet, Hesiod, whose corpse (as Plutarch related) was 'received by a float or troupe of Dolphins, and by them carried as farre as to the capes of Rhion and Molychria' (*N&Q*). Robert E. Jungman annotates lines 165–73 by invoking Catullus (*Classical Folia*).

John E. Gorecki relates the last two lines of Sonnet XIII to Aeschylus's *Agamemnon*, 420–26 (*N&Q*). Sidney Greenbaum in 'The Poem, the Poet, and the Reader: An Analysis of Milton's Sonnet 19' (*L&S*) regards the poem not as static but as 'in flux, vibrant with alternative interpretations'. John J. Glavin juxtaposes Sonnet XIX and Hopkins's 'Patience' in ' "The Exercise of Saints": Hopkins, Milton, and Patience' (*TSLL*), and fascinatingly observes the formation of an antithetical dyptich.

3. 'Paradise Lost'

Noteworthy both in itself and as an interpretation of Milton's epic, Krzysztof Penderecki's opera *Paradise Lost* had its world premiere in Chicago's Lyric on 29 November 1978. Commissioned six years earlier as part of the bicentennial celebrations of the United States, the opera is based on a libretto by Christopher Fry. In an enthusiastic review, Michael Lieb describes the work as 'grand opera', records his essentially positive response, and praises in particular Penderecki's music, 'closer to oratorio than anything else' (*MiltonQ*).

As noted at the outset of this chapter, Roland Mushat Frye's *Milton's Imagery and the Visual Arts*[1] is an achievement of the highest excellence. Articulated with palpable clarity, the argument unfolds authoritatively from an initial assertion of Milton's visual imagination *pace* T. S. Eliot and others ('Milton may be said never to have seen anything') to a demonstration of Milton's full awareness of the visual arts as a direct result of his visit to Italy. The book's thesis is amply proven in the ensuing five sustained discourses on the visual dimensions of the demonic and celestial realms, of the created universe, of the human world, and of the world redeemed (the latter in relation exclusively to *Paradise Regained*). Each discourse encompasses some preliminary observations and an exposition of the changing patterns of visual representation, but finally centres on a wondrously detailed examination of Milton's adjustment of the inherited pictorial tradition to his purposes. Felicities abound. Thus the poet's delineation of the dolorous realm inclusive of Satan and his disciples cannot hereafter be discussed without reference to Frye's thesis about the decisive impact of the visual arts, witness *inter alia* his examination of the humanoid devils in relation to numerous paintings such as Beccafumi's stunning *Michael and the Fallen Angels* – or, where a lesser but highly-controverted subject such as Eden's 'vegetable gold' is concerned, the firm conclusion that Milton's representation was all too standard among painters. In short, no pattern is too small, as no pattern is ever too large, to be accommodated within Frye's alert devotion to those cumulative details that consistently enrich one's visual appreciation of Milton's eminently visual poetry. Whether he attends to the hair styles of Adam and Eve or to the grandiose vision of history in the last two books of *Paradise Lost*, Frye advances with the complete assurance of a scholar who commands his field in all its infinite complexity. Yet the issue is never forced; for where no substantial evidence is provided by the visual arts – as none is available either on the sex life of the angels or on Adam and Eve holding hands, for instance – Frye expressly states so (pp. 182, 282), and passes on to other vital thematic patterns. The compass of his study is even broader than one might have expected, in that the argument often expands to include a highly-compressed summary of the Renaissance garden in relation to Milton's Eden, or to provide a most suggestive account of topographical representations pertinent to the events in *Paradise Regained*. The eight plates in colour, and the 261 in black and white, are so well reproduced that, together with the book's overall design, they elicit one's admiration for the evident efforts of Princeton University Press to match visually the splendid argument of Frye's magisterial study.

U. Milo Kaufmann's monograph on *Paradise in the Age of Milton*[12] is concerned with 'those literary and scriptural constructions which feature the interpenetration of earth and heaven' in Milton as in Herrick and Marvell. The monograph aspires to annotate the Miltonic versions of paradise, culminating in 'that consummated union of earth and heaven which means beatitude not only for individuals but for nature and the entire community of man'; and next, it contextualises those versions by placing them within Milton's moral and aesthetic theodicies. The poetry *qua* poetry is kept largely at a distance; yet the monograph impresses because it is lucid in style and zestful in argument.

Shahla Anand's study of the emblem tradition in relation to *Paradise Lost*[13] begins with two testimonials on her behalf and ends with a synopsis of the book's argument, a full-page photograph of the author, and a full-page biographical sketch not devoid of some degree of self-praise. The typescript – for the book is offset from typescript – displays generous reading in the emblematic literature Milton could be claimed to have consulted; yet the book remains, when all is said, fundamentally a mere catalogue of the relevant material. Connections with *Paradise Lost* are not habitually ventured with much sophistication; and too many of the details appear to be regarded as more or less equal to all the other details. Nominally parallel passages are said to be 'like' Milton's, or else 'equivalent' or 'similar' to Milton's (pp. 177, 80, 111, 228, etc.); alternatively, one of Milton's descriptions 'brings to mind' an emblematist (p. 163), and he is

[12] *Paradise in the Age of Milton*, by U. Milo Kaufmann. English Literary Studies Monograph Series, 11. Victoria, B.C.: U. of Victoria. pp. 84. $3.75.

[13] *Of Costliest Emblem: 'Paradise Lost' and the Emblem Tradition*, by Shahla Anand. Washington, D.C.: University Press of America. pp. ix + 297. $10.25.

also said to share 'the same allegorical tradition' of one of his contemporaries (p. 165) who in turn has 'much in common' with others (p. 57). Where Milton is unlike others, he is expressly claimed to be just that: 'unlike' (p. 95). Generalisations are even more improbable. Adam's 'dramatic flaw', for example, is identified as his 'inordinate love for Eve' (p. 252). Before the creation of Eve, we are also assured, Adam was a hermaphrodite (p. 38) – or, as we are later informed, 'androgynous. . .like the primeval God of the Hindu pantheon, Brahma' (p. 219). The book is, clearly, stillborn.

In a composite volume on *The Author in his Work*[14], three essays address themselves to *Paradise Lost*: George de F. Lord's 'Milton's Dialogue with Omniscience in *Paradise Lost*', which dwells on the invocations to Books I, III, VII, and IX, in order to comprehend the nature of Milton's 'unabashed projection of himself into his epic'; Janet Adelman's 'Creation and the Place of the Poet in *Paradise Lost*', which explicates Milton's 'anxieties about his own creative process and about the special status of his poem' as reflected in his sustained concern with modes of creativity; and Louis L. Martz's '*Paradise Lost*: The Solitary Way', which emphasises the marked amendments Milton introduced into the traditional representations of the expulsion.

Milton Studies XII[8] includes four studies of the epic: Douglas A. Northrop's 'The Double Structure of *Paradise Lost*', which confirms the significance of the poem's sequential and spatial aspects by resorting to the perspectives of time and eternity; Don P. Norford's 'The Separation of the World Parents in *Paradise Lost*', which dwells on some intriguing ramifications – most particularly on Eve as the poem's 'creative principle' – with a rather self-conscious invocation of Kierkegaard, Buber, Marcuse, *et al.*; Diane McColley's 'Eve's Dream', which zestfully argues that the dream (V, 28–93) is an opportunity for Eve ('a free agent in a perilous world') to exert her 'freely willed obedience by means of a fully informed imagination'; and Dennis Danielson's 'Milton's Arminianism and *Paradise Lost*', which attends to the theological dimension that informs the transition from the later part of Book X to the earlier one of Book XI.

Douglas Chambers in 'Darkness Visible' (in the Barker volume)[10] discourses on the seventeenth century's taste for chiaroscuro and tenebrism as a way of comprehending 'the principle of definition by absence by which Satan and hell are delineated in *Paradise Lost*'. C. Herbert Gilliland in 'Limitary Patterns in *Paradise Lost*' (*SAB*) argues energetically that the 'active tension between the establishment of boundaries and their violation' is one of the fundamental aspects of the poem's organisation. Herbert F. Tucker Jr in 'Gravity and Milton's Moral Physics' (*MiltonQ*) touches on some instances of the poem's 'numerous descriptions of individual falls, drops, ruins, descents, lapses, and cadences'. Albert C. Labriola in 'The Titans and the Giants: *Paradise Lost* and the Tradition of the Renaissance Ovid' (*MiltonQ*) discerns by way of George Sandys's edition of the *Metamorphoses* (1632) connections between the actions of the fallen angels

[14] *The Author in his Work: Essays on a Problem in Criticism*, ed. by Louis L. Martz and Aubrey Williams, intro. by Patricia Meyer Spacks. New Haven, Conn. and London: Yale U.P. pp. xix + 407. $22.50.

and the evil deeds of fallen men. Robert J. Wickenheiser resolutely proclaims that 'Milton's Pattern of a Christian Hero' is the Son of God (*MiltonQ*).

Virginia R. Mollenkott in 'Some Implications of Milton's Androgynous Muse' (*BuR*) meditates on some of the distinctly androgynous elements in *Paradise Lost*, inclusive of the Muse who inspires the poet. Margaret M. Byard in 'Divine Wisdom – Urania' (*MiltonQ*) notes that Andrea Sacchi's ceiling fresco of 'Divine Wisdom' with its central figure of Urania, already *in situ* when Milton visited the Barberini Palace in Rome for a performance of Giulio Rospigliosi's *Chi soffre, speri* (February 1639), may be relevant to the poet's later invocation of 'Heav'nly Muse' in *Paradise Lost* (I, 6, and III, 19) – always provided, of course, that Milton had in fact seen the fresco. Albert C. Labriola in '*Christus Patiens*: The Virtue Patience and *Paradise Lost*, I–II'[15] surveys the epic in terms of Christ's heroic patience and its demonic counterpart in Satan. John Wooten in 'Satan, Satire, and Burlesque Fables in *Paradise Lost*' (*MiltonQ*) sketches Satan's development from a potentially tragic figure to one that 'becomes enmeshed in the coils of God's satiric punishment and the traps of Milton's burlesque debunking'. Michael Lieb in 'Further Thoughts on Satan's Journey through Chaos' (*MiltonQ*) stresses the 'excremental vision' – 'almost Swiftian in its repulsiveness' yet Rabelaisian in its effects – that appears to stalk Satan's mission to destroy man. Philip C. Kolin dwells on 'Milton's Use of Clouds for Satanic Parody in *Paradise Lost*' (*ELWIU*) and concludes that the image illustrates both infernal folly and divine providence.

Stephen Wigler in 'The Poet and Satan before the Light' (*MiltonQ*) cleverly juxtaposes the poet's invocation to Book III and its 'unintentional parody' by Satan in Book IV (32–113) in order to emphasise, through their very differences, the intended celebration of the Son's decision to save man. Linda Davis Kyle in 'Milton's Eden: Cyclical Amplification of Spenser's Gardens' (*SELit*) revisits the Spenserian dimension of Milton's poetry in terms of the structurally significant 'moralized landscapes' of the Gardens of Proserpina and of Adonis on the one hand, and the Garden of Eden on the other. Kathleen Blake in 'Towards a Utopian Psychology: The Quality of Life in Milton's Eden' (*NDQ*) defends the poet's conception of the prelapsarian state as a creditable realisation of humanity's potential. Diane McColley in '"Daughter of God and Man": The Subordination of Eve' (in the Barker volume)[10] revisits the familiar arguments about Eve's dignity and freedom, and somehow manages to sound more sombrely moralistic than Milton ever is.

Cheryl F. Fresch in 'Milton's Eve and the Problem of the Additions to the Command' (*MiltonQ*) attends to the discrepancy between the original command not to eat the forbidden fruit (VIII, 329–30) and Even's different version of it (IX, 659–63). Robert L. Entzminger in 'Michael's Options and Milton's Poetry: *Paradise Lost* XI and XII' (*ELR*) examines the contours of the epic's final movement in terms of the new mode of revelation necessitated by the Fall, the eventually attained wisdom centred on the Word. William J. Dowie in '*Paradise Lost*: A Hypothetical Fall' (*Innisfree* 1977) briefly and superficially opines that Adam's behaviour in Book

[15] In *The Triumph of Peace: Medieval and Renaissance Studies*, ed. Gerald J. Schiffhorst. Orlando, Fla.: U. Presses of Florida.

IX is 'a brave fall of love' (a thesis long since argued by A. J. A. Waldock) and the like. Finally, there are annotations of I, 609, by Carter and Stella Revard (*MiltonQ*); IX, 648, by Robert F. Fleissner (*AN&Q*); X, 578–84, by Philip J. Gallagher (*MiltonQ*); and X, 325–29, by John E. Gorecki (*ELN*). It should also be recorded that *Paradise Lost* has been translated into Japanese by Akira Arai[16].

4. 'Paradise Regained' and 'Samson Agonistes'

Milton Studies XII[8] includes four essays on *Paradise Regained*: Mary Christopher Pecheux's 'Milton and *Kairos*', which studies the poet's concern with the concept of time in advance of its reappearance in *Paradise Regained*; David Renaker's 'The Horoscope of Christ', which annotates Satan's astrological prognostication (IV, 382–93) with a learned examination of the abundant materials on astrological lore and astronomical theories; Edward Le Comte's 'Satan's Heresies in *Paradise Regained*', which catalogues the numerous points of dogma touched by Satan ('a would-be Christologist who grapples with some real problems – and loses'); and Malcolm Kelsall's 'The Historicity of *Paradise Regained*', which dwells on the actual historical background to the temptations in the wilderness and remarks on a number of the more fascinating implications of the confluence of history and poetry.

Richard D. Jordan in '*Paradise Regained*: A Dramatic Analogue' (*MiltonQ*) argues that Milton's poem belongs within the tradition of biblical drama as represented by Jean Michel's *Le Mystère de la Passion*. A. Burnett annotates the gathering of sticks by the disguised Satan (I, 316) in terms of Numbers 15.32–36 (*N&Q*). Kathleen M. Swaim in 'Hercules, Antaeus, and Prometheus: A Study of the Climactic Epic Similes in *Paradise Regained*' (*SEL*) attends to 'the major thrust of the themes and artistry' of the poem by way of its concluding analogies (IV, 562–81), where Milton meaningfully shifts 'poetic gears' (*sic*) to accommodate mythological implications as they relate to the redemption of man.

Mary Ann Radzinowicz's *Toward 'Samson Agonistes': The Growth of Milton's Mind*[17] is, beyond any doubt, the most ambitious study of Milton's play to date, comparable in its generous compass to Barbara K. Lewalski's equally massive study of *Paradise Regained* (*Milton's Brief Epic*, 1966). Radzinowicz has clearly expended many years – one suspects a decade but it was actually more than two – marshalling and mastering her encylcopaedic details into one sustained performance. The authority with which she discourses is so overwhelming that by the time one reaches the last of her appendixes – an expert demolition of all theories against, and a cumulatively persuasive argument in favour of, a late composition date – one is tempted simply to surrender. The book's subtitle is certainly awe-inspiring, for who would today dare to encompass within a single study the development of a poet's mind? But the daring is securely grounded on a thorough familiarity with the sum of Milton's works in poetry as in prose, while the approach itself is by way of a 'contextual' study of the

[16] *Rakuen no Soshitsu*, translated by Akira Arai. Tokyo: Taiskukan. pp. 411.

[17] *Toward 'Samson Agonistes': The Growth of Milton's Mind*, by Mary Ann Radzinowicz. Princeton, N.J.: Princeton U.P. pp. xxiii + 436. $27.50; £17.50.

play in the light of Milton's logic or dialectic, his conception of history, his politics, his ethics, his theology, and his poetics. Profuse in detail and ever-expansive in perceptions, the argument often pauses long enough to attend to a single work – the pages devoted to *Lycidas*, for example, contribute the finest single study of its political orientation – even as the ultimate goal is never misplaced en route ('[*Lycidas*] strikingly prepares for the strategy of *Samson Agonistes*'). Radzinowicz's claims will not be accepted in every case, especially where she avers *inter alia* that *Samson Agonistes* contains Milton's 'most advanced theological position' and enacts his 'most revolutionary poetics'. Yet the claims will continue to command our respect for the committed way they are articulated, while most of us will learn habitually to consult her considered views on the individual works she discusses and the intellectual patterns she delineates. Justly selected by the Milton Society as one of the year's two recipients of the Hanford Award, *Toward 'Samson Agonistes'* is clearly a book for all seasons.

Samson Agonistes has not benefited only from Radzinowicz's highly recommended study, however. It is further illumined by several excellent essays, especially the three in *Milton Studies XII*[8]: Joan S. Bennett's 'Liberty under the Law: The Chorus and the Meaning of *Samson Agonistes*', which studies Milton's views on the experience of a people in bondage to the law and applies them to his delineation of the developing attitudes of the Chorus; John N. Wall's 'The Contrarious Hand of God: *Samson Agonistes* and the Biblical Lament', which considers the impact of the lament-psalm ('a clearly defined genre of Hebrew poetry') on the play's dramatic movement; and Helen Damico's 'Duality in Dramatic Vision: A Structural Analysis of *Samson Agonistes*', which argues the play's bipartite organisation with its pivot in the Dalila episode, and thereafter attends to a number of intriguing speculations, especially the astonishing parallels with the form of the Old Comedy. Damico's energetic essay is one which students of Milton will wish to study with care.

Elsewhere, Joan S. Bennett in '"A Person Rais'd": Public and Private Cause in *Samson Agonistes*' (*SEL*) focuses on the political dimensions of the episodes of Dalila and Harapha in order to emphasise the balanced vision of 'a universe governed by wisdom and virtue' eventually achieved by Samson. William Slaymaker in 'Tragic Freedoms: Milton's Samson and Sartre's Orestes' (*Studies in the Humanities* [Indiana University of Pennsylvannia]) posits that the two dramatists, in spite of their differences, alike upheld that 'a sense of freedom is not necessarily communicated to others by heroic example'. Finally, James L. Crenshaw in *Samson: A Secret Betrayed, A Vow Ignored* (Atlanta: John Knox Press) glances at *Samson Agonistes* from the standpoint of a theologian in five rather unsophisticated pages.

5. Prose

Robert T. Fallon in 'Filling the Gaps: New Perspectives on Mr. Secretary Milton' (*MiltonS*) concludes after a detailed re-examination of the available documents that Milton was much more than a mere 'translator and interpreter for monolingual bosses', as William R. Parker had claimed; for to heed the tangential and circumstantial evidence, Fallon avers, is to confirm that Milton's role was distinctly substantive in a variety of directions.

Thomas N. Corns in 'Punctuation in Milton's Vernacular Prose' (*N&Q*) touches on some reasons that might have led Milton's readers in the mid-seventeenth century to regard his punctuation as containing 'aberrant' elements. Leo Miller in 'Milton cited in Germany, 1652' (*MiltonQ*) invokes a relatively uncommitted oration delivered at the University of Wittenberg by Wilhelmus a Kospoth. Julian Mason in 'Milton modifies a Metaphor: "Veritas Filia Temporis"' (*MiltonQ*) annotates the reference in *The Doctrine and Discipline of Divorce* to Time as 'the Midwife rather than the Mother of Truth'. Michael West in a brief but lively article notes the Ciceronian antecedents to the celebrated refusal in *Areopagitica* to praise that virtue which 'slinks out of the race, where that immortal garland is to be run for, not without heat and dust' (*RES*).

XII

The Later Seventeenth Century

JAMES OGDEN

This chapter has four sections: 1. General; 2. Dryden; 3. Other authors; 4. Background. The treatment of philosophy in section 3 and of background studies in section 4 is highly selective, and depends mainly on what was sent for review.

1. General

The first two volumes of the new series of *The Eighteenth Century: A Current Bibliography*[1], dealing with work published in 1975 and 1976, became available in 1979. Readers of this chapter may consult these volumes for specialist book reviews and fuller coverage in the areas of bibliography, philosophy, and background studies; readers of these volumes may consult this chapter for fuller coverage of work on Restoration literature, especially learned articles. They exclude 'highly technical' articles, but I note some they omit which cannot be so described, and my comments are almost always more detailed, though theirs are quite often more dismissive. Work on Restoration literature in 1976 was also covered in *PQ* (1977) in three review-essays: Robert D. Hume's 'Studies in English Drama, 1660–1800', Philip Harth's 'Studies in Restoration Literature', and J. Paul Hunter's 'Studies in Eighteenth-Century Fiction'. Hume's essay is characteristically thorough and even describes his own work at some length. Harth's is clearly meant to exclude drama, but largely excludes prose too. He says 1976 was 'a lean year' and 'the only important publishing event in Restoration nondramatic literary studies' was the completion of the Latham-Matthews edition of Pepys's *Diary*; this is to ignore the inaugural volume of the Oxford edition of Bunyan's *Miscellaneous Works*. In *SEL* G. S. Rousseau reviews 'Recent Studies in the Restoration and Eighteenth Century', and he too finds little of interest in work on the Restoration. As he complains of receiving review copies of only two-thirds of the books he wants, I may as well record that I generally receive review copies of less than half the books I discuss.

Restoration[2] is now a journal rather than a newsletter, but remains my major source of news and comment on recent work. As well as the critical

[1] *The Eighteenth Century: A Current Bibliography, N.S. 1 – for 1975*, ed. by Robert L. Allen. Philadelphia and Los Angeles: American Society for Eighteenth-Century Studies. pp. [viii] + 438. *N.S. 2 – for 1976*, ed. by Robert L. Allen. New York: AMS Press, Inc., for the Society, 1979. pp. [viii] + 448. £15.85. (Vols. 3 and 4 for 1977 and 1978 are announced for publication in 1980.)

[2] *Restoration: Studies in English Literary Culture, 1660–1700*, ed. by J. M. Armistead. Knoxville, Tenn.: U. of Tennessee. Twice yearly. Six issues, $6 inside USA; $8 outside.

essays noted elsewhere in this chapter, the second volume included annotated lists of 'Some Current Publications', by Catherine L. Blecki and Laura B. Kennelly; essays on 'Essential Studies' of Clarendon, Burnet, Halifax, and Temple, by Joel Blair, and of the Restoration Anglican sermon, by Gerard Reedy; a critique of anthologies of Restoration literature, by J. M. Armistead; accounts of lectures and conferences; and 'Projects, News, and Queries'. The lists of current publications are admirably comprehensive and up-to-date. The British Society for Eighteenth-Century Studies also transformed its newsletter into 'a serious forum for criticism and scholarship', *The British Journal for Eighteenth-Century Studies*[3], though the first volume included nothing directly relevant to our period.

I note several articles about Restoration books, booksellers, and libraries. B. J. McMullin's 'A Peripheralist View of *Wing*' (*PBSA*) concludes that the second edition of Wing's *S.T.C.* is appearing prematurely; a much more careful revision, taking proper account of libraries outside the British Isles and the United States, is wanted. M. J. Jennetta's 'English Books 1641–1700' (*BLJ*) is an interestingly annotated list of British Library acquisitions from 1965 to 1975. J. L. Gaunt's 'Popular Fiction and the Ballad Market in the Second Half of the Seventeenth Century' (*PBSA*) shows that two syndicates of booksellers virtually monopolised the trade in broadside ballads and published most of the popular fiction, consisting of old jokes, romances of chivalry, and tales of folk heroes. Prose versions of the ballads began to appear, and several such works can be dated more accurately than Wing and other bibliographers have thought. Harold Love's 'Preacher and Publisher: Oliver Heywood and Thomas Parkhurst' (*SB*) suggests that in the later seventeenth century the country clergy may have done more than the provincial booksellers to circulate books outside London. Heywood wrote for the edification of his flock, distributed copies at his own expense, maintained a private lending library of devotional works, and publicised new books; other clergymen may have done the same. Wayne H. Phelps's 'The Will of Randall Taylor, a Restoration Bookseller' (*PBSA*) gives biographical facts and a transcript of the will. A. K. Dalby's '"Weekly Memorials for the Ingenious": An Error Corrected' (*N&Q*) clarifies the publishing history of 'the first English book review'. An editorial in *BC* (1977), 'Sion, Evelyn, and What Now?' comments on the sale of books from the Sion College Library and the dispersal of John Evelyn's library, and urges Government action to keep together such historic collections.

(a) Poetry

Pierre Danchin's *The Prologues and Epilogues of the Restoration*[4] is a checklist of all such poems so far discovered. It is arranged chronologically, and aims at giving the title and author of the relevant play; the date and venue of the first performance; and information on the poems themselves (their authors, the actors who recited them, their publication). Indexes of persons, plays, and first lines add to the book's usefulness. It is itself a

[3] *The British Journal for Eighteenth-Century Studies*, ed. by Joan Pittock; from January 1980 ed. by Dennis Fletcher. British Society for Eighteenth-Century Studies. Thrice yearly. By subscription: £4 for ordinary members, £1 for students.

[4] *The Prologues and Epilogues of the Restoration (1660–1700): A tentative Check-list*, by Pierre Danchin. Nancy: Publications de l'Université de Nancy II. pp. x + 216; 1 illustration. No price stated. (Reviewed by Sybil Rosenfeld, *TN*, 1979).

prologue to a forthcoming edition, but although over a thousand poems are listed Professor Danchin believes there are more to be found, and needs more information about some of them. Scholars who can help are asked to write to him at the Université de Nancy II; the project certainly deserves encouragement.

Raman Selden's *English Verse Satire*[5] begins with an account of Horace and Juvenal, as the basis for a study of most of the great tradition of English verse satire. His attempt at comprehensiveness commits him to generality, but this is well supported by quotation and analysis, and the work of Oldham, Butler, Rochester, Marvell, Dryden, and some minor writers is thus illuminated. Dr Selden is especially good on the Roman influence, but less helpful on the origin and development of the practice of writing satire in heroic couplets. Was Chaucer remembered? Certainly he was by Spenser, whose *Mother Hubberd's Tale* seems to have revived the practice and was known to Dryden, though Selden does not mention it.

(b) Drama

Steven John van der Weele's *The Critical Reputation of Restoration Comedy in Modern Times up to 1950*[6] is divided into three parts. The first (over one hundred pages) surveys critical opinion before 1900; the second (nearly three hundred) 'presents the substance of critical materials' published between about 1900 and 1950 dealing with Restoration comedy in general; the third (only two hundred) presents the criticism in the same period of particular dramatists, namely Etherege, Wycherley, Congreve, Vanbrugh, and Farquhar. The book is perhaps the longest contribution to the 'Salzburg Studies' so far, and might be called a dissertation without a thesis, since van der Weele concludes that 'it is not to be expected that in a finite world such diverse opions' as those surveyed 'should be satisfactorily reconciled'; no, but they might have been more succinctly described. The period chiefly studied is, as we are shown, one in which criticism of this drama became more sophisticated, but still much of the best criticism is missed by stopping at 1950. As the author has been immured with the writings of many forgotten or half-remembered academic authorities, part of the interest of his study lies in seeing if he is still sane; happily, in his conclusion he notes 'the elusively obvious fact that criticism, valuable as it is, cannot ultimately do full justice to literature generally, and that comedy suffers especially when criticism is not complemented by a reading of the plays'.

More directly concerned with the plays is Ursula Jantz's *Targets of Satire in the Comedies of Etherege, Wycherley, and Congreve*[7]. This dissertation is mainly about 'Targets of Mimetic Satire', or characters who are presented satirically; various sorts of hypocrites, fops, and fortune-

[5] *English Verse Satire 1590–1765*, by Raman Selden. George Allen & Unwin. pp. 193. £8.50.

[6] *The Critical Reputation of Restoration Comedy in Modern Times up to 1950*, by Steven John van der Weele. SSPDPT 36. Salzburg: Institut für Englische Sprache und Literatur. 2 vols., not separately paginated; pp. viii + 637.

[7] *Targets of Satire in the Comedies of Etherege, Wycherley, and Congreve*, by Ursula Jantz. SSPDPT 42. Salzburg: Institut für Englische Sprache und Literatur. pp. vi + 242.

hunters are distinguished. There is also a chapter on 'Targets of Satiric Comments', including marriage, the clergy, and the law, though – as Dr Jantz points out – such comments, being often voiced by characters who are themselves satirised, are less indicative of the playwrights' own views. The heroes of these plays are those who are aware of the world's imperfections and have learned to live gracefully with them; hence the honest rake and even the honest boor may not be scorned. The playwrights are not anarchists, but do value such virtues as honesty, tolerance, and generosity. This is not a bad dissertation, though predictably Dr Jantz's focus on satire limits her awareness of the mixed feelings we may have about characters in these plays.

Several articles had to do with the development of drama in the later seventeenth century. Robert D. Hume's book on the subject (*YW* 57.188–9) prompts Brian Corman's question, 'What is Restoration Drama?' (*UTQ*), though he hardly answers it. R. A. Zimbardo's 'Imitation to Emulation: "Imitation of Nature" from the Restoration to the Eighteenth Century' (*Restoration*) is an ambitious attempt at describing changes in the theory of drama from about 1660 to 1730. In 1660 the emphasis was on the dramatist's 'imitation of nature', understood to mean the representation of abstract ideals; but in the early eighteenth century it was on the audience's 'emulation' of exemplary characters. The new emphasis led to the replacement of drama by the novel, since 'we can "enter into" the characters in a novel much more easily and fully than we can those in a play'. A more specific and palpable development, that of the repentance scene from Shadwell to Cibber, is examined in Paul E. Parnell's 'The Etiquette of the Sentimental Repentance Scene, 1688–96' (*PLL*). It was Cibber's *Love's Last Shift* that gave this sort of scene its typical eighteenth-century form.

There were two good essays on the rise and fall of English opera. Richard Luckett's 'Exotic but Rational Entertainments: the English Dramatick Operas'[8] is the more comprehensive, ranging from the Restoration to the first decade of the eighteenth century. The immediate models of English opera were French, and its chief distinguishing features were the use of spoken dialogue, choruses, and dances; the best of Purcell's operas were unified works showing real insight into the nature and possibilities of a native opera. Its fall had several causes: the waning love of things French; the rage for the 'exotick and irrational' Italian opera; the lack of royal patronage and growth of subscription finance; and above all the death of Thomas Betterton, who alone had the imagination, knowledge, and practical ability needed for a successful production. But in 'The Critical Decade for English Music Drama, 1700–1710' (*HLB*) Curtis A. Price takes a rather different view. He believes English opera was the casualty of efforts to accommodate Italian opera in London without ejecting English spoken drama; the two theatres had to specialise in one or the other, and there was no room for the hybrid form. But perhaps a large share of the blame for the end of English oprra should be borne by Vanbrugh, who built the Haymarket theatre with Italian opera in mind.

That brings me to studies of theatre history. Arthur H. Scouten's '*Julius*

[8] pp. 123–41 of *English Drama: Forms and Development*, ed. by Marie Axton and Raymond Williams. C.U.P., 1977. (Reviewed by Roam Gill, *EIC*, 1979).

Caesar and Restoration Shakespeare' (*SQ*) shows that *Julius Caesar* was a stock play from 1663 to 1702. It was unaltered, so its popularity should help to correct the prevailing view that Restoration audiences saw Shakespeare's tragedies chiefly in adaptations. In fact, the numbers of performancies of the tragedies from genuine texts and adaptations are about the same. Judith Milhous's 'The Duke's Company's Profits, 1675–1677' (*TN*) reconsiders the evidence of Leslie Hotson's *The Commonwealth and Restoration Stage*. Hotson perhaps exaggerated the profits; Milhous thinks the company was at this time 'a solidly profitable operation – but it was no goldmine'. She speculates on the dates of premieres of plays by Otway and Shadwell. Bruce Podewell's 'Thomas Betterton's Roles' (*TN*) corrects and adds to Milhous's survey (*TN*, 1975; *YW* 56.224). Podewell believes Betterton played Hotspur, though the point cannot be decisively proved. He also throws 'New Light on John Downes' (*N&Q*): Downes the prompter is satirised in an anonymous broadside, *The Players Turn'd Academicks* (1703). Edward A. Langhans discusses 'More Restoration Manuscript Casts and a New Restoration Promptbook' (*TN*).

(c) Prose

In 'An Early Appreciation of *Paradise Lost*' (*MP*) James M. Rosenheim transcribes passages about Milton's poem from letters by Sir John Hobart, of Blickling Hall, written early in 1668 and now in the Bodleian. Hobart says *Paradise Lost* is 'in ye opinion of ye impartiall learned, not only above all moderne attempts in verse, but equall to any of ye Antie[nt] Poets'. Rosenheim does not remark on the similarity of this to Dryden's alleged comment, 'this man cuts us all out and the Ancients too', but his article is of exceptional interest to the student of Restoration literary taste.

2. Dryden

A selection of Dryden's work was edited by John Conaghan[9]. It includes most of his better known poems and critical essays, some translations, and two plays, *Marriage à la Mode* and *All for Love*. The questionable omissions of *The Medal* and the second and third parts of *The Hind and the Panther* do allow the range and variety of Dryden's work to be better exhibited; Conaghan's would seem to be the most comprehensive selection available. It has a brief critical introduction, helpful but not lavish annotation, and a bibliography. As its success will depend on persuading the student to down Dryden like Guiness rather than sip him like medicine, Conaghan does well to note some ways of getting from one work to another; but he might have noted more. Of course he is not prepared to lead them from *Absalom and Achitophel* to *The Medal*, but he might have directed them from 'To the Memory of Mr. Oldham' to 'The Episode of Nisus and Euryalus' from the fifth book of the *Æneis*. The latter is included, and makes a strange gloss on lines 9–10 of the Oldham elegy, but Conaghan refers only to Virgil. Texts have been modernised, 'cautiously in respect of punctuation, and with deference to some of Dryden's spellings'. I would have emended pp. 296 line 3 ('cell' for 'dell') and 388 line 501 ('you' for 'your'). In the text of *Marriage à la Mode* more care might have been taken

[9] *Dryden: A Selection*, ed. by John Conaghan. Methuen. pp. xxiv + 632. pb £6.95.

with the italicisation of French words – see section 2(b) below – and an aside should be marked for most of Palamede's last speech. In general the text is good; I noted only two or three misprints ('dropping' for 'drooping' at p.67 line 896 may be termed quasi-emendation), and the large typeface is welcome.

George McFadden offers *Dryden: The Public Writer 1660–1685*[10] as 'a supplement' to Ward's biography, ' in the hope that it will lead to a more sympathetic understanding of the achievement of a great poet'. It follows Dryden through the intrigues of Charles II's reign, studies his relations with some public figures, and views his works, especially the plays, as attempts to influence them and the public at large. Dryden emerges as a conscientious, self-critical professional writer, who naturally made enemies of such ambitious, self-confident literary amateurs as Sir Robert Howard and Buckingham. There is much circumstantial evidence of animosity between Howard and Dryden after Howard's 'hijacking' of *The Indian Queen*. Dryden also emerges as essentially a Jacobite; the heroes of the heroic plays, notably Almanzor and Aureng-Zebe, are optimistic portraits of James Duke of York, while the various beleaguered, good-natured, but rather weak monarchs reflect Dryden's opinion of Charles. *Absalom and Achitophel* aims at encouraging the king to assert himself, frustrate the knavish tricks of his enemies, and secure the succession. This book supplements Ward with interesting biographical speculations, but whether its emphasis on Dryden's didacticism will lead to a more sympathetic understanding of how he transcends his age is open to doubt; some major poems, including *Religio Laici*, are virtually ignored, and in general Dryden sounds respectable but unexciting. It is doubtful, for instance, whether McFadden would move C. N. Manlove, whose chief criticisms in decidedly unsympathetic accounts of the satires and 'The Cock and the Fox' in his *Literature and Reality*[11] are that Dryden is 'moral only by restricting life' and that in his work we see 'fiction eroded by external fact'.

Two of this year's critical essays described Dryden's attitudes to greater writers. Earl Miner's 'Dryden's Admired Acquaintance, Mr Milton' (*MiltonS*) surveys the relations of the two men, adding no new facts, but claiming to distinguish knowledge from conjecture. Miner believes they got on well; Milton's attack on rhyme was not an attack on Dryden and not taken as such, and Dryden's rhymed version of *Paradise Lost* caused no disagreement. Though he quickly saw *Paradise Lost* as a classic, Dryden probably did not read the minor poems till their second edition in 1773. No doubt Dryden was Milton's 'poetical son', but Christopher Ricks (*YW* 58.217) need presume no Freudian uneasiness with the father. Dryden often borrows from Milton, but always wholly revising what he borrows, 'after the Miltonic manner'; he differs from Milton in not dismissing his sources 'with some "Satyricall" phrase'. He becomes completely independent only in the *Fables*, which, though inferior to *Paradise Lost*, is in its own way an epic. Two cavils: I think when Miner attributes to Dryden the information

[10] *Dryden: The Public Writer, 1660–1685*, by George McFadden. Princeton, N.J.: Princeton U.P. pp. xii + 305. £11. (Reviewed by Alan S. Fisher, *MLQ*, 1978, and by William Frost, *Scriblerian*, 1979.)

[11] *Literature and Reality, 1600–1800*, by C. N. Manlove. MacMillan. pp. x + 238.

that Milton was a 'temperate man' he misunderstands Aubrey, and I do not think the line from *The State of Innocence*, 'If this be dreaming, let me never wake' can be called 'distinctly Drydenian', since it paraphrases *Twelfth Night*, IV. i. 62. William Myers's 'Dryden's Shakespeare'[12] seeks to defend Dryden's attitude to Shakespeare, seen in his criticism and adaptations, against the attacks of F. R. Leavis (*YW* 56.229) and L. C. Knights. Leavis's case was that 'born into Dryden's age, when "logic" and "clarity" had triumphed, Shakespeare couldn't have been Shakespeare'. Myers's answer is that while Dryden's age was indeed limited in sensibility, thought, and idiom, Dryden himself was as aware of these limitations as Leavis was, and as able as Leavis and Knights to read Shakespeare's plays as dramatic poems. 'He accommodated neoclassicism to Shakespeare and not the other way round'. This is attractive but not wholly convincing; it could be argued that Dryden's admiration for Shakespeare's 'universal mind, which comprehended all characters and passions' led not to Knights but to Bradley.

Another general and stimulating essay was Harold Love's 'Dryden's "Unideal Vacancy"' (*ECS*), which develops Dr Johnson's remark that Dryden delighted 'to approach the precipice of absurdity, and hover over the abyss of unideal vacancy'. He and other Restoration poets evolved from Shakespeare, Donne, and Cowley what Dryden called 'Dalilahs of the theatre', or what Love calls heroic conceits; which were 'unideal' in the sense of not letting readers form coherent ideas, at least not as understood in the *Essay concerning Humane Understanding*. Readers were becoming more literal-minded anyway, so these conceits were more shocking than metaphysical ones had been. Love treats them more indulgently than Johnson could, and closely examines instances mainly from the heroic plays. One is the image of the sun becoming an earth in the opening lines of *Oedipus*; this is a fantastic extension of the Cartesian theory of planetary formation, as Harold and Rosaleen Love point out in 'A Cartesian Allusion in Dryden and Lee's "Oedipus"' (*N&Q*).

(a) Poetry

W. K. Thomas's *The Crafting of 'Absalom and Achitophel'*[13] is a critical commentary with chapters on the poem's historical background, characters, genre, and structure. By comparing *Absalom and Achitophel* with other pamphlets on the Exclusion Crisis and by close reading of the poem itself, Thomas hopes to enable us to see it as contemporaries did. In general his style suggests anxious awareness that his readers are not Dryden's contemporaries, and perhaps his title arises from this feeling; 'crafting' in the sense of constructing may be common American usage, yet I would have avoided it, since Dryden uses 'craft' in a pejorative sense in the very first line. Quite often I found the commentary laborious (on chiasmus, pp. 93–9), over-ingenious (the proof that Zimri connotes whoremaster, p. 93), or wrong (on 'cockle', p. 59, where Kinsley could have helped). But I was thankful for enlightenment on points previous commentators

[12] pp. 15–27 of *Augustan Worlds*, ed. by J. C. Hilson, M. M. B. Jones, and J. R. Watson. Leicester, Leics.: Leicester U.P. pp. 311.

[13] *The Crafting of 'Absalom and Achitophel': Dryden's 'Pen for a Party'*, by W. K. Thomas. Waterloo, Ontario: Wilfrid Laurier U.P. pp. viii + 239. $7.50.

have left obscure; the idea that by 'the Jews' we should understand not the English but the dissenters, for example, is new and seems valid. And major critical points, on how we should see Absalom compared with Achitophel, or on why we should see the poem as a whole as 'Varronian' satire, are persuasively argued. Thomas believes that writing a book like this is comparable to restoring a picture; removing the grime of centuries, not, as might be feared, merely varnishing it over. If this belief seems optimistic, at least the poem is not found to be a forgery.

Three essays on *Absalom and Achitophel* will have to be considered by future critics and editors. Dustin Griffin's 'Dryden's Charles: The Ending of *Absalom and Achitophel*' (*PQ*) argues that in supporting Charles, Dryden comes closer to the sceptical pragmatism of Halifax than to the extreme royalism of those who invoked divine right. At the end of the poem the king emerges not as God's anointed but as a politician who is clever enough to *appear* 'Godlike'. Hence Griffin convincingly attacks critics who favour an almost wholly unironic account of the ending; but a comparison of Griffin's reading with W. K. Thomas's leaves me conscious of problems of interpretation. Thomas admits that 'the final effect may well vary with individual readers'; is that what Dryden wanted? J. Douglas Canfield's 'Anarchy and Style: What Dryden "Grants" in *Absalom and Achitophel*' (*PLL*) is a long note on line 795, 'Yet, grant our Lords the People Kings can make'. Canfield maintains that we underestimate the irony if we say Dryden is granting for argument's sake the claim that people can make kings; rather, 'in the grammatical anarchy of the line', he is suggesting that Whigs are levellers who will reduce everything to chaos. Arthur Weitzman's 'An Overlooked Manuscript of Dryden's *Absalom and Achitophel*' (*PBSA*) is one now belonging to the Massachusetts Historical Society. It is perhaps basically a late seventeenth-century transcript of the second folio, but gives many readings not found elsewhere, and Weitzman wonders if these represent Dryden's own first thoughts. Weitzman says little about the literary quality of these readings; in my view most of them are inferior to the received text.

Other critical essays on Dryden's poetry varied in character and quality. Michael West's 'Dryden's *Mac Flecknoe* and the Example of Duffett's Burlesque Dramas' (*SEL*) shows that Dryden's satire has more than he cared to admit in common with Duffett's burlesques of plays by Settle, Betterton, and Shadwell. H. A. Mason's 'The Dream of Happiness' (*CQ*) interestingly relates Dryden's translation of Horace's second Epode to those of Jonson and Cowley, and to the whole tradition of poems in praise of country life. These poems seek to express an ideal of happiness that is both deeply desired by the suffering individual and common to mankind. G. Douglas Atkins's 'Dryden's *Religio Laici*: A Reappraisal' (*SP*) argues, long-windedly, against Harth that this poem is essentially propaganda for Anglicanism, and against Empson that it shows covert sympathy with Deism. Its sub-title suggests it is about 'A Layman's Faith' by a layman for laymen, and it is conspicuously anti-clerical. It seems to say God is found in the Bible, not through the mediation of priests or private illumination; Dryden thus reaches an uneasy compromise between authoritarianism and individualism. Ruth Smith's fine essay on 'The Argument and Contexts of Dryden's *Alexander's Feast*' (*SEL*) is a great improvement on previous critiques of this poem. Mrs Smith shows that Timotheus's pagan music arouses in Alexander vicious excesses of feeling and behaviour, though we should not entirely lose sympathy with him; Cecilia's Christian music composes the passions and gently leads us to the contemplation of divine goodness. This interpretation is supported by reference to the contemporary debate on the usefulness of church music, though in exploring the ambivalence of musical effect Dryden was ahead of his time.

Three notes from *N&Q* remain. In 'Dryden's Zimri and Juvenal' P. F. Hammond suggests that if the character of Zimri is partly inspired by Juvenal's sketch of the Greek virtuosi in his third satire, Dryden may have used Eilhardus Lubinus's edition of Juvenal (1603), since Lubinus glosses line 75 as 'non unus homo est, sed omnia promtus est & paratus', which looks like the source for 'Not one, but all Mankind's Epitome'. In 'Dryden's Borrowings from a Poem by his Son Charles' D. W. Hopkins notes borrowings in the *Æneis* and 'The Wife of Bath's Tale' from Charles Dryden's 'On the Happyness of a Retir'd Life'. In 'Dryden's "Metamorphoses" and Thomson's "Paraphrase of Psalm CIV" ' Thomas A. Reisner notes that lines 19–20 of Thomson's poem are practically a quotation from Dryden's 'The First Book of Ovid's Metamorphoses', lines 421–2.

(b) Drama

Volume XI of the California *Dryden*[14] appeared, consisting of *The Conquest of Granada, Marriage A-la-Mode*, and *The Assignation*. Texts are based on first editions, all emendations are noted, and variant readings from later editions down to Congreve's are listed. Accidentals are altered 'where it seems helpful to the reader', but punctuation remains distinctly rhetorical. The regular italicisation of Melantha and Palamede's French words in *Marriage A-la-Mode* is a real improvement. The headnotes usefully synthesise work on the sources, structure, and general character of the plays. There are also some more original contributions, notably Roper's on the relevance of casuistry to *The Conquest of Granada*, Loftis's on differences between *The Assignation* and Dryden's earlier plays of similar structure, and Rodes's essay on 'The Actors' of all three plays. The annotation is as usual thorough, but not beyond criticism. Quite often notes on individual words merely cite '*O.E.D.*', which I might have consulted anyway, and indeed had to for 'libration' (p. 142, l. 192). Some further notes are wanting; I was especially surprised to find nothing on 'noble Savage' (p. 30, l. 209), and I think the dialogue of Ascanio and Hippolita in *The Assignation*, III.i.90–5, gains piquancy if the reader is reminded that Ascanio was a breeches role (and played by Mrs Reeves, Dryden's reputed mistress); Hippolita says, 'I should have the strangest thoughts if I once wore Breeches'.

In 'Dryden's *All for Love* on the Restoration Stage' (*RECTR*, 1977) Michael Yots remarks that the original audiences saw well known actors and actresses in roles probably written to suit them. The successes of Hart,

[14] *The Works of John Dryden. Vol. XI: Plays: The Conquest of Granada, Marriage A-la-Mode, The Assignation*, ed. by John Loftis and David Stuart Rodes; textual editor Vinton A. Dearing; associate editors George R. Guffey, Alan Roper, H. T. Swedenberg Jr. Berkeley, Los Angeles, Calif. and London: U. of California P. pp. xii + 639; 5 plates. £24.50. (Reviewed by Edward L. Saslow, *Scriblerian*, 1979.)

Mohun, and Mrs Boutell as Alexander, Clitus, and Statira in Lee's *Rival Queens* earlier in the season would influence the writing and acting of their roles as Antony, Ventidius, and Cleopatra. Mrs Boutell would play a girlish Cleopatra to Mrs Corey's shrewish Octavia.

(c) Prose

In 'Dryden as Historiographer Royal, and the Authorship of *His Majesties Declaration Defended*' (*MP*) Edward L. Saslow claims there are no good grounds for supposing Dryden wrote this anonymous pamphlet on the Exclusion Crisis. As Historiographer Royal under Charles he did not undertake such work; and if he had, it is unlikely anonymity would have been preserved. Parallels of thought and wording with his known works are not so close as to prove common authorship. Saslow casts doubt on whether it should have been included in the California *Works*.

There were a number of contributions to the study of Dryden's criticism. Robert DeMaria Jr's 'The Ideal Reader: A Critical Fiction' (*PMLA*) considers notions of the ideal reader in Johnson, Dryden, Coleridge and Northrop Frye. Dryden's tendency to conceive of criticism as drama is related to his division of readers into groups, of which 'the most judicious' constitute his intellectual aristocracy. Richard Elias's '"Bayes" in Buckingham's *The Rehearsal*' (*ELN*) notes that Bayes's boast of his new play's having a plot which 'is a Virgin; 't has never yet been blown upon' echoes the *Essay of Dramatic Poesy*, where Neander says there is scarcely a humour, character, or plot which earlier English dramatists 'have not blown upon'. Dryden changed 'blown upon' to 'used' in later editions of the *Essay*, possibly to obscure Buckingham's satire. D. W. Hopkins's 'Dryden, Le Bossu and Ovid's Speeches of Ajax and Ulysses' (*N&Q*) points out Dryden's debt to Le Bossu's *Traité du Poème Epique* in *The Grounds of Criticism in Tragedy*. Albert Poyet discusses 'French Influence in Dryden's *Discourse concerning the Original and Progress of Satire*' (*Caliban*, 1976).

3. Other Authors

(a) Poets

The tercentenary of the death of Marvell occasioned a good many books and articles; some dealing with his life and work after the Restoration are noted here. *Andrew Marvell, Poet & Politician*[15], the catalogue of the commemorative exhibition at the British Museum, usefully supplements the late Pierre Legouis's biography. Hilton Kelliher summarises Marvell's life with the aid of seventy-six nicely reproduced illustrations, including manuscript facsimiles, pictures of places associated with the poet, and portraits of his acquaintances. Some new information is incorporated, and is set forth more fully in *BLJ* by Kelliher's 'Some Notes on Andrew Marvell' and Pauline Burdon's 'Marvell after Cambridge'. Kelliher throws some new light on Marvell's death but there is still no proof that

[15] *Andrew Marvell, Poet & Politician, 1621–78*, compiled by Hilton Kelliher. British Museum Publications Ltd. pp. 128; 1 coloured plate and 75 black-and-white illustrations. £7.

'Mary Marvell' was his widow. The Marvell volume in the 'Critical Heritage' series[16] anthologises contemporary comments on his polemical prose; comments on the verse satires are largely excluded, on the ground that their authorship is uncertain. The rude remarks on Marvell in *His Majesties Declaration Defended* should not be attributed to Dryden, if Edward Saslow is right (see 2(c) above). However, the remarks which can be attributed to him are equally rude; although the two men were among the first to acknowledge the greatness of *Paradise Lost*, Dryden may have taken offence at what seem to be sarcastic references to him in Marvell's commendatory verses to Milton's poem.

Three essays dealt directly with Marvell and Milton. The two by Christopher Hill and Joseph Anthony Wittreich Jr are versions of tercentenary lectures at York University[17]. Hill's 'Milton and Marvell' emphasises their political accord, and sees Marvell as Milton's disciple. The commendatory verses to *Paradise Lost* suggest to Hill that Marvell thought the epic a disguised lament for the end of the Commonwealth and England's happiness. Wittreich's 'Perplexing the Explanation: Marvell's "On Mr. Milton's *Paradise Lost*" ' claims that Marvell's 'evident uneasiness with his subject' and 'modesty in the face of Milton's achievement' are 'strategies calculated to portray Marvell as a poet different in kind from Milton, with an integrity of his own'. Yes, but I do wonder why he would not portray himself by publishing his own best poems. Judith Scherer Herz's 'Milton and Marvell: The Poet as Fit Reader' (*MLQ*) analyses the commendatory verses in the context of an account of Milton's influence on Marvell, and concludes that they make their own existence evidence of the epic's success, and show that 'the truest reading is re-creation'.

In another tercentenary volume Milton hovers over two essays on Marvell's satires[18]. Warren L. Chernaik's 'Marvell's Satires: The Artist as Puritan' maintains that 'Marvell, like Milton, is centrally a Puritan'; the witty poignancy of his early poetry gives way first to indelicate satire and then to the plain prose of *The Growth of Popery*. Joseph Messina's 'The Heroic Image in *The Last Instructions to a Painter*' suggests that in this satire Marvell both ridicules the sham heroism of the Royalists and creates, in the description of the death of Captain Douglas, an image of what Milton called 'the better fortitude/Of patience and heroic martyrdom'. This may be what Marvell tries to create, but I am not persuaded that he succeeds. A. S. G. Edwards's 'New Texts of Marvell's Satires: II' (*SB*) is complementary to the essay by Edwards and R. M. Schuler (*SB* 1977; *YW* 58.220). Edwards draws attention to some apparently hitherto unexamined manuscripts of Marvell's satires in Nottingham University Library. These are copies of 'The Statue-in-Stocks-Market', 'Nostradamus, a Prophecy', 'Upon the Statue at Charing Cross', 'Britannia and Rawleigh', 'Last Instructions to a Painter', and 'Further Advice to a Painter'. Full lists of variants are given.

[16] *Andrew Marvell: The Critical Heritage*, ed. by Elizabeth Story Donno. Routledge & Kegan Paul. pp. xvii + 385.

[17] pp. 1–30 and 280–305 of *Approaches to Marvell: The York Tercentenary Lectures*, ed. by C. A. Patrides. Routledge & Kegan Paul. pp. xviii + 354.

[18] pp. 268–310 of *Tercentenary Essays in Honor of Andrew Marvell*, ed. by Kenneth Friedenreich. Hamden, Conn.: Archon Books, Shoe String Press Inc., 1977. pp. 314; 7 illustrations.

There was nothing on Butler this year, apart from the brief but acute comments by Selden in his book on satire (see 1(a) above), but one article omitted previously deserves mention. Nicholas H. Nelson's 'Astrology, *Hudibras*, and the Puritans' (*JHI*, 1976) throws light on the Sidrophel episode. Nelson describes the bitter controversy over astrology during the interregnum, and shows that Butler satirises both the pseudo-science as such and its abuse by politicians, including Presbyterians who did not believe in it, and sectarians who did.

Rochester has generally been seen as more a case than a poet. This tradition was still influential in the first avowedly critical study, Griffin's *Satires against Man* (*YW* 54.266–7). David Farley-Hills's *Rochester's Poetry*[19] is, as a sub-title insists, *A Study of Rochester's Poetry*; its emphasis not psychological but critical. It divides his poems into lyrics, burlesques and lampoons, and satires, and shows how he modified the conventions of these genres to become a poet of rare quality. Dr Farley-Hills has an enviably wide knowledge of relevant poetry, both English and French, and describes Rochester's literary context well. He makes acute discriminations among the lyrics, but finds the best of the poet's work in the satires. I found the book stimulating but had two recurrent worries. One was that Farley-Hills has a streak of wanton originality which makes him refuse to quote or even correct Vieth's and Pinto's editions, but go back to early editions which he believes are textually reliable; I would have more confidence in this procedure if his own book did not have so many misprints, including a glaring one in a quotation from Rochester (p. 182). Admittedly, at line 18 of *A Ramble in St James's Park* the verb 'frig' has a capital letter in the 1680 edition, thus for Farley-Hills bringing out its connection with Frigga the Scandinavian Goddess (pp. 107–8); but the etymology, though clear to him, has eluded Partridge and other scholars, and anyway another well known slang verb beginning with 'f' is capitalised in the next line but one. My other worry was that Farley-Hills is not original enough when praising the poems. He often says something to the effect that their orderly manner triumphs over their disorderly matter; but I doubt if this sufficiently distinguishes them from good poetry generally, and I am sure it does not deserve so much repetition.

Two articles on Rochester deserve attention. Peter Beal's 'Ben Jonson and Rochester's *Rodomontade on his Cruel Mistress*' (*RES*) shows that these eight lines, which Vieth included in his edition as 'possibly by Rochester', were first published in the 1640 folio of Jonson's *Works*, as part of 'A Satyricall Shrub'. They often appear in seventeenth-century commonplace books, and the version in *The Westminster Drollery* (1671) is 'a deliberate adaptation', but there is no reason to think the alteration was by Rochester – or by anyone else. Carole Fabricant's 'The Writer as Whore: Rochester's "Letter from Artemisia to Chloe" ' (*Essays in Literature*, 1976) disagrees with Vieth (*Lang&S*, 1972; *YW* 54.267) and Weinbrot (*SLitI*, 1972), and sees Artemisia as a sympathetic figure who adopts attitudes close to those of Rochester himself in his letters.

(b) Dramatists

In 'The Earl of Orrery and Cowley's *Davideis*: Recovered Works and New Connections' (*MP*) Ted-Larry Pebworth prints in full for the first

[19] *Rochester's Poetry*, by David Farley-Hills. Totowa, N.J.: Rowman & Littlefield; London: Bell & Hyman. pp. viii + 230. £8.95.

time Orrery's poem '*To Mr.* Cowley *on his* Davideis', which confirms the attribution to Orrery of *The Tragedy of King Saul*. Pebworth sees many links between *Saul* and the *Davideis*, and suggests that Cowley's unfinished epic may also have influenced Orrery to write the first of the heroic plays, *The Generall*, in pentameter couplets rather than hexameters after the French model.

Parodies of the heroic plays prompted a number of articles. David M. Vieth's 'Bayes and Bardolph: An Unnoticed Allusion in Buckingham's "The Rehearsal"' (*N&Q*) points out that Crane and other editors have missed an allusion in *The Rehearsal* which associates Bayes with Bardolph in *Henry IV Part I*. Richard Elias's '"Bayes" in Buckingham's *The Rehearsal*' (*ELN*) is noted in section 2(c) above. His 'Political Satire in *Sodom*' (*SEL*) contends that the play was inspired by court politics following the Declaration of Indulgence in 1672. 'What little artistic merit *Sodom* possesses arises mostly from the author's inventiveness in peopling his imaginary kingdom of Sodom with characters whose sexual perversions reflect what other satirists regarded as the increasingly unnatural political condition of the kingdom of England'. Bolloxinion is of course Charles II, Pockenello the Duke of York, Borastus probably Buckingham, and the rule of sodomy a metaphor for the feared imposition of popery. Elias concludes that 'we cannot laugh as heartily, or as maliciously, as the Restoration could'; which is perfectly true, as no text is available. Peter Lewis's 'A Note on "Chrononhotonthologus"' (*N&Q*) concerns a speech by Bombardion in this play which parodies one by the Earl of Essex in Banks's *The Unhappy Favourite*.

Lee's *Sophonisba* is perhaps now remembered mainly from parodies in Fielding's *Tom Thumb*, but in 'Hero as Endangered Species: Structure and Idea in Lee's *Sophonisba*' (*DUJ*) J. M. Armistead argues that in tracing the development of heroic drama 'into something resembling genuine tragedy' this play must not be overlooked. Its two plots are effectively unified, and if in structure it seems to look back to *The Conquest of Granada*, really it looks forward to *All for Love*. Certainly in the latter play Dryden keeps Octavius offstage as a 'shadowy force', while in *Sophonisba* Lee brings Scipio on as a strong central character 'to articulate the new heroics', but Scipio's closing speech expresses 'the tragic loss of old-fashioned love and honour'. In 'Nathaniel Lee's *The Rival Queens* and the Psychology of Assassination' (*Restoration*) David M. Vieth asserts that here Lee delineates 'the social psychology of assassination' by having Alexander the Great as the central character, to whom four groups of what Vieth calls 'reflectors' are related more directly than they are to each other. He is a 'charismatic leader' who creates the opposite responses of love and envy.

The development from heroic drama to something resembling genuine tragedy can be traced in the work of Otway too, though that is only hinted in Bhupendranath Seal's 'The Theme of Jealousy in Otway's *Alcibiades*' (*Calcutta Review*) and 'Otway's Tragic Vision in *Venice Preserved*' (*Parnassus*). Taking little account of recent criticism, Seal writes about these plays with engaging enthusiasm, but does not say what if anything Otway's 'tragic vision' owes to his earlier work. Ronald G. Shafer deals at length with problems in the interpretation of *The Orphan* in a review for *SCN* of Aline Mackenzie Taylor's edition (*YW* 58.224). J. A. Downie's 'Swift's Dismal' (*N&Q*) registers disagreement with A. J. Varney (*YW* 58.225): Swift was not indebted to *Venice Preserved* and probably did not know Otway's work at all. James Ogden's 'Literary Echoes in Otway's Comedies' (*N&Q*) catches echoes of *Macbeth* in *The Souldier's Fortune* and of *Absalom and Achitophel* in *The Atheist*. The quotation from the latter contains misprints, and should read 'to raise an Estate for a Blockhead of his own begetting, as he thinks, that shall waste it as scandalously as his Father got it'. Otway improves on Dryden's abuse of Shaftesbury in suggesting that his son was illegitimate.

Restoration comedies prompted relatively few articles. Stephen D. Cox's 'Public Virtue and Private Vitality in Shadwell's Comedies' (*RECTR*, 1977) claims that despite some self-righteous pronouncements and edifying scenes Shadwell was not a conventional moralist. Rather, he 'exalts the raw vitality which makes some of his heroes successful rakes as the source of a type of public virtue', namely the defence of civilised society against both pious drudges and violent criminals. In 'The Deserted Mistress Motif in Mrs. Manley's *Lost Lover*, 1696' (*RECTR*, 1977) Candace Brook Katz argues that unlike the cast mistresses of earlier comedy, Belira in *The Lost Lover* is treated sympathetically; although her schemes to win back her lover are defeated she does not have to endure public humiliation. In 'Mercury and Syphilis: Word-play in Sedley and Congreve' (*N&Q*) Bernard Richards suggests that the use of mercury to cure syphilis is alluded to in Sedley's *Bellamira* (V.i.33–42) and Congreve's *The Old Bachelor* (I.i.229–31).

I noted only one critical essay on Congreve. Arthur W. Hoffman's 'Allusions and the Definition of Themes in Congreve's *Love for Love*'[20] comments severely on interpretations by critics and editors of the play in general and some passages in particular. Allusions to Shakespeare are not 'random', as John Wain once said, but designed to 'give range and definition to the themes'. Yet despite several allusions to Hamlet's mad scenes, we are to see Valentine's madness as 'not merely a method of defence, but a voice adjacent to Lear'. And Hoffman is obliged to call a comparison of Sir Sampson Legend with Caliban 'anomalous', since all the other references to Caliban are meant to help us see his son Ben as an outsider. James Thompson's 'A Dance from *Love for Love*' (*N&Q*) concerns music and an account of a dance entitled 'Love for Love: Danc'd in the Play' which survive in John Playford's *The Second Part of the Dancing Master* (1696). The dance is the one near the end of the play; the music is reprinted in the article. Janet Ruth Heller's 'Congreve's "Contract Scene" and the *Satyricon*' (*PBSA*) suggests that what is normally called 'the proviso scene' in *The Way of the World* may be indebted to an episode in Petronius. David Gerard's review in *Lib* of D. F. McKenzie's Sandars Lectures (*YW* 57.186) queries the argument for an edition of Congreve based on a conflation of quarto and folio texts.

[20] pp. 283–96 of *The Author in his Work: Essays on a Problem in Criticism*, ed. by Louis L. Martz and Aubrey Williams. New Haven, Conn. and London: Yale U.P.

[21] *The Beaux' Strategem*, by George Farquhar, ed. by Michael Cordner. The New Mermaids. Benn. 1976. pp. xxxiv + 124. £1.75. Reviewed by Alan Roper, *YES*, 1979).

Farquhar's *The Beaux Stratagem* has been edited for the 'New Mermaids' by Michael Cordner[21], and for the 'Regents' series by Charles Fifer[22]. Q1 is the copy-text for both, but Fifer has collated several copies and examined many later editions. By reference to the Octavo edition of 1710 he makes better sense than Cordner of Archer's important speech about the beaux' finances in Act I (which should read, 'this two hundred pound. . .is a better estate than the ten thousand'). Fifer also has textual notes showing minor production changes, and an appendix showing what was done when the part of Bellair was omitted. In his introduction he elaborates on the play's textual and theatre history, whereas Cordner sketches the author's life. In their critiques of the play both editors seek to show why it should be thought a serious discussion of social problems; Cordner's argument that it questions its audience's assumptions about what constitutes gentility is rather the more convincing. Cordner's explanatory notes are generally better, and almost too helpful. To sum up, these are both scholarly editions; if Fifer's is the more interesting to the specialist, Cordner's is the more useful to the student.

In 'Farquhar, Wilks, and Wildair; or, the Metamorphosis of the "Fine Gentleman" ' (*PQ*) Shirley Strum Kenny holds that much of the credit – her word – for the change in comic heroes in eighteenth-century drama is due to Farquhar and the actor Robert Wilks, who together created the role of Wildair in *The Constant Couple*. The role underwent a further metamorphosis, I would have thought, when it was taken by Peg Woffington and other actresses, as Professor Kenny mentions in passing. The essence of the new hero was greater human warmth and *joie de vivre*.

Some articles on minor figures remain. Wayne H. Phelps discusses 'Simon Baylie (1644–1679) and the Date of *The Wizard*' (*PBSA*) and suggests that this play, which has been thought to date from the Caroline period, actually belongs to the Restoration. B. J. McMullin considers 'The Direction Line as Bibliographical Evidence: Sheet K in Crowne's *City Politiques*, 1683' (*SB*). G. J. Finch analyses 'Hawkesworth's Adaptation of Southerne's *Oroonoko*' (*RECTR*, 1977) and concludes that the play is improved by omission of the sub-plot and emphasis on the evils of slavery, but does not refer to the defence of *Oroonoko* as a unified play by Novak and Rodes (*YW* 58.225). Bruce Podewell offers 'An Identification of the Players in Vanbrugh's *Æsop, Part II*' (*RECTR*, 1977). Among the players satirised are Mrs Barry, Betterton, and his wife; Mrs Betterton perhaps had more influence than has been thought on the seceding players at Lincoln's Inn Fields.

(c) Prose

The Trial of John Bunyan & the Persecution of the Puritans[23] is an anthology of writings by and about Bunyan, edited by Monica Furlong. It comprises: selections from *Grace Abounding*; extracts from the minute book of the Bedford Meeting; *A Relation of the Life of Mrs Agnes Beaumont,*

[22] *The Beaux' Strategem*, by George Farquhar, ed. by Charles N. Fifer. RRestDS. Arnold. pp. xxxvi + 145. pb £3.95.

[23] *The Trial of John Bunyan & The Persecution of the Puritans, Selections from the writings of John Bunyan and Agnes Beaumont*, ed. by Monica Furlong. Folio Society. pp. 200; 10 illustrations. £7.95.

written by Herself; Bunyan's *Relation* of his imprisonment; his sermon, *A Few Sighs from Hell*; and *A Continuation of Mr Bunyan's Life*, by Charles Doe. Some of these are not easily accessible. With Ms Furlong's substantial introduction they help us to admire the courage and faith of Bunyan and the Puritans in the face of the malice and ignorance of their persecutors. The unwary reader might have been told that only about half the text of *Grace Abounding* is given.

I noted four articles on Bunyan. David Renaker's 'John Bunyan's Misattribution to Francesco Spira of a Remark by Nathaniel Bacon' (*N&Q*) notes a reference in *Grace Abounding* to Bacon's *Relation of the Fearefull Estate of Francis Spira* (1638). A. Richard Dutton's ' "Interesting, but tough": Reading *The Pilgrim's Progress*' (*SEL*) sympathises with Huck Finn's response to the first part of *Pilgrim's Progress*, and maintains that it is not 'in conception, a work of "universal faith": it does not address itself to mankind as equals, but is very much the product of an exclusive sect'. This may be true of the book's conception, but is surely not true of its effect, so its universal appeal is less puzzling than Dutton says. Bridget Puzon sees 'The *Bildungsroman* of Middle Life' (*HLB*) 'as a distinct narrative form, describing the personal journey to self-integration of a man in the middle stage of life', and *Pilgrim's Progress* as one of several examples. James F. Forrest doubts 'The Authenticity of the 1684 Edition of Bunyan's *Holy War*' (*PBSA*): it is a cheap edition with many abridgements that Bunyan is unlikely to have approved.

The Illustrated Pepys[24] is an attractive series of extracts from the diary and reproductions of contemporary paintings, engravings, and drawings. Only about one-twelfth of the diary is left, so editorial interpolations complete the story. Pepys the lover of wine, women, and song is well represented; Pepys the organisation man is less prominent, as his activities would need too much editorial explanation. The many illustrations really do illustrate the text. Lady Castlemaine, of whom Pepys dreamed 'the best that ever was dreamed – which was that I. . .was admitted to use all the dalliance I desired with her', appears in colour; his wife, whom he tried to love, appears in black-and-white; and his mistresses, always women of lower social status, appear only in the text, and then of course chiefly in polyglot pidgin. There is an index and glossary, from which however most foreign words are excluded.

Pepys's is the earliest private library in England to survive complete, a collection of great interest to the Pepys enthusiast and real value to the historian of English culture. The 3000 volumes were chosen by Pepys, housed in his own book presses, and left to Magdalene College, Cambridge. A definitive catalogue is being issued in seven volumes, of which the first, the catalogue of printed books, was published this year[25]. The books are listed alphabetically under authors, or where authorship is uncertain under titles, with an appendix on incunabula. There are brief notes on points of interest, and cross-references to other printed catalogues and bibliographies.

[24] *The Illustrated Pepys: Extracts from the Diary*, ed. by Robert Latham. Bell & Hyman Ltd. pp. 240; about 100 illustrations, 14 in colour. £8.50.

[25] *Catalogue of the Pepys Library at Magdalene College, Cambridge*, ed. by Robert Latham; *Vol. I: Printed Books*, compiled by N. A. Smith, H. M. Adams, and D. Pepys Whiteley. Ipswich, Suff.: D. S. Brewer. pp. xiv + 201. £35.

Browsing through, I found Pepys had most of the English literature I expected, but not (*pace* Christopher Hill) Milton's minor poems, and not two of the most popular works of the time, *Pilgrim's Progress* and *Absalom and Achitophel*. Indeed Pepys seems to have had none of Dryden's poetry except the *Fables* and the *Æneis*.

Less surprisingly, Pepys kept Aphra Behn's novels out of his library too. They are the focus of attention in Larry Carver's 'Aphra Behn: The Poet's Heart in a Woman's Body' (*PLL*). The essay derives its silly title from Mrs Behn's description of 'the Poet in me' as 'my Masculine Part' in the preface to *The Lucky Chance*, where she pleads to be considered as an artist rather than as a woman. Her contemporaries did not grant the plea, and in her novels she comments on what was expected of women in 'an ironic voice at once self-effacing and assertive'. More straightforward comments on this subject, and on what was expected of men, are to be found in Dorothy Osborne, as Genie S. Lerch-Davis reminds us in 'The Rebellion against Public Prose: The Letters of Dorothy Osborne to William Temple (1652–54)' (*TSLL*). As fine examples of 'private artistic prose', their artistry should not be judged according to criteria appropriate to letters written for publication. I admire her artful account of the 'ingredients must go to the making me happy in a husband' (ed. Smith, letter 44). 'He must not be a thing that began the world in a free school, was sent from thence to the University, and is at his furthest when he reaches the Inns of Court', she declared, and could well have told Temple that much ado about learning often results in the advancement of nothing. In 'Sir William Temple, the Idea of Progress, and the Meaning of Learning' (*DUJ*) Roberta F. S. Borkat interprets the *Essay upon the Ancient and Modern Learning* as an attack on the idea that modern learning was necessarily evidence of progress, and a warning that if learning was not seen as a means of moral improvement or humanitarian usefulness, it could only increase man's pride and greed.

It is hard to tell where literature ends and philosophy begins. Right on this unmarked frontier is W. R. Albury's 'Halley's Ode on the *Principia* of Newton and the Epicurean Revival in England' (*JHI*), drawing parallels between Halley's poem and Lucretius's *De Rerum Natura* which help us to understand Halley's intentions. Lucretius had of course expounded the theories of Epicurus, and Halley meant to convince fashionable Epicureans of the importance of Newtonian science. When Epicureanism went out of fashion, his ode was altered by Richard Bentley so as to make the new science support the idea of divine providence. The spread of the new science is also considered in G. A. J. Rogers's 'Locke's *Essay* and Newton's *Principia*' (*JHI*). Rogers believes that Newton did not influence Locke as much as has been thought, that Locke may indeed have influenced Newton, and that his philosophical work did much to make Newton's ideas acceptable. *The Locke Newsletter*[26] includes a list of recent publications, articles (including 'Locke and Glanvill: A Comparison', by Sascha Talmor), and a reply by J. L. Mackie to R. S. Woolhouse's review of his *Problems from Locke*.

[26] *The Locke Newsletter*, No. 9, ed. by Roland Hall. York: Dept. of Philosophy, University of York. pp. 124. Free to Locke scholars and Libraries in U.K., or by subscription £3.50.

Articles of more specialised interest included William Dean's ' "The Widow's Tears": The Earliest Critical Reference and an Analogue for Lysander's Pretended Journey' (*N&Q*), noting P. M.'s allusion to Chapman's play in *The Ephesian and Cimmerian Matrons* (1668); A. J. Turner's 'Andrew Paschall's Tables of Plants for the Universal Language, 1678' (*BLR*), showing that these manuscripts are part of the Rev Paschall's development of the ideas of John Wilkins's *An Essay towards a Real Character and a Philosophical Language*; and Grant Carr-Harris's 'The Ancestry of John Harris (1667–1719) – Father of the Encyclopaedia' (*N&Q*), tracing the genealogy of the author of the first English encyclopaedia.

4. Background

What did the Restoration restore? I. M. Green's *The Re-establishment of the Church of England 1660–1663*[27] gives part of the answer. The conservatism of the ecclesiastical settlement was not what was at first intended. Charles II did his best to bring about a compromise; 'any expedient that embroyling Episcopacy, will not advance Presbitery', as one of his Roman Catholic friends put it. It was not the clergy of the so-called 'Laudian' party who forced Charles to abandon this policy; there is little evidence for the existence of such a party. Nor was it Clarendon; he did not like the policy, but did his duty as the king's minister, and lost friends trying to operate it. Charles was thwarted by the strong Anglicanism of the most powerful of the laity, motivated more by political than theological considerations. The Cavalier Parliament passed the series of intolerant measures known to Whig historians as 'the Clarendon code', and the country gentry found various ways of harassing the Puritans. The ecclesiastical authorities were less fierce, and finally 'far more Commonwealth clergy conformed to the Restoration settlement, at least outwardly, than were ejected for nonconformity'. This book is likely to be regarded as the standard work on its subject. It is straightforwardly written and accessible to non-specialists, but readers of *YW* should be warned that it is a history of administration, rather than of ideas and personalities; its relevance to literary studies is limited. It can help us to read the autobiographies of Clarendon and Baxter, making due allowance for their bias; but there is no hint that the revised *Book of Common Prayer* of 1662 was a literary masterpiece that graced the Anglican Church for three centuries.

In his *Child's History of England* Dickens gives the Whig interpretation of James II, that the one object of his reign was to restore Catholicism, 'and this he doggedly pursued with such a stupid obstinacy, that his career very soon came to a close'. In his *James II*[28] Maurice Ashley promises to get James off the charge of stupid obstinacy, and to see his downfall as a personal tragedy. He maintains that James truly believed in religious toleration and had some respect for other people's views, but finally has to

[27] *The Re-establishment of the Church of England 1660–1663*, by I. M. Green. O.U.P. pp. x + 263. £8.50. (Reviewed by Geoffrey F. Nuttall, Journal of Ecclesiastical History, 1979).

[28] *James II*, by Maurice Ashley. Dent. pp. 342; 22 illustrations; 3 maps. £7.50.

attribute his downfall to his 'habitual stupidity'. This might just be seen as a fatal flaw, I suppose, though James's behaviour lacked the dignity normally associated with a tragic hero. The book gives a good account of his career, but the corridors of power become claustrophobic; I would like to have seen more of James the man, and the life of the times. The principal essay in characterisation (chapter 7) does tell us he said no woman's leg 'was worth anything without green stockings', but makes nothing of his patronage of the theatre. It is a comment on academic specialisation that Dryden and Aphra Behn are ignored; doubtless Tory panegyrics are as bad as Whig interpretations, but the poets need not go wholly unacknowledged, and would have enlivened the book.

Three essays dealt with events leading from the fall of James to the lapse of the Licensing Act. In 'The Idea of Conquest in Controversies over the 1688 Revolution' (*JHI*, 1977) M. P. Thompson shows that till 1693, when Parliament ordered that Charles Blount's *King William and Mary Conquerors* should be publicly burned, ideas of conquest were prominent in constitutional arguments, especially those defending William and Mary's accession. Jeremy Collier and others undermined such defences, putting forward the idea that a conquest merely replaced one regime based on force with another. In 'Charles Blount's Intention in Writing "King William and Mary Conquerors" (1693)' (*N&Q*) Mark Goldie argues that Macaulay's story about this book is almost certainly false, and should not be repeated uncritically by modern scholars. Macaulay said Blount wrote it as a parody of the conquest theory, and so contrived to discredit Edmund Bohun, the licenser of the press, and bring about the abolition of censorship. Goldie says Blount could have actually believed in the theory, and anyway the episode has little to do with the end of censorship. In a very detailed study of 'The Renewal of the Licensing Act in 1693 and its Lapse in 1695' (*Lib*) Raymond Astbury shows that there were many reasons for the lapse of the Act, and evidently Blount's contribution was much smaller than John Locke's. The end of licensing did not cause literature to be 'emancipated for ever from the control of the Government', as Macaulay asserted, but did encourage 'the trend towards a more diversified literature in the early eighteenth century'.

Keith Thomas's 'Age and Authority in Early Modern England' (*PBA*, lxii) considers basic assumptions about the rights and duties of different age-groups in England between the sixteenth and eighteenth centuries, when 'stratification by age increased, the anomalies of youthful advancement were reduced, and the redundancy of the elderly was increasingly emphasized'. This essay illuminates the literature, especially the drama, of our period in various ways. Possibly Lady Wishfort's love of Protestant authors arose from their doctrine that the end of matrimony was 'comfortable society', not just procreation, which tended to justify the marriage or re-marriage of the elderly.

XIII

The Eighteenth Century

K. E. ROBINSON and CLARE WENLEY

1. General

As usual the eighteenth century was well served by the annual *PQ* bibliography, by the selective notices of books and papers in both *The Scriblerian* and the *Johnsonian News Letter*, and by the annual *SEL* review article, this year by G. S. Rousseau.

The most challenging book to appear this year was Howard D. Weinbrot's *Augustus Caesar in 'Augustan' England: The Decline of a Classical Norm*[1]. Weinbrot offers his work as revisionist. It questions the assumption that Augustus was the focus of positive norms for the Restoration and the eighteenth century, suggesting instead a 'firm tradition of Augustus as usurping tyrant. . . [with] roots in the classical historians themselves'. The tradition runs through the Renaissance, passes into temporary abeyance during the ascendency of sixteenth- and seventeenth-century divine monarchy, and reasserts itself in the later seventeenth century. By the early eighteenth century it had 'become entrenched in libertarian commonplaces, historical discussions and practical politics'. Weinbrot's revision of the received notion of Augustan literature has massive implications for criticism of the period, ranging from general questioning of the place of Horace and Juvenal in eighteenth-century poetry to a particular assault on Pope's *Epistle to Augustus* which becomes a rejection of 'most of the non-literary, especially political, standards that Augustus and Horace had come to represent'. But the revision cannot be accepted as it stands. Weinbrot has amassed a formidable body of support for his thesis but he is less scrupulous about the counter-evidence, though he admits that it, too, bulks large. Similarly, where texts do not quite fit the argument they are interpreted to agree. This is not least the case with the *Epistle to Augustus*. If Weinbrot challenges, he does not wholly oust the received understanding: we must now wait for a more scholarly, circumspect synthesis of the received view and Weinbrot's revision.

Less challenging but more well-rounded and sound is the eighteenth century volume in the Methuen *Context of English Literature* series, edited by Pat Rogers[2]. Rogers' brilliantly lucid introduction, which unpacks a lot of information in a limited space with tact and discrimination, sets the tone for the other contributions. Any editor of such a collection

[1] *Augustus Caesar in 'Augustan' England: The Decline of a Classical Norm*, by Howard D. Weinbrot. Princeton, N.J.: Princeton U.P. pp. xii + 270. £10.10.

[2] *The Context of English Literature: The Eighteenth Century*, ed. by Pat Rogers. Methuen. pp. xvi + 246. £3.95.

faces the problem of whether to deal in detail with the connections between the literature and its background or to sketch in the background, leaving it to the reader to make the connections for himself. Rogers has resolved the problem by providing an introduction to the literature, its forms and readers, against which his contributors have portrayed various aspects of the background, touching here and there on the most obvious links with the literature. W. A. Speck accounts for the politics, John Vladimir Price for religion and ideas, G. S. Rousseau for the science, and Peter Willis for the visual arts. The result is a splendid introduction for the undergraduate.

Max Byrd's *London Transformed: Images of the City in the Eighteenth Century*[3] focuses on several recurrent images of London at key points in the century. Byrd traces an increasing effort to humanise the city as it grew so that it is imaged, for example, as a body (as a diseased body in Defoe's *Journal of the Plague Year*). Three chapters are relevant to this section of *YW*. In his first chapter Byrd concentrates on Defoe's vision of London as 'a body torn by fever, a body diseased, plague ridden, and misshapen', a vision born out of his sense that commerce and crime were near allied. When Byrd turns to Pope in his second chapter it is to a contrast which brings out no less the unideal side of London. He contrasts the ideal Augusta of *Windsor Forest*, the city of order, with that of the *Dunciad* which 'overturns the fabulous, yearning idealism of the earlier poem and replaces it with a nightmarish contraction of the moral life'. Here the dominant images are of the theatre, the river, and the language of the Dunces. 'Pope's London. . .has simply grown too real – too vast, too full of problems, too insistently itself – to serve as epic symbol any longer'. In the third chapter Boswell and Johnson present another contrast, between the figure of the rake as a traditional adventurer urbanised and an epitome of compassion alert to the sufferings of poor city dwellers but engaged by the city's vitality. Boswell undergoes a Fieldingesque moral descent into London, his *Journal* identifying the city and the self; but Johnson, denying the decline of London without creating an ideal, sees London as a 'tribunal for the moral life'. Johnson's rootedness in London suggests to Byrd the rootedness of his thought in the concrete, the living, the capacious, as opposed to the simply academic and the cloistered. Two further chapters deal with Wordsworth's and Blake's responses to London. Although Byrd covers much familiar material under the banner of his central topic, he does offer a good deal of fresh illumination.

Georges Lamoine's two-volume *La Vie Littéraire de Bath et de Bristol 1750–1800*[4] started life as a Paris thesis. It charts the literary, theatrical and intellectual life of the two cities with separate chapters on the circle of Lady Miller at Batheaston, Chatterton, and Hannah More, and three chapters devoted to the stirrings of Romanticism in Bristol from 1794 to 1800. The whole work is readable and well evidenced, and it is rounded off with a helpful bibliography.

[3] *London Transformed: Images of the City in the Eighteenth Century*, by Max Byrd. New Haven, Conn. and London: Yale U.P. pp. x + 202. £9.

[4] *La Vie Littéraire de Bath et de Bristol 1750–1800*, by Georges Lamoine. Paris: Librairie Honore Champion. 2 vols. pp. vi + 937. 100 frs.

Among the papers of general interest, Peter Hughes[5] offers an unduly obscure but still suggestive account of the strategy of allusion. One summatory sentence should bring out the strengths and weaknesses of Hughes's style: 'Allusion robs the past of its mystery, turning it into mock-epic and anti-heroic, but it also confers on the past an increasingly literary modernity, turning the sacred books of the ancients into the mock-books of the Scriblerians'. Hughes shows an attractive willingness to generalise, but his essay cries out for more examples and sharper definition. With more clarity, H. Grant Sampson (*ESC*) discusses three styles of Augustanism, the baroque, the rococo and the picturesque, and in a second article (*CentR*) focuses on the rococo in England. In his contribution to *Studies in Eighteenth-Century Culture*[6] Patrick Brady discusses an allied topic, the unlikely relationship between atomistic empiricism and the rococo mode of vision.

Herbert M. Atherton (*ECS*) and James Sherry (*ECS*) take on more particular aspects of the period's art. Atherton comments on the mob in eighteenth-century caricature, and Sherry wrestles with Rowlandson's blend of distance and humour. Robert C. Holub (*CLS*) is exercised by the century's own thinking about art, charting the genesis of aesthetics in the period; but for a view of the eighteenth-century aesthetician at work there is the Scholars' Facsimiles and Reprints version of William Duff's *Essay on Original Genius and its Various Modes of Exertion in Philosophy and the Fine Arts, Particularly in Poetry* (1767) introduced by John L. Mahoney[7], or the same publisher's re-issue of its facsimile of the third edition (1780) of Alexander Gerard's *An Essay on Taste, together with Observations Concerning the Imitative Nature of Poetry*, introduced by Walter J. Hipple, Jr[8]. No doubt John Kerslake's two-volume *Early Georgian Portraits*[9] will prove a fruitful hunting ground for future art historians and theoreticians. Essentially a catalogue of the National Portrait Gallery's holdings of portraits of sitters important between 1714 and 1760 Kerslake's volumes include more than nine hundred and fifty plates.

Anyone curious about the domestic background of the Georgian period would do well to read John Woodforde's *Georgian Houses for All*[10]. It explores domestic architecture of the period in general but it is especially notable for its demonstration of just how speculative was much domestic building and just how much jerry-building such speculation inevitably

[5] *The Author in His Work: Essays on a Problem in Criticism*, ed. by Louis L. Martz and Aubrey Williams. New Haven, Conn. and London: Yale U.P. pp. xix + 407. £16.20.

[6] *Studies in Eighteenth-Century Culture*, Volume 7, ed. by Roseann Runte. Madison, Wisc.: U. of Wisconsin P. pp. 576. $19.95.

[7] *An Essay on Original Genius and Its Various Modes of Exertion in Philosophy and the Fine Arts, Particularly in Poetry*, by William Duff, intro. by John L.Mahoney. Delmar, New York: Scholars' Facsimiles and Reprints. $33.

[8] *An Essay on Taste, together with Observations Concerning the Imitative Nature of Poetry*, by Alexander Gerard, intro. by Walter J. Hipple Jr. Delmar, New York: Scholars' Facsimiles and Reprints. $32.

[9] *Early Georgian Portraits*, by John Kerslake. HMSO. 2 vols. pp. [xv + 391] 953 plates. £50.

[10] *Georgian Houses for All*, by John Woodforde. Routledge & Kegan Paul. pp. xiv + 177.

brought with it. Woodforde has provided a mine of information about the details of Georgian housing, from brick bonds to sewage arrangements.

Two background books of a very different sort also deserve mention – Lester S. King's *The Philosophy of Medicine: The Early Eighteenth Century*[11] and F. F. Madan's *Critical Bibliography of Dr. Henry Sacheverell*[12]. King's book is not about specific diseases or cures but about the theoretical underpinnings of medical practice from 1650 to 1750. As such it will be useful to those interested in the general scientific and philosophical background of the period. Madan's *Bibliography* is an enlarged version of his father's 1884 bibliography, completed by W. A. Speck, which provides a full and clearly organised research tool. John O. Lyons' *The Invention of the Self: the Hinge of Consciousness in the Eighteenth Century*[13] has not yet come to hand.

2. Poetry

The one general book on eighteenth-century poetry to appear in 1978 is important. Richard Feingold's *Nature and Society: Late Eighteenth-Century Uses of the Pastoral and Georgic*[14] concentrates on Cowper's *The Task* and Dyer's *The Fleece* to explore the attempts of pastoral and georgic poets to reconcile their art with the actuality of England's emergence as an economically advanced power. Feingold takes as his starting point Donald Davie's remark that 'in literature the Industrial Revolution is recorded exclusively in its effect upon agrarian England. The poets saw what was happening to rural England without understanding why it was happening'. His study does not rescue the poetry, but it does shed light on Cowper's and Dyer's responses to change. It is not so much that they did not think enough or could not adopt a larger perspective but that they tried to interpret their complex world in terms of a mode whose social and political implications belonged to an earlier and pre-industrial context. Cowper's *The Task* emerges 'not as a simple and sentimental statement of the pleasures of retirement, but as a tortured, and often self-contradictory attempt to speak in a public voice'.

An altogether simpler piece on public poems comes from Roger Stephens Jones (*AWR*) who comments upon some Anglo-Welsh poems in honour of George III, Queen Charlotte and the Prince of Wales; and, also on a Welsh subject, Trevor Johnson (*N&Q*) reports on epitaphs in Abereduw church, Radnor, believing two which show poetic promise to be the work of one James Davies. Traversing more mapped but no less obscure ground Phyllis J. Guskin (*N&Q*) redates 'An Elegy on the Death of Pamphlets' which is assigned to September 1712 in Volume VII of the Yale POAS series. This Whiggish attack on the Tory press (especially Abel Roper and his *Post-Boy*)

[11] *The Philosophy of Medecine: The Early Eighteenth Century*, by Lester S. King. Cambridge, Mass.: Harvard U.P. pp. vii + 291. $17.50.

[12] *A Critical Bibliography of Dr. Henry Sacheverell*, by F. F. Madan, ed. by W. A. Speck. Lawrence, Kan.: U. of Kansas Libraries. pp. xi + 343. $15.

[13] *The Invention of the Self: the Hinge of Consciousness in the Eighteenth Century*, by John O. Lyons. Carbondale and Edwardsville, Ill.: U. of Southern Illinois P. pp. 268. $12.95.

[14] *Nature and Society: Later Eighteenth-Century Uses of the Pastoral and Georgic* by Richard Feingold. Hassocks, Sx.: Harvester Press. pp. x + 209. £11.50.

was first printed in the *Protestant Post-Boy*, no. 101 (April 22–24, 1712). Cynthia S. Dessen (*TSLL*) is concerned with a later political attack on the corrupt state of Walpole's England. In *Walpole and the Wits* Bertrand Goldgar remarked that Pope's *Epilogue to the Satires*, dialogues I and II, and Johnson's *London* spawned a number of similar verse satires: Miss Dessen comments on one of these, Benjamin Loveling's (*circa* 1738) imitation of Persius.

As one might expect, studies of particular poets divide up very unevenly into those on Pope and Swift and those on the others. First amongst the others comes Matthew Prior whose poems addressed to Cloe are the subject of a paper by Ronald Rower (*BSUF*). Rower distinguishes between the earlier (1709) and later poems to Cloe, finding in the latter a note of 'delicate whimsy' as the nymph is warmly and intimately teased. Gay is another nymphologist, but Dianne S. Ames (*SP*) pays attention not to his nymphs but to his parody. She reveals *Trivia* to be 'a highly successful exercise in the art of classical allusion'. A major source of its humour derives from an artful mangling of snatches of Virgil, Horace, Ovid and Juvenal. Maynard Mack (*Scriblerian*), however, is concerned with Gay and nymphs, not the nymphs of his poetry but the Blount sisters. Mack comments on a letter from Gay in 1715 written to the Blount sisters from a journey into Devon. Gay's adoption of the persona of a gelding from the Mapledurham stables perhaps explains why his authorship has escaped notice for so long.

Bernard Fabian's (*Wolfenbütteler B*) addition to our knowledge of Young's correspondence with his translator Johann Arnold Ebert is less remarkable but none the less noteworthy. The editors of this part of Young's correspondence have used the text in Eschenburg's edition of Ebert's *Episteln and vermischte Gedichte*. Fabian has located Young's first letter in the Herzog August Bibliothek, Wolfenbüttel. He transcribes the text and comments on Eschenburg's misdating and its consequences for the order of the Young–Ebert letters. Less prosaically, Merrill D. Whitburn (*ELWIU*) discusses the rhetoric of other-worldliness in *Night Thoughts*.

Judging by the rate of publication, interest in Swift's poetry continues to grow. There are two books and a bevy of papers to report for 1978. Peter J. Schakel's *The Poetry of Jonathan Swift: Allusion and the Development of a Poetic Style*[15] has not yet been seen but John Irwin Fischer's *On Swift's Poetry*[16] has. It is focused on 'the ways Swift sought to temper his hubristic indignation with the world into a morally responsible reaction to it'. Fischer's determination to take Swift's poetry seriously is both a strength and a weakness. It leads to careful and sometimes challenging readings but it also brings with it an underestimate of the strength of the comic and it forces moral interpretation on to unwilling material. Fischer seems more interested in foisting on to Swift a providential view of human nature or in showing him to be a champion of intellectual humility than in rendering the complex experience of reading. His approach is usefully off-

[15] *The Poetry of Jonathan Swift: Allusion and the Development of a Poetic Style*, by Peter J. Schakel. Madison, Wisc.: U. of Wisconsin P. pp. 224. $25.

[16] *On Swift's Poetry*, by John Irwin Fischer. Gainesville, Fla.: U.P. of Florida. pp. 207. $10.

set by Colin J. Horne's interest in Swift's 'flair for comic situation and dialogue'[17]. Horne finds in the poetry 'abundant instances of his love of fun and nonsense, of jokes and amusing trifling, never wholly nonsensical, for it is always charged with intellectual activity as well as verbal wit, and mostly has some moral concern in it'. But it may be that Horne overemphasises the comic as much as Fischer the moral. In Horne's reading of *A Beautiful Young Nymph*, for example, gusto undermines disgust: 'the verve of the realistic details of her toilette transforms potential horror and pity into a rich apprehension of the ludicrous plight of the "nymph" '. This is to underrate the note of revulsion at the poem's end. Richard H. Rodino (*PLL*) grapples more surely with the complex mixture of *A Beautiful Young Nymph*. Rodino tackles the reader's involvement in the unprintables, showing them to contain an uneasy blend of blasphemy and blessing. For him *A Beautiful Young Nymph* elicits sympathy as well as disgust. More modestly, Arthur Sherbo (*Scriblerian*) reminds those who have forgotten about the usefulness of the *Fop Dictionary* appended to *Mundus Muliebris* as a glossary for *A Beautiful Young Nymph*.

Swift's women are the subject of several further essays in *PLL*. A. B. England looks into the relationship between emotional turmoil and rhetorical order in *Cadenus and Vanessa*, whilst John Irwin Fischer, pursuing much the same line as he does in his book, comments on the triad of faith, hope and charity in the poems to Stella. Peter J. Schakel deals with the scatalogical poems in general and Thomas B. Gilmore Jr offers a Freudian reading of *Strephon and Chloe*. Although David Sheehan is concerned, like Fischer, with the Stella poems, he is less interested in Swift and women and more in Swift and Voiture. Sheehan argues an affinity between the French writer in his letters and Swift's poems: both, he claims, display 'a spectrum of raillery, from the simplest modes of praise-by-blame to the more complicated modes in which praise and blame exist in fine balance'.

The only discussion of *Verses on the Death of Dr. Swift* comes from David M. Vieth[5] who faces up to the problem of locating Swift in the *Verses* in view of the poem's 'dazzling multiplication of identities'. This is a densely argued paper difficult to summarise: suffice it to say that Vieth finds the *Verses* a hoax, of a sort, in which Swift 'managed to predict, project, and even predetermine the kind of official image that would make the *Verses* come alive for posterity. . .imposing his semi-fictitious self-image on the future'. The complex artistry proposed by Vieth is very different from the priority of sense over sound which James L. Tyne (*PLL*) finds characteristic of Swift's poetry in general. Finally, William K. Wimsatt[5] tries to illuminate Swift's preference for the short rather than the long couplet by way of a synchronic digression into Goliardic verse.

No abatement in the rate of publication on Pope was seen in 1978. Four critical books appeared as well as a reprinting of Herbert Davis's Oxford Standard Authors edition of the poetry with a fine introduction to the life and works by Pat Rogers[18]. Morris R. Brownell's *Alexander Pope*

[17] *Augustan Worlds: Essays in Honour of A. R. Humphreys*, ed. by J. C. Hilson, M. M. B. Jones and J. R. Watson. Leicester, Leics.: Leicester U.P. pp. 311. £10.

[18] *Pope: Poetical Works*, ed. by H. Davis, intro. by Pat Rogers. O.U.P. pp. xxix + 754. £2.95.

and the Arts of Georgian England[19] is a splendidly produced book with eighty-three plates which aims to chart Pope's ' "virtuosoship" and taste in the arts'. Its account of Pope's relationship with artists, architects, designers and others is valuable both as a summary and an extension of our knowledge; but Brownell is less helpful about their theories. He describes his approach as empirical and descriptive: its fruits are a welter of facts and details, but one is often left wishing for a stronger clue through the dense undergrowth. On balance this is a useful, workmanlike study lacking in flair and energy except in those few places (like the appendix on 'The Myth of Pope's Insensitivity to Music') where there is something to show rather than facts to accumulate.

John M. Aden's *Pope's Once and Future Kings: Satire and Politics in the Early Career*[20] has the advantage of a stronger thesis, that there is a strong strain of political satire in Pope's early work. Aden's book is in two sections. The first plots Pope's own religion against the background of the treatment of Catholics from Elizabeth to George I and conjectures about the possible influence of the *Poems on Affairs of State* on Pope; the second turns to analysis of political elements in the early verse. In this second half Aden offers some especially interesting remarks on Pope's adaptation of translation to the needs of political satire, but elsewhere he can be a little over-ingenious in the pursuit of his thesis and too fond of the high-sounding critical phrase. But Aden's is an altogether more reliable and acute book than George S. Fraser's *Alexander Pope*[21]. Fraser's study shares all the faults of James Reeves' *The Reputation of Alexander Pope* without its compensating virtues. Writing as a non-specialist Reeves sounded some important caveats about tendencies in academic criticism of Pope and rose to some fresh commentary on the poetry, but Fraser's self-pronounced amateur approach is fraught with inaccuracies, misrepresentations, and simple ignorance. It is difficult to see why any publisher should want to add such a study to his list with much better introductory books, of very different tempers, already in print from Pat Rogers and Yasmine Gooneratne. Unlike both these studies Fraser's is ill-organised and fundamentally unsympathetic to, or critically obtuse about, large parts of the Pope *oeuvres.*

The last of the year's books deserves much more respect. Dustin H. Griffin's *Alexander Pope: The Poet in the Poems*[22] is an autobiographical exploration which sets out to 'recover some of the personal energy that invigorates Pope's greatest poems and makes them vividly self-expressive'. In his first section Griffin attempts to establish Pope's picture of himself from the correspondence and to square it with an objective view of the poet. Within Pope's view of himself Griffin distinguishes several component and contradictory roles. His findings are applied to related poems in the second section of the book. Like Aden's work Griffin's is useful in patches,

[19] *Alexander Pope and the Arts of Georgian England*, by Morris R. Brownell. Oxford: Clarendon. pp. xxvi + 401.

[20] *Pope's Once and Future Kings: Satire and Politics in the Early Career*, by John M. Aden. Knoxville, Tenn.: U. of Tennessee P. pp. xiv + 218. $12.50.

[21] *Alexander Pope*, by George S. Fraser. Routledge & Kegan Paul. pp. x + 134.

[22] *Alexander Pope: The Poet in the Poems*, by Dustin H. Griffin. Princeton, N.J.: Princeton U.P. pp. xvii + 285. $17.50.

for its readings of individual poems rather than for the light that it sheds on Pope the man and his works in general. As an object lesson in how to deal with the man in his work, and as a piece which keeps its eye sensitively on the poetry, pursuing truth rather than thesis, Maynard Mack's essay in *YR* is preferable to Griffin's. Mack discusses with great tact and insight the ways that Pope's physical disability affected the character of his verse, not just his self-projections but his responses to those around him. This is a paper that stops nowhere for long, but it always illuminates its subject and suggests fruitful avenues to follow. A second paper by Mack[17] also invites comparison with Griffin's book. It deals with Pope's claims to high seriousness in the 1717 Preface in the context of the publication of his Homer. Where Griffin finds in the Preface a blend of contradictory roles, Mack presents it as a more human and deliberate attempt to shed publicly the knavish side of his wit. His case is strengthened by a manuscript version of the image-making Preface, which includes alterations designed to give an air of greater detachment. Mack prints a transcription of the manuscript. By contrast Wolfgang E. H. Rudat (*DUJ*), ever hot on the trail of the sexual in Pope's poetry, offers yet another ingeniously inept account of hidden meanings in *Rape of the Lock*. Rudat diagnoses a Pope busy sublimating his sexual problems. A diagnosis of Rudat using his own approach might be far from complimentary. Vincent Carretta's *Scriblerian* note on a portrait of Pope comments upon the print that serves as a frontispiece to the anonymous poem *A Tryall of Skill Between a Court Lord, and a Twickenham 'Squire, Inscrib'd to Mr. Pope*.

Pat Rogers' treatment of Pope's rambles[17] is both simpler and more illuminating of the man. Placing the rambles in the context of early eighteenth-century tourism Rogers catalogues Pope's equipment as a tourist: his connoisseur's interest in the visual arts, weakness for 'romantic' moods, feeling for loss and mutability, and his antiquarian bent. Amongst Pope's motives for rambling Rogers finds self-education and nervous and physical renewal, as well as a more mundane compliance with social obligations. In a second paper Rogers (*MP*) focuses not on the poet but on those around him, listing identifications of contemporaries in Pope's letters. In the same vein Margaret Maison (*RES*) advances possible models for characters in *Of the Characters of Women*. Rufa is paired with Catharine Trotter (later Mrs Cockburn), and Sidia with Elizabeth Singer (later Mrs Rowe), whilst good Simplicius suggests to Miss Maison Isaac Watts. Pope's unfortunate lady on the other hand defies identification, according to Ian Jack[17]. Half of Jack's essay is given to a survey of discussions of her identity from Caryll to Reuben Brower to make the point that the lady cannot be traced. It is not that there are not sufficient clues but that Pope was writing in the Roman elegiac manner in which the poet only *suggests* that he is writing directly of his own experience.

Tom Woodman (*EIC*) sees much of Pope's poetic career as a dialogue with the tradition of the 'polite'. In the early work Pope is polished and displays polite assurance, but by the fourth book of the *Dunciad* he is 'both using and transcending the themes and techniques of the polite mode'. Those not sure about the complexion of the polite mode will get some help from Woodman but not enough. Few, however, will grumble at J. S. Cunningham's elegant and wide-ranging essay on the laughter of the gods in Milton, Pope, Johnson *et al*[17]. Cunningham trains his sights on the antithesis of the festive and the derisive notes of laughter in Christian literature. On a more scholarly, less critical, note Edward Heuston (*RES*) inserts the closing lines of *Windsor Forest* into the history of the so-called Pope–Philips quarrel. Heuston holds that Pope's lines commenting on the reception of his pastorals provoked Tickell to reply in his *Guardian* essays, Tickell's essays drawing in turn *Guardian* no. 40.

Belinda's character is the centre of two essays on *Rape of the Lock*. Frank L. Huntley (*ECLife*) finds Belinda's abilities at ombre replete with significance for her character; and Robert N. Gosselink (*PLL*) comments on what the name Belinda would have suggested to contemporary readers. Because of an overwhelming tendency in Restoration verse and comedy for female names ending in 'inda' to belong to coquettes, Pope's readers would be disposed to find Belinda coquettish.

Pope's Homer draws a more substantial contribution from Matthew Hodgart who elucidates the 'striking religious, political, and social features' of the subscription list for Pope's *Iliad* in 1715[23]. Amongst other things he finds a large number of Catholic and Protestant Jacobites in the list. The presence of their names probably explains the absence of Townshend and Walpole, though the Holdernesses, Rockinghams and so on were represented. Townshend and Walpole were to subscribe to the *Odyssey* in 1725, as were other notable absentees from the earlier list. The scholarly sharpness of Hodgart's essay is absent from George Fraser's discussion of Pope and Homer[17]. Throughout Fraser's essay biography mixes uneasily with criticism, though the comparison of Pound's and Pope's handling of the Elphenor passage from *Odyssey* XI promises more. This is a disappointing contribution to a volume which contains much of high quality, including Mack's essay on the 1717 Preface. More respectable is Vincent Carretta's (*JEGP*) attempt to account for Bathurst's being the addressee of a moral essay. Carretta believes that the poem might be more occasional than has been thought. Published 15 January, the day before Parliament convened in 1733, Pope's *Epistle* might well have appeared to many of its readers as a party piece recapitulating the political issues of the day from the Opposition point of view.

Finally, on Pope, there are two bibliographical papers. Phillipa Hardman (*Library*) records an addition to Griffith's bibliography, and David Foxon (*Library*) comments on Greg's rationale and the peculiar difficulties facing editors of Pope.

The remaining poets of the period receive much less, even scant, attention. Robert Halsband represents Lady Mary Wortley Montagu[23], discussing her career as a feminist and writer by way of a commentary upon his own and Isabel Grundy's edition of her prose and verse. Gray fares a little better with papers from John Ferguson (*N&Q*), Dustin Griffin (*EIC*) and Howard D. Weinbrot (*SEL*). Ferguson's is the least pretentious and most useful. Amongst the 'Poems of Doubtful Authenticity' in Starr and Hendrickson's *Complete Poems* is an 'Imitation of Martial' (Fulvia *formosa* est multis. . .). Ferguson points out that it is in fact a transcription of

[23] *The Dress of Words: Essays on Restoration and Eighteenth-Century Literature in Honour of Richmond P. Bond*, ed. by Robert B. White Jr. University of Kansas Publications Library Series, 42. Lawrence, Kan.: U. of Kansas Libraries. pp. 220. $12.

Catullus 86 with two slips and two alterations. Griffin differentiates the audiences presupposed by Gray's poetry, concerning himself especially with sympathetic and uncomprehending audiences. When these co-exist in the same poem they go some way towards overcoming Gray's sense of alienation and poetic failure. Weinbrot starts from R. S. Crane's account of the *Elegy* as 'an imitative lyric of moral choice rather than of action or mood' to show that the poem 'which begins as an elegy for the speaker's unfulfilled promise ends as an elegy. . .for a man who learns to accept and praise his limited world and its people, and thus hopes to be accepted and praised in the limitless world of God and His people'.

After Griffin and Weinbrot, Roger Lonsdale's paper on Goldsmith is welcome for its common sense. Lonsdale evaluates the critical reception of *The Traveller* and *The Deserted Village*, balancing the nineteenth century's interest in biographical reading against the more recent emphasis on the rhetorical strategies of the poems which separates the author from the speaker of the poem. Allowing that the rhetorical treatment casts light on certain aspects of the poetry, Lonsdale prefers a reading in which Goldsmith was moving towards membership of what Wordsworth describes as 'that class of poets, the principal charm of whose writings depends upon the familiar knowledge which they convey of the personal feelings of their authors'.

In *RES* David Fairer provides a postscript to his 1975 essay on Thomas Warton in which ten poems from *Poems on Several Occasions* (1748) were re-attributed to Thomas Warton the Younger. Fairer argued that this re-attribution signalled both a need to look afresh at the character and reputation of the elder Warton and doubts about the authorship of other poems. He now reports a manuscript draft for one of those doubtful poems, *Retirement: An Ode* in the unmistakable hand of Joseph Warton. Morris Brownell (*N&Q*) and John D. Baird (*N&Q*) are on the track of unmistakable sources for Cowper. Brownell finds a source for Cowper's description of himself as a 'stricken deer' in *The Task* (1784) in Pope's *To Mr. Gay, who wrote him a congratulatory letter on the finishing of his house* (*circa* 1722); and Baird spots an allusion to Terence, *Eunuchus* 54–55 in Cowper's letter of 21 August 1781 to John Newton. Still on Cowper, Lodwick Hartley[23] deals with Cowper's venture into satire in *Anti-Thelyphthora*, an attack on his cousin Martin Madan's advocacy of polygamy as a solution to the problem of prostitution. Relating it to *The Progress of Error* Hartley aruges that Cowper wrote to please Evangelical friends by combining Evangelicalism with formal satire. Cowper's authentic satiric voice outcropped again in *The Task* which resumed the mock-heroic for its mild opening parody of the *Æneid* and *Paradise Lost*.

Finally, on the poetry, a paper on Beattie, one on Smart, and another on Macpherson. In *N&Q* James R. Irvine sheds light on the relationship between James Beattie and John Ogilvie; in *RES* Christopher M. Dennis enters the debate about the structure of Smart's *Song to David* with a demonstration of its 'structural conceits akin. . .to the shape poems of Herbert or Donne's *La Corona*'. The most important (and hitherto unnoticed) 'structural conceit' for Dennis is the harp of David. Wolfgang G. Müller (*Anglia*) discourses on the devices of asyndeton and archaism in Macpherson's *Ossian*.

3. Prose

The only book of a general nature to report is Charles R. Batten Jr's *Pleasurable Instruction: Form and Convention in Eighteenth-Century Travel Literature*[24]. Batten outlines the form of the eighteenth-century travelogue and the conventions which governed it, plotting their changes in response to shifts in taste and intellectual background. He charts well a lot of familiar and unfamiliar territory ranging from the cold objectivity of Addison's *Remarks on Several Parts of Italy* through to Smollett and Sterne and the late picturesque. This is a book which needs to be appreciated as a whole: its strength lies in a comprehensive picture rather than startling *aperçu* on individual works. Other recent approaches to travel literature of the period are reviewed by Percy Adams (*TSLL*).

A handful of papers deal with the general, the peripheral, or with minutiae. In a paper thin on detail George May[5] searches for the origins of modern autobiography in the eighteenth century, suggesting that 'the autobiographical urge. . .with its stress on childhood, on obscure instincts, and on the mysterious recesses of the psyche, may well have been part of the spontaneous search for an antidote to the excessively rational side of the Enlightenment'. Focusing on detail David S. Wiesen (*Classical World*) finds allusions to Juvenal and Ovid in a speech before the House by the Earl of Chatham, whilst Simon Varey (*Library*) comments on the publication of *The Craftsman*. Two papers have to do indirectly with Pitt's relationship with the periodical literature. Daniel L. McCue (*ECLife*) gives an account of Eaton, the phamphleteer whom Pitt's Government could not silence, and Karl W. Schweizer (*N&Q*) defends Bute against the theory that he orchestrated attacks on Pitt in 1762 as part of a deliberate attempt to publicise his pension and undermine his reputation for disinterestedness. Schweizer demonstrates that only 'after the "Gutter Press" had arrayed its forces against him in October 1761 did Bute retaliate in kind, though even then he did so with caution and restraint'. Finally, of general interest, there are two facsimiles from the Augustan Reprint Society. William Warburton's *A Letter to the Editor of the Letters on the Spirit of Patriotism* (1749) and Bolingbroke's *A Familiar Epistle to the Most Imprudent Man Living* (1749) are reprinted together in one pamphlet, introduced by Donald T. Siebert Jr[25], and Sir William Chambers' *An Explanatory Discourse, by Tan Chet-qua of Quang-chew-fu, Gent.* (1773) is introduced by Richard E. Quaintance Jr[26].

In 1701 a new periodical appeared, the *Post Angel*, edited by John Dunton. Annibel Jenkins[23] describes its 'exceptional. . .form and design as well as. . .diversity and length'. It was aimed at middle-class Dissenters 'as messenger between heaven and earth'. On more familiar ground Lillian D.

[24] *Pleasurable Instruction: Form and Convention in Eighteenth-Century Travel Literature*, by Charles R. Batten Jr. Berkeley and Los Angeles, Calif.: U. of California P. pp. xii + 170. $13.95.

[25] *A Letter to the Editor of the Letters on the Spirit of Patriotism &c.*, by William Warburton, and *A Familiar Epistle to the Most Impudent Man Living*, by Henry St. John, Viscount Bolingbroke, intro. by Donald T. Siebert Jr. ARS No. 192. Los Angeles, Calif.: U. of California P. pp. 64.

[26] *An Explanatory Discourse by Tan Chet-qua of Quang-chew-fu, Gent.*, by Sir William Chambers, intro. by Richard E. Quaintance, Jr. ARS No. 191. Los Angeles, Calif.: U. of California P. pp. 71.

Bloom[5] places Addison's *Paradise Lost* papers in the context of both the spectatorial aesthetic as a whole and Addison's aim to create men and women of 'Polite Imagination'. Miss Bloom is espcially concerned with the rhetoric of the papers in the face of a popular audience. The same writer, in conjunction with Edward A. Bloom, is responsible for a valuable paper on Steele[23]. In the belief that 'men have a natural prejudice in favour of those who are strugglng against difficulties', Steele was careful to cast himself as 'the victim courageous in faction's cause' in his journalism between May 1709 and February 1714. The Blooms trace the attacks which made such a stance credible, starting from Mrs Manley's attack in the first volume of *The New Atalantis* which set a pattern for anti-Steele diatribe as *vituperatio hominis*. Concerned with much the same period Henry L. Snyder[23] deals with Abel Boyer's contributions to the *Protestant Post-Boy*, 1711-2, which share the Whig zeal of the *Political State* and the *Annals*. Snyder's paper is intended to whet the appetite of those who might investigate further Boyer's collaboration with more than one of the more notable Whig writers of the day.

On Defoe, J. Huddleston (*N&Q*) finds evidence of an affinity between Charles Morton's thoughts on English composition in his lecture 'Advice to Candidates for the Ministry, under the Present Discouraging Circumstances' (printed in Calamy's *Continuation* [1727]) and Defoe's journalistic style. Also concerned with affinities Gilbert D. McEwan[23] compares Benjamin Franklin, Cotton Mather and Defoe on conduct. Jean Bèranger[27] is more interested in Defoe's views on political stability than in his norms of social conduct, discussing the consistency of Defoe's attitude towards a permanent armed force, based on English soil, at the service of the sovereign and his Government. The work of Huddleston, McEwan and Bèranger relies on a bedrock of work on the notoriously problematic Defoe canon. John J. Perry (*N&Q*) busies himself making this bedrock more solid, querying Moore's dating of the publication of *Atalantis Major* (before 28 December 1710) and proposing instead that the pamphlet was seen through the press 11-13 February 1711.

Modern discussions of the irony of *The Fable of the Bees* can easily neglect or run counter to the book's historical context, but W. A. Speck's valuable essay in *ECS* sets *The Fable* firmly in its background. Speck finds the seeds of the notoriety of the third edition of *The Fable* in its presentment by the Middlesex Grand Jury. He concludes that the sentiments of the presentment 'were the political manifesto of the Country opposition to Walpole'. The Grand Jury 'was not merely getting its own back on Mandeville for his snide remarks on charity schools; they were censuring what has been called the most telling critique of the humanist values dear to the Opposition'. What Speck does for *The Fable* J. A. Downie does for *The Conduct of the Allies*[28], assessing the influence that Swift felt from St. John and Harley and redrawing the picture of the relationship between the ideas of the two men. Downie concludes that 'if St. John was the "inspiration" behind Swift's attack on the conduct of the allies in 1711, there is more than enough evidence to suggest that Oxford provided the

[27] *Hommage a Emile Gasquet (1920–1977)*, Annales de la Faculte des Lettres et Sciences Humaines de Nice No. 34. Paris: Les Belles Lettres. pp. 228.

[28] *The Art of Jonathan Swift*, ed. by Clive T. Probyn. Vision. pp. 215. £6.40.

stimulus for the attack on the conduct of the Godolphin ministry'. Interested in a different aspect of Swift's relationship with Harley, John A. Vance (*Scriblerian*) finds evidence of Swift's anger at Harley when not preferred to a vacant deanery in an omitted sentence in his sketch of Harley included in the *History of the Four Last Years*.

Several papers on Swift focus upon details of the life and works. Two are by J. A. Downie who in *N&Q* comments on Swift's pre-occupation with being impecunious, and, again in *N&Q*, queries A. J. Varney's notion that the portrait of Nottingham as Dismal in *An Excellent New Song being the Intended Speech of a famous Orator against Peace* is probably modelled on Antonio in Otway's *Venice Preserved*. Downie doubts Swift's reading of Otway. At greater length C. P. Daw (*MP*) speculates on the date of Swift's sermon on the *Excellency of Christianity*. Daw thinks that it was probably preached before Swift's award of D.D. by Trinity College, Dublin in February 1701/2 as part of the requirements for that degree.

Angus Ross's article in *The Art of Jonathan Swift*[28] is more critically speculative. Ross asks whether the Hibernian Patriot's pre-1714 prose pieces might be in any sense Irish writing. The question is asked to cast light on both Swift's apprenticeship and the problem of his Irishness as a writer. Ross deals with the four obviously Irish pieces, *The Story of the Injured Lady* (1707), *A Letter from a Member of the House of Commons in Ireland* (1708), *A Letter to a Member of Parliament in Ireland* (1710) and *A Short Character of. . . Wharton* (1710), and he locates elements of Irish temper in others. 'It is clear that Swift's notion of prose style is a social one, that would commend itself to a brilliant and skilful outsider wishing to make his mark in the metropolis'. By the side of Ross's tactful speculations J. R. Crider's paper (*SEL*) on the *Mechanical Operation of the Spirit* is pedestrian. Crider supplies the background to Swift's argument in his 'History of Fanaticism' that fanatics have always been inspired by Eros rather than the Holy Spirit. Even more pedestrian is Eugene Korkowski's reading (*ECLife*) of *A Tale of a Tub* against the backcloth of the place of the tub in iconography and in proverbs 'as a type of enigma, an emblem for all objects of materialistic human curiosity'.

Of the three pieces on *A Modest Proposal* only one is significant. In *Eire* Edward Craney Jacobs finds echoes of Micah in *A Modest Proposal*, whiles Charles Pullen (*DR*) offers an unconvincing and critically unsure account of the effect of Swift's treatment of the insane projector. But Claude Rawson's 'A Reading of *A Modest Proposal*'[17] is splendidly argued, carefully evidenced and critically sensitive. Properly impatient with humane readings of the *Proposal* which ignore its disturbing texture, Rawson holds that if there is mimicry of projects concerning the poor it is 'only a seasoning, not the main point'. Swift is neither 'liberal' nor 'humane' in any modern sense. As David Nokes before him, Rawson uses Swift's other writings, especially his sermons, to show his unironical attitude to beggars, his intense hostility. For Rawson the 'complicated interplay of compassion and contempt is not to be taken as a finely-textured, sensitively judicial blend, a mellowly pondered product of the liberal imagination. It is an explosive mixture'.

Just as Rawson tries to cut through modern presupposition to render accurately the disturbing texture of *A Modest Proposal* so Frank Brady

(*MP*) elucidates three problem areas of which critics have fallen foul in *Gulliver's Travels*: jokes, Swift's view of deterioration, and his techniques and attitudes in the fourth book. Unfortunately Brady is better at spotting the faults in others than in repairing them; nor does he see the pitfalls against which Rawson's criticism is aimed. But the besetting sin of many studies of *Gulliver's Travels* this year lies in treating the book as a *roman à clef*. In *Gulliver's Progress* L. J. Morrissey[29] hunts for the meaning of the *Travels* in the collects and lessons assigned to the calendar of Gulliver's life. The result is a mish-mash of references which are made to add up to a religious significance. Fitting a fiction to the church calendar can be very fruitful for Joyce's work, but it is critically tactless for *Gulliver's Travels*. James E. Gill[23] looks for the key to the relationship of the Yahoos and Houyhnhnms to man in the dialectical confrontation between Gulliver and the Master Houyhnhnm as they try to comprehend each other's worlds. The problem with Gill's key is that it is insensitive to the affective complexities of the fourth book, making it a complex of intellectual distinctions. But even with this reservation Gill's paper is preferable to Ann Cline Kelly's (*ELH*) exploration of Swift's thoughts on universal language in *Gulliver's Travels* against the background of seventeenth-century linguistic theory. Beneath the top-dressing of scholarship there lurks an uncritically twentieth-century view of the Yahoos as an oppressed minority.

From the background of linguistic theory we move to the background of logic. Clive Probyn[28] tries to apply the logical apparatus of Swift's intellectual milieu to Book IV on the basis of Swift's distinction between man as *animal rationale* and man as *animal rationis capax* to arrive at the far from surprising conclusion that 'Swift showed in *Gulliver's Travels* that man's animal nature was not merely part of a traditional logical definition but an undeniable imperative in his conduct'. By the way, Probyn tries his hand at a new etymology for Houyhnhnm: from homonym. Swift the moralist figures, too, in Françoise Lapraz's reading of *Gulliver's Travels*[27]. Lapraz charts the motif of death, arguing that though Swift was no stranger to death and loss, his treatment of death is not intimate or personal. *Gulliver's Travels* moves from death as the 'instigator' – it is the death of James Bates that pushes Gulliver into his travels – to death in Book IV as 'la conséquence, la preuve et le symbole des limitations humaines'. On Lapraz's reading Swift recommends facing up to death and human limitations to achieve human dignity. In Dennis Todd's view (*SP*) the clue to Book III lies not in death but parallels with Babylon and Jerusalem which lie behind the foreground of science. The difficulty with Todd's approach rests not so much in its parallel hunting as in novelistic reading. Todd transmutes Gulliver into both 'a parodic Ezekiel' and 'an unregenerate Crusoe', into one whose 'self is turned into an object of its own observation and is consequently locked in a paralysis which is eternally poised for response but which does not respond'.

After such a clutch of journeyman papers it is refreshing to turn to three pieces on *Gulliver's Travels*, all from *The Art of Jonathan Swift*[28], each of which in its different way is fine. First there is Jenny Mezciems' comparison of *Gullivers Travels* with *Robinson Crusoe* on the one hand

[29] *Gulliver's Progress*, by L. J. Morrissey. Hamden, Conn.: Shoe String. pp. 199. $12.50.

and the *Dunciad* on the other to bring out Swift's use of the heroic. Whereas the *Dunciad* presents us with a hero, Swift in spite of many heroic allusions carefully excludes 'a heroic concept which will allow us to juggle the parts around so that we can call this figure a hero'. Miss Mezciems is particularly stimulating on these allusions, contrasting Pope's methods of referring to heroic norms to stress the degeneration of contemporaries. Pope's allusions are specific and direct, Swift's are silent. 'Swift leaves his reader to do [the work], to guess a range of targets and to draw from his own literary experience, without authorial guidance, the models by which they are to be judged'. The outcome for Miss Mezciems is a satire which turns in on the 'gentle reader' and his allusions about himself. Pat Rogers' essay is much less dense but much more urbanely witty. Rogers finds Gulliver's reliance on his spectacles symptomatic of a larger concern with perception in *Gulliver's Travels*. 'The glasses are the badge of his meddling and inquisitive nature'; they represent an 'over-intent scrutiny of what is better left unexamined, because it causes pain and revulsion when pried into by the modern empiricist'. Finally, on *Gulliver's Travels* there is David Woolley's magisterially definitive, detailed (and illustrated) account of the 'Armagh' copy, and the Hyde edition shown to incorporate a significant number of the 'Armagh' alterations. Woolley finds for Swift's hand.

There remain two general articles on Swift, again from *The Art of Jonathan Swift*[28]. W. B. Carnochan finds that although Swift 'was hard put to maintain composure and was often far less than stoical himself', in his art he was capable not only of rational distance but of discovering 'compensatory remedies' in the world of his satire. *A Modest Proposal*, for example, 'yields a perverse but generous comfort, even elation' through jokes, rhetorical extravaganzas and therapeutic mock-cruelty. Carnochan singles out *Gulliver's Travels* as alone amongst the satires in not cancelling pain and loss. It is a shame that this densely stimulating essay should so underestimate the negative and disorienting vigour of Swift's satire. More disappointing is David Nokes's essay, which argues that Swift's puns are derived from language under the pressure of change.

I have not seen a copy of Ricardo Quintana's *Two Augustans: John Locke, Jonathan Swift*[30].

The most important Johnson publication of the year was Jean Hagstrum and James Gray's edition of the *Sermons* for the Yale edition of the Works[31]. That apart the year brought nothing startlingly original on Johnson's prose but there were several sensible and respectable pieces. William Bowman Piper (*TSLL*) presents Johnson as an exemplary critic and as an antidote to structuralism; whilst James Engell (*MP*) tries to show that Johnson 'recognised that only a thin line separates pleasantly familiar accounts from hackneyed ones and concluded that good writing is fresh; that is, challenges our willingness to believe without itself degenerating into something unbelievable'. Engell holds that 'originality' came to mean for Johnson 'the ability to reflect the inner drama and process of a mind

[30] *Two Augustans: John Locke, Jonathan Swift*, by Ricardo Quintana. Madison, Wisc.: U. of Wisconsin P. pp. 160. $17.50.

[31] *Sermons. The Yale Edition of the Works of Samuel Johnson Volume XIV*, ed. by Jean Hagstrum and James Gray. New Haven, Conn. and London: Yale U.P. pp. 354.

charged with feeling'. If Piper opposes Johnson to structuralism C. T. Probyn (*MLR*) explores an antipathy which Johnson himself felt, toward James Harris and his work, the antipathy of a common reader to a cultural classicist. The collision between Harris and Johnson is that 'between the philosopher-scholar and the man of the world, between the mind which defines everything in the proper forms of scholastic logic and the mind to which even "the most sublime and important precepts require no uncommon opportunities, nor laborious preparations" '. At the same time Harris was as convinced as Johnson of the importance of ethics over logic. Probyn locates some points of contact between Harris's *Concering Happiness: A Dialogue* and *Rasselas*. Frank H. Ellis[5] is more concerned with tragedy than happiness. Ellis believes that two failed tragedies, Savage's *The Tragedy of Sir Thomas Overbury* and Johnson's *Irene*, dominated Johnson's mind when he wrote his *Life of Savage*. Johnson portrays Savage as a failed tragic hero in best Aristotelian fashion except that his catastrophe stops short of anagnorisis. Savage was 'never made wiser by his sufferings'.

Patrick O'Flaherty (*SEL*) writes on *The Rambler*, claiming that the absence of 'any readily perceived symmetry among the numerous meditations in *The Rambler* can be explained and offset by keeping in mind the area of experience Johnson is exploring and by focusing upon the weighty and complicated purpose behind his writings'. Peter T. Koper (*Style*) is less interested in Johnson's weighty moral temper in *The Rambler* and more in his rhetorical stance. In a more scholarly essay Irma S. Lustig (*MP*) provides a history of the publication of John Ker's Latin *Donaides* and David Malloch's English imitation by way of background to Johnson's interest in Malloch's poem, recorded in Boswell's journals but not in the *Life*. In a related piece Miss Lustig (*PBSA*) redates Malloch's published letters to Ker.

In two rather more ephemeral papers Brian Vickers (*N&Q*) questions George Steevens' reliability as a reporter of Dr Johnson, and Giles Barber[23] catalogues 'the very personal but not untypical' views of Johnson on food and cookery. Finally, Johnson's reception is explored by William Kenney[6] who discusses parodies and imitations of Johnson in the eighteenth century and by Lawrence Lipking and Frederick S. Troy who consider recent studies in review articles in *YR* and *MR* respectively.

In the remaining papers on prose J. C. Hilson[17] relates the style and fictive techniques of the first volumes of Hume's *History of England* to the sentimental tradition in mid-eighteenth-century philosophy and literary criticism, and Martin Price[17], James D. Garrison (*MP*) and Melvyn New (*N&Q*) deal with various aspects of Gibbon the historian. Price explores Gibbon's treatment of 'the dark and implacable genius of superstition', at its most powerful in monasticism as treated by Gibbon in chapter XXXVII of his *History*. According to Price, Gibbon held that 'the faculties of the mind must be exercised to remain strong, and for their exercise they require the stubborn resistance of a world outside. That world may seem intractable to the weak mind and may send it in search of a more comfortable realm of its own making'. Hence superstition, to which Gibbon opposes facing up to a reality which can be changed. Garrison plies a very different argument. He finds the footnotes to the *History* to constitute a metahistory, an interpretative survey of Western historiography from

Herodotus and Thucydides to Robertson and Hume. Garrison is especially concerned with characterisations of the historians in the notes. New focuses on the influence of Conyers Middleton on Gibbon. Conyers' earlier history 'had paved the way for both the religious scepticism and the cultural nostalgia which together form the cornerstone of Gibbon's view of the fall of Rome'.

Sir John Hawkins remarked that 'the avowed end of the *Adventurer*, being the same with that of the *Rambler*, and the plan and conduct thereof so little different from it, the latter may be considered as a continuation of the former'. Philip Malone Griffith[23] investigates the reception of Hawkesworth's *Adventurer*, showing that high regard for it was not confined to Hawkins: 'it had become part of the edifying literature recommended for young people, and. . .through private reading societies and circulating libraries, it had established a prominent place for itself among that group of "classical essays" often reprinted during the later part of the eighteenth century and into the nineteenth century'.

A facsimile of Beckford's *Biographical Memoirs of Extraordinary Painters* (1780) is now available from the Oleander Press with an introduction by Philip Ward[32]. The facsimile is clear, the introduction brief but sure, setting the necessary guidelines for new readers; and the whole is garnished with George Romney's, John Hoppner's and William Hoare's (?) portraits. Walpole, too, attracts an edition, of his *Miscellany 1786–1795*, edited by Lars E. Troide[33]. This is the first of the three most important notebooks to be published. The introduction describes its compilation and its contents which range over many topics from poetry to politics to the picturesque. Troide does not exaggerate when he sums up the miscellany as a 'microcosm of Walpole's life and thought'. It will be found especially useful for Walpole's remarks on poets and poetry, not least for the challenging definition of poetry as 'a beautiful way of spoiling prose, & the laborious art of exchanging plain sense for harmony'. The whole is splendidly annotated and indexed. And, finally, a paper by the doyen of Walpole scholars: W. S. Lewis[23] comments on Walpole's account of his visit to Stowe in July 1770 when Lord and Lady Temple entertained Princess Amelia there.

4. Novel

Among the works of general interest that have appeared this year, there are several research aids. Jerry C. Beasley's *English Fiction, 1660–1800: A Guide to Information Sources*[34] is Vol. 14 of the American, English, and World Literature in English Information Guide Series, and it contains lists of general resources, introductory studies, lists of specialised books and articles. It also manages to cover twenty-nine major authors of the period. *The English Novel: Twentieth-Century Criticism: Vol. I Defoe through Hardy*[35], edited by Richard J. Dunn, provides a comprehensive biblio-

[32] *Biographical Memoirs of Extraordinary Painters*, by William Beckford, intro. by Philip Ward. Cambridge, Cambs. and New York: Oleander Press. pp. [xiv] + 158.

[33] *Horace Walpole's Miscellany 1786–1795*, ed. by Lars E. Troide. Yale Studies in English, 188. New Haven, Conn. and London: Yale U.P. pp. xli + 174. £10.60.

[34] *English Fiction, 1660–1800: A Guide to Information Sources*, by Jerry C. Beasley. Detroit: Gale. pp. 313. $22.

graphy. Of a more specialised interest in this field is Madeleine Blondel's article, in *PBSA*, which deals with the disreputable habits of eighteenth-century publishers in rehashing old works. The second volume of Clifford R. Johnson's *Plots and Characters in the Fiction of Eighteenth-Century English Authors*[36], which covers Fielding, Smollett, Sterne, Johnson, and Goldsmith, is available. This needs to be treated with the same reservations as the first volume (see *YW* 58.248). General criticism on the novelists of the age can be found in the collection of essays by Jean Ducrocq, Suzy Halimi, and Maurice Lévy in *Roman et Société en Angleterre au XVIIIe siècle*[37]. As the introduction points out, this is primarily a descriptive work, planned for a wider audience than the specialist. It contains general articles on the novel, and the background of the age, and particular discussions of Defoe, Richardson, Fielding, Smollett, Sterne, and Matthew Lewis. In *Augustan Worlds*[17], Isabel Rivers pays attention to the religious tradition of spiritual autobiography, and describes the unique literary subculture created by Wesley for his itinerant preachers. Methodist literature offers an interesting contrast to the tradition of secular pilgrimage as it developed in the eighteenth-century novel: Isabel Rivers ends by indicating some of the similarities and differences between these two traditions.

Autobiography is also the subject of George May's article in *The Author in His Work*[5]. In the absence of a working definition of autobiography, May isolates certain aspects of the form which indicate its origin in the eighteenth century, examining the writings of Rousseau, Gibbon, Franklin, and Goethe. Patrician Meyer Spacks, in *ECS*, studies the theme of adolescence in the major writers of the period. Ms Spacks's concern with adolescence as a form of social criticism takes her examination of self and society a step forward. G. D. Kelly (*EA*) continues his study of the English Jacobin novel by exploring the influence of *Intellectual Physics* by Thomas Pownall (?) on the fiction of Thomas Holcroft and William Godwin.

The Paddington Press reprint of the 1853 edition of *Robinson Crusoe*[38] is more significant for its illustrations by J. J. Grandville than for its text or its introduction by Edward Lucie-Smith. Shirlene Mason's book *Daniel Defoe and the Status of Women*[39], which I have not seen, presumably is another feminist interpretation of Defoe. Less grand but probably of more use to the researcher is Frederick N. Nash's 'Additions and Refinements to Moore's *A Checklist to the Writings of Daniel Defoe*' in *PBSA*. *N&Q* also contains several interesting pieces on Defoe of a bibliographical and biographical nature. John J. Perry deals with the date of the publication of 'Atalantis Major' by examining the letters between Defoe and Robert Harley. J. Huddleston is concerned with the possible influence of the

[35] *The English Novel: Twentieth Century Criticism: Vol. 1. Defoe through Hardy*, ed. by Richard J. Dunn. Chicago: Swallow. pp. 202.

[36] *Plots and Characters in the Fiction of Eighteenth-Century English Authors, II: Henry Fielding, Tobias Smollett, Laurence Sterne, Samuel Johnson, and Oliver Goldsmith*, by Clifford R. Johnson. Plots and Character Ser. Hamden, Conn.: Shoe String (Archon); Folkestone, Kent: Dawson. pp. 243.

[37] *Roman et société en Angleterre au XVIIIe siècle*, by Jean Ducrocq, Suzy Halimi, Maurice Lévy. Paris: Presses Universitaires de France. pp. 256.

[38] *The Life and Adventures of Robinson Crusoe*, by Daniel Defoe. Illustrated by J. J. Grandville. Paddington Masterpieces of the Illustrated Book. Paddington Press. pp. 325. £3.50.

educational theories of Charles Morton on Defoe's journalistic style. Geoffrey M. Sill investigates Defoe's name. He suggests that the addition of the prefix 'De' was not a sign of aristocratic pretensions, but evidence that Defoe was the first in a family of immigrants to feel secure enough to reveal his roots. Another interesting short note on Defoe can be found in the *Dickensian*, where L. I. Michaelson maps the London journeys of Moll Flanders and Bill Sikes. His comparison both indicates the differing motivation of the characters, and illustrates the technique, quasi-cartographical and, otherwise, of the authors. Defoe's commercial writings on trade, geography, economics and international relations are the province of John McVeagh in *DUJ*. He points out that the nineteenth-century emphasis on Defoe's realism ignores the vision of beauty and excellence of creation present even in Defoe's practical thought. Christopher W. Gray appears to contradict this theme in his article 'Defoe's Literalizing Imagination' in *PQ*. Gray shows that Defoe's narrators display a verbal analogue of their isolation from society. Defoe's literalising imagination is an unwillingness to see things except in their most public aspects. Isolation from society, and problems of identity in Defoe are also the themes of Thomas M. Kavanagh's article in *TSLL*, which in attempting to unravel *Robinson Crusoe* succeeds in doing the opposite.

More psychology can be found in Gerald Levin's *Richardson the Novelist: the Psychological Patterns*[40]. Analysing the novels in the light of Freud's theories of psychic masochism, Levin diagnoses the psychosis in most of Richardson's characters. June Sigler Siegel's more comprehensible article (*Diderot Studies*) compares and differentiates the two anti-heroes, Lovelace and Rameau's nephew, thereby studying an aspect of Diderot's relationship with Richardson which has previously escaped notice. The only work specifically on *Pamela* that I have seen is Anna-Marie Kovac's essay (*RLV*) on 'Pamela's Poverty'. *Clarissa* is used by Nancy K. Miller in her article in *ECS* on 'Novels of Innocence: Fictions of Loss'. Ms Miller's terminology is obstructive to an understanding of her subject: how 'innocence and initiation in the novel are taken up by the allegory of fiction itself'. Coral Lansbury in *Thalia* writes on 'The Triumph of Clarissa: Richardson's Divine Comedy', but I have not seen it. A. D. Harvey's article in *EIC* looks anew at the problem of Puritan tradition and *Clarissa*. Harvey questions Christopher Hill's thesis that the novel is about the economics of marriage, and suggests that the emphasis on virginity and the reification of feminine sexuality marks a change of attitude from earlier Puritanism to the essentially Victorian notion of sexual passivity in women. The general trend of the novel is therefore prurient not puritan. Another discussion of Clarissa's motivation is in *PLL*, where Shirley Van Marter traces the correspondence between Hester Mulso and Richardson, and indicates the textual changes he made on her advice. These delicately alter the character of Clarissa, transferring some of the guilt from Clarissa to her father when he curses her. Another piece concerned with Richardson's correspondence is Elizabeth Bergen Brophy's identification of a word in *N&Q*. In a letter to Lady Bradshaigh, Richardson calls the reader 'carpers'

[39] *Daniel Defoe and the Status of Women*, by Shirlene Mason. Monograph in Women's Studies. Montreal: Eden. pp. 129.

[40] *Richardson the Novelist: The Psychological Patterns*, by Gerald Levin. Amsterdam: Rodophi N.V. pp. 177. Price not set.

or 'carvers'. Ms Brophy believes it to be 'carvers' on the evidence of a similar use of the word in *Sir Charles Grandison*.

There has not been very much on Fielding this year. Two papers deal with Fielding's politics: Thomas R. Cleary's 'Henry Fielding and the Great Jacobite Paper War of 1747–49' in *ECLife*, and M. C. and R. R. Battestin's 'Fielding, Bedford, and the Westminster Election of 1749' in *ECS*. The latter uses new evidence from the documents of the Bedford Estate Office to examine the relationship between Fielding and Bedford. Bedford helped to obtain for Fielding the Westminster and Middlesex magistracy, and Fielding repaid the debt as a magistrate and a writer in the Westminster election of 1749. *Tom Jones* is Ronald Paulson's subject in *Augustan Worlds*[17]. He shows how the methodology of euhemerism, reducing mythology to history, used by Abbé Banier in 'Mythology and Fables of the Ancients explained from History', is relevant to Fielding's work in both the *Jacobite Journal* and *Tom Jones*. 'The poet mythologizes historical facts, the historian tries to establish what really happened, and the mythologist analyses the myth in the light of history'; *Tom Jones* is the result of this three-part process. Also on *Tom Jones* Leland E. Warrens (*ELWIU*) writes on Allworthy and authority.

This year the Oxford University Press edition of Smollett's *Ferdinand Count Fathom*[41] has come out in paperback. There is also a useful addition to Smollett scholarship in Francesco Cordasco's *Tobias George Smollett: A Bibliographical Guide*[42]. Lance Bertelsen's article (*Novel*) on 'The Smollettian View of Life' is a work of general critical interest. It deals with Smollett's episodic technique where form reflects theme in physical chain-reactions. Bertelsen sees this style as 'a kind of comic choreography'; and he shows how Smollett has mastered it in the character of Matt Bramble in *Humphrey Clinker*. Sophia Andres in *SSL* also concentrates on Bramble, seeing him as Smollett's satiric spokesman. For Ms Andres *Humphrey Clinker* is a fusion of two genres, satire and novel, and the epistolary style helps to enhance Bramble's satiric distance from the moral disorder he sees around him. Also in *SSL* Richard Bjornsen writes on 'Victimization and Vindication in Smollett's *Roderick Random*', by which he means the way the narrator's consciousness functions as a screen through which objective reality is filtered. Satire and sentiment in *Roderick Random* are not incompatible but expressions of the same moral vision, hence what Bjornsen sees as sequences of victimisation and vindication. In *EA* Ian Campbell Ross is similarly concerned with moral disorder and the episodic style of *Roderick Random*. The style is not evidence of Smollett's inability to handle his material, but a reflection of the moral disorder in the world of the novel. Verbal repetition of this disorder give the novel a structural, if not a thematic, unity. On *Peregrine Pickle* there is Joel Weinsheimer's article in *Ariel* on 'Defects and Difficulties in Smollett's *Peregrine Pickle*'. He finds that the novel fails to be a satire, and also fails to be a comic-picaresque *Bildungsroman*. According to Weinsheimer Peregrine Pickle cannot be both a satirist and a comic hero, and he fails to be

[41] *Ferdinand Count Fathom*, by Tobias Smollett, ed. with an Introduction by Damian Grant. O.U.P. pp. 384.

[42] *Tobias George Smollett: A Bibliographical Guide*, by Francesco Cordasco. AMS Press. pp. 157. £15.95.

either. The novel is an uneasy combination of the Swiftian and the Fieldingesque. Amonst the short notes on Smollett Guillaume Sutherland (*EA*) notes and explains some of the deficiencies of John Moore's biography of Smollett. He sees the vague nature of this work as the result of Moore's intention of resisting personal reminiscences and loyalty to the memory of the dead. In *N&Q* there is a hypothetical addition to the list of Smollett portraits. J. C. Hilson suggests, from the evidence of a letter from Sibylla Dixon to the educationalist James Elphinston, that Smollett sat for Sibylla's father, the miniaturist Charles Dixon. Also in *N&Q* Earl F. Briden draws parallels between *Sir Launcelot Greaves*, and Smollett's views on specific inequities in the bankruptcy laws.

Two volumes of *The Florida Edition of the Works of Sterne*[43], edited by Melvyn and Joan New, have appeared. The volumes, bound differently for some reason, contain a facsimile reproduction of the first edition of *Tristram Shandy*, and comprehensive appendixes of textual notes, emendations, word division, historical collation, a bibliographical description by Kenneth Monkman, and the copytexts of 'memoire presenté a Messieurs les Docteurs de Sorbonne' and 'The Abuse of Conscience Sermon'. This promises to be the definitive edition of Sterne's works. Another addition to Sterne scholarship is *Laurence Sterne: An Annotated Bibliography 1965–1977*[44]. Its editor, Lodwick Hartley, provides an introductory essay and a review of the scholarship it covers. It is planned as a supplement to Hartley's earlier work, *Laurence Sterne in the Twentieth Century*, whose format it shares. New works of criticism on Sterne include William Freedman's *Laurence Sterne and the origins of the Musical Novel*[45]. Although I have not seen a copy it is presumably on the same lines as his article in *MLQ* (1971). Peter Conrad's *Shandyism: The Character of Romantic Irony*[46], is, as Conrad states in his preface 'a book less about than around *Tristram Shandy*'. This work examines the novel's relationship with the tragicomic ambiguity of Romantic thought and thereby establishes a tradition for the novel. Conrad continues by looking closely at *Tristram Shandy*'s influence on the other arts, and he discusses the aesthetic theories of Hogarth, Fuseli, and John Soane. The somewhat tangential approach to *Tristram Shandy* provides stimulating criticism. Two shorter pieces on *Tristram Shandy* occur in *N&Q*. Anthony Coleman uses Edmund Ferrer's annotated copy of *Tristram Shandy* to elucidate Sterne's use of the Motteux-Ozell 'Rabelais'; and Mark Sinfield proves Uncle Toby's potency by a close examination of the text. Sinfield demonstrates how an error in Work's edition and Sterne's deliberate authorial confusion have led to critical misunderstanding of Uncle Toby. Also on *Tristram Shandy* is Robert G. Walker's article, ' A Sign of the Satirist's Wit: The Nose in *Tristram Shandy*' in *BSUF*. In *Augustan Worlds*[17] Martin C. Battestin sees *A Senti-*

[43] *The Florida Edition of the Works of Laurence Sterne*, ed. by Melvyn New and Joan New. University Presses of Florida. Vol. I pp. 487. Vol. II pp. 997. $37.50.

[44] *Laurence Sterne: An Annotated Bibliography, 1965–1977 with an introductory essay-review of the scholarship*, ed. by Lodwick Hartley. Boston, Mass.: G.K. Hall. pp. 103. $12.

[45] *Laurence Sterne and the Origins of the Musical Novel*, by William Freedman. Athens, Ga.: U. of Georgia P. pp. 213. Price not set.

[46] *Shandyism: The Character of Romantic Irony*, by Peter Conrad. Oxford: Blackwell. pp. 190. £9.50.

mental Journey as more hopeful than *Tristram Shandy* about the possibility of communication. Battestin sees this communication as the syntax of things, which means both the logical process of grammatical prediction and the universal grammar of Nature herself. *A Sentimental Journey* seeks connections and relationships. James W. Garvey writes on 'Translations, Equivocation, and Reconciliation in Sterne's *Sentimental Journey*' in *SHR*. In *ESC* James Downey writes on 'The Sermons of Mr Yorick: A Reassessment of Hammond'. Finally, there is a brief section on Sterne in Stanley Meltzoff's article on Hogarth in *NLH*.

There is an interesting article in *MLN* on Mackenzie and others by Sander L. Gilman, 'Seeing the Insane: Mackenzie, Kleist, William James'. Gilman uses Mackenzie to illustrate changes in the reaction to madness, showing how the novelist is indebted to Hogarth in his description of Harley's visit to Bedlam in *A Man of Feeling*. Volume VII of the Oxford edition of *The Journals and Letters of Fanny Burney*[47] has appeared. This volume, edited by Edward A. and Lillian D. Bloom, covers the period 1812 to 1814. William Godwin has attracted some attention this year. In the *TLS* George Woodcock deals with Godwin and Spanish anarchists. Jacqueline T. Miller in *Criticism* writes on 'The Imperfect Tale: Articulation, Rhetoric, and Self in *Caleb Williams*', and G. A. Starr in *N&Q* finds a source for the name of Falkland's antagonist in *Caleb Williams*. In the third volume of Henry Brooke's *The Fool of Quality*, there is a Barnabas Tirrell who has a similar character and is involved in similar deeds to Godwin's Barnabas Tyrrell. There are two articles on Godwin's disciple, Elizabeth Inchbald. In *PBSA* Janice Marie Cauwels deals with the influence of Godwin and Holcroft on Inchbald's novel *Nature and Art*. Ms Cauwels demonstrates how the revisions made at the request of Godwin and others put difficulties in the way of establishing a copytext. Patricia M. Taylor's concern (*N&Q*) with amendments to *Nature and Art* is rather different. In the alterations to the 1810 edition she finds evidence that Inchbald is a more disciplined writer than is often thought.

5. Drama

There is less than usual to report on the drama and theatre in 1978, in part because at the time of writing *RECTR* has only just struggled into its 1977 volume. There was no book of a general critical nature and in the periodicals there was only L. W. Conolly's (*ESC*) exploration of the English drama and the slave trade and Robert D. Hume's *PQ* review article of studies of drama between 1660 and 1800. We move therefore to items on particular writers.

Though most readers derive their sense of Cibber as 'the careless coxcomb' from Pope, it was Cibber himself who created the image. Lois Potter[17] points out that he not only wrote and acted the parts of fops but in his non-dramatic writings adopted the persona of a fop. Miss Potter concludes that Cibber exploited the fop as hero with his taste for 'dashing rascality' without seeming to condone it. In a related vein John E. Sitter

[47] *The Journals and Letters of Fanny Burney*, ed. by Edward A. Bloom and Lillian D. Bloom. Vol. VII 1812–1814. Letters 632–684. Oxford: Clarendon Press. pp. 634.

(*N&Q*) notes that when in his *Apology* Cibber reflects on a schoolboy ode 'not much above the merry style of *Sing! Sing! the Day, and Sing the Song*, in the Farce', he is quoting Fielding's parody of a Cibberian New Year ode in *The Historical Register for the Year 1736*. On Fielding himself T. W. Craik[17] finds evidence for the Age of Reason as an Age of Nonsense in the 1731 version of *Tom Thumb, Tragedy of Tragedies; or the Life and Death of Tom Thumb the Great*. This expanded and revised version shows a marked increase in the quantity of stylistic parody, parody written with enthusiastic gusto rather than with satiric animus. Also concerned with parody, Peter Lewis (*N&Q*) draws attention to an occasion on which Henry Carey's *Chrononhotonthologus* departs from its general burlesque to parody a specific source in John Banks's *The Unhappy Favourite: or The Earl of Essex* (1682).

On Goldsmith Oliver W. Ferguson[23] questions the unchallenged assumption that *The Good-Natur'd Man* is an anti-sentimental drama. Where other critics have found parody of the sentimental Ferguson finds the sentimental, especially in the play's ending. The stir caused by the low humour of the bailiff scene and the success of Hugh Kelly's *False Delicacy*, produced in rivalry with *The Good-Natur'd Man*, prompted in Ferguson's view Goldsmith's 'cheerful revenge' in the anti-sentimental *She Stoops to Conquer*.

Sheridan is the only dramatist to be blessed with a book-length study. His achievement can still tend to be evaluated relative to that of Restoration comedy. In *Sheridan's Comedies, Their Contexts and Achievements* Mark S. Auburn[48] tries to supply a fresh context of Georgian drama, critical debate and professional theatrical practice. Co-author of *Drama through Performance*, it is not surprising that Auburn should put especial emphasis on staging. He dons historical spectacles to see Sheridan's works 'primarily as products of a practical playwright working within the theatrical tradition of the late eighteenth century'. Although there is evidence that Sheridan's contemporaries saw his work as marking a return to the witty drama of Congreve, Auburn suggests that seen within the tradition of Georgian drama *School for Scandal*, for example, becomes not 'a brilliantly witty play exposing hypocrisy and foolishness in the cynical and often punitive manner of high Restoration comedy' but 'a comedy representative of its time. . .employing attitudes typical of the doctrine of sentimentalism. . .appealing more to the emotions than to the intellect'. It is useful to have Auburn's account of Sheridan's context, but his assumptions about Sheridan's relation to that context are suspect. They serve him well enough for *The Critic* where what is needed is elucidation of topical hits and some account of Sheridan's ability to pull together burlesque and parody into a coherent structure; but they are less viable for *School for Scandal*. John Loftis's *Sheridan and the Drama of Georgian England* offers a much more acute and fluid sense of Sheridan in his time.

Despite their contemporary popularity Cumberland and Lillo get little critical attention from modern critics. This year they receive attention from Elizabeth M. Yearling (*N&Q*) and Stephen L. Trainor (*SEL*). In the absence of a tradition of Creole mockery in drama before Cumberland,

[48] *Sheridan's Comedies, Their Contexts and Achievements*, by Mark S. Auburn. Lincoln, Neb. and London: U. of Nebraska P. pp. x + 221. £7.70.

Miss Yearling finds a likely source for Cumberland's complaint that Creoles 'had been *usually* exhibited on the stage, as the butts for ridicule and abuse' in Foote's *The Patron* and its Sir Peter Pepperpot. Trainor argues that in *The London Merchant* Lillo developed a new tragic form by adapting his structure to Puritan homilectic theory and by basing his dramatic world view on the doctrines of Calvin.

Garrick attracts attention as both a playwright and a subject for portrait painters. Those who have approached Colman and Garrick's *The Clandestine Marriage* have been concerned with apportioning responsibility for various parts of the play. M. A. Goldsmith and J. D. Hainsworth (*RES*) take up the problem of its relation to James Townley's *False Concord*. Lance Bertelsen (*ECS*) on the other hand writes on Garrick's influence on English painting as patron and as man of the theatre. According to Bertelsen 'his arresting presence (and direct patronage) stimulated the production of an unprecedented number of theatrical conversation pieces and helped establish that genre; and 'his innovative staging and direction. . .not only altered the way in which certain literary scenes were visualised, but provided models for later works painted entirely outside the theatrical field'.

Finally we turn to the remaining managers, actors and others associated with the theatre. In *TN* Julia Curtis gives an account of Tate Wilkinson's costume notebook, whilst Robert B. Resnick (*StHum*) discusses James Quin as actor and man. For stage personnel from Eagan to Garrett and Garrick to Gyngell there are the two latest volumes (5 and 6) in the *Biographical Dictionary of Actors, Actresses, Musicians, Dancers, Managers, and Other Stage Personnel in London, 1660–1800*[49].

[49] *A Biographical Dictionary of Actors, Actresses, Musicians, Dancers, Managers, and Other Stage Personnel in London, 1660–1800*, by Philip H. Highfill Jr, Kalman A. Burnim, and Edward A. Langhans. Volume 5: Eagan to Garrett; Volume 6: Garrick to Gyngell. Carbondale and Edwardsville, Ill.: Southern Illinois U.P. pp. 480 per vol. $25 each.

XIV

The Nineteenth Century: Romantic Period

BRYAN BURNS, PHILIP DODD and J. R. WATSON

The chapter has three sections: 1. Verse and Drama, by J. R. Watson; 2. Prose Fiction, by Bryan Burns; 3. Prose, by Philip Dodd.

1. Verse and Drama

The most useful bibliographical aids to the study of the romantic period are the *MLA* bibliography and the annotated 'Selective and Critical Bibliography' in *ELN*. The summer number of *TWC* reviews books, mainly on the first-generation romantics, and provides 'Annual Registers' of Wordsworth and Coleridge scholarship by Eric R. Birdsall and Jane Matsinger respectively. Thomas L. Minnick and Detlef W. Doerrbecker present 'A Checklist of Recent Blake Scholarship' in *Blake*. J. P. Wearing edits a bibliography of drama criticism and scholarship in *NCTR*. *KSJ* has a bibliography (for 1976) on the second-generation romantics and their circles, principally compiled by Robert M. Ryan and Andrew P. Glassman. A useful guide to information sources, *Irish Literature, 1800–1875*[1], seeks, in its own words, 'to reflect the development and variety of Irish Literature in English in these years. . .and to give a sense of their literary world'. This it does by listing works by and about the more prominent and representative authors: it also lists periodicals, anthologies and other useful items. I find the type-face ugly and difficult to read, but the information is fully annotated and indexed.

Images of Romanticism[2] is a collection of distinguished essays on verbal and visual affinities within the romantic movement, edited by Karl Kroeber and William Walling. The volume begins, however, with an essay by Rudolph Arnheim, 'Space as Image of Time', which transcends the period in considering the presentation of history and time, and ends with a moving tribute to the permanence of art. After this, the volume takes shape around a number of pictorial and poetic features of the romantic movement, with particular reference to the dominating figure of Turner. Lorenz Eitner's 'Cages, Prisons, and Captives in Eighteenth-Century Art' deals with the theme of liberty which reaches a climax in the fall of the Bastille: Eitner relates this to Piranesi, to birds in cages, and to Sterne's *Sentimental Journey*. Jean Starobinski takes up Arnheim's theme in

[1] *Irish Literature, 1800–1875*, by Brian McKenna. Detroit, Mich.: Gale. pp. xviii + 388. n.p.

[2] *Images of Romanticism*, ed. by Karl Kroeber and William Walling. New Haven, Conn., and London: Yale U.P. pp. xvi + 288. £13.65.

'André Chenier and the Allegory of Poetry', which deals with the aesthetic clarity which represents and contains violence. Jean H. Hagstrum's 'Blake and British Art: The Gifts of Grace and Terror' sets Blake in the context of contemporary British painting, with particular reference to the work of George Romney. L. J. Swingle writes of 'Wordsworth's "Picture of the Mind" ', dealing with the pictorial imagination of Wordsworth and its function in his poetry. Carl Woodring traces Coleridge's knowledge of pictures and his theories about them in 'What Coleridge Thought of Pictures', an essay which emphasises the importance of his acquaintance with Sir George Beaumont and Washington Allston. The book then takes a slightly different direction with William Walling's 'More Than Sufficient Room: Sir David Wilkie and the Scottish Literary Tradition', which compares Wilkie with Fergusson, Burns, Scott and Galt, and argues for a critical approach that is less exclusively concerned with formal considerations in literature and art. James A. W. Heffernan writes on 'The English Romantic Perception of Color', with particular reference to Wordsworth, Coleridge, and Turner; he concludes that the Romantic use of colour is distinct from the Augustan, in that colours need no longer be absolutely distinct, and they need not be uniformly warm. Karl Kroeber's 'Romantic Historicism: The Temporal Sublime' deals with the treatment of history by Turner and Carlyle, among others, who are seen by Kroeber as aesthetically interpreting the confusing experience of detailed historical experience. Turner is also the centre of Ronald Paulson's 'Turner's Graffiti: The Sun and Its Glosses', which deals with the painter as both creator and revolutionary, presenting the sun as sublime, yet also with a collection of verbal associations which radically alter the simple interpretation. R. F. Storch writes of the veil in Shelley and of indistinctness in Turner in 'Abstract Idealism in English Romantic Poetry and Painting', an essay whose title does not do justice to the psychological and artistic subtlety of its content. By contrast, Martin Meisel's 'The Material Sublime: John Martin, Byron, Turner and the Theater' is concerned with a palpable or outer sublime, the use of catastrophic and infernal themes in the nineteenth-century theatre. In spite of its variety and its absence of structure, *Images of Romanticism* is a coherent and useful book, if only because it eschews the abstractions of theoretical discussion and remains, for the most part, firmly attached to the practice of painting and poetry in the period.

William Vaughan's *Romantic Art*[3] is like a tight, well-run ship: there is a substantial cargo on board, properly stowed, and everything is in its place and in good order. Vaughan is particularly good at relating one part of the romantic movement to another, connecting Greek Revival with Gothic Revival, heroism with the prophetic, landscape, atmosphere and sensation. Vaughan has a strenuous and individual view of romanticism which is inclined to underplay the dreamy side: even such painters as Fuseli and Friedrich are seen as concerned with expressing feelings rather than dream-images, while the inheritors of romanticism, the Pre-Raphaelites, are seen as romancers rather than true romantics. Such a position gives the book a flavour, and prevents it from becoming just another survey of romantic painting and sculpture. Vaughan is also very good at analysing

[3] *Romantic Art*, by William Vaughan. Thames & Hudson. pp. 288. £5.50.

the formal characteristics of a work of art; in fact, the whole book is shaped by the disciplines of the art historian in a very effective way.

The double (1977–78) number of the proceedings of the *Centre du Romantisme Anglais* from Clermont-Ferrand is entitled *Nature et Surnature*[4]. It begins with an eloquent piece 'Immanence et Transcendance dans "Tintern Abbey": Tradition et Innovation' by Jean Raimond, which deals with the presence in the poem of the 'here and now' and the interaction of this with the transcendent; Raimond places this in its eighteenth-century tradition, and concludes that the originality of the poem lies less in the quality of the emotion than in the language used to express that emotion. M. J. Vosluisant chooses an unusual topic in 'Nature et Surnature dans les Poèmes Dramatiques de Coleridge, *Remorse* et *Zapolya*'; she suggests that the plays ridicule conventional or gothic manifestations of the supernatural, and puts forward the idea of a union between natural and supernatural as the true imaginative act. Jacques Blondel writes of the 'Ode to a Nightingale' in terms of the self and the other, the centre and the circumference, the transitory and the transcendent, in 'L'Ode au Rossignol: Nature et Surnature'. In 'Keats et Proust', Bernard Brugière makes a series of subtle comparisons, beginning with psychology and continuing (naturally) with the treatment of time and beauty, ending with a suggestion that both writers saw the immanence of beauty in the world, and the encounter with death as implicit within this. Immanence is also the centre of Jacques Blondel's 'Romantisme Anglais, Religion et Transcendance', which surveys the religion of natural beauty in romantic poetry, the substitution of beauty and joy for the traditional Christian God, the inner excitement replacing the outer formulation. In 'Blake, Peintre du Sublime et Critique de la Transcendance' François Piquet contrasts Blake's conception of the exact and energetic sublime with Burke's obscurity, and Blake's transformation of eighteenth-century concepts of the sublime such as loudness and the prophetic. Jean Perrin writes on 'La Symbolique de la Transcendance dans la Poésie de Shelley', dealing with symbols of light, ascension, the wing (of a bird and of the soul), of dew, and of a combination of these. Marcel Isnard, in 'Wordsworth Pédagogue', points out that 'guide' is a key word in Wordsworth, and examines his educational theory in relation to those of Rousseau and others. Finally, Brigitte Bordessoules-Preumont examines 'Le Mal et la Rédemption dans la Pensée de Coleridge', with particular reference to his conception of an 'anti-Faust', and the relation of this to man's guilt and to the problem of evil.

August Wilhelm Hoffmeister's *Die Blume in Der Dichtung der Englischen Romantik*[5] is a thorough, if heavy-handed, survey of the use of flowers by the major English romantic poets from Blake to Shelley (no flowers in Byron). Edward Proffitt's 'Romanticism, Bicamerality, and the Evolution of the Brain' (*TWC*) is a peculiar attempt to apply the ideas of Julian Jaynes on the origin of consciousness to the romantic period, which Proffitt now sees as marking the final transition from a right brain

[4] *Nature et Surnature*. Clermont-Ferrand: Centre du Romantisme Anglais, Université de Clermont II. pp. vi + 164. n.p.

[5] *Die Blume in Der Dichtung der Englischen Romantik*, by August Wilhelm Hoffmeister. SSELRR No. 76. Salzburg: Institut für Englische Sprache und Literatur.

hemisphere to a left brain-hemisphere, from which man no longer hears inspirational voices. In a more orthodox way, Marshall Brown's 'The Pre-Romantic Discovery of Consciousness' (*SIR*) attempts to understand the coming of romanticism through Cowper, who is seen as extending the boundaries of 'The Urbane Style' (the title of another article by Marshall Brown, on eighteenth-century style, in *ELH*), and whose poetic process is seen as embodying ideas by Rousseau and Kant. The transition from the eighteenth century is also the subject of 'The Romantic Emergence', subtitled 'Multiplication of Alternatives and the Problem of Systematic Entrapment' (*MLR*), in which L. J. Swingle casts doubt upon some recent theories of romanticism as a 'subtler language' replacing insensitive eighteenth-century epistemologies. Swingle prefers a romanticism which is indeterminate between opposed systems, and directs our attention to the play of language in which the counter-claims are debated.

R. K. Raval's 'The Picturesque: Knight, Turner and Hipple' (*BJA*) discusses the function of light in romantic art and its function in making Turner a 'poetical painter', in addition to examining the theories of Richard Payne Knight (which Raval sees as fruitful). In 'Other People's Faces: The English Romantics and the Paradox of Fraternity' (*SIR*), Paul Hamill deals with the underside of the ideal of fraternity: the presence in poetry of lost souls and ghastly shapes.

Janice L. Haney looks back to the ideas of the romantic, and especially the Germans, in ' "Shadow-Hunting": Romantic Irony, *Sartor Resartus*, and Victorian Romanticism' (*SIR*). This sees the work as concerned with romantic attitudes and their application to the Victorian historical situation. Another general article, by John E. Reed, begins 'The earliest major Victorian writers were William Wordsworth and Samuel Taylor Coleridge'. In his 'Inherited Characteristics: Romantic to Victorian Will' (*SIR*), Reed draws some interesting parallels and distinctions around the problems of self-consciousness and free will.

Morton D. Paley's *William Blake*[6] is a beautifully produced introduction to the illuminated work of the poet. It is tied very loosely to Blake's biography, and to the literary productions; but Paley's chief concern is with the illustrated books, and his rapid survey will put many students of Blake on the right road, even if they have to supply the other details for themselves. Paley goes straight to the point, directing the reader's attention to the key figures of Blake's imaginative world, and to his most necessary symbols: the book is well illustrated, with both colour and monochrome plates.

W. J. T. Mitchell's *Blake's Composite Art*[7] begins with a brave, and I think successful, attempt to identify the precise status of poem and illustration in Blake, and the relationship of one to the other in his work. Mitchell argues that Blake was writing against the tradition of *ut pictura poesis*, and that he regarded poem and illustration as complementary but having their own life. In this, and in other respects, Mitchell treats the interaction of poem and illustration in Blake 'from the inside', that is from the standpoint of Blake's ideas on space and time: these are seen as

[6] *William Blake*, by Morton D. Paley. Phaidon. pp. 192. £11.95.

[7] *Blake's Composite Art*, by W. J. T. Mitchell. Princeton, N.J.: Princeton U.P. pp. xx + 232. £10.40.

contraries which are reconciled only by the imagination, but in ways which respect their difference. Thus Mitchell relates Blake's artistic practice to his aesthetic theories, with particular interpretations of *The Book of Thel, Urizen*, and *Jerusalem*. Mitchell is particularly interesting on the recurrent forms of Blake's pictorial style, the circle, the spiral or vortex, the s-curve, and the inverted u: his perception and application of this is an example of the book's great virtue, an understanding of Blake in theory and in practice. Mitchell seems to me convincing in his understanding of the principles of Blake's art, and in his reading of individual examples; moreover, the individuality of Blake's methods ensures that Mitchell's approach is often more illuminating than that of art historians.

Blake's 'Four Zoas', The Design of a Dream[8], by Brian Wilkie and Mary Lynn Johnson, is an explicatory reading of Blake's manuscript poem, written with a commendable clarity and a straightforward orthodoxy: this is not, the authors maintain, either a new reading of the poem or an eccentric one. They take the reader gently but firmly by the hand, encouraging him to use his instinctive interpretations, and taking him through the poem's complex surface to the central themes beneath. An appendix deals with the relationship of VIIa to VIIb; marginal drawings are reproduced as illustrations. The result is a scholarly work that is informative and humane: it is reassuring to find critics who base one of their modes of interpretation on 'the adducing of analogies from personal and familiar experience'. Nelson Hilton's 'The Sweet Science of Atmospheres in *The Four Zoas*' (*Blake*), examines a passage from the poem on increasing atmospheres and nets, an adaptation from Swedenborg. Several other articles on *The Four Zoas* appear in the same issue of *Blake*: Terence Allan Hoagwood's '*The Four Zoas* and "The Philosophic Cabbala" ' focuses on the influence of the Neoplatonist Henry More, and Andrew Lincoln's '*The Four Zoas*: The Text of Pages 5, 6, and 7, Night the First' discusses the revisions and their significance. David Erdman, accepting Lincoln's reconstruction, examines the implications for other variants on the same pages. Mary Lynn Johnson and Brian Wilkie consider 'The Spectrous Embrace in *The Four Zoas*, VIIa' (*Blake*), identifying two planes of action; and John Kilgore examines the puzzle of two 'seventh nights' in the poem (*Blake*), arguing for a plan of revision which Blake never carried out. Andrew Lincoln agrees, relating this to problems of the eighth and ninth nights. Mark S. Lefebvre and David V. Erdman make further contributions. Cettina Magno presents a translation, 'The Four Zoas for Italy' (*Blake*). Isak Bouwer and Paul McNally write on ' "The Mental Traveller": Man's Eternal Journey' (*Blake*), showing the poem as concerned with successive states of fall and return, sleeping and waking, and relating the pattern to *The Four Zoas*.

Interpreting Blake[9] is a collection of essays based on an Edinburgh symposium of 1974. It provides a series of close analyses of specific texts, representing a variety of Blake's modes or techniques, and relating these to the wider implications of Blake's poetry. It begins with a *tour-de-*

[8] *Blake's 'Four Zoas', The Design of a Dream*, by Brian Wilkie and Mary Lynn Johnson. Cambridge, Mass. and London: Harvard U.P. pp. xviii + 302. £10.50.

[9] *Interpreting Blake*, ed. by Michael Phillips. Cambridge: C.U.P. pp. x + 270. £14.50.

force by E. P. Thompson, entitled simply 'London', which enriches our understanding of the poem in several ways. Not only does it consider the relation of the finished poem to an earlier draft, but it also interprets the multiple meanings with convincing thoroughness as both literal and apocalyptic, placing the literal meanings in their contemporary context and suggesting biblical and Swedenborgian allusions in the apocalyptic references. In 'Blake's Criticism of Moral Thinking in *Songs of Innocence and of Experience*', Heather Glen demonstrates Blake's antinomianism, and his deep sense of conventional moral precepts, such as duty and pity, as upholding a corrupt society. Frank M. Parisi examines the plates of *The Gates of Paradise*, concluding that the vision of life presented is two-fold, that of melancholy, and that of renewal through vision. Harold A. Kittel, in '*The Book of Urizen* and *An Essay Concerning Human Understanding*' examines the way in which Blake's opposition to Locke's theory of knowledge, with its emphasis upon sensation and reflection, affects the structure and unity of the poem. Peter Butter asks some very direct and trenchant questions about Blake's Prophetic Books in '*Milton*: The Final Plates', in which he points to ambiguities and apparent contradictory impressions in descriptions of Satan and of Ololon. James Ferguson writes on the 'Prefaces to *Jerusalem*', indicating the poem's status as a national epic, and emphasising the poet's control over details of expression and organisation. In the last essay of the collection, John Beer studies 'Influence and Independence in Blake' in a graceful and stimulating discussion, especially of the illustrations of Ugolino and his sons, and of individual works or passages, in which Beer traces some surprising influences but concludes that Blake creates his own highly individual artefact.

Michele Leiss Stepto distinguishes between 'Mothers and Fathers in Blake's *Songs of Innocence*' (*YR*), noting the closeness of the mother–child relationship and the way fathers are often involved in the abandoning of their children; but she concludes that Blake had little use for either, since they prolong the state of infantile helplessness. James Harrison points out the importance of the ingenuous metre in 'The Chimney Sweeper' from *Songs of Innocence* (*Expl*).

In 'Why Ezekiel ate Dung' (*ELN*), Randel Helms suggests that such an act contravenes the Mosaic Law, and so would be attractive to Blake in the *Marriage of Heaven and Hell*. In 'Holbach and Blake's Philosophical Statement in "The Voice of the Devil" ' (*ELN*), Terence Allan Hoagwood suggests that the *Marriage of Heaven and Hell* owes some of its ideas to Holbach's *System of Nature*.

There are several general articles on Blake. In 'Blake's Idea of Brotherhood' (*PMLA*) Michael Ferber points out that Blake his conception on men's natural friendship, goodness and mercy, and not on any traditional Christian sense of the fatherhood of God. Blake's humour, and his attitude to satire, are charmingly discussed by Irene Tayler in 'Blake meets Byron on April Fool's' (*ELN*). She argues that while Blake loved laughter, he sought always the constructive side of satire. Hand-printing from the original wood blocks is interestingly described by Iain Bain and David Chambers in 'Printing Blake's Engravings for Thornton's *Virgil*' (*The Private Library*). 'Blake's Epic Meter' (*SIR*) by William Kumbier begins with some heavy stuff out of Roman Jakobson which could have been more economically found in T. S. Eliot; between this overweight preamble and a complex conclusion is an interesting exercise in scansion using musical notation, often across two or more lines.

Kurt Heinzelman's 'William Blake and the Economics of the Imagination' (*MLQ*) reflects interestingly on the relationship between money, labour, and imagination in Blake's vision, and on the commercial metaphors which exist in his concept of the relationship between poet and audience. Elsewhere Heinzelman wrestles with a gnomic utterance in Blake's notebook of 1810 in 'Blake's Golden Word' (*ELN*, 1977).

Robert F. Gleckner suggests an origin of Blake's interest in fourfoldedness in the biblical allegory in 'Blake and the Four Daughters of God' (*ELN*, 1977). Edward J. Rose's 'The Gate of Los: Vision and Symbol in Blake' (*TSLL*) notes the gate of Los as present everywhere as symbol of the transforming vision that sees (for instance) a world in a grain of sand. Nancy M. Goslee's 'From Marble to Living Form: Sculpture as Art and Analogue from the Renaissance to Blake' (*JEGP*) is a wide-ranging account of sculpture as an art-form; the discussion is used to illuminate the passage from Blake's *Milton*, in which the poet struggles to put 'new flesh' on Urizen. Goslee identifies the particular significance of sculpture in this context, where it appears as living form, uniting tactile, visual and verbal. Among the Blake items in *N&Q* are Robert N. Essick's 'William Blake and Sir Thomas Lawrence', which shows Lawrence being very generous, and A. W. J. Lincoln's 'Blake's "Europe": an Early Version', which refers to the copy in the British Museum.

'A Supplement to *Blake Books*', by G. E. Bentley Jr, appears in *Blake*. Other supplements are found in 'Some Minor Additions to Bentley's "Blake among the Slavs" ' (*Blake*), by Detlef W. Doerrbecker and Marta Slowikova (see *YW* 58.258); and in 'A Bibliography of William Blake in Japan, 1969–1977', by Kazumitsu Watarai (*Blake*). Also in *Blake*, R. W. Peattie writes on 'William Michael Rossetti's Aldine Edition of Blake', emphasising the problem created by the Prophetic Books in 1874. Robert N. Essick's 'The Figure in the Carpet: Blake's Engravings in Salzmann's Elements of Morality' (*Blake*) uses the recurrence of a carpet pattern to argue for Blake's hand. Another attribution problem is dealt with by Christopher Heppner in 'Blake and *The Seaman's Recorder*: The Letter and the Spirit in a Problem of Attribution' (*Blake*), which reveals an E. Blake who was doing journeyman work at the time. Mary Clarke describes (with illustrations) 'The Job Ballet of 1931' (*Blake*), and Robert N. Essick describes the state of the Blake book and print market (*Blake*).

'Minute Particulars' in *Blake* include Martin Butlin's 'An Illustration to Robert Bage', concerned with Bage's *Hermsprong*; Nelson Hilton's 'A Note on Cowper and "A Poison Tree" ', which notes an odd parallel from Cowper's 'On the Death of Mrs Throckmorton's Bullfinch'; Dwight E. Weber's 'William Blake's *Visions of the Daughters of Albion*: A Poem Based on Doubt', which suggests that Daughters, Oothoon, Urizen, Bromion and Theotormon are a first-letter formation of Doubt, with Urizen at the centre; G. E. Bentley Jr's ' "New" Blake Engravings after Blake's Designs, 1837, 1859, 1861'; David Bindman's 'A New Blake Drawing in the Boston Museum of Fine Art'; G. E. Bentley Jr's 'Echoes of Blake's *Grave* Designs in 1838' found in the Book of Common Prayer; and E. B. Bentley's curious item, 'Vision in Fiction: Two Novels about William Blake', one of which is clearly not about *the* William Blake.

Christopher Heppner takes up a suggestion made by Rodney M. and Mary R. Baine about William Nicholson, the probable original for Inflammable Gass (see *YW* 57.241). In 'Another "New" Blake Engraving: More about William Nicholson' (*Blake*), Heppner shows that Blake did engrave a plate in Nicholson's *Introduction to Natural Philosophy*, published in 1782. J. Karl Franson writes on 'The Serpent-Driving Females in Blake's *Comus* 4' (*Blake*), seeing them as Cotytto and Hecate in A and B respectively. Arnold Cheskin concludes that Blake knew some Hebrew but not much in 'The Echoing Greenhorn: Blake as Hebraist' (*Blake*).

The revision of *The Letters of William and Dorothy Wordsworth* continues with Alan G. Hill's *The Later Years, Part I*[10]. This contains letters from 1821 to 1828, including one or two (very lively) ones from Mary Wordsworth. Among the many newly-published letters are a whole series of sycophantic letters to Lord Lonsdale keeping him informed of the 1826 election; other regular correspondents include the Beaumonts (until Sir George's death in 1827), Henry Crabb Robinson and Samuel Rogers. In his introduction Hill shows himself a champion of the later Wordsworth, whose work of this period 'it is still the fashion to neglect'; his essay is graceful and kind, but it seems in many ways blind to Wordsworth's stodginess at this time. Hill's best tribute, however, is in the devoted editorial labour, which has brought to light more than six hundred unpublished letters: it is a measure of the size of the revision that *The Later Years* will occupy four volumes instead of three.

John Beer's *Wordsworth and the Human Heart*[11] is a warm and enthusiastic book which traces an apparently simple theme, that of Wordsworth's humanitarian feeling; and as so often with Wordsworth, what appears simple has deep and complex roots. Wordsworth's study of the human heart leads him in many different directions: the study of his own heart, for instance, leads him towards an understanding of others, but also towards a sense of solitude. His awareness of the importance of passion is tempered too, by the sense of a need to ground the passion in a common human morality. In other words, Beer is approaching some central problems in Wordsworth, concerning the relationship between man and men, and man and nature. The possibility of natural goodness in man is seen as vital, unlocking the isolation in which each may live; to this end Wordsworth explores the education of the heart, through the passions of beauty and the ministrations of fear. Beer is particularly good at incorporating his ideas into a chronological survey of Wordsworth's life and art: he sees the decline into conventionality which accompanies the loss of Coleridge, because Wordsworth comes to rely more on ordinary human and family love, and less upon passion and vision. By a feat of ingenuity, Beer even includes the later Wordsworth, and Wordsworth the landscape gardener, in his survey; while his fruitful comparisons with Blake and D. H. Lawrence make clear the absence of the daemonic in Wordsworth.

[10] *The Letters of William and Dorothy Wordsworth, III: The Later Years, Part I, 1821–1828*, ed. by Alan G. Hill, from the first edition by E. de Selincourt. Oxford: Clarendon P. pp. xxxii + 730. £20.

[11] *Wordsworth and the Human Heart*, by John Beer. Macmillan. pp. xx + 277. £10.

It is not easy to see the purpose of the Romantic Reassessment volume *Wordsworth Criticism since 1952: a Bibliography*[12], edited by Ronald B. Hearn and others. It is both incomplete and unannotated, and has too many errors and omissions; the job has recently been far better done by David H. Stam in his *Wordsworthian Criticism* (see *YW* 55.361). A more valuable 'Romantic Reassessment' volume is Karl R. Johnson Jr's *The Written Spirit*[13]; this is subtitled 'Thematic and Rhetorical Structure in Wordsworth's *The Prelude*'. It is a study of rhetorical and structural patterns in *The Prelude*, based on the thesis that the poem's structure is a sequence of five cyclic movements of loss and gain. This is an interesting hypothesis, but it leads Johnson into some difficult situations, such as having to explain away the later composition of the preamble after arguing that the whole poem springs from it. He has some useful things to say about recurring language, and about the residence of 'power' in Wordsworth's poetry: the treatment of the boat-stealing and ice-skating passages in Book I is illuminating and helpful. Sometimes the connections seem a little forced, as when Johnson compares the boat-racing of Book II 'inevitably' with the boat-stealing of Book I; but his cyclic pattern is certainly present in III and IV, and Johnson makes the most of it, in what is the best section of his book. The final contrast, between V and VI, is less convincing, but the whole exercise is a fresh and original approach to *The Prelude*.

Three essays (conference papers) on 'Wordsworth: The Psychoanalytic View' are printed in *TWC*. Richard E. Matlak's 'The Man in Wordsworth's Life' emphasises the death of Wordsworth's father and the longing for the love and presence of an adult male; Peter J. Manning's ' "My former thoughts returned": Wordsworth's *Resolution and Independence*' sees the leech-gatherer as embodying Wordsworth's anxieties, and reliance on others; and Michael H. Friedman's 'The Princely and the Contracted Wordsworth: A Study of Wordsworth's Personality in Terms of Psychoanalytic Ego Psychology', which posits two 'selves' in Wordsworth, one confident and the other anxious, neither of which allowed Wordsworth to enter into a stable relationship with the external world. Related to these is another essay by Richard E. Matlak, who studies 'Wordsworth's Lucy Poems in Psychobiographical Context' (*PMLA*), concluding that Wordsworth felt ambivalent towards Dorothy at the time of their composition; Wordsworth both loved her and wished to be rid of her, and the Lucy poems are an expression of this. The difficulty of this is similar to that concerning Hamlet and his father: if Hamlet says he loved his father, we are supposed not to believe him. In 'Principle and Whimsey: Thomas Holcroft and *Descriptive Sketches*' (*TWC*) Steven E. Sharp suggests that an early hostile review in the *Monthly* was written in haste by a reviewer who had not read the poems properly. In 'The Speaker as Questioner in *Lyrical Ballads*' (*JEGP*), Susan J. Wolfson shows not only how questions are answered in the ballad poems, but how some questions remain unanswered or unanswerable, and how some poems accept uncertainties, mysteries and

[12] *Wordsworth Criticism since 1952: A Bibliography*, by Ronald B. Hearn and others. SSELRR No. 83. Salzburg: Institut für Englische Sprache und Literatur. pp. viii + 93.

[13] *The Written Spirit*, by Karl R. Johnson Jr. SSELRR No. 72. Salzburg: Institut für Englische Sprache und Literatur. pp. viii + 302. n.p.

doubts. She is particularly interesting on the half-formed and hardly articulated questions which lie behind the assurance of 'Tintern Abbey'. *Lyrical Ballads* is also discussed in *JEGP* by James H. Averill, in 'Wordsworth and "Natural Science": The Poetry of 1798', in which Averill points to the stimulus of Coleridge's scientific interests, and the influence of Erasmus Darwin's *Zoonamia*. In 'A Fresh Comparison of "The Idiot Boy" and "The Idiot" ' (*N&Q*), Elizabeth Duthie compares the conventional response required by Southey's poem with the surprise created by Wordsworth's. Randel Helms suggests that the Jacob stories in *Genesis* are an influence on 'Michael'; in 'On the Genesis of Wordsworth's *Michael*' (*ELN*, 1977) he neatly suggests this as part of the successful rejection of the earlier ballad-poem on the sheepfold. Sydney Lea's 'Wordsworth and his "Michael": the Pastor Passes' (*ELH*) argues that Wordsworth aims (as the opening lines show) to transmit a legacy of pastoral values.

In 'Wordsworth's Metaphors for Eternity: Appearance and Representation' (*SIR*), Charles Sherry discusses the way in which Wordsworth uses images, notably those of the star and of light, as metaphors for eternity. Another general article is Colin Butler's 'Margaret Drabble: *The Millstone* and Wordsworth' (*ES*), which is primarily helpful in an assessment of Miss Drabble's fiction, but has some insights into ways of approaching Wordsworth. Another comparison occurs in 'Crisis and Recovery: Wordsworth, George Eliot, and *Silas Marner*' (*UTQ*), in which Peter Simpson produces some interesting biographical parallels, and suggests that *Silas Marner* is exploring the same pattern of crisis and recovery which is found in both writers' lives, and which attended the composition of the novel. David Simpson's 'Pound's Wordsworth; or Growth of a Poet's Mind' (*ELH*) is mainly about Pound, but it sees interesting parallels between Wordsworth's long poems and the *Cantos*.

In 'The Absent Dead: Wordsworth, Byron and the Epitaph' (*SIR*), Paul H. Fry treats of *The Excursion V–VIII* and *Childe Harold's Pilgrimage III and IV*; his essay is very much Yale-patterned, considering the epitaph as 'the intersubjective moment of the heart's writing' and as a point of meeting between life and death, or between the beholder and the inscriber. Infinitely more helpful, in my view, is an article by Helen Vendler, who gives a superb reading of the 'Immortality Ode', eloquent and convincing, in 'Lionel Trilling and the *Immortality* Ode' (*Salmagundi*): Ms Vendler pays close attention to the language of the poem and to the complexity of experience which is represented in it, rejecting Trilling's theory of the two answers to the question of the disappearance of glory.

In 'Ruskin on Wordsworth: The Victorian Critic in Romantic Country' (*SIR*), Elizabeth K. Helsinger examines Ruskin's arguments beyond the pathetic fallacy, showing the importance of Wordsworth to *Modern Painters*, but also Ruskin's distrust of the individuality of the romantic poet's response. In another article from *SIR*, 'Wordsworth among the Victorians: The Case Of Sir Henry Taylor', Lawrence Poston considers a disagreement between Taylor and Aubrey De Vere, each of whom considered himself a transmitter of the Wordsworth tradition: Taylor as a lover of Wordsworth the portrayer of nature, De Vere as preferring Wordsworth the mystic.

Three articles deal with episodes from *The Prelude*. In 'The "Home-

Amusements'' Scene in *The Prelude* and the Speaker's Residences' (*ELN*), James Holt McGavran Jr deals with Wordsworth's card games, and the relation of indoor and outdoor experiences. In 'The Artifice of Disjunction: Book 5, *The Prelude*' (*PLL*), Michael C. Jaye admits a lack of unity, but argues that it is a transitional book which explores problems of life as well as an ambivalent attitude to books. Gordon K. Thomas's 'Whither Wordsworth on His Elfin Pinnace' (*TWC*), defends the later version of the boat-stealing, but does so by interpretations which seem to me to be somewhat forced.

A number of articles deal with the later years. Gene W. Ruoff's title, 'Critical Implications of Wordsworth's 1815 Categorization, with Some Animadversions on Binaristic Commentary' (*TWC*) promises a lively essay: it has some splendid remarks on critics who create their own 'over-poem' in order to pull it to pieces, and some pregnant suggestions about Wordsworth's classifications as parts of a whole. These classifications are also discussed by Judith B. Herman, in 'The Poet as Editor: Wordsworth's Edition of 1815' (*TWC*), which investigates particularly the categories of 'Fancy' and 'The Affections'. In 'Blessing the Torrent: On Wordsworth's Later Style' (*PMLA*), Geoffrey Hartman takes an 1824 sonnet on a waterfall, and shows how it transforms clichés into profound suggestions about man and his relationship to nature and time. The poet is reminded of far-off Alpine waterfalls, and Hartman shows how his later style is subdued but charged with reflective meaning.

In *N&Q*, J. Don Vann discusses the newspaper publications (hitherto unregarded) of Wordsworth's poem on Grace Darling. Steven Allaback and Alexander Medlicott Jr give an account of 'A Visit with Wordsworth: From the Unpublished Journals of Anna Eliot Ticknor' (*TWC*), relating to a visit of September 1835.

Carl H. Ketcham gives an account of the journals which Dorothy Wordsworth kept at Rydal and elsewhere from 1824 to 1835 (*TWC*). This is the first of four articles on Dorothy Wordsworth in the Winter number of *TWC*: Richard Fadem's 'Dorothy Wordsworth: A View from "Tintern Abbey" ' is much more than its title implies, for it is a lengthy, and affecting, description of Dorothy's character and her relationship to William and his poetry. Susan Levin and Robert Ready continue with 'Unpublished Poems from Dorothy Wordsworth's Commonplace Book', which contains poems which she wrote in the 1820s and 1830s; and Robert Con Davis discusses 'The Structure of the Picturesque: Dorothy Wordsworth's Journals', in an article which emphasises the ordering of nature, and the relationship of man to the landscape in which he is found.

Kenneth R. Johnston's enquiries into *The Excursion* continue with 'Wordsworth's Reckless Recluse: The Solitary' (*TWC*), which deals principally with The Wanderer's sermon in Book IV: Johnston describes the Wanderer, indeed, as being 'like a kindly college chaplain' of the 1970s, and sees his consolations as operating imaginatively rather than logically. Annabel Patterson describes *The Excursion* as Virgilian in 'Wordsworth's Georgic: Genre and Structure in *The Excursion*' (*TWC*); her account has the great merit of explaining the patriotism of the poem, and accounting for its structure. Geoffrey Durrant, on the other hand, sees 'the question of death' at the heart of the poem, in 'The Elegiac Poetry of *The Excur-*

sion' (*TWC*). Other articles on the poem include David Q. Smith's 'The Wanderer's Silence: A Strange Reticence in Book IX of *The Excursion*' (*TWC*), which suggests that the Wanderer's ending is evidence of the strength of silence and solitude, and that it is a dramatic rendering of the need for inner strength; Stuart Peterfreund's ' "In Free Homage and Generous Subjection": Miltonic Influence on *The Excursion*' (*TWC*), which suggests complex patterns of allusion to and revision of *Paradise Lost*; Barbara T. Gates's 'Providential History and *The Excursion*' (*TWC*), which deals with problems of free-will and determinism in the poem, and suggests that for the Wanderer, the virtuous will is still vitally important; Jim Springer Borck's ' "The Bitter Language of the Heart" in Wordsworth's *The Excursion*' (*TWC*), which discusses the use of language in facing death and sorrow; and Peter F. McInerney's 'Natural Wisdom in Wordsworth's *The Excursion*' (*TWC*), which suggests that the Wanderer's indeterminacy of consolation is part of his adherence to the spirit rather than the letter, and a reading of nature rather than a perception of it.

P. M. Zall contributes an article to *TWC* with the extraordinary title of 'Reading Wordsworth at Off-Ramp U', which turns out to be 'a mammoth, urban, no-dorm institution' in Los Angeles where Mr Zall teaches. His brief account of his methods is part of a number of articles in a special number of *TWC* 'On the Teaching of Wordsworth'. Contributors include Frederick A. Pottle (who suggests an ingenious 'double' approach), Richard Wordsworth (on Grasmere), Karl Kroeber, Laraine Fergenson, Jeffrey C. Robinson, Carl H. Ketcham, Joan B. Gratz, Anya Taylor, and Marlene Longenecker. Some, like Geoffrey Durrant and Eugene L. Stelzig, write of 'strategies' for teaching Wordsworth; others, like William Stephenson (on Wordsworth and Turner) and Donald Wesling (on style and imagery) note the importance of specific issues; particular poems, or groups of poems, are the focus of pedagogical attention by James W. Christie (on 'Tintern Abbey'), John A. Hodgson ('To Joanna'), and James H. Averill (*Lyrical Ballads*). There are several descriptions of reading *The Prelude*, in parts or as a whole, by Kenneth R. Johnston, John T. Ogden, W. J. B. Owen, and Edward Proffitt; and there are other approaches (parody, structural anthropology) by other teachers. The occasional complacency ('Student reaction to the course has been almost entirely favourable') is balanced by an attractive awareness of the very real difficulties involved in teaching Wordsworth in modern conditions and an urban environment.

Two articles in *TWC* connect Wordsworth and Coleridge in relation to 'Christabel': Marilyn Katz, in 'Early Dissent Between Wordsworth and Coleridge: Preface Deletion of October 1800', considers the paragraph which referred to 'Christabel', and the removal of that poem from the volume; James Kissane argues that 'Michael' should be seen as an 'aesthetic alternative' to 'Christabel', and that the ruined sheepfold may be a symbol of Coleridge's inability to finish his poem. Another connecting article is by Don H. Bialostosky, who emphasises Coleridge's tendency to write about what he thought Wordsworth meant rather than what he said in 'Coleridge's Interpretation of Wordsworth's Preface to *Lyrical Ballads*' (*PMLA*). He shows how variable Coleridge's practice of interpretation is, and how distracting his critique has been.

The publication of *The Collected Works of Samuel Taylor Coleridge* continues with David V. Erdman's three-volume *Essays on His Times*[14]. These volumes reprint Coleridge's contributions to *The Morning Post* and *The Courier* from 1798 to 1818, and Erdman has collected almost one hundred essays never before published in book form, in addition to providing the original texts of essays published by Sara Coleridge in 1850. In his graceful and charitable introduction, Erdman is generous to Coleridge, describing his course as an 'oscillation' between his Pantisocratic radicalism and his demands for peace on the one hand and his hatred of Napoleon and defence of the war on the other. The introduction is packed with information and pregnant suggestion (such as the connection with Spinoza which Erdman gives a footnote to, but which others would have inflated into an article). Even Erdman finds it difficult to defend Coleridge when he joined the *Courier* of 1811, and the attacks of Cobbett and Hazlitt (printed by Erdman as an appendix to Volume III) seem fully justified, and, indeed, positively healthy beside the anti-democratic twistings and turnings of Coleridge's later journalism. The first of Erdman's three volumes carries the introduction and *The Morning Post* articles; the second those from *The Courier*; the third contains conjectural attributions, contemporary attacks, and verse contributions. There is a superb index, and the whole project is carried out in a masterly and modest way: as E. P. Thompson wrote in a review (*TWC*), 'congratulations, in fact, should be sent in every direction, except to the author of the *Essays*'.

John Spencer Hill's *Imagination in Coleridge*[15] is complementary to his recent anthology on *The Romantic Imagination* (see *YW* 58.257). This brings together passages on the imagination from various parts of Coleridge's work, including notebooks, letters, essays, and full-scale works. There are the extracts from *Biographia Literaria*, and substantial passages from the lectures of 1818 and 1819, together with prefaces, poems and even marginalia. It is a useful collection, well annotated and with a decent if traditional introduction, and sections illustrating Reason, Understanding, and Symbol. A useful appendix is an extract from Wordsworth's Preface to *Poems* (1815), which is the only non-Coleridge item in the collection apart from a rather unnecessary paragraph from Henry Crabb Robinson's diary. The extracts are cross-referenced, and Coleridge's unusual words are glossed; other passages are cited in support of those quoted, and the notes themselves make up a good annotated Coleridge bibliography.

George Dekker's *Coleridge and the Literature of Sensibility*[16] is lively, provocative, and scholarly. It begins with the unusual argument that the Letter to Sara Hutchinson is not the original of 'Dejection: an Ode', but rather a reshaping of lines and ideas already written. The letter thus becomes a deviation from the main tradition in which 'Dejection' should be seen, that of the greater ode in the age of sensibility. Dekker's theory involves him in extended and valuable explorations of the eighteenth-century literary themes and modes: he considers the role of despairing and

[14] *The Collected Works of Samuel Taylor Coleridge, 3: Essays on His Times*, ed. by David V. Erdman. Vol. I, pp. clxxx + 436; Vol. II, pp. xii + 489; Vol. III, pp. xii + 526. £15 each volume.

[15] *Imagination in Coleridge*, ed. by John Spencer Hill. Macmillan. pp. xviii + 232. £8.95.

[16] *Coleridge and the Literature of Sensibility*, by George Dekker. Vision P. pp. 270. £6.95.

failed poets, the inspirational emblem of the Aeolian Harp, the place and nature of Joy, and the formal qualities of the Ode. Occasionally Dekker seems over-persuasive, but he has an admirable ability to establish a complex tradition from which the Ode sprang. This is so much more valuable than a view of the Ode as occasioned by despair for Sara Hutchinson, that Dekker's account is inevitably more useful than most discussions of 'Dejection'. It has the merit, too, of making the reader look again at the poem, and allowing him to see it not as a rewritten love poem but as a masterpiece in its own right.

General articles on Coleridge include Joel Weinsheimer's 'Coleridge on Synonymity and the Reorigination of Truth' (*PLL*), a difficult but rewarding examination of Coleridge's attitude to synonyms, which is seen as allied to creation in poet or reader; and 'Coleridge and the Sublime: A response to Thomas Weiskel's *The Romantic Sublime*' (*TWC*), in which Raimonda Modiano argues that Coleridge was more interested in the sublime than Weiskel suggests, and traces his theories through Kant and Herder. In 'Herbert, Coleridge and the Vexed Work of Narration' (*MLN*), Barbara Leah Harman relates the work of the narrator to the consciousness of the world and the self within it, which she ingeniously connects to the theological assumptions of both poets. Jerome C. Christensen's 'The Symbol's Errant Allegory: Coleridge and His Critics' (*ELH*), suggests that Coleridge's practice subverts his theory in this instance, and that his definition of symbol needs to be seen poetically rather than literally.

Robert de Maria's 'Coleridgean Names' (*JEGP*), is concerned with the way in which Coleridge uses names, especially of poets, with a symbolic significance: each represents a kind of poetic life, just as the names of plants stand for an identifiable quality.

In ' "The Style and Spirit of the Elder Poets": The *Ancient Mariner* and English Literary Tradition' (*MP*), Richard Payne discusses Coleridge's use of archaic language in the 1798 version of the poem, concluding that Coleridge uses authentic forms, together with northern variants after the manner of Percy's *Reliques*. H. W. Piper writes on 'The Disunity of *Christabel* and the Fall of Nature' (*EIC*), stressing the differences between the two parts: in the first part Coleridge, while still believing in Nature as a source of joy, was investigating its fearful side; in the second, Nature is largely absent, and the result is a simple Gothic effect.

In 'The Genius in the *Biographia Literaria*' (*SIR*), Jerome C. Christensen uses a passage from Chapter IV, in which Coleridge quotes from his 1809 periodical *The Friend,* to make a complex and ingenious commentary on Coleridge's use of parody and quotation throughout. This should be read in conjunction with Daniel Mark Fogel's account of the actual composition of different parts of the work in 'A Compositional History of the *Biographia Literaria*' (*SB*, 1977).

Marshall Brown's 'Toward an Archeology of English Romanticism: Coleridge and Sarbiewski' (*CompL*) is an examination of a Coleridge translation from Sarbiewski, known as the 'divine Casimir' or 'the Polish Horace'. From a close examination of Coleridge's imitation, Brown makes far-reaching observations about the relationship of the mind to the external world, and the status of poem and language in the romantic period. In 'Coleridge et De Quincey face à l'inconscient' (*Romantisme* 1977),

François Moreux emphasises the similarity between the two writers in their approach to dreams and the unconscious, but notes De Quincey's belief that dreams could lead to the Infinite.

Corrections to the text of 'Coleridge's College Declamation, 1792' (see *YW* 58.265) are published by John Anthony Harding in *TWC*. Other minor Coleridge items include William P. Albrecht's 'An Annotated Copy of *The Watchman*' (*TWC*). Among the Coleridge items in *N&Q* are H. W. Piper's 'Coleridge's note on Unitarianism, Orthodoxy and Atheism', which traces a note of 1797 back to 1796 or 1795; Edgar C. Knowlton Jr's 'A Coleridge Allusion to Angelica Catalani (1790–1849)', which corrects Shawcross's printing of 'Catalina' in 'On the Principles of Genial Criticism Concerning the Fine Arts'; a piece of Coleridge marginalia to a copy of Scott's *Minstrelsy of the Scottish Border*, by Jeffrey Robinson; and 'A New Coleridge Letter' in Leicester University Library, by C. D. W. Sheppard. Gordon Cullum provides a review of several recent books on Coleridge in *SR*. P. M. Zall continues his 'cool world' series with an account of 'Joseph Priestley, Firebrand Philosopher' (*TWC*), and of 'John Reeves: The Perils of Public Service' (*TWC*), this latter being a government pamphleteer of the 1790s.

A Bibliography of George Crabbe[17], by T. Bareham and S. Gatrell, contains a great deal of information on the various volumes and editions of Crabbe's work, both during his lifetime and subsequently. There is also a chronological list of reviews of critical books and articles. The bibliography's only weakness seems to be in this section (Heath-Stubbes, *Studies in romanticism*; no mention of Raymond Williams, *The Country and the City* or John Speirs, *Poetry into Novel*). The bibliographical descriptions of such volumes as the present reviewer possesses are scrupulously correct.

Two of Crabbe's tales, 'The Natural Death of Love' and 'Procrastination' are discussed among others in W. K. Thomas's '*Mors Amoris*: When is Love Really Dead' (*DR*). An attractive suggestion by Sharon Footerman in 'The First Fanny Price' (*N&Q*) is that the heroine of *Mansfield Park* may have been suggested by *The Parish Register*.

A worth-while volume in the Romantic Reassessment series is J. H. Alexander's '*The Lay of the Last Minstrel*': *Three Essays*[18]. The essays are on the verbal and thematic texture, on the poetic craftsmanship, and on the notes of the poem. The first essay suggests that there is an intricate and complex interweaving of images of pride and love – 'pride is quelled, and love is free' – with religious attitudes to death. Alexander shows in this essay how well-ordered and subtle Scott's statement of the theme is: in the second he points out metrical skills, word-play, the use of rhyme, repetition and the interaction of the cantos with one another. In the third essay, Alexander points out the way in which the antiquarian notes reinforce the complex attitudes to time within the poem, and add yet another level to the dense layers of meaning. Throughout this is a well-written, helpful study, concentrated and workmanlike: it really does illuminate *The Lay* in ways which are unexpectedly rich. In 'Themes of Time and Art in *The Lay of the Last Minstrel*' (*SSL*), Ruth Eller sees the

[17] *A Bibliography of George Crabbe*, by T. Bareham and S. Gatrell. Folkestone, Kent: Dawson, and Hamden, Conn.: Archon Books. pp. vi + 194. £10.

[18] '*The Lay of the Last Minstrel*': *Three Essays*, by J. H. Alexander. SSELRR No. 77. Salzburg: Institut für Englische Sprache und Literatur. pp. vi + 220. n.p.

poem as concerned with the role of the artist in a changing world, and the artist's understanding of the Romantic ideas of time, change, and death.

Jack Stillinger's *The Poems of John Keats*[19] is described on the dust-jacket, though not in the book itself, as 'the definitive edition'. This is a dangerous thing to claim, and one which, it may be suspected, Stillinger would not have made himself. But if anyone has earned the right to make such a claim, it is Stillinger, whose work on the texts of Keats revealed a host of errors by earlier editors. He strongly defends the choice of printed versions in the volumes of 1818 and 1820 as opposed to holograph texts, even in the difficult case of *The Eve of St. Agnes*; though in matters of periodical publication he is rightly more cautious. The new text is sometimes a surprise, as in 'The Eve of St. Mark', where the 'organs' played loud and sweet (though this reading is found in John Barnard's Penguin edition); more often it is strongly familiar, though accurate in both substantives and accidentals, as in the textually complicated *Eve of St. Agnes*. It is a splendidly produced book, on fine paper and with good type: designed to last, as it presumably will, as a reference book for problems of Keats's text.

Luisa Conti Camaiora's *Il Primo Keats*[20] is a study of the poetry from 1814 to 1818. Signora Camaiora divides this period into three sections, corresponding roughly to the period of *Poems* (1817), of *Endymion* (spring to November 1817), and of the poems preceding the first work on *Hyperion* in November 1818. Her treatment of each period is sensible and straightforward, without being particularly stimulating or original: it recognises the importance of beauty in Keats's early poems, and the subsidiary preoccupation with happiness and permanence, followed by an increasing awareness of pain and transience. The epistle to J. H. Reynolds figures importantly in the last section, together with *Isabella*, as examples of Keats's increasing awareness of forces inimical to beauty. Signora Camaiora shows herself to be a judicious and careful critic, with a firm grasp of the central concerns of the early Keats. William Garrett's 'The Glaucus Episode: An Interpretation of Book III of *Endymion*' (*KSJ*) argues that Glaucus represents the movement of civilisation in time, enduring the curse of Circe before being redeemed by beneficence and knowledge. Paul Sherwin is concerned (in the sense pioneered by Harold Bloom) with Keats's attitude to Milton and Wordsworth. In 'Dying into Life: Keats's Struggle with Milton in *Hyperion*' (*PMLA*), Sherwin suggests that the revision of *Hyperion* is an attempt to escape from Milton's ethical order of good and evil, while retaining its sublime mythologies: if *Hyperion* fails, *The Fall of Hyperion* succeeds in exploring the complex nature of the poetic mind and its relation to the world. Also concerned with the influence of earlier poets is Robert F. Gleckner's 'Keats's "How Many Bards" and Poetic Tradition' (*KSJ*), which draws attention to specific and meaningful borrowings from Spenser, often through Milton. In 'Keats's "Truth" and "A Truth" ' (*PQ*), W. P. Albrecht connects Keats's distinction between a 'felt' truth and an abstract truth with the distinction between the chameleon poet and the egotistical sublime.

[19] *The Poems of John Keats*, ed. by Jack Stillinger. Heinemann. pp. xx + 769. £18.
[20] *Il Primo Keats*, by Luisa Conti Camaiora. Lecce: Milella. pp. 420. n.p.

Pratap Biswas aims some swinging blows at almost every critic who has ever written on the 'Ode on a Grecian Urn' in 'Keats's Cold Pastoral' (*UTQ*). Biswas's article is nothing if not controversial: its interpretation of the urn as illusive and artificial is as extreme as some of the other interpretations he condemns with such vigour. Mark Taylor suggests that the phrase 'emperor and clown' in the 'Ode to a Nightingale' may refer back to Alexander and Yorick in the grave-digger scene of *Hamlet* (*Expl*). Patrick Swinden, examining 'To Autumn' in *CritQ*, suggests that Keats is unusual in omitting falling leaves, and that this is related to a quality of rest and replenishment in the poem, though there is also a tender sharpness and sense of foreboding in the final stanza. In 'The Dialectics of Movement in Keats's "To Autumn" ' (*PMLA*), Virgil Nemoianu draws attention to a multitude of changes within the poem, though many would question the statement that ' "To Autumn" should be understood as a poem on the dialectics of movement', and the suggestion (tentatively put, of course) that the last stanza might be read as 'a criticism of a mechanical late phase of democracy in which man is a number rather than a being'. Andrew J. Kappel suggests that the nightingale's immortality is simply its ignorance of death in 'The Immortality of the Natural: Keats' "Ode to a Nightingale" ' (*ELH*).

In 'The Poet as Critic: A Reading of John Keats' (*KSMB*), Ernest Pereira discusses Keats's criticism in terms of its delighted enjoyment, its almost physical response to poetry, and its interest in his craft. Lawrence Kramer's 'The Return of the Gods: Keats to Rilke' (*SIR*) considers a longing for the classical gods that runs throughout the romantic tradition in poetry, and examines what he calls 'theophanic poetry'.

Bernard Richards in 'Keats and the Lives of the Cat' (*N&Q*) notes neatly that the cat's nine lives and the human's seven ages make sixty-three, the 'grand climacteric' of Keats's 'To Mrs. Reynolds's Cat'; also in *N&Q*, A. J. Flick notes an allusion to the first lines of Dante in a Keats letter. Nicholas A. Joukovsky prints a poem on the death of Keats from the *Newcastle Magazine* in 'New Verse on Keats and the Reviewers' (*KSMB*). Tohru Matsuura considers the influence of Keats on Japanese poets from 1871 in 'John Keats and his Influence on Modern Japanese Poetry' (*KSMB*). In 'The Date of "Lines on the Mermaid Tavern" ' (*ELN*), Leonidas M. Jones dates the poem in late January 1818. Jones also notes a reference to *Antony and Cleopatra* as Keats's favourite play (*ELN*, 1977). An examination of Haydon's relationship with, and contributions to, *The Examiner* is provided by Colbert Kearney in *KSJ*.

Several articles on Shelley appear in one number of *SIR*. In 'Prometheus Made Capable Poet in Act One of *Prometheus Unbound*', Daniel Hughes suggests that Prometheus is intentionally allowed to fade, becoming implicit in the creations of his own imagination. Bernard A. Hirsch writes on *Julian and Maddalo*, entitling his article ' "A Want of That True Theory": *Julian and Maddalo* as Dramatic Monologue'. He emphasises that the poem is a dramatic monologue, and that we should not rely on Julian's interpretations. E. B. Murray's 'The Trial of Mr. Perry, Lord Eldon, and Shelley's *Address to the Irish*' reconstructs the circumstances of a digression towards the end of the *Address*, and shows how the remainder of the work relates to the trial of James Perry, the editor of the *Morning Chronicle*. Carl H.

Ketcham writes on 'Shelley's Vision of the Sea', arguing that it shows Nature at its most destructive (in order to avoid a charge of facile optimism) before turning to a benevolent view of nature and man. He thus achieves 'a complete and utterly unsentimental view of Nature'. R. G. Woodman's 'Shelley's Urania' sees the figure as *Venus Genetrix* and also as lover and inspirer; Woodman cleverly sees an ambivalence in the figure of Urania which he associates with a Keats-like attitude to the world as it is found in the 'Ode to a Nightingale'.

In 'The Necessity of Response: How Shelley's Radical Poetry Works' (*KSJ*), Richard Hendrix emphasises the fusion of literary and political elements, the setting of practical revolutionary exhortation within a fictive structure. This is the only general article on Shelley: many of the others consider Shelley in relation to other poets. Richard E. Brown's 'The Role of Dante in *Epipsychidion*' (*CompL*) demonstrates a relationship between Dante, whose retrospective vision is complete, and Shelley's speaker whose awareness of love is more immediate and fragmentary; Brown also investigates other similarities of structure and imagery. Another article, Barry Weller's 'Shakespeare, Shelley and the Binding of the Lyric' (*MLN*), takes its origin from the phrase 'Ariel to Miranda', and examines the relationship between the late lyrics addressed to Jane Williams and *The Tempest*. Terry Meyers studies Swinburne's attitude to the lyric through Shelley in 'Shelley and Swinburne's Aesthetic of Melody' (*PLL*). Thomas A. Reisner points to a bird-image in *Prometheus Unbound* which owes its origin to Paracelsus (*Expl*).

Lisa M. Steinman's 'Shelley's Scepticism: Allegory in *Alastor*' (*ELH*) argues that Shelley not only offers scepticism as a stance within the poem but also 'offers a self-conscious examination of that stance'. Frederic S. Colwell's 'Shelley's "Witch of Atlas" and the Mythic Geography of the Nile' (*ELH*) stresses, as the title suggests, the poem's geographical background and setting, and proceeds to explore the mythological references which are contained in it.

Lloyd Abbey's 'Apocalyptic Scepticism: The Imagery of Shelley's "The Triumph of Life" ' (*KSJ*) argues that the poem produces image after image as a potential analogue of ultimate reality, only to reject each. P. M. S. Dawson clarifies Shelley's attitudes to Roman Catholics and to Irish Catholicism, and identifies a source of his opinions, in 'Shelley and the Irish Catholics in 1812' (*KSMB*).

In 'Shelley's *The Cenci*: the Ice Motif and the Ninth Circle of Dante's Hell' (*TSL*, 1977), Fred L. Milne examines the imagery of coldness and hardness in *The Cenci*, tracing its origin to the *Inferno*. James D. Wilson's 'Beatrice Cenci and Shelley's Vision of Moral Responsibility' (*ArielE*) argues that Beatrice's disintegration is unlike Prometheus's fortitude because in *The Cenci* Shelley is dealing with a real world as opposed to an ideal one. In 'Cenci as Corrupt Dramatic Poet' (*ELN*), Ronald L. Lemoncelli sees Count Cenci as the kind of corrupt dramatic poet that Shelley describes in *A Defence of Poetry*. Shelley's delight in classical drama is recorded by Stella P. Revard in 'Shelley and Aristophanes: "The Cloud" and *Clouds*, 269–290' (*ELN*). Judith Chernaik and Timothy Burnett describe 'The Byron and Shelley Notebooks in the Scrope Davies Find' (*RES*), with special reference to *Childe Harold's Pilgrimage* III, the 'Hymn to Intellectual Beauty', and 'Mont Blanc'. E. B. Murray identifies 'Shelley's Contribution to Mary's *Frankenstein'* (*KSMB*) from two manuscripts in the Bodleian Library. Mary Shelley's inhibitions about writing Shelley's life are the subject of Paula R. Feldman's 'Biography and the Literary Executor: The Case of Mary Shelley' (*PABS*). An unnoticed obituary of Shelley, in a Dorset magazine, is recorded in *ELN* 1977 by Nicholas A. Joukovsky.

The eighth volume of *Byron's Letters and Journals* is entitled *Born for Opposition*[21]. It contains letters from 1 January to 31 October, 1821, together with a 'Ravenna Journal' for January and February, and another, intermittent Journal entitled 'My Dictionary'. It shows Byron in a combative and buoyant mood, supporting the Carbonari insurrection, and trouncing Southey with *The Vision of Judgment*. Because he was living in Ravenna and seeing Teresa Guiccioli, the volume is much more concerned with English correspondence: about *Don Juan*, the stage presentation (against Byron's wish) of *Marino Faliero*, Keats's death, and 'a diplomatic puppy called Turner', who said that Byron had succeeded in swimming the Hellespont because the tide was in his favour.

New Light on Byron[22] is a series of essays published under the 'Romantic Reassessment' imprint; some of them are by the two figures whose names appear on every one of the series, Professor Erwin A. Stürzl and Dr James Hogg. Stürzl writes three essays, one in English and two in German; one is an agreeable account of some academic junketing, misleadingly entitled 'Byron's Portugal and Spain'; another is an account of the 1977 Conference of the German Byron Society at Constance, with abstracts of the papers delivered there; a third, 'Byron – Unser Zeitgenosse' deals with Byron as our contemporary in his thoughts on social questions, politics and religion. Dr James Hogg studies 'Byron's Revisions to the "Ocean Stanzas" in *Childe Harold's Pilgrimage*, Canto IV, clxiv-clxxxvi', showing that the work of revision was taken more seriously by Byron than is sometimes supposed. There are three other essays in the volume: M. S. Kushawa's 'Byron: A Search for Identity' points out various features of the poet's character which are found in the *Letters and Journals*; B. G. Tandon's 'Dialogue in Byron's Plays' defends the dialogue from charges that it is empty and declamatory; and Zamiruddin's 'Manfred: Restudied as Drama' suggests that the necessary mystery of Manfred's character poses problems, but that otherwise *Manfred* has many dramatic qualities.

The Constance Byron Symposium, mentioned above, reappears in a further volume of the 'Romantic Reassessment' series, which is devoted to the papers whose abstracts are printed above[23]. These begin with Hans-Jürgen Diller's 'The Function of Verse in Byron's *Don Juan*', which looks at the style of *Don Juan* through theories of Jurij Tynjanov and Wolfgang Iser, and other more traditional poetic qualities known here as SPS ('specifically poetic signals') and PIS ('poetically intensified signals').

[21] *Born for Opposition: Byron's Letters and Journals*, Vol. 8. Ed. by Leslie A. Marchand. John Murray. pp. iv + 272. £7.50.

[22] *New Light on Byron*. SSELRR No. 74. Salzburg: Institut für Englische Sprache und Literatur. pp. 136.

[23] *The Constance Byron Symposium, 1977*, by various hands. *Manuscript Revision in Byron's Childe Harold's Pilgrimage, Canto IV, 1–29*, by James Hogg. SSELRR No. 80. Salzburg: Institut für Englische Sprache und Literatur. pp. 130.

Wolfgang Franke's '*Don Juan* and the Black Friar: a Byronic Variant of the Ghost Story' places the story of Canto XVI in the context of Byron's Gothic practices at Newstead. Jürgen Schlaeger, in 'Some Remarks on the Aesthetic Structure of *Don Juan*', argues that it is 'astoundingly modern' in its use of the self-reflecting narrator and in its conscious blending of truth and fiction. Rainer Schöwerling studies 'Lord Byron and German Literary Criticism. Some Remarks on the Reception and Influence of Byron and His *Don Juan*', which instances many strangely conflicting judgements, together with some politically interesting ones. Finally, Helmut Viebrock examines a number of levels of operation of the Fall motif in *Don Juan*, in 'The Fall from Perfection: a Major Motif in Byron's *Don Juan*'. Viebrock distinguishes seven levels: to reproduce them all here ('mythic-cosmological, mythic-anthropological') would make him seem like Polonius, which he clearly is not. An addendum to this collection of essays on *Don Juan* is James Hogg's 'Manuscript Revision in Byron's *Childe Harold's Pilgrimage*, Canto IV, 1–29' (the opening section on Venice).

In 'The "Desultory Rhyme" of *Don Juan*: Byron, Pulci, and the Improvisatory Style' (*ELH*), Lindsay Waters examines the reasons for the rediscovery of Pulci, the 'loose style' and the early epic; by using Pulci, Byron is seen as attacking Wordsworth and the reigning romantic orthodoxy.

Ina Schabert's '*Zur Ideologie der Poetischen Sprachstrukturierung: George Herbert und Byron*' (*Anglia*), is a structuralist study of opposition and chime in the use of contrast and rhyme. Charles Eric Reeves, in 'Continual Seduction: The Reading of *Don Juan*' (*SIR*) asks interesting questions about the reader's response to various effects of the poem, often those which strive 'to escape delimiting conceptions of poetic discourse'. A new periodical, *Quinquereme*, has a lively account by Herbert W. Smith of Byron's brief friendship in Milan with the Italian author of *Le Mie Prigioni* in 'Byron and Sylvio Pellico'.

Alice Levine's 'T. S. Eliot and Byron' (*ELH*) presents an ingenious comparison between *Childe Harold's Pilgrimage* and *The Waste Land* as poems of their age. Gloria T. Hull writes on 'The Byronic Heroine and Byron's *The Corsair*' (*ArielE*), emphasising the ideal beauty of the heroines, and contrasting the fair and dark Medora and Gulnare.

Byron matters discussed in *N&Q* include Peter J. Manning's 'Byron, Southey and Botany Bay', which notes a reference back in *Don Juan* to Southey's 'Botany Bay Eclogues' of 1794; Francis Doherty's 'Byron in Cephalonia', which prints a contemporary account of Byron's last days in Greece; and Doris H. Meriweather's attractively titled 'The Reeling Romaika', which corrects Leslie Marchand's annotation of this dance as a Highland Reel.

Anne Tibble claims that *The Midsummer Cushion*[24], now printed for the first time, is the most important of all Clare's books. This seems a strong claim, and yet it has some truth in it, for the new book contains some of Clare's greatest poems, such as 'Decay' and 'The Flitting', and a great abundance of superb sonnets. A selection of poems was printed by

[24] *The Midsummer Cushion*, by John Clare, ed. by Anne Tibble, associate editor R. K. R. Thornton. Ashington, Northumberland, and Manchester: The Mid Northumberland Arts Group in association with Carcanet P. pp. xxii + 520. £8.

Robinson and Summerfield in *Selected Poems and Prose*, but this edition prints the whole manuscript, complete with Clare's spellings, dialect words, ampersands, and punctuation. The text differs considerably from Robinson and Summerfield's, and since they were so critical of the pioneering work of the Tibbles, one can only rejoice that Mrs Tibble, and her associate editor, Dr Thornton, have had the last word. Reproducing ampersands really does make the poem on the page seem more authentic, and there are many new readings: 'mattock' in 'The Woodman' becomes 'mittins', in 'Angling', 'level meadows of oerhanging woods', which never seemed right, becomes '& oerhanging woods', and the heron now watches for 'coil' not 'spoil'. It is impossible in a review of this space to do more than indicate the kind of new text that is offered, and to say that *The Midsummer Cushion* really does present a Clare who is a poet of fertility, energy, and integrity. Timothy Brownlow's 'A Molehill for Parnassus: John Clare and Prospect Poetry' (*UTQ*) argues that Clare's poetry is not characteristic 'prospect' poetry, but that he takes a low viewpoint (which Brownlow ingeniously relates to Clare's position on the social scale), and his poetry is concerned with the multiplicity of small natural phenomena.

I am glad to notice, somewhat belatedly, Thérèse Tessier's excellent study *La Poésie Lyrique de Thomas Moore*[25]. It is notable because so little has been written on Moore, and because his lyrics are particularly resistant to modern critical techniques. Mme Tessier's particular skill is in discovering the relationship of the words to the music, not just in general but also in specific details of scansion, melody, quaver and appogiatura. The context and influence of *Irish Melodies* are not ignored: Mme Tessier points out that they were taken abroad by Irish emigrants, and became a vitally important source of Irish nationalism; they influenced such widely disparate figures as Yeats and Benjamin Britten, Dickens and Sean O'Casey. To complete the survey there is a substantial study of *Lalla Rookh, The Loves of the Angels* and other minor pieces.

In 'Regency Newspaper Verse: An Anonymous Squib on Wordsworth' (*KSJ*), Stanley Jones argues enjoyably and convincingly that Thomas Moore, rather than Hazlitt, was the author. An 1834 letter from Southey to an American poetess is printed by W. P. Albrecht in 'A Letter from Southey to Maria Gowen Brooks' (*ELN*).

Two books from Salzburg cover similar ground in surveying the awkward field of romantic drama. These are Om Prakash Mathur's *The Closet Drama of the Romantic Revival*[26] and Pratyush Ranjan Purkayastha's *The Romantics' Third Voice*[27], subtitled 'A Study of the Dramatic Works of the English Romantic Poets'. The titles imply the difference of method: Mathur is straightforward, interested in closet drama as a form; he gives a complete coverage, including sections on Southey, Scott, and minor figures such as Joanna Baillie. Purkayastha is more interested in romantic drama as a 'voice', even though a third one, for each individual poet. Since Mathur spreads his attention more widely, his attention to individual plays

[25] *La Poésie Lyrique de Thomas Moore*, by Thérèse Tessier. Paris: Didier, 1976. pp. xiv + 498. n.p.

[26] *The Closet Drama of the Romantic Revival*, by Om Prakash Mathur. SSPDPT No. 35. Salzburg: Institut für Englische Sprache und Literatur. pp. vi + 391. £4.60.

[27] *The Romanties' Third Voice*, by Pratyush Ranjan Purkayastha. SSPDPT No. 41. Salzburg: Institut für Englische Sprache und Literatur. pp. iv + 365. £4.60.

tends to be thinner, though nis style is simpler. This may also be due to Mathur's interest in external causes for the inadequacy of romantic drama: to some extent he blames the failure of Wordsworth and Coleridge on the unsympathetic response of theatrical management. Both writers struggle manfully with their unresponsive subject-matter: they protest the poet's interest in the drama, point to the 'dramatic' qualities in their lives and conversation, and plead for the importance of the plays either in terms of their intrinsic worth or of a certain historical significance. It is difficult, however, to see all their hard work as much more than a losing critical battle in the end, for the material remains stubbornly resistant to special pleading.

In 'Some Comic Circus Entrées' (*TN*), George Speaight describes various acts which became part of the circus repertoire in the late eighteenth and early nineteenth centuries. Yashdip Singh Bains and Norma Jenckes record 'Canadian Evaluations of Edmund Kean' (*TN*) on a tour of 1826 in Montreal and Quebec. An actor-manager with a string of provincial theatres, Henry Ford Thornton, is described by Paul Ranger in 'The Thornton Circuit, 1784–1817' (*TN*). Carol J. Carlisle disentangles confusions between Helen Faucit and her lesser-known sister Harriet in 'The Other Miss Faucit' (*NCTR*). A late eighteenth-century theatre at Wisbech is described by Richard Leacroft in *TN*. Y. S. Bains gives an account of 'The Articulate Audience and the Fortunes of the Theatre in Halifax in 1816–1819' (*DR*), which discusses Shakespeare performances by visiting companies.

2. Prose Fiction

An interesting but wordy book by Hubert Teyssandier[28] studies the relationships between major and minor novels of the Romantic period and traces their common links with the moral tale, whose rigidity they either modify or copy. Teyssandier begins by offering a detailed and orthodox account of the conventions governing the moral tale, and notes strains of irony and comedy which animate its general seriousness. He then studies *Mansfield Park* and *Emma* at length, carefully pointing out their symmetries of plot and situation, and discussing how Jane Austen moves away from romance and towards a more naturalistic treatment of her materials. The chapter on Peacock which follows is original and stimulating, and offers good close readings of *Headlong Hall* and *Melincourt*. Teyssandier does justice to the vigour and freshness of Peacock's novels, which he presents as works whose satire is counterpointed by a positive vision of the world, symbolically expressed by music and dancing. The chapter on Scott concentrates on *Waverley* and *Old Mortality* and gives a standard view of his 'vision historique d'un monde qui subit les effets de transformations irréversibles'. On the Gothic novel, where he mainly talks of *Frankenstein* and *Melmoth the Wanderer*, Teyssandier is acute and sympathetic, and comments interestingly on the moral disquiet which he sees as characteristic of the genre. In general, Teyssandier's thesis is unexceptionable, though it leads him to some very detailed writing on well-covered topics, and this rather detracts from the helpful insights into technique

[28] *Les formes de la création romanesque à l'époque de Walter Scott et de Jane Austen 1814–1820*, by Hubert Teyssandier. Paris: Didier (1977). pp. 432. 86, 80 fr.

and plotting which form his book's principal recommendation.

Jill Rubenstein's *Sir Walter Scott, a reference guide*[29] is a valuable research tool which presents a comprehensive and thoroughly annotated listing of virtually all of the criticism of Scott to appear between 1932 and 1977, together with a brief introductory study of his reputation. The summaries of both books and articles are clear and to the point, the range of material covered is wide, and efficient cross-referencing and an excellent index allow one to locate quickly whatever information one is looking for. This is a welcome work, and has been well done. Mark A. Weinstein has usefully edited *The Prefaces to the Waverley Novels*[30], with a short preface describing Scott as 'a novelist who has thought seriously about the practice of his profession' and adequate elucidatory notes on the text. In *MSE* Ernest Bevan Jr discusses how, in *Waverley*, Edward's moral growth is presented as a movement from 'an idealistic conception of self-determination to a realistic acknowledgement of the self as a time-conditioned entity whose actions can affect many lives'. Seamus Cooney has a study of 'The Two Drovers' in *SSF* in which he discusses the tale from the viewpoint of its surprisingly modern attitude towards the question of how far freedom is limited by cultural conditioning. Mary Cullinan's thoughtful article on 'History and Language in Scott's *Redgauntlet*' in *SEL* studies the control of perspective in the novel and comes to the conclusion that while its plot reveals 'the layers of fictions with which man clothes his meaning and his identity, the narrative structure demonstrates the difficulty with which one arrives at any truth'. Francis R. Hart surveys the conclusions of Scott's novels in *NCF* and points to their uncertainty and the way in which they appeal for authority to some force 'that must be re-created before it can function effectively and legitimately'. Richard E. Johnson discusses 'embedding' in Scott's fiction in *SSL*, in the course of which he offers an interesting restatement of our standard notion of Scott's attitude towards the past: 'A figure from the historic past, dissatisfied with his own environment, makes a journey into the mythic past. After a series of adventures, he re-enters the historical past, bringing back with him something out of the mythic past. As a result, the historic past is transformed and the hero is reconciled to his environment, but the mythic past is destroyed'. George Levine's fine study of *The Bride of Lammermoor* in *NCF* sensitively presents the relationship of Gothic and naturalistic elements in the novel, which for him 'shows us the past in the act of self-destruction that will distance it sufficiently to make it an object of nostalgia'.

No work of major importance on Jane Austen has appeared this year. David Cecil's *A Portrait of Jane Austen*[31] is a well-illustrated, attractively presented brief biography which also makes some mention of her novels and of the time in which she lived, and is aimed at the general reader rather than the specialist. Brian Wilks's *Jane Austen*[32] is an excellent introductory study of the novelist's life and period, and makes full and interest-

[29] *Sir Walter Scott, a reference guide*, by Jill Rubenstein. Boston, Mass.: G. K. Hall & Co. pp. xxiii + 344. £17.50.

[30] *The Prefaces to the Waverley Novels*, ed. by Mark A. Weinstein. Lincoln, Neb. and London: U. of Nebraska P. pp. xvii + 269. £8.40.

[31] *A Portrait of Jane Austen*, by David Cecil. Constable. pp. 208. £6.95.

[32] *Jane Austen*, by Brian Wilks. Hamlyn. pp. 144. £4.50.

ing use of background material and of her letters. The approach is fresh and lively, and much of the information on early nineteenth-century life is vivid and thought-provoking. The attitude towards Jane Austen herself is refreshingly clear-sighted, and a convincing portrait emerges. The book is very well produced, has many good illustrations, and can be highly recommended to the non-specialist reader.

I have been unable to read Juliet McMaster's *Jane Austen on Love*. In *PLL* Joseph Kestner writes on Jane Austen's letters, which he tries unconvincingly to present as being 'so much about themselves and their processes', and forming a kind of *grammaire* of the letter form. Terry Lovell's study of 'Jane Austen and the Gentry' in *The Sociology of Literature: Applied Studies*[33] gives an orthodox picture of the novelist as a thoughtful conservative concerned to fight off the '*internal* decay which undermined the traditional order'. A sensitive and discriminating article by Thomas Lockwood in *NCF* traces the difference, in *Persuasion*, between Jane Austen's sense of significance and Anne Elliot's, and concludes that 'Jane Austen does make the controlling truth of Anne's story, and of *Persuasion*, an emotional truth; and if Anne is never quite prepared with Jane Austen to tell this truth, at any rate she is allowed to live it'. In the same periodical David Monaghan writes an excellent reassessment of *Mansfield Park* and Evangelicalism in which he accepts a number of links between the novel and evangelical ideas but decides that 'at a very fundamental level the religious and social views expressed in *Mansfield Park* are completely incompatible with those of the Evangelicals'. Bruce Olsen's 'The Empiricism of the Imitator' (*Lang&S*) is principally concerned with imitation and has little to say about either Jane Austen or *The Watsons*.

John K. Crabbe, in his neat summary in *TSL* of the function of women in Peacock's novels, describes the importance of freedom and self-determination for Peacock's female characters, and notes that a warning threat of 'marital unhappiness' is often sounded for those who submit to arranged marriages. John Dixon Hunt discusses Humphry Repton's landscape designs in *SBHT*, and notes in passing that Peacock's Milestone mingles the ideas of both Repton and Capability Brown. In *The Evidence of the Imagination*[34] William Walling writes acutely on the deep sense of fracture in Peacock's novels, and comes in the end to see them as 'paradoxical creations of community in a contemporary world where the possibility of community no longer seemed to exist'.

The year has produced two interesting articles on Hogg's *Justified Sinner*, both of them appearing in *SSL*. Michael Mason carefully dissects the evidence as to the three burials in the novel, finds that the material is organised so that 'no complete fit is possible', and deduces an overall questioning of authority, even that of the author's own utterance. Michael S. Kearns sees much of the struggle of the book, especially in the case of the editor and Robert Wringhim, as resulting from an inability to accept the supernatural and to agree to the validity of intuition as a mode of perception.

[33] *The Sociology of Literature: Applied Studies*, ed. by Diana Laurenson. Keele, Staffs.: U. of Keele. pp. 283. £4.95.

[34] *The Evidence of the Imagination: Studies of Interactions between Life and Art in English Romantic Literature*, ed. by Donald H. Reiman, Michael C. Jaye, Betty T. Bennett, Doucet Devin Fischer, and Ricki B. Herzfeld. New York: New York U.P. pp. xvii + 409. $15.

Ruth Aldrich's *John Galt*[35] provides a comprehensive record of Galt's writings in all genres and includes a certain amount of information as to his life and times. Its main focus is on the novels, which are described systematically and clearly, with full synopses, and assessments of structure, characterisation, style, significance and criticism. There are interesting excerpts from contemporary reviews, and Aldrich is at pains to offer rounded views of Galt's relationship with his contemporaries and his reaction to their views. The book has a useful chronology of Galt's life and a bibliography both of primary sources and of criticism, the latter selective and helpfully annotated. Aldrich's purpose is informative rather than critical, and she amasses a good deal of material that is not conveniently available elsewhere, especially on the lesser novels and the large body of occasional writing with which few readers are nowadays familiar. Nevertheless, she also adduces evidence which supports her presentation of Galt at his best as a novelist of 'unsentimental tender realism'. Galt's stories have been selected and edited by Ian A. Gordon[36], with a short introduction and a minimum of annotation, but a full vocabulary explaining the meaning of his many Scottish dialect words. Keith M. Costain writes in *UTQ* that Galt focuses a pastoral point of view upon modern urban life so that 'city and village pass comment on each other, thus obliging the reader to enter into the process whereby, in the writing of his fictions, Galt was himself attempting to adjust their mutual claims upon his emotional allegiance'.

John Cronin's elegant and judicious critical biography of Gerald Griffin[37] throws light both on the career of this successful and enigmatic figure and on the dilemmas of the Anglo-Irish writer in general. The book begins by evoking the parlous state of Irish culture in the 1800s, and gives us information as to Griffin's early background and family life. It then summarises his unsuccessful attempts to make his name in London, first by playwriting and then as a contributor to the periodical press. A discussion of the early short stories on Irish themes, realistically treated, leads to a long, sharp analysis of Griffin's most famous work, the novel *The Collegians*, which Cronin presents as an intense and personal book offering 'a vivid depiction of a society in decay'. Griffin's later writing, which shows his compassionate interest in 'the wretched state of the Irish peasantry' is interpreted by reference both to his Commonplace book and to the increasing failure of his personal relationships. His subsequent creative decline and retreat into the Christian Brothers teaching order are treated with sympathy. A most interesting conclusion describes Griffin as 'a powerfully realistic depictor of the troubled Ireland of his time', and an author who explored contrasts between sentimentality and pragmatism which Cronin sees as being 'central to the Anglo-Irish tradition'. The book is lucid and well-balanced, and offers insights which are of interest not only to students of Griffin, but also to those more widely concerned with the general problems of Anglo-Irish literature.

The now considerable field of Mary Shelley studies is well represented

[35] *John Galt*, by Ruth I. Aldrich. Boston, Mass.: Twayne. pp. 172. £5.15.

[36] *John Galt, Selected Short Stories*, ed. by Ian A. Gordon. Edinburgh: Scottish Academic P. pp. ix + 213. £4.50.

[37] *Gerald Griffin (1803–1840), A critical biography*, by John Cronin. Cambridge: C.U.P. pp. xx + 163. £6.95.

this year, with a bulky biography and a number of articles of varying usefulness. Jane Dunn's *Moon in Eclipse*[38] is copious and accurate in its detailing of Mary Shelley's life, but its comments on her books are few and undistinguished and its writing is marred by carelessness of phrasing and frequent sentimentality. Peter Brooks has a superb article on language in *Frankenstein* in *NLH*, where he analyses the concept of monstrosity in the novel and the way in which it is transmitted to the reader, leaving 'a residue of meaning that cannot be explained, rationalized, but is passed on as affect, as taint'. Laura E. Crouch discusses Mary Shelley's probable borrowing from Sir Humphry Davy's *A Discourse, Introductory to A Course of Lectures on Chemistry* and indicates that Frankenstein's ideas were only slightly more presumptuous than those of other scientists of the time (*KSJ*). In an important article in *KSMB* E. B. Murray evaluates the evidence for Shelley's having some considerable hand in the writing of *Frankenstein* and concludes that 'the poet's contribution – particularly to the last few pages of the novel – may well have been substantial enough to require Mary's editorial carte blanche, whenever first given, and original enough to suggest that at times his creative impulse added its own initiative to the novel's effect, though always in keeping with Mary's conception and with her implicit sanction. In *SIR* Robert Lance Snyder offers an interesting discussion of *The Last Man*, whose power he sees as deriving from its perception of 'the fearful marginality of man in a disjointed and alien universe'. The same novel is well analysed by Lee Sterrenburg in *NCF* as a philosophical anatomy in which Mary Shelley is presenting her gloomy obituary of the meliorist view of social advance of her parent's generation.

Coral Ann Howells begins her serious and carefully balanced book on the Gothic novel[39] with a valuable chapter on themes, values and techniques which points accurately at the 'mixture of coyness and hysteria' with which genuine insights into feeling are often presented. The chapter on *The Mysteries of Udolpho* does justice to Mrs Radcliffe's technical adroitness and acutely identifies the underlying design of her fiction as resting on 'the contest between her imagination and her sense of reality'. On *The Monk* Howells is less interesting and substantial, treating it conventionally as a work primarily of 'male sexual fantasy'. The varieties of Gothic fiction are further illustrated in a well-informed discussion of two of the products of the Minerva Press, Regina Maria Roche's domesticated and sentimental *The Children of the Abbey* and Mary-Anne Radliffe's sensational *Manfroné*. The discussion of *Northanger Abbey* is sensible and leads to the unexceptionable conclusion that Jane Austen 'does not reject Gothic because it is different from life, but because it can so easily distort one's real life responses'. The long chapter on *Melmoth the Wanderer* is excellent, and offers a convincing reading of the novel's emotional intensity and psychological analysis of states of terror and suffering. *Jane Eyre*, in conclusion, is shown to differ from the Gothic novel in its 'acceptance of the need to take all kinds of experience into account in a realistic presentation of human experience'. Howells' book is commendable when it deals

[38] *Moon in Eclipse: A Life of Mary Shelley*, by Jane Dunn. Weidenfeld & Nicolson. pp. ix + 374. £8.50.

[39] *Love, Mystery, and Misery: Feeling in Gothic Fiction*, by Coral Ann Howells. Athlone P. pp. 199. £8.50.

with mainstream Gothic novels, on which it has many perceptive things to say, and about whose treatment of feeling it is often fresh and illuminating; the chapters on Jane Austen and Charlotte Brontë have less to offer.

3. Prose

Two useful bibliographical aids are: an annual annotated bibliography of work on nineteenth-century non-fiction in *Prose Studies 1800–1900*, a new journal devoted exclusively to the study of non-fiction; and *Keats, Shelley, Byron, Hunt, and Their Circles: A Bibliography: July, 1962 – December 31, 1974*[40], a collection of *KSJ* annual bibliographies. Haydon, Hazlitt, and Hunt are the prose-writers principally covered. A detailed index facilitates use.

The labours which have recently brought forth numerous scholarly editions of Mary Wollstonecraft's works have not been rewarded with critical accounts of her writings which would justify the expense of such editorial spirit. Of the articles mentioned here, only Elissa S. Guralnick's 'Radical Politics in Mary Wollstonecraft's *A Vindication of the Rights of Woman*' (*SBHT*, 1977) brings us nearer to an understanding of the nature of her achievement. *Rights of Woman* is not primarily a feminist tract, according to Professor Guralnick, but a radical political tract which more sustainedly and successfully than its overly polemical predecessor, *Rights of Men*, discovers in the figure of the woman a literary figure for all men (and women), 'high and low, who are implicated in social and political contracts which condone inequality of rank, wealth, and privilege'. At the heart of this lucid, persuasive piece is the welcome awareness that in Mary Wollstonecraft's writings literary and political matters are inseparable.

In 'Mary Wollstonecraft in Federalist America: 1791–1802', in *The Evidence of the Imagination*[41], Marcelle Thiébaux maps with care her subject's fortunes in America, from the first appearance of one of her translations, to the reviews and lampoons that appeared after the American publication of Godwin's *Memoirs*. Private correspondence as well as published writings are the source of her judgements. The recent discovery of Mary Wollstonecraft's missing anthology has brought to light two lost pieces – the preface and four prayers – which are reprinted in 'The Discovery of Mary Wollstonecraft's *The Female Reader*' (*Signs*) by Moira Ferguson, whose introduction sketches Wollstonecraft's role in the education campaigns of the time, discusses what light the anthology sheds on her literary tastes, and offers reasons for attributing certain parts of the anthology to her. Mary Wollstonecraft is one of several women who 'consciously used scientific advances and ideas in their battle for equality', according to Lois N. Magner in 'Women and the Scientific Idiom: Textual Episodes from Wollstonecraft, Fuller, Gilman, and Firestone' (*Signs*). The interesting section on Wollstonecraft, drawing primarily on *Rights of*

[40] *Keats, Shelley, Byron, Hunt, and Their Circles: A Bibliography: July 1, 1962–December 31, 1974*, ed. by Robert A. Hartley. Lincoln, Neb. and London: U. of Nebraska P. pp. xvi + 487. $18.50.

[41] *The Evidence of the Imagination: Studies of Interactions Between Life and Art in English Romantic Literature*, ed. by Donald H. Reiman, Michael C. Jaye, and Betty T. Bennett. New York: New York U.P. pp. xix + 409. $15.

Woman, concludes that 'the extrapolation of Newtonian theories from the physical world to the social realm formed the basis of Wollstonecraft's analysis of the human situation and her constant use of reasoning from the laws of nature'.

The most recent volume of *The Letters of Charles and Mary Anne Lamb*[42] not only covers a relatively uneventful period in Charles's life, but also finds him deprived, for the most part, of those few correspondents against whose personalities and convictions he defined himself. It comes as no surprise that some of the best letters are written to Wordsworth, whose celebration of rural life provoked Lamb into playful exposure of the pretension of his friend's claim for the country, and identification and definition of his own commitment to urban life and experience. On 'Lamb as dramatist, as critic of dramatic literature, as critic and experiencer of theatrical performance, and as critic of Shakespeare and painting', Wayne Mckenna's introductory summary to *Charles Lamb and the Theatre*[43] is just to the interests of the work and loyal to the infelicities of style which mar it. A useful opening chapter on the English theatre, 1737–1843, prefaces the detailed scrutiny of Lamb's writings.

Lamb's writings on Shakespeare are collected as *Charles Lamb on Shakespeare*[44] by Joan Coldwell, whose introduction and notes do not wholly provide the necessary context for comments which are sometimes no longer than a paragraph. J. E. Stevens's 'Charles Lamb, The Romantic Humorist' (*ChLB*) is one of several recent attempts, of which the most sustained and forceful is Fred Randel's *The World of Elia* (see *YW* 56.338), to see play as an important strategy in *Essays of Elia*. Stevens makes some useful remarks about Lamb's play with reality (his dramatic fictions), his play with logic (his mastery of inconsequence), and his play with words. In 'Lamb Recreates a Burney Wedding', in *The Evidence of the Imagination*[45], Joyce Hemlow compares Lamb's essay 'The Wedding' with other accounts of the same event to demonstrate how he transmuted fact into art. Finally, two readable if modest items are: 'Charles Lamb, The Apostate: 1796–1798' (*ChLB*), in which Jane Aaron offers an account of Lamb's developing independence from Coleridge during the 1790s, especially from his systems of theological and aesthetic thought; and 'Charles Lamb's "Golden Year"' (*ChLB*) by Charles A. Rance, who promises, in this and a succeeding article, to review the events in Lamb's life during 1821, the year in which perhaps the best of the Elia essays were published.

Two thoughtful pieces on Thomas De Quincey are included in a worthwhile collection of essays, *Interspace and the Inward Sphere*[46], devoted to the illumination and definition of continuities between Romantic and

[42] *The Letters of Charles and Mary Anne Lamb*, III, 1809–17, ed. by Edwin W. Marrs Jr. Ithaca, N.Y. and London: Cornell U.P. pp. xix + 274. £24.50.

[43] *Charles Lamb and the Theatre*, by Wayne Mckenna. Gerrards Cross, Bucks.: Colin Smythe. pp. 134. £4.95.

[44] *Charles Lamb on Shakespeare*, ed. by Joan Coldwell. Gerrards Cross, Bucks.: Colin Smythe. pp. 175. £6.95.

[45] *The Evidence of the Imagination: Studies of Interactions Between Life and Art in English Romantic Literature*, ed. by Donald H. Reiman, Michael C. Jaye, and Betty T. Bennett. New York: New York U.P. pp. xix + 409. $15.

[46] *Interspace and the Inward Sphere: Essays on Romantic and Victorian Self*, ed. by Norman A. Anderson and Margene E. Weiss. An Essays in Literature Book. Macomb, Ill.: Western Illinois University. pp. 146. $5.

Victorian prose. E. Michael Thorn's 'Speed, Steam, Self, and Thomas De Quincey' is to be welcomed not least for its willingness to see *Suspira* in its historical context, as, in part, a response to the startling technological changes of the early Victorian period. De Quincey's effort in *Suspira* is to perfect his escape from bewildering change through the creation of an 'aristocratic perspective' which will allow him to create a coherent, meaningful self. The cost of such creation is separation from the world around him. Thorn's argument makes one consider anew the familiar imagery and style which characterise and structure De Quincey's writings. In the same volume Robert Ready's 'De Quincey's Magnificent Apparatus' offers a persuasive account of the *Confessions*, especially its comic tone, claiming that its narrator is a 'utilitarian who has undergone the most extraordinary discoveries about his own "latent capacity for sympathy with the infinite" ', and who struggles to comprehend dreams, 'the most irrational experience normal consciousness has', in rational language. Division is also the subject of 'The Structure of De Quincey's *Confessions of an English Opium-Eater*' (*PS*) in which Roger Ramsey argues that De Quincey's unresolved ambivalence towards the opium habit – it is at once beatific and merely sensual – forces him to develop a structure which accommodates both perceptions. Richard Downing in 'De Quincey and the *Westmoreland Gazette*' (*ChLB*) details De Quincey's writings on the 1818 Westmoreland election campaign, his subsequent appointment to the editorship of the *Westmoreland Gazette*, and his contributions as editor to the paper, all activities which helped to heal the breach in his friendship with Wordsworth.

John Kinnaird's *William Hazlitt: Critic of Power*[47] is a major effort to comprehend its subject's achievements; 'a biography of the mind' rather than a record of his life in the conventional sense. It offers as its own unifying theme and that of Hazlitt's life and writings his 'vision of the continuity of "power" and its motives – of "power" both as *kratos* and *dynamis*, both in the political (that is, societal) sense as ruling force or authority, and in the natural, or broadly philosophical, sense as active, creative, or generative energy'. After tracing its genesis in his upbringing and youthful experiences, Kinnaird shows Hazlitt's vision of power growing in range and complexity in his philosophical criticism, in his political, literary and art criticism, and, finally, in his late writings, which are at once personal and broadly cultural. Amongst his aims are: to challenge the received belief that Hazlitt's thought was unalterably fixed in his youth; to establish his centrality in English romanticism; and to claim his place in the line of English critics from Johnson to Arnold. The achievement of *William Hazlitt: Critic of Power* is considerable, vitiated only by its author's undue assimilation of Hazlitt's way of viewing the world. John L. Mahoney's modest *The Logic of Passion: The Literary Criticism of William Hazlitt*[48] devotes chapters to the major themes that give shape and direction to Hazlitt's work: to the themes of nature, of emotional immediacy, of imagination, and of the ends of literature and criticism. If there is nothing new here, neither is there anything dreary or silly.

[47] *William Hazlitt: Critic of Power*, by John Kinnaird. New York: Columbia U.P. pp. xv + 429. $28.10.

[48] *The Logic of Passion: The Literary Criticism of William Hazlitt*, by John L. Mahoney. SSELRR No. 75. Salzburg: Universität Salzburg. pp. ix + 150. $22.75.

John Mahoney also edits *The English Romantics: Major Poetry and Critical Theory*[49]. Hazlitt is represented by nine pieces, five of which (including 'On Gusto') are given entire, and a critical essay, 'No Better Reality: New Dimensions in Hazlitt's Aesthetics' by Mahoney, who explores the character of Hazlitt's interest in poetry's 'basic roots, its connections with life, the peculiar mode through which it represents life, and the special character of its impact on human personality'. Norman Bryson in 'Hazlitt on Painting' (*JAAC*) situates Hazlitt's theory of the visual arts between Reynolds's and Ruskin's, arguing that in Hazlitt's work 'one encounters for the first time the claim that the function of the visual arts is to refine perception, and, the secondary, supportive claim that the agent of this refinement is a genius whose perception differs radically from that of other men'. In 'Hazlitt, Passion and *King Lear*' (*SEL*) W. P. Albrecht records the acknowledgement in romantic criticism of the power of passion to 'propel the mind – not merely out of selfishness, pride, or lethargy – but into a creative process of learning', and proceeds to describe Hazlitt's conviction that the passion aroused in tragic protagonist or audience 'by confronting a painful world may bring the whole mind to bear on a process of moral recordering'. Two articles are bicentennial tributes: there is no defence for their publication other than that they rehearse the orthodox view of Hazlitt's accomplishments. W. R. Niblett's 'William Hazlitt as Critic' (*ChLB*) surveys his achievements, including his contribution to novel criticism and his pioneering of the modern form of dramatic criticism; and Lillian Haddakin's 'William Hazlitt (1778–1830): A Bicentenary Assessment' (*ContempR*) discusses his various interests, concluding that the central problem for any critic of Hazlitt is that while his scattered and piecemeal writings demand an interpreter 'who must be a systematiser', Hazlitt himself, as his mode of writing itself testifies, distrusts ' "system" as falsifying'.

Francis Jeffrey wrote on philosophical, literary, and political matters, and Philip Flynn in his useful study, *Francis Jeffrey*[50], finds himself offering brief accounts of Jeffrey's convictions and writings on topics as various as: epistemology; moral sentiments and social progress; politics – the war; politics – reform; aesthetics and literary history; poetry, and prose fiction. Flynn is especially good on the Scottish philosophical context of Jeffrey's thought.

[49] *The English Romantics: Major Poetry and Critical Theory*, ed. by John L. Mahoney. Lexington, Mass. and Toronto: D.C. Heath. pp. xix + 828. $22.75.

[50] *Francis Jeffrey*, by Philip Flynn. Newark: Del.: U. of Delaware P.; London: Associated University Presses. pp. 218. £6.50.

XV

The Nineteenth Century: Victorian Period

LAUREL BRAKE and OWEN KNOWLES

This chapter is arranged as follows: 1. Verse, by Laurel Brake; 2. The Novel, by Owen Knowles; 3. Prose, by Laurel Brake; 4. Drama, by Owen Knowles. A very comprehensive Victorian Studies Bibliography appears in *VS*, annotated guides in *VP* and *SEL*, and specialist lists in *VPN, ELT, BIS*, and *NCTR*.

1. Verse

William T. Going's book[1] studies the phenomenon of the sonnet sequence in the Victorian period. He begins with a general chapter on the nature of the Victorian 'sequences', a term coined by D. G. Rossetti; essays on the sonnets of the Tennysons and the Rossettis, Robert Browning, Arnold, *Modern Love*, J. A. Symonds, and W. S. Blunt follow. The work maps Victorian authors of sonnets and their notions and employment of the genre, and a useful appendix lists the many eighteenth- and nineteenth-century sonnet sequences. But Going attempts too much; not enough is said about individual sequences and poems, and *Scanty Plot of Ground* seems a bad example of formalist genre criticism. The author is over fond of numerical analyses: what is the significance of Tennyson having written 'more sonnets than Arnold and more than Meredith if the seizains of *Modern Love* are excluded', particularly when in the Meredith chapter Going calls the poems of *Modern Love* 'sixteen-line sonnets'? Other aspects of the work manifest strain – an unrewarding chapter on Robert Browning's usually occasional and unremarkable sonnets is included while Elizabeth Barrett Browning's *Sonnets from the Portuguese* appear briefly in the introductory chapter where Going affirms that their 'significance. . . cannot be overemphasized in any account, however brief, of the sonnet-sequence in English'. This book, useful as its mapping is, has all the marks of a thesis which has not been rewritten for publication; nor has the bibliography been updated.

In *Swinburne, Hardy, Lawrence, and the Burden of Belief*[2], Ross C. Murfin concerns himself with a sequence of influence and the independent reaction of his three agnostics to Christianity and Romanticism. He illustrates the misprision and adoption of Romanticism by the Victorians,

[1] *Scanty Plot of Ground*, by William T. Going. The Hague, Paris, and New York: Mouton, 1976. pp. 174. DM40.

[2] *Swinburne, Hardy, Lawrence and the Burden of Belief*, by Ross C. Murfin. Chicago, Ill., and London: U. of Chicago P. pp. xii + 238. £10.50.

and the common effort of these three to build other faiths from the rubble of those destroyed. Murfin offers two chapters on Swinburne's poetry which are traditional in their method of close reading and exegesis, a chapter on Swinburne's and Hardy's poems, and another on Hardy's fiction. He concludes with essays on the relations of his authors to Romantic forms and to Christianity. Lawrence figures comparatively briefly. Throughout the author brandishes his knowledge of Romantic and Victorian poetry, and the argument consequently lacks grace, obscured as it is by side-long glimpses of others' lines, expression, and criticism. The book, which originates in a thesis, is sometimes busy, informed without finally being wise. Still, Murfin's contemplation of how Romanticism and faith fare – their death and revival – in the works of these authors will be suggestive to readers who are thoroughly conversant with nineteenth-century literature, and able to dismiss the overstatements, spot the lacunae, catch their breath, and rescue the truths.

Raleigh Trevelyan's *A Pre-Raphaelite Circle*[3], a biography of Pauline Trevelyan (1816–1866), draws on unpublished material from the Trevelyan manuscripts at Newcastle and on family papers. These include many letters from Ruskin, some of which pertain to the Ruskins' marriage. As writer for the periodicals, botanist, and an art collector and patron, Lady Trevelyan befriended beside Ruskin, William Bell Scott, Thomas Woolner, Swinburne, D. G. and Christina Rossetti, Francis Pattison, and Jane Carlyle; *A Pre-Raphaelite Circle* treats them all in some detail, but it is particularly full on Ruskin. Though not in a scholarly format, the narrative seems careful, accurate, and informed; sources are indicated for the most part, and the author has managed his multiple personae to good effect; the tone and complexity of the circle emerge clearly. It provides new material concerning lives of various Victorian writers, and artists, and it is absorbing to read.

In *Songs of the People*[4] Brian Hollingworth provides an annotated anthology, arranged by theme, of Lancashire dialect poetry of the industrial revolution. Unfamiliar words are glossed in the margins around the poems which are mainly Victorian, and a useful bibliography lists a wide range of sources. In the introductory essay, Hollingworth considers the outbreak of dialect writing in Lancashire between 1856 and 1870, a phenomenon which, along with the poems themselves, will interest the student of Victorian fiction and realism as well as the reader of Victorian poetry. The work of twenty-three poets is included, on subjects such as Fairs and Festivities, Home, Work, The Cotton Panic, and Old Age.

A pamphlet[5] of the Manchester Studies Group (Manchester Poly) by B. E. Maidment and A. S. Crehan reprints J. C. Prince's poem 'The Death of the Factory Child' for the first time since 1841, presents alternative contexts – literary and political – for it in two essays, and concludes with a bibliography. Maidment's interesting essay touches on important general questions surrounding the literary appreciation of Victorian working class

[3] *A Pre-Raphaelite Circle*, by Raleigh Trevelyan. Chatto & Windus. pp. 256. £8.50.
[4] *Songs of the People*, ed. by Brian Hollingworth. Manchester: Manchester U.P. pp. x + 166. £3.95.
[5] *J. C. Prince and 'The Death of the Factory Child'*, by B. E. Maidment and A. S. Crehan. Manchester, Lancs.: Manchester Studies Group, Manchester Polytechnic.

poetry. Crehan, who sees the poem as part of the renewed agitation for factory reform and the Ten Hours Hill in the Chartist period, offers a different notion of the poem's success. As a whole the pamphlet contains a well-defined debate which would serve as a useful stimulant of classroom discussions.

PQ (1977) prints the proceedings of an MLA Forum on the Arthurian literature of the nineteenth and twentieth centuries, and three items pertain to Victorian literature. James R. Kincaid argues that Tennyson casts romantic and exalted elements of the tradition into an ironic plot in the *Idylls*. The six Arthurian poems in Morris's *The Defence of Guenevere* similarly constitute a criticism of life according to Aubrey E. Calyon, although here Camelot itself is a world of moral ambiguities like the present, and not an idealised heroic world against which the flawed present is defined. James D. Merriman unearths Victorian Arthurians other than Tennyson, Morris, Arnold, and Swinburne, and surveys characteristics of some of the more than sixty authors he discovers.

In 'Science, Religion and Personification in Poetry' (*CERVE*) Jerome Bump notes the faltering of pastoral in 'Lines Written in Kensington Gardens'; its contemporary confident presence in Hopkins is coupled by Bump with Hopkins's recognition of the importance of personification through the ultimate personification: the cosmic Christ. The resistance and capitulation of poets and critics to the dictates of scientific rationalism are surveyed by Bump, from Marvell through Wordsworth and Ruskin to Wallace Stevens, in what is an interesting piece.

In 'Victorian Philology and Victorian Poetry', a noteworthy article in *VN*, Dennis Taylor considers the work of Hardy and Hopkins, which exhibits contrivance and archaism alongside the 'real language of men'. While the experimental language of both poets represents responses to Victorian philology, Hardy dramatises its 'gloomy paradox' and Hopkins its 'optimistic possibility'. Lloyd G. Siemens in 'The Poet as Huckster' describes the history of the nineteenth-century literary annual and the authors whose work became staples of the genre; they include Lamb, Thomas Moore, Southey, Lockhart, Scott, Wordsworth, and Tennyson (*ELN*).

As a conclusion to *VP*'s special number 'The Victorianism of Victorian Poetry' Wendell V. Harris considers Arnold's 'Philomela' as the essential Victorian poem and looks before, around, and after it for comparisons out of which he ekes a series of Victorian characteristics. In *Criticism* Charles Altieri regards lyrics of Arnold and Tennyson not 'as embodying representative Victorian beliefs' but as revelatory of the origins of modernism and in particular the problems of authority. Despite its verbosity and critical posture, this long article contains some interesting readings of the most well-known poems of Arnold and Tennyson. In an essay where aesthetics of the visual arts and literature vie for dominance with critical commentary on specific texts, Gerhard Joseph considers the iconography of the extensive 'looking glass' as window and the reflexive one as mirror in works of Browning, Arnold, and Tennyson (*VP*). He also views them as types of mediating and framing things. Also in *VP*, Dorothy F. Donnelly studies three poems by Spasmodics – *Festus, A Life Drama*, and *Balder* – as types of popular literature in order to explain the contrast between their Victorian and present-day reception. But Donnelly indulges in some whopping generalisations which come badly unstuck, and Browning is described as one of a number of poets who subscribe to a subjective poetry with little emphasis placed on art or craft; in successive paragraphs she argues that the Spasmodic poems appealed to the 'readers' desire for the realization of egalitarian principles' *and* the penchant for hero-worship.

With the shortage of texts for teaching Victorian literature so acute, it is sad to note that Dent (Everyman) has replaced K. Allott's edition of *Poems*, and the separate edition of *Essays in Criticism, First and Second Series* with one new volume of selected poems and prose edited by M. Allott[6]. Although the editor reflects on the inadequacies of such selectiveness, she attempts the task, keeping 'representativeness and centrality' and 'the interplay between Arnold's poetic achievement and his critical responsiveness' as her principal criteria. This volume does not include 'Sohrab and Rustum' (save for 18 lines) or 'Balder Dead', so that the new style heralded by the 1853 Preface is not to be seen. 'Obermann Once More' is also absent as is 'The Strayed Reveller', and 'Haworth Churchyard' is represented by a fragment. Poetry should not be read in this way. With the exception of the 1853 Preface and 'The Study of Poetry' *all* the prose consists of fragments – thirteen pages from *Culture and Anarchy* for example. This echoes the worst of academic publishing in America, where students get most of their undergraduate reading from such anthologies and fragments of texts. One would not complain so boldly, if this were not one of the very few paperback editions of Arnold's poetry available at a price students can afford. Beside the 'multitude of regrets' which haunt the editor lies a racy salesmanship in the otherwise learned introduction, where the editor also tries in vain to fill in the gaps in the text that follows. There are three pages of sound bibliographical information, short headnotes and annotation for each selection, and lineation for the poetry. One feels that the editor has been ill-served by the publishers here – insufficient space, inferior paper, and an American market firmly in mind.

Park Honan, in extracts from a forthcoming biography of Arnold in *VP*, traces Arnold's path from his experience at Fox How to the European sentimental school, effected in part through the agency of Mary Claude, a young contemporary neighbour of Arnold's from the late 1830s, and his friend in the late 1840s. Mary and the Sentimentalists helped Arnold to concentrate large spans of his emotional life in brief lyrics and to rid himself of English literary influences. Also in *VP*, using much of the same material, Honan goes on to connect Mary Claude with the Switzerland lyrics and Marguerite; she, not Clough, was Arnold's 'most suggestive' friend from 1847–1849.

In the same periodical Ruth apRoberts traces the theme of vocation in and through his use of symbols in the major poems in the same periodical: she discusses Glanvill's *Vanity of Dogmatising* as a symbol pervading Arnold's minor poems and through his use of symbols in the major poems tree; she examines closely the five songs of Callicles which impart figuratively a 'radical modification' of the meaning of the whole, the discourses

[6] *Matthew Arnold, Selected Poems and Prose*, ed. by Miriam Allott. London, Melbourne, and Toronto: Dent; New York: E.P. Dutton. pp. lviii + 296. £4.95 and £1.95.

of Empedocles, and the dialogue between the mode of Callicles and that of Empedocles. In *Expl* Patrick J. Creevy makes explicit the implications of the tidal metaphor in 'Dover Beach' – that nothing is permanent except love, but that at the same time everything returns upon itself and then withdraws. D. S. Neff contributes to the discussion of the influence of Empedocles on 'Dover Beach' (*VN*) by noting use of Fragment 20 of *On Nature* in the poem which takes its philosophy and setting from Empedocles' 'the surf-swept beaches and drear shores of life'. In *DUJ* Paul Dean and Jacqueline Johnson trace the recurring position of Limbo in the structure of Arnold's poems, first in poems with imagined figures and then in the elegies on real people.

In 'Undermined Metaphors in Arnold's Poetry' (*VP*) Elisabeth G. Gitter writes very interestingly on the theoretical implications of Arnold's transfer of emotion from tenor to vehicle, a movement from comparison of man and nature to their identification, found in 'To Marguerite-Continued', 'Self-Dependence', and 'Dover Beach'. For Arnold, the 'All' is hidden, not revealed by phenomena; to find it, the poet must look inward; Nature provides an example, but cannot furnish metaphors for human experience. Mark Siegchrist in *PLL* notes two elements in Arnold's construction of the action of 'Sohrab and Rustum', the symmetry of its structure, and the use of colour to focus attention on the climax.

Two critics consider Arnold in relation to other authors. In *VP* Dorothy Deering describes clearly and concisely the antithetical poetics of Arnold and Clough, and urges the application of Clough's and not Arnold's critical standards in criticism of Clough's verse. D. J. James's contrast in *Matthew Arnold and the Decline of English Romanticism* of Arnold and Baudelaire's views of the imagination is probed and endorsed by Norma Rowen in *CL* who also examines closely the two poets' treatment of nature.

Richard C. Tobias presents a study of Thomas Edward Brown (1830-1897)[7], who, writing in Manx dialect, is regarded as the national poet of the Isle of Man. Of the generation of Arnold, Clough, and Morris, his work was published by Macmillan in the 1880s in a form Brown disavowed. Tobias makes use of much new material in this well-written, succinct, and absorbing biography which also has much to tell us of Oxford in the 1850s, Victorian publishing, and Clifton College, Bristol.

If Morse Peckham has turned to photo-offset for accuracy with some success in his edition of *Sordello* (below), Cora Kaplan in her *Aurora Leigh*[8] has multiplied errors through photo-offset and, relying on an earlier edition to provide 'full annotations', also avoids that exacting task, and contents herself with 'sources of the more obscure references, where the context does not reveal the meaning. Place names and contemporary political and intellectual figures have not been included'. This shoddy practice seems inexcusable in an edition which is clearly aimed at students, and which announces itself as the 'first twentieth-century edition' (this despite the reliance on the 1900 American edition by Porter and Clarke for annotation). Every copy of this edition I have seen misprints the

[7] *T.E. Brown*, by Richard C. Tobias. Boston, Mass.: Twayne. TEAS 213. pp. 186. $9.95.

[8] *'Aurora Leigh' and Other Poems, by Elizabeth Barrett Browning*, introd. by Cora Kaplan. The Women's P. pp. 416. hb £4.95, pb £2.95.

sequence of the poem on pages 79–80, 83–85, and 170–173. From the narrow margins of the prelims, the rigorous use of every recto and verso, and the quality of the paper, it is clear that low price was a priority of The Women's Press, but mass access to an inaccurate and scantily annotated text is a doubtful virtue. Kaplan's ample introduction is polemical and informative in a brisk allusive manner, and best on the poem's literary context and sources.

EBB is currently one of the 'particular topics' of *BSN*; Lucien L. Agosta introduces and annotates a long unpublished letter (1864) to Mary Russell Mitford from EBB who comments on the 'inconvenience of celebrity' as a 'noble tax' which authors owe to their public. Also in *BSN* Althea Hayter writes on Thackeray's motives for refusing to publish 'Lord Walter's Wife' in *Cornhill* in 1861, and Malcolm Hicks pursues this by examining Robert Browning's involvement in the affair which hinged on his distaste for periodicals, his contempt for Thackeray's editorial prudery, and his comments on it in *Red Cotton Night-Cap Country*, which echoes 'Lord Walter's Wife'. Together these fascinating articles make a significant contribution to our knowledge of the relation between periodicals and authors. EBB's early poetics of the 1820s occupy M. Raymond, and Fred Thomson tackles the poet's vocabulary numerically, and compares her use of 'all' and 'light' with that of Matthew Arnold; both articles appear in *BSN*. In the same periodical, in 'EBB: the Natural and the Spiritual'' John Woolford, examines the progression from Romantic subjectivity to a Victorian appreciation of otherness; her difficulties are shown to exemplify the wider predicament of the Victorian poet. In *SBC* Rita A. Humphrey identifies the present whereabouts of E. F. Bridell's drawing of EBB, and traces its journey there. Anne Lohrli publishes three sonnets dedicated to EBB which appeared in the *New York Tribune* in 1853 (*BIS*). By Helen Whitman, a minor American poet, the sonnets indicate EBB's popularity in the U.S.

The editors of *The Brownings' Correspondence. A Checklist*[9] are engaged on the publication of the whole of the poets' correspondence; this checklist, 9789 entries, is a by-product of that project and an invitation for corrections and addition to it. The introduction briefly describes the history and scope of the work and its editorial method. The entries are listed chronologically, alphabetically, and by collection. A tentative calendar of each poet's travels based on information in the correspondence is appended. Extracts from some 1700 missing letters are quoted where known from catalogue descriptions in order to aid their identification and location.

Morse Peckham's marginally emended edition of *Sordello*[10] results from his unhappy experience of editing the Ohio Browning, as described by Peckham in several recent articles. Here he has retained the pagination of his copy-text, and moreover reproduced that text by photo-offset so that new errors are avoided. Peckham's thirty-eight emendations are

[9] *The Brownings' Correspondence. A Checklist*, compiled by Philip Kelley and Ronald Hudson. New York: The Browning Institute and Wedgestone P. pp. xxiii + 498. $95.

[10] *Sordello, by Robert Browning*, ed. by Morse Peckham. Troy, N.Y.: Whitson Pub. Co., 1977. pp. xxiii + 293. $15.

indicated in the margins and explained by notes. In an appendix he lists corrections to the Ohio Edition's Editorial Notes by Roma King which, though 'the most valuable notes for *Sordello* yet done. . .are marred by numerous errors, some. . .crucial'. The economy of labour involved in this method, the high degree of accuracy, and the relatively low price of the volume are commendable, but the lack of lineation and of full notes make this volume incomplete in itself. Presumably their inclusion would raise the price, though not to the level of the Ohio *Sordello*.

BIS includes an annotated bibliography by William S. Peterson for Browning studies in 1976 and 'Supplement No. 1 to *The Brownings' Correspondence. A Checklist*' by Philip Kelley and Ronald Hudson, compilers of the *Checklist*; it records some three hundred corrections and additions. All in all, the standard of articles in *BIS* is higher this year than ever before.

Numerous allusions to Carlyle's various works are found by Susan Hardy Aiken in 'Bishop Blougram's Apology' (*VP*) which Aiken links closely with the contemporaneous *Latter-Day Pamphlets*. References to Johnson and Boswell, the Carlylean model of the relation between hero and worshipper, clarify the relation between Blougram (as quack) and Gigadibs (as nascent hero). By recalling the pattern of history against which the same poem is set, Julia Markus, in a lively piece in *VS*, reveals the way in which Browning used living models in the poem. She accomplishes this in an informative examination of three periodicals in which Cardinal Wiseman and the Papal Aggression were debated in 1850–1, the *Dublin Review*, the *Globe*, and *Punch*; Browning refers to *Punch* in the poem, and Markus shows that in 1850–1 'Father Prout', long regarded as a possible model for Gigadibs, was editor of the anti-Wiseman *Globe*, and a friend of Browning's. Markus convincingly shows that neither Gigadibs nor Blougram had Browning's approval; rather the poem is concerned finally with the triumph of the life of faith over the life of doubt; the poem transcends its local inspiration. The same critic seeks to show the existence of a rapport between the Brownings by tracing the differences and marked similarities between the structure, imagery, and political content of EBB's *Casa Guidi Windows* (1851) and Robert's 'Old Pictures in Florence' (1853); the first poem emerges as 'the unacknowledged armature' of the second (*BIS*). Markus argues from an unpublished letter that 'Old Pictures in Florence' stems from 1853 circumstances different from those of 1850 which have generally been associated with the poem. Flavia Alaya in the same periodical makes a similar point about the rapport between the Brownings; in 'The Brownings' Italy' she attempts to unseat the truisms about Robert Browning's politics found in criticism of the poet, and to come to a better understanding of the politics and poetics of both Brownings; critics have also misrepresented the tone and intelligence of EBB's politics and the extent of disagreement concerning politics between wife and husband. Alaya treats 'Prince Hohenstiel-Schwangau', *Aurora Leigh*, *Casa Guidi Windows*, and *The Ring and the Book* as in part a memorial act. This long article is of interest with regard to the poetry and to critical method.

In *VP* Russell Astley examines a series of ill-thought-through prosodic experiments by Browning which are all logaoedic, a mixture of iambic and anapaestic feet which may point to any mingling of measures. In 'The Pied Piper of Hamelin', 'The Statue and the Bust', 'A Light Woman' and 'A Lover's Quarrel' Browning refuses or fails to decide whether he is writing in an accentual-syllabic or a strong-stress metre. 'Love Among the Ruins' exhibits a third more successful kind of logaoedic method.

William Baker has discovered an unknown manuscript by Browning which he transcribes and annotates in *BSN*. It treats William Charles Macready, and indicates that their disagreement during production of *A Blot in the Scutcheon* was, in Browning's opinion, due to the bad influence of John Forster and the *Examiner* on Macready. J. W. Binns shows that Browning's contrast of Tully's and Ulpian's Latin in 'The Bishop Orders His Tomb' is cited to point out a learned disagreement between Gandolf and his successor about Latin style, not to denigrate Ulpian (*SBC*). In *VP* Vincenta Colby notes that the ailing Saul of Browning's poem who is depicted as a Victorian melancholic does not derive from the Biblical source nor from Smart's *A Song to David*; he is Browning's creation, and Colby suggests that 'Saul' represents Browning's exorcism of romantic melancholy. Because Browning banished melancholy, he failed to command the affection of the reading public. The substance of this article is unfortunately introduced by a series of commonplaces and overstatements in which Browning's debt to Shelley is minimised to prepare for the author's stress on Browning's celebration of social healthy values.

In an investigation of Browning's response to Shelley in *VN*, Loy D. Martin stresses its Victorian nature. He closely compares the opening of *Pauline* with 'To a Skylark', 'Mont Blanc', and 'Letter to Maria Gisborne', even in the opening of *The Ring and the Book*, Browning uses a metaphor of 'mixing' and 'assimilation' for the poet's confrontation with his source that is surprisingly similar to the metaphors in his tribute to Shelley in *Pauline* in the consciousness of discontinuity and the desire for fusion.

Curtis Dahl shows that in the poems Browning associates moral values with architectural styles, and that the connotations of the styles echo the ideas of Ruskin (*SBC*). Conversely Ruskin's architectonics in 'The Nature of Gothic' can be applied to Browning's poems. Also in *SBC* Mario L. D'Avanzo discusses why Browning chose a Rabbi, of all possible models of piety, optimism, and hope throughout the Judeo-Christian world. He suggests that the Rabbi's doubt – his model, Ibn Ezra, was the first to write a higher criticism of the Bible – rather than his faith alone, attracted the poet. That Frederick Harrison's article 'On the Soul and Future Life', in the *Nineteenth Century*, June and July 1877, is an important unifying pre-occupation in the seemingly varied contents of *La Saisiaz: The Two Poets of Croisic* is Cory Breman Davies' contention in *SBC*. The poems reflect Browning's interest in the movement from knowledge to belief, and to an affirmation of life and love.

Margaret Doane argues in a note (*SBC*) that Caponsacchi's transformation by the good of Pompilia is instant rather than gradual, and similar to that of the patriot in 'The Italian in England', while in *BSN* Paul Turner discusses the opposition between the divination and mechanism of truth in the lawyer's monologues in *The Ring and the Book*. In ' "Childe Roland" and the Urban Wilderness' in *BSN*, Philip Drew compares the landscape of the poem and Roland's reactions to it with depictions of urban and rural slums in Dickens and Ruskin, and suggests that the territory of the poem is contemporary as well as medieval. This is a well-written and informative piece.

In *VP* Mark D. Hawthorne reveals systematic structural techniques in *Sordello* which are 'mechanical' and 'simple': repetition of phrases, clauses, lines, or images indicates digressive units and transitions, and repetition of descriptive details indicates development. These suggest that the poem is not fractured narratively and thematically in half as is usually thought. Ian Jack concerns himself with rare words or usage in *Sordello*, which he is editing and annotating for an Oxford English Texts edition (*BIS*). John Pettigrew, feeling noticeably acerbic, lists in detail the many erroneous notes on *Sordello* in the Ohio Browning volume edited by Roma A. King Jr (*Libr*). In *BSN* William S. Peterson reflects on the editing of past editions of the Brownings' correspondence in anticipation of the new collected edition edited by Phillip Kelley and Ronald Hudson (see their *Checklist* above).

While new editors are responsible for *BSN*, it continues to solicit and publish articles on particular topics. In 'Exploring *Asolando*' Donald S. Hair ranges through the volume, considering Browning's conception of fancies and facts, and related questions. Daniel R. Karlin locates sources for 'Which?' and 'Speculative' from *Asolando* in the poet's correspondence with EBB and, acting on Harold Bloom's suggestions in *Poetry and Repression*, W. David Shaw treats the 'Prologue' to the volume as Browning's Intimations Ode. Brendan Kenny pleads for more readers and texts for Browning's later poetry in 'Browning as a Cultural Critic: *Red Cotton Night-Cap Country*' (*BIS*). In *UTQ* Donald Hair regards the notion of the palace of art as an aspect of the nineteenth-century endeavour to contain within a single structure the whole of human knowledge and experience. Using 'Kubla Khan' as the seed of the nineteenth-century image, Hair argues that its attention to the role of memory, the link between music and architecture, and the figure of the inspired poet are important in the palaces of Tennyson and Browning. Comparison of 'The Palace of Art' and the one in 'Abt Vogler' shows Browning to be both traditional and self-expressive in his treatment of the theme, which is also discernable in early poems such as *Paracelsus* and *Sordello*. Browning's works attempt to contain within a single consciousness a whole world.

Adrienne Munich contends that in 'Cleon' Browning has invented an artist who fulfilled his own ambitions and shared his worries about immortality (*BIS*). The emblems of this poem suggest an approach to Browning's poetry in general, and the author compares 'Cleon' to earlier poems with Greek settings and elegiac themes: 'Ulysses', 'The Lotos Eaters', and 'Empedocles on Etna'. In *SBC* G. W. Spence shows how 'Cleon' contrasts with the Greek poets who anticipated the notion of the God proclaimed by St Paul. In the same journal James E. Neufeld explains the major musical references in the poems, in order to make clear Browning's technical knowledge of music. Through a reading of the poems and letters, Malcolm Richardson discerns the poet's taste in music as that of 'a musical reactionary' (*BIS*).

Ruth Roberts considers the functional similarities in Pippa's role and that of a Greek chorus (*SBC*), and there too, in a piece on 'A Grammarian's

Funeral', Mary W. Schneider stresses the importance of Renaissance scholarship to the poem and the art of poetry in Browning's view. That three poems of *Men and Women*, 'Master Hugues of Saxe-Gotha', 'Memorabilia', and 'Popularity' are indebted to a letter of Keats' is shown by Yao Shen in *SBC* where, in a note on 'An Epistle from Karshish', Joseph Solimine Jr considers the definition of science in the poem and its positive relation to religion; the same author stresses development as Browning's central paradigm, one which informs 'Johannes Agricola in Meditation' in which the static state of perfection is sought. In two more articles in *SBC*, C. F. Thomas identifies the painting of St Laurence at Prato in 'Fra Lippo Lippi' as an oil painting by two seventeenth-century painters, Mario Belassi and Carlo Dolci, rather than a fresco by Lippi, and T. P. Wolfe provides a detailed rhetorical and psychological analysis of 'Caliban upon Setebos' and a psychological explanation of the implicitly comic nature of the dramatic monologue as a form. John Woolford and Daniel Karlin provide in *BSN* a transcript and notes for the draft of an unfinished poem by Browning known as 'Aeschylus' Soliloquy', a facsimile of which appears. The editors date it later than DeVane, after EBB's death. In *BIS* Alan Gribben describes and analyses Samuel Clemens' public readings of and infatuation with Browning's poetry during and after the 1880s.

A new bibliography of Clough[11] is intended to meet the special needs of collectors, librarians, and textual scholars. It supplements the enumerative bibliography by R. M. Gollin, W. E. Houghton, and Michael Timko (N.Y., 1967) by filling out knowledge of individual Clough items and their printed form, and by bringing together summaries of earlier scattered comment. Title-pages are reproduced and some problems of dating or provenance of particular texts are discussed. Section A covers Clough's separately published works up to *Poems and Prose Remains* (1869) and Section B consists of an annotated checklist of Clough editions since 1869. In an account of Clough and his publishers in the introduction, Scott contributes to the increasing and wide-ranging explorations of Victorian publishing by contemporary critics. It is curious that such an experienced scholar as Scott should not have decided on one date for so important a source as the enumerative catalogue of Gollin, Houghton, and Timko which appears variously here as '1967', '1968', and 'n.d. 1968'. Where Dorothy Deering locates the roots of modernism in Clough's poetics as distinguished from Arnold's (see Arnold articles above), Scott in *VP* views the 'modernist' label as more evaluative than analytical, and instead stresses Clough's Victorianism. Scott uses the elements of Victorianism defined by Michael Timko (*YW* 56.301) to show Clough's quintessential qualities, and as an incriminating contrast to the modernist emphases of recent work, which have resulted in serious distortion of Clough's achievement. This is a learned and provocative piece.

Richard H. Taylor presents and edits four personal notebooks of Hardy[12] – two called 'Memoranda'; the 'School of Painting' notebook, and the 'Trumpet-Major' notebook; all are now at the Dorset County

[11] *The Early Editions of Arthur Hugh Clough*, ed. by Patrick Greig Scott. New York and London: Garland, 1977. pp. xiv + 106. $20.90.

[12] *The Personal Notebooks of Thomas Hardy*, ed. by Richard H. Taylor. Macmillan. pp. xxxii + 301. £15.

Museum. In a long appendix he introduces, reproduces, and annotates most of the typescript passages omitted from F. E. Hardy's *The Life of Thomas Hardy*, the author's disguised autobiography. The informative and full notes unfailingly help the Hardy reader, whom there is much to interest. In *The Older Hardy* [13] Robert Gittings takes up the biography where *Young Thomas Hardy* concluded, in 1876 when Hardy and Emma were both thirty-five. Gittings's subject is a life at the centre of which lies the literature, and he manages a wealth of material deftly; emphases, selection, and structure are clear, economical, and dramatically conceived without appearing to strive for the illusion of fiction. He offers lively interpretations of the prose fiction and poems, often using notebook material and correspondence for illumination. Among other chapters, those on 'The Original Tess', 'Jude and Tess', 'Dynasts and Destinies', and 'A Satire of Circumstance' reflect the considerable orientation of this balanced biography to the literature.

John Bayley's *An Essay on Hardy*[14] is a graceful, leisured, tough contemplation of Hardy, primarily his prose; but the author's refusal to restrict himself to a single announced theme, a resistance borne out in the chapter headings which are simply numerical, leaves him genuinely free to get to the quintessential elements of Hardy's creative procedures. The poetry is drawn on to bastion the steady succession of insights because Bayley views the prose and poetry as closely linked: 'The effectiveness of the poem is that it is written by a novelist. In various ways all Hardy's poems are'. But among early chapters of the *Essay*, the poetry figures importantly. Good criticism on Hardy is rare, but this is it.

H. L. Weatherby writes a thoughtful review article on recent criticism of Hardy's poetry in *SR*, and in *1837–1901* Chris Wrigley reviews the publications and events of 1978 which concern Hardy. These include the Dorchester Festival and the first volume of the *Letters*. Cynthia Sampson publishes a forgotten letter (1893) of Hardy's which concerns the naming of streets in Dorchester (*N&Q*).

In an *E&S* piece entitled 'Hardy's Poetical Metonymy' John Bayley suggests that animism signifies the way poetry in general works rather than the poet's attitude to the natural world. Unlike most poets, Hardy takes the literalness of his frequent anthropomorphic inventions for granted and makes no distinction between fact and metaphor. Bayley attributes Hardy's mixture of belief and the literalism which contradicts it to Hardy's unwillingness to have an audience, even though he wanted to publish his poems. In *BSUF* A. H. Harrison rambles through various perspectives on Hardy's uses of Nature in the poetry, and discovers 'a striking versatility of concept and technique in Hardy's poetry' which distinguishes him from the three previous generations of nineteenth-century nature writers. H. Neville Davies provides a gloss for 1.4 of 'In the Cemetery' where Pharisee refers not only to a religious sect but to the Sussex dialect word for fairy, 'Pharisee' or 'farisee' (*N&Q*). In 'Thomas Hardy's Poetry of Transcendence' Geoffrey Harvey discusses a small group of poems which achieve a 'transcending freedom'; Hardy manages to make in them an existential statement within the content of the Romantic tradition (*ArielE*). In 'Hardy's War Poetry' in

[13] *The Older Hardy*, by Robert Gittings. Heinemann. pp. xii + 244. £6.95.
[14] *An Essay on Hardy*, by John Bayley. Cambridge: C.U.P. pp. 237. £6.95.

FDP James Hazen examines poems concerning the Napoleonic, Boer, and Great Wars, and finds in them the emergence of an increasingly critical attitude toward war, and a deepening of the poet's sense of the importance of war in history.

Margaret Mahar begins her impressive 'Hardy's Poetry of Renunciation' (*ELH*) with a discussion of the discrepancy between Hardy's theory of narrative form as organic and his practice in which the future repeats rather than fulfils the past; out of this constraint Hardy escapes into the freedom of the lyric with its purely formal requirements. The distance between beginning and end of narrative in the novel is eschewed in favour of the identity of rhyme. Form and meaning are deliberately unjoined in the poems – rather he proliferated forms which dispel meanings. The relation between Hardy's divided vision and the style of his poetry is also discussed by Lloyd G. Siemens in *DR*. To the motif of unreconciled antinomies identified by Samuel Hynes, Siemens adds the rhetoric of negation as a second pattern which does no violence to Hardy's vision. Fluently, Siemens considers Hardy's use of devices of negation such as the debate, the sequence of negatives, the negative particle, the subjunctive, and an idiom of fatigue. Eugene Williamson probes the motives of Hardy's stated antagonistic reactions to Nietzsche in the face of the affinities with the philosopher seen in poems such as 'God's Funeral' and 'A Plaint to Man' (*CLS*).

Paddy Kitchen designates her biography of Hopkins[15] a 'personal rather than an academic study', which invites comparison with Philip Henderson's life of Tennyson noted below. But unlike Henderson, she brings a distinctive interpretation to her subject, in her assessment of unpublished confessional passages in Hopkins's diaries which concern his fascination with the 'physical beauty of choristers and certain of his fellow alumni'. Kitchen debates the significance of these passages without tendentiousness, and concludes that they may well indicate, as the poems do, sexual ambivalence rather than homosexuality. Hopkins's poems live today because in them he recreated the moment of arousing wonder at physical attraction and described the experience of barren despair. In his study of Hopkins[16], John Robinson rejects the opposing notions of the main camps of critics; Hopkins was neither an individual suppressed by the Jesuits, nor a man made by the Jesuits; for Robinson the verse and the religion are 'attendant on the same aspirations in the man'. Hopkins is of a piece, and completely involved with his extreme purposes, his 'choking aspiration to excellence'. Robinson's fresh and considered reassessments pertain to the interpretation by critics of the relation between poems and the life, with the poems sharing and usually dominating the foreground. This work is far more closely concerned with the poetry and the poetic sensibility and less with the life than Kitchen; it is tauter too. Robinson takes this same path, transcending and obviating received views, in connection with Pater whose positive rather than negative relation with Hopkins he stresses. But his reading of Pater is misleadingly selective, and he ends up contradicting himself and misrepresenting Pater's notions of the artist

[15] *Gerard Manley Hopkins*, by Paddy Kitchen. Hamish Hamilton. pp. 243. £7.50.
[16] *In Extremity. A Study of Gerard Manley Hopkins*, by John Robinson. Cambridge: C.U.P. pp. xii + 175. £6.90.

and the relation of life and art. But his positive point survives: Hopkins and Pater shared an interest in form. *In Extremity* is well written and clear; it wears its learning gracefully.

In the third number of *HQ* R. F. Giles presents a comprehensive bibliography of work published between 1974 and 1977. Research appearing in Japan, India, Holland, France, and Spain is included, as well as theses. Brief contact between Hopkins and Edward Dowden during the poet's years in Dublin is noted by David J. DeLaura in *HQ*; the Winter number of *HQ* is a double issue which reprints papers delivered at the MLA conference, on Hopkins biography by Alison G. Sulloway (her 'Study of Representative Biographical Materials, Priorities, and Techniques' reviews critically sixteen biographies which concern Hopkins), R. F. Giles (an assessment of progress and possibilities), R. K. R. Thornton (on the poet's conversion and isolation from his family), Norman White (on the 'Epithalamion'), Michael Allsopp (Hopkins's studies at Oxford), and Jerome Bump (an unpublished letter and a catalogue of the Texas Collection). In a letter to *HQ* Father Robert Boyle challenges the theology in 'The Science of Sacraments' by James Leggio (*YW* 58.292) who, in his reply, suggests that their disagreement stems from a basic divergence of interests between Catholic and non-Catholic scholars. In the same journal Nathan Cervo offers a new and illuminating reading of 'Plough Down Sillion Shine', and R. Gallet comments on 'The Windhover' and 'Hurrahing in Harvest' as paired poems. In *DUJ* John Pick reviews approaches to 'The Windhover'.

A link between 'Patience' and Milton's 'On his Blindness', of a kind which Harold Bloom terms *tessera* or 'antithetical completion', is revealed by J. J. Glavin in *TSLL*. Hopkins tends not to imitate Milton, but to alter and correct Milton's model. In *VP* Florence S. Boos considers from correspondence another debt of Hopkins to Richard Watson Dixon, and characterises it as 'Christian Pre-Raphaelitism'. Boos examines those of Dixon's poems which Hopkins copied out to take with him to the novitiate in relation to Hopkins's subsequent work, specifically *The Wreck*, and Hopkins's response to Dixon's narrative romances. In *Expl* R. F. Giles turns his attention to the word 'spell' in stanza 3 of *The Wreck* and searches for an 'explosive' rather than any single meaning; 'spell' is a verb which takes in the meanings associated with reading it as a noun. Joaquin Kuhn reveals a serious aspect of 'Pied Beauty' by noting its denotations as well as its connotations (*SEL*). Using 'prosodic arithmetic', she shows how the poet found enforced equilibrium in the poem, which both follows and breaks the rules of sonnet form.

In *HQ* G. D. Monsman detects an imagery common to the ten sonnets of 1877 expressing the experience of Nature as to the paradoxical condition of rising and falling simultaneously which echoes Christ's death and resurrection, and in *VP* J. F. Cotter writes on 'The Inscape of the Passion' and Hopkins's poetry. Edward Proffitt, in *HQ*, argues for a contrast at the end of the octave in 'The Starlight Night' rather than the customary interpretation that line 8 is a culmination of lines 1–7, and an ecstatic transition to the sestet. The same author in *VP* speculates on the significance of the word 'combs' in 'To R.B.' which he interprets as furthering the metaphor of gestation. In 'How Leaden is your Echo?' (*HQ*) R. K. R. Thornton takes issue with S. Bagchee's contention (*YW* 57.273) that Henry King's

'The Exequy' was a source for 'The Leaden Echo and the Golden Echo'. He shows that the 'close verbal and thematic echoes' are part of a well-known tradition, or belong to a different source: the Bible. In a careful and suggestive piece in the same journal, Thomas A. Zaniello explores 'The Origins and Use of Hopkins' "Scape" ' and relates them to the poet's study of Platonic epistemology as reflected in some of the unpublished 'Oxford Essays', his Journal, and his Oxford notebooks.

In *HQ* two critics approach Hopkins in connection with another poet. M. M. Holloway examines in a letter of 1886 Hopkins's defence of Wordsworth's Intimations Ode, and concludes that in Hopkins's stress on the aesthetic truth rather than the experience which occasioned the poem, he illuminates *The Wreck* as well as Wordsworth's Ode. Robert W. Hill makes 'A Phenomenological Approach to Hopkins and Yeats' in order to determine if the poets' art and subject matter are phenomenological. While Hopkins possesses greater vision than Yeats, Yeats's technique was less obtrusive; Hill locates Yeats's phenomenology in his concern with poetic language and Hopkins's mainly in his treatment of poetic consciousness as a subject.

Paul C. Boomsliter and Warren Creel examine Houseman's notion of the 'latent base, comprising natural laws by which all verification is conditioned' as implied in the poet's footnote in *The Name and Nature of Poetry* (*Lang&S*, 1977). The authors, who feel that Housman anticipates current work in linguistics, flesh out his points with contemporary developments in linguistics, phonetics, and the study of perception. The *Housman Society Journal* contains a full interpretation of 'Last Poems III' by G. V. M. Heap who relates it to *A Shropshire Lad*, specifically poems xliv and lxv, and a note on Housman and the *fin de siècle* by Robert W. Witt, who compares the poet's emphasis on feeling not thought with that of the aesthetes' emphasis on beauty rather than content. But Housman's stoicism distinguishes his work from that of Decadents such as Dowson. In the same journal the quality and degree of Housman's patriotism, as seen in the soldiers of his poems, are judged by Brian Gasser, and related to the military career of his brother Herbert. Another letter (1892) from Herbert is published and discussed by R. P. Graves. This volume also contains pieces on Clemence Housman's *The Unknown Sea* by Anne Borne, and on a connection between the Brontës and Housman's great-grandfather by John Pugh, as well as correspondence and a review.

The *Kipling Journal*, a quarterly, publishes addresses from the discussion meetings of The Kipling Society, reviews of current books, and news, notes, and correspondence. Also, A. L. F. Rivet writes on 'Rudyard Kipling's Roman Britain', John Coates on 'Religious Cross Currents in "The House Surgeon" ', Walter Allen briefly on 'Kipling's Place in Literature', and E. N. Houlton on Kipling's different depictions of Mr King in *Stalky & Co*, in 'Regulus', and in 'The Propagation of Knowledge'.

In *VP* are found three articles on poets whom scholars tend to overlook. Ina Rae Hark treats Edward Lear's 'nonsense' as a Victorian exploration of the conflict between the freedom of the individual and the stability of the society. The nature of nonsense precludes any clear, unequivocal statement, and Lear reveals Victorian *angst* about the capacity for irrationality and violence in the individual, his society, and his universe. Barry V.

Qualls reprints and introduces W. H. Mallock's undergraduate satire *Every Man His Own Poet* (1872) which takes the form of a cook-book for poets and contains recipes for 'how to make an ordinary Love poem', 'How to make a pathetic Marine poem', as well as suggestions on how to imitate Tennyson, Arnold, Browning, Morris, Buchanan, Byron, Swinburne, and the Pre-Raphaelites. Linda C. Dowling juxtaposes Yeats's 'Rosa Mundi', an early form of 'The Rose of the World', with Richard Le Gallienne's 'Beauty Accurst' which she regards as 'largely if unconsciously' a response to Yeats's poem, a misprision which reveals the dilemma of the late Victorian poet.

The handsome two-volume edition[17] of the poems of George Meredith edited by Phyllis B. Bartlett includes all the poetry Meredith is known to have written: poems collected by the poet, those uncollected but published by him, the posthumously published work, and that never published before. Drafts of poems are also included. The poems are printed in the order Meredith collected them, rather than chronologically; explanatory notes appear in the back of Vol. 2, and only textual variants and occasional headnotes are included on the page with the text. The result is a page cleaner in appearance than that of the Longman's Annotated Poets, but an edition which, for the student or scholar, is more inconvenient to read. The Introduction is informative but disjointed, consisting as it does of commentary text by text. Nevertheless, the edition is welcome and very useful; it should prove a stimulus to work on the poems. Michael Lund in *VP* shows that in its images of space which reflect a spiritual crisis, the disappearance of God, *Modern Love* resembles the imagery and preoccupation of other mid-Victorian works such as Arnold's Switzerland poems and *In Memoriam*.

In his two-volume study of 1972, now translated into English[18], Paul Meier confines himself to Morris's utopian writings, mainly those theoretical writings, lectures, articles, treatises and stories of 1880 and after; in his introduction he states his resistance to 'even the smallest literary digression'. He begins with an estimate of Morris's religious and class background. The greater part of Vol. I is devoted to sources in and influence from utopian literature, medievalism, and pre-Marxist socialism, and the rest of the work is an analysis of Morris's notions of a communist society of the future. In appendixes Meier includes three letters of the 1880s from Morris, and his notes for a lecture of 1885 to the Socialist League called 'Justice and Socialism'. For readers interested in Morris's prose fiction, Meier provides a detailed analysis of the context and nature of *News from Nowhere* and 'A Dream of John Ball', but even for readers of the poetry, the chapter on medievalism is stimulating in its abrasive dismissal of Pre-Raphaelitism and its greater attention to Carlyle and Ruskin.

Ian Bradley's book on Morris[19] is most suitable for younger secondary school students; it capitulates entirely to its visual element, and comment

[17] *The Poems of George Meredith*, ed. by Phyllis B. Bartlett. New Haven, Conn., and London: Yale U.P. 2 vols. pp. 1 + 1253. £57.60.

[18] *William Morris. The Marxist Dreamer*, by Paul Meier, transl. by Frank Grubb. Hassocks, Sussex: Harvester P.; Atlantic Highlands, N.J.: Humanities P. 2 vols. pp. xiv + 598 + xl + lxx. £28.50.

[19] *William Morris and his World*, by Ian Bradley. Thames & Hudson. pp. 127. £4.50.

on Morris's literary work is superficial and scanty, while the life, art, and design dominate. Some of the 130 illustrations are of interest, but the copy is reductive in its simplifications and critical judgements. Bradley seems to take delight in minimising Morris's later revolutionary socialism, and his book begins accordingly: 'William Morris owed a lot to the forces of capitalism against which he was to engage in "holy warfare" for most of his life.'

In *JWMS* Ralph Berry suggests that Morris's *œuvre* is oriented toward the symbolic poles of Paradise Lost and Paradise Regained, and shows certain common preoccupations. He demonstrates this with illustrations from *The Defence of Guenevere* poems to the latest prose work, as well as from Morris's designs. Ernest L. Fontana attempts to unravel the tangled interior monologue 'Judgment of God' which appeared in *The Defence of Guenevere* volume. Fontana sees the poem as the enactment of a struggle between a self searching for articulation and a violent, rigid, chivalric code (*PRR*); in the same periodical the rediscovery at the Houghton Library at Harvard of the copy of *Hypnerotomachia Poliphili* used by Morris and Burne-Jones as a model for the projected edition of *The Earthly Paradise* is reported by Mark Samuels-Lasner, and Stephen Sossaman usefully reveals the importance of the Pre-Raphaelite visual aesthetic in Morris's version of *Sigurd*.

Although the title of David Kent's 'W.M. Rossetti and the Editing of Christina Rossetti's Religious Poetry' suggests a focus on one area of the poet's verse, the article in *PRR* concerns her brother's failure to respect his sister's arrangement of her poems in general in the 1904 edition. Kent goes on to describe the circumstances in which *Verses* (1893), a volume of devotional poetry, was compiled and structured by Christina, and its subsequent re-ordering by William.

The Rossetti-Leyland Letters[20] is an attractive edition of 137 new letters not in the Doughty and Wahl *Letters* (1965–7); it contains 103 from Rossetti to Frederick R. Leyland, and thirty-four from patron to poet. The letters are lightly annotated. How Rossetti, who never exhibited in public after he was twenty-one, earned his living from his various patrons is indicated here. Also revealed are the vicissitudes of the artist's long and close relationship with Leyland, who proved both friend and patron. In the well-written introduction the editor suggests that Leyland's narrowness, as seen in the letters, is a possible explanation of the decline of Rossetti's work in his last years: he became a prisoner of his own business arrangements – his tiny circle of patrons.

The Poetry of Dante G. Rossetti[21] originated in a thesis which is updated to 1972. It has three chapters, 'Style in *The House of Life*', 'Evolution of a Narrative Ballad Style', and 'Reflective and Lyrical Poetry', and an appendix which consists of notes on 'Sources and Resemblances'. The book retains the unmistakable form of a thesis, but this accounts for its strength as well as its weakness; its strength is a systematic and relatively

[20] *The Rossetti-Leyland Letters. The Correspondence of an Artist and His Patron*, ed. by Francis L. Fennell Jr. Athens, Ohio: Ohio U.P. pp. xxxiv + 111. $11.

[21] *The Poetry of Dante G. Rossetti: A Critical Reading and Source Study*, by Florence Saunders Boos. The Hague, Paris, New York: Mouton, distrib. by Walter de Gruyter, Berlin and New York, 1976. pp. x + 311. DM72.

thorough covering of ground, and its weakness a resultant dearth of distinctive emphasis, focus, and room for flair and digressions. Certitude characterises the voice of the author; this contributes to the authority of her positive readings, but it grates in more questionable negative interpretations such as her dismissal of 'Jenny'. In *JWMS* the same author publishes and annotates two letters of Rossetti's, one of 1854 or 1855 to Thomas Keightley, the second of 1877 to W. Davenport Adams.

In *Expl* D. M. R. Bentley elucidates the allegory of 'Sunset Wings' written by Rossetti in 1870, and in *ELN* Bentley takes W. M. Rossetti's suggestion and explores the three 'Old and New Art' sonnets as Dante Gabriel's manifesto for the PRB. The recurring figure of 'Hope, with Eyes Upcast in Rossetti's poems of 1869–1871 and his later pictures is studied by Bentley in *Mosaic*. The vision behind these works is purgatorial, and the Hope eschatological. From 1870 hope for an afterlife of eternal love characterises Rossetti's poetry and pictures. In a fascinating bit of untangling James W. Christie establishes that William Bell Scott's poem 'Rosabell' on the theme of a fallen woman was neither an influence on 'Jenny' or on Rossetti's painting 'Found'. Rossetti was more committed to truth to nature than Scott's conventional sentimentalising and moralising would allow (*PRR*). In the same journal Lucien L. Agosta locates five studies for important visual works by Rossetti at the University of Texas Humanities Research Centre. Although these are described by Virginia Surtees in her *catalogue raisonné* of Rossetti's paintings and drawings (Clarendon, 1971), their whereabouts is described as unknown.

Steven C. Dittman offers a note on Swinburne's 'Herse', a poem representative of the large amount of child-worship verse Swinburne wrote between 1870 and 1894. Dittman locates a source for the flexibility of the word 'Herse' in the poem in Liddell and Scott's *A Greek-English Lexicon* (*PRR*). In *TSL* Antony H. Harrison examines 'The Aesthetics of Androgyny in Swinburne's Early Poetry'; *Atalanta in Calydon* and 'Hermaphroditus' receive close attention. Terry L. Meyers gathers Swinburne's scattered remarks on Shelley and other lyrical poets in order to recover Swinburne's aesthetic of lyric poetry (*PLL*). The weight Swinburne attributes to melody in his own and others' work explains the extent of his love for Shelley. In *ELH* George M. Ridenour asks 'What does it mean. . .to live in and through literature in the way that Swinburne so evidently did?'. His reading of five poems by Swinburne reveals the poet's strong faith in poetic language which Ridenour suggests helps answer the question. Using Blakean criteria of criticism throughout, Ridenour first examines closely three poems on the death of artists – 'The Last Oracle', 'Ave Atque Vale' and 'In Memory of John William Inchbold', and then 'On the Cliffs'. Swinburne's poems involve both the universality associated with eternity and the specificity associated with time.

In undertaking a reassessment of the 'magnificent' 'On the Cliffs' in *VP*, David G. Riede wishes to scotch the notion that Swinburne's late work is unrewarding and emanates from a period of stagnation in the poet's creative life. Swinburne, Riede argues, tries to generate a myth within the poem, and by examining closely a seven-line sentence from the poem Reide illuminates Swinburne's methods and enters the hermeneutic circle. His re-iterated comparison of 'On the Cliffs' with 'Tintern Abbey', and his suggestion that Swinburne succeeds in reviving the dying tradition of poetry where in *The Wasteland* Eliot fails, seem inflated, but the article makes an otherwise convincing argument for reconsideration of the poem. Swinburne's Arthurian poetry and its medieval sources are David Staines's concern in *SN*. Initially prompted to entertain Arthurian subjects by Pre-Raphaelite interest in Malory, he persisted with Arthur in (angry) reaction to Tennyson's reworking of the material, and selected from his sources according to his own lights, while generally and increasingly keeping much closer to them than Tennyson does.

In his informative pamphlet, 'The Making of the Memoir'[22], Philip L. Elliott describes the timing, selection of materials, and method of composition of Hallam Tennyson's *Memoir* of his father, which seems to have first taken form in 1894 in an ur-manuscript now lost. Its successive drafts, which were published in trial runs by Hallam as part of the process of composition, are part of its publishing history, which is also recounted here. Hallam's erratic editorial practices, the roles of other contributors and editors (such as F. T. Palgrave, Emily Tennyson, James Knowles, Aubrey de Vere, Henry Sidgwick), and the image of Tennyson which Hallam created by omissions and suppressions, are Elliott's subjects for the second half of this unfailingly interesting essay.

Philip Henderson's biography[23] of Tennyson is, as he claims in his introduction, not more than a 'personal interpretation, the record of the rediscovery of a great poet'. His debts are pervasive and explicit, and he offers little that is new. It is not as abrasive and critically acute a biography as that of Christopher Ricks, and seems on the whole to be a commercial rather than a scholarly venture. Remarks and observations, 1870–92, of the poet, compiled by Audrey Boyle Tennyson, Hallam's wife, are published and annotated for the first time by James O. Hoge Jr in *JEGP*. In revealing the extreme rigours of the water-cure taken by Tennyson near Cheltenham in 1843–4 to cure his depression, Ann C. Colley adds to Elizabeth Jenkins's account of its nature in *Tennyson and Dr. Gully* (*YW* 55.411) and attests to Tennyson's strong nature and the extent of his fears for his sanity at the time (*TRB*). Sir Francis Hill in 'a cold blooded survey of the family's financial relationships' reconsiders the 'Disinheritance Tradition' and shows that Hallam Tennyson's original description in the *Life* is mitigated by the contents of two unpublished letters, one from Ellen Elizabeth Tennyson, the other from Hallam (*TRB*).

Gerald L. Bruns examines the reversals at the end of *In Memoriam*, where expectations of a generic response seem inadequately fulfilled (*JEGP*). Resisting the model of the poem as a problem-solving mechanism which either yields or fails to yield a solution, he describes convincingly in *PQ* a characteristic rupture of imagination and idea in the poem (dwelling particularly on 126, 127 and 128), a rupture which reflects Tennyson's considered positive idea that time is not homogeneous, but breached by opposition. The poet's 'lesser faith' is inseparable from hope, as well as love; history indicates the incompleteness of God's design. Also discon-

[22] 'The Making of the Memoir', by Philip L. Elliott. Greenville, S.C.: Furman U. pp. 33. n.p.

[23] *Tennyson, Poet and Prophet*, by Philip Henderson. Routledge & Kegan Paul. pp. xx + 225. £6.95.

tented with current views of the structure of *In Memoriam* is James Kilroy, who feels that an exclusive emphasis on thematic unity has obscured the importance of the central group of discomforting poems (50–58), in a book which exhibits a chiastic pattern (whereby parallel units are set in reversed order) from its smallest unit (the quatrain) to its largest. Within each quatrain, section, and the poem as a whole, the greatest weight is toward the centre: the proper emphasis is neither on 95, nor on the division of the poem at Christmasses or anniversaries, but on the nadir of the speaker's experience lying in the middle section of the fifth of the 'nine natural groups' which Tennyson described in a letter to James Knowles. After a brief review of the history of comment on Tennyson's revision of *In Memoriam*, Susan Shatto draws conclusions about the major types of revisions Tennyson made and about his methods (*VP*). The objectification of personal references is the only type of major revision which runs through the whole poem. Sections 31, 32, 59, 123, 124, 128, and 130 were substantially altered, and Shatto finds that these indicate a variety of methods of composition and revision: 'Where he expanded sections, he added an intellectual toughness and depth. Where he abbreviated them, he intensified our focus' and suggested rather than delineated. From Notebook 17 at Trinity College, Cambridge, Shatto (*N&Q*) is able to identify indisputably at least some and perhaps all of the first sections of *In Memoriam* written after 9 (Fair ship). These fragments (1833–5) form the skeleton of poetic sequences built up later, and diminish the force of Tennyson's disavowal of initial plans for a single poem or for publication. Also clarified is how Hallam came to make five conflicting and inaccurate lists of the first sections of the poem. Ways in which *In Memoriam* echoes *Job* are enumerated by J. J. Savory in the same periodical.

In a note in *VP*, Nancy R. Comley examines 'The Islet' which appeared in the *Enoch Arden* volume in 1864 as an inversion of pastoral, specifically as a parody of Marvell's 'A Dialogue Between Thyrsis and Dorinda'. With the intent of determining whether Percivale has a vision of the Holy Grail in *Idylls of the King*, Kathryn Crabbe, in 'Tennyson, Faith, and the Fantastic', attempts to establish the generic conventions by which 'The Holy Grail' operates (*TRB*). J. M. Gray briefly considers Tennyson's repeated use of the Biblical expression 'lifted up his eyes' in the *Idylls* (*Expl*), and the same critic notes some literary echoes in *Guinevere*, ll. 21–52 (*TRB*). In *VPN* John Bush Jones records the strange circumstances by which Tennyson's 'The New Timon, and the Poets' and 'Afterthought', both attacks on Bulwer, were intentionally misattributed by John Forster to J. W. Ferguson and soon after properly attributed to Tennyson in the house annals of *Punch*, in which periodical they first appeared. Jones's investigation of Ferguson reveals him to be Forster's *Punch* connection in this affair: to him Forster passed on the first poem.

In *TSLL* Priscilla Johnston tackles anew Tennyson's use of the Demeter and Persephone theme, and argues that Persephone is not so much a symbol for lost artistic creativity as the essence of a lost past in general that the artist needs to revive. Pastoral landscape represents lucid vision and the solid familiarity of the past in contrast to the 'unreal and indistinct present' created by the repeated Aidoneus figures in Tennyson, who abduct Persephone from the world of the living to that of the dead, and who leave behind a wasteland bereft of growth. Also central in Tennyson's use of the myth is Demeter as an agent of memory and imagination which together, as in the poet, reverse temporal sequence and extract a banished ideal out of the past into life. In this cogent article the author details the working of the Demeter-Persephone myth in *In Memoriam* where it, rather than Christianity, predominates, and in *Maud*. For Tennyson it expressed simultaneously antithetical concepts of change and decay – dynamic and mechanical progress – between which he could not choose.

Ian H. C. Kennedy chronicles the interests and readings of Tennyson's fellows at Cambridge: the pre-occupation of the Apostles with Coleridgean transcendentalism, German literature, and Goethe (*PQ*). He specifies extraordinary correspondences between parts of *Wilhelm Meister's Apprenticeship* and *Wilhelm Meister's Travels* and a number of Tennyson's poems of the Cambridge period including 'Mariana', 'The Palace of Art' and 'The Lover's Tale', and echoes of Bulwer Lytton's Wertherian novel *Falkland* (1827) in 'The Kraken', 'The Palace of Art' and the Mariana poems. Deborah B. Mantell, who examines theatrical history and Shakespearean criticism in the 1830s and 1840s, concludes, in a very interesting article, that Shakespeare was an appropriate model for the handling of radical and feminist themes, and that *The Princess* is an eminently Shakespearean poem (*TSLL*).

In *E&S* H. A. Mason examines 'The First Setting of Tennyson's "Morte D'Arthur" ' through consideration of its contemporary reception, and reads it as a poem of disguised unmanly collapse. We are distracted from the real subject of 'exposure to and presentation of the death of a beloved object' by pedantic retention of turns from Malory and concentration on externals. But the Malory is shown to echo G. S. Faber's paraphrase in *The Origin of Pagan Idolatry* rather than the original, and reveals how the superimposition of innumerable figures over a single myth-hero suited Tennyson. Two rainbow allusions in 'Phrenology' by Charles Tennyson are identified by Robin S. McDowell, who suggests that they, along with other allusions in *Poems by Two Brothers*, reveal the Tennyson children's reading (*TRB*).

In *VS* Kerry McSweeney surveys Swinburne's reservations abou individual works of Tennyson and the Laureate's notions of the role of the artist and the function of poetry. The primary departure in 'Demeter and Persephone' from the pattern of *In Memoriam* is regarded as Tennyson's response to Swinburne's 'Hymn to Proserpine: but also to his strictures on *In Memoriam*. McSweeney notes that the animosity in the Prelude of *Songs Before Sunrise* towards the arguments of *In Memoriam* betrays an anxiety which betrays influence, while the younger poet's critique of the *Idylls* in *Under the Microscope* nevertheless proves suggestive. Swinburne's parodies in 1880 and 1881 of two Tennyson poems, 'The Higher Pantheism' and 'Despair', serve McSweeney as the basis for a critical evaluation of the poems.

Four shorter pieces from *TRB* conclude this review of Tennyson research. Priscilla Metcalf uses information from the papers of James Knowles at the Tennyson Research Centre to pinpoint places and dates of composition of some of Tennyson's poems from the years 1868–1877, and Patrick Scott draws attention to a possible new source for 'Is it peace or war?' in *Maud*: Martin Tupper's poem, 'A Commentary' (1851) contrasts the peaceful industry of the Great Exhibition with Wiseman's Papal Aggression. *TRB* reprints Frederick Waddy's caricature of Tennyson which appeared in *Once a Week* in 1872, and Jerold J. Savory supplies a short note; a photomontage caricature of Tennyson which appeared in *Life* magazine's 'Gallery of Beauties' in 1889 accompanied by a satirical biography also appears in *TRB* with commentary by Patricia Marks.

In a somewhat rambling essay in *VP*, Ian Campbell examines the means that James Thomson employs to transfer his private passion to public poetic utterance in 'The City of Dreadful Night'. In *ELT* Richard Benvenuto identifies a succession of poems in which Ernest Dowson explores the nature of language; the opposition of the futility of words to the efficacy of silence is a recurring motif.

2. The Novel

(a) General

Geoffrey Tillotson's survey of Victorian literature[24], originally designed to be part of the O.H.E.L. series but left unpublished after his death in 1969, has been edited as an independent volume by Kathleen Tillotson. It is both a fitting memorial to an outstanding scholar and a vivid reminder of the sensitivity and belletristic grace long associated with Professor Tillotson's name. The entire volume is marked by a polite deference to Victorian opinion, respectful homage to its authors, beautifully apt quotation, and a style which (to repeat Tillotson's comment on Thackeray) is 'unassuming, easy, comfortable. . . as limpid when its sense is profound as when not'. After an introduction to the period and its 'earnestness', Tillotson surveys the group of earlier generation Victorians of whom Carlyle is found to be the most influential member a group including Dickens, Thackeray, the Brontës, Mrs Gaskell, Trollope, Tennyson and Browning.

Published fourteen years after its original predecessor, *Victorian Fiction: A Second Guide to Research*[25], edited by George H. Ford, takes stock of the vast flood of materials appearing since 1963. Most of the contributors confront 'boom' conditions with commendable poise, and the *Guide* still remains one of the best single-volume reviews of primary and secondary materials. Contributors (and their subjects) are as follows: Richard D. Altick (General), Curtis Dahl (Disraeli and Bulwer-Lytton), Philip Collins (Dickens). Robert A. Colby (Thackeray), Ruth apRoberts (Trollope), Herbert J. Rosengarten (the Brontës), James D. Barry (Mrs Gaskell and Kingsley), Robert Ashley (Collins), Wayne Burns (Reade), U. C. Knoepflmacher (George Eliot), Gillian Beer (Meredith), Daniel F. Howard (Butler), Michael Millgate (Hardy), Robert Kiely (Stevenson), and Jacob Korg (Moore and Gissing).

Andrew Sanders undertakes a somewhat thankless task in attempting a

[24] *A View of Victorian Literature*, by Geoffrey Tillotson. Oxford: The Clarendon Press. pp. x + 396. £6.95.

[25] *Victorian Fiction: A Second Guide to Research*, ed. by George H. Ford. N.Y.: The Modern Language Association of America. pp. xxv + 401. hb $17.50, pb $9.

critical examination of Victorian historical novels between 1840 and 1880[26]. Denying himself the opportunity to write on Scott, he is left with three or four major novels, some lesser novels by major writers (such as George Eliot's *Romola* and Hardy's *The Trumpet-Major*) and a number of forgotten museum-pieces which hardly survive stringent critical analysis (such as Bulwer-Lytton's *Harold*, Wiseman's *Fabiola*, and Newman's *Callista*). Though Sanders writes knowledgeably on the ways in which history was 'contemporary, synchronic and enveloping' to the Victorians, and makes intelligent claims for their best historical novels, he only partially overcomes the problem of how to treat the lesser products of Scott's progeny: his project unfortunately commits him to much routine stocktaking of imperfect types.

In *Guardians and Angels: Parents and Children in Nineteenth-Century Literature*[27], David Grylls offers an ambitious socio-literary survey of changing attitudes to parent–child relations as revealed in periodicals, childrens' literature, and fiction (Jane Austen, Dickens, Butler and Gosse). He sets up a useful working definition of 'Puritan' and 'Romantic' ideals of nurture, and is at his most wittily perceptive in tracing the partial displacement of the first by the second in popular writings of the period. His treatment of the major novelists, with the exception of Dickens, is less satisfactory. In particular a final chapter on *Father and Son* and *The Way of All Flesh*, which rightly presents them as untypical family-histories, leaves the reader wondering why they were chosen to typify late Victorian attitudes.

In her survey of the New Woman as a character-type and polemical centre in late Victorian fiction[28], Gail Cunningham hurries through some large and familiar areas – nineteenth-century legal and educational reforms affecting the position of women, the characteristics of the well-regulated Victorian heroine, and so on. This provides her with a background against which to stress the revolutionary feminism of New Woman fiction, a body of novels which Cunningham then uses as a 'necessary context' in which to judge the 'feminist propaganda' in some major novelists of the period (Meredith, Hardy and Gissing). Neat though they are, Cunningham's selective contexts lead to some odd groupings (Charlotte Brontë finds herself in the unusual company of Mrs Henry Wood and Trollope, while Emily Brontë and George Eliot are omitted from the account of mid-century novelists), and they assume connections which invariably need to be argued out on a wider basis.

Jean E. Kennard establishes a bridge between feminist and formal criticism in *Victims of Convention*[29], a study highlighting the various effects of the 'two suitors' convention in novels with a leading female protagonist. Such a convention is found to have a fundamentally sexist bias, though Kennard is alert to both its successes and failures in a range of

[26] *The Victorian Historical Novel, 1840–1880*, by Andrew Sanders. Macmillan. pp. xi + 264. £8.95.

[27] *Guardians and Angels: Parents and Children in Nineteenth-Century Literature*, by David Grylls. Faber & Faber. pp. 211. £6.50.

[28] *The New Woman and the Victorian Novel*, by Gail Cunningham. Macmillan. pp. viii + 172. £8.95.

[29] *Victims of Convention*, by Jean E. Kennard. Hamden, Conn.: Archon Books. pp. 195. $12.50.

novelists from Jane Austen to Gissing: it is most likely to fail, she maintains, when it conflicts with a more modern view of female self-fulfilment and independence. Within the limits imposed by very narrow interests, this is a clear and balanced survey.

Proceedings of two conferences, centred upon widely different areas of study, are published this year. Papers from a University of Essex conference on *1848: The Sociology of Literature*[30] include Raymond Williams's 'Forms of English Fiction in 1848', David Musselwhite's 'The Novel as Narcotic', Gillian Beer's 'Carlyle and *Mary Barton*: Problems of Utterance', Patsy Stoneman's 'The Brontës and Death: Alternatives to Revolution', and other contributions on Le Fanu, Bulwer-Lytton and Dickens. *Editing Nineteenth-Century Fiction*[31], a collection of papers from a University of Toronto conference, edited by Jane Millgate, contains three essays on Victorian novelists: Sylvère Monod on Dickens, Michael Millgate on Hardy, and Peter Shillingsburg on Thackeray.

More conventional survey works include C. P. Snow's *The Realists*[32] which contains chapters on Dickens and Henry James. *Le roman anglais au XIXe siècle*[33] begins with an overview of the socio-cultural context and the evolution of various fictional kinds. Then follows a series of chapters on novelists from Jane Austen to Conrad, each writer represented by a notable work. Glen St John Barclay offers a brief sketch of the popular ingredients of occult fiction, particularly the Dracula myth and its accompanying sado-eroticism[34].

Michael Steig ranges interestingly through novels by Dickens, Thackeray and Hardy in his discussion of ' "Evasive" Narrative and Authorial Intention; or, Do Critics Make Style?' (*Lang&S*, 1977), 'evasiveness' being distinguished from 'elusiveness' and defined as the 'ability to imply the presence of meaning by its absence or denial'. Ambiguities of a different kind engage the attention of James R. Kincaid in ' "Why Unblooms the Best Hope?": Victorian Narrative Forms and the Explanation of Calamity' (*VN*). Considering the open-ended response to death and disaster characteristic of many Victorian poems and novels, he examines the rhetorical duality which results when writers both endorse *and* subvert the formal conventions they use.

(b) Individual Novelists

Though K. C. Phillipps's aim in *The Language of Thackeray*[35] is to catalogue items of habitual usage (which he conscientiously does under

[30] *1848: The Sociology of Literature: Proceedings of the Essex conference on the Sociology of Literature, July 1977*, ed. by F. Barker, J. Coombes, P. Hulme, C. Mercer, and D. Musselwhite. Colchester, Essex: U. of Essex. pp. 290. pb £3.50.

[31] *Editing Nineteenth-Century Fiction: Papers given at the thirteenth annual Conference on Editorial Problems, University of Toronto, 4–5 November 1977*, ed. by Jane Millgate. N.Y. and London: Garland. pp. 128. $18.70.

[32] *The Realists: Portraits of Eight Novelists*, by C. P. Snow. Macmillan. pp. 254. £6.95.

[33] *Le roman anglais au XIXe siècle*, by Pierre Coustillas, Jean-Pierre Petit, and Jean Raimond. Vendôme: Presses Universitaires de France. pp. 317. pb.

[34] *Anatomy of Horror: The Masters of Occult Fiction*, by Glen St John Barclay. Weidenfeld & Nicolson. pp. 144. £5.50.

[35] *The Language of Thackeray*, by K. C. Phillipps. The Language Library, general ed. Eric Partridge. Andre Deutsch. pp. 205. £6.50.

such headings as Regency English in the Victorian Period, Slang, Register, Proper Names, Modes of Address, and so on), his study has further bonuses. A rich selection of examples, in itself an enjoyable feature, enables Phillipps to stress Thackeray's more subtle comic and ironic effects. If his study lacks overall coherence, it has a fair measure of continuity – an introductory cross-section of Thackeray's style, a chapter on the language of *Henry Esmond*, and underlying interests in the class distinctions revealed by Thackeray's language, his 'subtle sense of solecism', and the standards of correctness underlying his usage and abusage. This survey brings a fresh touch to a number of issues: it has the added value of suggesting new possibilities for research.

The Book of Snobs is edited and succinctly introduced by John Sutherland[36], who outlines their cultural significance, journalistic context, and importance in confirming Thackeray's evolution from the typical *Punch* iconoclast towards a 'growing dedication to the novel and moral legislation'. He maintains that, despite Thackeray's often hobbyhorsical attitudes, *The Book of Snobs* as a whole attains to 'a respectably impersonal statement of social philosophy'. Also included are notes and an appendix devoted to the etymology of the term 'snob'.

Arthur Pollard's casebook on *Vanity Fair*[37] contains a good cross-section of critical opinion. The volume begins with a synopsis of criticism up to 1930 and commentary on source material and illustrations. Then follow more recent judgements by Gordon N. Ray, Dorothy Van Ghent, Kathleen Tillotson, G. Armour Craig, A. E. Dyson. Ioan M. Williams, Edgar F. Harden and Barbara Hardy.

NCF contains 'Thackeray's Pendennis: Son and Gentleman', in which Thomas L. Jeffers examines the currency of the expectations, unpretentious ideals, emotional and professional attitudes which make Pen a representative gentleman of the 1850s. Thackeray, he shows, accepts Pen's social accommodation with only a modified degree of comfort: the novel also acknowledges awkward sexual truths as well as 'the transient, unbalanced, feebly conventional nature of the Victorian establishment'.

'How Many Children had Barry Lyndon?' asks Winslow Rogers (*VN*), before going on to consider the wider issue of how seriously we should take the inconclusive factual discrepancies in Thackeray's novels. In a detailed survey of the influence of *The Newcomes* upon both *Roderick Hudson* and *The American* (*NCF*), R. D. McMaster concludes that despite their technical differences, James and Thackeray share a common interest in 'the tension between how the world is and how it is seen through the lenses of the shaping imagination'. *N&Q* contains two items on Thackeray: Richard W. Oram supplies details of 'Thackeray's Translations of German Poetry and his Weimar Commonplace Book', while Donald Hawes offers 'Thackeray and *The Battle of Blenheim*', noting the presence of echoes from Southey's poem in *Henry Esmond*. Finally, Albert Borowitz (*VN*) recreates 'The Unpleasantness at the Garrick Club' over the expulsion of Edmund Yates in 1858 which produced a rift in the already fragile relationship between Thackeray and Dickens.

[36] *The Book of Snobs*, by William Makepeace Thackeray, ed. by John Sutherland. New York: St Martin's P. pp. 237. $16.95.
[37] *Thackeray: 'Vanity Fair', A Casebook*, ed. by Arthur Pollard. Casebook Series. Macmillan. pp. 237. hb £5.95, pb £2.50.

'Disraeli: Politician as Novelist' is Arthur Pollard's theme in a succinct and balanced essay (*Disraeli Newsletter*) which examines not only 'the views from which Disraeli started but also the imagination and passion that energised his progress' as a political novelist, particularly in *Coningsby, Sybil* and *Tancred*. In *VN*, Lois E. Bueler writes on parallels in the treatment of popular insurrection which connect 'Disraeli's *Sybil* and Holinshed's *Chronicles*'. Thom Braun (*N&Q*) offers a note on '*Sybil*: A Misprint'.

Dickens criticism is as predictably abundant and varied as usual, and the appropriate place to begin is with John Romano's ambitiously theoretic *Dickens and Reality*[38]. Raising the question of how and in what sense Dickens is a realist writer, Romano finds a key in the form of his novels, and the kind of form in particular which is 'open' or vulnerable to the 'form-destroying activity of reality in the real world'. Realism is thus identified with a fiction which questions its own fictiveness and resents the unreality of its own conventions. Combining examples drawn from Tolstoy with later post-structural orthodoxies, Romano sees Dickens as needing 'models and formal constructs, and paradigms. . .in order to represent reality' and as even ready to embrace meaningful 'distintegration of the text'. Provocative and articulate as Romano is, he constantly elevates tendencies in Dickens's work into open-ended paradigms which seem more applicable to a Joyce or Beckett than to Dickens. Nor does he seem totally convinced that 'open' form *in itself* is sufficient to characterise Dickens's realism: he can be found to refer to the river in *Our Mutual Friend* as 'a substratum of reality' upon which the novel 'depends', and to Dickens as ' "realistic" or right' about things in a prophetic way. At points like these, Romano seems unknowingly to question the limits of his own thesis.

George J. Worth returns to basic considerations in a brief, well organised survey of the forms and functions of Dickensian melodrama[39]. The enquiry is conducted with a welcome respect for clear definition and a refreshing openness to the possibilities of melodrama. Its ethical and linguistic features are outlined in an introductory chapter, with illustrations drawn from Douglas Jerrold's plays and Dickens's *Sketches*. Worth then proceeds chronologically through the novels, showing the frequency of melodrama, Dickens's successive transformation of its devices, and his increasing control in using them.

Robert L. Patten is a literary historian with an enormous appetite for facts, and in *Charles Dickens and His Publishers*[40] offers a seemingly definitive statistical record of Dickens's publishing associations, the commercial history of his books, and the rise of the Victorian Dickens industry. Publishers' records provide Patten with amazingly detailed information about contracts, advertising, marketing, sales, profits and losses – information which he incorporates into a developing account of the progress of Dickens's own great expectations. Underlying conclusions are reserved for

[38] *Dickens and Reality*, by John Romano. New York: Columbia U.P. pp. xi + 187. $15.60.

[39] *Dickensian Melodrama: A Reading of the Novel*, by George J. Worth. University of Kansas Humanistic Studies 50. Lawrence, Kansas: U. of Kansas P. pp. ix + 147. pb $6.

[40] *Charles Dickens and His Publishers*, by Robert L. Patten. Oxford: The Clarendon Press. pp. ix + 502. £15.

a final chapter (which the reader might be advised to consult first): here our attention is drawn to how much the conditions of publishing influenced the shape and success of Dickens's career and how he, in turn, helped to establish professional standards, took advantage of serialisation and reprint series to be the first novelist to truly 'belong' (through ownership) to his audience, and thereby 'democratized fiction'. Concluding appendixes give further details of sales and profits, Dickens's income, and the printing history of his monthly serials.

In a stylishly produced volume[41], equally divided between commentary and illustrations, Michael Steig throws fresh light on the creative association between Dickens and Phiz. He sees this association as a subtle and developing collaboration in which Hablot Browne often seems to have the freedom to bring out aspects not overtly expressed in the text: Browne thus becomes, in effect, Dickens's creative partner and first interpreter. Steig's detailed reading of the various kinds of congruence between picture and text stresses the importance of Hogarthian and earlier traditions of iconography, and implicitly underlines the value of a graphic 'reading'.

Acknowledging a debt to the approach followed by Philip Collins in his studies of Dickens on education and crime, Norris Pope has produced a worthy successor in *Dickens and Charity*[42]. Pope's expert knowledge of evangelical philanthropy as an organised movement and shaping force in Victorian life allows him to measure very clearly the justice of Dickens's hostility to the movement as well as to show that, on matters of practical remedy for social ills, he and Exeter Hall could share common attitudes. Careful use is made of Dickens's letters, speeches and journalism to show his opinion (and the reliability of his opinion) on a wide range of issues – evangelicalism, sabbatarianism, missions and missionaries, the Ragged movement, health and housing – and Pope neatly emphasises how these add topical impact to the fiction.

Dickens Studies Annual, Volume 7[43] and *The Dickensian* contain so many varied articles that it is possible to mention only the more notable. The first volume contains two articles engaging fruitfully with the nature and importance of Christian elements in particular novels – Stanley Friedman's 'Dickens' Mid-Victorian Theodicy: *David Copperfield*' and Richard Barickman's 'The Spiritual Journey of Amy Dorrit and Arthur Clennam'. James A. Davies undertakes a sympathetic defence of Forster's *Life*, while David Paroissien writes on 'Dickens and the Cinema', discussing Dickens's cinematic appeal and his influence on later film-makers, notably Eisenstein. Finally, Thomas J. Rice offers a cogent reading of domestic-civil analogies in '*Barnaby Rudge*: A Vade Mecum for the Theme of Domestic Government in Dickens'. Among its many articles and brief notes *The Dickensian* includes Philip Collins's 'Dickens's Public Readings: The Kit and the Team', Andrew Sanders's ' "Come Back and Be Alive": Living and Dying in *Our Mutual Friend*', Joanne Shattock's 'The Entertainers: Dickens and Thackeray on Tour', Donald Hawes's 'David Copper-

[41] *Dickens and Phiz*, by Michael Steig. Bloomington, Ind., and London: Indiana U.P. pp. x + 340 (including 126 illustrations). $12.50.

[42] *Dickens and Charity*, by Norris Pope. Macmillan. pp. xi + 303. £8.95.

[43] *Dickens Studies Annual, Volume* 7, ed. by Robert B. Partlow Jr. Carbondale and Edwardsville, Ill.: S. Illinois U.P. pp. xviii + 268. $17.50.

field's Names', and Michael Hollington's 'Dickens and the Dance of Death'. Finally, the collection of Dicken's supernatural short stories is usefully compiled and briefly introduced by Michael Hayes[44].

There are several articles of a general nature this year, including two lengthy comparative studies in *CompL*. Kenneth R. Ireland writes on 'Urban Perspectives: Fantasy and Reality in Hoffman and Dickens', examining such shared features as the grotesque, the *Doppelgänger*, humanisation and reification. In 'City Life and the Novel: Hugo, Ainsworth, Dickens', Richard Maxwell draws attention to the importance of Hugo as a key figure behind much of the popular fiction of the 1840s. Examining links between his three chosen writers, he goes on to show the genesis of urban gothic as a standard fictional mode. Richard Barickman writes attractively on 'The Comedy of Survival in Dickens' Novels' (*Novel*), ranging over a wide number of eccentrics whose quirks and mannerisms provide them with strategies for protecting the beleaguered self and asserting vital human energies in a world of deadening social routine. Approaching *Dombey and Son, The Old Curiosity Shop* and *Little Dorrit* by way of mid-century ideas of 'servanthood', N. N. Feltes (*L&H*) examines Dickens's response to social and historical pressures affecting master–servant relations. In tracing the development of Dickens's pastoralism and garden-images, Roselee Robison (*ES*) grazes in some familiar pastures. She notes, however, the incongruity and irony which arise when the garden is located in the city, though often 'as its dimensions contract, its vitality paradoxically increases'. Ranging over a number of Dickens characters, Charles I. Schuster (*ELN*) considers the connections between inarticulacy and social alienation, while Aida Farrag (*RomN*) offers a brief note on 'Zola, Dickens, and Spontaneous Combustion Again'.

Michael Slater's enjoyable introduction to the Penguin *Nicholas Nickleby*[45] is very just in its emphasis on theatricality and role-playing as the 'living heart' of the novel. These features, he shows, underlie both its inexhaustible comic vitality and the satire upon a society of poseurs and self-interested 'actors'. Comparisons with *Oliver Twist* and *Sketches* allow Slater to stress the satiric and parodic verve of the novel and the mythic power it seems to lack. William T. Lankford (*PMLA*) discerns an evolving form in *Oliver Twist*, its deepening tension between innocence, evil and the law being 'enacted as a conflict in its mode of representation'.

David S. Marcus (*VN*) offers an interesting analysis of the 'multidimensional view of man and society' in *Martin Chuzzlewit*, emphasising Dickens's tendency to confront the schism between morality and experience, and to explore 'opposed sides of human experience that must be seen in terms of each other'. Open-ended and problematic in its moral debate, the novel 'conveys an awareness of how very limited the basis of any final judgment must be'. Mark M. Hennelly Jr (*SNNTS*) maintains that Dickens successfully reconciles change and changelessness in *David Copperfield*. Through an analysis of the novel's narrative method and co-ordinating images (sea, seasonal change, and ripening process), Hennelly shows

[44] *The Supernatural Short Stories of Charles Dickens*, ed. by Michael Hayes. London: Calder; Dallas: Riverrun P. pp. 159. £4.95.

[45] *Nicholas Nickleby*, by Charles Dickens, ed. with intro. by Michael Slater. Hardmondsworth, Middx.: Penguin. pp. 974. pb £1.75.

the Wordsworthian basis of Dickens's reconciliation of protean 'lunar' change and 'solar' permanence. In 'Time and Design in *David Copperfield*' (*ES*), Albert A. Dunn considers the meaning of time as process, and process as structure. Peter Bracher (*SNNTS*) discusses 'Muddle and Wonderful No-Meaning: Verbal Irresponsibility and Verbal Failures in *Hard Times*'. Albert D. Hutter (*PMLA*) combines literary, historical and psychoanalytic approaches to show how Dickens correlates 'Nation and Generation in *A Tale of Two Cities*'. Special emphasis falls on character-doubling or 'splitting' as the basis of a structure which links psychic, generational and social conflict.

An outstanding item of Dickens criticism this year is Garrett Stewart's splendidly imaginative meditation on 'The New Morality of *Bleak House*' (*ELH*), in which he probes Dickens's response to death and the grim shadow cast upon life by the novel's embracing 'rhetoric of death'. Death conceived by Dickens as both synopsis and synonym for life, as 'inward eventuation' for a life gone defunct, and as 'merely life unfurling' for those already dead at heart – these and other implications are beautifully woven together in an argument which arrives at the following conclusion: 'In the ordering and portent of his death scenes Dickens tapped as no writer of fiction before him the profound, sometimes meliorating, more often astringent relation between the antonyms latent in the noun "mortality", a functional pun denoting both the condition of human life and, in a definition only recently obsolete for Dickens, its end in death. This linguistic curiosity suggests at once a pervasive narrative strategy, a fictional psychology, and an entire satiric method.'

For Allon H. White (*CritQ*), *Bleak House* contains a 'deferred' or 'anterior' narrative which enacts the process by which characters move forward by moving backwards – in the quest for origins and by tracking down the past in order to repeat it. Through this retrospective 'nostalgia for origins' and the recovery of bonds already established but temporarily obscured, the novel asserts a vision of restored order and security equivalent to the Victorian ideal of family unity. Lowry Pei (*ELN*) impinges upon this same area in 'Mirrors, The Dead Child, Snagsby's Secret, and Esther', where she shows that the characters' efforts to sustain unnatural lifelessness are a corollary of repression and guilt – an unnameable guilt deriving, as with Snagsby, from 'the fact of having been born at all'. Forced self-repression rules Esther's conduct and underlies her unnamed illness: she must painfully confront what has always been 'secretly' known – the fact of her own self-deprivation and the meaning of having died to 'a child's state of being'.

A special edition of *NCF* devoted to narrative endings includes two essays on Dickens's later novels. John Kucich writes on 'Action in the Dickens Ending: *Bleak House* and *Great Expectations*', while Alistair M. Duckworth considers '*Little Dorrit* and the Question of Closure'. Philip Collins (*L&H*) uses the Sunday-in-London passages in Chapter 3 of *Little Dorrit* to illustrate how such topical issues as the sabbatarian controversy operate – and operated for Dickens's readers – in his mature fiction. George Holoch (*VS*) argues that *Little Dorrit* is Dickens's bleakest study of the fate of the individual in a society where mystifying fictions (particularly the pretence of gentility) universally safeguard the perpetuation of injustice, parasitism, and oppression. The novel's ending offers no possibility of spiritual or political transformation, since 'exploded ideologies reconstitute themselves'. Even moral action made possible by retreat is based, he maintains, upon values 'explicitly asserted in hypocritical fashion by society'. J. G. Schippers (*DQR*) shows how the collapse of language as a medium of communication relates to problems of identity, falsity of vision and depersonalisation in *Little Dorrit*.

Barry V. Qualls (*SNNTS*) traces the influence of Carlyle and Carlylism in *Our Mutual Friend*, particularly in its treatment of mammonism, past and present, and the mechanistic society as life-in-death. He concludes that the novel is 'at once Dickens's final attack on the Age of Machinery and his last affirmation of Carlyle's importance to his work'. In 'The Completed Story in *The Mystery of Edwin Drood*' (*Criticism*), Roy Roussel maintains that the question of completion raised by the unfinished state of the novel is also intrinsic to its theme and mode of narration.

Kirk H. Beetz's *Wilkie Collins: An Annotated Bibliography, 1889–1976*[46] is divided into three sections: editions of Collins's works, criticism (including theses), and selected book reveiws. He provides a useful and much needed compilation, though the introductory bibliographic essay is disappointingly scrappy.

The incidental merits of Cynthia A. Linder's *Romantic Imagery in the Novels of Charlotte Brontë*[47] seem substantially outweighed by haphazard focus, pedestrian method and much wooden prose. No definition of 'romantic imagery' is offered: instead the elusive twin companions, Realism and Romanticism, guide our progress. Eliot's idea of the 'objective correlative' is inappropriately seen as 'a particularly Romantic mode' and subsequently proves a blunt critical tool. Nor is much attention given to problems raised by Charlotte Brontë's figurative language, the author being always ready to stray into peripheral issues. Earnestly literal analysis often combines with eccentric conclusion, as when *Villette* is seen as 'an epic poem written in the form of a novel'.

Two recently discovered stories from Charlotte Brontë's juvenilia, 'The Secret' and 'Lily Hart' (dated 1833) are presented in a sumptuous showcase-volume[48]. The editor, William Holtz, provides a facsimile of the minute manuscript, an edited transcript for the non-specialist, plus photographic enlargement and exact transcript for the specialist. In more senses than one, a great deal is thus made from a very little, and even the most ardent Brontë-lover may find the cost of this edition prohibitive.

Articles on Charlotte Brontë are scarce this year. In 'Fairy Tale Elements in *Jane Eyre*' (*JPC*), Paula Sullivan coincidentally covers much of the same ground as Robert K. Martin in an article of last year (*YW* 58.314). Literary, feminist and psychoanalytic perspectives are combined by Mary Jacobus in her sophisticated reading of '*Villette*'s Buried Letter' (*EIC*), in which she

[46] *Wilkie Collins: An Annotated Bibliography, 1889–1976*, by Kirk H. Beetz. The Scarecrow Author Bibliographies 50. Methuen, N.J., and London: Scarecrow P. pp. viii + 167. £5.25.

[47] *Romantic Imagery in the Novels of Charlotte Brontë*, by Cynthia A. Linder. Macmillan. pp. ix + 138. £7.95.

[48] *Two Tales by Charlotte Brontë: 'The Secret' and 'Lily Hart'*, transcribed and ed. by William Holtz. Columbia, Mo., and London: U. of Missouri P. pp. 143. $28.

sees Lucy's repression and self-estrangement as endowing the novel with a displaced and 'ghostly sub-text'. Focusing initially upon the buried letter as an extension of the buried self, Jacobus traces in later Gothic episodes Lucy's attempt to exorcise repressed phantoms and reunite her divided self.

No serious student of the Brontës will want to miss Margaret Homans's boldly revisionist study of 'Repression and Sublimation of Nature in *Wuthering Heights*' (*PMLA*). Beginning with the proposition that the natural world is mainly present in the novel indirectly and figuratively, Homans goes on to interpret the pervasive figuration and symbolic landscape in Freudian terms. Nature, or the destructive reality it represents, must be repressed, while the figurative use of nature is a liberating and constructive sublimation. While Cathy provides negative confirmation in not being able to transcend repression, her creator's habit of figuration allows repressed material to return in a way that is 'radiantly creative'. Developing through analysis of the novel's narrative indirection and mediation, Homans's argument is both subtle and challenging.

Forcefulness is perhaps more evident than subtlety in Walter E. Anderson's 'The Lyrical Form of *Wuthering Heights*' (*UTQ*), in which he stresses the primacy of a single 'symbolic action progressing towards "lyric" revelation', that revelation being the strange reality of Heathcliff's and Cathy's existence together after death. Like Heathcliff, the novel is 'monomaniacal' in the singleness of its concern: hence, the two principals, who define the norms of the novel, are to be seen as dual manifestations of a single soul, Heathcliff's ferocity as the corollary of an overriding love, and the novel's second part as a symbolic 'reprojection of the original principals'.

BST contains a number of valuable articles, including Arthur Pollard's address on the relationship between Charlotte Brontë and Thackeray, Cecil Davies's 'Art Within a Tradition: *Wuthering Heights* and the German *Novelle*', and Edward Chitham's 'Emily Brontë and Shelley'.

There is little to record on Mrs Gaskell this year. Angus Easson (*VN*) discusses the significance of references and allusions to Thackeray (some of them from Charlotte Brontë's letters) which were omitted from the manuscript of Mrs Gaskell's *The Life of Charlotte Brontë* at an apparently late stage. In 'A Missing Gaskell Tale Found' (*SSF*), Ellen M. Laun adduces stylistic evidence to support her argument that the middle section of *The Poor Clare* (published in *Household Words*, 1856) resurrects the early missing Yorkshire tale referred to in the preface of *Mary Barton*.

The monumental Yale Edition of *The George Eliot Letters*, devotedly edited over a period of forty years by Gordon S. Haight, is brought to a conclusion with the publication of Volume VIII[49] and Volume IX[50]. Both are supplementary collections, printing newly-found letters (among them, an interesting correspondence between George Eliot and Herbert Spencer in 1852), other letters of which only fragments were included in earlier volumes, and all of G. H. Lewes's known correspondence between 1854 and 1878. Volume IX also contains addenda, corrigenda and index for the complete edition.

[49] *The George Eliot Letters: Volume VIII, 1840–1870*, ed. by Gordon S. Haight. New Haven, Conn., and London: Yale U.P. pp. xix + 491. £16.30.

[50] *The George Eliot Letters, Volume IX, 1871–1881*, ed. by Gordon S. Haight. New Haven, Conn., and London: Yale U.P. pp. 539. £16.30.

A large thesis is linked mainly to a single novel (*Middlemarch*) in Alan Mintz's *George Eliot and the Novel of Vocation*[51]. In one respect, this helps him to delineate very clearly the secularised version of Puritan vocation or 'calling' which suffuses George Eliot's treatment of the professions and growing professionalism in the society of her time. In another respect, *Middlemarch* alone is hardly sufficient to support Mintz's larger argument that George Eliot stands pre-eminent in a distinctive genre of fiction which depicts the shape of a life as a 'coming-into-vocation'. Though he fruitfully examines affinities between *Middlemarch* and the vocational design in Victorian autobiographies (Mill, Carlyle, Newman and others), there is little attempt to embrace George Eliot's other work or that of her contemporaries.

This same proviso applies to Dorothy Atkins's competent study of the kinship between *George Eliot and Spinoza*[52]. She begins with an outline of Spinoza's ethical doctrine (including extracts from George Eliot's translation of *Ethica*) and argues for its importance in providing George Eliot with a 'synthesizing ethical stance': she stresses their common emphasis upon the importance of knowledge in the moral governance of life, the need for a view of human suffering *sub specie aeternitatis*, and contrasting patterns of philosophic freedom and bondage to unreasoned feelings. However, Atkins's subsequent emphasis upon the Spinozan framework of *Adam Bede* is unduly limiting: it leaves unresolved the question of how pervasive and permanent Spinoza's influence was in George Eliot's life and work.

General articles include 'G.H. Lewes Revised: George Eliot and the Moral Sense' (*VS*), in which K. K. Collins considers the implications of George Eliot's revision of the posthumous later volumes of Lewes's *Problems of Life and Mind* (published in 1879). His two-part enquiry assesses George Eliot's contribution to the ethical doctrine presented in *Problems*, and compares her position with that revealed in her fiction. George Eliot's reformulations (some of which are printed in an appendix) show two powerful Victorian minds 'in sympathetic collision'. In 'A Russian View of George Eliot' (*NCF*), Raymond Chapman and Eleanora Gottlieb offer a translation of Sofia Kovalevskaya's recollections of two meetings with George Eliot, in 1869 and 1880. Janet K. Gezari writes on 'The Metaphorical Imagination of George Eliot' (*ELH*), surveying the various ways in which metaphors are 'a habit of meaning' in *Middlemarch*.

Peter Simpson (*UTQ*) sensitively probes the general affinities between George Eliot and Wordsworth, before going on to explore how *Silas Marner* – considered as both displaced autobiography and a rural fable patterned upon a process of crisis and recovery – 'combines the social truths of the lyrical ballads with the deep psychological truths of *The Prelude*'. In '*Silas Marner* and *Felix Holt*: From Fairy Tale to Feminism' (*SNNTS*), Richard Conway discerns connections between two novels written at about the same time. In particular, Eppie's choice of an adoptive father whose love offers freedom in preference to a natural father

[51] *George Eliot and the Novel of Vocation*, by Alan Mintz. Cambridge, Mass.: Harvard U.P. pp. xi + 193. £7.70.

[52] *George Eliot and Spinoza*, by Dorothy Atkins. SSELRR 78. Salzburg: U. Salzburg. pp. iv + 188. pb.

whose social traditions would limit her woman's potential provides a rough draft of what is to follow in Esther's story in *Felix Holt*.

In 'Dorothea's "Resartus" and the Palingenetic Impulse of *Middlemarch*' (*TSLL*), Rodger L. Tarr proposes similarities between Dorothea's progress and that of Teufelsdröckh in *Sartor Resartus*, similarities leading him to consider the possible ways in which *Middlemarch* is a branch of Carlylean root. Gordon S. Haight (*VN*) makes a case for Mary Garth as the true heroine of *Middlemarch*: she 'serves as a control, a standard of life, against which Dorothea and Rosamond must be measured'. *NCF* includes Richard D. Altick's 'Anachronisms in *Middlemarch*: A Note'. In the view of Deborah Heller Roazen (*ES*, 1977), Wordsworth's influence is persistent in *Middlemarch* and underlies George Eliot's pre-occupation with 'unifying vision', creative memory, and continuity of experience. Finally, *PMLA* includes Cynthia Chase's 'The Decomposition of the Elephants: Double-Reading *Daniel Deronda*'.

The three full-length studies of Trollope last year are now followed by four more – a remarkable rise of the critical barometer! In his compact author-guide[53], Arthur Pollard succeeds remarkably well in meeting the problems posed by Trollope's enormous output. Novels are considered chronologically, helpfully grouped, with a deft working-in of background information. Though Pollard's premises are familiar and friendly (Trollope's appreciation of the usual, his low-keyed realism, and uncompromising sense of moral purpose), they are applied with tact and forthrightness. He clearly recognises that the Trollope-critic, like Trollope himself, needs to have 'the gift of intimate communion with the reader'.

P. D. Edwards's *Anthony Trollope: His Art and Scope*[54] is a more searching and specialised *re*-evaluation of the entire oeuvre, with premises more challenging than Pollard's and more rigorously applied, with a view to discriminating between the best and the worst in Trollope. His dissent from the traditional view stems from a belief that 'Trollope at his most "realistic" is often Trollope at his dullest, and that in attempting to be serious he often becomes pretentious'. Without minimising Trollope's homogeneity, Edwards goes on to group the novels in a way allowing him to emphasise their variety (domestic realism, sensational aspects, comedy and tragic effects) and to estimate Trollope's success in handling this variety. He is throughout a sharply discriminating and tenacious critic, engaging freshly with Trollope's particular niceties, the evolution of his work, and the underlying qualities of his best fiction (such as the sense it conveys 'at once of the strangeness of common life and of the naturalness, the inherent ordinariness of seemingly out-of-the-way experience'). The result is a rewarding study of the limits within which Trollope succeeds and beyond which he is apt to fail strikingly.

Two further studies – by Robert Tracy[55] and Juliet McMaster[56] –

[53] *Anthony Trollope*, by Arthur Pollard. Routledge & Kegan Paul. pp. xi + 208. £5.50.

[54] *Anthony Trollope: His Art and Scope*, by P. D. Edwards. Hassocks, Sussex: Harvester P. pp. xi + 234. £8.50.

[55] *Trollope's Later Novels*, by Robert Tracy. Berkeley, Los Angeles, Calif. and London: U. of California P. pp. x + 350. £8.75.

[56] *Trollope's Palliser Novels: Theme and Pattern*, by Juliet McMaster. Macmillan. pp. ix + 242. £8.95.

make an approach to the later fiction with certain common objectives. Tracy argues for the maturity of Trollope's novels during the 1870s, emphasising the aptness with which his analogical and mutually referential plots embody a complex vision of society. He stresses Trollope's command of formal pattern and structure, his debt to the multiple plotting of Elizabethan and Jacobean drama, and the ways in which his formal experiments 'constitute a non-Jamesian attempt to achieve the Jamesian end of unity'. Juliet McMaster explores the congruence between theme and pattern in the Palliser novels, detailing the thematic bearing of sub-plots and imagery. Disconcertingly, she provides hardly any introductory guidance to her detailed readings: wider perspectives emerge only in her final chapters on Trollope's men and women, places and things, and authorial presence. Students of Trollope now have a comprehensive bibliography of books, articles and dissertations published between 1925 and 1975[57]. Entries are helpfully annotated and indexed, with a preface outlining the development of Trollope's reputation.

Articles on Trollope have a refreshing variety of approach this year. 'His double commitment to individuality and community is the conundrum that generates his fiction', writes William J. Overton in a subtle and wide-ranging study of 'Self and Society in Trollope' (*ELH*). Stressing Trollope's commitment to 'energy of the self' as a necessary condition of existence, Overton shows how strenuously the novels test the ways in which satisfying self-realisation is compatible with forms of social accommodation and integration. In partial contrast to Overton, Christopher Herbert (*PMLA*) emphasises a darker vein of imagination which leads Trollope to question the possibility of moral renewal and saving change of heart. *Orley Farm, He Knew He Was Right*, and *The Duke's Children* are shown to include a sombre emphasis upon the 'essentially tragic fixity of the self'. Shirley Robin Letwin's consideration of 'Trollope on Generations Without Gaps' (*Daedalus*) leads her to conclude that the ideals of the gentleman and gentlemanly integrity govern Trollope's view of change resulting from political and generational conflict. Treading a narrow divide between 'crass indifference and a nice sense of proportion', the gentleman-politician shows a 'readiness to acknowledge the disparity between the urgency of what has to be done today and its unimportance in the future'. John Halperin (*SAQ*) explores the basis of Trollope's opposition to organised feminism and female careerists, citing examples of his 'independent' women who are shown to be 'unfeminine in their aggressive hardness and, ultimately, embittered failures'. In 'Trollope on the Sublime and Beautiful' (*NCF*), Susan L. Humphreys publishes and helpfully introduces Trollope's earliest known piece of writing, his marginal annotations of 1833 in a copy of Burke's *Philosophical Enquiry*.

In *ES*, John Halperin discusses 'Trollope's *Phineas Finn* and History', identifying the politicians who serve as Trollope's models and help to make *Phineas Finn* 'a political novel whose people and issues reflect and revise various historical realities' of the 1860s. While acknowledging the satiric power of *The Way We Live Now*, J. D. Coates (*DUJ*) feels that its

[57] *The Reputation of Trollope: An Annotated Bibliography, 1925–1975*, by John Charles Olmsted and Jeffrey Egan Welch. Garland Reference Library of the Humanities 88. New York and London: Garland. pp. xxiii + 212. $27.

subtlety as a moral exploration has been underestimated. He goes on to examine its frame of moral reference and the major problem posed – that of maintaining a middle ground between 'the extreme assertion of one's own code or nature and complete insouciance or too ready an acceptance of "realistic" or conventional values'. In '*The Duke's Children*: Reflection and Reconciliation' (*MLQ*), Lowry Pei discusses the novel as 'the cadence of the Palliser series', a work turning on what has gone before and moving towards muted reconciliation of past conflicts.

Items of Meredith criticism from 1925 to 1975 are listed and helpfully annotated in John Charles Olmsted's bibliography[58]. Maaja A. Stewart (*NCF*) shows how analysis of Sir Willoughby's self-image in *The Egoist* combines with a dissection of country house ideals, the failure of the man being 'also a failure of one dream of an ideal life within a changing historical reality'. Meredith's comic reformulation of pastoral mythology stresses how remote, outdated, and divorced from vital civilisation is the sentimental dream of being 'arcadian by aesthetic route'. Unfortunately there is little to recommend in Renate Brückl's monograph on the themes and structure of *Diana of the Crossways*[59] : it is a study which clings tenaciously to received opinion and contains a good deal of mechanical itemisation. Michael Collie (*YES*) draws interestingly upon manuscript evidence to show Meredith's protracted difficulties in composing what he felt to be a new type of psychological fiction in *The Amazing Marriage* (1895) and other late novels. In *N&Q*, M. Y. Shaheen publishes 'Two New Meredith Letters', one to Walter Besant, the other to Leslie Stephen, and both dated 1889.

Meticulously edited by Richard Little Purdy and Michael Millgate, *The Collected Letters of Thomas Hardy: Volume 1, 1840–1892*[60] is, in its contents, a muted opening to the projected seven-volume series. Given the probable loss of important letters from this period of Hardy's life combined with the scarcity of family-letters, there remains a heavy percentage of brief notes to editors, publishers and other acquaintances. The self-conscious formality of the young writer is always evident, and we shall have to wait (say the editors) for the more intimate and expansive letters of the later Hardy. The present collection does at least show the emergent man of letters in varied contact with the late Victorian literary establishment.

In his critical survey of Hardy's major fiction and poetry[61], Lance St John Butler announces a leading theme – the tragic complications brought about by love between men and women. He pursues it spasmodically, however, preferring to multiply approaches and talking-points. This leads to a book which, while it constantly stimulates, rarely gets down to sustained and coherent reading of the texts. It is a study which also presents the beginner with some oddities – a discussion of *The Return of*

[58] *George Meredith: An Annotated Bibliography of Criticism, 1925–1975*, by John Charles Olmsted. Garland Reference Library of the Humanities 99. New York and London: Garland. pp. xix + 158. $20.

[59] *Structural and Thematic Analysis of George Meredith's Novel 'Diana of the Crossways'*, by Renate Brückl. SSELRR 73. U. Salzburg. pp. v + 191. pb.

[60] *The Collected Letters of Thomas Hardy: Volume One, 1840–1892*, ed. by Richard Little Purdy and Michael Millgate. Oxford: The Clarendon Press. pp. xxii + 293. £12.50.

[61] *Thomas Hardy*, by Lance St John Butler. Cambridge: C.U.P. pp. 181. £7.50.

the Native with hardly any reference to Clym, a defence of authorial commentary in an early novel where it is not really problematic, and some cryptic references to Samuel Beckett.

Two volumes reprinted this year are *Thomas Hardy: The Critical Heritage*[62], edited by R. G. Cox (reviewed in *YW* 51.333), and Vere H. Collins's *Talks with Thomas Hardy at Max Gate, 1920–1922*[63], originally published in 1928.

In *SNNTS*, Lawrence Jones examines the effect of compromises Hardy was prepared to make in *Far from the Madding Crowd* to meet the demands of serial publication in *Cornhill*. Hardy's attempt to be 'a good hand at a serial' is traced in his concessions to Victorian sexual decorum, inclusion of sensational and melodramatic event, and arrangement of plot to maintain suspense. Frank R. Giordano Jr writes appreciatively of 'Farmer Boldwood: Hardy's Portrait of a Suicide' (*ELT*), drawing upon Durkheim and Freud to show Hardy's skill in depicting the obsessional logic of the suicidal mind.

In a long and searching article on 'Sue Bridehead, "The Woman of the Feminist Movement"' (*SEL*), Kathleen Blake claims that Sue's contradictoriness, if seen as a reflection of larger divisions between hedonist and ascetic impulses in Victorian feminism, can be defended as part of a consistent 'experiment in self-creation'. In Sue's dangerous combination of 'gravitation and rejection' in her relations with men, Hardy dramatises 'a daring and plausible try at personal liberation' which eventually 'fails of its own divisions'.

Among smaller items on Hardy, Edward C. Sampson and Cynthia R. Sampson draw attention to 'A Forgotten Letter by Thomas Hardy' (*N&Q*), first printed in *The Dorset County Chronicle*, 1893. Also in *N&Q*, R. P. Corballis offers 'A Note on Mumming in *The Return of the Native*'. A final item is Blake Morrison's review of 'Hardy televised: the BBC's *Mayor of Casterbridge* series' (*CritQ*).

George Moore is the subject of a welcome study by Anthony Farrow[64], who surveys his whole output from early poems to late novels. Farrow judiciously combines exposition and evaluation in his attempt to show the internal consistency of Moore's works as determined by 'the sustaining patterns of their creator's mind' and to retrieve what is of lasting value. Another full-length work, R. A. Cave's *A Study of the Novels of George Moore* (Gerrard's Cross: Colin Smythe), has not been available for review. In *ELT*, Eileen Kennedy offers 'George Moore to Edward Elgar: Eighteen Letters on *Diarmuid and Grania* and Operatic Dreams', letters illuminating the background of the ill-fated production of 1901 and showing something of Moore's commitment to the Irish Literary Movement. Elliot L. Gilbert (*Novel*) discusses the kinds of affirmation possible in naturalistic novels, before going on to examine 'In the Flesh: *Esther Waters* and the Passion for Yes'.

[62] *Thomas Hardy: The Critical Heritage*, ed. by R. G. Cox. The Critical Heritage Series. Routledge & Kegan Paul. Second edition. pp. xlvii + 473. £12.

[63] *Talks with Thomas Hardy at Max Gate, 1920–1922*, by Vere H. Collins. Duckworth. Second edition. pp. xv + 85. £5.95.

[64] *George Moore*, by Anthony Farrow. London: George Prior; Boston, Mass.: Twayne (TEAS). pp. iv (unnumbered) + 169. £5.25.

Peter Berresford Ellis follows the unfolding career of H. Rider Haggard as man of letters, imperial adventurer, public servant and social reformer[65]. His portrait has a wealth of factual detail, but is too slight in literary acumen to give a very intimate view of Haggard as man and writer. Norman Etherington (*VS*) offers a more searching analysis of Haggard's romances in 'Rider Haggard, Imperialism, and the Layered Personality': he emphasises the ways in which Haggard anticipates Freud and Jung in using Africa as 'a special psychological terrain in which European man confronts and nearly succumbs to his deepest fears'. Edinburgh City Libraries publish a catalogue of post-1950 publications added to their Stevenson collection, with a guide to holdings at Lady Stair's House Museum[66]. *NCF* contains an unusual item, 'Memory in the Alice Books', in which Lionel Morton shows how Carroll engages in a *recherche du temps perdu*.

A notable event for Gissing scholars is the publication of the writer's diary[67], ably edited (with introduction and notes) by the indefatigable Pierre Coustillas. Covering fifteen years of Gissing's life (1887–1902), it provides a detailed record of daily activities – working routine, reading, literary contacts, travel and, above all, the endless struggle to combat solitude and discouragement. Though Coustillas makes interesting claims for the cultural importance of the diary, he seems nearer the mark in describing it as a record of the writer's vocation considered as 'a trade of the damned'. 'I never enjoy anything now – *never anything*' – Gissing's own entry of 1888 might act as a rubric for the diary's overall tone.

Rod Edmonds (*L&H*) discusses the interwoven strands which give 'The Conservatism of Gissing's Early Novels' its distinctive character – the artist's own struggle to survive in the London of the 1880s, an attraction to social Darwinism which helped to strengthen his anti-working-class bias, and the adoption of Schopenhauerian tenets. Such a position, in Edmonds's view, does not forbid compassion for individual suffering, but it does neutralise 'any criticism of particular social forms or institutions' and results in 'ideological deformation'.

Harvester Press continues to reprint Gissing's novels in handsome modern editions, each with an introduction, notes and bibliography. This year's volumes include *Born in Exile*[68], edited by Pierre Coustillas, *The Crown of Life*[69], edited by Michel Ballard, and *Denzil Quarrier*[70], edited by John Halperin. Among many articles in *The Gissing Newsletter*, the most notable are Ivan Melada's 'George Gissing's Anti-Jingo Book: *The Crown of Life* and the "Question of Peace" ', John Peck's '*New Grub*

[65] *H. Rider Haggard: A Voice from the Infinite*, by Peter Berresford Ellis. Routledge & Kegan Paul. pp. xiv + 291. £7.95.

[66] *Robert Louis Stevenson: Supplementary catalogue of the Stevenson Collection in the Edinburgh Room with a select list of books and manuscripts in Lady Stair's House Museum*. Edinburgh City Libraries. pp. 40. pb £0.50.

[67] *London and the Life of Literature in Late Victorian England: The Diary of George Gissing, Novelist*, ed. by Pierre Coustillas. Hassocks, Sussex: Harvester P. pp. vii + 617. £16.50.

[68] *Born in Exile*, by George Gissing, ed. with intro. by Pierre Coustillas. Hassocks, Sussex: Harvester P. pp. xxi + 521. £7.50.

[69] *The Crown of Life*, by George Gissing, ed. with intro. by Michel Ballard. Hassocks, Sussex: Harvester P. pp. xx + 341. £8.50.

[70] *Denzil Quarrier*, by George Gissing, ed. with intro. by John Halperin. Hassocks, Sussex: Harvester P. pp. xx + 355.

Street: Some Suggestions for an Approach Through Form', R. D. Best's 'Alice Ward and the Gissings', and Alison Cotes's 'New Women and Odd Women'. In *EA*, Pierre Coustillas offers a useful survey, '*New Grub Street*: Esquisse de Panorama Bibliographique et Critique'.

Lord Birkenhead's biography of Rudyard Kipling[71], delayed for over thirty years by the refusal of Kipling's daughter to allow its publication, is at last in print (introduced with an account of its controversial background by the author's son). Neither an unkind nor even unattractive portrait, Birkenhead's work is simply a more authoritatively personal one than any other, shedding fresh light on Kipling's background, life in India, and his more personal relationships. He had full access to Kipling's papers and, when the study was written in 1948, the advantage of being able to interview still-surviving friends of the writer. With revisions incorporated at a later date, this posthumous volume deserves to stand as a worthy complement to Carrington's authorised biography.

Coincidentally, a third edition of Charles Carrington's biography[72] has appeared this year. Like good wine, it has also matured over the years: in this edition new material is mainly restricted to a series of appendixes which bring the study up to date. One of his appendixes provides a background for Kipling's *The Light that Failed*, a story which is also reassessed by Robert F. Moss in *ELT*.

3. Prose

This section has the following parts: (a) Bibliography, and General and thematic works. (b) Individual authors. (c) Periodicals and Publishing History.

(a) Bibliography and General

In *Primary Sources for Victorian Studies*[73] Richard Storey and Lionel Madden provide basic information about the location and use of manuscripts and other unpublished source materials in Britain. Succinct chapters on the Historical Manuscripts Commission, national and local repositories, general published guides, special subject interests, and organisation and description of materials indicate the scope of this guide, which will be of great use to research students of history, the history of science, literature, and business history. Linda C. Dowling's *Aestheticism and Decadence*[74] is a 'selective annotated bibliography' of books, articles, and dissertations written between 1882 and 1975. The annotations are reasonably full and disinterested, and the introduction, if breezy, attempts to define and summarise.

CERVE devotes one number to a bibliography of ongoing theses in French Universities which concern the Victorian and Edwardian periods.

[71] *Rudyard Kipling*, by Lord Birkenhead. Weidenfeld & Nicolson. pp. xi + 423. £7.95.

[72] *Rudyard Kipling*, by Charles Carrington. Third edition. Macmillan. pp. 652. £8.95.

[73] *Primary Sources for Victorian Studies*, by Richard Storey and Lionel Madden. Chichester, Sussex: Phillimore, 1977. pp. 81. £3.50.

[74] *Aestheticism and Decadence*, by Linda C. Dowling. New York and London: Garland, 1977. pp. 140. $24.

They are listed by subject, theme, and author. In *Publishing History* Alan Bell reports on the recent acquisition of publishing archives by the National Library of Scotland, some of them Victorian. A detailed description of the additional Blackwood papers, the Oliver and Boyd archives, and the Smith, Elder papers is tendered. In *VS* Leslie G. Bailey provides 'An Update' to the previous listings of Victorian Studies programmes in English speaking countries.

In the first volume of *Authors by Profession*[75] Victor Bonham-Carter combines an account of the early years of the Society of Authors with an outline of the growth and nature of professional authorship from the introduction of printing until the Copyright Act of 1911. The bulk of the narrative treats the nineteenth century, with only one chapter on the period between 1500 and 1800. The author particularly concerns himself with the business arrangements of novelists and playwrights. But this book suffers from its diverse interests – in the Society of Authors, in development of copyright, and in authorship as a profession and it has been overtaken in the last category by more specialised, and thus more detailed works such as John Sutherland's *Victorian Novelists and their Publishers*. But the history of the Society of Authors is welcome.

In *Guardians and Angels*[76] David Grylls traces the development of thought in the nineteenth century on the subject of parent–child relations, and finds a 'growth of childhood independence and the decay of parental power'; 'the Victorian father is probably a myth'. The author expresses interest in the methodological problems of such a study, and besides examining attitudes in imaginative literature – such as the novels of Dickens and Jane Austen, *The Way of All Flesh*, and *Father and Son* – he also looks carefully at nineteenth-century children's books, and periodical articles about parent–child relations. *Guardians & Angels* is an integrated ruminative book on a theme, rather than a series of essays on individual texts, and only Gosse's and Butler's autobiographies are treated as artistic wholes. But Grylls does create a lively, coherent and wide-ranging essay on the subject which usefully provides a context for more detailed study of specific children and parents in literature.

Ben Knights, in a work which combines literary criticism and intellectual history, studies *The Idea of the Clerisy in the Nineteenth Century*[77]. Chapters on Coleridge, Carlyle, Arnold, Mill, and the idea of a university are preceded by a substantial introduction in which Knights provides for them both a background and a framework. He concludes in an epilogue, 'Cultural studies without a clerisy', that 'We might with advantage learn to look on outstanding cultural works as voices contributing to and arising from ongoing social dialogue' rather than regarding culture as requiring deference. This cogent argument ends by renouncing the clerisy as the vehicle of a society's values and by examining the implications for the academy.

[75] *Authors by Profession, Vol. I*, by Victor Bonham-Carter. The Society of Authors. pp. 252. £5.95 and £2.95.

[76] *Guardians and Angels: Parents and Children in 19th Century Literature*, by David Grylls. Faber & Faber. pp. 211. £6.50.

[77] *The Idea of the Clerisy in the Nineteenth Century*, by Ben Knights. Cambridge: C.U.P. pp. x + 274. £12.50.

The Victorians[78] contains essays on aspects of the social context of Victorian literature, as well as two initial statements, 'The novel' by Geoffrey Hemstedt and 'Poetry' by the editor, and two final comparative essays by the editor on *Dombey and Son* and on *The Princess*. In the middle section Barry Supple writes on 'Material Development: the condition of England 1830–1860' and 'The governing framework: social class and institutional reform in Victorian Britain', Carol Dyhouse on 'The condition of England 1860–1900' and 'The role of women; from self-sacrifice to self-awareness', J. W. Burrow on 'The sense of the past' and 'Faiths, doubt and unbelief', and Geoffrey Hemstedt on 'Painting and illustration'. Short bibliographies accompany each piece. On the whole, the standard of the essays is high and *The Victorians* can be recommended to the intelligent newcomer to the period with confidence.

In *The Child Figure in English Literature*[79] Robert Pattison suggests from interpretation of children in English literature before 1914 that the child figure tends to appear in thematic surroundings which discuss the Fall of Man, and that the norm against which we have become accustomed to measure these discussions is that of Original Sin. Pattison examines the child figure from Homer to Augustine and the pre-Romantic English tradition in two chapters, but the remainder of the book treats nineteenth-century authors – Wordsworth, Dickens, George Eliot, and Henry James. For the child's perspective he turns to Gosse, and Dickens and James again; finally he looks at children in children's literature from James Janeway in the seventeenth century to Lewis Carroll.

Susan S. Tamke considers hymns as a reflection of the social concerns of Victorian Christians in *Make a Joyful Noise Unto the Lord*[80]; liturgical, theological, and devotional hymns which largely defy sociological analysis are ignored. In chapters on the history of hymns, evangelicalism, the didactic church, hymns for children, the condition of England question, foreign mission, and imagery, Tamke reveals a wealth of source material, as well as providing interesting commentary. There are extensive notes and a full and useful bibliography.

Geoffrey Tillotson's *A View of Victorian Literature*[81] is essentially a draft of material intended for the mid-nineteenth-century volumes of the *Oxford History of English Literature*, edited knowledgeably and tactfully by Kathleen Tillotson, after her husband's untimely death. It contains essays on six novelists – Dickens, Thackeray, Charlotte and Emily Brontë, Elizabeth Gaskell, and Trollope – on Tennyson and Browning, and on Carlyle. It is emphatically worth having because the author's profound familiarity with the literature of the period means that the essays are concrete and wide-ranging, full of comparisons which command assent and offer illumination. Geoffrey Tillotson's style is leisurely, ruminative, and

[78] *The Victorians*, ed. by Laurence Lerner. Methuen. The Context of English Literature. pp. vii + 228. £8. and £3.95.

[79] *The Child Figure in English Literature*, by Robert Pattison. Athens, Ga.: U. of Georgia P. pp. xiv + 190. $10.50.

[80] *Make a Joyful Noise Unto the Lord*, by Susan S. Tamke. Athens, Ohio: Ohio U.P. pp. x + 209. $12. and $5.

[81] *A View of Victorian Literature*, by Geoffrey Tillotson. Oxford: Clarendon P. pp. x + 396. £6.95.

clear – old-fashioned qualities which make for much additional pleasure in the text.

Noting that Victorian narrative forms are neither coherent nor indeterminate, James Kincaid suggests that while Victorian authors characteristically employ forms which can encompass calamity, they then deny that form or tradition, and resort to the explanation that explanation is lacking (*VN*). Repeated use of an incompetent reporter reflects this rhetorical duality. For illustration Kincaid draws on the poetry and fiction of Hardy, on *Wuthering Heights*, and on the work of Tennyson, Hopkins, Edward Lear, Browning, Trollope, and Samuel Butler. In *PRR* symbolism and point of view in 'Mariana' and Holman Hunt's 'The Awakening Conscience' are compared by Michael C. Kotzin who wishes to stress links between Tennyson's attitude toward setting and that of Pre-Raphaelite painters. Stanley Weintraub discusses autobiography and authenticity through considering memoirs and fiction of Shaw, Yeats, and George Moore (*CERVE*). Concluding that as memoirist Shaw could be relied on for his facts, Yeats for his essential truth, and Moore for his impressions, Weintraub suggests that the truth of documentation is only one dimension of autobiographical authenticity.

(b) Authors

Leslie Brisman shows how Arnold's conception of God as seen in *God and the Bible* and *Literature and Dogma* inspired Mordecai Kaplan, the great modern philosopher of Judaism. This is one of three papers delivered at an MLA special session on these texts of Arnold's and published by *The Arnoldian*. In 'The Gospel According to Arnold' Jerold Savory denies that Arnold's religious books were either a break from his earlier concerns or less important than his other works. Briefly noting how Arnold in these works anticipates later theologians, Savory concentrates on the effects on *God and the Bible* of the simultaneous appearance of Walter Cassel's *Supernatural Religion*; in the same periodical Ruth apRoberts in 'Arnold and the Metaphor of Religion' regards *Literature and Dogma* as a landmark study of the relationship of religion to language. In a well set out argument, apRoberts convincingly shows the element of metaphor which distinguishes Arnold's notion of religion from the literalness of secular ethics.

In *ES* Dennis Douglas reminds readers not to trust Arnold's vociferous arguments with other critics by documenting his curious half-reliance on them. Arnold's limitations for Douglas are manifest in his insufficient awareness of the historical dimension of his critical assumptions which prevented him from bridging the gap between their historical and non-historical elements. Thomas S. Snyder examines the extent to which Arnold's political beliefs conform to the recognised factions of the Liberal Unionists, the secessionists who left the Liberal party in 1886, ostensibly over the issue of Home Rule. Arnold's singularity demonstrates the lack of Liberal Unionist homogeneity (*Arnoldian*).

Eloise Behnken's book on Carlyle[82] is a study of his religious thought;

[82] *Thomas Carlyle: 'Calvinist Without the Theology'*, by Eloise M. Behnken. Columbia, Mo., and London: U. of Missouri P. U. of Missouri Studies LXIV. pp. x + 149. $12.50.

he is seen 'as more radical than he is usually thought to be, for his world view. . .has much more in common with the death of God theology of the 1960s and 1970s than with the Calvinism he is often said to have inherited'. Where Charles Frederick Harrold in *Carlyle and German Thought* views Carlyle as more Calvinist than anything else, Behnken stresses the distinction between Carlyle's beliefs and Calvinism. This short work is comprised of chapters on the significance of labour, the early and later heroes, and eschatology and social theory. But there is little new here, and the high proportion of restatement of the texts is unfortunate. W. W. Waring's TEAS volume on Carlyle[83] is firmly aimed at American undergraduates, providing as it does, for example, book-by-book summaries of *Sartor Resartus*. It is written in a clipped matter-of-fact style suitable for its purpose. Waring regards Carlyle as neither a saint, nor a literary man, but as a moralist. As a succinct introduction for young people, preparatory to reading, this will do.

In '*Past and Present* as Literary Experience' (*PS*), William E. Buckler contrasts the imaginative sense of fact in that work with the contemporary *The Condition of the Working Class in England* by Engels, which is 'hardly literary'. He goes on to speculate about the concern with the relationship between poetry and truth shared by Carlyle in *Past and Present*, Browning in *The Ring and the Book*, and Tennyson in *In Memoriam*. Carlyle anticipates Pater here in making literature out of literature. James Hill draws attention to an allusion to Paul's epistle to the Romans in 'Shooting Niagra' (*Expl*). K. J. Fielding constructs from letters of the Wedgwoods a rich account of the Carlyles' long and warm friendship with Erasmus Darwin which, deliberately suppressed by Froude in his biography, serves to humanise the Carlyles (*E&S*). Among the influences on the young Charles Darwin studied by Edward Manier in *The Young Darwin and his Cultural Circle*[84] is Wordsworth's *The Excursion*. Notebooks, manuscripts, and marginalia of 1837–44 are the basis of this assessment of overlooked influences. This work, which treats such subjects as Darwin's employment of the metaphors associated with the words 'selection' and 'struggle', and his relation in his youth to the ideas of Lyell, Paley, and Malthus, should interest readers of *In Memoriam* especially. Stephen E. Tabachnick prods the first sentence of Charles Doughty's *Travels in Arabia Deserta* (1888) in order to divine Doughty's motives for the journey (*PRR*).

An annual, *The John Forster Newsletter*, edited by Alec W. C. Brice (38 Lewis Rd, Chipping Norton, Oxon.), made its first appearance this year. It includes 'Some Recent Work on the Forster Collection' by Anthony Burton and a progress report on Forster research (1876–1977), by James A. Davies; Engelina David publishes and comments on a letter of 1885 written by George Washington Putnam, Dickens's secretary on his 1842 American visit, who alludes to Forster as 'low and brutish' and his biography as unjust to Dickens. In *N&Q* Edmund Gosse's silent corrections to impressions and editions of *Father and Son* are located and revealed by

[83] *Thomas Carlyle*, by W. W. Waring, Boston, Mass.: Twayne, G. K. Hall. TEAS 238. pp. 146. $8.95.

[84] *The Young Darwin and his Cultural Circle*, by Edward Manier. Dordrecht, Holland, and Boston, Mass.: D. Reidel Publishing Co. Studies in the History of Modern Science. pp. xii + 242. $24.50 and $11.95.

Douglas Wertheimer who suggests that the author's reticence about errors in the text stemmed from his fear of John Churton Collins, virulent critic of Gosse's *From Shakespeare to Pope* in 1885.

Richard Holt Hutton's literary criticism concerning Arnold's poetry and prose is delineated in its characteristic aspects by Patrick J. Creevy in *VP*. Hutton judges Arnold's poetry sane, his criticism over-intellectual, and his theology sentimental. For Hutton, Arnold as a critic was avoiding even more of himself than he did as a poet. Creevy's claim that Hutton is Arnold's best Victorian critic is unproven as no comparisons are offered, but from what Creevy has amassed, Hutton is undeniably good and full on Arnold's 'sweet reasonableness'. In *PS* Donald Watt suggests that T. H. Huxley's sharp sense of humour and versatile figurative language are vital agents in his prose.

Faber and Faber mark the centenary of Edward Thomas's birth with a new edition of his much praised 1909 biography of the essayist, novelist, and working journalist, Richard Jefferies (1848–1887)[85].

John Griffin contributes to our knowledge of John Keble's early writing in the attribution to Keble of two early reviews for the *Quarterly* in 1816 on Wordsworth and Chateaubriand on the basis of letters to John Taylor Coleridge. Keble emerges unexpectedly as a vigorous critic of Wordsworth's practice and theory, of the *ancien régime*, and of the *Quarterly* itself for its intolerance of Socinianism (*RES*).

Andrew Lang is Eleanor de Selms Langstaff's subject in the Twayne series[86]. Lang as poet, novelist, classicist, critic, writer of children's tales, anthropologist, and journalist is described and assessed here, and the book acquaints the reader new to Lang with the contours of his achievement.

Hock Guan Tjoa's *George Henry Lewes*[87] provides an analysis of Lewes's 'major intellectual pre-occupations', which Tjoa believes to be moral and philosophical rather than literary: he includes a discussion of the social setting of Lewes's journalistic career to show the circumstances within which a man of letters was forced to advance his career. Thus we have three chapters: The Making of a Man of Letters, the Man of Letters as Moralist, and The Construction of a Victorian World-View. In the second Tjoa discusses Lewes's criticism of society and of literature, and in the third his philosophical and scientific writing. This study (rightly) assumes that most of its readers will be unfamiliar with Lewes's work, and thus includes a certain amount of description and explanation, which in a short work takes its toll. But the essay is to be welcomed as the beginning of a re-assessment of Lewes's contribution to Victorian intellectual life. Appended are a short bibliographical essay and full notes. K. K. Collins's description of George Eliot's preparation and revision of Lewes's manuscripts for the third series of *Problems of Life and Mind* in *VS* is largely concerned with how George Eliot writes about ethics; but the article also necessarily considers Lewes's moral philosophy. In an appendix the author presents in parallel a transcript of the Lewes MS. and Eliot's revised text.

[85] *Richard Jefferies*, by Edward Thomas. Faber & Faber. pp. x + 306. £4.95 and £2.25.

[86] *Andrew Lang*, by Eleanor de Selms Langstaff. Boston, Mass.: Twayne, G. K. Hall. TEAS 241. pp. 176. $9.50.

[87] *George Henry Lewes: A Victorian Mind*, by Hock Guan Tjoa. Cambridge, Mass. and London: Harvard U.P. Harvard Historical Monographs LXX. pp. xii + 172. £7.

An unpublished memoir of Lord Macaulay probably written by his sister Frances *circa* 1875 is offered by Randolph J. Bufano as a likely source of G. O. Trevelyan's *Life* and a supplement to it (*N&Q*). It tells us domestic details of Macaulay as a child and young man, and stresses his 'unexampled powers of conversation'. In the same journal A. K. Bacon makes some additions to E. D. LeMire's calendar and bibliography of William Morris's speaking career in his edition of the unpublished lectures (*YW* 50.288), and a newspaper report of Morris's otherwise unknown speech for the opening of an annual art exhibition in Whitechapel in 1884 is reprinted from the *East London Observer* by Frances Borzello. Catherine Buckley considers some of the criticism of Morris's notions of art during the 1880s and 1890s in *JWMS*. In *PS* Elizabeth Strode examines the propaganda style evident in Morris's prose after he became a socialist and joined the Democratic federation in 1883. *Lectures on Art and Industry, Signs of Change, Lectures on Socialism*, and *Art and Crafts Essays* Strode finds the 'most consistently well-produced of all his works'. In 'Art and Society in the Late Prose Narratives' N. J. Tyson distinguishes between the didactic socialism of *A Dream of John Ball* and *News from Nowhere* and the escapism and delightfulness of the other eight non-didactic prose narratives (*PRR*). But at the same time she detects various reflections of Morris's socialism in details of these non-didactic pieces. The pyrotechnical correspondence in *DUJ* between E. P. Thompson and John Y. Le Bourgeois about the depth of Morris's Marxism continues.

Robert Pattison suggests that questions raised for Newman by the Arian heresy and its confutation by St Athanasius became after 1830 the frame of Newman's historical perspective on other events. The heresy served as his model of the danger of the usurpation of religion by philosophy, and Pattison shows how other aspects of anti-Arianism are reflected in specific tenets of Newman's dislike of liberalism (*Mosaic*).

John J. Conlon publishes three uncollected letters (1882–3) of Walter Pater to D. S. MacColl, the editor of the *Oxford Magazine*, from the Glasgow University Library; in them Pater refuses and then agrees to review *Love in Idleness* (*N&Q*). For Olivia C. Ayres in *SEL*, *Marius the Epicurean* is the epitome of Pater's works that discuss the fusion of form and spirit because the novel takes the form of dialectic, Pater's conception of truth; the truest mimetic form of the dialectic in the novel is Marius's repeated journeys. Though interesting, this article is tendentious, and skimpy on the origins of the fusion of form and spirit; Heraclitus as well as Plato figures in Pater's earliest thoughts on fusion in the 1860s. In '*Marius the Epicurean*: Beyond Victorianism' (*VP*) William E. Buckler notes the pervasive Lockean underpinnings in Pater's epistemology and psychology, the first principle of which is *sentio ergo sum*. Buckler treats *Marius* as the focal document for the study of the transformation of the creative spirit of the nineteenth century into that of the twentieth, and regards it as the most accomplished product of the nineteenth century's highly developed 'science of origins'. Buckler looks in detail at the 'White Nights' sections of *Marius* and the ironies of the novel's conclusion.

In *PRR* Earl F. Bargainnier considers the 1868 essay 'Aesthetic Poetry' from which the 'Conclusion' to *Studies in the History of the Renaissance* was drawn, and what its treatment of Morris reveals of Pater's relationship to Pre-Raphaelitism. It is true, as Bargainnier states, that 'Aesthetic Poetry' has not been a common subject of Pater criticism, but this article fails to offer new perspectives on the essay. Richard Dellamora suggests that Pater's interpretation of Leonardo in his early essay is a modernist attempt to define a self-consciously modern, homoerotic idea of beauty and to celebrate Leonardo's pagan rather than Christian elements. Pater's version is compared with those of Michelet, Arsène Houssaye, Gautier, and Charles Clement, and Pater's comments on four paintings are assessed in detail (*UTQ*). The succession of androgynes and images of self-awareness and of self-fulfilment in Pater's piece on Leonardo were seen by younger contemporaries of Pater as norms for the enquiring artist.

In a closely argued and interesting essay in *NCF* Gerald Monsman examines the structure and build-up of psychological urgencies in *Gaston de Latour* in order to explain Pater's inability to complete it. Monsman regards *Gaston* along with the other imaginary portraits as autobiographical. Pater's sense of dualism is dramatised in the fiction as the separation of the hero from his double (echoing Pater's relation to his brother William) and resolved in harmony only in the realm of the text. But in *Gaston* Monsman suggests the resolution appeared sinister, and Pater turned to his most impersonal work, *Plato and Platonism*, instead. In *N&Q* I. C. Small identifies two sources for Pater's portrayal of Spinoza in 'Sebastian Van Storck': a rare book, Andala's *Apologia pro vera et saniore philosophia* (1719), and John Colerus's *Life of Spinosa* (1706) which had recently been republished by Frederick Pollock, whose commentary also helped Pater. Pater's debt in the critical vocabulary of *Studies in the History of the Renaissance* to British psychology of the 1860s and 1870s, revealed by I. C. Small in *BJA*, clarifies the relation between the 'Preface' and 'Conclusion' of that work. H. Spencer, James Sully, Alexander Bain, and the literary and art criticism of the time shared a highly specialised vocabulary, a jargon. *News of Pater Scholarship*, a newsletter, appeared for the first time this year; it is available from its editors, Billie Inman (University of Arizona, Tucson) and Laurel Brake (University of Wales, Aberystwyth).

In *Looking at Architecture with Ruskin*[88] John Unrau considers Ruskin's ideas about architecture in the light of his contemporaries' theories and practice, and of twentieth-century concepts and criteria of architecture and art criticism. Ruskin's approach can enrich modern study of architecture claims Unrau, especially if his architectural writings are studied from a point of view which disregards his 'sweeping ethical and historical pronouncements'. Illustrations of Ruskin's drawings help Unrau convince the reader of how much Ruskin knew about architecture. Quentin Bell's succinct monograph on Ruskin[89] appears in a new edition for which the author tells us there were few passages that he was tempted to rewrite. But the bibliography is updated from the original in 1963. Quentin Bell's book represents the old-fashioned alternative to the Twayne monographs which serve the new generations of American students as introductions.

[88] *Looking at Architecture with Ruskin*, by John Unrau. Thames & Hudson. pp. 180. £7.50.

[89] *Ruskin*, by Quentin Bell. Hogarth P. pp. 164. £3.75.

But the combination of Bell's light touch, wisdom, and reading experience is palatable and difficult to better.

John Hayman traces Ruskin's developing pre-occupation with myth in the shifting foci of *Modern Painters* as a preface to comment on Ruskin's concern with the 'natural myths' in *The Queen of the Air*, which he saw as an aspect of 'natural history', of continuity (*PQ*). Remarking on the ways in which a dark dualism pervades the conception of myth in *The Queen of the Air*, Hayman notes also the frequent Blakean transcendence of that dualism which distinguishes Ruskin's understanding of reality from that of the natural scientists. In *MLN* John Dixon Hunt calls attention to Ruskin's debts to eighteenth-century aesthetics of the picturesque and their persistence in his views of the experience of landscape and reading landscape painting until at least 1860, despite public renunciations of the picturesque. A fascination with ruins, a fresh alliance of word and picture in the wake of the eighteenth-century rejection of *ut pictura poesis*, and a repeated use of mirrors became 'the signature of Ruskin's imaginative world'. Adopting Todorov's notion of genre, Clinton Machann examines *Praeterita* in terms of codes associated with Romantic autobiography and shows how the author's use of these codes is related to his use of similar codes in other non-fictional prose: 'expectations based on the conventional codes are foregrounded and subverted' (*ELN*).

James G. Kennedy denies nearly all claims to interest of Herbert Spencer, the subject of his TEAS volume[90]. 'One goes to Spencer. . .to review errors that were plausible a century ago. . .He was neither a creator of fictions nor a great philosopher. Not an artist, he does not invite suspension of disbelief. . .Not a profound thinker, he does not face fundamental issues without logical errors. . .What Spencer's works still do is admonish all general writers. . .to be circumspect'. They are immoderately successful with Kennedy whose distilled interpretation has the force of fact and analysis alone. Among the nine chapters are essays on Spencer's prose style, his metaphysics, philosophy of mind, ethics, biology, sociology, economics and political philosophy, and his audience and influence. The index is scanty but the notes are ample.

Alan P. Johnson's informative bibliographical review essay of *The Memoirs of Arthur Symons* by Karl Beckson (*YW* 58.333–4) appears in *ELT*. For *Oscar Wilde*[91] E. H. Mikhail recklessly provides an introduction bristling with indignation at the errors and inadequacies that have characterised previous bibliographies, editions, and dissertations, but the first thing I noticed in his edition was a misprint. In addition, it should be remarked that the annotations indicated in the title are very light. Nevertheless, Mikhail gives us a selected 3500 entries in the following categories: bibliographies, published books by Wilde and their reviews, criticism on Oscar Wilde – books, periodicals and reviews of play productions, disserations, discography, and satires on Oscar Wilde in *Punch*. This work corrects and updates Mason, and modern students and scholars are likely to find it very useful.

[90] *Herbert Spencer*, by James G. Kennedy. Boston, Mass.: Twayne, G. K. Hall. TEAS 219. pp. 163. $8.95.

[91] *Oscar Wilde: An Annotated Bibliography of Criticism*, by E. H. Mikhail. Macmillan. pp. xii + 249. £15.

Bruce Bashford, in a sustained discussion, considers the criticism of Oscar Wilde as an example of subjectivist criticism as a type, and compares it with its anti-type, the new criticism notions of Northrop Frye. Those at present concerned with the reader as individual will find Wilde one of the few British critics of the past in this tradition (*ELT*). In their paper 'Anarchy and Culture' in *TSLL* Michael Helfand and Philip Smith II argue that ethnology and the study of human evolution have influenced the writing of English cultural critics such as Matthew Arnold and Oscar Wilde, but that Arnold's and Wilde's applications of these sciences to theories of cultural improvement are contrasting. Wilde's notions are representative of a group of radical social scientists and writers such as A. R. Wallace and Grant Allen. The authors discuss 'The Chinese Sage' and 'The Soul of Man Under Socialism' in some detail.

(c) Periodicals and Publishing History

Caught in the Web of Words[92] is the biography of James Murray (1837–1915), the first editor of the *O.E.D.* and the creator of modern historical lexicography. The author, Murray's granddaughter, has drawn extensively on privately-held sources and family oral tradition as well as correspondence and files for this well-written account. The nature of the endeavour and achievement of this largely self-educated man makes a significant contrast with the story of other great Victorian editors, such as Leslie Stephen or R. H. Hutton, who stemmed from the universities. The full account of the struggle for publication of the *O.E.D.* makes *Caught in the Web of Words* as pertinent to the history of publishing as it is to that of lexicography.

In *BSUF* E. M. Behnken reports on the feminine image in the monthly *English Woman's Journal* (1858–63), a periodical edited by Emily Faithfull, an activist for woman's employment. From this article it seems clear that the *Journal* which discussed employment, education, suffrage, and biography would be an illuminating background to fiction, poetry, and essays of the period. In a rag-bag in *Libr*, James S. Stone stresses Emily Faithfull's efforts to further education and the vote for women as well as employment; many articles in her periodical *The Victoria Magazine* attest to this. Stone's other addenda to Fredeman's article on the Victoria Press (*YW* 55.391) include more on Faithfull and the Codrington divorce case, on the connection between Faithfull and Austin Holyoake, and on Faithfull and her partner W. W. Head. In *VPN* Myra Stark reports on work in progress for the Garland edition of *The Englishwomen's Review of Social and Industrial Questions* (1866–1910), and Darwin F. Bostick reprints a mid-Victorian account of the *Examiner* by Charles Reynell found in the collection of Albany Fonblanque's papers at Princeton.

In *Libr* H. Neville Davies finds Tauchnitz collections (1862 and 1867) of Christmas stories from *All the Year Round* that antedate the first British collection and attributions in 1868. In an informative piece, he considers the accuracy of the Tauchnitz dates and the authority of their attributions of authorship for these editions, which were undoubtedly

[92] *Caught in the Web of Words. James A. H. Murray and the Oxford English Dictionary*, by K. M. Elisabeth Murray. New Haven, Conn., and London: Yale U.P., 1977. pp. xiv + 386. £6.95.

published by arrangement with the periodical. In 'Science in *Household Words*' Nancy A. Metz contests the view developed by Gordon Haight that Dickens remained indifferent or hostile to the scientific developments of his age (*VPN*). She points to the number and variety of articles on scientific subjects published under Dickens's editorial direction and analyses in some detail the role of science and the scientist in *Household Words*. Richard Elia provides a short list of post-Reform leaders from the *Morning Post* of 1833, each devoted to an individual, including Macaulay, Brougham, John Russell, and Wellington (*VPN*). Piracy is suspected by John Hodgson in the publication in *Harper's Weekly* of three stories by Elizabeth Gaskell which appeared in each case shortly before in *Household Words* or *All the Year Round* (*VPN*). However, from circumstances surrounding two other Gaskell stories in the same periodical, it appears that *Harper's Weekly* maintained a balance between piracy and purchase. How Richard Bentley and Sons recovered solvency between 1855 and 1857 by selling off their Standard Novels to the book trade is related by Elizabeth James in *Libr.*

An index of artists who created the cuts for the large cartoons in *Punch* between 1843 and 1848 and the 'suggestors' who proposed them is another result of John Bush Jones's (here with Priscilla Shaw) combing of the *Punch* files (*VPN*). K. A. Manley offers insight into the problems of Victorian librarians of the Bodleian in the enforcement of legal deposit under the Copyright Acts (*BLR*). In *VPN* Peter C. Noel-Bentley minutes in some detail the Research Society for Victorian Periodicals papers at the 1978 R.S.V.P. and Midwest Victorian Studies Association Conference. Also in *VPN* Gerald Olsen provides a profile of the *Church of England Temperance Magazine* (1862–1873), edited by Robert Maguire, William S. Peterson publishes a list of attributions for articles in *The Working Men's College Magazine* in 1859–60, and Rosemary T. Van Arsdel considers the growth of scholarship concerning Victorian periodicals by reviewing the first decade of *VPN*, in the same journal J. Don Vann reports on the resistance of the *United Service Gazette* of 1840 to efforts by Bentley to influence reviews of works of Fenimore Cooper, and to ruin authors who had left them for another publisher. An acrimonious correspondence between Robert Lee Wolff and J. A. Sutherland concerning the accuracy of Sutherland's *Victorian Novelists and Publishers* appears in *PBSA*. In 'Advertisements in Periodicals as a Means of Dating Eighteenth and Nineteenth Century Publications' in *VPN* James P. Woodruff and H. B. de Groot show that dates in advertisements must be treated with caution. The history of the phrase 'This day is published' is traced from the eighteenth century.

Deborah Gorham undertakes an examination of the contradictions within the agitation for the Criminal Law Amendment Act of 1885, the legislation which raised the age of consent to sixteen, after W. T. Stead's series on child prostitution in the *Pall Mall Gazette* of that year (*VS*). The ambiguity of aim among the reformers – control or protection of the children – reflects contradictions in the Victorian ideology of childhood and youth. Readers of Dickens, Thackeray, and Gaskell will find the author's probing apposite. J. O. Baylen publishes for the first time Gerald Massey's poem 'Greeting to W.T. Stead' which the author sent to Stead in 1886 after his release from prison, to which he had been sent in connection with his research for the 'Maiden Tribute of Modern Babylon' series (*VPN*), and in the same journal Ann Robson gauges the significance of the series; it 'ended the conspiracy of silence which had protected the double standard'. Stead was not merely exposing vice. He was challenging Victorian society.

4. Drama

Pride of place this year belongs to Michael Baker's informative and meticulously researched social history, *The Rise of the Victorian Actor*[93], in which he traces the growth of the actor's status and the emergence of acting as a respectable middle-class profession in Victorian England. The value of his study lies in the fresh evidence he adroitly synthesises from a remarkably wide number of sources – Select Committee Reports, census forms, diaries, religious tracts, memoirs, and even theatre novels. Such width of reference allows Baker varied perspectives upon the changing social character of the theatre and enables him to follow the interacting relationship between conditions within the theatre and changes of attitude outside it. Thus, while most of his chapters revolve round specific aspects of the actor's world (salary, contract, community, ethics, working conditions and so on), they also embrace wider changes in Victorian society – in moral and religious attitudes, the rise of middle-class professions, and the evolving identity of the theatre as a cultural institution. This illuminating survey concludes with appendixes giving family trees and biographical details of three generations of actors and actresses.

Meticulous scholarship, though of a more specialised kind, is also a feature of Terence Rees's *Theatre Lighting in the Age of Gas*[94], a definitive history of the period's stage-lighting. Rees follows the remarkable technical and operational changes brought about in all parts of the theatre by developments in the technology of illumination (as oil was superseded by gas, and gas by electricity). Scientific manuals, engineering records and theatre inventories supply a wealth of factual detail, through which Rees guides us with the help of diagrams and illustrations. His later chapters also helpfully show the effect of these technological changes upon production methods, scene- and costume-design.

L. W. Conolly and J. P. Wearing have compiled a comprehensive bibliography embracing all important aspects of nineteenth-century English theatre and drama[95]. Entries are listed chronologically in ten chapters which cover such topics as Victorian and modern criticism, individual authors, theatres, acting and management, anthologies, and critics. With its useful annotations and bibliographical details, this volume will be an indispensable aid to scholars and teachers working in the area.

[93] *The Rise of the Victorian Actor*, by Michael Baker. London: Croom Helm; Totowa, N.J.: Rowman & Littlefield. pp. v (unnumbered) + 249. £6.95.

[94] *Theatre Lighting in the Age of Gas*, by Terence Rees, with Foreword by Michael R. Booth. London: The Society for Theatre Research. pp. x + 238. £7.50.

[95] *English Drama and Theatre, 1800–1900: A Guide to Information Sources*, by L. W. Conolly and J. P. Wearing. Gale Information Guide Library 12. Detroit: Gale Research Co. pp. xix + 508. $18.

In *Queen Victoria Goes to the Theatre*[96], George Rowell draws upon hitherto unpublished material in the Queen's journal to construct a valuable record of her theatrical tastes and opinions, theatregoing, and patronage. Though ballet was her first love and opera her most constant, she was an assiduous playgoer with tastes ranging from French tragedy to contemporary melodrama. Windsor theatricals as well as later Command Performances also figure prominently in Rowell's account of relations between Crown and theatre. Attractive illustrations and a calendar of the Queen's theatregoing are supplementary features. A second edition of Rowell's study of the Victorian theatre (first published in 1956) has appeared this year, with a revised title and from a new publisher[97]. Additional material includes an afterword and an enlarged bibliography.

Raymond Mander and Joe Mitchenson evoke the world of Victorian and Edwardian entertainments through a compilation of finely reproduced photographs[98]. Theatre, ballet and opera are included as well as fairs, circuses and street performers. Accompanying captions give interesting information about the practitioners and techniques of theatrical photography.

Specific Victorian actors and actresses attract the attention of several critics this year. A revised and enlarged version of Richard Findlater's 1955 study of Grimaldi appears in a new edition under the title, *Joe Grimaldi: His Life and Theatre*[99]. Eleanor Ransome performs a valuable editorial service in distilling from the mass of Fanny Kemble's autobiographical writings (letters, memoirs and journals) a compact self-portrait[100] in which the actress emerges as a lively reporter of English and American life.

'His career not only spanned the whole history of the Victorian theatre . . .it *was* the Victorian theatre', writes Madeleine Bingham in her lively and sympathetic biography of Henry Irving[101]. She gives an intimate picture of Irving's life, career, and partnership with Ellen Terry both on and off stage, measuring the way in which Irving broke with and continued Victorian theatrical traditions. The trajectory of his career is also neatly interwoven with the story of the Lyceum's growing importance as a social and cultural institution in Victorian London. Further insight into the Lyceum's productions is provided by George Rowell who reproduces, describes and evaluates the contents of 'A Lyceum Sketchbook' (*NCTR*). Containing twenty-eight sketches made by a 'Marion Clarkson' between 1879 and 1883, these newly discovered illustrations offer rare glimpses of

[96] *Queen Victoria Goes to the Theatre*, by George Rowell. Paul Elek. pp. 144. £6.95.

[97] *The Victorian Theatre, 1792–1914: A Survey*, by George Rowell. Second edition. Cambridge: C.U.P. pp. xiii + 239. hb £10.50, pb £3.95.

[98] *Victorian and Edwardian Entertainment from old photographs*, by Raymond Mander and Joe Mitchenson. Batsford. pp. 120. £4.95.

[99] *Joe Grimaldi: His Life and Theatre*, by Richard Findlater. Second edition. Cambridge: C.U.P. pp. 260. hb £15, pb £4.95.

[100] *The Terrific Kemble: A Victorian Self-Portrait from the writings of Fanny Kemble*, ed. with intro. by Eleanor Ransome. Hamish Hamilton. pp. xv + 272. £7.50.

[101] *Henry Irving and the Victorian Theatre*, by Madeleine Bingham, with Foreword by John Gielgud. Allen & Unwin. pp. 312. £7.50.

such notable Irving productions as *Hamlet, The Merchant of Venice,* and *Much Ado About Nothing.* James Leggio compares 'Irving and Chaliapin' (*TN*), as a way of focusing the similarities between Victorian melodrama and opera, and to show how Irving's acting exploits 'the middle territory between speech and song'.

NCTR contains 'Edwin Landseer's Joke on Macready', in which A. H. Saxon shows how a Landseer painting of Van Amburgh and his performing animals contains an oblique joke directed at Macready's distaste for such popular spectacles. Carol J. Carlisle (*NCTR*) describes and evaluates the career of Harriet Faucit, a talented but less gifted actress than her sister, Helen.

Studies of Victorian plays, theatres and direction include Richard M. Ford's discussion of 'The Waverley Burlesques' produced between 1846 and 1885 (*NCTR*). He indicates the direct and indirect relationships between burlesques and original novels, and shows that in most productions literary travesty played a small part in the total comic effect. Sally Vernon (*NCTR*) discusses the controversy surrounding a play of 1840, James Haynes's *Mary Stuart*, to parts of which the censor took objection on the likely grounds that they reflected upon topical issues raised by the forthcoming marriage of Queen Victoria and Prince Albert. *TN* includes an examination by Christopher Calthrop of the brief, ill-fated partnership between Dion Boucicault and Benjamin Webster. Russell Jackson surveys 'Shakespeare in Liverpool: Edward Saker's Revivals, 1876–81' (*TN*), finding evidence of a vigorous provincial theatre whose manager professed the ideals of Charles Kean in Shakespearean production. Jackson also offers 'The Lyceum in Irving's Absence: G. E. Terry's Letters to Bram Stoker' (*NCTR*), drawing upon unpublished letters of 1883–4 which offer insights into the theatre's routine business and include Terry's opinion of Mary Anderson, the American actress who leased the theatre during Irving's absence. This same critic writes on the attitudes of 'J.F. Nisbet of *The Times*: A Conservative Critic of the 'Eighties and 'Nineties' (*ThRI*).

William Cox-Ife vigorously champions W. S. Gilbert[102] as an innovative stage-director who, while owing something to the example of T. W. Robertson, brought new standards of production to the theatre of his day. Gilbertian principles are clearly explained – particularly his rule that a farcical subject should be treated in a thoroughly serious way – and the meticulous planning of the author-director is traced in his iron supervision of actors, chorus, and setting. Earl F. Bargainnier (*JPC*) outlines one area of Gilbert's influence in 'W.S. Gilbert and American Musical Theatre'.

The Dickensian contains two items on the presence of theatrical elements in Dickens's novels. Jim Davis compares Dickens's caricatural techniques with the low-comedy performances of John Liston, while Valerie Purton suggests a possible Dickens debt to Lytton's plays, particularly *Not So Bad As We Seem* (1851).

Students of Wilde will welcome E. H. Mikhail's comprehensive and up-to-date compilation, *Oscar Wilde: An Annotated Bibliography of*

[102] *W. S. Gilbert: Stage Director*, by William Cox-Ife, with Foreword by William Darlington. The Student's Music Library. Dennis Dobson, 1977. pp. 112. £4.25.

Criticism[103]. Its contents include bibliographies, published books by Wilde, criticism, dissertations, play reviews, and even 'discography'. A full-length critical study, Philip Cohen's *The Moral Vision of Oscar Wilde* (Rutherford: Fairleigh Dickinson U.P.; London: Associated U.P.), has not been available for inspection.

Wilde's drama is the subject of two articles in *MD*. In 'Oscar Wilde's Game of Being Earnest', Tirthankar Bose approaches the play's serious social meaning through an examination of its formal design – its matched situations, games of combat and courtship rituals. William Green considers Wilde's fascination with names and his technique of naming characters, with particular reference to the source and significance of 'Bunbury'.

Other articles include 'Artist, Critic, and Performer: Wilde and Joyce on Shakespeare' (*TSLL*), in which R. B. Kershner Jr reviews the general kinship between Wilde and Joyce, before going on to elaborate the specific influence of Wilde's 'The Portrait of Mr. W.H.' (1889) upon Stephen's Shakespearean disquisition in *Ulysses*. He convincingly shows that 'Joyce takes Wilde – or at least the *idea* of Wilde – very seriously indeed'. Michael S. Helfand and Philip E. Smith II (*TSLL*) have a twofold purpose in their study of 'Anarchy and Culture: The Evolutionary Turn of Cultural Criticism in the Work of Oscar Wilde'. They draw attention to the influence of science, particularly ethnology and evolutionary theory, in the cultural criticism of Arnold, Wilde and others, and secondly contrast Arnold's and Wilde's application of these sciences to theories of cultural improvement. Wilde's *The Picture of Dorian Gray* figures in Laurence M. Porter's wide-ranging study of 'Literary Structure and the Concept of Decadence: Huysmans, D'Annunzio, and Wilde' (*CentR*).

[103] *Oscar Wilde: An Annotated Bibliography of Criticism*, by E. H. Mikhail. Macmillan. pp. xii + 249. £15.

XVI

The Twentieth Century

MAUREEN MORAN, SUSAN PAINTER
and JAMES REDMOND

The chapter has the following sections: 1. The Novel, by Maureen Moran; 2. Verse, by Susan Painter, 3. Prose Drama, by James Redmond.

1. The Novel

Some absorbing general studies on the state of contemporary fiction which have appeared this year will certainly stimulate further intense discussion about the nature of modern novels. Important editions of manuscript and unpublished material by Forster, Joyce, Lawrence, and Woolf have been printed, and some impressive critical work has been done on Conrad, Lawrence, and Joyce.

(a) General Studies

Among the excellent studies on modern fiction is Malcolm Bradbury's *The Novel Today*[1], an important collection of essays by major contemporary novelists and several critics, together with interviews. In a penetrating introduction Bradbury traces the evolution of the novel and shows the violent oscillation in contemporary fiction between novels as 'social documentation' and novels as 'form, fictionality, and reflexive self-examination'. He also outlines briefly the effect of new developments in philosophy and psychology on modern fiction and describes the revival of realist novels in the postwar period. The current interest in the theory of fiction complements a growing emphasis on 'structure, pattern, form', and the contemporary novel with its plurality of styles and techniques, its idiosyncratic mannerisms, and its frequent 'game-like' constructs becomes 'a sample case of self-conscious organization of experience'. Yet the withdrawal from realism so marked in, say, the *nouveau roman* is far less apparent in English fiction which is primarily anti-experimental. Nevertheless, the modern novel is still 'evolving and changing', and writers like Iris Murdoch and Angus Wilson are moving into mythic and disordered narratives in an attempt to question the status of the text. The first essay reprinted in the anthology is 'Against Dryness' in which Iris Murdoch voices her suspicions of a form which lures reader and writer away from reality: 'what we require is a renewed sense of the difficulty and complexity of the moral life and the opacity of persons'. Philip Roth considers the difficulty of writing fiction in America given that country's current social,

[1] *The Novel Today: Contemporary Writers on Modern Fiction*, ed. by Malcolm Bradbury. Fontana. 1977. pp. 256. pb £1.50.

political and cultural predicament. Michel Butor calls for an evolution of the concept of the novel 'toward a new kind of poetry at once epic and didactic' when he investigates differing notions of narrative and the relationship of narrative to the reality around us. Recent American fictional treatments of 'the individual and his society' are considered in a 1963 essay by Saul Bellow, while John Barth centres on Jorge Luis Borges' exhaustion of certain fictional possibilities. David Lodge's fine essay, 'The Novelist at the Crossroads', is included. Lodge reflects on the validity of claims that the novel is disintegrating into 'fabulation'. While he affirms his faith 'in the future of realistic fiction', he admits that scepticism concerning 'the aesthetic and epistemological premises of literary realism' is forcing novelists to turn to non-fiction novels, fabulation, and game fiction. Extracts from Frank Kermode's interviews with seven novelists are printed. He discusses the relationship between fiction and reality with Iris Murdoch, Graham Greene, Angus Wilson, Ivy Compton-Burnett, C. P. Snow, John Wain, and Muriel Spark. John Fowles' notes on technical difficulties encountered when writing *The French-Lieutenant's Woman* and Doris Lessing's Preface to *The Golden Notebook* are also to be found in the anthology. B. S. Johnson relates his fiction to his life in an introduction to *Aren't You Rather Young to be Writing Your Memoirs?* Philip Stevick describes and characterises the 'new fiction', and Gerald Graff defines post-modernism as the culmination of the romantic-modernist tradition. It is 'a reactionary tendency, one which reinforces the effects of technocratic, bureaucratic society'. The selection finishes with a good bibliography.

In the Summer issue of *New Review*, fifty-six novelists comment on developments in fiction in the last decade and make predictions on the state of the novel in the next ten years. Observations range from Kingsley Amis's 'I have no hopes worth going on about' to David Lodge's concern about 'the absence of any significant school or movement' and call for 'a reinvigoration of criticism' and 'the infusion of some new, genuinely original creative talent'. In *Novel* N. W. Visser writes on 'The Generic Identity of the Novel', and Franz K. Stanzel entertains some 'Second Thoughts on Narrative Situations in the Novel' in an attempt to derive a grammar of fiction. Mark Spilka conducts a symposium on character in modern fiction. In *PLL* Jeffrey R. Smitten looks at narrative structure and 'spatiality' in fiction. Johan Thielemans surveys representatives of the New Fiction in Britain in *RLV*. Giles Gordon, B. S. Johnson, John Noone, David Caute, and John Berger 'are all in their several ways concerned with a renewed investigation of the relation between experience and language'.

J. A. Sutherland has produced a timely, illuminating and entertaining survey of the British fiction industry[2] which will fascinate writers and readers alike. The current crisis in the book trade is vigorously examined; external factors such as inflation and the 'Americanizing' of British publishing are identified; possible state remedies are discussed (Public Lending Right and Arts Council subsidies, for example); revolutionary trends (book clubs, the 'telenovel') are assessed. Sutherland detects a serious decline in the book industry and a deterioration in the circumstances under which novels are produced today. Production needs and marketing styles take

[2] *Fiction and the Fiction Industry,* by J. A. Sutherland. Athlone P. pp. xxviii + 231. £6.95.

precedence over the desire to cater for minority tastes. Reduced public spending and the failure of government cultural agencies to resolve current problems mean that fewer books are available for the general reading public. Yet despite such gloomy findings, Sutherland remains hopeful that 'the crisis of the 1970s will probably take its place in a long series of critical episodes in the production of fiction none of which has yet proved final, however painful they seemed at the time'.

Stephen Hazell has gathered a number of critical essays on fiction from Henry James to the present day[3] in order to show developments in novel criticism. In a concise and comprehensive introduction Hazell identifies two critical extremes – either 'total absorption in a novel' or 'unceasing analytical consciousness'. The four parts of the anthology define these extremes and demonstrate varying positions between them. Part I begins with two essays by James showing his 'consciously-developed reading of novels' and greater awareness of the relationships between moral values and artistic modes. Lawrence's essays on 'Morality and the Novel' and 'John Galsworthy' manifest moral concerns as well and, like James's criticism, call for sincere, personally involved readers and critics; the autonomy of the work of art is also stressed. Essays by Trilling and Leavis round out the section. Leavis resembles James and Lawrence in his concern with the 'independent organic' world of the novel and its moral pre-occupations. He formally insists on the 'importance of evaluation' and argues that novels which have moral significance and pre-occupations are infinitely superior to novels which are simply life-like. Trilling's approach is rather different, for he emphasises the need to see literature in a much wider context of philosophical, political, intellectual, and psychological developments. Part II contains essays by Barbara Hardy, Wayne Booth, Robert Scholes, and David Lodge dealing specifically with George Eliot, Fielding, Durrell, and Beckett. These analytical critics are interested in the skills of the novelist and, in Hazell's words, try 'to increase awareness of verbal and formal artifice in the novel'. Essays by Frank Kermode, Norman Holland, Malcolm Bradbury, Raymond Williams, and David Craig cover subjects such as Golding, Hardy, and 'the Rising Industrial Classes' in Part III. Critical approaches here range through Freudian, liberal, and Marxist; some critics, such as Kermode, are not committed to any single ideology. All respond in their various ways to the present crisis in realism. Finally in Part IV, three novelists – Murdoch, Wilson, and Fowles – write about novels and their own work. Like the critics they too are concerned with such problems as form and the relationship of story to authorial intention. The essays in this collection have all been previously published, but by drawing them together and grouping them effectively, Hazell has provided much valuable comparative material as fuel for the critical debate between those who desire evaluation and those who seek explication in their novel criticism.

Several challenging articles on modernist fiction appear in *Modernism*[4].

[3] *The English Novel: Developments in Criticism since Henry James,* ed. with an introduction by Stephen Hazell. (Casebook Series). Macmillan. pp. 239. hb £6.95. pb £2.95.

[4] *Modernism 1890–1930*, ed. by Malcolm Bradbury and James McFarlane. Hassocks, Sussex: Harvester P.; New Jersey: Humanities P. pp. 684. hb £10.95.

John Fletcher and Malcolm Bradbury investigate the 'symbolist' character of modern 'introverted' novels which are pre-occupied with their own fictiveness, form, and technique. J. P. Stern compares Theodor Fontane and Thomas Mann. Mann uses Fontane's '*bürgerlich* realism' but gradually undermines the realistic tradition with his awareness and depiction of the isolated consciousness. Michael Hollington moves toward a useful definition of 'a basic Modernist mood' when he compares the treatment of time by Svevo and Joyce. *Ulysses* is a particularly modernist text with its comic vision and 'its aim to exorcise the enslaving structure language imposes on experience'. The fiction of Conrad, Musil, Kafka, and Mann suggests to Franz Kuna that modern novels emboy 'Nietzsche's formula of the "Janus face" of modern man, who is doomed to exist tragically'. Melvin J. Friedman writes intelligently on the symbolist novel from Huysmans to Malraux, Donald Fanger considers the 'anguished ambivalence toward the burden of the past' in Biely, Mandelstam, and Zamyatin, and David Lodge perceptively compares metaphoric and metonymic structures in modernist fiction.

Varying themes and genres discovered in modern fiction have interested a number of critics. John Orr's *Tragic Realism and Modern Society*[5] is intended both as 'an original contribution to the sociology of the novel' and a 'criticism of the anti-realist conventions which have recently dominated the sociology of literature'. In Part I, Orr provides a strongly argued case for viewing tragic realism 'as the dominant genre of modern literature'. He defines tragic realism in the novel by considering its evolution and relationship to political fiction. Tragic realism is characterised by 'the alienation of its heroes from bourgeois societies. . . within novels which are nevertheless produced for a predominantly bourgeois readership within liberal capitalist societies'. Relationships are destroyed, potential is lost, moral values prove unattainable. Yet by its very nature tragic realism entails 'an artistic vision of the transformation of modern society' and Orr thus sees a connection between tragic realism and political fiction. In the political novel of tragic realism, 'its sense of the new, its prophetic character, emerge from a sense of loss and perhaps more decisively, a feeling of damnation in a secular world'. As well as emphasising the importance of the genre, Orr also suggests that anti-realist theorists, formalists, and structuralists are actually more dependent on 'a realist paradigm' than they admit. Such a suggestion is enticing and, while Orr does not develop it at length, it remains one of the more interesting issues which he raises. Part II involves a consideration of the political novel of tragic realism by writers working from 1848 to 1948: Tolstoy, Dostoevsky, Zola, Conrad, Mann, Sholokhov, Hemingway, Malraux, Orwell, and Solzhenitsyn. This section yields few surprises and though less confused by jargon than is usual in sociological literary studies, it generally fails to assess the literary merits or artistic strengths of the works discussed. Conrad is viewed predictably as rejecting 'from a thoroughly humanitarian yet tragic viewpoint, the bourgeois ideology of progress'. Orwell's *Nineteen Eighty-Four* is more interestingly described as 'a novel about the destruction of human freedom which is also a parable about the destruction of the novel'. Orr concludes with a short discussion of the decline of tragic realism. Sociological reasons

[5] *Tragic Realism and Modern Society: Studies in the Sociology of the Modern Novel*, by John Orr. Macmillan. 1977. pp. x + 204. £8.95.

for its disappearance are advanced, but he suggests that its resurgence may come from countries still emerging 'from a colonial or traditional past'.

David Smith's examination of Socialist propaganda in modern British fiction[6] is in essence a survey of the 'political propaganda novel' from about 1906 to 1956 (although more recent works are mentioned). Some important novelists who advocated the Socialist cause do appear; Robert Tressell, H. G. Wells, Grassic Gibbon, Wain, and Lessing are mentioned. But many unremarkable authors and novels march grimly and relentlessly through the pages in order to demonstrate the rise and fall of the socialist novel. Smith describes the gradual evolution of the working class novelist with his first-hand experience of 'social hardship', and he outlines the ways in which the writers of the 1930s tried to fictionalise their dogmatic beliefs, incorporating romance, suspense, and autobiography into their fiction as a means of persuasion. The middle-class, too, responded to social challenge in its novels, urging the need for Socialism as a weapon against Facism. Historical settings, surrealistic effects, and allegory were all pressed to serve the Socialist cause, as Smith exemplifies. But the revolutionary beliefs were only imperfectly grasped and gradually even those who espoused the left in the 1950s became ambivalent and aware of the deficiencies of their ideology. Smith concludes rather limply that the best Socialist propaganda novels are those with a 'blend of passion and hopefulness' which operate as both art and propaganda. It is worthwhile remembering Orwell's claim that Socialist literature was 'dull, tasteless and bad'. There is little here which proves that he was wrong, for few novels discussed are highly successful in an artistic sense.

David B. Espey considers the notion of the great white hunter in literature. Writing in *RS* he glances at the treatment of this sportsman and his relation to primitive natives in the work of Kipling, Conrad, Orwell, John Master, and Romain Gary. Bridget Puzon (*IILD*) argues that the *Bildungsroman* of middle life is 'a distinctive narrative form'. Robert M. Adams has an article in *SR* on a significant pattern which he finds in some modern novels – that of characters who form 'dynamic duos', 'magnetic centers within the same field of force, with attractions to and repulsions from one another that are not to be defined in terms of intrigue or plot'. Stephen and Bloom, Clarissa Dalloway and Septimus Smith, Molloy and Moran, and Benny Profane and Herbert Stencil are cited in evidence. John Z. Guzlowski and Yvonne Shikany Eddy offer a selected checklist in *MFS* on 'studies of the modern novel and the city'.

The literature of writers who form minority groups has also been examined this year. In the 1976 series of Clark Lectures at Cambridge Donald Davie considered the writing of English Dissenters since the seventeenth century, 'the heroic age of English Dissent'. These lectures are now collected in book form[7]. Davie surveys the relationship between literary themes, techniques, and dissenting belief and outlines the literary achievements of dissenters like Isaac Watts, Blake, Elizabeth Gaskell, George Eliot, and Mark Rutherford, before turning to the twentieth-century dissenter,

[6] *Socialist Propaganda in the Twentieth-Century British Novel,* by David Smith. Macmillan. pp. x + 203. £8.95.

[7] *A Gathered Church: The Literature of the English Dissenting Interest, 1700–1930,* by Donald Davie. Routledge & Kegan Paul. pp. viii + 152. £4.25.

D. H. Lawrence. Although brief, Davie's account of the failed Congregational tradition (which Lawrence inherited and which never satisfied his craving for ceremonial) offers new insights into the novelist's religious background and his later interest in ritual. Davie also considers the dissenters' art in *Father and Son*, 'an undoubted masterpiece' of the tradition. 'Simplicity, sobriety, and measure' emerge as the major characteristics of the great literary works by dissenters from Isaac Watts to Rutherford; and, Davie concludes, these qualities mark the chief contribution of the dissenting tradition to English cultural life.

A wide-ranging collection of previously published essays on contemporary women novelists has been edited by Patricia Meyer Spacks[8]. She introduces her book with an astute essay which suggests some of the problems facing the critics of women novelists and which provides an overview of the essays in the volume. Virginia K. Beards explores Margaret Drabble's interest in 'bungled and achieved female self-definition'. Ultimately, she concludes, though Drabble is both a 'compassionate pessimist' and 'feminist', the questions she explores are 'finally human and impartial to sexual distinction'. Dagmar Barnouw studies the different forms of narrative organisation in Lessing's *The Golden Notebook* and *The Four-Gated City*. Narrative structure is related to 'the development of the protagonist's consciousness' and most significantly supports the movement to self-knowledge in *The Four-Gated City* and *Briefing for a Descent into Hell*. The 'multiperspectivity' of *The Golden Notebook* is a failure. Frederick R. Karl also assesses Doris Lessing. Considering her as a writer of the 1960s, he detects a mythic pattern enhanced by images and symbols in the work of this period; the pattern of 'the descent into hell' is used to investigate the 'dislocation and fragmentation' of life for female characters in the 1960s. Such honesty about women is the perfect 'corollary of her political fervor in the fifties'. Norman Mailer and Patricia Meyer Spacks both write on Mary McCarthy, and Linda Kuehl energetically examines magical techniques and 'metaphysical fantasy' in the works of Iris Murdoch. Kuehl finally concludes that Murdoch's characters are dehumanised. They are forced to play predetermined roles and are crushed by 'weighty and unrealized philosophical concepts and mythic-literary allusions'. Her narrative designs are too playful and sensational. In the last analysis, Murdoch betrays her own 'wit, intelligence and inventiveness'. Thelma J. Shinn considers 'Women in the Novels of Ann Petry', and Elgin W. Mellown investigates connections between the novels of Jean Rhys. Rhys's ability to realise a particular character type is praised in glowing terms. 'Relentlessly she develops her single vision of a world in which free will is a myth and the individual has no power to control his destiny'. Technique and content in the novels are brilliantly matched. Malcolm Bradbury's interesting essay on Muriel Spark demonstrates a significant development in her fiction. *The Public Image*, *The Driver's Seat*, and *Not to Disturb* 'are all novels of ending'. *The Driver's Seat* in particular has an elegant and sophisticated movement 'not only to the aesthetic but also to the moral extreme of its own substance'. Two essays on Eudora Welty by John

[8] *Contemporary Women Novelists: A Collection of Critical Essays*, ed. with an introduction by Patricia Meyer Spacks. (Twentieth Century Views). Englewood Cliffs, N.J.: Prentice-Hall; London: Prentice-Hall International. 1977. pp. viii + 183.

Edward Hardy and Joyce Carol Oates round out this collection which ends with a helpful select bibliography.

Readers interested in modern women novelists will also wish to consult the Fall number of *SLitI* which is devoted to 'the female novelist in twentieth-century Britain'. Angus Wilson assesses the changing impact of Virginia Woolf on his own work as a way of suggesting her excellence and defects. Carol Ames stresses the importance of the relationship between nature and aristocracy in the work of Vita Sackville-West, finding that 'the nurturing unity between the true aristocrat and nature can lead him to a broader love of the world, can become destructive through his selfishness, or can lead to a deep sense of displacement'. Philippa Tristram suggests that Ivy Compton-Burnett 'precedes' Lawrence and Woolf with her interest in nineteenth-century life, particularly its decay and death. Hers is an 'embalmer's art' for she prepares 'the corpse of the nineteenth century for burial'. *Wide Sargasso Sea* is an impressionist masterpiece, according to Todd K. Bender, who relates the novel's patterns and themes to Rhys's other work. Frank Baldanza also looks at the work of Jean Rhys; he analyses her concern with the helpless woman victim. Robert O. Evans surveys the work of Sybille Bedford to substantiate his claim that she is an important twentieth-century novelist. Robin Grove appreciates the stylishness and clear-headedness of Elizabeth Taylor's work. Her use of middle-class speech to dramatise moral problems of loneliness and exclusion is exceptional. Peter Wolfe argues that Murdoch's *Black Prince* is her 'most celebrated novel', and Jack I. Biles provides a lively and entertaining interview with Murdoch. Finally, Joan Manheimer notes (with little originality) the struggle of Margaret Drabble's feminine characters towards identity. Drabble's work is branching out to the public realm with its complex but less radical heroines.

Woman in contemporary fiction between 1953 and 1975 is the subject of an extensive study by Georg Festerling[9]. It examines the extent to which twentieth-century extensions of the woman's role in society have or have not been reflected in recent fiction. The novels under discussion are selected from authors of the first post-war generation publishing in the early 1950s. Only novels actually set in the England of the last three decades are considered in an attempt to compare fiction and contemporary reality. Three types of fictional heroine emerge: the traditional wife and mother, the twentieth-century equivalent of the *femme fatale* in the figure of the 'domineering woman', and the new 'free woman' who refuses to conform to conventional role expectations. Particular attention is paid to works by Kingsley Amis, Stan Barstow, John Braine, Margaret Drabble, Doris Lessing, Alan Sillitoe, Muriel Spark, John Wain, and Angus Wilson. [H.C.C.]

Two studies based on particular periods of twentieth-century life and experience have appeared. John Lucas has reprinted a number of essays on and poems from the 1930s[10] which first appeared in a 1976 *RMS* Special Number (*YW* 57.320). The previously published critical articles are by

[9] *Die Frau im zeitgenössischen englischen Roman (1953–1975)*, by George Festerling. Bonn: Bouvier. (Studien zur englischen Literatur 18). pp. 341. DM 58.

[10] *The 1930s: A Challenge to Orthodoxy*, ed. by John Lucas. New York: Barnes & Noble; Hassocks, Sussex: Harvester P. pp. viii + 268. £9.95.

John Lucas, H. Gustav Klaus, Roy Johnson, Tom Paulin, P. J. Widdowson, and Arnold Rattenbury, and range over writings by Auden and MacNeice, Patrick Hamilton, and Grassic Gibbon as well as over intellectual and political commitments of the 1930s and socialist fiction of the period. Edgell Rickword is intereviewed. There are a few minor changes in some of these essays, and Lucas also includes some James Boswell satiric drawings and two new essays. Michael Draper glances at Christopher Caudwell and his writing. Caudwell was neither a 'hack' nor an 'intellectual curiosity'. Although he attempted 'a premature synthesis' of ideas through Marxist theory, 'the issues he raised and the answers he proffered nevertheless constitute a vision from which sustenance can be drawn'. William Myers sees *Black Mischief* as a deeper work than either *Decline and Fall* or *Vile Bodies*. He detects a new coherence and seriousness in 'its central pre-occupation with barbarism and civilisation'.

Women and Children First[11] is an amusing and informative survey of the effect of the two world wars on fiction. Mary Cadogan and Patricia Craig have examined adult and children's fiction, as well as popular and serious writing in an effort to detect the themes, intentions, and changing attitudes inherent in war literature. Such diverse writers as Dorothy Richardson, Berta Ruck, John Buchan, Iris Murdoch, Jennifer Johnston, Evelyn Waugh, Elizabeth Bowen, Graham Greene, and Beryl Bainbridge are considered, as are sentimental fashion magazine stories and 'bestsellers'. Cadogan and Craig reach several interesting conclusions from their lively descriptions of storylines and succinct summaries of character types. They discover that war fiction seems to have many purposes – it can serve as reassurance, propaganda, nostalgic reminiscence; it may shock romantic notions and underline the social and emotional challenges which war brings. On the whole, the more imaginative and 'literary' the work the more serious is its purpose. While popular fiction incorporated war as a background giving topical interest, serious novels tended to use war as an opportunity to reveal social corruption or investigate the inner fragmentation and dislocation of individuals. The changing role of women and their increased autonomy are also demonstrated in a comparison of World War One and World War Two novels and stories. Gradually women were involved heavily in reconstruction; war also brought them face to face with a challenging double sexual standard. Recurrent themes (such as the loss of innocence), traditional images, and 'ironic connections and transpositions' are all duly noted by Cadogan and Craig. Most significant of all, however, is the developing attitude to war which is reflected (in both adult and children's literature) in content and technique. The idealism and patriotism encouraged by fiction in the early days of the First World War gave way to bitter disillusionment. World War Two fiction is thus more subdued, and tends more often to a realistic assessment of the problem of war. However, although this realistic shattering of conventional ideals is present in the retrospective war literature of post-1945 Britain, Cadogan and Craig point to a distinct optimism for a better society. Admittedly, many of the works dealt with in this survey are slight; but the study provides an illuminating account of changing social attitudes and suggests some of the

[11] *Woman and Children First: The Fiction of Two World Wars*, by Mary Cadogan and Patricia Craig. Victor Gollancz. pp. 301. £7.50.

ways in which literature responds to shifting contexts and radical challenges.

A number of general studies on the modern novel deal with literature written outside Britain. David Cook's *African Literature*[12] is both an eloquent plea for a more sophisticated approach to African literature and also a demonstration of how this might be accomplished. The first section of this book attempts to place African fiction and poetry in helpful perspectives. Cook draws attention to the primary differences between Western and African novels. Whereas the lone individualist in Western fiction 'is representative of the inescapable position in which all mankind. . .finds itself', the African novelist portrays a sensitive protagonist who must try to separate himself from the group in order 'to assert individuality'. Rebellion, loneliness, or re-absorption seem the only possibilities. Cook also relates African poetry to the oral tradition, and suggests some of the difficulties encountered by the African poet who tries to assimilate both his own traditions and those of the West. Part Two comprises a series of 'close-up studies'. Chapters are devoted to brief but succinct thematic and stylistic analyses of works by Achebe, Ngugi, Soyinka, Palangyo, and Ekwensi. Cook provides concise judgements on merits and weaknesses. The final part is a persuasive call for an expanded definition of literature. Important contemporary non-fiction work by Oculi, Kenyatta, Fanon, and Nkosi which deals with African 'protest and human challenge' is vigorously defended as deserving critical attention. Cook is never tempted to stray down political, anthropological, or sociological paths. His concern is vehemently literary, and it is refreshing indeed to see such dedicated concern for means of presentation as well as for subject matter.

Kenneth Parker has edited a collection of lively essays (some previously published) on the South African novel in English[13] which, he hopes, will demonstrate a South African desire for self-discovery and a radical, non-racial society. He opens the collection with a general essay on the relationship 'between political perspective and literary creation in South Africa'. The political climate is hostile to creative work and this means that South African novelists will 'increasingly resort to exoticism of one kind or another'. Those in exile will 'become increasingly propagandistic'. Ursula Edmands surveys the life and work of Olive Schreiner, pointing to influences such as Emerson. She insists that Schreiner was primarily concerned with the 'moral effect' of her writing. Although the elusive Pauline Smith was not popular, she was a significant influence on writers like Alan Paton, according to an admiring Arthur Ravenscroft who offers an appreciation of her life and work. Tim Couzens studies Sol Plaatje's *Mhudi* as a warning 'to the whites that what they are doing could lead to ultimate revolution'. He finds the novel illuminated by an examination of Plaatje's character, beliefs, and other writings. David Rabkin compares *God's Stepchildren* and *Turbott Wolfe* as contrasting answers to the questions posed by racial problems and liberalism in South Africa. Michael Wade treats Peter Abrahams as 'South Africa's first proletarian writer', and Kenneth Parker explores Nadine Gordimer's portrayal of 'the dilemma of the white South

[12] *African Literature. A Critical View*, by David Cook. Longman. 1977. pp. xiv + 240. pb £3.50.

[13] *The South African Novel in English: Essays in Criticism and Society*, ed. by Kenneth Parker. Macmillan. pp. xiv + 202. £12.

African liberal'. Michael Wade also looks at Nadine Gordimer in an essay on *A Guest of Honour*: 'The book may be said to embody some African lessons on the history of Europe'. Finally, the same critic analyses *A Walk in the Night* to show the 'complexity and integrity' of Alex La Guma's aesthetic. The rough 'realistic surface texture' is the novel's strength; its weakness lies in 'simplistic politico-moral truisms'.

David Rabkin also considers the South African novel in the *Journal of Commonwealth Literature*. He examines its origins and discusses the problems of writers who had to consider different races in Africa. Racial clichés were often the result. 'Few South African authors have been able to subsume the consideration of these problems of a plural society within a wider structure of intellectual and moral convictions.' Olive Schreiner is one of few exceptions. Stephen Gray (*Theoria*) traces changes in the shape and effect of 'Hottentot Eve' in South African fiction. Also in *Theoria* Robin Hallett considers the combined efforts of Roy Campbell and William Plomer in the production of the literary magazine *Voorslag*.

Helen Daniel (*Southerly*) analyses the picaresque mode in modern Australian fiction, showing how the novels of writers like Sumner Locke Elliott and Thea Astley reflect 'a profound mistrust of society and a radical uncertainty about the possibilities of meaningful existence in the midst of disorder'. Daniel also compares the handling of the part-Aborigine by David Ireland and Thomas Keneally in the same journal.

In *Meanjin*, D. R. Burns surveys the Canadian novel from 1940 to 1973 and suggests why so many Canadian novels seem to fail. In *Canadian Literature*, P. L. Surette, Roderick W. Harvey, Francis Mansbridge, R. P. Bilan, Elizabeth Marsland, Donald R. Bartlett, and Robert A. Lecker write on Albertan novelists such as W. O. Mitchell, Rudy Wiebe and Henry Kreisel. In the same journal Ofelia Cohn-Sfectu chastises those who find Canadian prose and poetry gloomy and pessimistic. The way in which time is viewed vertically in Canadian literature is both mature and stimulating. David Williams (*DR*) writes about protagonists who accept their 'aboriginal inheritance' in the work of Laurence, Wiebe, and Mitchell. A. R. M. Lower replies in *DR* to Anne Boutelle's 1977 article in that journal on 'the Dorian Gray phenomenon' in Canadian fiction. Lower irritably suggests that Canadian characters wear masks because they are 'immature people in an immature society'.

Dublin as 'metaphor and subject' is Terence Brown's concern in *IUR*. He finds that Irish writers are increasingly fond of exploiting Dublin as a subject that allows reflection on the Irish mind; it is no longer simply a setting.

Elizabeth Nunez-Harrell (*ConL*) suggests a few aesthetic criteria for evaluating third-world fiction. She examines the work of George Lamming and V. S. Naipaul to show that such literature 'claims a new way of seeing; and thus allows a new way of representing the formerly peripheral character. Its future depends on its avoidance of mimicry, in spite of its connections to a European tradition'.

The Annual Bibliography of Commonwealth Literature (1976–7) can be found in the April and December issues of the *Journal of Commonwealth Literature*, and *IUR* has a bibliography for Anglo-Irish literature.

There are several critiques of writers who are related in one way or another. The most important of these is *Personality and Impersonality*[14] in which Daniel Albright considers three writers who undermined the nineteenth-century novel tradition and used their fiction to express their own personalities. He argues cogently that D. H. Lawrence, Virginia Woolf and Thomas Mann conceived their characters as versions of themselves, 'fractured into some fable only because the mind is dynamic and can never conceive itself in its totality'. Such striking attempts at self-expression necessitated new stylistic and syntactical forms, and Albright convincingly demonstrates the connection between 'self-disclosure' and technique in the works of the three novelists. His primary aim, however, is 'to comprehend the entire work of each author as a single act, and to describe in a single, long and complicated statement the indivisible meaning. . .which the author presents from youth to old age'. For Lawrence, this entailed a gradual subtraction of accidentals from his characters and an increasing interest in ritual and myth to accommodate his own refined vision of the 'inside world'. Virginia Woolf, on the other hand, chose a multiplicity of perceivers, each representing a different aspect of self. Taken together they emerge as a 'personality swollen and conglomerated into paradise'. Thomas Mann adopted a character type – the gifted genius – to explore his own personal growth. This is a dense and difficult work. At times it seems that Albright himself can only frankly admit the elusiveness of the selves before him. Nevertheless, his conclusion that the modern novel is singularly marked by its intimate connection 'to the central ego of its author' is a point well worth further investigation, and it is heartening to read his claim that such subjectivity really encourages rather than hinders the growth of human sympathy. Through it we discover in others 'minds analogous to our own'. Yet the real value of Albright's work must surely lie in his attempt to define a new way of approaching subjective characterisation where 'every literary act is at once self-disclosure and self-evasion'

John Carswell's *Lives and Letters*[15] is a curious beast. 'Neither straightforward biography nor a work of literary criticism', it attempts to show the complex relationships between a number of bohemian 'literary people' – A. R. Orage, Beatrice Hastings, Katherine Mansfield, John Middleton Murry, and S. S. Koteliansky. The tale which emerges is an intricate one of political commitment and literary ambitions, fevered animosities and jealous rivalries, joyful successes and depressing failures. In essence, Carswell's work is a group biography of a 'literary underworld'. Lacking advanced formal education and academic interests, this literary set reacted against the Victorian background, but in the constant travels, the flamboyant behaviour and the studied self-consciousness of the group, Carswell also discovers a desire for a new authority or certainty to replace what had been discarded. There are many brief appearances by other noteworthy figures such as Lawrence, Modigliani, and Virginia Woolf, and some interesting accounts of contributions to and involvements with *New Age*,

[14] *Personality and Impersonality: Lawrence, Woolf, and Mann*, by Daniel Albright. Chicago and London: U. of Chicago P. pp. viii + 320. £13.65.

[15] *Lives and Letters: A. R. Orage, Beatrice Hastings, Katherine Mansfield, John Middleton Murry, S. S. Koteliansky: 1906–1957*, by John Carswell. Faber & Faber. pp. 307. £7.95.

Rhythm, *Signature*, the *Athenaeum*, and the *Adelphi*. Carswell seems as interested in the ideas and campaigns of these five figures as in their artistic achievements, but he does conclude that a 'mixture of high principles, genuine craftsmanship, and gullibility was characteristic of their world of letters'. The appendix is devoted to 'The Wills of Katherine Mansfield and D. H. Lawrence'.

David Higham's *Literary Gent*[16] is the autobiography of a literary agent whose career spanned six decades – but it is also much more. Higham offers a gossipy and frank description of his late Victorian family, amusing and vivid impressions of a London cluttered with horse-drawn vehicles, and much inside information on publishing and the book trade in general. There are sketches of various writers whom he knew (Paul Scott, Harold Nicolson, Galsworthy, Ackerley, the Sitwells, Dorothy Sayers, and Dylan Thomas) and comments on the relationships between authors, agents, and publishers. Marred only by a scattering of coy remarks, this is a lively account of a highly interesting and generally forgotten profession.

Minor genres and areas of modern fiction are also well represented this year. D. L. Kirkpatrick has compiled an invaluable reference guide to over six hundred twentieth-century writers of children's literature in English[17]. Each entry contains biographical notes, bibliographical information, and a short critical assessment. Naomi Lewis highlights significant developments in works for children, Anthea Bell supplies an essay on 'children's books in translation' with a check-list of selected translations, and an appendix contains information on influential late nineteenth-century children's writers.

Colin Wilson's *Science Fiction as Existentialism*[18] is a short essay on the relationship between existentialism and science fiction (with emphasis on self-discovery, the immensity of the universe and 'the terrifying untapped powers of the subconscious mind'). Really an apologist for science fiction, Wilson asserts that this genre should 'serve as a catalyst in the evolution of a new human consciousness'.

Peter Hühn's and Wulf Künne's book on contemporary light fiction for women[19] is intended as an introduction to the subject and offers a very thorough analysis of two short articles from recent issues of two women's magazines. The authors attempt 'to investigate possible implications of the findings for the teaching of English through the medium of such texts' and appear to address themselves primarily to teachers and students of English as a foreign language. [H.C.C.]

In *KanQ* John McAleer surveys modern detective fiction and scholarly writings about it, while G. Jay Rausch and Diane K. Rausch consider some of the distinctive characteristics of spy fiction. The following general books have not been seen: Alan Kennedy's *Meaning and Signs in Fiction* (Macmillan), John Pearson's *Facades: Edith, Osbert and Sacheverell Sitwell* (Macmillan), Eric S. Rabkin's *The Fantastic in Literature* (Princeton U.P.,

[16] *Literary Gent*, by David Higham. Jonathan Cape. pp. vi + 334. £7.95.

[17] *Twentieth-Century Children's Writers*, by D. L. Kirkpatrick with a preface by Naomi Lewis. Macmillan. pp. xvi + 1507. £17.50.

[18] *Science Fiction as Existentialism*, by Colin Wilson. Hayes, Middx: Bran's Head Books. pp. ii + 16.

[19] *Englische triviale Frauenliteratur*, by Peter Hühn and Wulf Künne. Königstein/Ts.: Athenäum. (Europäische Literaturwissenschaft 3). pp. 190. DM 29.90.

1977), and Barbara Hill Rigney's *Madness and Sexual Politics in the Feminist Novel* (U. of Wisconsin P.).

(b) Authors

Jim Davidson talked to Margaret Atwood about the implications of being a Canadian woman writer, and prints his interview in *Meanjin*.

Samuel Beckett informed Deirdre Bair that he would neither help nor hinder her efforts to write a detailed study of his life. Deciding that this was Beckett's way of granting permission, Bair embarked on an extensive research project, interviewing those close to Beckett, studying published and unpublished writings and letters, and conversing and corresponding with Beckett himself. The result is a massive biography[20] which attempts to establish the context in which Beckett's works were produced. Bair provides a detailed account of Beckett's fragmented and often unhappy life, dealing straightforwardly and sympathetically with his domestic traumas, moody isolation, his psychosomatic illnesses, and his crippling bouts of depression. The rather exploitative relationship which existed between Joyce and Beckett is considered at length, and Bair recounts in agonising detail the passionate and embarrassing pursuit of Beckett by Lucia Joyce. From this biography it is quite clear that Beckett's real life problems, experiences, and anxieties lie at the heart of his work. Only when he accepted his dark inner world where 'alienation, isolation, exile, and the separation of mind and body' exist, could he use his life as a source of creative inspiration. Bair deftly identifies the origins and traces the development of Beckett's major thematic and stylistic concerns, and provides helpful, low-key critiques of the novels and plays. There is little new light shed on the fiction, but Bair does try to account both for Beckett's own dissatisfaction with some of his works such as *Murphy* and also for his gradual movement from fiction to drama. When his fictional 'characters became too upsetting for Beckett, too terrifying because of the exploration and confrontation of himself, he turned to theatre as release and salvation'. The wealth of detail concerning Beckett's life, habits and pre-occupations together with Bair's sensible attempts to relate life and work, make this biography one of the most significant works on modern writers this year.

In *Commonweal*, Vivian Mercier urges readers to note Biblical influence in the work of Beckett and to remember that all aspects of his development 'possess a religious dimension'. Eric P. Levy writes in *ELH* on the one speaker who lies behind all the disguises in *Molloy*, *Malone Dies*, and *The Unnamable*. In fact, this narrator is used by Beckett to express a vision of mankind. Since he has 'no definite personal features, [he] is recognizable only in so far as he belongs to the species and is, therefore, the embodiment of Beckettian Man'. Two articles have appeared on 'Still'. Paul J. Corr suggests in *Expl* that it 'highlights the disparity between fiction and reality by focusing the reader's attention on the reality the observer/ narrator tries to evade'. In *EIC* John Pilling views 'Still' as 'the most approachable and satisfying of Beckett's prose texts since *How it is*'. It perfectly expresses the calm of 'the mind quietly communing with itself'.

[20] *Samuel Beckett: A Biography*, by Deirdre Bair. Jonathan Cape. pp. xiv + 736. £8.50.

In *ConL* James Acheson defends the brilliant originality of Beckett's essay on Proust with its demonstration that Proust adapted Schopenhauer's theory of music to fiction. Acheson also directs attention to the importance of Proust and Schopenhauer for Beckett's fiction.

Frank Swinnerton's 'portrait of Arnold Bennett as he was known to his friends'[21] is a rather heavy-handed attempt to destroy the myth that Bennett was self-important, ostentatious and money-hungry. Swinnerton provides a lively description of himself and his friendship with Bennett and his wife Marguerite. Those whom Swinnerton feels betrayed Bennett are soundly repudiated, and Bennett's humour, modesty, generosity, and integrity vociferously extolled. The relationship between the novelist and Dorothy Cheston is also described – generally as one in which Bennett was misled by an unoriginal and unintelligent woman. Bennett emerges from this short memoir as an 'avuncular and fundamentally romantic' man, given to writing pot-boilers simply as a release for 'his fertile humorous inventiveness'. Swinnerton includes as an appendix a 1917 publicity piece on himself written by Arnold Bennett.

Hermione Lee's article on Elizabeth Bowen's *To the North* in *EIC* probes the treatment of loss and betrayal in the novel. The most outstanding feature of the work is the way in which Bowen uses place as a 'complex vehicle for the novel's deeper meanings'. Two articles in *Southerly* draw attention to the work of Martin Boyd. Susan McKernan studies the relationship between Boyd's non-fiction and later novels in an attempt to account for the lack of seriousness in his fiction. Kenneth Moon acknowledges the slushy, pulp writing in *Lucinda Brayford* but also detects a powerful tragic vision which redeems Boyd's novel.

In *MFS* Rubin Rabinovitz looks at Burgess's original ending for *A Clockwork Orange* which was omitted in American editions. It is not sentimental as some have claimed but clarifies Burgess's ideas on free will. John Mowat suggests in *ConL* that Burgess is worthy of greater recognition as a disciple of Joyce, as *Napoleon Symphony* so amply illustrates.

Diana Farr's workmanlike biography of the neglected Gilbert Cannan[22] is the account of a life characterised by 'poignant tragedy' and 'strange quirky brilliance'. The second son of a Manchester shipping clerk, Cannan showed great promise as a writer of novels, plays, poems, short stories, essays, translations, and critical articles. He contributed to little magazines and associated with prominent literary figures such as Lytton Strachey, Ottoline Morrell, Katherine Mansfield, and D. H. Lawrence. Praised by Henry James and befriended by Galsworthy and James Barrie, Cannan became involved in a series of romantic entanglements. He was cited as co-respondent in Barrie's divorce case, became increasingly unbalanced, and died a madman. Farr quotes liberally from Cannan's writings to demonstrate his intense emotional states, and she succeeds in bringing the highly-strung young writer to life. However, there is no critical evaluation of his work. Such would indeed have been helpful in view of Lawrence's own

[21] *Arnold Bennett: A Last Word*, by Frank Swinnerton. Hamish Hamilton. pp. vi + 120. £4.95.

[22] *Gilbert Cannan: A Georgian Prodigy*, by Diana Farr. Chatto & Windus. pp. 220. £8.50.

assessment of Cannan – 'very crude, very shockingly undisciplined, and consequently inarticulate'.

In *ArielE* Virginia U. Ola registers her distaste for Joyce Cary's African women and their connection with violence. His portrayals of Africans fail because they attempt to force characters 'to fit into an already constructed set of beliefs' about racial superiority. Brian McFarlane offers a good defence of a novelist often dismissed as 'artificial' and 'brittle' in *SoRA*. He uses Ivy Compton-Burnett's *A House and its Head* to demonstrate her talents and the way in which her technique served her vision. Compton-Burnett emerges from this closely argued account as a skilful penetrator of 'the darkest recesses of the human mind'.

Trevor H. Hall has prepared a collection of essays on Arthur Conan Doyle[23] which will appeal primarily to Sherlock Holmes devotees, although some of the essays are rather insubstantial. A speculative biography of Moriarty reveals potential inconsistencies from story to story. A discussion of Nicholas Meyer's *The Seven-Per-Cent Solution* pinpoints numerous inaccuracies. There is the now standard consideration of possible sources for the character of Holmes, and an attempt to 'place the chronological sequence of the events of the duel between Sherlock Holmes and Arsène Lupin'. Echoes from the Holmes stories in the works of T. S. Eliot are noted and a lengthy essay investigates Conan Doyle's interest in spiritualism. Charles O. Ellison contributes a piece on Holmes's chemical experiments, and also decides that there is no clear proof that the detective knew Yorkshire. In *TQ* Peter V. Conroy argues that Watson is significant as a narrator, not just as a 'foil' for Holmes. Indeed, an examination of the narrative method in the Holmes stories illuminates the great sleuth's 'method of detection'. In *AN&Q* Dominick A. Labianca and William J. Reeves briefly observe that 'The Disappearance of Lady Frances Carfax' is flawed since 'the chemical knowledge of Holmes, and of Watson, is suspect'. The following were not made available: Walter Shepherd's *On the Scent with Sherlock Holmes* (A. Barker), and Jack Tracey's *The Encyclopaedia Sherlockiana* (New English Library).

Several absorbing book-length studies of Conrad have been issued. Jacques Berthoud[24] approaches the major phase of Conrad's work by attempting to understand Conrad's own vision of himself. *A Personal Record* reveals Conrad's view of the relationship between life and art and the role of the artist. It also shows Conrad's belief in the practical need for moral values such as 'restraint', 'solidarity', and 'fidelity' in both writer and seaman. Using this as a starting-place, Berthoud goes on to consider Conrad as a writer with a coherent tragic vision such as is 'vouchsafed only to those capable of moral commitment'. The novels are filled with the awareness of the tragic grandeur and the tragic contradictions of a life in which scepticism undermines faith, fact destroys dream, and detachment and commitment seem 'at once necessary and incompatible'. The tragic dilemmas in Conrad's fiction are thus related to his own personality as

[23] *Sherlock Holmes and His Creator*, by Trevor H. Hall with contributions by Archdeacon Charles O. Ellison. Duckworth. pp. xii + 155. £7.95.

[24] *Joseph Conrad: The Major Phase*, by Jacques Berthoud. Cambridge: C.U.P. pp. viii + 191. hb £7.50, pb £2.95.

both romantic and realist. Strikingly responsive to the modern sense of reality as rooted in the outer and the public life, Conrad also realised the inevitable tragedy for the inner self which is challenged, overruled, and isolated by the needs of the outer world. Berthoud offers elegant appraisals of the major novels from *The Nigger of the 'Narcissus'* to *Under Western Eyes*, demonstrating constantly and convincingly that the power and coherence of Conrad's art lie in his treatment of the tragic contradictions in life. Intellectually and emotionally torn by these contradictions, Conrad wrote novels which were neither 'philosophically pretentious' nor 'morally nihilistic'. Rather they show the tragedy of man who 'seems capable of discovering the reality of his own values only through their defeat or contradiction'.

R. A. Gekoski's *Conrad*[25] is intended largely for those unacquainted with the novelist. Gekoski identifies Conrad's moral viewpoint as one which attempted to hold in balance 'the facts of existence (autonomy and isolation) and the necessities of existence (social responsibility)'. It is on Conrad's ability to present these contradictory visions with equal sympathy that his artistry depends. The conflicting perspectives, if taken to their logical conclusions, might easily give way to nihilism, but Gekoski views Conrad as a writer who avoided anarchy and disintegration by relying on certain values, even if they were 'in fact only arbitrary props'. Fidelity, 'a stern code of conduct', 'stoical acceptance of life's hardships, and avoidance of introspection' give men honour and dignity and 'become the bases of a renewed hope for human intercourse'. Yet the tension between social virtues and inevitable isolation accounts for the underlying ambivalence in Conrad's fiction, according to Gekoski who neatly discusses Conrad's novels in turn, paraphrasing plots and commenting on the threat of meaningless chaos which constantly challenges human solidarity and social responsibility. Unfortunately, Conrad could not maintain the balance indefinitely. In *Nostromo* Gekoski detects the seeds of Conrad's decline, for Decoud's insight is undercut by a 'feeling that one really cannot afford such insights'. Scepticism is finally rejected for 'an increasingly severe affirmation of ethical standards and social responsibility'. The last novels lack the delicate poise of the greatest work in which ironic acceptance of purposelessness counterbalances brave aspirations and ideals.

Sanford Pinsker sets out in a brief monograph[26] to consider the metaphoric texture of Conrad's language. He notes that different 'languages' 'filter preoccupations. . .through radically disparate sensibilities' and goes on to define and characterise four Conrad 'languages' or ways of ordering and expressing experience – the languages of the east, of narration, of the sea, and of politics. In every case, Pinsker suggestively notes the 'contrapuntal rhythms' which are created when different languages confront each other or when the 'chaos of silence' and the Incomprehensible challenge one particular language. Pinsker argues energetically that it is in his treatment of language that Conrad most certainly anticipates later twentieth-

[25] *Conrad: The Moral World of the Novelist*, by R. A. Gekoski. (Novelists and Their World Series). Paul Elek. pp. x + 208. £7.50.

[26] *The Languages of Joseph Conrad*, by Sanford Pinsker (Costerus: Essays in English and American Language and Literature). Amsterdam: Rodopi. pp. 87. pb Hf 120–.

century trends in fiction. Conrad's thematic concerns and 'alternating attractions/repulsions to the irrational and anarchistic' can be seen as firmly within the modern relativist movement, but his handling of language which threatens to fragment into nothingness most intriguingly foreshadows modernism. Conrad was well aware of 'the gaps that language either creates or cannot bridge' and this brooding about the possibilities and instabilities of language makes him 'an important precursor of Modernism's finest achievements'.

The complex ambiguity of *Heart of Darkness* is the subject of an enjoyable critical discussion by Cedric Watts[27]. Watts examines the tale in a variety of contexts in order to reveal its essential mystery. Themes, imagery, the use of the 'antipathetic fallacy', the tale-within-a-tale convention, literary allusions, absurdist descriptive techniques, characterisation, and Marlowe's narrative voice are all considered in an effort to reach the 'heart' of the story. A central paradox is discovered there: 'the tale creates a powerful sense of evil while at the same time conveying a powerful scepticism about matters of religion and morality'. The reasons for such an effect are legion. Characters shift in their commitments; ironic structuring and complex stylistic techniques undercut the initial impact made by the story. Indeed, Watts takes pains to point out that the tale contains an unusually rich mixture of narrative modes – naturalistic, satiric, symbolic – which suggests the complexity of truth and the different ways by which it may be attained. Thorough and level-headed in his approach, Watts also takes into account the various interpretations of *Heart of Darkness* (mythic, archetypal, psychological) before deciding that 'no one allegorical meaning is possible'. Yet despite its ambivalence, the tale conveys a keen sense of the absurdity and futility of action.

Conradiana contains some particularly cogent pieces. In the first number, Andrzej Braun examines Conrad's treatment of 'the kingdom of Wadjo' in works like 'Karain', *The Rescue*, *Lord Jim*, and 'The Lagoon'. The kingdom became for the novelist 'a question of conscience, of honor, and of loyalty'. William W. Bonney considers Tom MacWhirr in *Typhoon*. The gale dramatises 'the irruption of the disorderly unconscious that MacWhirr experiences personally'. That he cannot comment on his situation is ironically appropriate since 'there is in Conrad's universe ultimately nothing to be said anyhow'. Frances B. Singh's close analysis of *Heart of Darkness* shows that Marlow is really a colonialist, not because his creator was 'reactionary' or 'racist', but because Conrad was limited by current anthropological notions of his age. Conrad was familiar with the legendary characteristics of the Finns, according to Ernest J. Moyne who looks intently at Wamibo in *The Nigger of the 'Narcissus'*. Ernest Bevan Jr explores Conrad's portrayal of 'the dynamic relationship between private and public history' in *Nostromo*. The novel clearly proves the impossibility of knowing or understanding 'the human substance of the past'. David Leon Higdon and Floyd Eugene Eddleman offer 'A Glossary of Malay Words in Conrad's *Almayer's Folly*', and John Feaster adds a note on the 'Privileged Man' who receives Marlow's written account of the end of Lord

[27] *Conrad's 'Heart of Darkness': A Critical and Contextual Discussion*, by Cedric Watts. Milan: Mursia International; London: Wildwood House. 1977. pp. viii + 171. £7.50.

Jim's life. He thinks it might be Tom Lingard. Raymond T. Brebach surveys the manuscripts and typescripts of *Romance*, the product of collaboration between Ford and Conrad.

The second number of *Conradiana* opens with a rather curious article by Todd Gray Willy who argues that the Russian Harlequin's cry that Kurtz was 'shamefully abandoned' is probably connected to the notorious 'abandonment' of General Gordon in Khartoum. Such an allusion would add to the ambivalence and irony of *Heart of Darkness*, since it would encourage a contemporary reader to pity and possibly forgive Kurtz. G. W. Kennedy usefully examines Conrad's recasting of the Crusoe myth. He tries to prove that Conrad found the notion of the victorious solitary man 'a potentially subversive influence', since it undermines the important notion of community. Sister Mary Sullivan's essay on 'meaningful silences' in *Lord Jim* is filled with perceptive and sensitive observations. Rosemary Pitt opts for a rather unusual comparison between *Heart of Darkness* and *The Voyage Out*, two powerful depictions of the 'exploration of the self'. Robert R. Owens ghoulishly considers the displayed heads in *Heart of Darkness* and suggests their possible significance for Kurtz. Hans van Marle demonstrates from a review of *Almayer's Folly* and a letter to the *Straits Times* that Conrad was read in the East and used characters based on personalities easily recognisable there. Mario Curreli also considers early reviews of the same novel and writes about interest in the real Lingard, while John Patterson compares the characters who hate to be named in *Under Western Eyes* and Tolstoy's *Resurrection*.

The third number is devoted to papers from the 1977 Conrad Conference in Miami. Frederick R. Karl offers some useful reflections on the problems involved in using Conrad's letters. He shows how difficult it is to separate subjective personas from objective data. Todd K. Bender wonders what Ford Madox Ford meant when he referred to Conrad as an impressionist. William W. Bonney investigates the connection between Conrad and Schopenhauer with regard to the use of Oriental concepts and attitudes in the fiction. Adam Gillon interestingly considers Conrad's fiction in relationship to painting, emphasising the significance of visual imagery in the novels. An area of increasing importance to comparative scholars is highlighted by Elsa Nettels when she notes resemblances between Conrad and Stephen Crane. The chief difference between these writers lies 'in the kinds of mental experience they represent'. As usual, sound reviews accompany each number.

Other articles which have appeared this year vary greatly in importance. David Gill writes briefly in *N&Q* on Conrad's inscription in a first edition of *The Children of the Sea*. Gill argues that it shows Conrad's pride in his work and his 'ingrained sense of rank'. Tony Tanner's *PR* article connects cannibalism in *Falk* and *Heart of Darkness* to Conrad's awareness of 'the insoluble problematics of utterance'. In *ES* David L. Higdon offers his usual sensible fare in a discussion of the Macmillan reader's report on *Almayer's Folly*. Ian Milner's essay in *Prague Studies in English* is a rather limited attempt to relate image, content, and theme in Conrad's work. The analysis of imagery in *Heart of Darkness* leads to the unoriginal conclusion that the novella treats 'the darkness of colonial exploitation and the degeneration by that darkness of an enlightened man'. Janis P. Stout's comparison in *PQ* between *Heart of Darkness* and *Henderson the Rain King* is useful in its insistence that the attitude to hope in each novel is more qualified than has been suggested. Bellow's optimism is limited; Conrad's despair is 'moderated', 'so that the two novels in their own ways finally make very similar arguments about the possibility for a hopeful view of human life'.

Ian Watt has produced two absorbing essays on *Heart of Darkness*. In *PR* he explores Conrad's double vision. Through his portrayal of Marlow and Kurtz, Conrad shows that he 'wanted both to endorse the standard Victorian moral positives, and to express his forebodings that the dominant intellectual directions of the nineteenth century were preparing disaster for the twentieth'. Watt's article in *NCF* is less original, centring as it does on Marlow as 'Conrad's most persuasive fictional embodiment of that human solidarity which he had affirmed as his essential authorial purpose'. But within this essay is an interesting comparison of Conrad and James and their methods of handling narrative approaches. Stein's function in *Lord Jim* is the subject of Elizabeth Brody Tenenbaum's piece in *SNNTS*. She investigates similarities between Stein and Jim as doubt-tormented men, and points to the pathos of the last paragraph of the novel 'if we assume Stein to be Jewel's father'. Fritz Gysin attempts to right a minor wrong in critical work on *Lord Jim* by examining the hitherto ignored grotesqueness of the Patna skipper. By comparing the skipper to Doramin, Gysin feels that we can see 'the two extreme positions between which Jim, as a human being, is bound to move'. Donald W. Rude speculates about the reasons for Conrad's letter to Crane denouncing W. L. Courtney's review of *The Nigger of the 'Narcissus'* (*ELT*). Peter L. Hays takes up the current interest in Conrad and Crane in *EA*, concluding that 'Crane did influence Conrad's early work, possibly without Conrad's full awareness'. Christine W. Sizemore (*MFS*) pursues that 'small cardboard box' in *The Secret Agent*. Like all symbols of boxes and containers in the novel, it represents 'the paradoxical and threatening secrecy that pervades the city, the female protagonist, and the very structure of *The Secret Agent*'. Terry Otten (*SHR*) sees the myth of the Fortunate Fall in 'The Secret Sharer'. In *SNNTS* H. S. Gilliam analyses *Under Western Eyes*, concentrating on 'the Russian and the Western' as 'symbols of states of consciousness'.

Brian Masters' study of Marie Corelli (*Now Barabbas Was a Rotter*, Hamish Hamilton) was unavailable. In *TSLL* Janet H. Burstein's essay on 'selfhood and "otherness"' in the writings of Isak Dinesen is a sound treatment of a neglected Danish author writing in English. Susan Spitzer challenges the surface reading of Drabble's *The Millstone* in *Novel*. Even if unintended, the presentation of Rosamund's unconscious 'infantile fantasy' is effective. Colin Butler looks at the same novel in *ES* comparing it to Drabble's critical account of Wordsworth. While similar interests and themes are found in both works, the comparison is primarily useful for its revelation of a weakness in *The Millstone* – 'it has no social dimension worth the name'.

Kenneth Seib argues that the sketches in Dylan Thomas's *Portrait of the Artist as a Young Dog* are both autobiographical and shaped artistic experience (*MFS*). *CritQ* contains a persuasive statement on the importance of Firbank by Shaun McCarthy who investigates the striking originality of

Inclinations and its relationship to the *nouveau roman*. James Hurt writes unconvincingly in *JNT* on a possible key to *The Good Soldier* and the character of Dowell. Dowell's perception is distorted by his 'infantile theory of sex' which 'is the one Freud identified with the primal scene fantasy'. Much more useful is Hilda D. Spear's consideration of the novel in *DUJ*. She argues that the book is about interpretations of truth and shows 'that no one can know the whole truth about another human heart and that final judgment must be left to God'.

Two volumes in the Abinger Edition of E. M. Forster's works have appeared, both dealing with *A Passage to India*[28]. Volume 6 is the final published version of the novel; its companion volume, 6a, contains extant manuscript material pertaining to the novel and comes complete with page and line references to Volume 6 and a 'line finder' to enable readers to compare draft material with the final version. The painstaking editing of Oliver Stallybrass is up to its usual high standards, and his introductions to both volumes are perceptive and sympathetic. In his opening remarks on the published version, for example, he neatly destroys speculations about Forster's indebtedness to Whitman at the same time as he traces the genesis of the novel and describes Forster's doubts about it. He also quietly draws attention to the novel's stylistic perfection, quoting Forster's own comment that he wished the novel to be 'philosophic and poetic'. Appendixes include Forster's 1957 prefatory note and Peter Burra's introduction to the Everyman edition as well as 'Forster's programme note to Santha Rama Rau's dramatized version'. Textual notes are helpful and precise; Stallybrass points to the gradual deterioration of the text through various editions. Notes supplied by Forster and others for the Everyman edition are reprinted together with a most useful glossary of Anglo-Indian words. Volume 6a with its complete manuscript version, earlier draft material, working notes, and few pages of typescript is really designed as a tool for the scholar and critic. Stallybrass has correlated the manuscript material with the final version to show divergences from the published text and from this draws several interesting conclusions about Forster's intentions and method of writing. Stallybrass's careful comparison of manuscript and final text provides ample proof of his judgement that the writing of the novel 'was a long, painful and complicated process'. What is even more striking is the way in which such an impressive final version could emerge from the rather pedestrian early drafts. There are two appendixes: 'Miscellaneous Fragments and Working Notes', and 'Forster's Corrections to the Typescript'.

P. N. Furbank's second and final volume of the life of E. M. Forster[29] deals with Forster's life from 1914 to 1970 and commences with Forster in his World War One role as a cataloguer at the National Gallery. Unhappy about this 'unjust and unnecessary' war leading 'to panic and herd-instinct, to slogans and bogus "cheeriness" ', he found comfort in the hope that sincere friendship would become the underlying foundation of the future

[28] *A Passage to India*, by E. M. Forster, ed. by Oliver Stallybrass. (Abinger Edition, Volume 6). Edward Arnold. pp. xxviii + 371. £12.50. *The Manuscripts of A Passage to India*, by E. M. Forster, ed. by Oliver Stallybrass (Abinger Edition Volume 6a). Edward Arnold. pp. xxvi + 589. £37.50.

[29] *E. M. Forster: A Life. Volume Two: Polycrates' Ring (1914–1970)*, by P. N. Furbank. Secker & Warburg. pp. xx + 348. £7.50.

world. At the same time he cultivated his own friendships – with Lytton Strachey and the Bloomsbury Circle, with D. H. Lawrence and Frieda and later, with Constantine Cavafy, Siegfried Sassoon, J. R. Ackerley, and T. E. Lawrence. Some of these friendships were brief but intense and a select few (such as that with D. H. Lawrence) encouraged Forster to express his own feelings more openly. Furbank treats Forster's later life and career with the same tactful attention to detail and the same honesty as pervade the first volume. There are absorbing chapters on Forster's time in Alexandria as a Red-Cross 'searcher' and in India where he was a temporary secretary to the Maharaja of Dewas. Much of Forster's experience in India and Alexandria is shown to permeate *A Passage to India*, and Furbank writes intelligently about other possible influences on this novel. Personal doubts about creative sterility, homosexuality, and his relationship with his mother troubled Forster throughout his later life and Furbank deals sensitively with these. There is some speculation about Forster's failure to produce a novel after *A Passage to India*, and attention is usefully drawn to Forster's singleness of inspiration and boredom with men–women relationships. But Furbank performs an even greater service by considering Forster's emergence as broadcaster and social critic and by pointing to the remarkable productivity of his last years. The biography concludes with a delightful portrait of Forster as Furbank knew him – a timid but attentive listener, marked by generosity and a discrete oriental courtesy. There is an appendix on the Maharaja of Dewas. Scholars, critics, and general readers alike will be grateful for Furbank's thoughtful, well-balanced, and sympathetic approach to his subject as well as for the wealth of intimate and revealing details about Forster's personality, experiences, and preoccupations.

The Writers and Their Work monograph on E. M. Forster[30] takes the usual form of a brief biographical section followed by short accounts of the works. Philip Gardner makes his own position clear from the outset when he describes Forster as 'one of the finest novelists of his generation'. Such broad generalisations are repeated throughout. *Howards End* is cited as 'a remarkable piece of work', for example, and *A Passage to India* is viewed as 'profound and poignant' in its contrasts. There is much plot summary and little analysis of technique, but the book serves to draw attention to major issues of connection and self-discovery and Forster's deft handling of symbol and social comedy. One wonders about the audience for whom such a work is intended. Mature readers – even first-time readers – would find the summaries unnecessary and sixth-formers would also find the commentary too brief. Even Gardner admits that the pamphlet can be nothing more than 'the précis of a précis'. Students searching for an introduction could more profitably be directed elsewhere (as Gardner's up-to-date select bibliography ironically suggests).

Dennis Altman and Wilfred Stone both consider Forster's homosexuality. In *Meanjin* Altman's superficial and derivative article touches on the general relationship between Forster's homosexuality and his art. In *MLQ* Stone more perceptively studies the homosexual fiction, searching for links between Forster's sexuality and his concern for connection. Love offers no answer; separation and frustration abound. But the real failure

[30] *E. M. Forster*, by Philip Gardner (WTW). Longman. pp. 43.

to connect lies in Forster's 'class-boundedness'. Walter Evans writes briefly in *Expl* about the neglected Oniton setting in *Howards End*. Gary Brock reads *A Passage to India* in *SNNTS* as a dramatisation of the difference between 'verbal truth' and 'truth of mood'. The inability of people to understand one another is much more significant than religious, national, or ideological differences. Derek Peat (*SoRA*) takes issue with a previous article on *A Passage to India* in that journal. He finds Edwin Thumbro's 1977 response to the novel over-simplified and argues that what characters think and say should not be confused with what Forster wishes us to think. Peat rejects the view that Adela achieves salvation, insisting instead that Forster emphasised 'her continuing limitations'. J. R. Ebbatson (*N&Q*) points to 'striking resemblances of language, imagery and meaning between the Marabar sequence and a passage in Richard Jefferies' *The Story of My Heart*'. In *New Quest* (1977) S. V. Pradhan shows how Forster exposed and transcended the conventions of the Anglo-Indian tradition of fiction. Judith S. Herz identifies the energy which enlivens *A Room with a View* and *The Longest Journey*. In a brisk article in *ELT* she locates it in 'the tension generated by the collision of two story lines, the surface heterosexual romance and the interior homosexual romance'.

The linear presentation of flux in Galsworthy's *The Man of Property* forms the subject of a well-argues article in *ELT* by David L. Higdon. Jacqueline Ann Ariail looks at the ways in which *Cold Comfort Farm* 'mocks and honors' the English regional novel tradition (*ArielE*). Jeanne Delbaere handles a complex subject well in *RLV* when she explores the significance of the 'crossing motif' in Golding's *The Inheritors*. This motif occupies a position of singular importance in the narrative, and encourages Delbaere to define the difference between Tuami and Lok. 'It is the awareness of his guilt together with his capacity to give it a meaningful shape that makes Tuami fully human'. Hal Colebatch examines a neglected aspect of *Pincher Martin* in *SoRA* when he considers 'the extent to which Pincher Martin has physically caused his own destruction'. He tentatively suggests that a will to self-destruction in Martin may be 'a will towards the destruction of that evil self'. Kolawole Ogungbesan analyses Nadine Gordimer's narrator in *The Late Bourgeois World* (*ArielE*). S. T. Fisher compares various printings, issues, and editions of *Father and Son* and records his findings in *N&Q*. Gosse took painstaking care with even minor corrections.

Keith C. Odom's chronological survey of the writings of Henry Green[31] is a good starting-place for the reader seeking outlines of major themes and key techniques. There is no attempt at in-depth discussion, but Odom manages to touch on central issues for Green such as isolation, the quest for love, and the disintegration of society. His emphasis on Green's symbolism and poetic techniques suggests some of the stylistic subtlety of the novels. The conclusion is a rather perfunctory re-iteration of earlier points with emphasis on Green's 'solid achievement', but the few paragraphs devoted to the reception and influence of Green's work are interesting, albeit sketchy.

Antonie Weber offers a most interesting study of the narrative structures

[31] *Henry Green*, by Keith C. Odom. (TEAS). Boston, Mass.: Twayne/G. K. Hall. pp. 155. $9.50.

of Greene's Catholic novels *Brighton Rock* and *The End of the Affair*[32]. The relationship between religious theme and novelistic form is explored and the author elaborates the results of her analyses in a chapter on the major narrative patterns that occur throughout Greene's work. All his novels are shown to share more or less the same underlying structure. [H.C.C.]

In *DR* D. S. Savage presents a hostile examination of Greene's religious belief and the extent to which his Catholicism is mere trapping to conceal his 'aberrant view of the world as objectively real'. Greene's notions of sin and evil are castigated as extraordinarily narrow, and the imaginative sustenance which he offers his readers is dismissed as paltry. Greene is viewed as having 'an obsessional concern with the same inescapable issue, the situation of the inadequate loner whom the author. . .both wants to present with honest realism and yet to justify as some sort of superior being'. David Karnath compares Bernanos' *Diary of a Country Priest* and Greene's *The Heart of the Matter* in *ConL*. He finds that in both novels the 'literary form' overrides the world view and forces its reshaping 'in the direction predictable from the artistic form employed'. In *SB* Philip Stratford replies to David L. Higdon's 1977 article on changes between the first and final editions of *The Heart of the Matter*. Higdon seemed to forget that Greene made revisions even earlier than the extensive 1971 revision for the Collected Edition. Jesse F. McCartney considers different political viewpoints in 'The Destructors' in a readable *SHR* essay which attempts to account for the ambiguity of the story.

Rudy Wiebe offers some personal memories of reading Frederick Grove in *UTQ*. In *DR* Margaret Stobie comments on the development of Grove's animal fable, *Consider Her Ways*, and Henry Makow connects Grove's treatment of sex and his tragic vision in *The Yoke of Life*. In *TSLL* Nathaniel Mackey argues forcefully that Wilson Harris's *The Eye of the Scarecrow* is the pivot 'on which Harris' work turns decidedly self-reflexive'

Edward T. Jones[33] relies on extensive quotation and summary in an effort to establish the distinctive contribution which L. P. Hartley made to British fiction. Although there is a rather strained and pretentious attempt made to compare Hartley to writers like Huxley and Greene, Jones for the most part tries to delineate the major areas of Hartley's art which are worthy of note. He approaches Hartley's characters through the psychological notion of 'the crisis of Identity' and draws attention to the novelist's insistence on individuality and 'traditional bourgeois values'. Hartley is also briefly discussed as a moralist akin to the transcendentalists. Jones admires Hartley as a careful craftsman exploiting both romantic and realistic traditions and all fictive modes between. To substantiate this view, descriptions of the short fiction and novels with little analysis are supplied together with a short chapter on Hartley as a fastidious and sensitive literary critic. Jones concludes that Hartley is a significant writer for contemporary readers since his 'ethos offers an alternative to mass society and conformity to a life-style bereft of moral definition'. But despite Jones's

[32] *Die Erzählstruktur von Graham Greenes Katholischen Romanen*, by Antonie Weber. Bern: Francke. (Schweizer Anglistische Arbeiten 95). pp. 173. SFr. 28.

[33] *L. P. Hartley*, by Edward T. Jones (TEAS). Boston, Mass.: Twayne/G. K. Hall. pp. 221. $9.50.

sometimes inflated claims, Hartley remains an interesting but most definitely minor writer.

J. R. Ebbatson accounts for the neglect of Maurice Hewlett's 'Senhouse' trilogy in *ELT* when he discovers that the work is a simplistic failure. Ebbatson does show, however, that Hewlett's work offers a useful portrait of Edwardian thought.

Dennis Shrubsall's biography of W. H. Hudson[34] is a very readable work based largely on unpublished personal papers and letters. Shrubsall provides a straightforward and simple introduction to the man and his work, including the classic *Green Mansions*, and his quiet approach seems eminently suited to the sensitive naturalist. There is no attempt made to discuss Hudson's writing in detail or to assess his literary achievements, but two final chapters on 'The Naturalist and the Man' and 'The Writer' draw attention to Hudson's stylistic development and amply illustrate his ability to create charming word pictures. His sense of whimsy and pathos is also acknowledged. There are three appendixes: 'Select Bibliography', 'The Published Books and Letters of W. H. Hudson', and 'Contents of Books of English Essays not Related to Any One Country'. In *UTQ* Mervin Nicholson analyses Hudson's *Nature in Downland* as a good example of his nature books. But Nicholson also points out that it has the same imaginative power and technical skill as *Green Mansions*.

Piero Ferrucci has edited Aldous Huxley's *The Human Situation*[35], a series of lectures delivered at the University of California (Santa Barbara) in 1959. The book is a monument to Huxley's vast learning. Throughout the lectures he draws on an immense fund of knowledge about many disciplines in order to discuss the possibility of the survival of civilisation and the fulfilment of man's potential. R. Wajc-Tenenbaum draws attention to a forgotten story by Huxley in *RLV*. 'Consider the Lilies' is best understood with reference to the '*Four Noble Truths* of Buddhism'.

Paul Piazza's analysis of the strange relationship between the life and the writings of Christopher Isherwood[36] is a thought-provoking study of an 'intensely personal world'. Piazza begins with Isherwood's past, drawing attention to his dominant 'holy widow-mother' and the memory of the ideal heroic father-soldier which she forced upon him. It is Piazza's contention that Isherwood rebelled against 'the constricted existence' which his mother's authority presented by creating – and living – an 'anti-myth' of himself, that is, a personality which was the antithesis of what was expected. Throughout his life Isherwood has constantly re-assessed and re-interpreted this anti-myth so that a number of personas emerge – the 'Cambridge-Mortmere Isherwood', 'Berlin Herr Issyvoo, the American Vedantist Isherwood, the recent homosexual Isherwood'. These anti-myths people his fiction and branch out to include images of the anti-heroic anti-father, and the anti-heroic pacifist. Even more interesting is Piazza's assured account of the ways in which the changing anti-myths influenced the

[34] *W. H. Hudson: Writer and Naturalist*, by Dennis Shrubsall. Tisbury, Wiltshire: Compton P. pp. xiv + 127. £5.50.

[35] *The Human Situation: Lectures at Santa Barbara*, by Aldous Huxley, ed. by Piero Ferrucci. Chatto & Windus. pp. x + 261. £4.95.

[36] *Christopher Isherwood – Myth and Anti-Myth*, by Paul Piazza. New York: Columbia U.P. pp. xiv + 245. $15.60.

narrative styles in Isherwood's fiction. This is one of the best studies in recent years on the ' "essential Isherwood", always investing his life with epic proportions, always creating his ironic anti-myth, the subject of which is, always, the anti-son of Kathleen and Frank'.

In a biographically based and generally descriptive essay, Hanna Behrend reminds us of the existence of Storm Jameson (*ZAA*). Philip Pacey points to the importance of Wales and things Welsh for B. S. Johnson as poet and novelist (*AWR*).

Two general studies, more detailed accounts related to specific works, and a manuscript transcription are among the book-length critical works offered on Joyce this year. Matthew Hodgart's *James Joyce*[37] is a lively but lightweight introduction to Joyce as man and writer. There are general chapters devoted to Joyce's biography, attitudes of mind and artistic milieu, the history of Ireland, and the novelist's sexual interests, alcoholism, and mental state. The chapters devoted to the works are primarily descriptive. There is a great deal of summary and historical background in the section on *Dubliners* together with a concentration on rather idiosyncratic points (such as the suggestion regarding tertiary syphilis in 'The Sisters'). A greater concern with stylistic achievements and artistry can be noted in the chapters on *A Portrait* and *Ulysses*, and first-time readers of the latter novel will probably be glad of Hodgart's plot summaries and thematic descriptions. There is a sketchy account of *Finnegans Wake* and brief treatments of Joyce's other writings. Little new thought on Joyce is evidenced here and the subtleties of that author are scarcely accounted for by the retelling of events and the noting of literary techniques, but new readers will find the section on *Ulysses* a helpful if not stimulating starting-place. The bibliography is limited, and more seriously, rather dated.

Colin MacCabe's *James Joyce and the Revolution of the Word*[38] is an intense and convoluted study of the relationship between politics, sexuality, and language in Joyce's writings. Since Joyce involved the reader in a new way in his works, MacCabe argues that a new kind of literary criticism is needed for Joyce study. Joyce's texts (especially *Ulysses* and *Finnegans Wake*) 'are concerned not with representing experience through language but with experiencing language through a destruction of representation. Instead of constructing a meaning, Joyce's texts concern themselves with the position of the subject in language'. Since the texts 'refuse the subject any dominant position from which language could be tallied with experience', the writings do not lend themselves to a simple exercise in decoding. Instead, they demand a different approach to the intertwined formal and substantial elements and MacCabe finds that approach in psychoanalysis. By using psychoanalytic concepts based on theories of Freud and Lacan, MacCabe attempts to show 'how the work relates to the forms in which it is written and how those forms can be understood in relation to fantasy – to the figuration of desire and sexuality', since there is a significant relationship between language and the unconscious. There is much to be appreciated in MacCabe's contention that the mature Joyce

[37] *James Joyce: A Student's Guide*, by Matthew Hodgart. Routledge & Kegan Paul. pp. viii + 196. hb £5.95, pb £2.95.

[38] *James Joyce and the Revolution of the Word*, by Colin MacCabe. Macmillan. (Language, Discourse, Society Series) pp. x + 186. £8.95.

departed from the 'classic realist text' and deprived his reader of any one dominant authorial stance offering a position of judgement. Instead, Joyce's fiction subverts 'any promise of origin in an author, coherence in itself, or correspondence with a given reality, in order to engage with the subject in a distancing from any final identification'. But to discuss this narrative or linguistic subversion in terms of sexual perversion and to consider Joyce's works as linguistic expressions of an oedipal complex seems far-fetched and unhelpful. It is one thing to describe 'the struggle against narrative'; it is quite another to identify it with the attempt 'to evade paternal identification and, in that evasion, to let the desire of the mother speak'. The connection established between Joyce's language and politics is also seen in sexual terms: 'central to his commitment to socialism was his ferocious opposition to the institution of marriage, bourgeois society's sanctified disavowal of the reality of desire'. In MacCabe's analysis, Joyce's language reflects his rejection of identities imposed in an authoritarian way and his desire to deconstruct 'the mechanisms of identification'. This deconstruction inevitably involves separation from a fixed point of reference, and such indeed is the reader's own experience of *Ulysses* and *Finnegans Wake* where no authoritative authorial position emerges. But one must ultimately argue with MacCabe's method of analysis. To substitute psychoanalytic interpretations for traditional textual criticism is not to reject 'decoding' but to exchange one kind of decoding for another.

Suzette A. Henke employs phenomenology, existential approaches, new criticism, psychoanalysis, and the Geneva 'criticism of consciousness' in order 'to re-create *Ulysses* as an existential act of mind and a phenomenological life-world'[39]. Jargon and a strident tone mar what is otherwise a most engaging consideration of the relationship between the creative imagination and a 'revolutionary view of consciousness' in the novel. Henke develops her argument from two basic premises: first, that Stephen, Bloom, and Molly are all artists who improve on and cope with life through the efforts of creative imagination; and second, that Joyce rejects the old moral view of 'sin' and 'guilt', substituting the principles of 'existential humanism' instead. Indeed, the novel can best be understood by combining these premises. Joyce's characters transcend the outmoded and stifling moral perceptions of their environment 'by virtue of the intellectual imagination made possible by language'. Consciousness is liberated if the individual can become an ' "artist of life" through myth, sympathy, and creative fantasy'. Once the psyche transcends and re-creates its world, Joyce's 'interindividual relations' are possible, for the liberating creative imagination activates that enlarged sympathy on which successful relationships depend. Although this study is dense and disjointed, Henke's analysis of the redemptive power of artistic or creative imagination in *Ulysses* is an important one. An extensive bibliography encourages further investigation of a fascinating area of Joyce criticism.

Joyce's Voices[40] is derived primarily from Hugh Kenner's T. S. Eliot Memorial Lectures delivered at the University of Kent in 1975. Kenner boldly attempts to come to terms with 'the apparent stylistic caprice that

[39] *Joyce's Moraculous Sindbook: A Study of 'Ulysses'*, by Suzette A. Henke. Columbus, Ohio: Ohio State U.P. pp. xii + 267. $15.

[40] *Joyce's Voices*, by Hugh Kenner. Faber & Faber. pp. xiv + 120. £5.50.

seems to invade and subvert' *Ulysses*. To this end he detects two 'voices' – one which is tied to the nature of a character and his idiom, and one which is that of the narrator, deft, inventive, and idiosyncratic. At first, the character voice (such as Bloom's) is 'garrulous, the narrative concise and economical'; but gradually these positions are reversed and the detached narrator takes over, '*reading* the narrative, and reserv[ing] the privilege of letting us know what he thinks of it'. This accomplished, ironic, and malicious technician is identified by Kenner as 'a counterpart of the fate that presides over the universe of farce'. In fact, Kenner concludes that it is not character but language as manipulated, distorted, and controlled by this voice which provides the key to meaning in the novel. The reader is forced to confront a language which is 'playing roles, striking postures, contorting itself into expressive patterns which offer to clarify what is going on and instead. . .mislead'. This rhetoric of deceit, evasion and imposture which permeates *Ulysses* is a truth and 'objective' in the purest sense since it destroys our illusions about the separateness of 'fact and perception, event and voice'. This is a gracefully discursive work. Kenner ranges over a number of authors as well as works by Joyce and supports his argument with entertaining and illuminating observations. He has smoothed the way for yet further consideration of Joyce's narration and language. The supplementary notes on matters raised in the text (such as 'Flaubert's mimesis') are helpful and precise.

James H. Maddox Jr opens his examination of character in *Ulysses*[41] with an acknowledgement of certain similarities between his book and Marilyn French's earlier *The Book as World*. Certainly, both studies of *Ulysses* draw attention to the co-existence of opposites inherent in Joyce's characters and to the importance of 'Joyce's stylistic variations' signifying the world's 'refracted signatures'. Given this, however, Maddox's work emerges as a highly readable and convincingly argued treatment of Joyce's indirect and 'unspoken' method of conveying his characters' souls. Maddox believes that for Joyce, the soul is 'mysterious, unknowable'; it can be suggested only by 'an art of surround and periphery, implying and evoking but never naming the center'. Various styles, such as stream of consciousness, are used to establish the inner rhythm, the 'emotional curve which is the shape of a character's being'. Style in *Ulysses* is not simply a means of relaying specific thoughts. The many different narrative modes of the novel provide a 'variety of perspectives' revealing 'the mystery of being'. To this end, Maddox groups the chapters of the novel as 'different movements' or 'perspectives by which character is seen'. Gradually developing from specific 'Stephen-chapters' and 'Bloom-chapters', the novel moves to the opaque and general with chapters in which characters merge into 'the background of humanity' or in which 'the author's style most insistently intrudes between us and the characters'. The resulting diminution in the importance of individuals forms the central movement of the novel and prompts Maddox to conclude that, by the end, 'everyone is willy-nilly a hero'. More significantly, as the style moves away from intimate contact with the character, readers are reminded once again that being can never be named, but only suggested. A distanced or intrusive authorial style

[41] *Joyce's 'Ulysses' and the Assault Upon Character*, by James H. Maddox Jr. Hassocks, Sussex: Harvester P. pp. xii + 244. £11.50.

enables us 'to see the abstract configurations' which the characters form without awareness. And, at the same time, the limitations of a style which loses contact with subject matter reflect the inadequacies of 'the elaborate intellectual dodges by which both Stephen and Bloom rule their lives'. Maddox's discussions of 'Oxen of the Sun', 'Ithaca', 'Penelope', and 'Circe' are particularly illuminating and his conclusion that 'Joyce acknowledges the final superiority of unformed experience to any of the shapes which the preceding chapters have attempted to impose upon it' develops logically and coherently from his general premise that personality in the novel is 'an unfathomable mystery'. All those seeking a stimulating analysis of the self-contradictory characters in *Ulysses* and a distinctive account of profuse styles in the novel will welcome Maddox's approach.

John Henry Raleigh has performed a useful service by collecting and organising information about the Blooms. His study of Leopold and Molly[42] is 'a compendium of the Blooms' own thoughts on their respective and mutual pasts', arranged chronologically after a brief account of the Bloom ancestry. Drawn from Joyce's chronologies of the Blooms and the chronology of *Ulysses* itself, this summary of events usefully emphasises 'the immense and detailed naturalistic base upon which *Ulysses* is constructed' and also serves as an introduction to figures and episodes in the novel. Bloom emerges as a character of many 'metamorphoses' – 'child-boy', suitor and married man, 'aggressive maladroit', Molly's protean husband, and the Bloom of June 16, 1904. While the multi-layered nature of Bloom has often been remarked upon, this chronicle helps to distinguish and define the different personas. Raleigh's painstaking amassing of facts about the Blooms also enables a fuller picture of Molly to emerge. The genealogy of Bloom and Molly is traced, and notes are provided on the Blooms' future and undatable past. There are two appendixes – one on Bloom's addresses, and another on Bloom's jobs, as well as maps and diagrams of Gibraltar, Dublin, Bloom's neighbourhood, and 7 Eccles Street.

Finnegans Wake manuscripts are of two kinds – workbooks which contain rudimentary material and drafts which rework the original notes. Danis Rose has capably edited the Holograph Workbook VI.B.46[43] which was 'compiled by Joyce in 1938 as the work in progress came to a conclusion'. Units of words or phrases were listed in the workbook; despite their random ordering all were related to various 'Indexes' or distinct themes. Rose identifies each unit by page and line number as it appears in the finished novel, and groups the units in their appropriate indexes. Clarifying annotations and comments on the individual units are arranged after each index. Rose has also coded each unit to show Joyce's coloured marks indicating that the workbook entry had been transferred to the draft. Certain conclusions can be drawn from the transcription, the most significant of which is related to the over-all structure of the novel. Rose claims that the final text 'is an ordered aggregate of elements each of which can be identified with a unit entered in one of the notebooks'.

[42] *The Chronicle of Leopold and Molly Bloom: 'Ulysses' as Narrative*, by John Henry Raleigh. London and Berkeley, Calif.: U. of California P. pp. xii + 282. £8.75.

[43] *The Index Manuscript: Finnegans Wake Holograph Workbook VI. B. 46*, by James Joyce, transcribed, annotated and with an introduction by Danis Rose. Colchester: Wake Newslitter P. pp. xviii + 379. pb £12.50.

Moreover, by establishing the relationship between notebook units, drafts, and external sources 'the primary meaning of the units upon which the textual element is structured can be established and the implied sense of each passage mapped out'. This transcription is an essential text for all concerned with the *Wake*, and students will appreciate Rose's bibliography which includes sources used by Joyce himself.

Articles published in *TriQuarterly* in 1977 (*YW* 58.382) in dealing with writers 'in the wake of the *Wake*' have been collected in book form by David Hayman and Elliott Anderson[44]. In addition to interviews with writers such as Maurice Roche and Philippe Sollers conducted by David Hayman, there are fictional extracts and poems (by Augusto de Campos, Maurice Roche, Hélène Cixous, Philippe Sollers, Arno Schmidt, Christine Brooke-Rose, Samuel Beckett, Raymond Federman and William Gass) supplying concrete demonstration of the influence of and reaction against *Finnegans Wake*. John Cage offers a mesostic on James Joyce, David Hayman considers the impact of the *Wake*, and Michael Finney writes on Eugene Jolas's linguistic distance from Joyce.

The following were not seen: Robert H. Deming's *A Bibliography of James Joyce Studies* (G. K. Hall), Phillip F. Herring's *Joyce's Notes and Early Drafts for Ulysses* (U.P. of Virginia). Kathleen McGrory and John Unterecker's *Yeats, Joyce, and Beckett* (Bucknell U.P.), and Brendan O'Hehir and John M. Dillon's *A Classical Lexicon for Finnegans Wake* (U. of California P.).

This was also a rich year for Joyce work in periodicals. Yet another query about Stephen on the rocks in the last section of 'Proteus' opens the first number of *JJQ*. David Hayman has an answer which equates Stephen's action with his 'deepest moment of self-absorption'. William B. Warner's sophisticated study of the movements of language in *Ulysses* shows that there is a logic to the changing styles. Brook Thomas insists on reading *Ulysses* as 'a detective story' in which an author hides behind his text and 'a detective reader' tries to unveil him. No new conclusions are drawn, for Thomas sees the narrator as 'a fictional James Joyce', not the flesh and blood man. Alan M. Cohn's 'Supplemental JJ Checklist, 1975', and William M. Schutte's index of recurrent elements in 'Lestrygonians' are invaluable tools for the Joyce scholar. Notes are supplied by Fergal Gallagher, John A. Rea, Stephen Tapscott, William D. Jenkins, Fitz Senn, Hugh Staples, Victory Pomeranz, and David F. Ward on minor aspects of *Ulysses*.

In the Winter issue, David E. Jones has a sound accessible piece on the unity of *Dubliners*. The characterisation of Richard is the focal point for Theo Q. Dombrowski's essay on the problem of love in *Exiles*. Elaine Unkeless looks at those threatening bats in Joyce's work. The association of the bat with someone who entices and seduces apparently demonstrates Joyce's 'fear of sexual power'. Corinna del Greco Lobner studies Joyce's reference to the basilisk in 'Scylla and Charybdis'. Joyce modified Brunetto Latini's definition in order to suggest another father–son relationship (between Dante and himself). There is a review essay of Richard Finneran's *Anglo-Irish Literature: A Review of Research* by Ellsworth Mason, a current JJ checklist from Alan Cohn, and an index of recurrent elements

[44] *In the Wake of the 'Wake'*, ed. by David Hayman and Elliott Anderson. Madison, Wisc. and London. U. of Wisconsin P. pp. 210 £11.05.

in 'Scylla and Charybdis' by William M. Schutte. Karl Beckson compares a passage in *A Portrait* with a section in *The Ordeal of Richard Feverel* to suggest indebtedness. B. D. Boyd finds a parody of George Moore's *The Lake* in *Ulysses*, Christine St. Peter sees a Jonsonian echo in Joyce's use of 'artificer' in *A Portrait*, and Scott Giantvalley notes an allusion to Goethe's *Faust* in the 'Circe' section of *Ulysses*.

Number Three opens with a rewarding essay by Craig Carver on Joyce's interest in the occult and its implications for his vision of the artist as an alchemist or magician. Anita Gandolfo notes that Joyce's knowledge of Blake was filtered through Yeats and argues that this has significance for any interpretation of Joycean symbolism. Karl Beckson discusses the important influence of Arthur Symons on Joyce. John Gordon continues the discussion initiated by Michael Seidel's 1976 article on *Ulysses*' 'black panther vampire', and provides his answer to the question about Stephen's refusal to stay with Bloom for the night. Alan M. Cohn's current checklist, William Schutte's index to recurring elements in the 'Wandering Rocks' episode, and notes from Bernard Benstock and Phillip F. Herring on Leopold and Molly Bloom round out the selection of articles.

In the final number, F. L. Radford's long and detailed essay on the 'labyrinth' of Irish history in *Ulysses* suggests the way in which Joyce coped with the past through parody. 'In the process, the most ordinary events and characters are invested with a weight of historical inheritance that gives a significance of religious dimensions to the pettiest words and actions.' A poem by David Citino is followed by a look at Joyce's treatment of the press and newspapers in *Ulysses*, Carol Shloss reveals that Joyce was hostile to the press but fully aware of its power. He even found in newspapers 'an analogue of form for his book'. He realised that newspapers could err and was disturbed 'that Dublin's citizens should shape their lives according to pre-packaged desires and opinions'. She concludes that 'Joyce's allegiance was not to the goal of Realism continually augmented by details. . . [but to] understanding correlations between one form of cultural representation and another'. William Hutchings offers a challenging piece on Chapter Four of *A Portrait*. He sees Stephen's visionary experience at the end of that chapter as representative of a like culmination 'in the history of western man, whose collective experience has been symbolically recapitulated in his own growth and maturation'. Hutchings also argues that Stephen's self-dedication to art 'is an ironic indication' of his hubris and egotism that will lift his earnestness into 'comic proportions'. Alan Cohn presents another current checklist, and William Schutte looks at 'Sirens' for recurring elements. Charles Skinner prints two letters from Joyce to Carl Bleibtreu about the latter's Shakespearean theory. Mary T. Reynolds writes on the editions of Dante which Joyce possessed, Robert Boyle provides evidence about Molly's age and her superstitious faith, and Erwin R. Steinberg reveals that an American inventor actually patented a device for awakening people buried alive, such as Bloom imagines. Each number contains reviews, letters and other notes of interest to Joyce readers. There was also a supplement this year to *JJQ* – John Cage's mesostic based on sentences and phrases from the *Wake*.

In *Bulletin of Research in the Humanities* (formerly *BNYPL*) Myron Schwartzman turns his attention to John Quinn's letters to Joyce. He transcribes some of these letters which cover the period from the American publication of *Dubliners* to the serialisation of *Ulysses* in *Little Review*. He also summarises and quotes letters from Joyce and Nora to Quinn, a lawyer, patron, manuscript collector, and friend. Bernard Benstock detects yet another unifying element in *Dubliners* – this time in the notable absence of the Holy Ghost. In *SoR* he demonstrates how symbols usually associated with the Holy Ghost are given sinister or repugnant expression. In *TCL* Marilyn French also studies *Dubliners*, arguing that it has 'both the moral standards and the technical approach that Joyce would maintain throughout his life'. There are two articles on particular stories in *SSF*. John J. Brugaletta and Mary H. Hayden try to account for the boy's great anguish at the end of 'Araby', and Thomas Dilworth considers Joyce's symbolic connection between the heroine and Helen of Troy in 'Eveline'. Some difficult but entertaining articles on *Ulysses* have appeared, among which is one by Ralph W. Rader in *UTQ*. Rader argues that Joyce sought 'to objectify and know himself as he was without thought of purgation or change' by creating Bloom who is none other than 'the mature Joyce imagining another in a different body as himself'. Marilyn French (*JNT*) centres on language in the novel. Concentrating on the 'Sirens' section she shows Joyce's mastery over tone. The 'linguistic surface' of the novel is complex but brilliantly achieves Joyce's intention 'to speak obsessively of a certain sort of emotion, to express it brilliantly, and to mock it with equal brilliance'. Shari Benstock (*MFS*) feels that Bloom survives hidden perils and risks by adhering to an 'evasion principle'. Phillip F. Herring tests the accuracy of Joyce's claim to have kept close to facts in *Ulysses*. In *ELH* Herring studies Molly Bloom as a woman from Gibraltar and comes to the conclusion that she is quite unconvincing. 'Exigencies of time plus his growing preoccupation with stylistic experimentation perhaps increased Joyce's intolerance of whatever rules of verisimilitude he might earlier have followed'. A very interesting article by R. B. Kershner Jr appears in *TSLL*. Kershner selects Stephen's disquisition on Shakespeare in the 'Scylla and Charybdis' episode in order to discuss the influence of Wilde on Joyce, and to show that Wilde's 'The Portrait of Mr. W. H.' served as 'a parallel and a model'.

Sidney A. Pearson Jr concentrates on the fiction of Arthur Koestler in his attempt to define Koestler's vision[45]. Pearson discusses several themes which are central to Koestler's novels. The political fiction frequently deals with the individual's responsibility for choices ultimately dictated by 'an inscrutable and irrational universe'. The conflict which thus emerges between deterministic and indeterministic views of the universe and the painful dilemma of choosing means or ends as the basis for political action account for the key moral issues and organising principles in Koestler's novels. Pearson offers a more general discussion of the science writings, arguing that they are the logical extension of the political fiction: 'a new, nondeterministic, nonmaterial science of the mind was the first order of business in the restoration of reason to politics'. Indeed 'the search for a rational source of order in the human condition' lies at the heart of Koestler's vision, for it offers man a chance to escape from the irrationality

[45] *Arthur Koestler*, by Sidney A. Pearson, Jr. (Twayne's English Author Series). Boston, Mass.: Twayne/G. K. Hall. pp. 171. $8.95.

of his universe. Yet, as Pearson sadly remarks, the application of reason in politics only further reveals 'the absurdity of the human condition' since reason rarely triumphs. In this way he accounts for Koestler's ultimate pessimism. This is a straightforward introduction to Koestler; there is some treatment of technique but the basic emphasis is on a sensible but simple description of themes, attitudes, and beliefs. Students who wish to examine Koestler's work at a more sophisticated level will in fact appreciate Pearson's concluding account of major critical objections to Koestler's writings.

Murray A. Sperber introduces his collection of critical essays on and reviews of Arthur Koestler[46] with a discussion of Koestler as a protean writer and a call for greater consideration of the autobiographical element in his work. The first section of essays deals with 'politics and literature'. George Orwell's review of *Spanish Testament* and his overview of Koestler's fiction are both included. Malcolm Cowley equates the power in *Darkness at Noon* with its 'ritual of sacrifice and atonement'. There are reviews of *Arrival and Departure* by Saul Bellow and Harold Rosenberg, and F. O. Matthiessen considers the significance of 'acute feeling' in Koestler's essays. Edmund Wilson praises *Thieves in the Night* for its psychological insight, and Isaac Rosenfeld's consideration of the Jewish problem in the same work is also printed. V. S. Pritchett writes on Koestler as a theatrical journalist rather than a novelist. Maurice Merleau-Ponty criticises Koestler's inadequate grasp of Marxism and revolution in *Darkness at Noon*. Two reviews of *The God That Failed* are supplied by Rebecca West and Isaac Deutscher, and Stephen Spender's review of Koestler's autobiography is included. Murray Sperber's study of Koestler's differing versions of his Spanish Civil War experience concludes the section. The essays in Part Two treat 'science and mysticism' in Koestler's works. James R. Newman and A. J. Ayer both write disapprovingly about *Insight and Outlook*. Stuart Hampshire praises the readability of *The Sleepwalkers* but criticises the old-fashioned synthesis of science and faith. William Empson's review of *The Lotus and The Robot* shows Koestler moving from faith to faith. *The Act of Creation* is treated by George Steiner as 'popularization' and by Henry David Aiken as vision, not science. Leslie Fiedler interprets *The Ghost in the Machine* as embodying Koestler's 'concealed hatred and resentment of the young'. Finally, Stephen Toulmin puts Koestler's scientific ideas in historical perspective. A selected bibliography is appended.

Some enjoyable overviews of Lawrence's fiction, a penetrating study of short stories in evolution, and the facsimile of a manuscript number among the exciting works on Lawrence this year. F. B. Pinion sets out to provide a companion to D. H. Lawrence's life, thought, and works[47]. The result is a sturdy introductory volume which offers useful summaries for general readers or students but has little for the more advanced scholar. Pinion's basic premise is that Lawrence's life and works are intimately connected. For this reason, his book opens with a biographical account which strains somewhat to relate writing to life wherever possible. Despite obvious drawbacks to such an approach, however, there are helpful observations on

[46] *Arthur Koestler: A Collection of Critical Essays*, ed. with an introd. by Murray A. Sperber. (Twentieth Century Views). Englewood Cliffs, N.J.: Prentice-Hall; London: Prentice-Hall International. pp. x + 189. pb £2.55.

[47] *A D. H. Lawrence Companion: Life, Thought, and Works*, by F. B. Pinion. Macmillan. pp. xii + 316. £15.

Lawrence's state of mind when writing various works as well as information on his reading, friends, and relationships with women. The novelist's 'thought-adventures' are also touched on, but not in a very sophisticated way. Such basic points as Lawrence's 'belief in blood-knowledge, instinct, and intuition', the connection between his views on sex, human awareness, and individuality, and his constant attempts to cope with the contraries of male and female, sensual and spiritual consciousness are covered. There are also chapters devoted to the poetry, the novels, and the shorter stories, in addition to a general chapter on 'other writings'. For the most part, Pinion outlines central ideas, attitudes, and themes, provides succinct plot summaries where applicable, and comments on dominant images and symbols. Technical and stylistic analysis is kept to a minimum and there are only a few attempts to evaluate literary merits and weaknesses. Pinion concludes that Lawrence grasped the 'weakness and corruption in our modern society' with remarkable acumen. The artistry of Lawrence is seen to lie in his imaginative ability to extend 'metaphor to scene and action which communicate attitudes and feelings, life forces and anti-life forces'. Appendixes on moon and rose imagery in Lawrence's writings and people and places in the novels together with a rather limited select bibliography complete the work. The limitations of such an ambitious undertaking are legion, since the desire to touch on all aspects of Lawrence in an accessible way inevitably has the effect of reducing a very complex author to his simplest (and most simplistic) terms. Still, the reader who requires a general introduction to Lawrence's basic pre-occupations and problems will find Pinion's work helpful and will no doubt be encouraged to pursue his investigations further.

Alastair Niven's introduction to the novels of Lawrence[48] offers a sensible account of the major fictional works in basic thematic and stylistic terms for the purpose of demonstrating 'that Lawrence contributed in a major way to the nature of the modern novel'. Standard interpretations are advanced; Niven usefully reads the novels as fiction rather than disguised autobiography. At the same time he tactfully hints at key relationships between themes, style, and personal circumstances in particular periods of creative activity. Moreover, Niven gives sympathetic attention to frequently neglected works such as *The White Peacock*, *The Trespasser*, and *Kangaroo* taking care, as with the other novels, to relate them to Lawrence's artistic development. The analyses of *The Rainbow* and *Women in Love* are particularly well handled and calculated to provide the new student of Lawrence with a comprehensive and stimulating appraisal of the texts. Changes in technique and themes are seen in terms of Lawrence's own feelings and responses to the challenge of attaining wholeness of being and to the importance of 'integrity in personal relationships'. Niven's conclusion is in keeping with his straightforward approach; he sees Lawrence as a writer finally 'in sad rebellion against the drift of modern life' but testifying 'to the possible endurance of the best human values'.

The Art of the Self in D. H. Lawrence[49] is a complex psychoanalytic

[48] *D. H. Lawrence: The Novels*, by Alastair Niven. Cambridge: C.U.P. (British Authors Introductory Critical Studies Series) pp. x + 188. hb £7.50, pb £2.95.

[49] *The Art of the Self in D. H. Lawrence*, by Marguerite Beede Howe. Athens, Ohio: Ohio U.P. 1977. pp. x + 164. $12.

study of the novels. Marguerite Howe believes that Lawrence's main theme is neither blood consciousness, nor the evils of industrial society, nor the glory of sex. Rather, she finds the key issue to be 'identity, and the fragmented self'. With a keen eye for patterns, Howe explores each novel as representative of a particular concept of self and personality, appropriate to particular stages of human development (from childhood to death) and dealing with different ways of creating and maintaining self in the face of reality. Thus, *Sons and Lovers* reflects the mother–son relationship and 'the oedipal personality' which evolves in *The Rainbow* into a new identity that is split between a social self and an essential core. The self must in the later novels do battle with 'disintegrative' cosmic chaos and struggle for the integration of its sensual and spiritual, masculine and female elements. Overall Howe detects a crucial change in Lawrence's treatment of the self, for he moves from a stance in which the self depends on others to a position in which the self is really located in and maintained by the unconscious. Lawrence's struggle for the self's autonomy is concluded in the 'elegiac' *Lady Chatterley's Lover* which, in Howe's terms, presents the novelist's final statement about 'the modern dilemma, the self in isolation'. The scientific 'insentient iron world' which determinedly fragments self seems triumphant. Lawrence's 'philosophy of existence' which originally promised life and salvation is finally and bleakly acknowledged to be impotent. Nevertheless, Howe argues, Lawrence's vision is extremely relevant to 'modern ego psychology' especially in its attempts to integrate 'rational and non-rational experience'. One might challenge Howe's essentially allegorical approach for she sets out to treat 'character primarily as idea, and the material world as symbol', ostentatiously avoiding comment on the artistry inherent in the fiction. But she makes a spirited defence of this method and contends that Lawrence himself used psychic allegory to explore and present that unconscious psychic life which defies logical analysis.

A. H. Gomme has collected a number of essays by the younger generation on the major novels and selected writings of Lawrence[50]. Only one essay has been previously published and Gomme suggests that the critics represented here supply the fresh look at Lawrence which is desperately needed. Eleven essays follow a chronological table of Lawrence's life, writing and publication. Some cover rather well-worked ground; others deal in a stimulating way with neglected areas of Lawrence's work or with 'new openings' to the major novels and themes. Ian Robinson writes suggestively on Lawrence's effect on English prose style and the relationship between Lawrence's style and thought. A. H. Gomme takes the relationship between Jessie Chambers and Miriam Leivers as a starting point for discussion of *Sons and Lovers*. The novel is seen as 'a tragedy whose heart is in the very tension between aim and achievement, what is said and what is shown' since 'the living Miriam who is directly revealed to us tells against and even undermines the Miriam who is described and interpreted'. Jacques Berthoud thoughtfully treats *The Rainbow* as an experimental novel in which Lawrence's stylistic attempts to portray unconscious experience are in part

[50] *D. H. Lawrence: A Critical Study of the Major Novels and Other Writings*, ed. by A. H. Gomme. Hassocks, Sussex: Harvester P.; New York: Harper & Row. pp. 224. £10.50.

strained and incoherent. Richard Drain argues that *Women in Love* should be approached as a study of the contradictory impulses to which the twentieth-century self is subject – 'from the rigidities of alienation to the outbursts of released repression'. A similar line is taken by R. E. Pritchard who considers 'the theme of the isolated outsider, and particularly, the concept of "singleness" and some of its implications' in Lawrence's work following *Women in Love*. D. Kenneth M. Mackenzie usefully reminds us that 'England, My England' involves not just an examination of personal relationships but also a study of the modern disease of ennui and its antidote, affirmative energy. *The Ladybird* tales are seen by H. M. Daleski as 'exploratory ventures' finally leading to *Lady Chatterley's Lover*. However, while the tales deal with the need for 'woman's submission to the "power-soul" in man', *Lady Chatterley's Lover* is based on 'a reciprocal tenderness'. G. R. Strickland is also concerned with *Lady Chatterley's Lover* and emphasises the importance of the first version of the novel. It is among the best works of Lawrence and serves as a touchstone for judging the artistry and moral beliefs of the disastrously uncontrolled third version. R. T. Jones sees Lawrence's poetry as an attempt to make 'the fact (not the subjective impression). . .real, made apprehensible as experience, by the creative imagination'. John and Ann Remsbury provide the most thought-provoking contribution in their essay on Lawrence's neglected paintings and writings on art. In their terms, Lawrence's consideration of the problems of perception, reality, imagination, and the theoretical nature of art should guarantee him a place with Hegel, Wittgenstein, and Merleau-Ponty. The bibliography which concludes this collection is, disappointingly, dated.

Lawrence and Women[51] is a collection of nine energetic essays which respond in various ways to Lawrence's treatment of the relationships between men and women. Anne Smith ransacks letters, memoirs, and Lawrence's poetry in order to analyse 'Lawrence's inability to come to terms with women as full human beings, and his inability to show a satisfactory, fulfilling marriage between two articulate people'. Her biographical approach emphasises Lawrence's own sickly, self-pitying and narcissistic being against which he struggled in his life and writings. Faith Pullin takes a similar line when she turns her attention to the women in *Sons and Lovers* and angrily argues that 'Lawrence never emerged from the infantile state in which other people are merely instruments'. Women in the novel are stereotypes, used by Paul as an aid to self-definition and stripped of credibility to assuage Lawrence of 'guilt and responsibility'. 'Mothers and Daughters in D. H. Lawrence: *The Rainbow* and Selected Shorter Works' is Lydia Blanchard's attempt to demonstrate that female relationships in these works are the key to relationships between men and women since they are the 'central impetus' to maturity for many of Lawrence's female characters. The metaphor of sex in Lawrence's fiction is explored by Mark Kinkead who isolates four scenes from *Sons and Lovers, The Rainbow, Women in Love*, and *Lady Chatterley's Lover* in an effort to show that language reveals 'both the erotic and its metaphysical extensiveness'. The sexual act becomes a vehicle for Lawrence's treatment of 'wider and wider

[51] *Lawrence and Women*, ed. by Anne Smith (Vision Critical Studies). Vision P. pp. 217. £6.40.

relationships, within people, between them, throughout society, and the connection of man to the universe'. Julian Moynahan adopts an original approach when he studies Lawrence's understanding of the Celtic character in relation to the presentation of women in the fiction. He believes that Lawrence's work with 'the Celt-woman' was an expression of his concern 'for women's liberation and the liberation of all from the fettered past'. *The Rainbow, Women in Love*, and *Aaron's Rod* form a progressive account of a personal crisis, according to Philippa Tristram. However, in Lawrence's battle for singleness of being and the maintenance of self in these novels, he was wrong 'to identify the enemy with women, not with the enemy within'. T. E. Apter tries to defend Lawrence against the now clichéd charge of male chauvinism in *The Plumed Serpent* by asserting that the novel is primarily an attempt to redefine 'male' and 'female' and to be responsive to a woman's real needs. 'Kate's success is only moderate, but the cultures in which she seeks fulfilment are uncongenial to the realisation of a woman's deepest needs – and that is the point of the novel.' Harry T. Moore offers a rather discursive consideration of Lawrence's attitudes to women and love, accusing Kate Millett of over-simplification. Moore believes that Lawrence essentially regarded women and love in a 'religious way'. Lawrence's antipathy to women is explored in a lively essay by Mark Spilka who suggests it is really centred on wilful women. In *Lady Chatterley's Lover* Lawrence discovers that Connie's world and way of life 'deplete her volition'. Moreover, Mellor's anger, 'an instance of wrongheaded wilfulness. . .can be accommodated by Connie's yielding love'.

Keith Cushman's *D. H. Lawrence at Work*[52] is a lucid account of *The Prussian Officer* stories and their relationship to Lawrence's own thematic and technical development. By examining the extant versions of these stories, Cushman convincingly demonstrates that the essential coherence and artistic success of the volume are intimately related to Lawrence's own perfection of personal vision. In 1914 Lawrence reached a significant point in his development as an artist. It was in this year in *The Rainbow* that he at last coherently formulated his own essentially dualistic vision of the universe, of the 'connectedness of the everyday world and the unknown beyond it'. A detailed study of the extensive 1914 revisions of *The Prussian Officer* stories reveals a similar concern on the part of Lawrence to show the 'integration of the daily and the cosmic'. Cushman's careful analysis of such stories as 'Odour of Chrysanthemums' and 'The Shades of Spring' supports his argument that 'the final revisions of the best stories are exciting because they seem to be an integral part of the moment in which he became the Lawrence we know'. In addition Cushman also discusses the stories as expressions of Lawrence's own family and love relationships and his Germanic experience. Again the revisions are significant since the changing emphases they reveal powerfully suggest Lawrence's growing ability to accept his past and his self and to express his feelings about the 'essential "man-life" and essential "woman-life" '. This engaging study concludes with appendixes on 'The "Prussian Officer" Texts', 'The Origins of "The Christening" ', and 'A *Prussian Officer* Calendar'.

[52] *D. H. Lawrence at Work: The Emergence of the 'Prussian Officer' Stories*, by Keith Cushman. Hassocks, Sussex: Harvester P. pp. xvi + 239. £10.50.

A facsimile of the final holograph manuscript of *Sons and Lovers* has appeared, edited by Mark Schorer who also contributes the succinct introduction on the history of the manuscript[53]. This is a beautifully produced volume consisting of the final (printer's copy) version of the novel and six fragments from the early chapters of 'Paul Morel' (penultimate draft). The final version emerges as a crucial guide to Lawrence's own stylistic aspirations. Lawrence's alterations are for the most part quite readable and show his constant striving for the specific, the dramatic, and the profound. Schorer also directs attention to the major changes which Edward Garnett made to the manuscript. Unlike the few Duckworth deletions made for moral reasons, Garnett cut numerous passages for artistic purposes. He tightened Lawrence's verbose style and excised awkward authorial intrusions with a keen eye for 'matters of tone, texture, thematic unity, reader response, even plausibility'. The 'Paul Morel' fragments highlight Lawrence's achievement in *Sons and Lovers*, for their cumbersomeness demonstrates by contrast the remarkable vitality of the published version. Bibliographers will welcome Schorer's supplement at the end which lists significant variations between the manuscript and the first British and American editions. The very high price of this facsimile edition means that few will be able to purchase it, but all serious students of Lawrence will wish to consult this splendid instance of 'work in progress'.

Keith Sagar's *D. H. Lawrence: A Calendar of His Works* (U. of Manchester P.) and Elizabeth Brody Tenenbaum's *The Problematic Self: Approaches to Identity in Stendhal, D. H. Lawrence, and Malraux* (Harvard U.P., 1977) were not seen.

In the Spring issue of *DHLR* Allan R. Zoll discusses the influence of 'vitalist metaphysics' on Lawrence's concept of love and his thought in general. He sees Lawrence as strikingly indebted to Schopenhauer. Gerald Contiff finds *The Widowing of Mrs. Holroyd* a typical Lawrentian work in its presentation and handling of the 'failed marriage' theme, though the emphasis is not on the sociological but on the physical aspect. R. P. Bilan challenges Leavis's 'claim for the normative bearings of Lawrence's art': 'it is possible to think of Lawrence as an essentially moral, affirmative, writer yet recognize that his work does not always, or even necessarily, have normative bearings.' 'Song of a Man Who Has Come Through' is read as a pivotal poem by Erwin R. Steinberg, who sees it as a tense autobiographical reflection of Lawrence's own hopes and fears with respect to Frieda and his artistic creativity. Paul Delany briefly examines the relationship between Forster and Lawrence. He concludes that Forster probably found Lawrence's integrity too intense and provocative. Sonja Miletić and Miroslav Beker compile a bibliography of Lawrence criticism in Yugoslavia (1926–76), and Richard D. Beards offers his 1977 checklist of Lawrence criticism and scholarship. Notes of interest to students of Lawrence and a checklist of research in progress are appended to this and each following issue.

The second number contains an article by Peter H. Balbert decrying the current neglect of *Sons and Lovers* as a study of a 'tripartite phallic

[53] *Sons and Lovers: A Facsimile of the Manuscript*, by D. H. Lawrence, ed. with an introduction by Mark Schorer. London and Berkely, Calif.: U. of California P. pp. iv + 624. £52.50.

struggle. . .for sexual emancipation'. Balbert identifies Paul's energy with his 'phallic imagination'. Deborah Core contrasts male/male and female/female relationships in Lawrence's writings. While ideal relationships between men seem possible, 'a woman must have energy directed and flowing from a man in order even to begin her redemption from the mechanistic, dead world'. An important essay from Robert H. MacDonald establishes the significance of Lawrence's 'The Two Principles'. The essay is crucial for an understanding of 'the structure and dynamics' behind Lawrence's complex system of cosmology and psychology based on sexual duality and polarity. The system is explored in terms of fire and water symbolism in the fiction and illustrates the fundamental belief that 'sexual duality, in all its manifest variety, is the basic constituent of life'. Lawrence's critical perception is discussed by Richard L. White who sees Lawrence's perspectives on English and American fiction as ahead of his time. Keith Sagar recounts the true history of *The Daughter-in-Law*. Information of interest to Lawrence readers is contained in the *D. H. Lawrence Newsletter* appended to this issue.

The Fall number has several perceptive pieces. John W. Haegert writes well on Lawrence's treatment of erotic love as an 'inexorable fate' leading either to bondage or higher freedom. This is seen particularly in *Women in Love*. Michael Squires offers a close textual study of the three manuscripts and surviving typescript of *Lady Chatterley's Lover* as a means of shedding light on the gamekeeper. Revisions in his presentation show 'Lawrence's concern with layers of character' and also reveal a movement 'toward self-portraiture' because Lawrence 'needed to justify himself to Frieda', and 'to discover an appropriate manhood'. Lydia Blanchard provides a much needed analysis of feminine response to *Lady Chatterley's Lover* and looks closely at Lady Chatterley herself. Again revisions in the novel are useful for they show that Lawrence was primarily interested in the growth to understanding. Lawrence gradually came to see that 'the self cut off from others is an impossibility'; Lady Chatterley learns this through sexuality. From this Blanchard argues that to miss the connection 'between sex and perception' is to misread the novel. Dennis Jackson concentrates on echoes of ancient myth and ritual in the same novel. Motifs such as 'underworld travels' and the 'dying-reviving god' archetype help to create 'a magic, vital ancient world starkly and ironically contrasted to the profane and meaningless life of modern man depicted in many parts of the novel'. Billy T. Tracy unearths Lawrence's travel books to consider them, not in the light of the novels, but in the tradition of Victorian and Edwardian travel book literature. Lawrence's travel writings are of the first order due to his profound penetration of 'the connections between culture and place'. There are several notes on *Lady Chatterley's Lover*. David Leon Higdon speculates on the possibility that Lawrence 'used Bertha Mason, Rochester's mad wife, as a source for Bertha Coutts, the gamekeeper's wife'. Daniel J. Sheerin finds that Lawrence's blasphemous and parodic use of Psalm 24 in Chapter XIV of the novel has 'two antecedent analogues in sacred literature'.

In *SoRA* John W. Haegert focuses on 'the creative and exploratory aspects of sex and friendship' in Lawrence's writings. He objects to John Edge's *SoRA* article on comradeship in Lawrence (1976) and asserts the 'naturalness of fraternal love' in the fiction. It is synonymous neither with homosexual desire nor Oedipal guilt. Alice Bloom explores the significance of 'dailiness' in Lawrence's life and art in *YR*. The notion of 'dying into being' or dying into a 'deeper consciousness' occupies Donald Gutierrez in his *TCL* Lawrence article. Even Lawrence's poetry is permeated by death-rebirth, mortality-immortality themes. Louise Wright (*TSLL*) discovers that *The Trespasser* 'is deeply rooted in Lawrence's own life', and does not depend solely on material supplied by Helen Corke. Gary Sloan's note in *AN&Q* is on *Sons and Lovers* and the way in which a passage from the Emersonian essay 'Experience' sheds light on the novel's ending and title. Discovering that his grief for his mother was transitory, 'Lawrence then let biographical truth root out artistic continuity'. Jeffrey Meyers devotes his *LMag* article to a consideration of the friendship between Lawrence and Katherine Mansfield. He argues that Katherine was transformed into Gudrun in such a way that 'the negative aspects' of her character were emphasised. R. P. Draper's detailed analysis of *The Rainbow* (*CritQ*) concentrates on the struggle for self-fulfilment, while Evelyn J. Hinz's essay on that novel in *DR* probes the influence of Jane Ellen Harrison's *Ancient Art and Ritual* on the religious elements of Lawrence's work. Janice Harris writes clearly in *MLQ* on the relationship between *The Plumed Serpent* and three Lawrence tales – 'The Woman Who Rode Away', 'St. Mawr', and 'The Princess' which were written between the first and final drafts of the novel. A comparison of the tales and novel drafts shows the organic evolution of Lawrence's struggle to 'many-centered consciousness'. In *CR* David Parker compares *The First Lady Chatterley* to the final version and finds it a superior work, 'more deeply and completely imagined'. *GaR* has an interesting article by William Wasserstrom on the elusive 'The Woman Who Rode Away'. Wasserstrom sees the work as a comment on the 'problem of American progress' and a response to Henry Adams who linked 'industry and inertia'. Charles Koban favours a mystical-religious interpretation of 'The Rocking-Horse Winner' in *SSF*. The story can be read allegorically as Paul is 'a symbol of the child in his mother'. His death is tragic, but 'just as tragic is the death of innocence and love, symbolized by Paul, in his unfortunate mother'. Cheng Lok Chua sees significance in the 'phallic image of the pipe' in 'The Shadow in the Rose Garden' (*Expl*) and in the same journal, Judith Mitchell finds mythic and biographical elements in 'Ballad of a Wilful Woman'. Iris Strohschoen analyses 'Snake' as an example of Lawrence's poetic style in *Estudos Anglo-Americanos.*

Revived interest in T. E. Lawrence has no doubt prompted Penguin to issue an unexpurgated version of *The Mint*[54], based on notes which Lawrence made when in the RAF under an assumed name. Consisting of short, sharply observed chapters, the book details the day-to-day activities of Lawrence as a recruit and aerial photographer. He hated the anonymous uniformity of the Air Force and here tellingly exposes the crude and sadistic world of the camp. J. M. Wilson's preface is an interesting one which urges recognition for Lawrence as a shrewd observer and brilliant descriptive writer. Lawrence, who created the book from a painstaking expansion of his notes, managed to retain a striking air of immediacy and sincerity. Although he felt it was 'an iron, rectangular, abhorrent book,

[54] *The Mint*, by T. E. Lawrence. Penguin. pp. 232. pb £0.95.

one which no man would willingly read' it cannot fail to grip the attention.

Clare Sydney Smith's record of her friendship with T. E. Lawrence first appeared in 1940. It has been reissued[55] and remains a very warm, informal, and affectionate portrait of Lawrence the man. Homely details of Lawrence's favourite food blend with rather reverential accounts of his quick-thinking, heroic actions in an emergency. The general impression given of Lawrence is that of a quiet kind man, ostensibly choosing to live 'the life of the spirit' and remaining to the end elusive and somehow aloof.

Two excellent critiques on the work of Doris Lessing have appeared. Mary Ann Singleton's major study of Doris Lessing[56] is a closely argued and commendably thorough account of Lessing's attempt to deal with the impending catastrophes of our civilisation and the responsibility of human beings for the collapse of their society. Lessing uses a number of narrative techniques to accommodate her vision of humanity's weaknesses and potential, but Singleton isolates three particular motifs (and their associated images) which recur regularly in Lessing's portrayals of a warped civilisation heading for disaster. The first of these motifs is the veld which symbolises the vast and impressive unity of nature. It is a world of instinct, not reason, where the individual is unimportant and subsumed by 'the ceaseless round of natural repetition'. The city stands for modern, fragmented consciousness, capable of using reason but partially destroyed by 'strife-torn society'. The protagonists in Lessing's fiction struggle in these worlds, yearning for a unification of city and veld. Such harmony is associated only with the final motif, that of the Ideal City which suggests 'unified consciousness. . .expressed as a harmonious society of unified citizens'. Neither reason nor instinct can bring about this state. Only through the exercise of imagination can the full potential of human nature be realised. Singleton persuasively demonstrates Lessing's connection of these motifs with mythic patterns, realistic and symbolic narrative methods, even with a semi-allegorical approach to the problems of individual and social fragmentation. She also sensibly warns against a simplified view of the integrated man: 'unification of the city and the veld involves something more than personal integration of the conscious with the unconscious, the rational with the intuitive and emotional. It also implies responsibility for one's actions and for the welfare of others', and lifts man above violence, instinctual behaviour, or actions governed by suppressed knowledge. Lessing's mature and deft handling of the Ideal City 'of the spirit' in *The Memoirs of a Survivor* is sensitively discussed in an afterword.

Michael Thorpe's study of Doris Lessing[57] dispenses with tedious plot summaries and discussions of other critics. Instead Thorpe plunges into a thoughtful account of Lessing's Africa with its ingrown colonial atmosphere before going on to analyse the part played by Africa in her writings. Lessing's work on Africa has a remarkable clarity, sureness, and scope, and Thorpe briskly demonstrates her wide-ranging concern for Africa. The

[55] *The Golden Reign: The Story of My Friendship with 'Lawrence of Arabia'*, by Clare Sydney Smith. Cassell. pp. 190. £4.25.

[56] *The City and the Veld: The Fiction of Doris Lessing*, by Mary Ann Singleton. Lewisburg, Pa.: Bucknell U.P.: London: Associated University Presses. 1977. pp. 243. £6.50.

[57] *Doris Lessing's Africa*, by Michael Thorpe. (Modern African Writers Series). Evans Brothers. pp. x + 117. hb £3.95, pb £2.75.

racial issue alone does not occupy her thoughts. Instead it offers a framework for a more profound consideration of the failure of white civilisation and the development of individual consciousness. What is particularly illuminating is Thorpe's meticulous concern for relating narrative techniques to theme. Lessing's skill in manipulating perspective and her use of both traditional forms (such as the *bildungsroman*) and experimental methods (such as distorted chronology) are sensitively handled. At the end Thorpe looks briefly at Lessing's non-African work, but argues convincingly that she must remain 'a writer Africa made': 'her passionate psychic and physical response to Africa contributed that romantic "conscience" which blends, most unusually in a modern writer, with a more contemporary analytical social and psychological realism.' In *MFS* Charles and Leibetraut Sarvan detect echoes of D. H. Lawrence in *The Grass is Singing*, although destruction in Lessing's work replaces what can be fulfilment for some of Lawrence's female characters. Judith Mitchell criticises those who find Wyndham Lewis anti-feminine (*MFS*). He attacked women who did not use their intellects, but equally, he did include some sympathetically drawn female characters in his fiction.

Malcolm Lowry: A Reference Guide[58] is a checklist of Lowry manuscripts, major Lowry writings (including translations), and criticism about his work from 1927 to 1976. In a splendid introduction William H. New offers some useful observations based on the checklist. Critical sympathy for Lowry is beginning to emerge, and his 'international reputation' is starting to grow. While early critics of Lowry searched for the curious and sensational, current trends indicate a more sophisticated appreciation of Lowry's style and the polarities and tensions in his work. New gives some idea of the wide range of critical approaches to Lowry: sources, landscapes, political and social frameworks, allusions, symbolism, and characterisation are all currently under investigation. Developments in the theory of fiction will broaden the critical response to the novelist, and New looks forward to future Lowry criticism based on phenomenological approaches, the influence of film, and the detection of musical analogies. He concludes by extolling Lowry's 'technical versatility and textural density'. This bibliography will be a major tool for Lowry scholars and those who use the book will be grateful for New's concise annotating of the entries on criticism.

Anne Smith has collected nine intriguing essays[59] which explore the growing critical awareness of Lowry's 'tragic relevance to our own disjointed times'. Lowry's brother, Russell, corrects much information which Lowry himself put about concerning his early life. Autobiographical readings of the fiction are neither accurate nor helpful, he believes. Richard Hauer Costa traces the critical reception of *Under the Volcano* over the last thirty years. Stephen Tifft capably analyses the 'reflexive' tragedy of the same novel. After an interesting consideration of allusions, motifs and parallels in the work, he concludes that the Consul destroys himself: 'knowing his tragic identity to be at once authentic and delusory, [the Consul] is paralysed – and through his paralysis the tragedy becomes

[58] *Malcolm Lowry: A Reference Guide*, by William H. New. (Reference Publication in Literature Series). Boston, Mass.: G. K. Hall. pp. xxx + 162. $18.

[59] *The Art of Malcolm Lowry*, ed. by Anne Smith. (Vision Critical Study). Vision P. pp. 173. £5.40.

authentic by default.' Brian O'Kill usefully relates the language and sentence construction of *Under the Volcano* to the structure of the novel. The overloaded style is uniquely related to 'Lowry's widening conception of the novel' and reflects his own ambivalence and scepticism concerning the efficacy of language. Lowry's use of expressionist techniques and the influence of expressionist films on his style are considered by Sherrill E. Grace who concludes that expressionism 'shaped Lowry's vision and his technique'. Lowry's sense of place, ultimately stronger than his sense of person, is the subject of George Woodcock's absorbing essay. Perle Epstein reads 'The Forest Path to the Spring' as 'a character's regeneration through the medium of Nature'. M. C. Bradbrook studies manuscript drafts, notebooks, and the typescript of 'October Ferry to Gabriola' in an effort to understand Lowry's unconventional prose form. Finally, T. E. Bareham offers a guide to the major themes and stylistic methods of Lowry's short stories, directing attention to 'an allusive inter-connecting thought-stream technique'. A discerning article by Barry Wood in *ConL* treats metafictional elements in Lowry's output. The story, 'Ghostkeeper', is an effective paradigm for all Lowry fiction 'about the process of writing fiction'. Ian Hamilton interviews short story writer and novelist Ian McEwan in *New Review*.

The Autumn number of *MFS* was an exciting Katherine Mansfield Special Issue. Jeffrey Meyers reprints and discusses Mansfield's elegy on the Polish painter and playwright Stanislaw Wyspianski. T. O. Beachcroft writes about Mansfield's literary milieu and briefly discusses the reaction of students to her today. Geraldine L. Conroy examines the friendship between Mansfield and S. S. Koteliansky, reprinting two of his letters on their translation of Chekhov. Ann L. McLaughlin compares the similar early visions of Virginia Woolf and Mansfield, Richard F. Peterson praises Mansfield's ability to let the reader *experience* the truth, particularly in 'Prelude', and Mary Burgan considers the thematic importance of child-bearing and fecundity in Mansfield's fiction. Autobiographical elements in 'Bliss' are noted and discussed by Marvin Magalaner who stresses Mansfield's belief that art should ultimately transcend the personal. Don W. Kleine wonders why 'The Daughters of the Late Colonel' should seem so modern and decides that it is because of Mansfield's handling of time and space in the story. Adam J. Sorkin defines tension in 'The Garden Party'. The rich texture of the story relies on the dialectical poise between 'the narrative world of vivid realistic clarity and specificity' and 'a symbolic, internalized world of metaphorical perception implicit in human reactions'. Toby Silverman Zinman concentrates on the ironic vision of victimisation in Mansfield's life and fiction, Cherry Hankin studies Mansfield's endings which entail the 'confrontation between fantasy and reality', and Jeffrey Meyers adds a supplement to his bibliography of international Mansfield crticism published in *BB*. The following have not been made available: Jeffrey Meyers' *Katherine Mansfield: A Biography* (Hamish Hamilton) and Mary H. Rohrberger's *The Art of Katherine Mansfield* (University Microfilms, 1977).

Robin Maugham's *Conversations with Willie* (W. H. Allen) and R. Toole Stott's *A Bibliography of the Works of W. Somerset Maugham* (U. of Alberta P.) were not seen. A minor novelist and short story writer of the turn of the century, Leonard Merrick, is brought to readers' notice by

William Baker, David Lass, and Stephen E. Tabachnick (*ELT*) who provide 'an annotated bibliography of writings about him'. Michael West argues in *HLB* that Moore's *The Untilled Field* contains interesting parallels to *Dubliners* and helps us to get Joyce's work in perspective as 'the product of its immediate cultural milieu'. In *ELT* Eileen Kennedy reprints eighteen letters from George Moore to Edward Elgar which usefully illuminate the background of the 'ill-fated' production of *Diarmuid and Grania.*

The art–love theme in Irish Murdoch's *The Black Prince* interests Jack F. Stewart who writes in *RS* about the ways in which Murdoch's fiction 'tries to combine a love of real, contingent human beings with the illuminating orders of myth and art'. Complex symbols in *A Severed Head* are used to explore 'the evolution of consciousness', according to Isaiah Smithson in *SoRA*. The novel effectively presents 'the dynamic nature peculiar to psychic processes'. L. H. Myers's tetralogy set in Akbar's India is examined by V. A. Rao. Religious and ethical meanings as well as complex structure and patterning form the bases of Rao's *RLV* essay.

V. S. Naipaul is the subject of several entertaining essays. In *ES* Linda R. Anderson compares the treatment of the individual's relationship to society in the works of Conrad and Naipaul. Unlike Conrad, Naipaul cannot see beyond alienation. The influence of Wells on Naipaul is investigated by John Carthew who usefully points out similarities between *The History of Mr. Polly* and *A House for Mr. Biswas*. Naipaul brilliantly adapts Wells to Trinidad. Another helpful article is to be found in *ArielE* where Alastair Niven compares Nirad C. Chaudhuri's *A Passage to England* with Naipaul's *An Area of Darkness*. Both essays 'could only have been written by men fascinated with Britain, with India, with the links between them and the language one bestowed upon the other'.

In a disjointed *Journal of Commonwealth Literature* article S. C. Harrex demonstrates the importance of R. K. Narayan's miscellaneous writings. Since they show how Narayan uses his experience and how his fictive modes and techniques develop, they enhance our understanding of his novels. Patrick F. Sheeran's *The Novels of Liam O'Flaherty* (Wolfhound P. 1977) was unavailable. Angela Praesent[60] pursues the themes of disgust, failure and escape as expressions of Orwell's Weltanschanuung in a monograph on the author. [H.C.C.]. In *YR* David Kubal argues that Orwell, like Freud, 'was never driven from the position of asserting that man's best hope lay in his reason and that the self grows to its fullest freedom in intimate, erotic touch with others'. To this end Kubal investigates Orwell's handling of bourgeois values and the bourgeois domestic family environment. Paul Roazen (*VQR*) also looks at Orwell and Freud, finding similarities between them in *Nineteen Eighty-Four*. Both men saw 'it is sometimes necessary to disproportion reality in order to heighten our perception of certain aspects of it'. A rather superficial article by Gordon B. Beadle in *TCL* looks at Orwell's pre-occupation with poverty and its 'de-humanizing effects'.

The second volume of Anthony Powell's memoirs[61] deals with his early career in publishing and his first novels. Through his association with

[60] *George Orwell,* by Angela Praesent. Winter: Heidelberg (Anglistische Forschungen 134). pp. 119. DM 46.

[61] *To Keep the Ball Rolling: The Memoirs of Anthony Powell.* Volume II: *Messengers of Day*, by Anthony Powell. Heinemann. pp. x + 209. £6.

Gerald Duckworth he met many in the literary set (Galsworthy, Ford Madox Ford, and Wyndham Lewis among others). Powell provides sharp vignettes of friends and acquaintances such as the role-playing Evelyn Waugh; he also comments on certain publishing decisions regarding these figures, noting for instance that Duckworth failed to publish *Decline and Fall* because Waugh refused to make the suggested alterations. The London background in this autobiography is vividly suggested with numerous asides about deb dances, 1920s: parties and Rosa Lewis's Cavendish Hotel ('already in its decadence'). In addition to offering such details which contribute to a striking portrait of the contemporary scene and its personalities, Powell also comments on his early literary aspirations, significant influences (such as E. E. Cummings, Hemingway, and Flaubert) and his 'lyrical' first novels. Dry and perceptive, his comments evoke an era of great interest to students of the modern world, but the essential Powell remains hidden behind the practised and aloof observer.

'Gossip, memory and speculation about his friends' are central to Nick Jenkins's life in Powell's *Dance to the Music of Time*. In *TQ* Stephen J. Tapscott argues that they also contribute to the integral nature of the work. Characters, locked into a social order where gossip, rumour and appearance are central, 'dance in the tension between centripetal social manners and centrifugal personal needs, "unable to control the melody, unable, perhaps, to control the steps of the dance" '.

G. Wilson Knight's intricate study of John Cowper Powys's prose works[62] has been revised to take account of new work. Knight's book provides a critical introduction to and interpretation of Powys's writings. He concentrates on the 'elementalism', sexual pre-occupations, and occultism of the fiction and philosophy of Powys, seeing them as related to the writer's desire to investigate 'the human psyche in interaffected relationships with natural surroundings'. The fusion of mind and nature is 'a kind of sexual union, having its own "sensuality" ' which emerges in all of Powys's writings be they filled with dark intuitions or 'pluralistic optimism'. Indeed, an embracing of phenomena 'with all the senses simultaneously' and the waking of 'sex-located instinct, whatever the nature of its fantasies' promise a 'greater consciousness for man'. Knight is not simply concerned with Powys's ambiguous and complex metaphysic, however. He also attends to Powys as artist, discovering in *Owen Glendower* the pinnacle of Powys's literary achievements. While Powys has many limitations – not least of which is his repetitive and cumbersome technique – he ranks for Knight as a supreme literary giant. 'Shakespeare alone has left us literature of so vast and intricate a comprehension.' Knights' treatment of Powys's search for a healthy, fulfilled 'psychic-physical being' is as difficult and complex as its subject. Nevertheless, his enthusiasm for Powys is communicable, and he has fulfilled part of the objective of a good introduction by encouraging a further study of Powys and his strange quest.

Kenneth White's monograph[63] offers a brief account of Powys's 'life-

[62] *The Saturnian Quest: John Cowper Powys: A Study of His Prose Works*, by G. Wilson Knight. Hassocks, Sussex: Harvester P; Atlantic Highlands, N.J.: Humanities P. pp. 139. £5.50.

[63] *The Life-Techniques of John Cowper Powys*, by Kenneth White. Swansea: Galloping Dog P. 1977. pp. 31. pb £0.60.

desire' dependent on a 'life-technique' or philosophy which encompasses a movement back to primal life and forward to a 'superhuman' life. Essential to Powys's vision was a '*rapport* with the elemental powers'. The self had to be virtually recreated 'by the sovereign mind in actual relation with primordial energies and elements'. 'Psycho-sensual enjoyment' of the cosmos, erotic contemplation and 'psycho-physiological rites and rituals' are all advocated by Powys as a means of attaining an immediate sense of 'the body of the universe itself'.

A reprint of Kenneth Hopkins' 1977 essay on Hal Trovillion and the Powys brothers has been issued[64]. An American who ran a small private press, Trovillion first encountered the Powys family in 1938 when he published some autobiographical essays by Llewelyn Powys. After printing letters from Llewelyn and John Cowper to Trovillion, Hopkins urges the publication of the correspondence between Trovillion and John Cowper as the letters form 'an outrageous largess of wisdom and speculation and knockabout fun'. In a two-part article in *ContempR* G. Wilson Knight examines the relationship between serpent symbolism, sexual energy, and vision in John Cowper Powys's works.

V. S. Pritchett's reflections on the art of autobiography[65] delivered as the English Association Presidential Address for 1977 have been published. Pritchett's observations include a very brief account of his own venture into autobiography. 'When I had finished the books I saw that I had rid myself of the mutilating part of my obsessions. . .in breaking out of one's solitude one may draw others out of what may be poisoning theirs.' Symbolism and the inner meaning of Herbert Read's *The Green Child* are considered by D. S. Savage (*DUJ*) who finds the novel 'a symbolic projection of the poet's inner life-and-thought pattern'. The symbolic core of the work is 'a myth of incestuous regression to the mother, earth and death'.

Jean Rhys's *Quartet* has stylistic elements very close to modernist technical innovations, and Thomas F. Staley argues in *TCL* that it is worth close inspection. Rhys's 'narrative focus and technique relieve the intense subjectivity in *Quartet* and offer a dramatic, human portrait of the female consciousness in the modern world'. Mordecai Richler's *Son of a Smaller Hero* is unjustly neglected, according to Michael Greenstein (*Canadian Literature*) who points to the novel's satire, unity, and process of 'initiation and self-discovery' as reasons for its importance. Emlyn Williams has chosen fifty-four stories and one account of bird life by Saki[66] as a comprehensive display of H. H. Munro's talents. Ranging as one would expect from the ironic to the fantastic and macabre, the selection includes many of the most famous stories, such as 'The Open Window', 'The Interlopers', and 'Tobermory'. Saki's use of the practical joke is discussed by Miriam Quen Cheikin in *ELT*. In *Crit* Francine S. Weinbaum praises the wide scope and solid values of Paul Scott's *The Raj Quartet*.

Ronald Dee Vaverka's Marxist critique of Alan Sillitoe's political

[64] *Hal Trovillion and the Powys Brothers*, by Kenneth Hopkins. North Walsham, Norfolk: Warren House P. pb £1.05.

[65] *Autobiography*, by V. S. Pritchett. English Association, 1977. pp. 10. pb £0.50.

[66] *Short Stories*, by Saki, chosen with a preface by Emlyn Williams. Dent. pp. 250. £1.50.

fiction[67] centres on Sillitoe's 'aesthetic of realism' which is used 'to depict critically contemporary English Reality'. There is, predictably, much discussion of working class protagonists who are 'in opposition to an exploitative and politically repressive social system'. Sillitoe's works are deemed successful because of his realistic method of rendering the conflicts inherent in bourgeois society today. And his 'socio-aesthetic perspective', his realistic technique, is sound because he 'has personally experienced the problems and struggles of the life of a worker'. While Vaverka insists that Sillitoe is not creating propaganda but an artistic interpretation of reality, that very interpretation is seen as intimately connected to Sillitoe's social experience and his ability to 'contribute significantly to increasing the social consciousness' of his readers.

May Sinclair's use of the term 'stream of consciousness' is thoughtfully probed in Diane F. Gillespie's article on a much neglected author (*ELT*). While Sinclair eventually abandoned the term as imprecise, she remained vitally interested in the presentation of reality and consciousness as is evident in her own fictional portrayals of psychological novelists.

Suguna Ramanathan's fresh assessment of C. P. Snow[68] is a rather superficial and awkwardly written summary of the central aspects of Snow's fiction. Ramanathan sees Snow as one who stands 'outside the literary tradition' of metaphor and myth. His works are reflective and discursive analyses of contemporary social life which reveal a darkening vision of man and his world. Snow's realistic portrayal of the social scene, his concern with 'a morally examined life', and his interest in the individual confronted by a group are all noted in a descriptive way with little attempt at rigorous analysis. Characterisation and style are also dealt with in a perfunctory final chapter. Ramanathan's description of Snow's increasing pessimism over the growth of unreason and the failure of science and liberalism is fairly accurate, but on the whole this introduction suffers from a lack of close textual reading. Some facile comparisons to writers such as Jonson are unhelpful and distracting.

The interest which C. P. Snow and Daniil Granin have in 'the impact of science on human and social values' is considered by A. G. Waring, writing in *FMLS* on science, love, and the establishment in the writings of these two authors. Snow seems to see scientific and human values in conflict while Granin believes that scientific values must be informed by human ones. Yet Granin's latest story shows that he has accepted Snow's belief that scientific values are inadequate 'balanced against the myriad complexities of life'.

The fourth number of *Southerly* is devoted to the work of Christina Stead. Joan Lidoff surveys the fiction, with special emphasis on Stead's treatment of 'the international realm of human fantasy'. Grant McGregor looks at the significance of Sydney in *Seven Poor Men of Sydney*. The same novel is the subject of Judith Barbour's obtuse article on Stead's stylistic representation of the sublime. Susan Higgins writes about material

[67] *Commitment as Art: A Marxist Critique of a Selection of Alan Sillitoe's Political Fiction*, by Ronald Dee Vaverka. (Studia Anglistica Upsaliensa). Uppsala, Sweden: Uppsala P. pp. vi + 136.

[68] *The Novels of C. P. Snow: A Critical Introduction*, by Suguna Ramanathan. Macmillan. pp. xii + 125. £7.95.

and spiritual poverty, 'ignorance and sexual repression' in *For Love Alone*. Teresa's achievement of freedom cannot be universalised. Pamela Law sees *Letty Fox, Her Luck* as 'a modern picaresque novel' and analyses the character of Letty. R. G. Geering offers an extended review of *The Little Hotel* and *Miss Herbert (The Suburban Wife)*. In *Meanjin* Veronica Brady examines *The Man Who Loved Children* in order to support her claim that Stead is a prophetic writer. The novel expresses a vision which suggests that society over-emphasises 'the merely notional and material'.

Robert Foster has produced a revised alphabetical guide to characters, places, events, languages, objects, and species related to Tolkien's Middle-earth and mentioned in writings by Tolkien published to date[69]. Entries are followed by coded references to the subject's principle appearance in the fiction. Some speculation concerning various subjects is inevitable for Tolkien himself did not always make the details of his Middle-earth world consistent. Nevertheless this handbook is invaluable for the reader who wishes a quick summary of facts, relationships, and chronologies not always clear from the texts. Foster has included two appendixes – a chronology of the First Age and various genealogical tables. Robert A. Hall Jr outlines similarities between Tolkien's Hobbit tetralogy and *Der Ring Des Nibelungen* (*WHR*). William Ready's *Understanding Tolkien and the Lord of the Rings* (New English Library) was not made available.

Jeffrey M. Heath's 'Year's Work in Waugh Studies' opens this year's *EWN*. Robert Murray Davis links Dick Hirst (a character in Dudley Carew's *The Next Corner*) with Waugh and there is a transcription of a letter clarifying the origins of *Wine in Peace and War*. Robert Murray Davis irritably corrects errors in Heath's transcriptions of Waugh material from the University of Texas and Heath responds in kind. There is a brief note on American editions of *Brideshead Revisited* and some pertinent book reviews. In the second number Paul A. Doyle gives an account of Robert Tallman's adaptation of 'The Man Who Liked Dickens' for television. John Riley re-assesses Waugh at war with a piece on *Put Out More Flags* as artful propaganda, and Jeanne Clayton Hunter sees the end of *Decline and Fall* as serious. In a strained article she claims that Paul is 'a modern day Christ figure'. Robert Murray Davis discovers a possible source for Captain Grimes' faked suicide in Lennox Robinson's *The Far-Off Hills*. A supplementary checklist of Waugh criticism is provided by Hans Otto Thieme, Auberon Waugh explains the relationship between Eyre Methuen and Waugh's publishers Chapman & Hall, and notes of various kinds for Waugh readers are appended. In the Winter issue Robert Murray Davis examines the process of Waugh's revision of *Scott-King's Modern Europe* to show how Waugh attained meaning in his novels. John Riley continues his re-assessment of Waugh at war with a discussion of *Brideshead Revisited* which stresses morality. There are brief notes, letters and comments of interest. Richard Jones in *VQR* dismisses Waugh's diaries as marred by a sad eccentricity. In *RMS* William Myers notes the 'serious concern with issues' in *Black Mischief* and argues persuasively that the novel marks a period of advance in Waugh's progress due to its 'coherence and seriousness'. 'It is not a "Catholic" work but its power and purpose are intimately

[69] *The Complete Guide to Middle-Earth: From 'The Hobbit' To 'The Silmarillion'*, by Robert Foster. Unwin Paperbacks. pp. xiv + 441. pb £1.50.

connected with that sense of himself and of fallen mankind which the Church gave him.' *EIC* has an interesting essay by Martin Stannard on *Work Suspended*. Stannard finds it 'enigmatic' but is impressed by Waugh's technical experimentation and sees the novel as 'a discussion of deep-rooted personal aesthetic problems which the revisions attempt to disguise and objectify'. Ultimately Waugh had to abandon the work because he failed to find a way 'of rendering the subjective objectively'. Alain Blayac in *SSF* sees in 'Bella Fleace Gave a Party' an 'archetype of Waugh's earlicr fiction – that of the decline and fall of Man in these, our modern times'. Finally, Richard J. Voorhees draws attention to the value of Waugh's travel books in *DR*. While entertaining in themselves, they can reveal much 'about Waugh's principles and convictions'.

The unhappy story of Mary Webb has been told this year by Gladys Mary Coles[70] who draws attention to a much neglected writer. Awarded the *Prix Femina Vie Heureuse* for her novel *Precious Bane*, Mary Webb achieved little public recognition during her life and even less after her death in obscurity. Using first-hand accounts by friends, family diaries, letters, and other material, Coles has attempted to redress the balance by providing a skilful and sympathetic critical biography. Mary Webb was a sensitive, elusive, and mystical woman whose refined and bizarre sensibility is reflected in her work. Her pantheistic and rapturous response to the creative force in all living things prompted her desire for a unity with the natural world, an escape from the fragmented uncertainty of everyday life. Coles shows the development of this mystical consciousness in Webb's life and writing, suggesting the importance of Shropshire, personal memories and symbolic awareness in her works. The illness, mental anguish, and guilt which dogged Webb's path are poignantly described, and Coles also reveals the 'passionate pity' and mystical joy which informed Webb's later life. There are unpretentious comments on her creative work as well. Coles summarises plots, notes major themes (such as the agony and wonder of experience), and describes technical achievements. Clearly a more detailed and rigorous analysis of Webb's writing is necessary before any claim for her 'special place' as a novelist of country life can be established. But the need for a re-appraisal is made clear by this interesting and well-written biography of a mystical and regional writer who possessed 'a twentieth-century consciousness'. Agate Nesaule Krouse sees Fay Weldon as more than a pessimistic feminist. In *SMF* Krouse notes Weldon's humour, experimental techniques and conviction that change is possible.

Darko Suvin believes that the science fiction of H. G. Wells needs to be examined in terms of the genre as a whole. His edition of selected essays on Wells and science fiction[71], the result of a 1971 symposium in Montreal, sets out to view Wells from this new perspective, investigating the writer's 'affinities and influences'. In a well-argued introduction, Suvin makes a case for seeing a three-phase division of Wells's science fiction writings into 'evolutionary science fiction', 'short-range sociopolitical extrapolation',

[70] *The Flower of Light: A Biography of Mary Webb*, by Gladys Mary Coles. Gerald Duckworth. pp. xxii + 352. £7.95.

[71] *H. G. Wells and Modern Science Fiction*, ed. by Darko Suvin with Robert M. Philmus. Lewisburg, Pa.: Bucknell U.P.; London: Associated University Presses. 1977. pp. 279. $15.

and 'momentary political peeves and enthusiasms'. It is the first phase which interests Suvin; here, by using a temporal evolutionary context, Wells was able to present issues with a 'more immediate and urgent' flavour. Suvin concludes with some selective book lists on Wells's early science fiction. He also translates Tatyana Chernysheva's essay on the influence of folktale motifs, plots, and themes on Wells. David Y. Hughes writes well on the use of the garden metaphor in Wells's scientific romances which 'have the form of quests (or would-be conquests) where the revelation of the limits of the human condition – expressed in terms of the garden – is brought about heuristically through the eye-opening of initially blinded narrators'. J. P. Vernier looks at the way in which Wells incorporates the theme of evolution into his writings, Darko Suvin argues that *The Time Machine* is 'at least one of the basic historical models for subsequent science-fiction structuring', and R. D. Mullen considers the consistency between early and late Wellsian interest in the 'crisis of man's destiny'. Patrick Parrinder identifies the Wellsian model for a science fiction work ('the humanist-narrative fable in which a man confronts the biologically and anthropologically unknown'). Such a model can be compared to Zamyatin's attempts 'to create the experience and language of an alien culture directly'. Orwell's *Coming Up for Air* is discussed as a parody of Wellsian utopian fiction by Howard Fink, and Robert M. Philmus argues the case for seeing Borges as profoundly indebted to 'the Wells who outlines the past and future history of the mind' as well as to 'the Wells who plausibly traces the absurd consequences of a more or less improbable idea'. Sakyo Komatsu asserts that the same factors which retarded the appreciation of Wells's science fiction ideas are hindering the development of science fiction in Japan. The 'selective bibliography (with abstracts) of H. G. Wells's Science Journalism, 1887–1901', compiled by David Y. Hughes and Robert M. Philmus, demonstrates shifts in Wells's scientific beliefs. Finally, R. D. Mullen offers 'an annotated survey of books and pamphlets by H. G. Wells'.

In *Criticism* William J. Scheick applies his belief that Wells constantly 'sought new fictional strategies more appropriate to his social and artistic beliefs' to the novels of the 1920s. Scheick concludes that Wells tried 'to subject the spatial norms of exhausted fictional forms to the warp of timeliness (human relativity) in order to derive four-dimensional novels evincing a tentative, potential form in the very process of evolving'. William G. Niederland (*AI*) asserts that the stages in *The Time Machine* parallel Wells's own response to his tuberculosis. In *MLQ* Geoffrey Galt Harpham analyses *Tono-Bungay* as 'an extended anatomy of a tumour, an elaborate analysis of the diseased condition of England'. Quap serves as a symbol of 'anarchy, social cancer'. Robert M. Philmus in *TSLL* establishes that it is misleading to divide Wells's work into early and late categories or to see him inflexibly as either novelist or polemicist, optimist or pessimist. In *The Anatomy of Frustration* Wells's many concerns are brought together in form and content. '*The Anatomy* defines the complementary aspects of Wells's fundamental and abiding theme: frustration.'

Lyndon Harries explores Patrick White's vision and achievements in *ConL* insisting that a better critical analysis of the relation between style and theme in White's work is called for. Annegret Maack (*Southerly*) thinks that the Shakespearean references in *The Tree of Man* and *The Eye of the Storm* are not simply allusions. They stand structurally at the heart of the novels and point to a 'cycle of birth, maturation, death and renewal'. An excellent article by David Tacey (*SoRA*) is devoted to White's neglected second novel. Tacey sees *The Living and the Dead* as an important expression of White's concern with 'the spiritual crisis' and 'psychic sickness' of modern man. William Walsh's *Patrick White's Fiction* (Rowman & Littlefield, 1977) was not made available for review.

Richard J. Schrader feels that he has found a significant motif in Charles Williams' *War in Heaven*. In a sensible article in *Renascence* he investigates the different varieties of religious experience in the novel in terms of '*Sehnsucht*, the intense yearning for something no material object can satisfy'. David Cannadine (*SAQ*) thinks it worthwhile to set Wodehouse's works in their historical, social, and cultural context. He believes that Wodehouse was really a late Victorian. Shirley Chew gives a brief account of Leonard Woolf's 'Pearls and Swine' in *Journal of Commonwealth Literature*. The story demonstrates Woolf's 'understanding of the nature of imperialism' and capacity 'to place the achievements of empire within a larger context of significance'. Duncan Wilson's *Leonard Woolf: A Political Biography* (Hogarth P.) was not seen.

Excellent editions of Virginia Woolf's unpublished writings continue to be produced. General studies adopt a psychological approach. Virginia Woolf once claimed to Gerald Brenan that letters ought, at least in part, 'to give back a reflection of the other person'. Such a comment suggests her acute awareness of her friends and correspondents, and in the new volume of letters from 1929 to 1931[72] there is ample evidence of her passionate interest in others and her vulnerable need to give and receive affection. One friend in particular seems to dominate this period – Ethel Smyth, the composer. In her relationship with this fellow artist, Virginia Woolf found both solace and the stimulus of irritation and disagreement. Yet friendships are not the only pre-occupations of these letters. *The Waves* also entered Virginia Woolf's life at this time, and there are many useful letters about her difficulties and ambitions while 'writing to a rhythm, not to a plot'. Once again Nigel Nicolson has ably edited the correspondence, offering succinct annotations where necessary and contributing a quietly pointed introduction.

The second volume of Virginia Woolf's diary has appeared this year[73]. Capably and unpretentiously edited by Anne Bell, this volume deals with the period 1920 to 1924 when Virginia Woolf received increasing public acclaim and was more confidently developing her new approach to fiction: 'no scaffolding; scarcely a brick to be seen; all crepuscular, but the heart, the passion, humour, everything as bright as fire in the mist'. *Jacob's Room* and *Mrs. Dalloway* were written during these years, and the diary entries record Virginia Woolf's own responses to the problems which her writing presented to her. At the same time there are frank judgements on

[72] *A Reflection of the Other Person: The Letters of Virginia Woolf: Volume IV: 1929–1931*, by Virginia Woolf, ed. by Nigel Nicolson with Joanne Trautmann. Hogarth P. pp. xxii + 442. £11.95.

[73] *The Diary of Virginia Woolf: Volume II: 1920–1924*, by Virginia Woolf, ed. by Anne Olivier Bell with Andrew McNeillie. Hogarth P. pp. xii + 371. £9.50.

her family and many friends, observations about her own illnesses, lively descriptions of her daily domestic life, and vivid accounts of her personal reactions to London and the natural world. Her involvement with the Hogarth Press and her growing feminist stance are also chronicled. Unlike the letters, the diary entries are more open and self-revealing. They lack the effective exaggeration and lively personas of the correspondence, but fascinate and entertain nonetheless. Although Virginia Woolf did not intend her diary to 'reveal her soul or her inner life', the entries are permeated by her personality, her great zest for life, her marvellously perceptive awareness of the people and places around her, and her unflinching confrontation of the problems of morality and isolation. Indeed courage is the quality which one most readily attributes to her after reading this volume. Acutely sensitive to the 'death & tragedy' of life which constantly puts 'down his paw, after letting us run a few paces', she resolved repeatedly to persevere with her art, isolated as she might feel in her unique visionary world: 'many people are saying that I shant last, & perhaps I shant. So I return to my old feeling of nakedness as the backbone of my existence, which indeed it is'. There are also valuable appendixes including biographical outlines of persons mentioned and reprints of several energetic replies written by Virginia Woolf in response to criticisms of vain and intellectually inferior women.

A Writer's Diary[74] has been issued in paperback. This is Leonard Woolf's selection of extracts from Virginia Woolf's diary and contains many of her memorable comments on family and friends, her own work and surroundings, current novels and novelists, the tortures of writing, and her moments of despair. Although censored by Leonard, the entries reveal much about Virginia Woolf's life, thoughts, and experience and her clipped, pointed diary style conveys an immediacy of response which is invigorating. Of course, the new edition of the diaries by Anne Bell supersedes this selection, but for anyone who esteems Virginia Woolf and has no access to the new Bell edition, this paperback is a reasonably priced alternative.

Virginia Woolf's *The Years* gradually evolved from an experimental 'novel-essay' written to consider 'the restrictions imposed upon a woman who chooses writing as a profession'. Mitchell A. Leaska has painstakingly edited this 'novel-essay', *The Pargiters*[75], printing for the first time the six explanatory essays and five accompanying fictional illustrations which eventually became the core of the 1880 section of *The Years*. Leaska has also included Woolf's 1931 speech to the National Society for Women's Service about her experience as a woman writer. This speech served as the basis for a more complex examination of sexual repression and attitudes in *The Pargiters*, a work which Virginia Woolf began in exhilaration and ended in despair over the impossible task of uniting fact and fiction in a new way. As Leaska points out in his introduction and explanatory notes, *The Pargiters*, although incomplete, is a most revealing volume. The 'expressive systems of interlocking symbols and complex orchestrations of interrupted metaphor' here used to dramatise her explicit prose ideas

[74] *A Writer's Diary*, by Virginia Woolf. St. Albans, Herts.: Triad/Panther. pp. 350. pb £1.95.

[75] *The Pargiters: The Novel-Essay Portion of 'The Years'*, by Virginia Woolf, ed. with an introduction by Mitchell A. Leaska. Hogarth P. pp. xliv + 167. £6.50.

become the key means of implicit presentation of themes in *The Years*. Moreover, *The Pargiters* offers a unique opportunity to see a major novelist analysing and explaining (in the prose interchapters) her own fictional specimens; and indeed, a close relating of essay to fictional episode in *The Pargiters* helps to clarify the 'governing ideas which guided the novelist in the selection of her material for the fictional portions'. Leaska has preserved Virginia Woolf's own deletions and alternatives and one can thus observe at first hand the speed with which her ideas came and the difficulties which she encountered struggling to unite 'granite' and 'rainbow'. This is a major publication for all those interested in Virginia Woolf's creative method; it also provides background material crucial to a detailed reappraisal of *The Years*.

Jean O. Love's first volume of a two-part psychological biography of Virginia Woolf[76] has finally appeared for review. Relying primarily on personal documents and using the fiction to clarify material from other sources, Love considers Virginia Woolf's first twenty-five years in a detailed way and demonstrates the paradoxical elements of the novelist's personality. Virginia Woolf's life was characterised by opposing tendencies and attitudes. She was both practical and imaginative, tough and fragile, life-loving and death-seeking. But in addition to these inner polarities, Love detects other influences and tensions which affected her as a woman and as a writer. A love–hate relationship with her father, a repressive family life, tension in her parents' marriage, sexual traumas inflicted by her step-brothers, and the deaths of those on whom she relied for affection gradually overpowered her. Wounded by the brevity and tragedy of life, betrayed by 'the vividness of her own sensations', and demoralised by the lack of a developed sense of self, she resorted to fantasy, either through insanity or through imaginative writing. In this way, both her madness and her art 'emerged from common ground'. This biography provides an impressively detailed portrait of the tense and claustrophobic Stephen home. Moreover, Love's treatment of the young Virginia Woolf as an intense creature, dominated by an inability to separate objective and subjective thought is both a sensitive and significant analysis of a writer who wrote in a desperate effort to combat death and nothingness and 'to reconcile her varying experiences of the world'.

Phyllis Rose has also written an interpretive biography of Virginia Woolf[77] as a counterbalance to the current emphasis on textual and formalistic studies. Rose's approach is very similar to that of Jean Love for she too notes the contrasting impulses in Virginia Woolf's personality. She views Woolf as a woman torn between maternal and independent desires, between social duties and creative impulses, between 'the urge to affirm life by creating social bonds' and 'the urge to despair in isolation'. Rose examines the details of Virginia Woolf's life and background but is ultimately more concerned with the stories which she composed about herself and which inform her writings. The details of the stories vary from telling to telling and, Rose maintains, constitute a personal mythology

[76] *Virginia Woolf: Sources of Madness and Art*, by Jean O. Love. Berkeley, Los Angeles, Calif.: U. of California P. 1977. pp. xiv + 379. £10.50.

[77] *Woman of Letters: A Life of Virginia Woolf*, by Phyllis Rose. Routledge & Kegan Paul. pp. xxii + 298. pb £2.95.

rather than an established set of facts. The myths which evolved demonstrate Virginia Woolf's developing sense of self and her struggle for a stable identity. Again, like Love, Rose identifies Virginia Woolf's madness as a means of release 'from the realm of the merely rational', but she also asserts that it was instrumental in teaching 'her to know the self in alienation and in terror, and it taught her to observe, with sensuous apprehension, the passing moment, unconnected to other moments'. Rose's biography also treats Woolf's feminism which strangely appears as therapeutic, for it was the novelist's 'only acceptable way of stating publicly the sense of oppression and persecution she suffered from' and was the sole means by which she could 'see herself as part of a group whose problems could be traced to common sources'. This is a well-presented account of themes and attitudes inherent in Virginia Woolf's life and art, and Rose has adopted a very original mode of approach in her suggestion that Woolf's personal experiences and biographical memoirs have their own distinctive fictional and psychological truth. But, at some points (such as the analysis of Woolf's suicide note as a literary document) Rose seems to move into a realm of somewhat callous speculation, and it is difficult to agree with some of her contentions (that the suicide was really 'a supreme and final attempt at discipline', for instance). The main value of this work must be its emphasis on Woolf's own artistic ordering of her life.

Roger Poole disagrees with the usual view of Virginia Woolf as insane or mad, and has examined her works 'as records of a life' to trace the sources and meanings of her mental distress[78]. To this end, he calls for a new kind of literary study which is neither biographical nor psychoanalytical but which depends on 'permutating perspectives' in order 'to apply phenomenological method to a life and to a series of novels'. Poole discusses the usual conflict and traumas in Virginia Woolf's life and comments extensively on the failure of her marriage. The deep intellectual hostility and sexual incompatibility which he feels existed between Virginia and Leonard are established by a close reading of Leonard Woolf's *The Wise Virgins* and Virginia Woolf's own novels. In addition, *The Voyage Out, Night and Day*, and *Mrs. Dalloway* are thoroughly probed to demonstrate the isolation which Virginia Woolf felt when associating with unsympathetic, exploitative, and merciless men with whom she could not communicate. Poole argues vigorously that each of Virginia Woolf's breakdowns had 'a localised cause and an entirely explicable origin'; even her final suicide could be traced to her fear that with the rise of Hitler, the 'male arrogance' she hated would become unendurable. Poole also dismisses her own references to madness in her suicide note, seeing them as her attempt to use Leonard's idiom and thus preserve him from guilt. Yet, despite many detailed analyses of the fiction and quite interesting suggestions (on the significance of water imagery in her writing, for example) Poole's argument fails to convince. Too often people are described in simple or exaggerated terms of black and white. Even so, by the end of the book, no clear answer is given concerning the reasons behind Virginia Woolf's inability to communicate and her self-destructive nervous states. The pinpointing of crises which caused nervous distress to erupt is no substitute for an

[78] *The Unknown Virginia Woolf*, by Roger Poole. Cambridge: C.U.P. pp. vii + 285. £6.95.

explanation of the tendency to mental distress in the first place. The subtle complexities of Virginia Woolf's psychological life must continue to defy analysis.

Mitchell A. Leaska's *The Novels of Virginia Woolf From Beginning to End* (John Jay P.) and John Lehmann's *Thrown to the Woolfs* (Weidenfeld & Nicolson) were unavailable. *VWQ* also did not appear for review.

In *New Review* Nigel Nicolson offers an unsurprising but pleasant personal memoir of Virginia Woolf. A character sketch of her is the subject of Phyllis Rose's *PE* essay. As in her book-length study, Rose concludes that we should see Woolf's madness as valuable. Elizabeth W. Pomeroy has a rather insubstantial article in *MFS* on the influence of Woolf's passion for the Elizabethans on her writing. John G. Hessler writes in *Renascence* on the ethical stance of Mrs Dalloway. He claims that Clarissa retreats into private experience and avoids confrontation with Doris Kilman and Septimus Warren Smith 'whose works call into question her own'. She is part of a traditional set of protagonists – a heroine in a bourgeois society 'determined by money and class' and struggling 'for a self-definition that in part accepts and in part defies those determinants'. Mrs Dalloway suffers 'more rarefied states of alienation' because 'she tries to suppress rather than to change her morally ambiguous relation to her world'. *RS* contains a speculative article by Lotus Snow who wonders why Virginia Woolf developed a minor character in *The Voyage Out* into the eponymous heroine of *Mrs. Dalloway*. Allusions to Shelley in 'Mrs. Dalloway in Bond Street' prompt Judith P. Saunders (*SSF*) to consider the ways in which Clarissa's meditations on the 'contagion' of life connect with her feelings 'about gender and sexuality'. 'Her revulsion from our common mortality goes hand-in-hand with her rejection of her tainted gender, as she shrinks from sexuality and life processes'. 'Futility and resignation' characterise the story. Vita Sackville-West's memoir is an important key to *Orlando*, according to Frederick Kellermann in *ES* who identifies Orlando with Vita, Sasha with Violet Trefusis, and Shelmerdine with Harold Nicolson. Aside from this decoding he also relates the novel to Woolf's writings generally. Woolf was engaged in 'a penetrating search for that spiritual and artistic wholeness which requires the coalescence of masculine rational faculties with the feminine domain of feeling and intuition'. Paul G. Arakelian attempts a rigorous 'feature analysis of metaphor' in his comparison of *The Waves* to *Manhattan Transfer* in *Style*. He suggests that '*The Waves* is woven into a reiterative style while *Manhattan Transfer* is strung into a serial style'.

2. Verse

Anthony Thwaite's *Twentieth-Century English Poetry*[79] is an expanded and revised version of his *Contemporary English Poetry* (1959). An introductory chapter sketches in the background of the subject with emphasis on the complex role of the modern poet. Individual studies are made of G. M. Hopkins, W. B. Yeats, Wilfred Owen, Edward Thomas, D. H. Lawrence, T. S. Eliot, W. H. Auden, Louis MacNeice, C. Day Lewis, Stephen Spender, Dylan Thomas, Robert Graves, William Empson, Edwin Muir, Philip

[79] *Twentieth-Century English Poetry: An Introduction*, by Anthony Thwaite. London: Heinemann; New York: Barnes & Noble. pp. x + 134. pb £1.80.

Larkin, and Ted Hughes. Roy Campbell, George Barker, John Betjeman, and other poets of the 1930s and 1940s are examined in one chapter; a final section looks at poetry since 1965, mentioning among others R. S. Thomas and Geoffrey Hill. A select bibliography and a list of anthologies and criticism are usefully provided. This is a sound survey that provides a good and wide-ranging introduction to a large subject.

Veronica Forrest-Thomson's *Poetic Artifice*[80] is a fascinating and intricate study of 'the most distinctive yet elusive features of poetry: all the rhythmic, phonetic, verbal, and logical devices which make poetry different from prose'. In an attempt to formulate a developed theory about the 'relations between the different strata of poetic artifice' critical processes are defined by isolating and entitling them: 'Naturalisation', for example, is the term used to define the process of reducing the strangeness of poetic language by translating it into 'a statement about the non-verbal external world, by making the Artifice appear natural'. The introduction clarifies the use of such terms by using them in relation to a Shakespeare sonnet. Subsequent chapters illustrate different modes of artifice, taking examples mainly from twentieth-century poets, often from T. S. Eliot and Pound, and especially concentrating on William Empson. It is suggested that 'As poet, theorist, and critic Empson illustrates the most fruitful tensions in the poetic culture of this century and provides many suggestive points of departure'.

Catherine W. Reilly's remarkable *English Poetry of the First World War*[81] is a bibliography wide in scope: 'It is a guide to comment on the war in poetry or verse, whether meritorious or not'. It encompasses servicemen and civilian war poets of England, Ireland, Scotland and Wales, and verse published from 1914 to 1973. Printed material in the form of book, pamphlet, card, and broadside is taken into consideration. The compiler excludes war poems published in periodicals, patriotic Irish war poetry, American and British Empire poets (but a list of these is appended), and the work of contemporary poets who have written of World War One although they were born after the war ended. An astonishing 2,225 English poets are included, at least 532 of whom were women. The corpus of English First World War poetry is quantified here for the first time and many English minor poets hitherto unknown are identified.

I. M. Parsons's selection of First World War poetry[82] is now available in paperback. Among the well-known inclusions there are some fresh names: poems by Charlotte Mew and Fredegond Shove present women's viewpoints. Another perspective is given by those poets indirectly involved in the war: Hardy, Yeats, D. H. Lawrence, and Walter de la Mare. Arranged in sections representative of a mood or subject connected with the war, the bulk of the poems are from those with experience of trench warfare, including Owen, Rosenberg, Sassoon, and Ivor Gurney.

Bernard Bergonzi's *Reading the Thirties*[83] approaches some writers as

[80] *Poetic Artifice: A Theory of Twentieth-Century Poetry*, by Veronica Forrest-Thomson. Manchester, Lancs.: Manchester U.P. pp. xiv + 168. £9.95.

[81] *English Poetry of the First World War: A Bibliography*, by Catherine W. Reilly. George Prior. pp. xxxi + 402. £14.95.

[82] *Men Who March Away: Poems of the First World War*, ed. by I. M. Parsons, Chatto & Windus. pp. 192. £1.50.

[83] *Reading the Thirties: Texts and Contexts*, by Bernard Bergonzi. Macmillan. pp. xi + 157. £5.95.

'a collective subject, even a collective text'. The group considered (including Auden, Spender, Day Lewis, Betjeman, Lehmann, and MacNeice, among poets) shared formative experiences: they went to public schools and to either Oxford or Cambridge. The opening chapter charts the common background; subsequently 'the emphasis is on common elements of style and structure, verbal and cultural'. Personal, intellectual, literary, linguistic and social determinants of the text are seen to be '*in* the text, as constituent elements. . . . The uniquely personal element that we look for in a literary work would consist in the form, the configuration or particular vortex, that informs all these constituents'. Correspondencies between texts are looked for and recurrent elements are seen to be the school, the frontier, the aeroplane, the popular song, and the cinema. It is concluded that 'These writers.. .were the first literary generation in England to have to face mass civilisation directly, though with a sensibility formed by traditional, minority culture. That encounter, or that frontier, I believe, a major determinant of the literature of the time'.

The Thirties and After[84] is a collection of essays, passages from journals, reviews, and reminiscences that document Stephen Spender's personal, literary, and political views over a period of nearly fifty years. Divided into sections according to decades, each is prefaced by an essay on the literary and political background of the time. Spender has tried to retain throughout the themes of the 1930s 'going beyond them, but relating always to them'. The reviews of W. B. Yeats's *A Vision*, Wyndham Lewis's *One-Way Song*, and Auden and Isherwood's drama are of especial interest to readers of these pages. The book ends with remembrances of Eliot, Auden, Cyril Connolly, and MacNeice. This absorbing record of the poet and the times concludes with the conviction that 'Perhaps, after all, what really maintained continuity from 1928 onwards was a dialogue between generations which had a certain mutual respect for one another: between that of Yeats and Eliot, Lawrence and Virginia Woolf, with ours. If this book shows anything I hope it will be that we looked through the eyes of an earlier generation as well as through those of our own'.

There are two valuable additions to the Writers of Wales series. W. Rhys Nicholas's *The Folk Poets*[85] is an investigation of the *bardd gwlad*: in a literal sense 'a poet in a rural community, reflecting the character of his society, its personalities, and its varied activities, its crafts and its diverse interests'. We cannot, however, confine the folk poets to an entirely rural context: colliers and quarrymen, among others, fall into this category. It is shown how the folk poetry tradition has gained a new lease of life in the last fifty years. Gwyn Williams has written *An Introduction to Welsh Literature*[86]. This survey indicates a continuous tradition in Welsh poetry, shown by the present day roles of Eisteddfod poet, academic poet and *bardd gwlad*.

Richard Fallis's *The Irish Renaissance*[87] is a survey of Irish literature

[84] *The Thirties and After: Poetry, Politics, People (1933–75)*, by Stephen Spender. Macmillan. pp. 285. £7.95.

[85] *The Folk Poets*, by W. Rhys Nicholas. Cardiff: U. of Wales P. pp. 79. £1.50.

[86] *An Introduction to Welsh Literature*, by Gwyn Williams. Cardiff: U. of Wales P. pp. 123. £1.50.

[87] *The Irish Renaissance: An Introduction to Anglo-Irish Literature*, by Richard Fallis. Gill and Macmillan. pp. xvi + 319. £3.60.

from 1885 to 1940 with a short final chapter that attempts to assess Irish writing since 1940. A huge amount is covered: the early development of the literary movement in Ireland, the Irish social and political scene, and the drama, poetry, and fiction of the period. For the purpose that the book was written, that is, as an introduction for the undergraduate, a 'basic history of modern Irish writing' that will direct its readers to the writers mentioned, it seems worthy.

Herbert V. Fackler's *That Tragic Queen: The Deirdre Legend in Anglo-Irish Literature*[88] deals with the versions of Sir Samuel Ferguson (*The Death of the Children of Usnach* of 1834, and the 1880 *Deirdre*), Robert Dwyer Joyce, Patrick Weston Joyce, Aubrey de Vere, William Sharp, Herbert Trench, Lady Gregory, A.E., W. B. Yeats, J. M. Synge, T. W. Rolleston, James Stephens, and 'J.J. Jones'. A preliminary chapter deals with sources of the Deirdre legend in early nineteenth-century Ireland. Final judgements are made as to the comparative literary worth of the works considered. A chronological listing of major versions of the Deirdre legend by Anglo-Irish writers is appended, and there is a selected bibliography.

In *IUR* Terence Brown examines 'Dublin in Twentieth-Century Writing: Metaphor and Subject'. For Yeats 'Dublin is an element in a debate about the nature of Irish life' and later Irish writers have continued the debate. MacNeice found that 'the random images of the city suggested a timeless receptivity'; Seamus Heaney has developed MacNeice's sense of Dublin's imperviousness to change. Thomas Kinsella, Patrick Kavanagh, and Austin Clarke also attempt to make Dublin more than a setting for their poetry. Seán Lucy writes on 'Metre and Movement in Anglo-Irish Verse' (*IUR*), noting the great effect of Irish music and song on Irish writing in English; Yeats, Clarke, and Montague are included in his study. In *AWR* Desirée Hirst comments on 'The Poetic Scene in Ireland Today' and Richard Burnham's '*The Dublin Magazine's* Welsh Poets' explores Seumas O'Sullivan's encouragement of several young Anglo-Welsh poets in the 1930s and 1940s. In *Éire*, Éamon Grennan has a paper: 'View from the Bridge: Irish Writing, 1977–78'.

Michael Schmidt brings together a substantial collection of C. H. Sisson's essays, reviews, introductions, and editorials spanning the years 1937 to 1977[89]. Political, religious, literary, and general cultural essays are gathered chronologically to provide insight into the development of the poet's thinking. Michael Schmidt sums up the work of forty years when he states that 'There is no embracing dogma, no international or class programme, no generalizations about the necessary conduct of writers or states. Instead we have in his work an escape from reductive generalization, a door that opens back on to the particular world'. General pieces include the topics 'Leisure and the Arts', 'Art and Morality', 'Poetry and Myth' and 'What is Culture?'. Writings on individual poets include commentaries on Wyndham Lewis, W. B. Yeats, T. S. Eliot, Edward Thomas, Geoffrey Hill, and David Jones.

[88] *That Tragic Queen: The Deirdre Legend in Anglo-Irish Literature*, by Herbert V. Fackler. SSPDPT No. 39. Salzburg: Universität Salzburg. pp. x + 161.

[89] *The Avoidance of Literature: Collected Essays*, by C. H. Sisson, ed. by Michael Schmidt. Manchester, Lancs.: Carcanet. pp. ix + 581. £7.90.

Christopher Middleton's collection of writings[90] is primarily concerned with German literature. However, the essays on translation will be of interest to readers of English verse and the entire volume will be stimulating to admirers of Middleton's work. 'Notes on Some Poems' and 'Notes on Rhythm' comment directly on Middleton's creative process: 'My poems aren't what I'd like to be able to write. They are what I've been able to write so far, with much time spent in fumbling and confusion. They aren't written with readers in mind, or to assail people with calculated effects.'

John Paul Russo edits the uncollected essays of I. A. Richards[91]. These are placed in three categories: historical (essays that help to show Richards's philosophical and critical background, and his relations to other disciplines), practical criticism pieces, and humanistic essays of general interest. The volume is interesting both for its relevance to the development of Richards's thinking, and for readers fascinated by subjects such as 'Art and Science' and 'Emotion and Art'. I. A. Richards prefaces each essay with a note that places that piece in the development of his thought and an interview with him concludes the volume.

In *TLS* Blake Morrison's 'A Place for Poetry' (16 June) looks at the relation between British and American poetry by examining how far English poetry magazines are interesting themselves in American poetry, and vice versa. There are letters in response in the 23 June and 30 June issues. In *Shenandoah* Donald Davie has an article: 'Poetry as Taking a Stand'.

Carcanet New Press continues to publish volumes of new verse. This year their output includes *Solent Shore* by Jeremy Hooker[92], *Third Person* by Paul Mills[93], *The Pleasure Steamers* by Andrew Motion[94], *New and Selected Poems* by I. A. Richards[95], and *Heart's Desire* by Jeffrey Wainwright[96]. Three other presses deserve mention for their endeavour to disseminate new verse. Anvil Press has published Peter Levi's *Five Ages*[97]. Ceolfrith Press has some beautifully produced paperback volumes: *Contentions* by Alistair Elliot[98] (1977), *Men Homeward* by A. A. Cleary[99] (1977), *Alibis and Convictions* by Glyn Hughes and Norman Adams[100] (poems by Hughes, and paintings and drawings by Adams), *The Way of It* by R. S. Thomas with drawings by Barry Hirst[101] (1977), and '*The Kestrel*'

[90] *Bolshevism in Art and Other Expository Writings*, by Christopher Middleton. Manchester, Lancs.: Carcanet. pp. 309. £6.

[91] *Complementarities: Uncollected Essays*, by I. A. Richards, ed. by John Paul Russo. Manchester, Lancs.: Carcanet. pp. xxiv + 293. £6.

[92] *Solent Shore*, by Jeremy Hooker. Manchester, Lancs.: Carcanet. pp. 61. £2.

[93] *Third Person*, by Paul Mills. Manchester, Lancs.: Carcanet. pp. 79. £2.

[94] *The Pleasure Steamers*, by Andrew Motion. Manchester, Lancs.: Carcanet. pp. 58. £2.

[95] *New and Selected Poems*, by I. A. Richards. Manchester, Lancs.: Carcanet. pp. 124. £2.90.

[96] *Heart's Desire*, by Jeffrey Wainwright. Manchester, Lancs.: Carcanet. pp. 56. £2.50.

[97] *Five Ages*, by Peter Levi. Anvil P. Poetry. pp. 54. £3.25.

[98] *Contentions*, by Alistair Elliot. Sunderland: Ceolfrith P. 1977. pp. 60. £1.75.

[99] *Men Homeward*, by A. A. Cleary. Sunderland: Ceolfrith P. 1977. pp. 53. £1.50.

[100] *Alibis and Convictions*, by Glyn Hughes and Norman Adams. Sunderland: Ceolfrith P. pp. 42. £1.75.

[101] *The Way Of It*, by R.S. Thomas. Sunderland: Ceolfrith P. 1977. pp. 35. £1.50.

and Other Poems of Past and Present by George Woodcock[102]. Mid Northumberland Arts Group publish *Tyson* by Irvine Hunt[103] and *The Shadow of Black Combe* by Norman Nicholson[104]. The little magazine *Outposts* continues to flourish in its brave attempt to publish new verse.

In *FDP* (1977) Keath Fraser has 'A Note on Aldington and Free Verse'. Edward Callan's 'W. H. Auden's Plays for the Group Theatre: from Revelation to Revelation' (*CompD*) analyses *The Dance of Death, The Dog Beneath the Skin, The Ascent of F6*, and *On the Frontier*, concluding that 'The Auden of "Sonnets from China"...would tend to find some of the shrillness of the Auden of the Group Theatre plays embarrassing'. Edward T. Callan's 'Auden and W. B. Yeats: from Singing-Master to Ogre' (*Commonweal*, 1977) demonstrates that 'The stages of his [Auden's] growing disenchantment with Yeats mark the hardening of his conviction that the greatest threats to individual freedom in the modern world were a direct legacy of the Romantic outlook on which Yeats prided himself'. The successive stages of disenchantment are demonstrated by analysis of the revisions of 'In Memory of W. B. Yeats' and 'September 1, 1939', and of the opera *Elegy for Young Lovers*. 'Auden's Eden', by Doris L. Eder (*SHR*) examines Auden's attraction to the *paysage moralisé*, dealing with 'Paysage Moralisé', a part of *New Year Letter*, the *Bucolics* and 'In Praise of Limestone'. Elizabeth Jones's 'Auden's "Lullaby"' (*N&Q*) draws a comparison between Oberon's last speech in *A Midsummer Night's Dream* and 'Lullaby'.

Ronald Carter's 'Auden Forty Years On: "City Without Walls"' (*Agenda*) linguistically analyses '1929' and 'City Without Walls' in order to demonstrate that there is not a great division between the early and the later work. In both poems Auden is trying 'to make language fit experience', and 'City Without Walls' is 'a poem as seminal and substantial as anything written by him in the Thirties'. In *PN Review* John Haffenden has an article on 'Early Auden'. In *RES* Lucy S. McDiarmid analyses 'W. H. Auden's "In the year of my youth..."', a poem unfinished and unpublished that draws on Dante, Langland, and Pope. Willard Spiegelman's '*The Rake's Progress*: An Operatic Version of Pastoral' (*SWR*) is concerned with the opera as 'an effort on Auden's part to recapture the myths and language of an earlier, more optimistic world, and to examine that world from the perspective of our own'. A close analysis reveals that 'the opera is an Empsonian pastoral in two distinct ways: first its basic fable explores the themes of paradise and potential rebirth; and second, the libretto is Auden's attempt to adapt certain poetic styles to the conditions of twentieth century literary life'. The evocation of a past age is coupled with a hope for a future golden age of human goodness. In *MQR* Robert L. Chapman writes on 'Auden in Ann Arbor'. In *Quadrant* David Malouf has an article: 'The English Auden'. Edward Mendelson notes '"An Auden Letter about *The Orators*": A Correction' (*CLQ*).

[102] *'The Kestrel' and Other Poems of Past and Present*, by George Woodcock. Sunderland: Ceolfrith P. pp. 54. £1.50.

[103] *Tyson*, by Irvine Hunt. Ashington, Northumberland: MidNAG Publications. pp. 23. £1.

[104] *The Shadow of Black Combe*, by Norman Nicholson. Ashington, Northumberland: MidNAG Publications. £1.50.

In *FDP* (1976) John Studley writes on 'Motion and Stillness: Antithetical Imagery in Edmund Blunden's Early Poetry'. Donald E. Stanford's *In the Classic Mode: The Achievement of Robert Bridges* has not been available for review[105]. Basil Bunting's *Collected Poems*[106] is published by O.U.P. This is a revised edition of the 1968 Fulcrum Press collection, with four new poems. *Agenda* has a special issue to mark this publication. The ten contributions include an interview with Bunting about *Briggflatts*, Kenneth Cox's commentary on *Villon*, Jeffrey Wainwright's 'William Wordsworth at *Briggflatts*', and Peter Makin on 'Bunting and Sound'.

In *Éire* Parkman Howe records an interview with Brian Coffey. Arthur E. Salmon's study of Alex Comfort[107] contains a section on the verse, concluding that 'The general drift of Comfort's development as a poet, like that of Thomas and Treece, is from obscurity towards clarity. Death and power are his pre-occupations as a poet, but in *Haste to the Wedding*, as in *Come Out to Play*, are partially transmuted into their opposites. Rather than focusing predominantly on human impotence, despair, death, and external, institutionalised power, Comfort celebrates the individual, particularly his sexual abilities, and joyously affirms life rather than death'.

Roger Little's 'Saint-John Perse and Denis Devlin: A *Compagnonnage*' (*IUR*) analyses the translation of *Pluies*; Devlin's own annotations are brought usefully into the discussion. Stan Smith's 'Precarious Guest: The Poetry of Denis Devlin' (*IUR*) is an interesting and complex piece exploring the choice of a diplomatic career as a key to the poet's identity and examining the Jansenist elements in the poetry. Desmond Graham edits *The Complete Poems of Keith Douglas*[108]. The collection aims to be definitive and draws on manuscript material not available to previous editors. As a result there are significant alterations to earlier editions both in the chronological arrangement of the poems and the form of individual poems. A helpful introduction and notes on each text contribute to a valuable volume which is intended as a companion book to the editor's 1974 critical biography of Keith Douglas. In *ArielE* David Ormerod's 'Keith Douglas and the Name of the Poem I Can't Write' views Douglas's work as 'an evolving entity', analysing the corpus to indicate the poet's perceptual dilemma and his position as the 'solipsist or the Berkeleian'.

Helen Gardner's *The Composition of 'Four Quartets'*[109] is the most admirable work on T. S. Eliot to be published this year. Dame Helen's great achievement is that, by presenting the drafts and correspondence relevant to *Four Quartets*, she has made available for scholarly use Eliot's process of composition: 'Taken together the drafts and the correspondence allow us to see his mind moving towards his final text, give information about the sources and the concerns that lay behind the poem, and clarify the poet's intentions.' There is a very large amount of such material

[105] *In the Classic Mode: The Achievement of Robert Bridges*, by Donald E. Stanford. Newark, N.J.: U. of Delaware P.; and Associated U.P. pp. 343.

[106] *Collected Poems*, by Basil Bunting. O.U.P. pp. 152. £3.75.

[107] *Alex Comfort*, by Arthur E. Salmon. Boston, Mass.: G. K. Hall & Co. TEAS. pp. 167. $8.95.

[108] *The Complete Poems of Keith Douglas*, ed. by Desmond Graham. O.U.P. pp. xiv + 145. £3.95.

[109] *The Composition of 'Four Quartets'*, by Helen Gardner. Faber. pp. viii + 239. £9.50.

because of the unique war-time circumstances: 'Correspondence had to take the place of conversation and drafts had to be sent by post and commented on by letter.' John Hayward's comments were especially important to Eliot, and it is Hayward who collected the drafts of *Four Quartets* and relevant letters; this material was bequeathed to King's College, Cambridge. There are other drafts at Magdalene College, Cambridge; these Dame Helen has also drawn upon. Prior to the presentation of the draft material we are given detailed information on the documents as well as on the evolution and sources of *Four Quartets*. Above all 'The poems are poems of experience and are not built upon literary sources'. The bulk of the book presents the text of the first (1944) English edition of *Four Quartets* with a critical apparatus that gives readings from all available texts prior to that. The only subsequent editions collated are *Collected Poems 1909–1962* (1963) and the paperback edition of this. The text and commentary are very clearly laid out. It is stressed that this is not an 'edition' of *Four Quartets*, therefore 'many passages that an editor would annotate are left without annotation'. Both in the background essays and in the immediate commentary Dame Helen has quoted from articles that are not easily available, including uncollected articles by Eliot. To counteract the cutting up of the text and the letters so that all commentary relevant to a particular section is immediately presented, an appendix prints in full the first draft of *Little Gidding* with Hayward's letter about it. That this is an extraordinarily valuable volume does not need emphasis.

David Newton-De Molina edits a volume of stimulating new essays on T. S. Eliot as literary critic[110]. The area is thoroughly explored: Eliot's rôle as a poet-critic is examined by Graham Hough; Denis Donoghue considers 'Eliot and the *Criterion*'; Samuel Hynes assesses 'The Trials of a Christian Critic'; R. Peacock looks at 'Eliot's Contribution to Criticism of Drama'; William Righter discusses Eliot as a 'philosophical critic'; W. W. Robson investigates 'A Poet's Notebook: *The Use of Poetry and the Use of Criticism*'; Roger Sharrock takes for his subject 'Eliot's "Tone" '. The opening essay by F. W. Bateson surveys the criticism, making a comparison with Wordsworth: 'If Wordsworth and Eliot are exceptional in beginning their critical careers with their masterpieces in the genre [the *Preface* to the 1800 Lyrical *Ballads* and 'Tradition and the Individual Talent'], may it not be that their finest creative work also came early, and that their best criticism is essentially devoted to expounding and justifying what their own poetry merely implies?' The final contribution by C. K. Stead reads Eliot's criticism against the background of Matthew Arnold's, discovering that, because Eliot's most original work was on the Metaphysicals and on the verse of the Jacobean dramatists, his failure to come to terms with the Romantic poets leaves Arnold's assertions on their behalf critically unchallenged.

The third Eliot volume in the valuable Casebook series[111] is devoted to 'Prufrock', 'Gerontion', *Ash Wednesday*, and other shorter poems. The

[110] *The Literary Criticism of T. S. Eliot: New Essays*, ed. by David Newton-De Molina. The Athlone P. 1977. pp. vi + 216. £6.50.

[111] *T. S. Eliot: 'Prufrock', 'Gerontion', 'Ash Wednesday', and Other Shorter Poems*, ed. by B. C. Southam. Macmillan. pp. 255. hb £5.95, pb £2.50.

volume documents some of the ways in which Eliot's work has been approached over the last sixty years. B. C. Southam comments: 'If a single truth emerges from this body of opinion, it is a testimony to the necessary independence of critical judgement and the obligation that rests on each individual reader to arrive at his own understanding of what he reads'. The collection takes it starting-point from Eliot's own reviews and critical essays, from which extracts are presented. Extracts from Eliot's reflections on criticism and his comments in the 1959 *Paris Review* interview conclude this section. 'Perspectives 1917–1966' includes Pound on 'Prufrock', and commentaries by I. A. Richards, Hugh Kenner, and W. B. Yeats among others. A final section on criticisms of individual poems and groups of poems spans the years 1915–1973. The poems fall into three divisions here, as follows: ' "Prufrock" to "Gerontion" ', 'The Quatrain Poems', and ' "The Hollow Men", *Ash Wednesday* and the Ariel Poems'; critics include F. R. Leavis, F. W. Bateson, Dame Helen Gardner, and Northrop Frye.

Ann P. Brady studies *Lyricism in the Poetry of T. S. Eliot*[112]. Eliot's theory of lyric verse and his early use of lyricism are examined as a starting-point. Development in the genre is investigated and it is seen that, as Eliot progresses from *The Waste Land* to 'Ash Wednesday', his lyricism becomes 'more pervasive and more varied in function from poem to poem' and culminates in *Four Quartets*. The lyrics in *Four Quartets* are given close and detailed analysis; it is then shown that they are used 'not simply as lyric interludes in a philosophical meditation, but rather as distillations of the entire content of each separate quartet'.

Keith Alldritt considers *Four Quartets* as a symbolist work[113], assessing 'the extent to which its procedures, meaning and value may be illuminated by relating them to some of the principal ideas in the symbolist poetic'. *Four Quartets* is placed in a tradition that stems from Baudelaire, Verlaine, Rimbaud, and Mallarmé, influenced Yeats, and continues in contemporary poetry: 'The methods of *Four Quartets* refer back to seventy years of difficult poetic endeavour; they also point forward to, and help to explain the concerns and endeavours of the important poetry of the present time.' Each of the three sections of the book deals with an important aspect of the tradition. The quartet form of the poem is examined; the experiences that are presented in the poem are studied; the verbal textures of the poem are detailed. Finally *Four Quartets* is not seen in terms of autobiographical or philosophical statements; what is most important is the theme of the language usage: 'The poem assesses the reality of the experiences which it recalls and the possibility of communicating them. In the *Quartets*, as in so many of the poems of Mallarmé, the sense of the reality and of the recoverability of experience remembered shifts continually and often disconcertingly.'

Marianne Thormählen's *'The Waste Land': A Fragmentary Wholeness*[114] approaches the poem from several angles. The verse techniques are examined. The critical interpretations that stemmed from an examination of

[112] *Lyricism in the Poetry of T. S. Eliot*, by Ann P. Brady. Port Washington, N.Y.: Kennikat P. (National University Publications). pp. 120. $8.95.

[113] *Eliot's 'Four Quartets': Poetry as Chamber Music*, by Keith Alldritt. The Woburn P. pp. 141. £6.95.

[114] *'The Waste Land': A Fragmentary Wholeness*, by Marianne Thormählen. Lund: Liber Läromedel. Lund Studies in English 52. pp. 248.

Eliot's notes rather than from the text are discussed and are found to impede rather than enlighten. The dramatic element, the conception of time and history, and the erotic dimension are analysed. The symbolic imagery is closely attended to. Interpretations of the poem in its entirety are given, and it is suggested that 'Whether the poem is experienced as a unity or a succession of unrelated fragments or anything in between is determined by the individual reader'. This careful study is refreshing in its close focus on one work.

Hans Osterwalder applies a linguistic critical method to Eliot's plays[115]. His study follows Roman Jakobson's theory of the metaphor-metonymy dichotomy. The theory is presented in detail; Eliot's critical essays are analysed in terms of the metaphoric and the metonymic principles, then the plays are turned to. It is seen that 'Generally speaking, Eliot's dramatic work is a good illustration of the complete shift from an almost purely metaphoric type of drama to a predominantly metonymic one'.

Peter Reinau makes a stylistic analysis of Eliot's work[116]. It is argued that the stylistic features are not to be seen as devices or techniques 'but rather as the natural consequence of a basic aesthetic impulse; that there is a relation among the patterns resulting from this impulse; and that there can be perceived a development towards greater frequency of such patterns as well as a shift of emphasis from certain forms to others'. Both the prose and the verse are analysed in this context. In *Die Struktur des Dramas bei T. S. Eliot*[117] Gerd Schmidt discusses Eliot's criticism and some dramatic elements in his poems before analysing the plays and considering some aspects of the concept of 'form' in Eliot's work.

T. S. Eliot Review is now incorporated in *Yeats Eliot Review. YER* is an uninterrupted continuation of the former periodical and appears twice a year. Its scope is not restricted to comparative Yeats–Eliot studies; there is an equal interest in scholarship on Yeats and Eliot. The editor mentions that 'Though we will publish results of textual scholarship, biographical studies and discovery of sources, we will be slightly more receptive to articles which shed light on the workings of the imagination and creative process of Yeats and Eliot, or relate these poets to larger issues of literary criticism'. This year there is an abundance of interesting Eliot material. Bruce Bailey considers some literary burlesques of *The Waste Land*. Hans Borchers suggests, as a new source of 'Prufrock', 'In Hospital' by William Ernest Henley. George Whiteside makes 'A Freudian Dream Analysis of "Sweeney Among the Nightingales" ', finding that 'The movement of events in this poem is typical of a nightmare's'. William Harmon's 'Visions of Perfection: Some Recurrent Figures in the Poems of Eliot and Pound' finds that for Eliot and Pound visions of perfection 'culminate in epiphanies that bring, along with a glimpse of peace and love, powerfully validated moral imperatives'. David G. Mead notes that in 'Prufrock':

[115] *T. S. Eliot: Between Metaphor and Metonymy: A Study of His Essays and Plays in Terms of Roman Jakobson's Typology*, by Hans Osterwalder. Bern, Switzerland: Francke Verlag Bern. Swiss Studies in English 96. pp. 144. SwF 28.

[116] *Recurring Patterns in T. S. Eliot's Prose and Poetry: A Stylistic Analysis*, by Peter Reinau. Bern, Switzerland: Francke Verlag Bern. The Cooper Monographs 28. pp. 114.

[117] *Die Struktur des Dramas bei T. S. Eliot*, by Gerd Schmidt. SSPDPT No. 38. Salzburg: Universitat Salzburg.

'Eliot's choice of "arms" as a symbol of female sexual attractiveness is particularly effective. Arms suggest the dynamic aspect of lovemaking which Prufrock desires, permit a suggestive allusion to Donne's "The Relique", and prepare the reader for Prufrock's desire to have been "a pair of ragged claws" '. I. B. Cauthen Jr presents 'An Unpublished Letter by T. S. Eliot (1962)' concerning an allusion to Webster's *The White Devil* in *The Waste Land*. Christopher D. Murray suggests a source for 'Prufrock' in a letter by Elizabeth Barrett Browning. Bernard F. Dick relates 'Sartre and *The Cocktail Party*'. Brian Green suggests a context for the reference to Phlebas in *The Waste Land*: the eighteenth-century novelette *Le Sopha* by Crébillon fils. Vincent Daly identifies the source of *The Waste Land*'s thunder fable: a translation by Charles Lanman of the Sanskrit fable. J. Peter Dyson finds Prufrock's 'overwhelming question' in the line 'No! I am not Prince Hamlet, nor was meant to be'. Jean MacIntyre finds 'A Source for the Rose-fires in Eliot's *Four Quartets*' in George MacDonald's fantasies for children. Aileen Shafer finds a reference to Donne's 'Valediction: forbidding Mourning' in 'Prufrock'. Douglas Fowler looks at the relationship between Nabokov and Eliot, finding that 'one of our century's greatest prose stylists could not stand the work of one of our century's greatest poets'.

In *CJ* James P. Condon has a paper: 'Notes on T. S. Eliot's "What is a Classic?": The Classical Norm and Social Existence'. Frances White Fry considers 'The Centrality of the Sermon in T. S. Eliot's *Murder in the Cathedral*' (*C&L*). In *Renditions* (1977) Charles Hartman writes on 'Han Yü and T. S. Eliot: A Sinological Essay in Comparative Literature'. There are two papers in *EA*: Bernard Brugière writes on 'Conscience et Temporalité dans *The Waste Land* de T. S. Eliot', and D. Lojkine-Morelec considers 'Persistance et avatars d'un mythe dans la poésie de T. S. Eliot'. John Clare's 'Form in Vers Libre' (*English*) examines the recurrent pattern of *vers libre*, taking examples from Eliot as well as from Pound and Lawrence. Melvin J. Luthy's 'The Case of Prufrock's Grammar' (*CE*) argues that the first line of 'Prufrock' is grammatically correct. Visvanath Chatterjee has a short article in *The Calcutta Review* (1977): 'T. S. Eliot and Buddhism'. He notes Buddhist references in *The Waste Land, The Cocktail Party, Ash-Wednesday*, and *Four Quartets*.

Stephen J. Adams's 'T. S. Eliot's So-Called Sestina: A Note on "The Dry Salvages", II' (*ELN*) identifies the form of the lyric as that of the Provencal *coblas estrampas* or 'isolated stanzas'. Eliot knew this form through Ezra Pound who both translated Arnaut Daniel's poems in the form and wrote an original series of *coblas estrampas*. It is argued that 'Eliot's lyric, in all its visible technique, means to call attention to both the attractions and the limitations of conscious artifice'.

Nancy K. Gish's 'Thought, Feeling and Form: The Dual Meaning of "Gerontion" ' (*ES*) analyses that poem as 'poetry of thought', 'that which offers ideas and concepts directly as well as through image or symbol', rejecting the view of the poem as a series of non-rational musings in the mind of Gerontion. The relation between Gerontion and history is all important; in history's decay Gerontion sees the meaning of his own decay. Alan Weinblatt's 'T. S. Eliot and the Historical Sense' (*SAQ*) deals with Eliot's attitude to past art and the dilemma provoked by it. Eliot's uses of the literary past in parallels and identifications with his own work, in essays that qualify the achievement of major writers, in essays that embrace minor figures, and in essays that attempt to trace a recurrent pattern in literature, all speak of Eliot's 'anguished struggle. . .to hold at bay the whelming tide of the past' in order to stave off silence in the present.

In *Encounter* Robert Craft examines the relationship between 'Stravinsky and Eliot: "Renard" and "Old Possum"' quoting extensively from their correspondence. Alice Levine writes on 'T. S. Eliot and Byron' (*ELH*). The poets are compared as social satirists, as classicists in literary taste, and as seekers after aesthetic means of ordering their poetic expression. A close analysis of a side-by-side reading of *Childe Harold's Pilgrimage* and *The Waste Land* is made in order 'to clarify the general statements of the two poems, to discover in Byron's mass of verse an implicit form that may be seen to provide a tradition for such a poem as *The Waste Land*; to deepen our awareness about the relationship between the nineteenth- and twentieth-century sensibilities as represented by Byron and Eliot'. It is concluded that 'Both poets confront conditions unpropitious, a wilderness where there is no solid recourse to a classical or a romantic form of faith'. B. Rajan's 'Milton and Eliot: A Twentieth-Century Acknowledgement' (*MiltonS*) explores Milton's presence in Eliot's poetry, finding that *East Coker, Little Gidding, The Dry Salvages, The Family Reunion*, and *The Cocktail Party* are related to Milton's work and thought. In *CE* Charles O. Hartman's 'Condensation: The Critical Vocabulary of Pound and Eliot' attempts to find a system behind the distinctive terms used by Pound and Eliot to distil their critical ideas. Circumambience, concentration, and detachment are essential parts of the system espoused by these poets and 'The core of what Eliot and Pound ask us to think about with respect to poetry is the notion that poems are not created out of nothing by the poet, but somehow exist before he writes them down'. In *PLL* Nicholas Joost and Alan Brown consider 'T. S. Eliot and Ernest Hemingway: A Literary Relationship'. Despite Hemingway's antagonistic attitude towards Eliot, he reveals his indebtedness to *The Waste Land* in his own work. Hemingway's theory of writing is related to Eliot's imagist technique; he imitated Eliot's depiction of sexual relationships and shared Eliot's interest in traditional Christianity. In these and other ways, Joost and Brown show us how 'Eliot filled the role of a tutor from whom Hemingway learned many valuable lessions'.

Jeffrey L. Spear's '"The Burial of the Dead": Eliot's Corpse in the Garden in a Christian Context' (*AL*) argues that the 'Stetson!' passage, usually placed in the context provided by the study of comparative religion, also 'fits in a complementary context that is specifically Christian'. In *MLR* Michael Hancher's 'The Adventures of Tiresias: France, Gourmont, Eliot' suggests that Anatole France was responsible for the presence of Tiresias in *The Waste Land*. A passage in the prefatory letter to *La Vie littéraire* includes mention of Tiresias and introduces the metaphor of the self as a prison. Sidney Poger's 'Eliot's *The Waste Land*' (*Expl*) finds an overlooked allusion to Dante. In Canto 18 of the *Inferno* Dante refers to crowds in Rome in 1300; the London rush-hour crowd in Eliot's poem is similarly defined and evokes similar associations: 'These English and Roman crowds, like the one in Hell, are all intent on the same subject:

pandering and seducing.' In *Mosaic* Paul Lewis has a paper: 'Life by Walter: Characterization and Salvation in *The Waste Land*'. In *AN&Q* (1977), Ira M. Miller finds an 'Implicit Allusion: Charles Lamb's *Specimens* in *The Wasteland*'.

In *The Practical Vision: Essays in English Literature in Honour of Flora Roy*[118], William Blissett writes on 'Wagner in *The Waste Land*'. Several books on Eliot have not been available for review: *T. S. Eliot Criticism in English, 1916–1965: A Supplementary Bibliography* by Mechthild Frank, Armin Paul Frank, and K. P. S. Jochum[119], *Landscape as Symbol in the Poetry of T. S. Eliot* by Nancy Duvall Hargrove[120], *La Question du moi: T. S. Eliot, Paul Célan, Yves Bonnefoy* by John E. Jackson[121], and *Sprachhermeneutik und Literatur: Ein Interpretationsversuch zu T. S. Eliots 'Four Quartets'* by Walter Weihermann[122].

William Empson and the Philosophy of Literary Criticism by C. C. Norris[123] is the first full-length study of Empson's work. A chapter on Empson and present-day criticism presents an analysis of 'how far Empson's outlook has opposed itself to the various orthodoxies in modern criticism'. Despite Empson's resistance to symbolist and Christian poetry he has found his most interesting subjects in these spheres; in this context, emphasis is placed on Empson's outlook of humanistic rationalism. Opposed to this is the opposite set of ideas of Hulme, Eliot, and the New Critics, 'the formalist notion of poetry as an autonomous verbal structure', which philosophy is seen as equally tending to add its ethical shading to critics' reading. The concept of Pastoral and its place in Empson's development is then turned to and discussed in detail. *Complex Words* is set in the context of modern ideas about the meaning of literature and the proper aims of critical interpretation. It is shown that *Complex Words* 'can be read. . .as a commentary on the whole enlightened effort of humanist re-interpretation, given its cultural and semantic starting-point, the disappearance of God'. *Milton's God* is seen to continue in the same vein of rationalisation, but Empson's interest is now moral rather than semantic. The general truths that *Complex Words* reveals are explored in a chapter that carries the reader into a specialised region of linguistic and philosophic enquiry. This book argues the logic and consistency of Empson's work, but the inherent limitations are also dealt with. Finally, Empson's worth as a critic is estimated: 'He has steadily refused to go along with literary movements of fashion which evade the problem of rational belief in an age of dominant scepticism. For this, and much besides, he will surely go down as one of the finest and most resourceful critics of his time.'

[118] *The Practical Vision: Essays in English Literature in Honour of Flora Roy*, ed. by Jane Campbell and James Doyle. Waterloo: Wilfred Laurier U.P. pp. 163.

[119] *T. S. Eliot Criticism in English, 1916–1965: A Supplementary Bibliography*, by Mechthild Frank, Armin Paul Frank, and K. P. S. Jochum. Edmonton: *Yeats Eliot Review*. YER Monograph 1. pp. 108.

[120] *Landscape as Symbol in the Poetry of T. S. Eliot*, by Nancy Duvall Hargrove. Jackson, Miss.: U. of Mississippi P. pp. 234.

[121] *La Question du moi: T. S. Eliot, Paul Célan, Yves Bonnefoy*, by John E. Jackson. Boudry: Baconnière. pp. 344.

[122] *Sprachhermeneutik und Literatur: Ein Interpretationsversuch zu T. S. Eliots 'Four Quartets'*, by Walter Weihermann. Frankfort: Lang. p. 296.

[123] *William Empson and the Philosophy of Literary Criticism*, by Christopher Norris. The Athlone P. pp. viii + 222. £8.95.

In *ShawR*, Timothy J. Kidd studies the relationship of 'James Elroy Flecker and Bernard Shaw'. Flecker submitted *Don Juan* to Shaw for criticism: in this play Flecker echoes *Man and Superman* and throws taunts at Shaw. Shaw pointed to the play's failings, indicated a course of action for Flecker, and encouraged him to persevere. Flecker's and Shaw's views are shown to be in many ways opposed, yet, after their meeting, Flecker modified his views on education and on the war with Germany. It is tentatively suggested that *Hassan* influenced *Saint Joan*.

In *MD*, Diane Filby Gillespie writes on 'Language as Life: Christopher Fry's Early Plays'. James Woodfield's ' "The Figure of a Dance": Christopher Fry's *A Phoenix Too Frequent*' (*ArielE*) explores the death and resurrection archetype in the play, showing how the perspective has shifted from the tragic treatment in *The Firstborn* to the comic mode in *Phoenix*. Robert Gittings's 'The Smell of Sulphur: *The Lady's Not for Burning* Now' (*Encounter*) investigates 'the play's literary and topical sources, in particular showing how much Fry absorbed from Charles Williams's *Witchcraft*. It is concluded that the play perhaps owes its deepest qualities to the unique personality and experiences of Fry himself, in the epoch when he first wrote it thirty years back'.

In *Agenda* Michael Hamburger makes an assessment of W. S. Graham's volume *Implements in their Places*. Jascha Kessler has an article on W. S. Graham in *Parnassus*: 'Coming Down'. John E. Gorecki's 'Graves' "The Naked and the Nude" ' (*Expl*) notes that in that poem 'Graves reduces both "the naked" and "the nude" to the same plight to indicate that the words do after all denote the same thing'. The words are equal in meaning 'but only in death, i.e., only when their vivid sensuous life in the poet's imagination (stanzas two and three) has been removed'. Samuel Hynes's 'Observations of the Ordinary' (*TLS*: 10 November) examines Grigson's *The Fiesta*. In *Parnassus* (1977) Donald Hall's 'A Nation of Poets' looks at the work of Seamus Heaney and John Montague. In *Éire*, Arthur E. McGuiness has an article: ' "Hoarder of Common Ground": Tradition and Ritual in Seamus Heaney's Poetry'. In *ELT* J. R. Ebbatson looks at 'Maurice Hewlett: The Senhouse Trilogy'. In *Éire*, Richard Burnham considers ' "Where the road from Laracor leads": On F. R. Higgins'.

Christopher Ricks's 'Geoffrey Hill and "The Tongue's Atrocities" ' (*TLS*: 30 June) is a long, intricate analysis of Hill's poetry, being the text of the W. D. Thomas Memorial lecture given at University College, Swansea, in February 1978. William S. Milne's ' "Creative Tact": Geoffrey Hill's *King Log*' (*CritQ*) illustrates how that volume explores perennial human paradoxes; it is demonstrated that the balance is preserved between concern with the details of contemporary and historical actuality and the abstraction of the imagination.

Keith Sagar has revised and extended his excellent study of Ted Hughes[124]. The first edition was reviewed with admiration in Volume 56 of *YW*. We now have chapters on *Season Songs, Cave Birds* and *Gaudete*, a bibliography that takes us into 1978, and minor revisions in the earlier text. The final chapter on *Gaudete* is now the most important in the book; it is this work that Sagar sees as 'perhaps the summit of his [Hughes's] achievement so far', a book of poems 'not to be explicated but to be

[124] *The Art of Ted Hughes*, by Keith Sagar. C.U.P. pp. vii + 277. hb £12, pb £3.95.

possessed by'. *Gaudete* occupies a crucial position in Hughes's quest: 'Hughes is searching for a position which cannot be outflanked, which maintains human dignity and purpose without falsifying the facts, which recovers the sane and sacred without evasion, abstraction or doctrine. In *Gaudete* he has come close to achieving that.' Keith Sagar promises future updated editions of his book; they will be very welcome, as will his forthcoming comparative study of Hughes and his predecessors and contemporaries. In *CP* Stuart Hirschberg writes 'Hughes's New "Rough Beast": The Malevolent New Order in "Song of a Rat" '. Geraldine Moyle has a paper in *Parnassus*: 'Hughes's *Gaudete*: A Poem Subverted by Its Plot'. In *BB* Janet H. Pocock makes 'An Addition to the Ted Hughes Bibliography'. In *DQR* Neil Roberts writes on 'Ted Hughes: Encounters with Death'.

Philip Pacey's 'B. S. Johnson and Wales' (*AWR*) shows how awareness of Wales affected the poet's achievement, leading to 'a feeling for the mysterious, and especially the mystery of the feminine and maternal'. Samuel Rees's *David Jones*[125] has not been available for review. In *ELN* Thomas R. Dilworth's 'David Jones's Use of a Geology Text for *The Anathemata*' explores the significance of adaptations of terms and categories from Watts's *Geology for Beginners* in 'Rite and Fore-Time'. There are two papers in *AWR* concerning David Jones. Roland Mathias introduces and annotates three letters from David Jones. Edward Levy's 'David Jones's "Life-out-there" and the Limits of Love' explores Jones's affirmation 'of a world, both animate and inanimate, always most truly itself when most entirely beneficient – a world which each man enriches by his own particular showing forth of that which he loves'. *In Parenthesis* and *The Anathemata* are cited in this connection.

Bruce K. Martin's study[126] examines Philip Larkin's work, providing social and biographical detail as well as textual analysis. Larkin's poetic theory and The Movement poets are discussed; *The Less Deceived, The Whitsun Weddings*, and *High Windows* are examined. The prose writings are evaluated. Larkin's overall development is considered and critical assessments are looked at. Finally Larkin is placed in the English poetic tradition. It is cautioned that 'his distaste for modernism does not make him an enemy of the major voices in British literature usually claimed by the extreme modernists as their own. Nor does it make him simply a throwback to an earlier way of writing or looking at life'. In *DR* Roger Bowen writes on 'Death, Failure, and Survival in the Poetry of Philip Larkin'. In *AWR* there are two papers on Alun Lewis. John Pikoulis's ' "East and East and East": Alun Lewis and the Vocation of Poetry' takes as its starting-point an analysis of 'The Mountain over Aberdare'. The tension between man and writer emerges as a crucial subject: 'The Jungle' is also explored in this context. It is seen that there is for Lewis a separation from the world and a withdrawal into art to find a 'scarcely human sense of confidence in himself, a serenity which is instinct with a sense of death'. Death is seen as a fulfilment, a climax to a 'long struggle to achieve his being': 'He has chosen perfection of the work by making his life into art and needs death to seal it'. Jacqueline Banerjee's ' "Living More Lives Than

[125] *David Jones*, by Samuel Rees. Boston, Mass. G. K. Hall & Co. TEAS.
[126] *Philip Larkin*, by Bruce K. Martin. Boston, Mass.: G. K. Hall & Co. TEAS. pp. 166. $8.95.

Are'': Three of Alun Lewis's Poems from India' comments on 'The Mahratta Ghats', 'In Hospital: Poona' and 'The Jungle', showing that 'the ability to enter into the experiences of those around him, as well as to understand the full implications of his own, always allows him to range far beyond the confines of the self'.

The Hogarth Press publishes Norman MacCaig's *Old Maps and New*[127]. The volume includes the *Selected Poems* of 1971 (with some changes and corrections), and selections from *The White Bird* and *The World's Room*. Basil Bunting's 'Hugh MacDiarmid Lost' (*Agenda*) is a short but moving account of recognition of the poet by a group of workmen: 'What other poet is there, or has there been these many, many years, who would be recognised and spontaneously honoured by men of no education and no pretension whatever?' Columbia U.P. have issued the catalogue of an exhibition to celebrate the centenary of John Masefield's birth. In *TLS* (November 17) T. J. Binyon's 'The Glory of Defeat' reviews at length *Selected Poems*. In *HC* Benedict Kiely writes on 'John Montague: Dancer in a Rough Field'.

Allie Corbin Hixson's *Edwin Muir*[128] (1977) aims to be a definitive study of the life and work, attempting to show 'how it has happened that a major poet came to maturity without benefit of a large following of biographers and critics'. It is seen that the childhood environment of the Orkneys made an indelible impact and the importance of the *Autobiography* is stressed. The various stages of Muir's career are documented: the early Nietzschean phase, the 1930s' 'time of testing, both of philosophy and of artistic technique', the critic and reviewer, the man who alienated Hugh MacDiarmid (both with his advice, in *Scott and Scotland*, to writers to forget Scots and to absorb the English tradition and his later 'debunking' of John Knox), the translator, and the poet. We are reminded that 'In recognizing his talents as a poet, we should also remember his contribution to world literature in discovering exceptional works for English translation'. These works included plays by Hauptmann, and novels by Feuchtwanger, Herman Broch, and Kafka. It is concluded that there can be no 'ready label' for Edwin Muir as man or poet: 'Muir had some of Milton's grandeur of vision, some of Wordsworth's kinship with nature', but it was with Kafka that he shared the most: 'As "exile", Kafka was his contemporary in spirit as well as in time'. The 'attainment of a universal voice' was Muir's final achievement.

Christopher Wiseman's *Beyond the Labyrinth*[129] places Edwin Muir's poetry in the post-symbolist tradition. The belief that dominates Muir's thought is that 'man is immortal and that the soul exists'; a pattern of symbols was developed to embody this belief. A careful distinction is made between 'symbolist' and 'symbolic', showing that a system of symbols is associated with 'symbolist' poetry. The key symbols for Muir are the journey, the Fall, Eden, and the labyrinth. The specialised symbolist techniques used by Muir are an indirectness and a suggestiveness, and (in

[127] *Old Maps and New: Selected Poems*, by Norman MacCaig. The Hogarth P. pp. 160. £3.50.

[128] *Edwin Muir: A Critical Study*, by Allie Corbin Hixson. New York: Vantage P. 1977. pp. xiii + 247. $8.95.

[129] *Beyond the Labyrinth: A Study of Edwin Muir's Poetry*, by Christopher Wiseman. Victoria, British Columbia, Canada: Solo Nis P. pp. 252. £8.

key poems only) fractured syntax, tense-shift, disorientation of place, language that comments on itself, and 'the elocutionary disappearance of the poet'. In this context, the early poetry is evaluated, and *The Labyrinth*, *One Foot in Eden*, and the last uncollected poems are closely analysed. In *One Foot in Eden* Muir found 'a mature poetic technique which wonderfully expressed the spiritual synthesis he had aimed at'. Christopher Wiseman's study should fulfil his hope to 'shift the emphasis from heavily biographical criticism to the individual poems'.

Ritchie Robertson's 'Two Bibliographical Notes on Edwin Muir' (*N&Q*) suggests that, in Elgin W. Mellown's bibliography, an essay on Spengler is wrongly attributed to Muir, and that a *TLS* review of Hofmannsthal is omitted. Roger J. Porter's 'Edwin Muir and Autobiography: Archetype of a Redemptive Memory' (*SAQ*) examines Muir's two autobiographical works to show how 'Autobiography for Muir was a genre which would not so much recapture the past. . .as give the past a special "plot", so that his "return" would function largely in a compensatory realm of art'. Muir's necessity to 'reconstitute the past and to see his entire life as an extension and product of the contradictory nature of that past' leads into comment on autobiography as a reflective literary art. Thus the 'redemptive autobiographical imagination' comes into play; autobiography is not merely the study of the perceived past. In *FMLS* P. H. Gaskill writes on 'Edwin Muir as a Critic of Hölderlin'.

Dennis Welland has completed a revised and enlarged edition of his familiar 1960 study of Wilfred Owen[130]. It is enlarged by a final chapter where Welland discusses changes of critical attitude since 1960, and assesses the biographical and background material now available. In this chapter too we find the revisions: the book is re-issued in substantially its original form. One quality that Welland finds he passed over rather easily in 1960 is the homo-eroticism of the poetry. The author also recognises that, were he re-writing the book, there are several changes of emphasis he would choose to make: for example, he 'would restate more fully the case for seeing protest as one of the main motivating forces behind Owen's poetry'. In *FDP* (1976) Dominic Hibberd considers ' "Rival Pieces on a Chosen Theme": A Note on Some of Wilfred Owen's Minor Poems'; in *SN* Hibberd also writes on 'Wilfred Owen's Rhyming'.

In *Lang&S* Christopher C. Norris has a paper: 'Laura Riding's *The Telling*: Language, Poetry, and Neutral Style'. In *FDP* (1976) Joyce Wexler has a checklist of Laura Riding's work, and Hilda D. Spear notes 'An Unrecognized War Poem by Siegfried Sassoon'. In *Parnassus* John Burney has 'An Interview with C. H. Sisson'. Arnold Rattenbury presents 'Poems and a Play by Montagu Slater' in *The 1930s: A Challenge to Orthodoxy* edited by John Lucas[131].

Dent notes the twenty-fifth anniversary of Dylan Thomas's death by issuing a very welcome paperback edition of *The Poems*[132] and another volume in the Miscellany series of selected poems and stories[133]. Included

[130] *Wilfred Owen: A Critical Study*, by Dennis Welland. Chatto & Windus. pp. 192. £3.50.

[131] *The 1930s: A Challenge to Orthodoxy*, ed. by John Lucas. Hassocks, Sussex: Harvester; New York: Barnes & Noble. pp. 268.

[132] *The Poems*, by Dylan Thomas, ed. by Daniel Jones. Dent. pp. xix + 291. pb £3.50.

[133] *Miscellany Three: Poems and Stories*, by Dylan Thomas. Dent. pp. 119. £0.95.

in both is a 'pub poem', 'Sooner than you can water milk', recently discovered by Wynford Vaughan Thomas and never before published in any anthology. Daniel Jones, editor of *The Poems*, provides a note to elucidate the poem and its genre. Donald Hall's *Remembering Poets: Reminiscences and Reflections: Dylan Thomas, Robert Frost, T. S. Eliot, Ezra Pound*[134] has not been available for review. George P. Weick finds 'An Error of Transcription in *Selected Letters of Dylan Thomas*' (*N&Q*); in *Expl* he examines 'Thomas' "The Spire Cranes" '. Jadwiga Dudkiewicz writes on 'Dylan Thomas's *Under Milk Wood*' (*KN*, 1977). In *PBSA* Mary Dee Harris Fosberg examines 'Dylan Thomas's Use of *Roget's Thesaurus* during Composition of "Poem on his Birthday" '. In *Innisfree* Rosemary A. Raynal looks at 'Tradition and Imagination in "Fern Hill" '. In *MFS* Kenneth Seib examines '*Portrait of the Artist as a Young Dog*: Dylan's *Dubliners*'. Denys Val Barker's ' "A Strange Country to Me" – Dylan Thomas and Cornwall' (*ContempR*) examines Thomas's attitude to Cornwall. Several essays have been gathered together in *AWR* in acknowledgement of the anniversary. The editors note that 'There is, it seems, an endless fascination with textual analysis, and Dylan still absorbs many American academics as the number of typescripts coming from the United States shows. The interest inside Wales today seems rather less fervent, and his place in this nation's literature is not yet clear'. Ian Hilton's ' "The Poetic Medicine Man": Dylan Thomas and Germany' discusses Thomas's impact on post-war Germany. Tom Costello's 'Dylan Thomas and the October Wind' makes a detailed analysis of 'Especially when the October wind'. David E. Middleton's 'The Ultimate Kingdom: Dylan Thomas's "Author's Prologue" to *Collected Poems*' stresses the importance of 'Author's Prologue' as Thomas's 'final comment on poetry, his major themes and the human predicament at mid-century'. Brother Benilde Montgomery's 'The Function of Ambiguity in "A Refusal to Mourn the Death by Fire of a Child in London" ' analyses that poem as 'not only a poem of deliberate ambiguity which affirms life by denying the reality of physical death, but. . .also a comment on the nature of the poetic process itself'.

Jan Marsh's *Edward Thomas*[135] places the writings in three contexts: the literary, the historical, and the biographical. The main approach is made through consideration of Thomas's love of the countryside and his sense of melancholy. The turn-of-the-century pastoral impulse is given full attention; it is made clear that the movement was linked with the need for religion in a scientific age. The period 1912–3 is seen as a watershed in Thomas's life. Prior to this period he had idealised the countryside, expressing his feelings in a correspondingly idealised language. After it he came around to a more realistic view and altered both his form and his style of writing. The crucial shift came in 1914: from prose to poetry. The radical literary change taking place is usefully elaborated here; the idealistic Aesthetic Movement-inspired work was giving way to the direct and the colloquial, seen most obviously in W. B. Yeats's career. With the advent of the First World War a new and pervasive subject was found for Thomas.

[134] *Remembering Poets: Reminiscences and Reflections: Dylan Thomas, Robert Frost, T. S. Eliot, Ezra Pound*, by Donald Hall. New York: Harper & Row.
[135] *Edward Thomas: A Poet for his Country*, by Jan Marsh. Paul Elek. pp. xiv + 225. £7.95.

We see how love of the country was transformed into patriotism, and Thomas's enlistment in the army followed. Thomas is placed in the mainstream of modern English poetry and is shown to be close in spirit to Thomas Hardy and Philip Larkin. This is an excellent and lucid study.

The youngest daughter of Edward Thomas edits the memoirs and letters of Helen Thomas[136]. Through these writings we view Helen Thomas's life in its entirety, we appreciate her relationship with Edward Thomas, and light is cast on the literary figures that are called to memory. An encounter with William Morris, friendships with W. H. Davies, Eleanor Farjeon, and Robert Frost, a visit of D. H. Lawrence, and a visit to Ivor Gurney are vividly described. Myfanwy Thomas knits together her mother's writing throughout, providing a sensitive commentary.

With a new edition of Thomas s biography of Richard Jefferies[137] Faber marks the 130th anniversary of Jefferies's birth and the centenary of Thomas's birth. First published in 1909, the re-issue is testimony of Thomas's talent as a biographer. Clearly written with love and enthusiasm, this biography is highly enjoyable to read. *AWR* celebrates the centenary with several papers. R. George Thomas's 'Edward Thomas s Poetry Now' looks at the progress of his verse career, implying that the decision to become a soldier 'ensured that his poetry, especially his later poems, would continue to live for subsequent generations of readers'. Maire A. Quinn's Ballad and Folk-Song in the Writing of Edward Thomas' explores the poet's enthusiasm for those forms 'as intermediaries between past and present'. Jan Marsh's 'Rid of This Dream' shows how Thomas cast off the language of illusion and dream. Robert Lumsden writes on 'Thomas in Wales' and Lawrence W. Hockey looks at 'The Gwentian Associations of Edward Thomas'. In F. G. Atkinson's 'Hilaire Belloc: Four New Letters and a Note on Some Literary Friendships' (*N&Q*) the relationship of Thomas and Belloc is elaborated. In *FDP* there are two articles: William Cooke's 'Edward Thomas, E.M., and the Georgian Anthologies' and Michael Kirkham's 'Edward Thomas and Social Values'. The latter is included in the 1977 *FDP*.

A. E. Dyson makes an intricate examination of the poetry of R. S. Thomas (*CritQ*). A close analysis of many poems is made in order to investigate 'the nature of Thomas's religious sensibility, as it moves increasingly into the foreground in his later work, and to define its centrality to his art itself'. The poet is discovered to be 'a believer in the free acceptance of life, whatever its offered terms'. Vimala Herman's 'Negativity and Language in the Religious Poetry of R. S. Thomas' (*ELH*) asserts that 'The God of Thomas does not reside in regions of ineffable plenitude, but in a context of alienation'. This manifests itself in a crisis of language: 'For what can a priest say about a God he cannot know? And how would language articulate such negation?' Several poems are analysed to demonstrate that 'The attempt to embody an Ultimate Reality in language has in fact resulted in the exploration of the terrain of the absence of that Reality'.

[136] *Time and Again: Memoirs and Letters*, by Helen Thomas, ed. by Myfanwy Thomas. Manchester: Carcanet. pp. 159 + X. £4.

[137] *Richard Jefferies: His Life and Works*, by Edward Thomas, introd. by Roland Gant. Faber. pp. x + 306. hb £4.95, pb £2.25.

Ruth A. Grogan's 'Charles Tomlinson: The Way of His World' (*ConL*) analyses the verse to show how 'Tomlinson's poetry has moved from a primarily visual orientation in which self and world are related by way of eye. . .to one which allies muscular and tactile modes of apprehension to the visual. . .and then to one which begins an oblique acknowledgement of the oneiric and unconscious life'. In *Agenda* Reginald Gibbons examines *The Shaft*, finding that 'A peculiar sense of contained energy, of taut oppositions, marks the best poems'. In *TLS* (1 December) Michael Schmidt reviews at length *Selected Poems* and *The Shaft*. In *HC* Edward Hirsch has a paper: 'The Meditative Eye of Charles Tomlinson'.

William M. Murphy introduces his *Prodigal Father*[138] as 'quite simply, the story of a man's life, an account of what happened to him from day to day and year to year. . .the very human story of a lovable, brilliant, and distressingly improvident man'. Access to John Butler Yeats's letters and manuscripts has given the author an unparalleled opportunity to do justice to his subject. This is a handsomely presented volume containing an abundance of illustrations, including many sketches by John Butler Yeats, and fascinating photographs of the Yeats family and their friends and associates. There is no doubt that the book is scholarly, searching, and full of love for the subject, whose quirky character comes alive in these pages. The word 'money' echoes disturbingly throughout, and it is made clear that W. B. Yeats found his father 'a failure, a mere dreamer unable to make his mark in the real world'. This reaction is perhaps understandable, yet it is in some ways easier to identify with Murphy's point (and this is characteristically put, in a tone tactful and sympathetic to father and son alike): 'in a perfect world in which "getting on" has become unnecessary and irrelevant, John Butler Yeats might be its perfect citizen, the end product of a beneficent evolution, wise, tolerant, liking and likable, witty, intelligent, full of shifting but always exciting ideas, a delight to the hearts and minds of those around him. Perhaps it was not he who was defective but the world he lived in. . .JBY's noninvolvement in causes, in "opinions", left him free to live as a whole person, and, paradoxically to enrage his son into the kind of action he himself rejected. Each life bore its own fruit, one chiefly in the literary remains, the other – neglecting for the moment its considerable achievements in art – in the life itself.' This is a book to be read by all enthusiasts of the Yeats family and their work. Robert Gordon's *John Butler Yeats and John Sloan: The Records of a Friendship*[139] has not been available for review.

K. P. S. Jochum's bibliography of W. B. Yeats[140] contains more than 7,900 items, including about 350 additions to Allan Wade's bibliography of Yeats's own writings. It improves on the Cross and Dunlop bibliography in various ways: firstly, more than five hundred items of the period 1887–1965 are added. Moreover, subjects are included which are not or only sporadically

[138] *Prodigal Father: The Life of John Butler Yeats* (1839–1922), by William M. Murphy. Ithaca, N. Y. and London: Cornell U.P. pp. 680. £17.50. $27.50.

[139] *John Butler Yeats and John Sloan: The Records of a Friendship*, by Robert Gordon. Dublin: Dolmen P. New Yeats Papers 14. pp. 32.

[140] *W. B. Yeats: A Classified Bibliography of Criticism: Including Additions to Allan Wade's 'Bibliography of the Writings of W. B. Yeats' and a Section on the Irish Literary and Dramatic Revival*, by K. P. S. Jochum. Folkestone, Kent: Dawson; Hamden, Conn.: Archon Books, The Shoe String P. pp. xiv + 801. £18.

represented in the earlier bibliography. The subjects are the following: poems about Yeats, parodies, recordings, films, musical renderings and operas, interviews with Yeats, reports of his speeches and lectures, and reviews of first performances of his plays. All the entries have been numbered consecutively and cross-references are made to Wade. Many items are usefully annotated. Occasionally value judgements have been made as to those items which, in Jochum's opinion, are essential reading for any extended research on Yeats. The book includes material from 1972 and 1973, but is reasonably complete only up to the end of 1971. Deliberate omissions include perfunctory articles in encyclopaedias and histories of literature. This vast and diligently researched volume will prove invaluable to Yeats scholars – although Yeatsians might take note of the compiler's shrewd warning: 'Another lesson to be learned from reading or seeing so much literature on Yeats is that he himself was ever so much cleverer than most if not all of his critics, adulators, detractors, and just plain readers. It is something of a relief to return to a Yeats poem or play or essay (especially a less glamorous one) and simply enjoy it. I would like to warn the budding Yeats scholar not to read too much of the material assembled here.'

Andrew Parkin's rather unilluminating study[141] dissects W. B. Yeats's imagination and finds it to be religious and essentially dramatic. Using Yeats's own comments on the imagination, an estimate of the poetry and drama is made. The book concentrates mainly on the drama; the importance of Yeats as inventor of the modern Irish tradition of the one-act play is stressed. The subject of the imagination, often embodied in one character (for example, Aleel in *The Countess Cathleen* and Forgael in *The Shadowy Waters*), is seen to recur. *The King's Threshold* is seen to concern 'the politics of imagination'. *On Baile's Strand* is interpreted as the dramatisation of an internal conflict. *Deirdre* is 'about his [Yeats's] own dramatic imagination and its predilection for folk-lore and legend'. *The Player Queen* incorporates a discussion of the poet-dramatist. Similarly, the later plays are shown to dramatise aspects of the human imagination. It is concluded that 'Yeats's position, then, is that imagination thrives on the beliefs of the folk, the beliefs of poets, works of art, wild speculation, the heart in conflict, the mind in conflict, the heart and mind in conflict with each other. . .the turmoil and suffering of history and politics, when embodied in some great personality, and symbols and spirits which invade and dramatise themselves through the human medium of body and mind'.

Yeats Eliot Review is a new source of scholarly articles on Yeats. L. M. Findlay's 'W. E. H. Lecky and "The Second Coming" ' notes an echo in the poem of Lecky's *The Rise and Influence of Rationalism in Europe*. John C. Wilcox's 'Enticing Yeats to Spain: Zenobia and Juan Ramón Jiménez' traces Yeats's connection with the Spanish poet. F. C. McGrath's ' "Rosa Alchemica": Pater Scrutinized and Alchemized' argues that 'the story is not just a critique and a rejection of Pater's weaknesses, but a rather thorough assessment and accommodation of him into Yeats's own vision'. Norman Friedman's 'Permanence and Change: What Happens in Yeats's "Dialogue of Self and Soul"?' closely examines that poem. Robert O'Driscoll and Lorna Reynolds discuss 'The Untilled Field of W. B. Yeats',

[141] *The Dramatic Imagination of W. B. Yeats*, by Andrew Parkin. Dublin: Gill and Macmillan; New York: Barnes & Noble. pp. 208. £9.

commenting on the abundance of unpublished manuscript material in Dublin. James Lovic Allen's 'All in the Family: Artistic Interaction between W. B. Yeats and His Siblings' discovers a definite pattern: 'from a close and harmonious integration of the Yeats siblings' artistic activities and accomplishments in childhood, youth and young adulthood to an increasing separation, alienation, and deterioration of genuine aesthetic interaction in middle years and old age'. Stuart Hirschberg makes a close examination of 'All Souls' Night' to suggest that the 1920 poem 'may have served Yeats as a model or prototype for his highly acclaimed 1930 poem, "Byzantium" '. Shyamal Bagchee suggests that behind the 1914 poem 'The Fisherman' stands Wordsworth's 'Resolution and Independence'.

In *CP* Lucas Carpenter writes on 'Yeats' Crazy Jane Poems'. David R. Clark's 'The Manuscripts of W. B. Yeats' "Crazy Jane on the Day of Judgement" ' (*MHRev*) includes facsimiles of eight original drafts. In *CJIS* Stuart Hirschberg comments on 'The Shaping Role of *A Vision* on Yeats's "Crazy Jane" Poems'. In *MLQ* Herbert J. Levine has a paper: 'Yeats at the Crossroads: The Debate of Self and Anti-Self in "Ego Dominus Tuus" '. In *PQ* (1977) William C. Barnwell notes 'A Possible Italian Influence on Yeats's "Statues" '. Rob Jackaman's 'Black and White: the Balanced View in Yeats's Poetry' (*ArielE*) discusses 'Easter 1916' and 'Nineteen Hundred and Nineteen', pointing out their pattern of balanced opposites and finding 'a final balance in Yeats's poetry. . . the ephemeral everyday experience juxtaposed with, and often even coinciding with, archetypal experience: the world of historical linear time balanced against the world of cyclical recurrence'. Dwight H. Purdy's 'Singing Amid Uncertainty: Image and Idea in Yeats's "Memory" ' (*ELN*) analyses 'Memory' as a 'philosophical lyric on two of Yeats's favorite themes, the ambiguity of idealism and the inherent contradictions in a Romantic theory of poetic remembering'. Vilas Sarang's 'W. B. Yeats: "The Four Ages of Man" ' (*N&Q*) finds that the 'four ages' correspond with the four periods of individual life as prescribed by ancient Hindu tradition. Sarang also has a paper in *CP*: 'The Byzantium Poems: Yeats at the Limits of Symbolism'. Kenneth B. Newell writes on 'Yeats's Fergus as a Sun God' (*Éire*).

F. C. McGrath's 'Heroic Aestheticism: Yeats, Pater, and the Marriage of Ireland and England' (*IUR*) traces the influence of Pater on Yeats, showing how, particularly in the plays, Yeats sought to couple Irish subject matter with the English aesthetic tradition. Richard J. Finneran's 'W. B. Yeats and Wilfred Scawen Blunt: A Misattribution' (*IUR*) suggests that an unsigned report in *The Times* of 1914, long attributed to Yeats, may have been written by Richard Aldington. In *N&Q* T. P. Foley and Maud Ellman make 'A Yeats and George Moore Identification'. A reference to a priest by both Yeats and Moore is identified as the Reverend Jeremiah O'Donovan, friend of most of the leaders of the Irish literary revival. In *Éire* Ronald G. Rollins has a paper: 'Old Men and Memories: Yeats and Beckett'. In *VN* Gary Sloan writes on 'Yeats, Tennyson, and "Inisfree" '. In *PLL* Phillip L. Marcus explores the relationship between Eliot's 'Gerontion' and Yeats's 'The Tower'. A close comparison of the texts is made. It is established that 'The Tower' 'may in fact have been written partly or entirely as an intentional counterstatement to "Gerontion", or the response may have been subconscious. Even if there is no direct connection, there remains the no less interesting phenomenon of two writers independently using highly similar subject matter, organization, and in some places even language and imagery to express dramatically opposed world-views'. In *Mosaic* P. L. R. Brown considers 'Psychological Aspects of Some Yeatsian Concepts'. Yeats's system finds parallels in the Jungian theories of extrasensory perception, of the personal and the collective unconscious, and of archetypes and symbols. Towards the end of his career Jung could not definitely suppose that the world of spirits can be psychologically explained; Jung's statements here can be transposed into Yeatsian terms: 'the archetype-Daimons must be allowed the possibility of existence in us in their effects, and also existence outside and independent of us'. Thus we cannot 'exclude the possibility that Yeats's system is not an analogue but a direct representation of reality'. At the least the system reveals Yeats as a man gifted with great psychological insight because we can read it as an accurate dramatisation of the unconscious processes that Jung investigated. In *FDP* (1976) Ronald E. McFarland links 'George Herbert and Yeats's "Sailing to Byzantium" '.

In *RES* Ronald Schuchard investigates 'W. B. Yeats and the London Theatre Societies, 1901–1904'. Yeats's attempt to establish a 'Theatre of Beauty' in London between 1901 and 1904, the London personages who first put into practice Yeats's principles of theatrical reform, and Yeats's involvement with the Literary Theatre Club, the Stage Society, and the Masquers Society are examined. The roles of T. Sturge Moore, Laurence Binyon, Charles Ricketts, Florence Farr, Robert Trevelyan, A. H. Fisher, Pamela Colman-Smith, Gilbert Murray, Arnold Dolmetsch, Edith Craig, and others are brought into focus. Finally 'Yeats's London theatre societies gave way to the Abbey Theatre, but the dramatic experiments first worked out in those societies continued to have a significant impact on the course of English drama, as the artists that he brought into intimate contact carried their experience into other productions and new societies'. In *ETJ* there are two papers on Yeats: Gordon M. Wickstrom's 'Legend Focusing Legend in Yeats's *Deirdre*' and Bettina L. Knapp's 'From *Separatio* to *Coagulatio* in Yeats's *The Only Jealousy of Emer*'. Lynn Haims's 'Apocalyptic Vision in Three Late Plays by Yeats' (*SoR*) examines *A Full Moon in March, The Death of Cuchulain*, and *Purgatory*. Although the three plays share many features, *Purgatory* is seen to differ in a crucial sense: 'Unlike *A Full Moon in March* and *The Death of Cuchulain*, which hold out the promise, however muted, of self-transcendence as a way of overcoming the "desolation of reality", *Purgatory* only stresses the futility of human will and physical effort to alter reality or to accommodate to it. . . Apocalypse and apocalyptic vision are glimpsed as lost possibilities for renewal; they exist for a moment only, then vanish.' In *MHRev* (1977) Diane E. Bessai has a paper: 'Who Was Cathleen ni Houlihan?'. In *Eire* Audrey S. Eyler considers 'His Hour Come Round at Last?: W. B. Yeats as Playwright'. In *CJIS* Sidney Poger writes on 'Ritual and Parody in *The Herne's Egg*', and David G. Wright has an article: 'The Elusive Self: Yeats's Autobiographical Prose'. In *Boundary* (1977) Daniel O'Hara focuses on 'The Irony of Tradition and W. B. Yeats's *Autobiography*: An Essay in Dialectical Hermeneutics'. In *FDP* Warwick Gould has a paper: 'Yeats as Aborigine'. Deborah Tannen locates 'Celtic Elements in Three Works by William Butler Yeats' (*Folklore and Mythology Studies*). Robert Langbaum's *The Mysteries of Identity: A Theme in Modern Literature*[142] (1977) has not been available for review.

Roger D. Sell's study of Andrew Young[143] surveys the career in entirety, following a chronological approach from the juvenilia to the late prose works, while concentrating on the middle poetry. Stress is laid on Young's complexity and variety, and this book takes into account both his many revisions and relevant biographical material, as well as surveying Young's critical reputation.

3. Prose drama

Modern Drama offers a useful list of books and articles covering British, American, and European drama; *The Shaw Review* continues to supply a very comprehensive annotated checklist of work done on Shaw and his context.

Oleg Kerensky's *The New British Drama*[144] surveys the work of fourteen playwrights who have emerged since the late 1960s and whose achievements or promise are substantial; the narrative is mainly paraphrase of the plots enlivened by some remarks by the playwrights, most of whom were interviewed; there are separate sections on David Storey, Edward Bond, Peter Shaffer, Peter Nichols, E. A. Whitehead, Christopher Hampton, Alan Ayckbourn, Simon Gray, Tom Stoppard, David Hare, Trevor Griffiths, Howard Brenton, Howard Barker, and Stephen Poliakoff.

In spite of its title, Douglas Colby's *As The Curtain Rises: On Contemporary British Drama 1966–1976*[145] is an analysis of three plays, Tom Stoppard's *Rosenkrantz and Guildenstern Are Dead*, Christopher Hampton's *The Philanthropist*, and Harold Pinter's *Old Times*, using the stage image at the beginning of each play as 'the interpretive key' in the analysis. John Russell Taylor's *The New Wave*[146] is a reprint of *The Second Wave* (1971: *YW* 52.390) with a revised bibliography. Horst P. Priessnitz's *Das Englische 'radio play' seit 1945*[147] is a very strictly regimented treatment which will have some use as a work of reference, although it communicates none of the enormous warmth with which millions of listeners in Britain and throughout the world regard the BBC's truly admirable work in the areas of 'popular', 'classical', and 'avant garde' drama. *The Problem Play in British Drama 1890–1914*[148] appears without explanation in a series entitled 'Poetic Drama & Poetic Theory', although Elliott M. Simon in fact surveys some of the work of Henry Arthur Jones,

[142] *The Mysteries of Identity: A Theme in Modern Literature*, by Robert Langbaum. New York: O.U.P. 1977. pp. 383.

[143] *Trespassing Ghost: A Critical Study of Andrew Young*, by Roger D. Sell. Åbo, Finland: Åbo Akademi. Acta Academiae Aboensis, Series A. pp. 258. Fmk. 60.

[144] *The New British Drama*, by Oleg Kerensky. Hamish Hamilton. 1977. pp. 276. £6.95.

[145] *As The Curtain Rises*, by Douglas Colby. Rutherford, N.J.: Fairleigh Dickinson U.P. pp. 103. $10.

[146] *The New Wave*, by John Russell Taylor. Eyre Methuen. pp. 238. £2.95.

[147] *Das Englische 'radio play' seit 1945*, by Horst P. Priessnitz. Berlin: Erich Schmidt Verlag. pp. 244.

[148] *The Problem Play in British Drama 1890–1914*, by Elliott M. Simon. Salzburg: Institut für Englische Sprache und Literatur, Universität Salzburg. pp. viii + 340.

Pinero, Galsworthy, and Granville-Barker: these playwrights were chosen, the author tells us, 'because I feel that their works most clearly indicate the kinds of thematic, dramatic and theatrical preoccupations of English playwrights during the period. I do not wish to imply that such well-known figures as George Bernard Shaw, Oscar Wilde and John Synge do not have a place. . .' Clive Barker's 'From Fringe to Alternative Theatre' (*ZAA*) begins in 1960 with the formation of Centre 42 and the production of the John Arden–Margaretta D'Arcy *The Business of Good Government* at Brent Knoll in Somerset; the article gives a detailed and balanced account of the most interesting writers and groups of the 1960s and 1970s. In 'Political Theatre in England' (*Performing Arts Journal*) Theodore Shank covers some of the same 1970s ground, emphasising the degree of Marxist commitment in the writers and companies.

Irving Wardle's *The Theatres of George Devine*[149] is a study worthy of its subject. From the early 1930s George Devine played a central role in the development of modern English theatre. He died in 1966, but his influence is still crucial and will mark many aspects of our best theatrical work for the forseeable future. The English Stage Company at the Royal Court was his creation and remains his most obvious benefaction, but John Osborne extends our debt accurately when he says that 'The two big subsidized companies – the National and the Royal Shakespeare – owe a debt to him that is incalculable. Their existence is due directly to him. Hundreds of writers and actors owe their present fortunes and favour to him. I am in the greatest debt of all'. Irving Wardle's excellent study is sensitive, informative, and persuasive.

The History of the National Theatre[150], by John Elsom and Nicholas Tomalin, is a long but never tedious story. For the hundreds of people involved – between Effingham Wilson, who proposed the idea in 1848, and Lord Olivier, who did not after all lead the Company into the custom-built theatre-complex – there was much tedium and a great deal of heart-break. The delay of Office over those many decades was matched by its deviousness. For the reader, at a safe distance, the history is fascinating. The text of this account is exemplary, the format is handsome, and the generous illustrations are expertly selected. Richard Stoddard's *Theatre and Cinema Architecture: a guide to information sources*[151] offers a very wide-ranging and informative bibliographical guide, which will earn its place on any shelf of theatre reference books. The coverage is complete, and the annotations are extremely helpful.

The most interesting piece for some years on John Arden is Jean Jacquot's account in the fifth number of *Les Voies de la Création Théâtrale* of Jacques Rosner's production of *Armstrong's Last Goodnight* and of Guy Retoré's production of *Live Like Pigs*. In 'John Arden: the Promise Unfulfilled' (*MD*) Craig Clinton briefly surveys Arden's career, and discusses the effect of his collaboration with Margaretta D'Arcy.

[149] *The Theatres of George Devine*, by Irving Wardle. Jonathan Cape. pp. xiii + 295. £8.50.

[150] *The History of the National Theatre*, by John Elsom and Nicholas Tomalin. Jonathan Cape. pp. x + 342. £8.50.

[151] *Theatre and Cinema Architecture: a guide to information sources*, by Richard Stoddard. Detroit, Mich.: Gale Research Co. pp. xi + 368. $24.

The most substantial and most disappointing work on Beckett is Deirdre Bair's *Samuel Beckett: A Biography*[152]. Beckett did not want any biographical study to be written, and this one seems determined to realise all of his fears. The information is voluminous but is presented as gossip, and the discussion of its relevance to the creative writing is depressingly simplistic. Of course we have come to assume that writers, even in exercising 'negative capability' in composing plays, derive their best work from some level of personal experience; but biographies of this kind are irrelevant to our business of responding to the work. The 'critical' aspect of the book is superficial and often muddle-headed, and the embarrassing intrusions into his private life throw no useful light on his art (see p. 355).

In *A Student's Guide to the Plays of Samuel Beckett*[153] the authors supply a well arranged 'Select Bibliography', a 'Biographical Table' that places the main works in a framework of relevant information, an introductory discussion of 'The Context of Modernism' and of 'Problems of Interpretation', and a stimulating response to each of the dramatic pieces, mainly in the form of notes on difficult or interesting points in the texts. The student is well supplied with information and helpfully prompted to personal response by the critical questions. James Knowlson's bilingual edition of *Happy Days: Oh les beaux jours*[154] makes use of Beckett's notebook for his production of the German text at the Berlin Schiller Theater in 1971. The English text is the one used in the National Theatre Old Vic production of 1975, with Beckett's emendations. The student is supplied with a short general account of 'Beckett and his work', an interesting analysis of the play, and detailed information about productions and critical response.

Katharine Worth's very engaging *The Irish Drama of Europe from Yeats to Beckett*[155] traces some ideas and techniques from Maeterlinck and Wilde's *Salomé* through Yeats, Synge, and O'Casey and decides that Beckett as a playwright is their heir, since he achieved complete fulfilment of the dream 'of a drama of "most interior being". Such a drama was confined to corners of Dublin and of London in Yeats's day; it is a measure of Beckett's virtuoso skill and also of his humaneness that he has been able to give it this great extension into the public domain and in doing so change the course of modern theatre.' Ronald G. Rollins in 'Old Men and Memories' (*Eire*) relates Yeats and Beckett as playwrights with special reference to *Purgatory* and *Krapp's Last Tape*. Several studies connect Beckett with other writers. In *Poetica* Sang-Kyong Lee considers 'Samuel Beckett und das Nō-Theater: Mit besonderer Berücksichtigung von *Endgame* und *Krapp's Last Tape*'; Vera G. Lee has an account of 'Beckett on Proust' in *The Romanic Review*; James Acheson relates 'Beckett, Proust, and Schopenhauer' (*ConL*); in 'Form and the Void' (*French Studies*) J. P. Little compares *Fin de partie* with Ionesco's *Les Chaises*; Dominique

[152] *Samuel Beckett, A Biography*, by Deirdre Bair. New York: Harcourt, Brace, Jovanovich. pp. xiv + 736. $27.25.

[153] *A Student's Guide to the Plays of Samuel Beckett*, by Beryl S. Fletcher, John Fletcher, Barry Smith, and Walter Bachem. Faber. pp. 222. hb £4.50, pb £2.25.

[154] *Happy Days: Oh Les Beaux Jours*, ed. by James Knowlson. Faber. pp. 149. pb £1.95.

[155] *The Irish Drama of Europe from Yeats to Beckett*, by Katharine Worth. Athlone P. pp. 276. £10.50.

Iehl's 'Grotesque et signification dans le théâtre de Beckett et de Dürrenmatt' is in *Caliban*, as is John Fletcher's 'Beckett and the Medium: Rough for Radio?'. In *Michigan Academician* Michael B. Kline considers '*Waiting for Godot* as Entropic Myth', and in *American Scholar* John Romano offers 'Beckett without Angst'.

George H. Szanto's *Theatre & Propaganda*[156] is aimed primarily at the 'social scientist interested in information theory and the ways by which information may be distorted into propaganda', but as well as discussing Brecht's plays and the Wakefield Mystery Cycle it has an interestingly tendentious chapter on Beckett: 'Beckett's plays are empty. . .he fills his plays with carefully juxtaposed units of cultural junk.' The analysis is factually accurate, if expressed in stilted, abstract English, and the negative criticism comes from the author's determination to see the plays as ideological rather than aesthetic, emotional, or spiritual expressions. The book is one a Beckett student might easily miss, and its rigorously negative response can be challenging. In '*Endgame* and the Dialogue of King and Fool in the Monarchical Metadrama' (*MD*) P. Merivale relates Beckett's play to Ghelderode's *Escurial*, Pinget's *Architruc*, and Arrabal's *The Architect and the Emperor of Assyria*. In 'Earlier Endgames' (*MD*) Ruby Cohn considers the three distinct versions of the play. In 'A Footnote to *Footfalls*: Footsteps of Infinity on Beckett's Narrow Space' (*CompD*) Enoch Brater offers a tentative reaction to the play with reference to productions in London, Berlin, and New York. In '*Krapp's Last Tape* and Critical Theory' (*CompD*) SueEllen Campbell looks at the play with the purpose of finding in it 'thematic and structural parallels to several major issues addressed by twentieth-century critical theory: the nature of genres, the characteristics of literary and non-literary language, the importance of history in interpretation, and the role of readers and critics as creators of a work's meaning through interpretation and evaluation'.

There are two new volumes in Methuen's admirable series Master Playwrights: *Behan, The Complete Plays*[157] has an introduction by Alan Simpson, and the second volume of Edward Bond's plays[158] is issued. In 'Triviality and Dramatic Achievement' (*Modern British Literature*) Patrick A. McCarthy offers an evaluation of Behan's *The Hostage* and *Richard's Cork Leg*. Peter Holland considers 'Brecht, Bond, Gaskill, and the Practice of Political Theatre' in *ThQ* and in the same number Bond makes his reply. In *Edward Bond: A Companion to the Plays*[159] Malcolm Hay and Philip Roberts supply a 'chronology' of his life, a section with Bond's comments on his plays, a bibliography, and a record of the plays in production. Christopher Fry writes with warmth as well as subtlety in his partly autobiographical *Can You Find Me? A Family History*[160]. In 'Language as Life: Christopher Fry's Early Plays' (*MD*) Diane Filby Gillespie enjoys the

[156] *Theatre & Propaganda*, by George H. Szanto. Austin, Tex. and London: U. of Texas P. pp. x + 226. £7.70.

[157] *Behan, The Complete Plays*, introd. by Alan Simpson. Methuen. pp. 384. £1.75.

[158] *Bond Plays: Two*. Methuen. pp. xvii + 253. £1.50.

[159] *Edward Bond: A Companion to the Plays*, by Malcolm Hay and Philip Roberts. Theatre Quarterly Publications. pp. 100. pb £4.

[160] *Can You Find Me? A Family History*, by Christopher Fry. O.U.P. pp. xii + 267. £5.95.

'abundance and exhuberance' of the style, and in *ArielE* James Woodford's 'The Figure of a Dance' appreciates *A Phoenix Too Frequent.*

Gene A. Barnett's *Denis Johnston*[161] offers a competent, businesslike account of Johnston's career, analysing his plays and placing him in the context of the Irish theatre. The commentary is detailed and sympathetic. All students of O'Casey will be delighted by the thoroughness of research and effectiveness of presentation in *Sean O'Casey: A Bibliography*[162] by Ronald Ayling and Michael J. Durkan; this admirable exercise covers every aspect of O'Casey's career. In 'Liturgical Imagery in Sean O'Casey's *The Silver Tassie*' (*MD*) Jacqueline Doyle discusses the fact that characterisation is subordinated to 'the play's ritualistic structure and to its complex symbolic framework'. In *IUR* Bernice Schrank's 'You Needn't Say No More' considers some problems of communication in *The Shadow of a Gunman*, and in *ZAA* Jack Mitchell writes generally on 'The Theatre of Sean O'Casey'. The other articles appear in *The Sean O'Casey Review* number devoted to *The Silver Tassie*, which has contributions from Elisabeth Freundlich, Marguerite Harkness, Carol Kleiman, Richard F. Peterson, and Simon Williams. Ronald G. Rollins's *Sean O'Casey's Drama: Verisimilitude and Vision* (U. of Alabama P.) has not been seen. In *Federico Garcia Lorca and Sean O'Casey: Powerful Voices in the Wilderness*[163] Katie Brittain Adams Davis draws parallels between the plays of Lorca and O'Casey with respect to their 'dramatic techniques, characterization, diction, and thematic progression. . .and their joint (sic) contribution to European thought'.

Claude Combres in considering 'Osborne's Imagery in *Look Back in Anger*' (*Caliban*) concentrates on images of warfare, blood, and animal life. Georges Bas offers two papers on *A Patriot for Me*: 'Alfred Redl, le juif galicien' in *EA*, and in *Caliban* 'Fonction et signification d'un personnage secondaire', which compares Redl with his foil Jaroslav Kunz, the judge advocate.

Steven H. Gale's *Harold Pinter: an Annotated Bibliography*[164] is the most complete and useful work of its kind. The annotations are brief and well aimed, the student is guided to all of the information relevant to Pinter's work for the various media and to the different kinds of critical response. The appendixes offer chronologies of Pinter's writings, of his plays, first performances, and of his career as a director. There is guidance to annual bibliographical lists as further sources of information. Harold Pinter's *Poems and Prose, 1949–1977*[165] is welcome as an easily accessible and handsomely presented record of his non-dramatic writing. The prose memory of 'Mac', for example, demonstrates Pinter's most characteristic

[161] *Denis Johnston*, by Gene A. Barnett. Boston, Mass.: Twayne. (TEAS 230). pp. 169. $9.50.

[162] *Sean O'Casey: A Bibliography*, by Ronald Ayling and Michael J. Durkan. Macmillan. pp. xiv + 411. £20.

[163] *Federico Garcia Lorca and Sean O'Casey: Powerful Voices in the Wilderness*, by Katie Brittain Adams Davis. Salzburg: Institut für Englische Sprache und Literatur, Universität Salzburg. pp. v + 147.

[164] *Harold Pinter: an annotated Bibliography*, by Stephen H. Gale. Boston, Mass.: G. K. Hall & Co. pp. xxi + 244. $24.

[165] *Poems and Prose 1949–1977*, by Harold Pinter. Eyre Methuen. pp. viii + 102. £6.

virtues: the wit is subtle and warmed by his natural exuberance and unreserved affection for his subject, Anew McMaster. In 'Hutton and the Past' the enthusiasm for cricket is expressed with force and without self-consciousness. In the verse, however, there are many crystallisations of the grey clouds that darken most of the later pieces for the stage; the words ask for high estimation, but are oddly abstract and curiously self-regarding. Pinter's genius as a dramatist is clear when he is convinced of the human reality of his characters and of his audience; in this volume that conviction appears only in the prose.

Pinter's work for the screen has always been emotionally sensitive, and dramatically intelligent; his scripts for Joseph Losey have elicited that director's finest work. *The Proust Screenplay*[166] has not yet been realised on film, but Pinter found the extraordinarily demanding experience to be 'the best working year of my life', and that it is now published in advance of any treatment there may one day be for the cinema or television may encourage drama enthusiasts and critics to see it as parallel to the texts of the plays. Here is an important addition to the Pinter canon.

In 'Artifice of "Reality" in Chekhov and Pinter' (*MD*) Bernard Beckerman discusses a similar 'dislocation between demand and response' with specific reference to *Three Sisters* and *No Man's Land*, and in *QQ* that play is the subject of R. G. Collins's 'Pinter and the End of Endings'; Gerald M. Berkowitz examines 'The Destruction of Identity in Pinter's Early Plays' (*ArielE*), and in '*The Dumb Waiter*: Undermining the Tacit Dimension' (*MD*) Austin E. Quigley analyses the play with emphasis on the final moment when 'the tacit dimension of understanding between Ben and Gus is disturbed'. E. T. Kirby looks at 'The Paranoid Pseudo Community in Pinter's *The Birthday Party* (*ETJ*), in *QJS* Ricki Morgan considers 'The Multiple Nature of Reality in Pinter's *The Caretaker*', and the same critic's paper on *The Collection* examines 'The Range of Emotional States' (*ETJ*). Vicki Ooi offers 'Edward Agonistes or Anagonistes? Theme and Structure of *A Slight Ache*' (*ThRI*), and Bernard F. Dukore considers 'Pinter's Revised *Homecoming*' (*ETJ*). In 'Dance to a Cut-Throat Temper: Harold Pinter's Poetry as an Index to Intended Audience Response' (*CompD*) Christopher C. Hudgins discusses 'Pinter's recurrent use in the plays of motifs and image patterns initiated in his more openly didactic poems'.

In ' "God-Hunting": The Chaos of Worship in Peter Shaffer's *Equus* and *Royal Hunt of the Sun*' (*MD*) Barbara Lounsberry reads each play as 'an exploration of man's search for gods, what he does when he seems to find them, and how they ultimately elude him'. In 'Peter Shaffer's Recurrent Character Type' (*MD*) Joan F. Dean discusses 'the middle-aged man in a crisis of faith: Pizarro and Martin Ruiz in *The Royal Hunt of the Sun*, Martin Dysart in *Equus*, and Mark Askelon in *Shrivings*.

In *ShawR* John R. Pfeiffer's 'Continuing Checklist of Shaviana' comments usefully on a very wide range of material, including books and articles where Shaw is briefly but interestingly mentioned. Together with reprints and reviews of relevant books, *ShawR* also offers most of the good articles published on Shaw. In 'The Search for Good Government' Warren Sylvester Smith writes on that theme in *The Apple Cart, On the Rocks*, and *Geneva*; in 'The Passion of Dick Dudgeon' Robert F. Whitman offers

[166] *The Proust Screenplay*, by Harold Pinter. Eyre Methuen. pp. viii + 166. £7.

a persuasive reading of *The Devil's Disciple*; in 'Shaw's Caesar and the Mythic Hero' Timothy G. Vesonder argues that Caesar is Shaw's 'first fully drawn hero'; W. T. Jewkes considers 'The Faust Theme in *Major Barbara*'; in 'Unity and Diversity' Susan Stone-Blackburn writes on the treatment of the legend in *Androcles and the Lion*; in 'Did Bernard Shaw kill John Davidson?' Mary O'Connor quotes and annotates the very sad correspondence which charts the events which preceded – and which Shaw feared led to – Davidson's suicide; in 'James Elroy Flecker and Bernard Shaw' Timothy J. Kidd discusses Shaw's encouragement of Flecker and his possible indebtedness to him; in 'Undershaft's Challenge and the Future of the Race' Ken A. Baskin traces the superman theme in *Major Barbara*.

In 'Shaw's Own Problem Play' (*ESC*) J. Percy Smith analyses *Major Barbara*, and in 'Logic and Religion in *Major Barbara*: the Syllogism of Sir Andrew Undershaft' (*MD*) Stuart E. Baker writes interestingly on the play's discussion of the concepts of salvation, power, and money, praising it as 'a marvel of logical consistency'. In 'The Daimons of *Heartbreak House*' (*MD*) Rhoda Nathan considers the roles of Hesione and Ariadne, and in '*Heartbreak House*: Shaw's Ship of Fools' (*MD*) Sally Peters Vogt admires the didactic ordering of the play and its 'principle of coherence'.

Eldon C. Hill's *George Bernard Shaw*[167] is offered as an introduction to the study of his life and major plays for the beginning student: the discussion is enthusiastic, there is enough quotation from Shaw to whet the appetite, and there is a select bibliography which usefully directs new readers to the main works and commentaries. In 'Bernard Shaw, Ibsen, and the Ethics of English Socialism' (*VS*) I. M. Britain makes good use of *The Quintessence of Ibsenism*, and in 'Pygmalion: Myth and Anti-Myth in the plays of Ibsen and Shaw' (*ESA*) Errol Durbach compares *Pygmalion* and *When We Dead Awaken*. Daniel J. Leary in 'Shaw versus Shakespeare' (*ETJ*) discusses the 'refinishing' of *Cymbeline*, and in the theme of England being governed by 'character' Richard L. Newby finds 'An Arnoldian Allusion in *Major Barbara*' (*AN&Q*).

There are a few slight pieces on Tom Stoppard's plays. In 'Who Are the Dadas of *Travesties*?' (*MD*) Margaret Gold discusses the play's use of its source materials: Wilde is a 'dada' and so is Shaw. David Camroux labels Stoppard with his own phrase 'The Last of the Metaphysical Egocentrics' (*Caliban*) in noticing his determination to find some kind of purpose, pattern, or order in life, Philip Roberts asks 'Tom Stoppard: Serious Artist or Siren?' (*CritQ*), in the *New York Literary Forum* Coppelia Kahn writes on '*Travesties* and the Importance of being Stoppard', and in 'Nothing in Mind' (*LMag*) Stoppard discusses *Every Good Boy Deserves Favour* and *Professional Foul*.

The Abbey Theatre: The Years of Synge 1905–1909[168] is the third volume of *The Modern Irish Drama: A Documentary History*. It begins with the first full year of the Irish National Theatre Society in its new theatre in Abbey Street, and by means of five hundred or so substantial quotations from letters, diaries, and newspapers it succeeds in building up an

[167] *George Bernard Shaw*, by Eldon C. Hill. Boston, Mass.: Twayne. (TEAS 236). pp. 184. $8.50.

[168] *The Abbey Theatre: The Years of Synge 1905–1909*, by Roger Hogan and James Kilroy. Dublin: Dolmen P. pp. 385. £16.

intricate portrait through the words of those involved. Central in importance and fascination are the *Playboy* riots, the events and words off-stage doing as much to discredit the participants as Synge's vitriolic genius. The departure of Frank and Willie Fay from the Abbey is charted, and the appearance of such new playwrights as George Fitzmaurice, Lennox Robinson, and Daniel Corkery. The volume ends with the death of Synge and the production of Shaw's *The Shewing Up of Blanco Posnet*. The second number of *Cahiers du Centre d'Etudes Irlandaises* (1977) has a long section on Synge with contributions by Michel Bariou, Deirdre M. Laigle, Gérard Leblanc, Almire Martin, François Boulaire, Per Denez, and Mark Mortimer. Arthur H. Nethercot has a short piece on *The Playboy* in *Éire*.

There is a long interview with Arnold Wesker, conducted by Robert Skloot, in *Performing Arts Journal*; the discussion ranges over his attitudes to the effect on the individual of totalitarian governments in Eastern Europe, and many of his plays are mentioned. In 'The Defeat of Naturalism in Arnold Wesker's *Roots*' (*MD*) Tom Costello argues that there are 'romantic and mythopoetic elements' in the play which should be allowed to moderate the tone in production. There are two pieces on John Whiting in *Caliban*. In 'John Whiting et Aldous Huxley: une autre dette' Fernand Lagarde suggests that *Saint's Day* may be indebted to 'The Tillotson Banquet', and in 'John Whiting: The Tragic Failure' Marie-Hélène Larre discusses his characters who fail to find valid relationships and are driven to choose death.

XVII

American Literature to 1900

JOHN B. VICKERY
with the assistance of T. GIANNOTTI, N. MUIR, and J. C. VICKERY

Bibliographies of current articles are published quarterly in *AL* and annually in *PMLA* and the summer supplement of *AQ*. In addition, a number of other bibliographical works on various topics and authors have appeared during this review period. L. Oggel and R. Hewitt have edited an *Index to Reviews of Bibliographical Publications*[1], which covers the year 1976 and is to be an annual effort. The volume is organised according to author and subject keyed to one another by a simple numbering system. M. J. Bruccoli and C. E. Frazer Clark Jr, have edited, with considerable collaborative assistance, *First Printings of American Authors*[2], a four-volume compilation of over three hundred author checklists of first printings, of books, collections, and secondary items such as prefaces, introductions, forewords, and afterwords together with (where available) bibliographical references. In a related venture M. J. Bruccoli, J. Meyerson, J. Helterman, and R. Layman have produced three volumes of a proposed multi-volumed *Dictionary of Literary Biography*[3]. One deals with antebellum literature and literary figures, another with the American Renaissance, and the third with post-war novelists. The fourth and fifth are to deal with American expatriates 1920–40 and American screenwriters. All are handsomely done with generally sound and informative as well as sensible articles, which in many cases are accompanied by interesting period photographs, illustrations, and other visual material.

There are also a number of research aids organised on topical lines. D. Yanella's and J. H. Roch's *American Prose to 1820*[4] is an annotated guide to information sources on its subject. It has four major parts: one on general references and special studies; one each on the colonial and revolutionary periods; and one on principal authors arranged alphabetically. In the main, items are not included beyond 1975, but they are grouped as to whether they are bibliographical, biographical, or critical. A convenient and highly useful starting point for the teacher of American literature of

[1] *Index to Reviews of Bibliographical Publications, 1976*, ed. by L. Oggel and R. Hewitt. Boston, Mass.: G. K. Hall. 1977. pp. xv + 141.

[2] *First Printings of American Authors*, ed. by M. Bruccoli and C. Clark. Detroit, Mich.: Gale Research Co. (Vols. 1–4). Vol. 1, pp. 432; Vol. 2, pp. 407; Vol. 3, pp. 412; Vol. 4, pp. 397. $37.50 each, $140 set.

[3] *Dictionary of Literary Biography*, ed. by M. Bruccoli, J. Myerson, J. Helterman, and R. Layman. Detroit, Mich.: Gale Research Co. Vol. 1, pp. 224. $42; Vol. 2, pp. 555. $42; Vol. 3, pp. 382. $42.

[4] *American Prose to 1820*, ed. by D. Yanella and J. Roch. Detroit, Mich.: Gale Research Co. pp. xv + 653.

the period and for the graduate student, *Studies in the American Renaissance 1978*[5] edited by J. Myerson contains thirteen articles on bibliographical, textual, and historical matters of the period. Bronson Alcott's edited 'Journal for 1836', Melville's marginalia of Hawthorne, the popular reaction to *Uncle Tom's Cabin*, and L. Alcott's feminist letters are some of the items dealt with. A related volume edited by J. T. Williams is a checklist of scholarship on Southern Literature 1968–1975 arranged chronologically and subdivided into colonial, antebellum, postbellum, and contemporary sections[6]. It is based on the first eight annual bibliographies appearing in *MissQ*.

A useful reference guide of a more concentrated order is that of G. C. Longest[7]. It provides an annotated list of books and articles from the late nineteenth century to the present dealing with Mary Johnston, Thomas Nelson Page, and Amelie Rives Troubetzkoy. Additional guides of the same general format are those of R. B. Bickley Jr on Joel Chandler Harris; C. W. Ellison and E. W. Metcalf Jr on William Wells Brown and Martin R. Delany; E. N. Harbert on Henry Adams; J. DeBellis on Sidney Lanier, Henry Timrod and Paul Hamilton Hayne; R. E. Fleming on James Weldon Johnson and Arna Wendell Bontemps[8], J. Stronks provides 'Supplements to the Standard Bibliographies of Crane, Dreiser, Frederic, Fuller, Garland, London, and Norris' (*ALR*) with an annotation of each item. C. L. P. Silet augments his 1977 reference guide with his annotated 'Henry Blake Fuller: A Supplemental Listing' (*ALR*). A two volume collection of bibliographical essays on *Black American Writers*[9] edited by M. T. Inge, M. Duke, and J. R. Bryer seeks to survey and assess the state of scholarship on significant black writers from early ones such as Phillis Wheatley to contemporaries of the order of James Baldwin and Baraka. Account is taken in the essays of bibliographical, textual, and manuscript, as well as biographical and critical matters. In many ways, the volumes are modelled after Bryer's careful and informed *Sixteen Modern American Authors: A Survey of Research and Criticism* and so probably constitute the indispensable starting point of researchers in the field. E. Margolies and D. Bakish edit a useful bibliographical volume, *Afro-American Fiction, 1853–1976*[10], which in addition to relevant primary and secondary materials provides a chronological listing of germane short fiction and novels. C. Fairbanks and

[5] *Studies in the American Renaissance*, ed. by J. Myerson. Boston, Mass.: G. K. Hall. pp. ix + 491. $25.

[6] *Southern Literature 1968–1975: A Checklist of Scholarship*, ed. by J. T. Williams. Boston, Mass.: G. K. Hall. pp. 271. $40.

[7] *Three Virginia Writers: Mary Johnston, Thomas Nelson Page and Amelie Rives Troubetzkoy*, ed. by G. Longest. Boston, Mass.: G. K. Hall. pp. xv + 202. $22.

[8] *Joel Chandler Harris: A Reference Guide*, ed. by R. B. Bickley Jr. Boston, Mass.: G. K. Hall. pp. xix + 309. $30. *William Wells Brown & Martin R. Delany: A Reference Guide*, ed. by C. Ellison and E. Metcalf. Boston, Mass.: G. K. Hall. pp. ix + 276. $24. *Henry Adams: A Reference Guide*, ed. by E. Harbert. Boston, Mass.: G. K. Hall. pp. xi + 77. $12. *Sidney Lanier, Henry Timrod and Paul Hamilton Hayne: A Reference Guide*, ed. by J. DeBellis. Boston, Mass.: G. K. Hall. pp. 207. $20. *James Weldon Johnson and Arna Wendell Bontemps: A Reference Guide*, ed. by R. E. Fleming. Boston, Mass.: G. K. Hall. pp. vii + 145. $15.

[9] *Black American Writers*, ed. by M. T. Inge, M. Duke and J. R. Bryer. Macmillan. Vol. 1, pp. vii + 217; Vol. 2, pp. vii + 187. £12 each, £20 set.

[10] *Afro-American Fiction, 1853–1976: A Guide to Information Sources*, ed. by E. Margolies and D. Bakish. Detroit, Mich.: Gale Research Co. 1979. $22.

E. A. Engeldinger provide a helpful bibliographical approach in *Black American Fiction*[11]. Authors are listed alphabetically and under each their works are catalogued by genre together with separate listings of reviews of each work as well as biography and criticism, including dissertations. The critical material is not annotated.

The first volume of *American Women Writers*[12] is edited by L. Mainiero and covers its subject from A. to E. Three more volumes are projected. All entries provide essential biographical information, brief historical and evaluative essays, and selected primary and secondary bibliographies. It provides a succinct information source about important literary and other writers as well as many deservedly neglected figures. Barbara A. White's *American Women Writers*[13] is an annotated bibliography organised around ten very loose categories (e.g. 'Special Topics', 'Problems', 'Phallic Criticism') within which the progression is alphabetical according to the critic's name. Hence it is very difficult to use in connection with a single or specific author since only the critics are indexed.

D. L. Kirkpatrick has edited a mammoth reference work on *Twentieth Century Children's Writers*[14] which lists the writers alphabetically and for each provides brief biographical information, a list of publications according to genre and whether addressed to a child or adult audience, brief authorial comments when provided, and brief critical comments that attempt to sketch the author's subjects and style. It should be useful for teachers and parents. C. S. Kessner provides a potentially very useful annotated bibliography of 'Jewish-American Immigrant Fiction Written in English between 1867 and 1920' (*BHR*). It includes background materials dealing with the history and sociology of the subject as well as literary history and criticism.

In *The National Book Awards for Fiction*[15] J. F. Trimmer has prepared an index covering the first twenty-five years of the awards. It includes chronologically each year's winner, the contest judges, the nominees (when announced), the Pulitzer Prize winner for fiction, and a list of the year's best fiction as selected by the editors of *The New York Times Book Review*, as well as a list of the year's best selling fiction, news responses to the year's award, and reviews and critical commentary (down to 1976) on the winner each year.

E. L. Huddleston and D. A. Noverr devote their volume in the American Studies Information Guide Series to *The Relationship of Painting and Literature*[16]. It consists of a checklist of analogous American paintings and poems arranged chronologically, five appendixes reprinting pairings

[11] *Black American Fiction: A Bibliography*, ed. by C Fairbanks and E. Metuchen, N. J.: Scarecrow P. Engeldinger. Place & publisher pp. vii + 351. $15.

[12] *American Women Writers, A–E*, ed. by L. Mainiero. New York: Ungar. Vol. 1, pp. 654. $45.

[13] *American Women Writers: An Annotated Bibliography of Criticism*, ed. by B. White. New York: Garland, 1977, pp. xv + 119. $16.

[14] *Twentieth Century Children's Writers*, ed. by D. L. Kirkpatrick. Macmillan. pp. xv + 1507. $17.50.

[15] *The National Book Awards for Fiction: An Index to the First Twenty-Five Years*, ed. by J. Trimmer. Boston, Mass.: G. K. Hall. pp. 320. $35.

[16] *The Relationship of Painting and Literature: A Guide to Information Sources*, ed. by E. Huddleston and D. Noverr. Detroit, Mich.: Gale Research Co. pp. xv + 184. $24.

previously published by others, lists of poems on paintings and painters, and a bibliography of books and articles in general and specific aspects of the verbal–visual relationship. Another information guide is D. B. Wilmeth's *The American Stage to World War I*[17]. Because it aims to cover 'all aspects and phases of the American Theatre', it has not only sections of reference and historical surveys but also ones devoted to actors, scenery and lighting, and foreign language theatre. The items are annotated.

1. General

Certainly one of the most important books of the year is S. Bercovitch's *The American Jeremiad*[18] which continues his work of recent years on the religious and psychological dimensions of Puritan thought. He suggests that the American Puritan jeremiad differs crucially from its European equivalent in that it fuses secular and sacred history in an effort to save individuals and to guide societies toward national cities of God each of which represents the fulfilment of destiny. Bercovitch writes as a corrective to what he sees as Perry Miller's imbalanced emphasis on the dichotomy between the Puritans' sense of history and use of rhetoric. He argues cogently, and with a wealth of illustration, that the original Puritan vision survived because historical fact was mediated by a language which provided social cohesion by nourishing the imagination to sustained efforts at self-justification. The most controversial aspects of this thesis are likely to be those that extend this Puritan phenomenon into the eighteenth and nineteenth centuries. The increasedly secular, regional, and national emphasis of the culture together with its concentration upon progressive improvement – admitted by Bercovitch – makes it difficult to agree wholly with his assessment that this is a matter of extension and adaptation rather than transformation. Nevertheless, his is a seminal book that will likely spur further scholarly research into the American Enlightenment and Renaissance while affording a sustained and coherent – perhaps too coherent – interpretive argument concerning Puritan thought and attitudes in the New World.

J. F. Berens's *Providence and Patriotism in Early America, 1640–1815*[19] is a careful and persuasive argument for the continuing importance of the notions surrounding the idea of 'civil millennialism' down through the Enlightenment and at least as far as the war of 1812. Thorough rather than stimulating, Berens makes a deeply scholarly contribution to our understanding of the part played by Puritan religious thought in the emergence of a basically secular culture. A more sophisticated work that deals with Bradford as well as many others is W. Franklin's *Discoverers, Explorers, Settlers*[20]. In successive closely argued and richly illustrated chapters, he examines the differing and characteristic features of discovery,

[17] *The American Stage to World War I*, ed. by D. Wilmeth. Detroit, Mich.: Gale Research Co. pp. xv + 269. $24.

[18] *The American Jeremiad*, by S. Bercovitch. Madison, Wisc.: U. of Wisconsin P. pp. xi + 233. $15.

[19] *Providence and Patriotism in Early America, 1640–1815*, by J. F. Berens. Charlottesville, Va.: U. of Virginia P. pp. xi + 188. $9.75.

[20] *Discoverers, Explorers, Settlers: The Diligent Writers of Early America*, by W. Franklin. Chicago, Ill.: U. of Chicago P. 1979. pp. xi + 241. $19.50.

exploratory, and settlement narrative from Wood, Alsop, and Bartram to Byrd, Bradford, and White. In resisting the attempts of Bercovitch, Minter, and Slotkin to make the Puritan and Pilgrim experience the paradigm of American identity, Franklin argues for a more pluralistic approach sensitive to the cultural and ideological oppositions and polarities endemic to America from the beginning. Out of this emerges the recognition that the isolated self is the real centre in American experience and the traveller the multiform figure of its enactment and realisation alike. The book is augmented by a series of plates that are held to organise their visual space in ways similar to the writers' control of their verbal space. Each plate is accompanied by a brief comment on these parallels and on the plate's historical circumstances. The result is a series of highly suggestive remarks that hopefully Franklin will develop in a full-length study.

C. Bush's *The Dream of Reason* deals, as its subtitle indicates, with *American Consciousness and Cultural Achievement from Independence to the Civil War*[21]. Its thesis is the truism that American culture drew on its European predecessors while effecting adaptations required by the new world. The dream of reason is seen to fail through its distintegration into mass psychosis in the nineteenth century, a view based on a wide range of cultural evidence rather arbitrarily selected and interpreted. Its breadth – painting, literature, philosophy, technology, and invention – will interest many, though the more historically inclined will question its psychological reductionism. M. Banta makes a wide-ranging effort to debate the literary imagination's sense of *Failure and Success in America*[22]. The book is not the history of an idea but an on-going narrative 'that is continually revised by the participating consciousness into a fiction that contains its own reality about success because also intent upon recording what failure is like'. Emerson, Thoreau, Twain, Henry Adams, the James brothers, Stein, and Mailer receive the largest measure of attention, though Poe, Hawthorne, Melville, and Fitzgerald also figure prominently. Less argument than a series of meditative grapplings and less scholarship than a multi-voiced *débat*, this study will repay sustained reflection even if it finally stimulates rather more than it convinces.

N. Baym's *Woman's Fiction*[23] focuses on novels by and about American women from 1820 to 1870 with particular attention to such popular authors as Catharine Sedgewick, Maria McIntosh, the Warners, and Augusta Evans among others. She discovers that a kind of feminine Horatio Alger story predominates in which social, economic, and psychological achievement are reached after sundry covert as well as overt obstacles are overcome. Unlike other critics, she finds this body of work to reveal a moderate, pragmatic feminism that is aware of the subtle relationship of culpability obtaining between oppressor and oppressed. Not the least of this study's achievements is its revelation that 'women novelists dominated American reading habits for most of the nineteenth century'. David Schuyler's

[21] *The Dream of Reason: American Consciousness and Cultural Achievement from Independence to the Civil War*, by C. Bush. New York: St Martin. $29.95.

[22] *Failure and Success in America: A Literary Debate*, by M. Banta. Princeton, N.J.: Princeton U.P. pp. vii + 541. $30.

[23] *Woman's Fiction: A Guide to Novels by and About Women in America 1820–1870*, by N. Baym. Ithaca, N.Y.: Cornell U.P. pp. 316. $15.

article 'Inventing a Feminine Past' (*NEQ*) is a devastatingly negative, well-documented, review of Ann Douglas's book *The Feminization of American Culture*. Despite the book's good reception, Schuyler finds that Douglas is projecting her own feminist-Marxist views backwards to the nineteenth century. Schuyler mounts a convincing attack on Douglas's thesis: that between 1820 and 1870 American culture was split into a masculine-economic culture and a feminine-domestic and sentimental culture by an alliance of 'disestablished' liberal clergy and middle class New England women. Evidence of Douglas's failure to prove her 'thesis' includes use of unrealistic time frames; mis-use of evidence; inadequate, or just plain wrong, literary criticism (she badly misreads Melville and Stowe); and distortion of historical records.

In *Myth and Literature in the American Renaissance*[24] R. D. Richardson Jr eschews contemporary theories about myth in favour of those concepts available to writers such as Emerson, Thoreau, Whitman, Hawthorne, and Melville. His focus is their conscious literary uses of myth seen against the period's multiplicity of 'myth-minded undertakings'. The subtlety and complexity of these uses Richardson traces to the historical dialectic between sceptical and positive attitudes toward myth, which produced a deep-seated but delicate ambivalence toward the activity of myth-making. Contributing to this dialectic are Enlightenment rationalism, pre-romantic intuitionism from Vico to Herder, the rediscovery of Nordic and Indic mythological materials, and the higher criticism of Biblical scholars. This is a valuable contribution to the history of ideas that discriminates sensibly and usefully between the diverse responses to myth by the major figures of the American Renaissance.

In 'The Shape of Death in American Autobiography' (*HR*) G. T. Couser suggests the genre reveals authors either seeking to come to terms with death or writing a conclusion which somehow will be equivalent to their death. Solutions to these problems are diverse. Among those dealt with are Jonathan Edwards's progressive transformation into the eternal, Woolman's conscious involvement in the world, Franklin's replaying and recreating of his life through his *Autobiography*, Thoreau's and Whitman's transcendence of time and individual identity and defiance of death, Henry Adams's use of irony and his view of autobiography as literary suicide, and finally, Malcolm X's deployment of the martyr's vision. E. Rovit's article 'The American Literary Ego: An Essay in Psychohistory' (*SR*), examines both the general social and political background of the theme of isolated selfhood in American literature and the influence of this theme on the writings of the authors of the American Renaissance. The authors of this renaissance period influenced the following 'Lost Generation', in that the latter was obviously overly concerned with 'Self' and had a great deal of difficulty reconciling self and society. The idea of a 'Self' that can and should stand alone, Rovit sees as a departure from the earlier Americans such as John Adams and Thomas Jefferson who saw individuality as containing a social element. After an examination of the lives of the members of the renaissance, and their works, Rovit finds ample evidence that these writers left a

[24] *Myth and Literature in the American Renaissance*, by R. D. Richardson Jr. Bloomington, Ind.: Indiana U.P. pp. ix + 299. $15.

heritage of the 'song of myself' that was impossible for the next generation to adhere to.

Bert A. Bender writes on 'Let There Be (Electric) Light!: The Image of Electricity in American Writing' (*ArQ*). American literature is shot through with images of electricity from Franklin's lightning-rod to Henry Adams's dynamo. Earlier writers ranging from Edwards to Whitman tended to use electricity as a positive image of personal or cultural salvation, while those of the mid-nineteenth century, like Hawthorne and Melville, took a more tentative view of its symbolic value. For Adams and most of his twentieth-century heirs, the wonder of electrical energy has passed off, and such images are more commonly used to convey a sense of horror and darkness. William C. Spengemann poses the hoary question 'What Is American Literature?' (*CentR*). Spengemann believes that the conventional definition of 'American Literature' is too narrow and has been chosen by those who would wed it to English literature. He calls for a redefinition which will abandon equating 'American' with places which are now part of the United States.

The Enchanted Country[25] by A. E. Rowe claims that Northern writers familiar with the South between 1865 and 1910 presented it in two main ways, either critically or encomiastically. Authors such as Stowe, DeForest, Tourgee, Hearn, Wister, and James are drawn on to trace this thesis and to reveal the individual variations upon it of particular authors. Though resolutely unoriginal, the study draws together effectively a range of attitudes and opinions that deepens our sense of the South's image and imaginative role in the nineteenth century. D. Fisher and R. B. Stepto have edited *Afro-American Literature*[26], essays that explore issues of literary history, language, and folklore, including a threefold perspective on Frederick Douglass' *Narrative of 1845*. Their aim as well as that of the concluding comments on survey, genre, and interdisciplinary courses, is to focus attention on the central critical issues bearing on what the editors call 'the reconstruction of instruction' in this area. *Transatlantic Mirrors* is edited by S. D. Braun and S. Lainoff[27]. It is a collection of essays from Crèvecoeur and Sainte-Beuve to Gide and Henry Miller, which seeks to document American and French writers' views of each other, their cultures, and their influences on each other.

America's Humor[28] by W. Blair and H. Hill is only partially concerned with literature, for in endeavouring to write a history of the subject from Franklin, Jarvis, and Harris to the present, they include not only creative writers but essayists, performers, story-tellers, and artists or cartoonists. The book is written in a relentlessly breezy, popularised manner, which probably represents the academic's notion of the light touch. There is a welter of anecdotal examples as well as some illustrations, which taken

[25] *The Enchanted Country: Northern Writers in the South, 1865–1910*, by A. E. Rowe. Baton Rouge, La.: Louisiana State U.P. pp. xxi + 155. $11.95.

[26] *Afro-American Literature*, ed. by D. Fisher and R. B. Stepto. New York: MLA. pp. vii + 256. $8.

[27] *Transatlantic Mirrors: Essays in Franco-American Literary Relations*, ed. by S. Braun and S. Lainoff. Boston, Mass.: G. K. Hall. pp. 271. $15.

[28] *America's Humor*, by W. Blair and H. Hill. New York: O.U.P. pp. x + 559. $17.50.

together make for an engaging introduction to the subject. Given the range of materials and time covered, analysis, unfortunately, is limited. *American Humor in France*[29] is J. C. Austin's effort to follow the French effort to comprehend and assess the literary manifestations of the American comic spirit. He differentiates shrewdly between the Gallic wit and the American sense of humour and then considers the various historical manifestations of the latter and their impact on French readers. The treatment is sensible, informed, and very alert to the sociological and psychological shifts involved.

'Wordsworth and His American Friends' by A. G. Hill (*BRH*) argues that the poet's impact and reputation in America stemmed not only from his works but from an extensive network of personal contacts. He appends a select list of Wordsworth's American visitors and contacts.

E. M. Eigner sees *The Metaphysical Novel in England and America*[30] as a subgenre of romance whose traits of arrogant authorial stance, static or stylised characterisation, and loose structure are a function of their antipathy to nineteenth-century positivism, materialism, and associational psychology, and their conviction of the cultural necessity of the imaginative energies embodied in visionary literature and German idealism. The writers dealt with are Hawthorne, Dickens, Melville, and Bulwer-Lytton who are considered not so much historically as part of an international genre in which character and structure play a primary role. Henry Nash Smith's *Democracy and the Novel*[31] demonstrates the compatibility of brevity, lucidity, and high intelligence in its examination of the relationship between serious fiction and the popular audience from Hawthorne to Henry James. The disappearance of Hawthorne's and Melville's audience, the efforts of Howells and Twain to retain theirs, and James's ironic disengagement from his are all argued shrewdly out of a deep but unobtrusive scholarship.

C. R. Larson's *American Indian Fiction*[32] surveys his subject's development from the turn of the century and Chief Simon Pokagon through D'Arcy McNickle and down to Momaday and Dallas Chief Eagle. In the process the gradual movement toward cultural self-awareness and aesthetic matters of technique are limned in neatly. In *From Hopalong to Hud* C. L. Sonnichsen[33] provides some 'thoughts' (a number of the essays have appeared separately) on Western fiction as a kind of regional cultural autobiography. Though most of the subject matter is popular literature, he notes interesting differences in treatment by hardback and paperback authors and makes some shrewd assessments and analyses of reasons for certain elements, such as sex and social protest, appearing and disappearing from the genre.

[29] *American Humor in France: Two Centuries of French Criticism of the Comic Spirit in American Literature*, by J. C. Austin. Ames, Iowa: Iowa State U.P. pp. x + 177. $9.50.

[30] *The Metaphysical Novel in England and America*, by E. M. Eigner. Berkeley, Calif.: U. of California P. pp. x + 237. $13.75.

[31] *Democracy and the Novel*, by H. N. Smith. New York: O.U.P. pp. 199. $13.95.

[32] *American Indian Fiction*, by C. R. Larson. Albuquerque, N.M.: U. of New Mexico P. pp. 208. $9.50.

[33] *From Hopalong to Hud: Thoughts on Western Fiction*, by C. L. Sonnichsen. College Station, Tex.: Texas A. & M. U.P. pp. 201. $9.95.

2. Poetry

B. Duffey's *Poetry in America*[34] surveys the major currents from the nineteenth to the mid-twentieth century in sensitive and undogmatic fashion. It identifies three phases: poetry as celebratory expression (Bryant, Emerson, Longfellow, Poe, Whittier), as contradiction, search, or question (Lowell, Whitman, Dickinson, Robinson, Crane), and as awareness of itself (Eliot, Pound, Stevens, Williams). Duffey stresses that these phases are part of the poetic flow and so not to be hypostatised into rigidity. They are loci of emphasis against which the alteration and variety of poetic voices can be most clearly seen. This concern with the continuity of poetry from one century to the other and the serious historical attention to the intentions and achievements of earlier poets often slighted these days are most welcome. At the same time, one hesitates to accept the notion that fitting such diverse poets as Aiken, Sandburg, Roethke, Millay, and Schwartz under a single phasal umbrella carries us very far in the direction of ultimate critical discriminations.

Much more modish and with a quite different focus is Michael Clark's ' "The Crucified Phrase": Sign and Desire in Puritan Semiology' (*EAL*). Clark maintains that 'uncertainty about visible signs of election [to Grace] belies the heuristic power attributed to Puritan symbols by scholars such as Robert Daly'. The latter 'blurs the Puritan's careful distinction between epistemological certitude and moralistic confidence in the sufficiency of our knowledge'. This distinction, Clark feels, is 'crucial' because while the Puritans were confident about the legibility of this world – i.e., its existence as a group of characters written by God's hand – they seldom confused that legibility with intelligibility. Clark further contends that the fact that 'their insistence on the gaps in the text of the world led them neither to a nominalistic pessimism nor to a mystical optimism is, perhaps, the Puritan's greatest philosophical achievement'. For evidence he analyses the writings of John Cotton, Thomas Shepard, and Thomas Hooker primarily, but also takes into account William Ames and William Perkins. Presumably Clark would level many of the same strictures against Daly's *God's Altar: The World and the Flesh in Puritan Poetry*[35] which develops the above thesis in much greater detail. Unfortunately, the exhaustion of the publisher's allocation of review copies made it unavailable for detailed consideration.

More limited or narrowly focused treatments of Puritan poetry take up aspects of Edward Taylor's verse. One is Michael Schuldiner's 'Edward Taylor's "Problematic" Imaginery' (*EAL*). On the theory that 'there are image sources which lie outside a strictly defined literary tradition but which, when understood, clarify the structure of a poem and demonstrate the resource and craft of the poet', Schuldiner examines some of the imagery in Taylor's poems. He finds that Taylor drew images from various sources such as books in his own library. An example is the use of 'mamillary' in reference to smell, which he points out is used in connections with a headcold and in the times in which Taylor was writing *was* used to refer to smell. Taylor also uses this word in connection with the breasts much as

[34] *Poetry in America*, by B. Duffey. Durham, State: Duke U.P. pp. xi + 355. $14.75.

[35] *God's Altar: The World and the Flesh in Puritan Poetry*, by R. Daly. Berkeley, Calif.: U. of California P. pp. ix + 253. $12.

more modern usage would do. Another is Karen Grube's 'The Secret Sweet Mysterie of Numbers in Edward Taylor's "Meditation 80", Second Series, (*EAL*). This article is about number symbolism as a tradition in Christian literature and how Edward Taylor used this symbolism in his 'Meditation 80'. Grube has analysed Taylor's 'Meditation 80, Second Series' and finds number symbolism used to underline the mystical union between the believer and Christ, a belief celebrated by the sacrament of the Lord's Supper. She links this use of traditional symbolism to that observed in Hardt's study of the *Divine Comedy*. In connection with the above general topic one should also point out J. E. Eberwein's rich and useful collection of *Early American Poetry: Selections from Bradstreet, Taylor, Dwight, Freneau, and Bryant*[36].

Land and Sea by R. C. Vitzthum[37] is a welcome though somewhat plodding examination of the lyric poetry of Philip Freneau. He reverses the conventional view of Freneau as a poet: Vitzthum finds him engaged in a coherent search for meaning but one conducted on a private level distinct from his public concerns and expressed in lyrics using a system of private symbolism unique in late eighteenth-century poetry. Dominating the last mentioned are the contrasting symbols of land and sea which are associated respectively with the benign, harmonious, and passive aspects of nature, on the one hand, and with the destructive, chaotic, and aggressive impulses. Vitzthum further argues that Freneau is more concerned to express his own private state of mind than to copy nature or manipulate an audience. This state of mind he finds to have three major phases. During the 1770s it was marked by a vague idealism and eighteenth-century romanticism rooted in fancy. For the next decade the poetry comes to reflect a pragmatic realism and rationalistic stoicism in which the sea's capacity to dissolve illusions produces a universe devoid of meaning, empathy, and promise. The final phase resolves the extremes of the first two and of the symbolic polarity dominating the poetry. By 1791 Freneau has cast his lot with an unchanging reason that sees natural contrasts of whatever order as but contributory elements to the cosmic design of an inherently stable universe. One may question the notions of a private symbolism and deliberate concealment of intent while still commending the effort to give full scholarly attention to the poetry, including its revisions.

In 'Emerson's "The Sphinx" and the Perception of Identity' (*ESQ*) J. B. Reece contends that an 'acceptance of Emerson's statement [about his poem "The Sphinx"] that the poem's meaning concerns the "perception of identity" leads to some fresh conclusions, among them the view that virtually all criticism of the poem has incorrectly identified The Sphinx's riddle, a mis-step which places on questionable grounds the subsequent search for meaning and coherence in the poem'. He concludes that Nature's riddle in the Sphinx is her challenge to man to find a 'ground unconditional and absolute', in the style of Plato. A much more far-reaching examination of Emerson considers both the poetry and the prose. D. Porter's *Emerson*

[36] *Early American Poetry: Selections from Bradstreet, Taylor, Dwight, Freneau, and Bryant*, ed. by J. E. Eberwein. Madison, Wisc.: U. of Wisconsin P. pp. 383. $20.

[37] *Land and Sea: The Lyric Poetry of Philip Freneau*, by R. Vitzthum. Minneapolis, Minn.: U. of Minnesota P. pp. v + 197. $12.50.

and Literary Change[38] addresses the enduring question concerning the differing recognition afforded Emerson's poetry and prose. The explanation resides, he feels, in the dynamics of Emerson's thought or philosophy: 'though the consciously deployed imperatives of his philosophy impoverished his poetry, the aesthetic sweep generated by the deep structure of that philosophy created in his prose the principle of heuristic form by which poetry after his perceived a richer and denser reality.' This structuralist approach involves some pretentiousness of language, but the ideas are stimulating and help us see more precisely why Emerson is a major factor in the American literary imagination. The variety of poetic voices and prose persona, the emphasis on open rather than closed verbal structures, and Emerson's disposition toward the spontaneous and improvisational as conceptual and imaginative strategies are all worth sustained consideration. At the same time, one may hesitate at endorsing the view that Emerson was quite as crisis-ridden and anxiety-haunted a figure as Porter suggests or that his writing betrays a characteristic latent sexuality.

Two efforts to reassess aspects of Jones Very's poetry reveal in general terms current critical pre-occupations. J. A. Levernier's 'Calvinism and Transcendentalism in the poetry of Jones Very' (*ESQ*) takes a new look at the poetry of Jones Very and finds him not as 'mad' or 'inscrutable' as some critics have presented him. Very used poetry to explore the problem of being an orthodox Christian and yet a Romanticist. He apparently believed that 'to be a Transcendentalist meant first to be a Calvinist, for as an epistemological mode for learning about the truth, Calvinism subsumed Transcendentalism'. David Robinson in 'The Exemplary Self and the Transcendent Self in the Poetry of Jones Very' (*ESQ*) notes other critics' differing views yet maintains that the identity of the speaker in the poems of Very remains problematic. He, however, concentrates on what he deems the more important question: that of 'conscious artistry'. Was Very conscious of his audience or not, did he compose as much for an audience as for release of some sort of inspiration? Robinson maintains that carefully examined, Very's poems show an evidence of 'a careful strategy of composition based not only on a poet's felt inspiration. . .but also on a conscious attempt to create an impact on his readers'. Robinson finds evidence for this view in the poems and in Very's life.

A different sort of reconsideration can be found in connection with Longfellow. Robert A. Ferguson examines 'Longfellow's Political Fears: Civic Authority and the Role of the Artist in *Hiawatha* and *Miles Standish*' (*AL*). He proposes that Longfellow, far from his usual portrayal as a poet of serenity, optimism, and repose, was actually well-informed concerning American political crises, and that his emotional reaction to these national conflicts can be detected in a careful reading of his poetry. *Hiawatha* reveals a world eventually scaled down to human size, in which the artist needs a stable civic authority to function, and in *Miles Standish* 'Longfellow has left us with an overall portrayal of civic authority that is openly dangerous and frequently wrong'. A similar subject is addressed in J. Harris' 'Longfellow's *Poems on Slavery*' (*CLQ*).

Though no full-length studies have appeared this year, the poetry of

[38] *Emerson and Literary Change*, by D. Porter. Cambridge, Mass.: Harvard U.P. pp. xiii + 232. $15.

Emily Dickinson continues to engage the attention of scholars. Lois Cuddy in her 'The Latin Imprint on Emily Dickinson's Poetry: Theory and Practice' (*AL*) proposes that Dickinson's syntax and grammer may 'derive from the rules in her Latin textbook' which she employed to create 'a new aesthetic theory'. Apparent errors in syntax and grammar are correct according to the Latin rules she adopted, which are, significantly, exceptions themselves within Latin syntax, such as *hyberbaton*, the 'transgression of usual order of words or clauses'. Dickinson's personality was suited to such a procedure, Cuddy argues, as she was likely to seek freedom and individuality through a creative implementation of an already existing structure. S. Carter acknowledges in his 'Emily Dickinson and Mysticism' (*ESQ*) previous observations about the mystical qualities in Emily Dickinson's poetry and then tries to clarify *the way* she uses mystical ideas and themes. Carter finds that she was influenced by Emerson's and Whitman's kind of transcendentalism: 'a oneness with the power that "rolls through all things" ' although he finds that there are also differences because her themes concern renunciation as well as ecstasy in living. Mystical qualities of her verse are not easily explained by any single philosophical or religious system and Carter sees her poems as a balancing of the sacred and the secular. He finds evidence of this in an examination of her poems and concludes that she uses mystical ideas as a bridge between the secular and the religious.

'Emily Dickinson, Emerson, and the Poet as Namer' (*NEQ*) by John S. Mann, contends that although Emily Dickinson was unusually reluctant to reveal her 'name' to a reading public, she was, nevertheless, fascinated by names themselves. He believes that detailed attention to her belief that names held special imagination and creative power will tell us much about her special forms and vision. He here finds strong links to Emerson's writings. This essay probes yet another link between Emerson and Dickinson and Emerson's influence, and makes specific references to the poems themselves. Mann concludes: 'In the poems cited here and in so many others, the mind's effort to name, to comprehend, and to possess give Emily Dickinson's work a depth shared by few of her American contemporaries. Not even Emerson, finally, who taught her so much, had her poet's eye, so tuned an instrument to discover the stark beauty and strangeness of common things. Naming the objects of our world with loving precision, she was a true daughter of earth.'

In ' "A Loaded Gun": Dickinson and the Dialectic of Rage' S. Cameron compares 'narrative and lyric conceptions of temporality' in Dickinson's poetry in order to shed light on a group of her poems in which a story, once begun, is broken into and disrupted. Based upon a definition of life as a series of alternatives, the poems establish a dialectic only to dismiss it as inadequate. Cameron finds that the dismissal is often one of rage at all that is temporal and has a history of requiring sacrifice and choice. These Dickinson poems, which often end in disorder, are examined here in the context of other lyrics that also seem to 'pin their hopes on the belief that a verbal sabotage of sequence will trigger a temporal one, that, grown sufficiently desperate, the maneuvers of speech can stop time dead'. A companion piece is her 'Naming as History: Dickinson's Poems of Definition' (*CritI*) which addresses itself to naming as a strategy for dealing with the possibilities and impossibilities of revelation concerning the inner life.

Both essays will form part of her book on Dickinson scheduled to appear next year.

E. Carton's 'Dickinson and the Divine: The Terror of Integration, The Terror of Detachment' (*ESQ*) examines Dickinson's poems and finds that they 'dramatically manifest' the 'twin terrors of detachment and integration, reflecting ambivalent attitudes toward both the originating artist-self and the original text of nature or God'. These 'twin terrors' Carton maintains 'haunt the works of the American Renaissance'. It is the evidence of Dickinson's 'ambivalent' conduct of a poetic quest to establish a relation to the divine which Carton finds convincing. Other pieces of a less speculative order are C. L. Gohdes, 'Emily Dickinson's Blue Fly' (*NEQ*) and G. Monteiro's 'Love and Fame: or What's a Heaven For? Emily Dickinson's Teleology' (*NEQ*). The poet A. Hecht considers again 'The Riddles of Emily Dickinson' (*New English Review*). In addition numerous brief explications continue to appear.

Perhaps because there is a journal devoted exclusively to his work the poetry of Whitman receives sustained and diverse attention. Nor are related studies lacking. Thus *Walt Whitman's Champion* by J. Loving[39] is a literary biography of William Douglas O'Connor, an annotated edition of O'Connor's essays and letters on behalf of Whitman, and a bibliography of O'Connor's writings. A judicious and useful book, it suggests, interestingly enough, that O'Connor may have been an influence on as well as an advocate of Whitman.

A number of scholars continue to be absorbed by influences and comparative resemblances. For instance, S. Strom writes on ' "Face to Face": Whitman's Biblical Reference in "Crossing Brooklyn Ferry" ' (*WWR*). The opening 'face to face' image of 'Brooklyn Ferry' dominates the poem's congeries of image structures and serves to define a development of Whitman's role of poet-prophet. The contexts of six biblical passages are examined as contributions to Whitman's concept of prophecy, while the poem itself is interpreted as a poetic revelation of that concept. J. A. Herndon takes up 'Parallels in Melville and Whitman' (*WWR*). The possibility of mutual influence is discussed in terms of the scant external evidence available and, more conjecturally, in terms of hints supplied by internal evidence. The bulk of the argument is given to establishing a parallel between Melville's poem on John Brown, 'The Portent', and Whitman's 'Year of Meteors'. Though the similarity of these poems is supported by external evidence, much remains incidental and speculative, and the influence of Whitman on Melville seems merely plausible rather than probable. Wendy Greenberg compares 'Hugo and Whitman: Poets of Totality' (*WWR*). Ironically she proceeds by stylistic analysis of the prose which compares Hugo's preface to *Les Rayons et les ombres* with Whitman's preface to *Leaves*. The passages show that both conceive of the poet as contemplative spectator of 'the totality of the cosmos'. This shared conception of the poet's role depends on the ideal of 'liberty', though for Hugo liberty is still a utopian state which doesn't yet exist, while for Whitman it is an already existent condition.

'Walt Whitman and Kate Chopin: A Further Connection' by G. L.

[39] *Walt Whitman's Champion: William Douglas O'Connor*, by J. Loving. College Station, Tex.: Texas A. & M. U.P. pp. xix + 252. $11.50.

Candela (*WWR*) draws attention to the similarity in function between the mockingbird of 'Out of the Cradle Endlessly Rocking' and both the actual bird and the pervasive avian imagery of *The Awakening*. In 'Hopkins and Whitman' J. A. Herndon notes briefly the evidence for influence of 'On the Beach at Night' on Hopkins's 'Spring and Fall: To a Young Child'. Betsy Erkkila treats 'Walt Whitman and Jules Laforgue' (*WWR*). Laforgue's partial translation of Whitman in the 1880s gives rise to an adoption of Whitmanian themes and *vers libre* in Laforgue's final works, notably in *Derniers Vers*. Through Laforgue, Whitman became an important influence on the French Symbolists and, through the French, on the English moderns who professed to deplore Whitman. Finally, R. Arbur briefly considers '"Lilacs" and "Sorrow": Whitman's Effect on the Early Poems of D. H. Lawrence' (*WWR*), and argues that Lawrence's debt to Whitman extends beyond Whitman's liberation of language and prose as the poet of democracy to a dependence on the earlier poet's mode of utterance as a means of articulating Lawrence's emotional crisis over his mother's death. The puzzling image of Lawrence's 'Sorrow', 'her soft-foot malady', is traced to the 'Dark mother always gliding near with soft feet' of Whitman's 'When Lilacs Last in the Dooryard Bloom'd'. Unlike Lawrence's superficially allusive use of Whitman as democratic stereotype elsewhere, this and other death-poems suggest that Lawrence's earlier poetry relies significantly on the example of Whitman for its deeper levels of meaning.

'Walt Whitman and American Art' by K. Blaser (*WWR*) points out that except for his friendship with Thomas Eakins, Whitman's direct influence on American artists is minimal. There is a kinship, however, between Whitman's poetry and the painting of some of his contemporaries, notably, the artists of 'expansive' natural landscape, of 'human' landscape, and the genre painters whose subjects reflect an egalitarianism germane to the democratic vistas of Whitman's verse. His poetry has a posthumous effect as a source of inspiration in the painting of the 'new realists' associated with the 'Ashcan School' of George Bellows, John Sloan, and Robert Henri. Early modernists like Alfred Steiglitz and Joseph Stella were attracted to him as prophet of the bohemian struggle against authority and tradition. Generally, his appeal to American artists stems from one of two strains in his poetry: first, the insistence on a didactic relationship between artist and democratic society; and second, the uneasy ambivalence about the role of the artist's creative individuality in such a democratic society.

Leandro Wolfson considers 'The Other Whitman in Spanish America' (*WWR*). Whitman's reception in Hispanic countries, as in other parts of the world, has been determined by mythologising the poet, a confusion of Whitman with the speakers of *Leaves*. Reviewing the biographical sources with special attention to books written in Spanish, Wolfson tries to debunk some of the myths attached to the literary personage and to suggest something of the character of the man himself. Apparently this is intended as a corrective rather than revelatory article. D. C. Leonard studies 'Lamarckian Evolution in Whitman's "Song of Myself"' (*WWR*). Though Whitman's prose shows strong traces of Emerson and Hegel as sources for his evolutionary thought, the poetry is more deeply influenced by the naturalism of Lamarck and his four laws of evolutionary development. In 'Song', Whitman combines his 'perpetual journey theme' with a misinterpretation of Lamarckian materialism in order to create a teleological paradigm of evolutionary progress. By interjecting a conscious will in the form of his poetic persona into the natural scheme of unconscious evolution, Whitman is in effect romanticising the Lamarckian concept of nature for his own thematic purposes.

Others pursue thematic and formal questions in diverse ways. One is David Kuebrich's 'Whitman's New Theism' (*ESQ*). It contends that theistic best describes Whitman's theological orientation although many, if not most, critics consider Whitman pantheistic. The problem, Kuebrich thinks, is that Westerners tend to regard a representation of God present in nature as panthetistic rather than an aspect of a theistic system where God not only creates, but is immanently present in the world 'sustaining his creation and revealing himself through it'. He finds that Whitman advocates this view in his works. He examines passages of Whitman and concludes that not only is Whitman theistic but that Whitman is attempting to provide 'a new understanding of the divine-human relationship'. Jeffrey Steinbrink takes up ' "To Span Vast Realms of Space and Time": Whitman's Vision of History' (*WWR*). Whitman's 'understanding of history as a progressive phenomenon ratified and strengthened' his 'preference' of the present to the past and of American over European culture, yet his sense of the importance of historical antecedents is implied by the very enthusiasm of his frequent renunciations of the past. His belief in the continuity of history, in the interconnectedness of past, present, and future, is affirmed by his organic conception of temporal relationships. Hence, the American present holds promise of becoming a transcendent historical phenomenon, but only because it is a distillation and culmination of former ages, former cultures. By and large, Steinbrink's accumulation of evidence contributes significantly to a view of Whitman as a more level-headed historiographer than is usually supposed.

D. B. Stauffer discusses 'Walt Whitman and Old Age' (*WWR*) and finds that though Whitman's philosophical commitments dictate a view of old age as fulfillment of the life cycle, the poems of his last twnety years show a conflict between this ideal view and the reality of his own old age and invalidism. The tension results sometimes in contradictions of the idealisation of human life in his earlier work, but always in attempts to justify old age as the culmination (if not the zenith) of human experience. Stephen J. Tapscott writes an essay entitled 'Leaves of Myself: Whitman's Egypt in "Song of Myself" ' (*AL*). He proposes that Whitman's lifelong interest in Egyptian lore and myth influenced the development of the major political and spiritual themes of 'Song of Myself'. The myth of Osiris is especially influential, says Tapscott, since its themes – the incorporation of diversity in one body, germination and regeneration, and so on – are inherent in Whitman's concept of American democracy and the role of the poet, and he suggests that the Osirian myth is the underlying metaphor in the poem for the 'American federated democracy'.

In ' "The Body Electric": Science, Sex, and Metaphor' (*WWR*), H. Aspiz provides a survey of medical and pseudo-scientific lore of the mid-century which shows that Whitman is not alone in associating electrical energy with both the vivifying force of physical life and the germinating element in procreation. Whitman, with reputable medical opinion to support him, therefore advances his image of the 'body electric' at several levels: he identifies it with an underlying *élan vital*, with sexual transmission of the 'spark of life', and with the cosmic forces which control the movements of the celestial bodies. B. L. Lueck has a different focus in 'Whitman's "Mystic Deliria" ' (*WWR*). She explores the connotations and contexts of a typical word cluster which includes 'electric', 'mad', 'charge', 'deliria', 'magnetic', and 'ecstasy'. These words, used commonly in association with one another, assume a cumulative significance which relates to Whitman's major themes of companionship, freedom and democracy, and the 'passion of the soul and body unified'. This word cluster, when it occurs in conjunction with such themes, usually signifies a vision of what Whitman describes as 'mystic deliria'. William J. Sabo looks briefly at 'The Ship and Its Related Imagery in "Inscriptions" and "Song of Myself" ' (*WWR*) and finds that 'the unity of the two poems is enhanced by the poet's development of recurring imagery related to the ship and through the ship's connection with the following prevalent motifs: the perpetual journey; the absorption of experience; war; and initiation into death and suffering'.

Specific aspects of the poetry are also explored. R. W. French sees 'Whitman in Crisis: A Reading of "Scented Herbage of My Breast" ' (*WWR*). A brief, close reading, it represents the lyric as stating first the theme of poetry, its nature, purpose, and power. The 'leaves' of poetry are then recognised as inadequate and ephemeral monuments to reality, and the poet turns to a confrontation of the inevitability of death. The resolution, which leads him to acknowledge the inadequacy of art and to face directly the problem of death, marks this as a poem of crisis and resolved confrontation. Dennis K. Renner's 'The Conscious Whitman: Allegorical Manifest Destiny in "Song of Myself" ' (*WWR*) takes up the anecdote of the aristocratic lady and the twenty-eight young men in section 11 of 'Song'. It has been regarded as an inexplicable interlude within the structure of the poem. Whitman in fact meant the bathing scene to be interpreted as historical allegory: to wit, the aristocratic woman is a symbolic figure of Texas, which was then being 'wooed' into the Union as the twenty-ninth state. The allegory of this section, coming at a structural crux of the poem, suggests that other passages of 'Song' may employ the same mode of historical allegory, and that Whitman's historical consciousness is being slighted in favour of interpretations which search into the poet's unconscious for psychological explanations of his imagery. S. Carter examines 'The Metaphor of Assimilation and "Rise O Days from Your Fathomless Deeps" ' (*WWR*). The seeming contradiction between present perfection and self-realisation and the progression toward some future possibility of absolute perfection is resolved with Jung's notion of 'assimilation', whereby the conscious ego gradually becomes aware of the unconscious and seemingly external contents of the self. In 'Rise O Days', the self meets the challenge of assimilating the new experience of the Civil War: the irreducible quantity represented by the coming of war is successfully absorbed into the stuff the self is made of. The 'Symbolic Values in "The Dalliance of the Eagles" ' (*WWR*) are found by R. W. French to be a timeless experience in which the eagles are emblematic of 'the union of independent beings through nature's insatiable procreative urge'. The symbolic value of the eagles is seen in their embodiment or revelation of a natural magnificence which passes beyond the ordinary events of nature.

3. Prose

P. D. Westbrook provides a lucid but unoriginal introduction to the career and works of New Plymouth's most prominent early governor in his *William Bradford*[40]. In addition to a chapter assessing the literary significance and characteristics of *Of Plimmoth Plantation*, he also pays useful and welcome attention to the minor prose such as the *Dialogues* and the poetry. A more strenuous piece by S. Bercovitch is 'The Typology of America's Mission' (*AQ*). It traces the development of American millennialism according to the premise that the 'Puritans invented the sacred history of New England; the eighteenth-century clergy established the concept of America's mission'. The Puritan theology of the seventeenth century is related to the 'civil millennialism' of Revolutionary America with the crux of development coming with the Edwardsian rhetoric of millennialism and the Enlightenment influences of the Great Awakening. The typological construct of New England theology becomes, through the agency of the eighteenth-century pulpit, a secular typology. R. A. Bosco is more specific in 'Lectures at the Pillory: The Early American Execution Sermon' (*AQ*). The seventeenth-century execution sermon, as exemplified by Cotton Mather's *The Wicked mans Portion*, is described as a principal example of the jeremiad form. As both a means of plain-dealing with criminals and a means of reminding the congregation of the provisions of the covenant theology, it persists into the eighteenth-century with characteristic rhetorical form and social purpose.

Cotton Mather's biography is superbly unfolded by D. Levin in his *The Young Life of the Lord's Remembrancer, 1663–1703*[41]. He is particularly good in elaborating the interactions of a man eager to wield power with the socio-political forces of the age. Mather's role as a historian and his relations with his father are also admirably rendered. Mark Seltzer in 'Saying Makes It So: Language and Event in Brown's *Wieland*' (*EAL*) examines several patterns of lanugage and event in *Wieland* and explores the special effects these patterns create in the narrative and what the implications are in terms of word and action. His analysis of structural configurations discovers a concern within the novel of the act of writing and the effect of reading. A different issue is raised by Sydney J. Krause's '*Ormond*: How Rapidly and How Well "Composed", Arranged and Delivered' (*EAL*). Crucial to this article is whether the speed at which Charles B. Brown wrote his novels was detrimental to their structure and coherence. Krause examines the evidence and concludes that even though Brown wrote rapidly and worked on several novels at a time, his *Ormond* shows that Brown's white-heat method resulted in a remarkably well composed,

[40] *William Bradford*, by a P. D. Westbrook. Boston, Mass.: G. K. Hall. pp. 172. $8.95.

[41] *Cotton Mather: The Young Life of the Lord's Remembrancer, 1663–1703*, by D. Levin. Cambridge, Mass.: Harvard U.P. pp. xvi + 360. $16.50.

arranged, and delivered novel. Krause also maintains that Brown took longer than he is credited for in writing this novel and notes that perhaps the very speed of writing enhanced its intensity.

In 'Cotton Mather and the Meaning of Suffering in the *Magnalia Christi Americana*' (*JAS*) K. Halttunen claims that literary historians have generally overlooked the immediate historical context of Cotton Mather's ecclesiastical history of New England and see it as either a jeremiad or an effort to establish New England's central importance in world redemption history. She finds that a consideration of the combination of concern about what Mather felt was a decline in piety on the part of the people of New England and an equal concern about the decline in influence of the Mather family on the Church and political system of the colony left Cotton Mather facing a challenge to his role as godly leader of the New England people; for this reason, *Magnalia* is a justification not simply of New England's significance in redemption history, but also of Cotton Mather's own special place in the New England experience. B. Tipson's article 'The Routinized Piety of Thomas Shepard's Diary' (*EAL*) is an attempt to make the spiritual diary of Shepard more readable and understandable by placing it in its context: English Puritan spirituality. Tipson answers such questions as why the Puritans felt that their personal spiritual experiences were worth meditating upon. Diary keeping is seen to lead to divine revelation. Tipson concludes: 'The assumption, often supported by references to faculty psychology, that experience simply provided raw data upon which the Puritan intellect was discreetly to reflect, has misled scholars of Puritanism. In Shepard's case, intellectual expectations virtually created experience'. C. E. Jones investigates 'The Impolitic Mr. Edwards: The Personal Dimension of the Robert Breck Affair' (*NEQ*). Jonathan Edwards, newly succeeded to his grandfather's pulpit, evidently sided with his uncle, Williams Williams, who was determined to control the appointments, to prevent a certain Robert Breck from becoming pastor at Springfield in 1734. The eastern powers of the Church prevailed, and Breck was ordained.

Of a different order is 'Providence and the Apocalypse In The Early Writings of Jonathan Edwards' (*EAL*) by S. J. Stein. He examines 'theological reflections' on the significance of the Apocalypse in the early private notebooks (up to 1724) of Jonathan Edwards. He finds that Edwards was fascinated with the Apocalypse and interpreted the vision of the living creatures in Revelation, Chapter 4 as providing an 'organizing focus by disclosing theological and literary order in the Apocalypse relating to 'the theme of providence'. Stein feels that 'a monothematic portrayal of the eschatological thought of Edwards is no longer adequate and it is not acceptable to regard his pronouncements from one time period as a full reflection of his views'. He contends that not enough attention has been paid to opinions of Edwards related to the Apocalypse in toto and over time. Stein feels the 1723 apocalyptic formulations were. . .a high point in Edwards' changing views of the Apocalypse'. L. Ziff's 'Revolutionary Rhetoric and Puritanism' (*EAL*) considers John Adams's argument that, based on a history of Massachusetts, citizens had the right to argue their rights by historical precedent. Adams contended that the peopling of America was not based on religious freedom alone, but also on a love of universal liberty. Adams's portrait of Puritan history is, Ziff says, secular rather than providential. Pertinent here is his comparison of the rhetoric of Adams with that of Paine's *Common Sense*.

In ' "A Turn of Thinking": The Long Shadow of the *Spectator* on Franklin's *Autobiography*' (*EAL*). J. S. Lewis finds ample evidence in the *Autobiography* of Franklin's continuing emulation of Addison and Steele, the 'Old Masters'. The similarities between the *Spectator* and the *Autobiography* go beyond the common topics of the Enlightenment and confirm the influence of Addison and Steele on Franklin. Lewis observed that while the *Spectator* remains theoretical, the *Autobiography* shows Franklin practising (or saying that he did) what the *Spectator* preached. Franklin selected and adapted his reading to his own genius and his own country. Philip D. Beidler (*EAL*) finds that Franklin's *Autobiography* and Crèvecoeur's *Letters from an American Farmer* are 'characteristic American "fictions" which anticipate the works of nineteenth century novelists'. 'Both works address large conceptions of democratic life through narrative strategies predicated on the writer's attempts. . .to invest personally vouched-for recitals of experience with larger sanctions of discovered representative truth.' Based on the evidence of Franklin's incomplete plans for an ethical work entitled *The Art of Virtue*, an essay by N. S. Fiering (*AQ*) argues against Franklin's alleged inheritance from Puritan ethical thought and stresses his similarity of position with the pragmatic ethics of pre-Enlightenment and Enlightenment philosophers.

James M. Cox writes on 'Jefferson's *Autobiography*: Recovering Literature's Lost Ground' (*SoR*). Cox is lamenting that the *Autobiography* has not been considered literature, as it should be, along with a good deal of other non-fiction in the history of American literature. Cox would like to see a revival of the study of factual and ideological works in university courses. C. W. Lewis examines Jefferson's style in 'Style in Jefferson's Notes on the State of Virginia' (*SoR*) and finds it a blend, with the style of Tacitus being predominant. Lewis is concerned with telling us why 'Notes' should be considered more than a guide to Virginia in 1780. It is a stylistic and imaginative achievement.

Wesley T. Mott explores 'Emerson and Antinomianism: The Legacy of the Sermons' (*AL*). Mott proposes that Emerson's early sermons help resolve the contradictory views of the transcendental rebel versus the conservative, as they reveal his early caution concerning an exclusive Antinomian vision and his advocacy of transmaterialistic enthusiasm. Mott concludes that Emerson has a central place in the Puritan tradition, as his resolution was a process of synthesis of 'spirit and world, grace and effort, private revelation and communal destiny'. Joel Myerson looks at 'Convers Francis and Emerson' (*AL*). Most of this article consists of extracts from Francis' *Journal on Emerson* from August 1835 to January 1863. Myerson finds Francis' comments on Emerson valuable since, although Francis retreated from the Unitarian controversy of the early 1840s because it was disruptive, his altered feelings about the transcendentalists didn't change his feelings about Emerson. D. Robinson investigates 'Emerson and the Challenge of the Future: The Paradox of the Unachieved in "Circles" ' (*PQ*). He finds the essay revealing the first signs of Emerson's disenchantment with the possibility of self-culture and his recognition that the unachieved has itself a tragic dimension.

T. Woodson (*BRH*) argues against Wendell Glick's editorial decision to give Thoreau's essay its original title of 'Resistance to Civil Government' in his edition of *Reform Papers*. He favours accepting the 1866 'Civil Disobedience' essay and title, with the exception of one emendation, as the most 'definitive' text and title. N. Joy (*ESQ*) compares Thoreau's passages with Jonathan Carver's *Three Years Travels Through the Interior Parts of North America in the Years 1766, 1767 & 1768*, and the Rev Gilpin's *A Guide Through the District of the Lakes in the North of England with A Description of the Scenery, &c. for the Use of Tourists and Residents*, and Wordsworth's passages celebrating the value of the rural life. Joy suggests that Thoreau's readings of these works provided an underpinning for some of his own descriptive and imaginative work. J. Anhorn's article (*ESQ*) is concerned with the structural aspects of the language of *Walden*. She finds, by an examination of *Walden* in general and the seventh chapter in particular that Thoreau is often speaking 'in two tongues'. Thoreau uses physical labour and nature as 'a right source of metaphors which unite the worlds of nature and the mind'. She further believes this constitutes a harmony of a moral sort for Thoreau. C. C. Walcutt considers '*Walden* As a Response to "The American Scholar" ' (*ArQ*). Thoreau's doctrinal quarrels with Emerson and personal distaste at being represented as embodiment of the American scholar are responsible for a deliberate structuring of *Walden* as reaction to and modified restatement of Emerson's essay. An interpretation of *Walden* shows that the chapters are arranged with intentional parallels and specific criticisms of each of the sub-headings of 'The American Scholar'. F. Garber's *Thoreau's Redemptive Imagination*[42] uses Thoreau's concern with the imagination as a means of redeeming nature to examine his ideas of order and the self, their merging in the landscape, and its significance intellectually and emotionally. The intractability of nature and the inadequacy of imagination lead him to seek a secondary act of redemption that would free man from the multi-cyclical dimensions of his existence and from time on which they all rest.

'Channing's Unfinished Autobiographical Novel' (*ESQ*) is the subject of an article by F. B. Dedmon who has found a notebook at the Folger library containing a fifty-page fragment of a novel by Ellery Channing (Folger MS N.a. 77), which he thinks Channing's biographers have overlooked. Dedmon says this fragment sheds light on a formative period of Channing's life (1841–2). A. Slater goes *In Search of Margaret Fuller*[43] and finds pretty much what others engaged in much more scholarly research have discovered. The treatment is highly popularised and focuses on her role as quintessential feminist; it also engages in considerable psychological speculation about Fuller's feelings and attitudes at specific times.

Washington Irving is represented by two quite different editions. The first is two volumes in the ongoing textual edition of *The Complete Works* under the general editorship of R. D. Rust and a product of the Center for Editions of American Authors. *The Sketch Book* has been edited by Haskell Springer and the biographies of Goldsmith and Margaret Davidson

[42] *Thoreau's Redemptive Imagination*, by F. Garber. New York: New York U.P. pp. x + 229. $15.

[43] *In Search of Margaret Fuller*, by A. Slater. New York: Delacorte. pp. 215. $7.50.

by E. L. West[44]. Both are careful, highly professional efforts which agreeably enough also constitute clear, serviceable, and attractive reading editions. More than half of each volume is devoted to editorial appendixes which take up such matters as textual commentary, discussions of adopted readings, lists of emendations and the like. Of a rather different order is the other edition[45]. It is a facsimile edition of the 1875 *Bracebridge Hall* and *Old Christmas* volumes. The latter was Volume 5 of the original Sketch Book series. Included are the original R. J. Caldecott illustrations. Both make attractive books in which charm and nostalgia work hand in hand with a graphic rendering of Victorian tastes in reading and book production.

J. H. McElroy (*AL*) assesses and supports the reliability of Irving's biography of Columbus (*History of the Life and Voyages of Christopher Columbus*, 1826-1827) which he feels marked Irving's emergence as a writer working for his livelihood rather than creating at his leisure; however, he engages in no discussion of Irving's fiction. William Bedford Clark considers 'How the West Won: Irving's Comic Inversion of the Westering Myth in *A Tour on the Prairies*' (*AL*). Clark sees *Tour* as a 'mock heroic quest' enacted against the backdrop of the myth of westering, which 'presupposes that civilization must inevitably conquer the wilderness'. The quest involves an 'archetypal confrontation', a 'ritualistic casting off', a corruption of 'civilized' procedures, and a conflict between man and nature. That the West and nature win Clark sees as evidence not only of Irving's conviction of man's limitations, but of his own romantic desire that the wilderness remain impregnable. W. R. Kime attempts two related tasks: to provide a complete biography of Washington Irving's nephew, Pierre and to give a careful account of their long and intricate relationship[46]. In the process he endeavours to correct some of the traditional views concerning Pierre as a biographer and personality, and to throw more light on Irving as a private individual than have earlier critics like S. T. Williams and W. L. Hedges.

History and Utopia by A. M. Axelrad[47] has a somewhat misleading title. Actually it is a dissertation devoted largely to Cooper's *The Crater* and to a lesser degree *The Bravo* and the historical and cultural processes Cooper finds operative in the world. According to Axelrad, Cooper accepts a cyclical theory of history within which he locates utopian and anti-utopian traits in terms of which he appraises a given society at a given moment. Buttressed by the authority of Nisbet, Manheim, Arendt, Eliade, and others, Axelrad argues that Cooper not only never underwent any socio-political transformation but that from the time of *The Spy* in 1821 he possessed a fully coherent and consistent conservative view of the world, one sustained by his conscious adherence to the tenets of neo-

[44] *The Complete Works of Washington Irving*. Vol. 8, ed. by H. Springer. Boston, Mass.: G. K. Hall. pp. xi + 510. $25; Vol. 17, ed. by E. West. Boston, Mass.: G. K. Hall. pp. 654. $25.

[45] *Bracebridge Hall*, by W. Irving. Tarrytown, N.Y.: Sleepy Hollow Restorations. pp. 284. $12; *Old Christmas*, by W. Irving. Tarrytown, N.Y.: Sleepy Hollow Restorations. pp. 165. $10.

[46] *Pierre M. Irving and Washington Irving*, by W. R. Kime. Waterloo, Canada: Wilfred Laurier U.P. pp. xv + 362. $9.50.

[47] *History and Utopia: A Study of the World View of James Fenimore Cooper*, by A. Axelrad. Norwood, Pa.: Norwood Editions. pp. vii + 231. $35.

orthodox Christianity, which remained substantially unchanged for his last thirty years. But to demonstrate such a sweeping claim one would think that to start from and to focus on a novel of 1847 is scarcely the tack to take.

S. Railton's *Fenimore Cooper*[48] essays a Freudian explanation of his subject's shift from romance to satiric social works, but the intent is less doctrinaire and terminologically freighted than most such ventures. That the man and his works betray Oedipal drives of considerable and recurring intensity is Railton's central conviction. Unfortunately, immediate as distinct from what might be called mediate evidence is largely lacking, so that one is thrown back on either the inherent or cross-culturally documented plausibility of the Oedipal impulse. Whatever one's view on the historical reality of the parent–sibling relation, it does in this case suggest a more deep-seated and functional reason for Cooper's generic shift than the usual ones. Predictably, specific statements and attribution of psychoanalytic significance strain credulity, but that appears endemic to the declarative mode. More regrettable perhaps is Railton's failure to take sufficient account of the more recent contributions to Cooper studies, which might in some cases have modified or attenuated his views.

Martin Green's 'Cooper, Nationalism and Imperialism' (*JAmS*) is rather misleadingly titled. Considering the adventure novel as a genre, Green works with Cooper's forest books (Leatherstocking saga) and sea fiction (*Afloat and Ashore, The Pilot, The Sea Lions*). His point is that if Cooper hadn't been influenced by Scott, he could have developed the genre of the adventure novel into something important, which would have reflected the 'confusions of feeling about what America was turning into'. As it was, the apprenticeship to Scott ruined the genre, potential in the forest novels, which were compromised by romance plots and high rhetoric. The sea novels, more convincing because they didn't contain the conflicts inherent in the forest novels, were less significant for *not* containing them. B. L. St. Armand examines 'Harvey Birch as the Wandering Jew: Literary Calvinism in James Fenimore Cooper's *The Spy*' (*AL*). Literary Calvinism informs the 'Americanness of Cooper's vision': obedience and self-sacrifice parallel and invest a concept of 'two Americas – one about to die, the other. . .to be born'. Birch combines the self-sacrifice and avariciousness of the wandering Jew with the Calvinistic 'willingness to be damned'. This schizophrenia allows him to be 'anything the moment demanded', a kind of peddler Christ, son of a deified Washington, for whom he sacrifices himself, clutching in death Washington's exoneration, his 'certificate of election' to the 'heaven of. . .American patriotism'. In this connection he notes that *The Spy* anticipates *Billy Budd*.

Poe at Work edited by B. F. Fisher IV offers seven textual studies[49]. One deals with the never-published *The Tales of the Folio Club*, its planned format, missing portions, and subsequently published tales. The remainder examine specific instances of Poe's revisions and conclude, as one might expect, that they were for the better. Two biographical volumes

[48] *Fenimore Cooper*, by S. Railton. Princeton, N.J.: Princeton U.P. pp. xvii + 282. $16.

[49] *Poe at Work*, by B. F. Fisher IV. Baltimore: Edgar Allan Poe Society. pp. 110. $8.

have appeared on Edgar Allan Poe. One, entitled *The Extraordinary Mr. Poe*, is by Wolf Mankowitz[50]. It is a popular effort, making no pretense to scholarship or critical originality, but sensibly written. Noteworthy are its illustrations, photographs, and daguerrotypes which capture both the social realities and the Gothic imaginative propensities of the time. Another critical biography is *The Tell-Tale Heart* by J. Symons[51], who feels that Poe studies merge the life and the works excessively. To that end, he separates his book into two parts – the life and the work – though much of the latter nevertheless crops up in the former. The biographical portion is less overtly psychological and 'Gothic' than Mankowitz and stresses his primary commitment to poetry and magazine editing and that his fiction was largely an economic necessity. Symons takes vigorous issue with what he regards as the aberrant trend of Poe criticism toward symbolic readings.

'Hans Pfaall: A False Variant and the Phallic Fallacy' by B. R. Pollin (*MissQ*) explains that the titular name was changed from its original spelling by Poe in order to avoid any conceivable 'phallic' references, to underscore its Germanic nature, and to underline the play on the 'fall' of the balloonist of the tale. In passing, he attacks the ingenuities and tendentiousness of Freudian and what he calls pseudo-metaphysical readings of Poe. In Jules Zanger's 'Poe and the Theme of Forbidden Knowledge' (*AL*), 'Morella', 'Ligeia', 'A Descent Into the Maelstrom', and 'Manuscript Found in a Bottle' are linked by the shared theme of forbidden knowledge, which is more Adamic than Faustian in origin. The stories' destructive women Zanger finds more representative of nineteenth-century attitudes than of Poe's impotence.

B. S. Mouffe has edited *Hawthorne's Lost Notebook, 1835–1841*[52] in facsimile and transcript thereby providing hitherto unavailable and unknown manuscript materials for these notebook years. It provides significant information concerning the author's personal life and his creative outlook. C. Badaracco's 'The Night-blooming Cereus' (*BRH*) prints a letter, with brief introduction, from the 'Cuba Journal' of 1833–5 by Sophia Peabody Hawthorne, and appends a check list of her autograph materials held in American institutions.

In 'The House and the Railroad: *Dombey and Son* and *The House of the Seven Gables*' (*NEQ*), J. Arac is concerned with 'the profound institutional similarities in the literary backgrounds and early careers of Dickens and Hawthorne that continue to mark their methods, techniques, and concerns'. Authorial use of sources in *Dombey and Son* and *The House of the Seven Gables*, and the integration of such things as forms of the Gothic tale and sketches of contemporary life into the respective early novels are compared. J. Franzosa in ' "The Custom-House", *The Scarlet Letter* and Hawthorne's Separation from Salem' (*ESQ*) sees Hester as the maternal matrix, incorporating both masculine and feminine qualities (as did

[50] *The Extraordinary Mr. Poe*, by W. Mankowitz. New York: Summit. pp. 248. $15.

[51] *The Tell-Tale Heart: The Life and Works of Edgar Allan Poe*, by J. Symons. Faber. pp. ix + 259. £6.95.

[52] *Hawthorne's Lost Notebook, 1835–1841*, ed. by B. S. Mouffe. University Park Pa.: Pennsylvania State U.P. pp. 30 + 86 double pp. $10.95.

Hawthorne's own mother on an emotional level), and suggests that the fantasy of the 'phallic mother. . .dominates this romance'. The underlying themes are paternal loss and self-discovery: 'Hawthorne's fictions do not conceal truths, but. . .denote that here was some object which would fain have been, or at least ought to be, concealed'. In 'The Custom-House' Hwthorne articulates his dependency, and becomes himself the centre of the universe, bearing the whole ancestral burden. He needed to separate himself from Salem, but could do this only through transforming artistically the psychological dynamics of maternal possessiveness which allowed him to survive. Although he left Salem he never left psychologically. He created his own identity through an artistic separation. In 'Progress and Providence in "The House of the Seven Gables" ' (*AL*) J. Gatta suggests that the 'prosperous' ending of the novel raises the question of what 'progress' in Hawthorne means and whether its agent is the individual or fate. He delineates three levels of progress in the narrative, all linked by providence under the aegis of a benevolent God: personal, social-historical and transhistorical, or 'visionary history'. The *individual* can progress toward 'communion and trust' but cannot *change* social history and can only *assist* the providential plan. Only on the transhistorical level is 'teleological' progress assured: the 'underground stream of sacred history [is] progressing toward a final apocalyptic fulfillment' and he implies that this 'underground stream' is operating through the figure of Phoebe as transcending agent; thus the visionary informs the actual in the prosperous ending. However, Gatta feels that Hawthorne failed to 'fuse the visionary dimension. . .with a portrayal of present-day life in Salem'.

With 'Sexual Exploitation and the Fall from Natural Virtue in Rappaccini's Garden' (*ESQ*), K. Bales relies heavily on Crews, Baym, Male, and Rahv, seeing Beatrice as a sexual and political victim of a world which can never return to the purity of Eden. She is poisonous because she represents original natural virtue, which Giovanni and Rappaccini exploit in spite of themselves. Rather than a religious Eden, Bales suggests that the secular Eden of human consciousness is more nearly Hawthorne's arena, and the potential destruction of humanity as we know it is the natural result of a return to a pure state. D. P. Norford's 'Rappaccini's Garden of Allegory' (*AL*) advances the thesis that Hawthorne's allegorical figures are projections of his ambivalence about the moral implications of art, specifically its symbolic language. Thus symbolic language may be an almost moral transgression while functioning at the same time as a representation of truth which reality expresses imperfectly. The allegorical character becomes a projection containing demonic and divine aspects: this intermixture illuminates reality, but does not offer a resolution for the character, who remains divided. Norford concludes that Hawthorne was never able to resolve the ambivalence either, retaining the Puritan view of art as blasphemy. With his ' "My Kinsman, Major Molineux": The Playful Art of Nathaniel Hawthorne' (*ESQ*), E. H. Miller suggests that reading 'My Kinsman' with Hawthorne's spirit of play in mind reveals Robin as a comic-tragic portrayal of anxious adolescence. Hawthorne's characteristic ambiguity has in this story the artistic function of leaving Robin's choices of identity and autonomy open, allowing the reader to identify with the bittersweet retrospective of his own rite of passage.

B. Higgins' *Herman Melville: An Annotated Bibliography* is the first volume of a useful listing of books, essays, and reviews from 1846–1930[53]. Many of the annotations are quite substantial so that one can glean from them a sense of the tides of Melville's reception. An index allows one also to determine quickly the historical range of opinion concerning individual works.

James Barbour and Robert Sattelmeyer collaborate on 'The Sources and Genesis of Melville's "Norfolk Isle and the Chola Widow"' (*AL*). The sources, they find, are Melville's pre-occupation since 1852 with the story of the abandoned Agatha Robertson and an 1853 newspaper account of an abandoned Indian woman off the California coast. The story itself is an inversion of popular sentimentality (Hunilla may be heartless, providence is not benevolent) and Melville finally wrote it, after trying to get Hawthorne to write it, during a time when his writing was being refused; thus the combination of the themes of patient endurance and anti-sentimentality. 'Evolving the Inscrutable: The Grotesque in Melville's Fiction' (*AL*) is by R. M. Cook. Citing Wolfgang Kayser and Frances Barasch to support a definition of the grotesque as an expression of human reaction to the unknown and the human incapacity to order logically human experience, Cook explores the grotesque in Melville on three levels: in his narrative pattern, in the nature of his characters, and as the 'underlying aesthetic mode' of *The Confidence Man*. In *Typee, Redburn, Moby Dick*, and *Pierre* a vision of physical deformity warns characters of their ignorance; in *Mardi, White Jacket*, and *Moby Dick* distortions in nature emerge in the human mind and body, undermining concepts that could make sense of the world, and in *The Confidence Man* the grotesque transformations are a way of presenting pure reality, free from human attempts to explain it.

In sum, the grotesque in Melville imposes on man the necessary distortion, a blurring of man's artificial focus on mysteries which won't yield to epistemologies. A similar subject is developed by S. T. Ryan in 'The Gothic Formula of "Bartelby"' (*ArQ*). The contemporaneity of 'Bartelby' is explained by the adherence of its story form to a traditional Gothic formula, which is in turn related to the balance between surface reality and epistemological terror in J. C. Oates, John Gardner, Kosinski, and other contemporary writers. Bartelby's tale, like that of Poe's Roderick Usher, depends largely on Gothic tradition for the connotations attached to its language, development of character, setting, and plot. But Melville's story diverges from Poe's in a greater realistic displacement of Gothic elements, suggesting that 'Bartelby' may occupy a significant place in the development of later Gothic fictions.

The Body Impolitic by R. M. Blau[54] is an interpretation of Melville's *Typee, White Jacket, Moby-Dick*, and *Pierre*. The aim is to determine Melville's growing awareness of the relations possible between self and world. Blau's conclusion is that each work records a failure to rise above false contraries so that ultimately Melville despairs of human coherence and the Romantic dream of unified being. The method combines dramatic

[53] *Herman Melville: An Annotated Bibliography, Vol. 1: 1846–1930*, ed. by B. Higgins. Boston, Mass.: G. K. Hall. pp. xvii + 397.

[54] *The Body Impolitic: A Reading of Four Novels*, by R. Blau. Amsterdam: Rodopi. 1979. pp. 214. Hfl. 45.

and discursive discourse in an effort, neither wholly successful nor devoid of pretentiousness, to formulate the argument. More extravagant is G. M. Sweeney's 'Melville's Smoky Humor: Fire-Lighting in *Typee*' (*ArQ*). The description of Kory-Kory's native method of kindling a flame for Tommo's pipe is, at a level just subliteral, 'an amazingly graphic description of masturbation'. Though the scene is said to have links with the book's satiric themes and with revelations of Tommo's character, the auto-erotic episode is advanced more with a view to multiplying instances of Melville's aggressive sexual humour. 'Melville's *Typee*: Fact, Fiction, and Esthetics' (*ArQ*) is examined by M. Clark. The critical debate over whether *Typee* is fact or fiction, chronicle or novel, is largely irrelevant; its appeal as fiction can be accounted for only in terms of the aesthetic organisation imposed on it by the narrator, Tommo. Though undeniably a record of experience (whether Melville's or Tommo's), *Typee* succeeds as imaginative literature because the narrative is shaped by Tommo's 'esthetic' perception of his own experience, thus implying that 'his perceptions are of equal importance to the "facts" themselves'.

M. L. D'Avanzo has a much smaller but more precise point in ' "A Bower in the Arsacides" and Solomon's Temple' (*ArQ*). Ishmael's whimsical digression in Chapter 102, 'A Bower in the Arsacides', describes the measurements of a whale skeleton found in Tranque in the Solomon Islands. Aside from the central biblical association with the Jonah story, the chapter uses the Temple of Solomon as its dominant biblical image. The ironic treatment given the description of the skeleton's exact measurements, associated with the exact measurements of Solomon's Temple, suggests that Melville is parodying human efforts at understanding empirically the dimensions of 'the phantom that is God'. In a related vein is Nancy Roundy's 'Present Shadows: Epistemology in Melville's "Benito Cereno" ' (*ArQ*). Using Ishmael's parable of the whale heads as model, Roundy discusses Captain Delano and Benito Cereno as the opposed epistemological types of Melville's story. Delano, the representative of Locke's empiricism and optimism, is an acute observer of sensible fact, but remains incapable of the imaginative explorations required of him while aboard the *San Dominick*. Tottering on the edge of sanity, Cereno is nearly incapable of empirical judgment, but as representative of Kantian imagination retains the ability to read metaphors and to extract from perceivable fact a transcendental significance. Neither epistemological position is adequate in itself and, like Ishmael's whale heads, both are necessary for a balanced mode of perception. Another treatment is T. D. Zlatic's ' "Benito Cereno": Melville's "Back-Handed-Well-Knot" ' (*ArQ*). As in *The Confidence-Man*, the reader is forced to question his own conception of morality by comparing it with the value-system of the central character, Captain Delano. His faith and charity, when confronted with the inverted moral order of the *San Dominick*, become a form of credulity inadequate to the necessary recognition of human malevolence. Hence, the reader must either adopt a cynicism greater than Delano's (thereby denying the Captain's traditional morality of rational benevolence), or acquiesce in accepting the disastrous consequences of Delano's amiable optimism. Neither alternative – acceptance or rejection of Delano's values – is satisfactory, but Melville means to propose by this a satiric rather than a nihilistic ambiguity: the unravelling of Melville's 'knot' does not lead to a clear distinction of good and evil, but to a differentiation and redefinition of the degrees of morality. A similar puzzle is explored by M. Q. Cheikin, in 'Captain Vere: Darkness Made Visible' (*ArQ*). The ambiguities of *Billy Budd* centre around Melville's attitude toward Vere's act of condemnation: is Billy's execution to be affirmed as just, or is Vere – for Melville – of the devil's party? Melville's presentation of characters follows a sequence from Billy to Claggart which suggests that a moral hierarchy is implicit in the order of presentation. Vere is introduced at the latter end of the moral spectrum just before Claggart, shares more fully in Claggart's depravity than in Billy's innocence, and is therefore guilty by association. Although his rational nature allows him to contemplate a 'transcendent act' of mercy, Vere's darker side will out, and Billy is destroyed not by Claggart, but by 'the evil lying dormant in an ostensibly good man'.

T. A. Tenney has amassed 'Mark Twain: A Reference Guide, Second Annual Supplement' (*ALR*) to the guide published in 1977; the items are annotated. C. L. Anderson's 'Mark Twain in Sweden: An Interview and Commentary' (*ALR*) is his translation of a Swedish newspaper interview with Twain in 1899. Edgar M. Branch relates ' "The Babes In The Wood": Artemus Ward's "Double Health" to Mark Twain' (*PMLA*). Branch's article reproduces a reasonably accurate speaking text of Artemus Ward's comical oration 'The Babes in the Wood'. Branch finds that Ward had considerable influence on the growth of Mark Twain's comical art. Ward was helpful in aiding Twain in publication, in strengthening Twain's determination to be a humorist, and in furnishing Twain with a fine example of both technique and subject matter in topical burlesque and platform speaking. Of a quite different order is H. Hawkins's 'Mark Twain's Involvement With the Congo Reform Movement: "A Fury of Generous Indignation" ' (*NEQ*). Mark Twain's participation in the Congo reform movement was his final anti-imperialist effort. This is an account based on Twain's essays and letters concerning the Congo reform movement.

S. J. Kahn's *Mark Twain's Mysterious Stranger*[55] carefully examines the two versions (the older Paine-Duneka one and the current Gibson edition) of the tales in order to attack the former version. He argues trenchantly for the literary differences between 'The Chronicle of Young Satan' and 'No. 44', for the essential consistency and coherence of the latter, and for its being a unique instance of Twain's mastery of satire. D. Welland's *Mark Twain in England*[56] examines Twain's relations with his British publisher Chatto & Windus, the reception of his works in England, and, less directly, Twain's experiences in England. The treatment is careful, informative, and insightful. Despite an unpardonable editorial lapse by the journal, E. J. Burde's 'Mark Twain: The Writer As Pilot' (*PMLA*) is most interesting. Burde examines the influence of Twain's piloting experiences on the Mississippi on his development, both literary and emotional, as a writer. Burde finds that Twain's complex and sometimes contradictory feelings about his days as a steamboat pilot provide valuable insights into Twain's

[55] *Mark Twain's Mysterious Stranger: A Study of the Manuscript Texts*, by S. Kahn. Columbia, Mo.: U. of Missouri P. pp. xii + 252. $15.

[56] *Mark Twain in England*, by D. Welland. Atlantic Highlands, N.J.: Humanities P. pp. 267. $20.

imagination and identity problems. Burde sees the significance of Twain's piloting experiences as a factor in his entire creative career and plans to investigate further this relationship in the full context of Clemens' work.

Everett Carter considers 'The Meaning of "A Connecticut Yankee"' (*AL*) and asserts that Twain felt that the nineteenth century, technology and all, was better than the past. He proposes that Twain approved of Hank, notwithstanding his destructive peccadillos: he is humane, his investment in progress worthy, and he is committed to American liberalism and progress rather than to the European past. A more speculative treatment is S. B. Girgus' 'Conscience in Connecticut: *Civilization and Its Discontents* in Twain's Camelot' (*NEQ*). He discusses connections between Twain and Freud, and Twain's apparent life-long struggle with a guilty conscience. He uses Twain's story 'The Facts Concerning the Recent Carnival of Crime in Connecticut', to begin his probe of Twain's model of conscience and its relationship to culture. Girgus finds that Twain anticipates Freud's 'novel idea' concerning the way conscience most afflicts the virtuous rather than the sinful. He goes on to examine *A Connecticut Yankee in King Arthur's Court* and how the relationship between technology, civilisation, and conscience is handled by Twain in an essentially Freudian manner. J. I. Fischer considers 'Mark Twain, Mount Tabor, and the Triumph of Art' (*SoR*). Fischer discusses the possibility that Twain has a pattern of writing on two levels: 1) a single consciously-held philosophic idea and 2) a feeling reaction to ideas done unconsciously and independent of his conscious intellect. Fischer has chosen 'Mount Tabor and the Prodigal Son' because it was later revised into *Innocents Abroad* and this pattern can be traced through the revisions, for the parable of the Prodigal Son can be seen as Twain's blend of artist and philosopher. R. Tuerk examines 'Appearance and Reality in Mark Twain's "Which Was the Dream?" "The Great Dark" and "Which Was It?"' (*IQ*) and concludes the author consistently refuses to make facile distinctions between dream and reality, probably because he cannot ultimately differentiate them.

E. Moers' *Harriet Beecher Stowe and American Literature*[57] is devoted to arguing the greatness of *Uncle Tom's Cabin* as a novel. More specifically, it details most interestingly the novel's realism, its strain of black humour, and its indebtedness to Frederick Douglass. Lawrence Buell finds 'Calvinism Romanticized: Harriet Beecher Stowe, Samuel, and *The Minister's Wooing*' (*ESQ*). Buell is concerned with investigating the impact of conservative Calvinist theological mainstream thought on the American literary renaissance of the mid-nineteenth century. He feels that too few scholars have investigated the impact of the theological opinions of such as Joseph Bellamy and Samuel Hopkins. To further such a study Buell here examines Stowe's 'The Minister's Wooing' with particular attention to the character and actions of the fictionalised minister, Samuel Hopkins, a successor of Edwards whom Buell feels acted as a reconciler of Calvinism and Romanticism in Stowe's book.

'The Presentation of Post-Revolutionary Law in *Woodcraft*: Another Perspective on the "Truth" of Simms's Fiction' (*MissQ*) by L. L. Hogue argues that Simms's concern with decorum and code has one of its prime

[57] *Harriet Beecher Stowe and American Literature*, by E. Moers. Hartford, Conn.: Stowe-Day Foundation. pp. 47. pb $4.

sources in the law and that this is most fully exemplified in *Woodcraft* where it contributes to theme, structure, character, and comic relief. J. E. Kibler takes a look at 'Simms as Naturalist: Lowcountry Landscape in His Revolutionary Novels' (*MissQ*) and concludes that Simms had a sizeable familiarity with the blackwater swamp area of South Carolina; he showed himself to be not merely a writer of impossible romances but one with strong powers of observation and able to draw plausible conclusions about man's relation to nature. *Richard Malcolm Johnston*, the Southern local colourist, best remembered as the author of *Dukesborough Tales*, is shrewdly placed in his literary and cultural context by B. Hitchcock[58].

W. M. Armstrong has produced a carefully researched and meticulously documented biography of E. L. Godkin, the founder of *The Nation*[59]. Godkin emerges as a man of his time, a representative mugwump social critic, whose strengths entailed weaknesses that prevented him from coping or comprehending fully the technological changes and their ramifications taking place around him as the century moved to a close. R. B. Bickley Jr provides a useful overview of *Joel Chandler Harris*[60] and his career as humorist, journalist, short story writer, and novelist. Both biographical and critical portions are competently done, though the claim for Harris's complexity and rhetorical subtlety is not sustained or developed in any profound degree. Bickley is aware, as he shows, of the sociological and psychological approaches of critics like Rubin, Dauner, Glazier and others, but he does little to extend or deepen their perceptions.

J. W. Tuttleton's *Thomas Wentworth Higginson*[61] is an introduction to the life and works of the radical reformer, abolitionist, solider, author, and critic. It will be of use to those not needing the more detailed treatments of Edelstein and Wells. In 'The Tempered Romanticism of John Muir' (*WAL*) H. P. Simonson discusses Muir's Calvinist background as in conflict with his Darwinian, Emersonian, and Wordsworthian education. He calls Muir 'perhaps the last important [Romantic] of our nineteenth century national literature' and notes that while Muir could apprehend the world in a romantic way, achieving a spiritual union with nature, he was hesitant to write about himself until late in life, when his journals take on a Calvinist tone, pointing to 'a world that nature does not symbolize'.

D. A. Sears has written a brief but lucid account of John Neal's literary career as poet, novelist, short story writer, and essayist[62]. Though the nature of the volume permits no more than a survey, Sears judiciously indicates the energy and strength as well as the flawed and trite character of Neal's tumultuous productions. Particularly valuable are his suggestions concerning Neal's anticipations of later American developments in fiction, notably of self-parody, mixed styles, linguistic vigour, and controversial themes. Like Neal, John Hay dissipated his energies in a wide range of

[58] *Richard Malcolm Johnston*, by B. Hitchcock. Boston, Mass.: G. K. Hall. pp. 162. $9.95.

[59] *E. L. Godkin: A Biography*, by W. Armstrong. Albany, N.Y.: State U. of New York P. pp. xvii + 287. $33.

[60] *Joel Chandler Harris*, by R. B. Bickley Jr. Boston, Mass.: G. K. Hall. pp. 168 $8.95.

[61] *Thomas Wentworth Higginson*, by J. W. Tuttleton. Boston, Mass.: G. K. Hall. pp. 172. $9.50.

[62] *John Neal*, by D. A. Sears. Boston, Mass.: G. K. Hall. pp. 154. $9.95.

activities, public and private. R. L. Gale is the first to concentrate largely upon Hay's literary activities, though of necessity he devotes several chapters to the life[63]. He concludes that only the *Pike County Ballads* with their skilful diction, deft character sketches, and local colourist affinities merit attention in the history of American poetry. His fiction, Gale suggests, may be implicitly more significant as anticipating developments in the novel of manners, and, strikingly enough, naturalism, but it too was not pursued. The most notable thing about Gale's study possibly is the shrewd yet sympathetic way in which he details Hay's ambivalent involvement with the American Dream. In the same series is E. H. Foster's account of the life and prolific writing career of *Susan and Anna Warner*[64]. Foster recognises the literary limitations of his subject, but provides a useful sketch of the sisters' socio-cultural significance. He is particularly valuable in his treating of their contribution in *The Wide, Wide World* and other works to the rise of local colour writing, and his correcting of H. W. Papashvily's view that they were early espousers of feminist views.

T. A. Gullason's 'Stephen Crane's "The Wreck of the *New Era*": the First Known Printing' (*ALR*) corrects R. W. Stallman's attribution of the first printing by citing its appearance with minor changes in *The Biblio* for September, 1923. L. D. Linder provides the text for previously unpublished work in '"The Ideal and the Real" and "Brer Washington's Consolation": Two Little Known Stories by Stephen Crane?' (*ALR*).

Several critics consider aspects of Crane's canon. Robert Shulman examines 'Community, Perception, and the Development of Stephen Crane: From *The Red Badge* to "The Open Boat"' (*AL*). In *The Red Badge* the individual is isolated; in 'The Open Boat' men function together to confront the storm. Crane's developing vision is that man, unable to rely on himself alone or on an unknowable nature, must experience the community of man. The epistemological problems are rendered less important than the shared knowledge that man does have, incomplete as it is, for the integrity of human perception is not qualified, in Crane, by the impenetrability of the unknown. J. Robertson writes on 'Stephen Crane, Eastern Outsider in the West and Mexico' (*WAL*). Robertson proposes that the myth of the American West (no more specifically defined in the article than 'the neo-romanticism of Remington, Roosevelt and Wister') in Crane's Western stories is a medium for the expression of his essentially ironic perception of man's insignificance in the indifferent universe. The outsider, for whom the West is largely a literary creation, through confronting the myth of heroism and perceiving reality demythicised, learns that his real heroism comes from accepting his insignificance. Both outsider and Westerner are humbled and ennobled by their confrontation of the actuality of the West as unknown wilderness. Robertson's definition of the myth of the West is not specific, and he does not explore how the theme of reciprocal human responsibility, implicit in a story like 'The Blue Hotel', informs and qualifies Crane's ironic vision. In 'The Prophetic City in Stephen Crane's 1893 *Maggie*' (*ALR*), T. A. Gullason admits the novel's old-fashioned and outdated aspects, but argues that it

[63] *John Hay*, by R. L. Gale. Boston, Mass.: G. K. Hall. pp. 164. $9.50.

[64] *Susan and Anna Warner*, by E. H. Foster. Boston, Mass.: G. K. Hall. pp. 138. $9.95.

was the image and reality of the city which made the work seminal as the experimental, anti-novel of its day, revealing a City of unreality and a modern American tragedy.

Lillian Faderman's 'Female Same-sex Relationships in Novels by Longfellow, Holmes, and James' (*NEQ*) examines 'divested of our contemporary attitudes, the treatment of same-sex love in three nineteenth-century American novels – Henry Wadsworth Longfellow's *Kavanagh* (1849), Oliver Wendell Holmes's *A Mortal Antipathy* (1885) and Henry James's *The Bostonians* (1885)'. She argues that love-relationships between women were viewed with much less concern in the nineteenth century. The apparent lack of serious concern over deep same-sex relationships between women in the nineteenth cenutury was based on the lack of threat to society since most women had to marry anyway for economic purposes. Leon Edel's 'Portrait of the Artist as an Old Man' (*ASch*) consists of biographic sketches of Tolstoy, Henry James, and Yeats who are used to suggest some of the ways in which each overcame the crisis of age. Tolstoy's art ends in repudiation and despair; James and Yeats both emerge from periods of latent depression to end their lives with a reaffirmation of art. In 'Lady Into Horse: James's "Lady Barberina" and *Gulliver's Travels,* Part IV' (*JNT*), A. R. Tintner argues that 'in addition to the basic conceit of pitting horses against man. . .there are specific details in "Lady Barberina" that suggest that James was using Swift's tale as a model or a parallel'. Tintner first establishes that James is using the 'metaphor of horse-trading to analogize the Anglo-American marriage market' in 'Lady Barberina'. She finds proof of this in the names of the characters such as Lady 'Barb', Barb being a horse introduced into England by the crusaders, and figures of speech, puns, and so on. She then makes a sustained comparison of James's 'Lady Barberina' and Swift's *Gulliver's Travels,* Part IV 'A Voyage to the Country of the Houyhnhnms'. Ralph F. Bogardus studies 'Henry James and the Art of Illustration' (*CentR*) by investigating James' seeming ambivalence toward illustrations. He concludes that James was actually quite clear in his opinion of illustrations: 'he admired the work of certain illustrators and still believed that illustration was a threat to good literature'. Interestingly enough, James seemed to be more approving of photography in connection with literature because it did not so much interfere with the text and the photographer is not as limited as the artist in his own freedom.

Susan Wolstenholme writes on 'Possession and Personality: Spiritualism in *The Bostonians*' (*AL*). The literal occult in this novel merely stands for James's vision that the human mind is a void unto itself, merely made up of other personalities and sociological influences upon which it is functionally dependent. The chaos and formlessness of Bostonian culture moves at random, haphazardly plucking bits of Verena Tarrant to the surface. Wolstenholme concludes that, in *this* novel, James is stating that no meaningful conclusions may be drawn from studying the individual and the forces by which he or she is possessed. In 'The Ambassadorial Motif in *The Ambassadors*' (*JNT*) J. A. Higgins discusses the visual and diplomatic representation of a character or appearance to another. This enables her to see Strether's renunciation as an understandable act of self-acceptance. William R. Goetz in 'The Allegory of Representation in The Tragic Muse'

(*JNT*) argues that *The Tragic Muse*'s partial failure is due to its being James's first use of the allegorical mode while also being the story of his discovery of that mode. It marks the end of his pictorial phase and introduces his concern with the dramatic. Both phases and their tensions are dramatised therein. 'The "High Felicity" of Comradeship: A New Reading of *Roderick Hudson*' (*ALR*) by R. K. Martin argues that James is right to call the novel the drama of Rowland Mallet's consciousness, for it focuses on a homosexual relationship whose tragic ending is integral to the development of Rowland's consciousness and his loss of the ability to feel. J. Snyder in 'James's Girl Huck: *What Maisie Knew*' (*ALR*) strainedly invokes *Huck Finn* in order to pursue an interpretation of the James novel as a study of a child's moral and psychological development into a responsible adult, and as a crucial preparation for his later treatments of the issues involved in moral success or failure.

Henry James and Germany, by E. A. Hovanec[65], is a straightforward but pedestrian examination of James's contact with Germany and things German, his opinions, and his fictive renderings of them. The conclusion is that James's recoil from Germany and Germans was because their physical and spiritual aggressiveness represented traits he had found in the America he had left and also that lurked subconsciously in himself. B. Lee has produced a very slender volume on *Henry James*[66] stressing the primacy of James's effort to comprehend and judge his civilisation's values. His starting point is Lewis's Adamic myth, and his antagonist all who seek to impose philosophical theory on James, by whom he seems to mean principally Quentin Anderson. The career from *The Europeans* to *The Ivory Tower* he views as a parabola tracing the changes in American civilisation from 'spiritual lightness and vigour' to parasitic and predatory vulgarity and crudity prompted by an acquisitive mercantilism. Lee's thesis would appear to betray a lack of familiarity with James criticism since the mid-1950s work of Bewley, Lewis, and Anderson. This together with the brevity of treatment of individual works makes it of limited value, though the civilisation versus barbarism motif is of central importance.

A Rhetoric of Literary Character by M. D. Springer[67] approaches the general question of the nature of fictional character largely through the women of Henry James and especially those appearing in the novellas. An opening chapter defines character empirically but not oppressively in the manner of the Chicago School stressing that identity is revealed primarily through acts, speeches, and decisions and only reinforced by the devices of description and diction. Subsequent chapters take up the kinds of rhetorical functions of character (suppressed, extra, frame, main, and didactic) with specific reference to such works as *The Turn of the Screw*, *The Jolly Corner*, and *The Aspern Papers*. More thematic than rhetorical, D. J. Schneider's *The Crystal Cage*[68] argues in an interesting fashion that the figure in the Jamesian carpet is that of the free spirit's efforts to escape

[65] *Henry James and Germany*, by E. Hovanec. Amsterdam: Rodopi, 1979. pp. 149. $16.50.

[66] *The Novels of Henry James*, by B. Lee. Edward Arnold. pp. ix + 121. £5.50.

[67] *A Rhetoric of Literary Character: Some Women of Henry James*, by M. Springer. Chicago, Ill.: U. of Chicago P. pp. vii + 241. $17.

[68] *The Crystal Cage: Adventures of the Imagination in the Fiction of Henry James*, by D. Schneider. Lawrence: Regents P. of Kansas. pp. vii + 189. $13.

the enslavement wrought by the world in a variety of internal and external forms. Schneider begins by sketching James's sense of life by which he means the sense of detachment and emphasis on the variety of the imagination as well as passivity surrounded by active aggressors. This pattern is then traced in gradually expanding terms as it operates in character, action, and imagery. He stresses the role of the divided self in the former, the entrapments of convention, career, convictions, and psychic need in the second, and the images of aggression, appearances, and the cage in the last.

P. Merivale traces resemblances between Henry James's *The Turn of the Screw* (1898) and *The Sacred Fount* (1901) and Witold Gombrowicz' *Pornografia* (1960) and *Cosmos* (1965) (*PMLA*). She finds that these four books use familiar Gothic conventions such as ghosts, doubles, haunted houses, and psychological sadism to make serious statements about the Romantic position that the poet 'is accursed and the artistic process at best is morally dubious'. She further finds that these works are 'metaphysical detective stories and self-reflexive texts in the contemporary mode. as well as nineteenth-century Gothic artist parables. 'Their heroes manipulate other innocent characters into their own fictions: the creation of the texts is thus seen as a morally tainted. . .endeavor'. D. Gervais' *Flaubert and Henry James*[69] accepts the radical difference between the two authors and by focusing largely on *Madame Bovary* and *The Portrait of a Lady* goes on to argue that James' imagination, unlike that of Flaubert, seeks to avoid tragedy even when confronting an incipiently tragic subject. It does so because 'a certain intellectual duplicity is necessary to James if he is to bring his most personal feelings into the sphere of art, an impression of half-articulated depths which he is as bent on concealing as confronting'. Another comparative exercise is S. Donadio's *Nietzsche, Henry James, and the Artistic Will*[70], which argues that both writers found only in art the capability for creating values and endowing with meaning and, further, that both ground their views in the Emersonian notion of belief. For Donadio, James's familiarity, or lack thereof, with Nietzsche is irrelevant.

Henry James and the Experimental Novel by S. Perosa[71] argues that James's middle period consisted of two phases separated by the watershed of the theatre experiences of the early 1890s. Only the work of the second phase is unequivocally and avowedly experimental, for in the former the stress falls on subject and theme rather than techniques such as those of the scenic method and the limited point of view. The notion inherently has a good deal to recommend it, particularly since it allows us to chart more carefully and discriminatingly the emergence of modern experimentalism from the traditional nineteenth-century novel with its illustrative and pictorial method. Perosa writes incisively and well and shows an easy comparative command of the genre. Unfortunately, with the exception of *The Sacred Fount*, he devotes only half-a-dozen pages or so to each

[69] *Flaubert and Henry James: A Study in Contrasts*, by D. Gervais. Macmillan. pp. xii + 240. $22.50.

[70] *Nietzsche, Henry James, and the Artistic Will*, by S. Donadio. New York: O.U.P. pp. xvi + 347. $15.95.

[71] *Henry James and the Experimental Novel*, by S. Perosa. Charlottesville, Va.: U. of Virginia P. pp. vii + 219. $11.95.

of the other novels of the second phase, which is scarcely sufficient. At the same time, he devotes roughly half the book either to minor works such as *The Whole Family* or to later experimental works (*The Sense of the Past* and *The Ivory Tower*) which fall outside the concern of his central thesis.

T. F. O'Donnell offers 'Harold Frederick's "Cordelian and the Moon" Text, with Comment' (*ALR*) and claims it is important in showing a long, though tentative, step toward *The Damnation of Theron Ware*. The chief concern of J. Tavernier-Courbin's 'Towards the City: Howell's Characterization in *A Modern Instance*' (*MFS*) is with his vision of the city and the ways in which its characters appear as paradigms of its major aspects. A. F. Stein admits the inferior nature of his subject in 'A New Look at Howells's "A Fearful Responsibility" ' (*MLQ*). But he argues it is important not merely because it is Howells's first bleak work but also because it reveals his profound doubts about his essentially pragmatic fictive vision. An editorial blunder has resulted in two articles on Howells having their titles reversed. One by W. L. Stull entitled 'The Battle of the *Century*: W. D. Howells, "Henry James, Jr", and the English' (*ALR*) recounts the transatlantic battle between advocates of realism and of romance touched off by Howells's 1883 essay on James. The other, by T. Wortham, is 'W. D. Howells's 1899 Midwest Lecture Tour: What the Letters Tell' (*ALR*). It is essentially a correction of some of the suppositions and errors made by R. Rowlette in several essays on the same subject as a result of his apparently not consulting some fifty letters from Howells to his wife in the autumn of 1899, which are presently housed in the Houghton Library at Harvard.

After an initial biographical chapter, Hamlin Garland's main contributions to American fiction, which are grouped in accordance with subject matter and theme, are surveyed by J. B. McCullough[72]. The bibliography includes a useful list of Garland's articles, short fiction, and poetry and their place of first publication. J. C. Edwards takes up 'A Question of Priorities: Hamlin Garland and the Dilemmas of War' (*IllQ*) and sketches the novelist's hesitant, then energetic association with the 1914 preparedness advocates and his relieved disassociation following the Armistice. In 'Robert Herrick's post-War Literary Theories and *Waste*' (*ALR*) P. Franklin tries to show that the novel was influenced by its author's awareness of the time's trends to use autobiographical material, introspective or personal psychology, and allegory or parable.

In 'Frank Norris: A Biographical Essay' (*ALR*) J. R. McElrath Jr considers early newspaper and periodical information, the works themselves, and early posthumous writing about Norris as potential sources for modifying the biographical views of Franklin Walker. S. Tatum argues for 'Norris's Debt in "Lauth" to Lemattre's "On the Transfusion of Blood" ' (*ALR*). Very briefly D. Graham discusses 'Frank Norris and Les Jaunes: Architectural Criticism and Aesthetic Values' (*ALR*) and argues that their architectural values correspond to Norris's notion of the novel as being a matter of simplicity, naturalness, and harmony. This subject is part of his *The Fiction of Frank Norris*[73] which focuses not on his contributions to

[72] *Hamlin Garland*, by J. B. McCullough. Boston, Mass.: G. K. Hall. pp. 143. $9.50.

[73] *The Fiction of Frank Norris*, by D. Graham. Columbia: U. of Missouri P. pp. 172. $13.

naturalism but on his use of aesthetic documentation, that is, reference and allusion to art of all sorts. This he traces to a youthful interest continued into his San Francisco days in the 1890s when he associated with Les Jaunes. The book concentrates on the four major novels and demonstrates how this pre-occupation becomes a technique that not only creates 'a sense of specific density' but also is 'a method of characterization and a mode of symbolic narration'. The view is interesting and important if not original, but it is misplaced in connection with *Vandover*, at least as formulated, and is of no help in discriminating between or explaining the differences between the minor, popular works and those on which Norris' reputation rests.

4. Drama

James A. Herne by J. Perry[74] provides a full-scale biography of one of the most versatile and influential figures in nineteenth-century drama. His efforts to sophisticate the stage of his day through his efforts as director, producer, and author are traced in this careful yet lively study. F. Shuffelton hears 'The Voice of History: Thomas Godfrey's *Prince of Parthia* and Revolutionary America' (*EAL*). In this examination of the first play written by an American-born author Shuffelton probes the significance of the author's choice of subject matter. The reasons for Godfrey's choices have a lot to do with democracy and despotic power despite his use of an oriental setting for his play. Shuffelton finds that Godfrey produces a dramatised symbol of tyranny in his image of a monarch and asks what course an honest man shall take. In 'Royall Tyler's "Bold Example": *The Contrast* and the English Comedy of Manners' (*EAL*), D. T. Siebert Jr is challenging the assumptions upon which most criticism of *The Contrast*, America's first native comedy to be professionally produced, are based. These assumptions are: that *The Contrast* displays no formal originality and that the theme of the contrast between European and American values is an attempt to hold up American values as superior. Siebert finds it hard to believe that Tyler would use a form so at odds with the theme of the work. He also finds no evidence that the play actually holds up American values over European ones, but rather reveals the contrast between those who try to be something they are not and those who are themselves.

'The Englightenment View of Myth and Barlow's *Vision of Columbus*' (*EAL*) by R. D. Richardson Jr discusses how the eighteenth century looked at myth/mythology. He then examines Barlow's play and finds that it has a 'complex and intentional mythic structure'. Richardson believes that Barlow was trying, in effect, to create a myth for Americans to show that they need not look to Europe for their myths. *Vision of Columbus* has, he says, all the ingredients of myth: vision, prophecy, founding a new world, and so on. Jay Martin charts 'The Province of Speech: American Drama in the Eighteenth Century' (*EAL*). Martin examines eighteenth-century drama as the 'acte' of American society. He gives numerous examples of plays which set the example for Americans in matters of manners, social standing, and political justice. His examples run from 'The Masque of Alfred the Great', and 'The Prince of Parthia', to later, more

[74] *James A. Herne: The American Ibsen*, by J. Perry. Chicago, Ill.: Nelson-Hall. pp. ix + 343. $17.95.

political plays such as 'The Death of General Montgomery' and 'The Defeat'. Martin concludes: 'In the eighteenth century, then, the American drama started to represent various visions of the driving forces behind the making and reworking of relationships that would become the chief concerns in the fiction of Hawthorne and Melville. The art of eighteenth-century American drama created a network of assumptions, a series of significances, in short, a reality for men during 1740–1800, by improvising systems of possible response and perimeters of rationality for them.'

XVIII

American Literature: The Twentieth Century

JOHN B. VICKERY

With the assistance of T. GIANNOTTI, N. MUIR, and J. C. VICKERY

1. General

Bibliographies of current articles are published quarterly in *AL* and annually in the summer supplement of *AQ*. *JML* has an annual bibliographical issue and *TCL* provides a running bibliography in each issue. Related materials are a series of reference guides[1] devoted to a single author and consisting of an annotated list of books and articles about the work. Currently available are R. G. Noreen on Saul Bellow, N. C. Joyner on Edwin Arlington Robinson, B. M. Keegan on Joseph Heller, C. S. Abbott on Marianne Moore, L. Wagner on William Carlos Williams, and J. Bryer and M. Hatem on William Styron. And finally, N. Baldwin, and S. L. Meyers have compiled a useful descriptive catalogue of William Carlos Williams' manuscripts and letters in the Lockwood Memorial Library at the State University of New York at Buffalo[2]. It should enable Williams' scholars to use that most valuable collection more expeditiously and efficiently.

L. P. Blouin, organises her bibliography of May Sarton[3] into two parts. One itemises Sarton's work by genre; the other provides a list of critical and biographical books and articles and reviews organised according to specific titles. All items save the references to her poetry are annotated. Essentially the same format is followed in G. Lane and M. Stevens, *Sylvia Plath: A Bibliography*[4], except that no annotations are provided while several appendixes are included. Two of America's premier detective story writers, Raymond Chandler and Dashiell Hammett, are the respective subjects of precise, highly professional descriptive bibliographies by M. J.

[1] *Saul Bellow: A Reference Guide*, ed. by R. Noreen. pp. vii + 149. $18; *Edwin Arlington Robinson: A Reference Guide*, ed. by N. Joyner. pp. xv + 203. $22; *Joseph Heller: A Reference Guide*, ed. by B. Keegan. pp. xxxiv + 141. $24; *Marianne Moore: A Reference Guide*, ed. by C. Abbott. pp. ix + 133. $18; *William Carlos Williams: A Reference Guide*, ed. by L. Wagner. pp. xv + 155. $18; *William Styron: A Reference Guide*, ed. by J. Bryer and M. Hatem. pp. ix + 143. $18; all Boston, Mass.: G. K. Hall.

[2] *The Manuscripts and Letters of William Carlos Williams*, ed. by N. Baldwin and S. Meyers. Boston, Mass.: G. K. Hall. pp. xxxi + 333. $30.

[3] *May Sarton: A Bibliography*, ed. by L. P. Blouin. Metuchen, N. J.: Scarecrow P. 1977. pp. 263. $10.

[4] *Sylvia Plath: A Bibliography*, ed. by G. Lane and M. Stevens. Metuchen, N.J.: Scarecrow P. pp. v + 144. $7.

Bruccoli and R. Layman[5]. Both establish the canon of the author and provide facsimiles of title pages and the like, as well as important information about their writing for the movies.

W. Contento has amassed an *Index to Science Fiction*[6] in order to provide a means of locating stories printed in anthologies and collections. It possesses an author index, a story index and a listing of books by title. Of a more historical order is L. Del Rey's *The World of Science Fiction: 1926–1976*[7] which divides the development of the genre into five ages or phases ranging from wonder through acceptance to rebellion. The treatment is informative and clear though not particularly sophisticated. *The Critical Temper*, vol. 4, edited by Martin Tucker[8] et. al., is a supplement to the preceding three volumes which consisted of brief excerpts from modern criticism of all the periods of English and American literature. This volume updates the others by supplying critical samples from the past decade. It is of little apparent value to scholars.

Crosscurrents of Criticism is not quite so inclusive as the title suggests[9]. Actually it is a collection of essays edited by P. Heins that appeared in *The Horn Book Magazine* between 1968 and 1977. This origin means that all the pieces are focused on children's literature in one way or another. Some of them are too short or too personal to rise much above the ephemeral. Others are more substantial. Jane Langton has some sensible analytic things to say about kinds of fantasy for children and the editor struggles to provide some useful and meaningful terms and criteria for the criticism of the genre. A special number or part of it has been devoted to American Literature by *YES*. Essays by various English and American contributors deal with such topics as the expatriates (M. Bradbury), Melville, (L. Ziff), Williams (S. Tapscott), Pound (S. Fender), Lowell (C. Butler), and Ashbery and O'Hara (M. Perloff). The pieces by Tapscott, Fender, and Perloff are particularly valuable contributions to scholarship.

M. Cowley's *And I Worked at the Writer's Trade*[10] is a series of essays which informally, personally, and from the inside, sketch aspects of the literary history of America from World War I to 1978. Its use resides largely in its revelations of a professional writer's responses to individuals and socio-historical movements. *Tradition and Change in Jewish Experience*, edited by A. L. Jamison[11], consists of the B. G. Rudolph Lectures in Judaic Studies, one of which is offered annually. The only essay of immediate relevance is L. W. Schwartz's 'Mutations of Jewish Values in Contemporary Fiction', which deals briefly and generally with Bellow, Roth, Wallant,

[5] *Raymond Chandler: A Descriptive Bibliography*, ed. by M. J. Bruccoli. Pittsburgh, Pa.: U. of Pittsburgh P. 1979. pp. xiii + 146. $17.50; *Dashiell Hammett: A Descriptive Bibliography*, ed. by R. Layman. Pittsburgh, Pa.: U. of Pittsburgh P. 1979. pp. xi + 185. $17.50.

[6] *Index to Science Fiction: Anthologies & Collections*, ed. by W. Contento. Boston, Mass.: G. K. Hall and Prior. pp. vii + 459. $28, £15.95.

[7] *The World of Science Fiction, 1926–1976*, by L. Del Rey. New York: Garland. 1979. pp. xi + 392. $15.

[8] *The Critical Temper, Vol. 4: Supplement, A Library of Literary Criticism*, ed. by M. Tucker et al. New York: Unger. pp. xv + 582. $35.

[9] *Crosscurrents of Criticism: Horn Book Essays, 1968–1977*, ed. by P. Heins. Boston, Mass.: Horn Book. pp. vii + 359. $12.50.

[10] *And I Worked at the Writer's Trade: Chapters of Literary History, 1918–1978*, by M. Cowley. New York: Penguin. pp. 276. $3.95.

[11] *Tradition and Change in Jewish Experience*, ed. by A. Jamison. Syracuse, N.Y.: Syracuse U.P. pp. xi + 272. pb $5.95.

Singer, and Levine. A. R. Huseboe and W. Geyer have edited *Where the West Begins*[12], a collection of essays on Middle Border literature. It includes studies of Rolvaag, Garland, Cather, Momaday, three on Manfred as well as others on Scandinavian immigrant fiction and the like. *Essays in American Literature* edited by D. Pizer[13] is a memorial volume for the late R. P. Adams. There are essays on Poe, Twain, James, Henry Adams, and others including four on Faulkner. *Comic Relief* is a series of essays on contemporary American literary humour edited by S. B. Cohen[14]. It includes a definition of black humour by M. Schulz, and a group of general pieces on such topics as college, WASP humour, the urban tall tale, two interesting pieces on contemporary drama and poetry by R. Cohn, and J. Vernon, and treatments of Nabokov, Barth and Berger, Afro-American humour, science-fiction humour, southern humour as well as considerations of Bellow, Roth, and Mary McCarthy.

J. Fetterley's *The Resisting Reader*[15] approaches texts by Irving, Hawthorne, James, Hemingway, Fitzgerald, Faulkner, and Mailer from a feminist perspective conscious of alienation, exclusion, and manipulation from and by male-authored texts. Though the opening is shrill and simplistic ('Literature is political'), later analyses are often perceptive (for example, Nick Carraway's double standard, and *An American Dream* as both projection and parody). Central to this provocative and provoking book is the attempt to redress the critical imbalance with respect to *The Bostonians.*

Like a Brother, Like a Lover by G.-M. Sarotte[16] is an English translation of his 1976 study of homosexuality as a theme and force in the novel and drama from Melville to Baldwin. Beginning from Ferenczi's terminological discriminations, Sarotte takes up in turn the homosexual literary history; archetypes; theatre uses; settings, types, and threats; and concludes with an examination of latent forms in James, Fitzgerald, Hemingway, Bellow, London, and Mailer. The sociology is rather glib and the wide-ranging survey approach sometimes dissipates interest, but this is a useful thematic overview that carefully avoids sensationalising the issue. In a most curious study, *Narcissus and the Voyeur*, R. M. Maclean[17] argues that *Moby-Dick, Let Us Now Praise Famous Men*, and *Naked Lunch* as well as two European films 'make use of' John Locke, I. A. Richards, and Wittgenstein in developing aspects of an empirical epistemology. But since he also admits that he provides 'no historical argument' linking writers and philosophers, it is clear that he is the one making use of both to serve a strained thesis about the act and self-reflexive nature of reporting. L. D. Rubin Jr writes gracefully and insightfully in *The Wary Fugitives*[18] of

[12] *Where the West Begins*, ed. by A. Huseboe and W. Geyer. Sioux Falls. S.D.: Center for Western Studies. pp. 160. pb $4.50.

[13] *Essays in American Literature in Memory of Richard P. Adams*, ed. by D. Pizer. New Orleans: Tulane U.P. pp. xiii + 253.

[14] *Comic Relief: Humor in Contemporary American Literature*, ed. by S. B. Cohen. Urbana, Ill.: U. of Illinois P. pp. 339. $15.

[15] *The Resisting Reader: A Feminist Approach to American Fiction*, by J. Fetterley. Bloomington, Ind.: Indiana U.P. pp. xiii + 198. $12.50.

[16] *Like a Brother, Like a Lover: Male Homosexuality in the American Novel and Theatre from Herman Melville to James Baldwin*, by G.-M. Sarotte. New York: Doubleday. pp. 339. $10.

[17] *Narcissus and the Voyeur*, by R. Maclean. The Hague: Mouton. pp. vii + 239.

[18] *The Wary Fugitives: Four Poets and the South*, by L. D. Rubin Jr. Baton Rouge, La.: Louisiana State U.P. pp. xv + 376. $24.95.

John Crowe Ransom, Allan Tate, Donald Davidson, and Robert Penn Warren. He traces their involvement with and disengagement from agrarianism and its continuing impact upon their subsequent writing.

2. Poetry

Two anthologies of poetry are worth mentioning. The first, edited by E. B. Germain, collects under the title *English and American Surrealist Poetry*[19] samples from a number of poets ranging from the 1920s to the present, including many who are not ordinarily thought of surrealists. A lengthy introduction prefaces the collection, but there is no biographical information apart from dates of birth. The second is *Five American Poets*[20], edited by M. Schmidt and presents fairly generous samples of the work of Robert Haas, John Matthias, James McMichael, John Peck, and Robert Pinsky, all of whom studied with Yvor Winters at Stanford University.

Language and the Poet[21] by M. Borroff is a stylistic study of Frost, Stevens, and Marianne Moore. Starting from particular features of their poetic language – simplicity or variegation of diction and syntactic imbalance – she follows them out with a view to achieving understanding of rather than a comprehensive description of the styles in question. Her general conclusions are that all three poets achieve solemnity in part by virtue of their use of words alluding to or linked with Christian texts and teachings; and that each reacts to the figure of the poet in the 'high formal' tradition in distinctive ways. *The American Quest for a Supreme Fiction* by J. E. Miller Jr[22] is an ambitious book which seeks to trace or establish Whitman's legacy in the 'personal epic'. Authors covered include Stevens, Pound, Eliot, Williams, Crane, Olson, Berryman, and Ginsberg. The focus is on the deep personal and cultural involvement of these poets with Whitman rather than upon surface influences, for as Miller notes, the connections are seldom a matter of simple imitations. Yet the effort to deal with the Whitman legacy at the same time as with formal explorations of the genre of the long poem creates some significant difficulties. To deal adequately with the latter entails frequently dropping discussion of the former with the result that a loss of continuity ensues.

In *The American Moment*[23] G. Thurley argues that only with post-World War II did culture and poetry acquire its own centre of gravity and emerge from provincialism. Topics such as affluence, imagism, the avant-garde, and language are used to group poets from Wilbur and Lowell through Olson and Duncan to Wieners and Bly. Strangely enough, all, save Rexroth and Patchen, and Ginsberg, are said to have such lapses and incapacities that one is hard put to see wherein the new American poetic maturity actually lies. 'Impersonal Personalism: The Making of a Confes-

[19] *English and American Surrealist Poetry*, ed. by E. B. Germain. New York: Penguin. 1979. pp. 339. pb $3.95.

[20] *Five American Poets*, ed. by M. Schmidt. Manchester, Lancs.: Carcanet. 1979. pp. xii + 160 pb £3.25.

[21] *Language and the Poet*, by M. Borroff. Chicago, Ill.: U. of Chicago P. 1979. pp. ix + 198.

[22] *The American Quest for a Supreme Fiction: Whitman's Legacy in the Personal Epic*, by J. E. Miller Jr. Chicago, Ill.: U. of Chicago P. 1979. pp. 376. $20.

[23] *The American Moment: American Poetry in Mid Century*, by G. Thurley. New York: St. Martin's. pp. 249. $20.

sional Poetic' by S. K. Hoffman (*ELH*) recognises the problems involved in labelling such diverse poets, but argues that there are shared characteristics. These include the inclination to personalism and consciousness-building as well as elaborate making techniques and objectifications, both of which are shaped by the movement's time continuum extending as it does from the late 1930s to the Vietnam era. *Towards a New American Poetics* edited by E. Faas[24] is a combination of essays on and interviews with poets Olson, Duncan, Snyder, Creeley, Bly, and Ginsberg. In a polemical preamble Faas decries traditional Western aesthetics in favour of a new one, advocated and developed in one way or another by the above poets, that is based on 'a non-anthropocentric, a-teleological and frequently monistic understanding of life'.

Peter Easy considers 'The Treatment of American Indian Materials in Contemporary American Poetry' (*JAmS*). Noting that 'ethnopoetics' has become a legitimate term, embracing both the straight translation of original material and the use of Indian myth, etc., as the basis for original American poetry (notable borrowers including Rexroth, Rothenberg, Snyder, Gifford), Easy points out three major problems in the genre: inaccurate translations; material seen as a purely primitive entity not to be tampered with; no preservation of poems as poems of their own culture; and, concerning translations, a fuzzy linguistic accuracy. He concludes that ethnopoetics' importance as a movement will likely be as an influence, and not as it is often now, a kind of invasive appropriation and distortion of materials. Paul Breslin tells us 'How to Read the New Contemporary Poem' (*ASch*). The new poetry of the 1970s – W. S. Merwin, Robert Bly, James Wright, Galway Kinnell, Mark Strand, James Tate, and Charles Simic are the principal exponents – is informed by its borrowing of imagery from Jungian archetypes and its adherence to a conceptual model provided by the Jungian collective unconscious. The new poets, along with their predecessors the 'confessional' poets (Lowell, Ginsberg, Plath), are influenced in their attitude toward the self by the radicalism of the 1960s. The New Left 'psycho-politics' of Marcuse, R. D. Laing, and N. O. Brown attempts to relieve civilisation of its cultural guilt (over Vietnam, racial oppression, etc.) by jettisoning the ego as a repressive agency and welcoming instinct and unconscious motivation as salutary. Though influenced by this thinking, the confessional poets retain their hold on the self as an entity which interacts with reality; the new poets of the 1970s seem to reject the ego in favour of a collective unconscious which is most markedly identified by an absence of self. Jungianism, then, appears likely to drive the new poets into a blind alley of solipsism.

A. R. Ammons is seen by A. Holder[25] as a poet who variously seeks to assimilate the findings of science, to reconcile unity and diversity, order and motion, to maintain a process of openness to particulars, and to establish a poetic mode that democratises perception and consciousness into the linearity of continual thinking. G. Q. Arpin's slender volume takes up a better known poet in *The Poetry of John Berryman*[26], and argues,

[24] *Towards a New American Poetics*, ed. by E. Faas. Santa Barbara, Calif.: Black Sparrow P. pp. 296. $14.

[25] *A. R. Ammons*, by A. Holder. Boston, Mass.: G. K. Hall. pp. 179. $8.95.

[26] *The Poetry of John Berryman*, by G. Arpin. Port Washington, N.Y.: Kennikat. pp. 109. $7.95.

not very convincingly, that Berryman was always a modernist poet no matter how different the aspects of modernism that engaged him through his career. His style evolved in response to the Symbolist aesthetic, but he differs from it in that he and his poet-figures seek not an ideal realm of sensibility but a means of survival in a world of real difficulties. Though the bibliography is declaredly selective, it is difficult to believe that nothing after 1973 was of value to the author.

In 'Elizabeth Bishop's "Natural Heroism" ' (*CentR*), W. Spiegelman is looking at three types of Elizabeth Bishop's poems, all of which he finds 'tinged with her qualifying scepticism'. He is examining those poems which trace the outline of 'heroic situations and/or devices and then undercut or negate them. . .those which internalize an encounter or conflict and make learning a heroic process' and those 'in which the via negativa of denial implies Bishop's positive ("natural heroism") values'. Spiegelman is trying to aid understanding of Bishop's 'natural heroism' which he defines as 'a politely sceptical courage which neither makes outrageous demands on the world nor demurely submits to the world's own'.

A. Ford's *Robert Creeley*[27] is an introduction not only to the poetry but also the prose, which Ford himself prefers. Though the organisation of the book is slightly idiosyncratic, it economically, if with not overmuch originality, traces Creeley's relationship to New England, the tradition of American literature, and his involvement with the avante-garde movement for a quarter of a century. A somewhat similar volume is C. D. Edelberg's *Robert Creeley's Poetry*[28] which after a brief introduction pointing up Valéry's influence and discriminating between the creative impetus of Olson and Creeley, proceeds to a chronological examination of *For Love, Words, Pieces*, and the second, poetic half of *A Day Book*. Underlined are Creeley's involvement with the mind's activities confronted with tensions in human relationships, his wrestling with the claims of thought and intuition, his modulations of the concept of love and human isolation, and his investigations of the nature of poetry as product and process.

Hart Crane and Yvor Winters by T. Parkinson[29] examines their literary correspondence which extended from 1926 to 1930. Actually the correspondence is only that of Crane to Winters augmented by those of Winters to Allen Tate during the same period. Parkinson skilfully and straightforwardly sets the letters in their personal and historical context and in passing casts a sympathetic light on Winters' early career which may help to encourage serious scholarly attention to his poetry and criticism. R. Combs's *Vision of the Voyage*[30] is a largely undocumented claim that Hart Crane is a profoundly Romantic sensibility whose work can be understood only in relation to a philosophic tradition begun by Kant and most fully explored by Hegel. Key features in it are the impossibility of a constitutive metaphysics, the temporal obsolescence of explanations, and the provision of cultural and personal value and meaning through self-mediation. Apparently historical Romantics such as Coleridge and Wordsworth were

[27] *Robert Creeley*, by A. Ford. Boston, Mass.: G. K. Hall. pp. 159. $8.95.

[28] *Robert Creeley's Poetry*, by C. Edelberg. Albuquerque, N.M.: U. of New Mexico P. pp. ix + 185. $11.95.

[29] *Hart Crane and Yvor Winters: Their Literary Correspondence*, by T. Parkinson. Berkeley, Calif.: U. of California P. pp. xiii + 174. $11.95.

[30] *Vision of the Voyage: Hart Crane and the Psychology of Romanticism*, by R. Combs. Memphis, Tenn.: Memphis State U.P. pp. ix + 200. $9.50.

unable to maintain consistently the cultural- and self-alienation and irony requisite for Romanticism but Crane was, which is why Combs feels he is not a visionary poet like Blake and Shelley. Hegel's attempt 'to demonstrate how one stops being victimised by ideas' does not seem to have succeeded in this book's forced and strained thesis. W. J. Lockwood's article (*ConL*) focuses on what kind of 'new' materials constitute the 'real' for Ed Dorn, whose desire in poetry is to escape the 'sluggish beast of Europe'. Lockwood probes how well Dorn has accomplished his goal of making a new poetic mystique based on the 'new' world rather than on European backgrounds. Brief comments on *The Gunslinger* poems are accompanied by greater concentration on three pieces of prose by Dorn. 'The Echoing Spell of H. D.'s Trilogy' (*ConL*) by S. Gubar seems to be a critique of H. D.'s work that undercuts the Freudian interpretation because Gubar finds in the female's search for safety, security, and power a rejection of 'masculine' forms of power. Writings by H. D. which are analysed by Gubar include: *The Hedgehog*, 'Tribute to Freud', 'Writing on the Wall', 'Advent', 'Tribute to Angels', and, most of all, H. D.'s trilogy.

M. Beilke's *Shining Clarity*[31] is a handsome, curiously shaped volume which chronologically surveys the themes of God and man in the poetry of Robinson Jeffers, with special attention to the lyrics rather than the long narratives. It is the work of an enthusiast who sees Jeffers as a major poet because he was a profound thinker whose view of God altered not at all and of man scarcely in the course of his career. A related volume is *Rock and Hawk: Robinson Jeffers and the Romantic Agony* by W. H. Nolte[32]. Like Beilke, he is interested in the poet's thought and not at all in matters of influence, style, or earlier criticism. Nolte includes the narratives as well in his consideration which focuses on defining Jeffers' individualism, his struggle with the nature and fact of evil, and his sense of the beauty of the world as a whole. Neither book, unfortunately, really comes to grips with Jeffers' distinctive poetic qualities.

Marjorie A. Taylor's 'Vachel Lindsay and the Ghost of Abraham Lincoln' (*CentR*) traces the influence of Abraham Lincoln on Vachel Lindsey by examining Lindsey's childhood connections with Lincoln and the evidence of Lincoln in Lindsay's work. Taylor says 'Vachel Linday's work is haunted by the spirit of Abraham Lincoln. . . Lindsay sought strength and comfort in Lincoln's brooding presence'. Ellery Sedgwick III in ' "Fireworks": Amy Lowell and the *Atlantic Monthly*' (*NEQ*) is writing about the extended battle between Amy Lowell and Ellery Sedgwick, editor of the *Atlantic Monthly* (1908–1937) over the poetic orthodoxy. Although they remained friends during the twenty-five-year battle over what form poetry should assume, they never really came to an agreement despite Sedgwick's recognition of Lowell's early poems. Sedgwick was on the side of traditional tastes and Amy Lowell wished to re-make radically American poetry. This article contains many letters between the two. S. G. Axelrod's *Robert Lowell*[33] attempts the difficult but essential task of interrelating the poetry and the life. He argues that despite changing

[31] *Shining Clarity: God and Man in the Works of Robinson Jeffers*, by M. Beilke. Amador City, Ca.: Quintessence P. pp. ivi + 267. $25.

[32] *Rock and Hawk: Robinson Jeffers and the Romantic Agony*, by W. H. Nolte. Athens, Ga.: U. of Georgia P. pp. 201. $14.

[33] *Robert Lowell: His Life and Art*, by S. Axelrod. Princeton, N.J. Princeton U.P. pp. xiii + 286. $14.50.

styles and modes, the art coheres around the notion of experience which is the sum of interactions of psyche and environment. This notion is developed chronologically in terms of the major volumes which are seen severally as myths, photographs, and impressions of experience. The culmination of the art, if not the life, is held to come in *The Dolphin*. L. Stapleton's *Marianne Moore*[34] is a supplely written, intelligent study of the poet. Matters of biography and influence are dealt with but are carefully subordinated to characterising the poet's development and the relationships between poems with a view to encouraging critical attention to her work, particularly in its sustained and extended experimentation over almost fifty years. G. Woodcock examines the life of *Thomas Merton*[35] as poet, monk, essayist, religious writer, and social critic, concluding that Merton's contradictory impulses, his recognition of them and of the plurality of all things, enabled him to make the reconciliation of Eastern and Western spiritual perspectives his most notable contribution to his age.

N. Procopiow in 'Hands Across the Sea – The British and American Poetries of Philip Larkin and Frank O'Hara' (*IllQ*) thinks that both poets adhere to the standards of the other's literature and by their personae exhibit resemblances in tonality and point of view. J. Replogle's 'Vernacular Poetry: Frost to Frank O'Hara' (*TCL*) begins by differentiating vernacular voices and their components and then discusses Frost, Marianne Moore, Auden, and O'Hara in general terms. D. F. Sadoff's 'Mythopoeia, The Moon, and Contemporary Women's Poetry' (*MassR*) is an attempt to find a viable Jungian basis for a feminist re-interpretation of mythology and more particularly dualistic moon myths. Such re-interpretations are traced in the poetry of Levertov, Willard, and Wakoski.

G. F. Butterick provides an appropriately mammoth *Guide to the Maximus Poems of Charles Olson*[36], which judiciously used is likely to yield important critical formulations. After a substantial introduction informatively charting the problems of the canon and the materials consulted, Butterick annotates all three volumes of the Maximus poems page by page. Elucidation of geographical and historical fact, allusions, sources, and circumstances of composition are variously attempted with varying degrees of success, necessity, and relevance. *Meaning a Life* by M. Oppen[37] is the autobiography of the wife of the Objectivist poet George Oppen. The emphasis is on their life together rather than their artistic efforts and views, but there are some interesting personal vignettes of Zukofsky, Reznikoff, and Pound.

L. R. Smith provides the first full-length treatment of *Kenneth Patchen*[38] the long-time avant-garde poet, novelist, and graphics student. He focuses on Patchen's aesthetic and his experimental forms. The former revolves around the concepts of madness, engagement, and wonder while

[34] *Marianne Moore*, by L. Stapleton, Princeton, N.J.: Princeton U.P. pp. xvi + 282. $15.

[35] *Thomas Merton: Monk and Poet*, by G. Woodcock. Edinburgh: Cannongate. pp. 200. £5.95.

[36] *A Guide to the Maximus Poems of Charles Olson*, by G. Butterick. Berkeley, Calif.: U. of California P. pp. ix + 816. £28.

[37] *Meaning a Life: An Autobiography*, by M. Oppen. Santa Barbara, Calif.: Black Sparrow P. pp. 213. $14.

[38] *Kenneth Patchen*, by L. R. Smith. Boston, Mass.: G. K. Hall. pp. 195. $8.95.

the latter embrace the anti-novel, the prose poem, the concrete poem, the jazz poem, absurdist poem, and the 'picture-poem'. C. K. Barnard's *Sylvia Plath*[39] briefly sketches the life, examines the work, and concludes with brief reflections on the life in the work. It emphasises the honest awkwardness of the early poems, the movement from written to spoken language in the transitional period, and the savage intensity and feverish necessity of the later ones. Barnard finds Plath beginning with a death-dominated vision and gradually moving toward an apocalyptic vision compounded of the surreal, war, domestic tensions, and mythology.

P. Makin's *Provence and Pound*[40] examines not only the Provençal poets most influential on Pound but what he made of them and how that material was incorporated into *The Cantos*, particularly Canto VI. The examination is careful, judicious and thoughtful, showing an admirable concern with the functional adaptations Pound made of the material. In *Instigations* R. Sieburth[41] takes up the interesting and, to date, largely tantalising matter of the intellectual and aesthetic relations between Ezra Pound and Remy de Gourmont. He finds that they are less a matter of specific ideas shared than an affinity of attitude toward ideas and a qualitative texture of intelligence. Sieburth is particularly astute in suggesting how Gourmont continued to play a subterranean but significant role in Pound's later works after the decade of explicit influence (1912–1922). *Ezra Pound: The London Years, 1908–1920*, edited by P. Grover[42], consists of six papers delivered in the United Kingdom, five of them at the 1976 Pound conference held at the University of Sheffield. Subjects considered include Pound's involvement with Modernism, the art of translation, imagism, and the Provençal tradition, together with detailed consideration of 'Hugh Selwyn Mauberley' and Canto IV.

In a rather tenuous but long essay entitled 'Pound's Wordsworth; or Growth of a Poet's Mind' (*ELH*), D. Simpson advances the views that Pound and Imagism were concerned to displace the late Romantic aesthetic but that the original or early Romantic position provided a fundamental threat to their pre-occupation with an aesthetic of objectivity. Though recognising the dangers of attempting to schematise the random, Simpson nevertheless persists in the attempt. John Lauber grapples with 'Pound's *Cantos*: A Fascist Epic' (*JAmS*). Lauber asserts that once it's been accepted as a given that Pound was both Fascist and anti-semitic one must ask if the *Cantos* express a fascist ideology. In other words, are the *Cantos* to fascism as *Paradise Lost* is to Christianity? Noting that Pound assumes the validity of a purely 'poetic' authority, in which 'A single man's vision is elevated to a law valid for all men', Lauber concludes that the *Cantos* express a paranoid interpretation of history, and support authoritarianism and elitism, and are thus ideologically fascistic and totalitarian – in short, a fascist epic. He posits but doesn't explore the dynamics inherent within

[39] *Sylvia Plath*, by C. K. Barnard. Boston, Mass.: G. K. Hall. pp. 132. $9.95.

[40] *Provence and Pound*, by P. Makin. Berkeley, Calif.: U. of California P. 1979. pp. xiv + 428. $22.50.

[41] *Instigations: Ezra Pound and Remy de Gourmont*, by R. Sieburth. Cambridge, Mass.: Harvard U.P. pp. viii + 197. $12.50.

[42] *Ezra Pound: The London Years, 1908–1920*, ed. by P. Grover. New York: AMS P. 1977. pp. xvi + 167. $16.95.

the tension of the co-existence of an artistic aesthetic with its psycho/political origins and visions.

A Great and Glorious Romance by H. Sandburg[43] is a daughter's account of the marriage and family life of Carl Sandburg and Lilian Steichen. The book substantially ends with the publication of his Lincoln volume in 1926. Warm and affectionate and fleshed out with considerable family material, this account will be important to any future scholarly biographer. J. D. McClatchy has edited *Anne Sexton: The Artist and Her Critics*[44] ostensibly to focus attention more sharply on the work and less on the biography. Yet easily two-thirds of the book consists of reminiscences, interview, and reviews. The only sustained essays are by R. Howard, R. Boyers, J. McCabe, and the editor, and all are general assessments of the career as a whole. Fred Miller Robinson considers 'Poems That Took the Place of Mountains: Realization in Stevens and Cezanne' (*CentR*). This essay examines 'how Cezanne's ideas about realisation helped Stevens to articulate his own deepest needs concerning, and doubts about, his poetic achievement'. These similar concerns were a doubt about their ability to express what exists and how objective nature can be realised by the subjective artist, a concern that struck both men in their later years. Philip Furia and Martin Roth in 'Stevens' Fusky Alphabet' (*PMLA*) contend that Wallace Stevens reveals a combination of the child and the philosopher in his deliberate use of a child-like love of the alphabet in and for itself, and at the same time infuses his alphabetical code with philosophical concerns. Stevens' alphabet, often abbreviated, can be either 'murderous' if it represents a sterile process or 'fusky' if it represents relationships between imagination and reality. The authors believe that by understanding the significance of Stevens' alphabet, one can better understand his work. Examples include: 'The Comedian as the Letter C', and 'An Ordinary Evening in New Haven'.

In a brief and modest essay (*SoR*), Allen Tate recalls the circumstances and association of ideas attendant upon the composition of some of his poems. He purposely does not attempt to deal with how ideas become associated. Roy Fuller in 'Tate Full Length' (*SoR*) presents essentially his reaction to the publication of a volume of Allen Tate's complete poems which gives the reader, other poets, and critics a heretofore unavailable opportunity to read Tate in sequence and rediscover his talent, from his early, young poems to his later mature work. Fuller feels that Tate has not been appreciated and accorded the fame which he deserves. Fuller himself benefited by rereading Tate and believes others should do so also. In 'Brother to Dragons: The Fact of Violence vs. the Possibility of Love' (*AL*), R. G. Law proposes that the 'hybrid genre' of *Brother to Dragons* is the result of Warren re-assessing the 'relation of his art and his life', and that it is 'an inquiry into the nature of love'. Warren creates, within the frame of the story, a metaphor for the artistic process, and, by becoming a character in his own art, recreates himself.

B. F. Michelson's article 'Richard Wilbur: The Quarrel with Poe (*SoR*)

[43] *A Great and Glorious Romance: The Story of Carl Sandburg and Lilian Steichen*, by H. Sandburg. New York: Harcourt. pp. 319. $12.95.

[44] *Anne Sexton: The Artist and Her Critics*, ed. by J. D. McClatchy. Bloomington, Ind.: Indiana U.P. pp. xiii + 297. $12.95.

is an attempt to relate Wilbur the scholar to Wilbur the poet. Wilbur once remarked that much of his own poetry 'can be read as a "quarrel" with Poe's aesthetics'. Michelson maintains that this remark has been misunderstood and that Wilbur's poetry is not, in fact, a 'quarrel' with Poe but rather shows a 'pervasive presence of Poe' in Wilbur's use of the image of the whirling sea and the abyss. As evidence he points out similar uses of the whirling abyss and the sea in Poe's 'Marginalia', 'MS Found in a Bottle', and 'A Descent into the Maelstrom'. 'The Politics of Description: W. C. Williams in the "Thirties", by R. Von Hallberg (*ELH*) suggests that the poems of this period are located between the poles of flat referentiality and emblematic or parabolic description as his way of dealing with ideologically burdened subjects. Of 'Yvor Winters' Greek Allegories' (*SoR*) G. E. Powell says: 'By using known myth in place of natural detail, Winters brings post-symbolist imagery into poems which have a narrative base'. Powell calls this the 'allegorical method'. He traces Winters' use of death and oblivion in 'Chiron' and other poems. B. Ahearn's 'Origins of "A": Zukofsky's Materials for Collage' (*ELH*) is a curiously unfocused essay, perhaps because of the paucity of criticism on the subject and/or its difficulty. He suggests the notion of collage as a paradigm of Zukofsky's art and then considers the contribution of such elements as his ghetto upbringing, his early exposure to the Yiddish theatre, his interest in avant-garde artistic circles, and his education in philosophy at Columbia. The suggestions are interesting but rather inconclusive.

3. Prose

In 'Harriette Arnow's *The Dollmaker*: A Journey to Awareness' (*Crit*) Dorothy H. Lee argues that Arnow's fiction, usually considered as naturalistic fiction, 'may be considered more fruitfully within the context of heightened realism'. She finds beneath the 'deceptively simple surface of its narrative' a 'selectivity and shaping that transcends the reportorial naturalistic method'. Lee sees the journey of the central character from the Kentucky mountains to Detroit as an archetypal one, a descent into the city of Hell. She furnishes ample evidence of this in her examination of the novel. L. A. Westervelt's 'Teller, Tale, Told: Relationships in John Barth's Latest Fiction' (*JNT*) concentrates on the roles of the reader and narrator in *Lost in the Funhouse* and *Chimera*. It argues that Barth is engaged in educating his reader in the problems of self-consciousness and hence in creating a reader capable of reading his fiction.

'Artists and Opportunists in Saul Bellow's *Humboldt's Gift*' (*ConL*) by Ben Siegel argues for Bellow's continued involvement with humanism, liberalism, and social expectations. Indeed, Siegel believes that Bellow in *Humboldt's Gift* embraces moral, ethical, and spiritual problems and that in this work Bellow is once again using the artist to mend the rift between America's professed ideals and practiced compromises. S. Pinsker's 'Meditations Interruptus! Saul Bellows' Ambivalent Novel of Ideas' (*IllQ*) sees *Herzog, Mr. Sammler's Planet*, and *Humboldt's Gift* as a loose trilogy concerned with the contemporary impact of ideas on American culture and with their exaltation and deflation by an embattled but ironic spokesman. Herbert J. Smith takes up '*Humboldt's Gift* and Rudolf

Steiner' (*CentR*). Smith contends that *Humboldt's Gift* contains a significant variation of the Bellow theme of 'a dialectic which dramatizes the opposition between human ideals and human experience'. This is because in *Humboldt's Gift*, Bellow 'explores the dialectical tension between human ideals and human actuality, between the spirit and the void, within the framework of Rudolf Steiner's anthroposophy – a new influence on Bellow's fiction'. Smith says that the basic tenets found in three of Steiner's works (*The Philosophy of Spiritual Activity* (1894), *Theosophy* (1910) and *Knowledge of the Higher Worlds and Its Attainment* (1930)) offer the reader a valuable 'means of assessing Citrine's quest for higher knowledge' and attempts 'to understand death'. 'The Possibility of Affirmation in "Heart of Darkness" and "Henderson the Rain King" ' (*PQ*) is considered by J. P. Stout who would have it that the difference between the two works on this score is a matter of degree rather than of kind. Essentially, what this comes down to is that each text qualifies its dominant tone so that they 'finally make very similar arguments about the possibility for a hopeful view of human life'. For S. B. Cohen 'Saul Bellow's Chicago' (*MFS*) has a number of differing versions depending on the individual novel, its time period, the nature and age of its protagonist, the length of his residency in the city, and his knowledge of it. In 'The Quest and the Question: Cosmology and Myth in the Work of William S. Burroughs, 1953–1960' (*TCL*) W. L. Stull suggests that rather than breaking radically with the past Burroughs taps a primordial source of vitality by adhering to the quest pattern traced by the likes of Weston and Campbell.

In endeavouring to formulate 'The Art of Willa Cather's Craft' (*PLL*) C. Chaliff notes her indebtedness to Romantic notions of the artist and creativity as deriving from an unconscious impulse. This accounts for the awkwardnesses of structure so frequently noted in her work and particularly the bringing together of two disparate stories. Marilyn Arnold looks at 'One of Ours: Willa Cather's Losing Battle' (*WAL*). By making war into an ideal, and trying to believe in that ideal through the personification of the weak character, Claude, Cather fatally weakened her novel: she couldn't be honest, and thus the novel fails. James Woodress considers 'Willa Cather and History' (*ArQ*). Cather's shift to historical fiction with *Death Comes for the Archbishop* reflects a retreat into the past from a present which she found psychologically dispiriting. The cultural malaise of the twenties which drove the lost generation to Europe, along with her own emotional crisis, drove Cather into the exile of writing novels set in the past. A survey of her reading in history and historical fiction indicates that the novels of her later years reflect a long-standing taste and talent for historical romance in the manner of Hawthorne, although this inclination is already partly perceptible in the uses of memory, childhood experience, and the recent past in earlier works like *Antonia* and *O Pioneers*. While the transition in the mid-twenties from the Nebraska stories to historical fiction is the chief watershed, then, her development can and should be seen as organic and evolutionary. 'Narrative Technique in Cather's *My Mortal Enemy*' (*JNT*) is examined by S. J. Rosowski who contends that 'both internal and external evidence suggests that narrative technique is, rather than extraneous to the book's subject and theme, central to them and that, by this very centrality, Cather fulfills the requirements of the *novel de meuble* more fully than has yet been recognised'.

D. Commins has written *What is an Editor?*[45] which is a series of essays dealing with her late husband, Saxe Commins, and his editorial relations with many of the major figures of modern American literature. The information is personal and professional rather than critical and is particularly interesting on O'Neill and Faulkner.

J. Mason notes the lack of substantial awareness of 'Black writers of the South' (*MissQ*) in university literature courses and proposes a list of ones who might be used. He concludes with a brief treatment of Albert A. Whitman, whose long, melodramatic narrative poems were popular from 1870 until the end of the century. As the title indicates, E. E. Waldron's *Walter White and the Harlem Renaissance*[46] attempts to see the man's contributions to the movement in perspective. Brief biographical and historical sketches lead to sustained consideration of his rather mediocre novels, *The Fire in the Flint* and *Flight*, and his role as counsellor, advocate, and guide to Black artists seeking to publish their work. Given the importance of this last as well as his involvement with the National Association for the Advancement of Colored Peoples (NAACP), one wonders if Waldron has not devoted a disproportionate amount of attention to White's literary efforts, particularly since he had available to him the extensive NAACP correspondence files. *Amira Baraka/LeRoi Jones: The Quest for a 'Populist Modernism'* by W. Sollors[47] is a thorough attempt to chart and to produce some coherence in Baraka's bewildering changes in political and aesthetic positions. He shows the stages, perhaps over-schematically, by which Baraka moves from expressive concentration on aesthetic protest and avant-gardism to a pragmatic aesthetic dominated by Marxism of both Soviet (or Leninist) and Chinese varieties.

Zora Neale Hurston[48] is a scrupulously researched and honestly written biography of an important black novelist and folklorist that also provides a discriminating treatment of the novels and other literary works. Two other books dealing with Black authors are R. E. Fleming's *Willard Motley* and L. H. Pratt's *James Baldwin*[49]. The former competently traces Motley's extensive writing apprenticeship, his maturation, and struggle to explore new techniques on behalf of his social vision, and concludes that he deserves a distinct place in the history of twentieth-century nationalism. Pratt's volume is not concerned with biography at all but rather seeks to show that the novels, short stories, and essays have a number of critically unexamined facts worthy of sustained consideration. Both books attend to the issues of race but are rather more concerned with universals such as oppression and liberation, freedom and enslavement, and the struggle for identity as they work themselves out in a racially mixed world.

'Coover's *Universal Baseball Association*: Play as Personalized Myth' (*MFS*) by N. Berman examines the novel as one instance of the novel of

[45] *What is an Editor? Saxe Commins at Work*, by D. Commins. Chicago, Ill.: U. of Chicago P. pp. 243. $10.

[46] *Walter White and the Harlem Renaissance*, by E. Waldron. Port Washington, N.Y.: Kennikat. pp. x + 185. $12.50.

[47] *Amira Baraka/LeRoi Jones: The Quest for a 'Populist Modernism'*, by W. Sollors. New York: Columbia U.P. pp. xii + 338. $16.95.

[48] *Zora Neale Hurston*, by R. Hemenway. Urbana, Ill.: U. of Illinois P. pp. xxv + 371. $15.

[49] *Willard Motley*, by R. E. Fleming. Boston, Mass.: G. K. Hall. pp. 168. $9.50; *James Baldwin*, by L. H. Pratt. Boston, Mass.: G. K. Hall. pp. 138. $8.50.

play, which is contrasted to naturalistic versions by virtue of its complete internalisation of its game-world thereby creating its own myths and rituals rather than drawing on traditional ones as do Malamud and Roth. Allen Shepherd's 'Matters of Life and Death: the Novels of Harry Crews' (*Crit*) was written in the hope that it would 'establish some critical ground work for surveying the canon'. It focuses on three novels, *Car* (1972), *The Hawk Is Dying* (1973), and *A Feast of Snakes* (1976) which Shepherd claims are the best novels of Harry Crews (who writes about blue-collar southerners trying to escape their lives in books that are full of danger and violence). He finds them 'fast, mean, dangerous, extraordinarily violent and often horrifyingly funny' and yet 'surprisingly plausible and consistent'.

The Wages of Expectation by C. De Fanti[50] is a careful biography of the volatile and deliberately obscured life of Edward Dahlberg, naturalistic novelist, truculent essayist, and exuberant autobiographer. Should a critical evaluation of Dahlberg ever be embarked upon, this will be an indispensable starting-point. Michael Oriard's 'Don DeLillo's Search For Walden Pond' (*Crit*) is followed by a checklist which includes critical reviews of DeLillo's works. Oriard examines the major characters in DeLillo's novels and how they attempt to follow Thoreau's advice to 'simplify, simplify, simplify'. In *Americana, End Zone, Great Jones St.*, and *Ratner's Star*, Oriard finds DeLillo's characters searching for a Walden Pond type of isolation from the problems of modern life in order to be 're-born', something they don't completely achieve but rather embark on as a tentative course of possibility. Barbara Foley suggests in 'From *U.S.A.* to *Ragtime*: Notes on the Forms of Historical Consciousness in Modern Fiction' (*AL*) that a comparison of Dos Passos' and Doctorow's novels reveals a developing pessimism in modern fiction concerning the existence of historical reality, which results in either a 'subjective' approach in which the only history is that which the author's imagination 'reworks' as in *Ragtime*, or a 'slice' of history, isolated from a broader historical process, as in Truman Capote's *In Cold Blood*. In *U.S.A.* history functions as a frame within which and *for* which the characters function. In *Ragtime* history is only motif; the plot is fictional, and historical characters are subjected to outlandish situations. This implies, says Foley, that history isn't interesting or 'coherent' enough to provide pattern or plot. Even *Ragtime*'s hero, Coalhouse Walker, is a fictional rather than historical derivation; moreover, she notes that the events surrounding him are more typical of the sixties than the pre-war years, suggesting that Doctorow is implying that the existence of the past in the present modifies contemporary 'superiority'. Foley finds Dos Passos more 'inspiring' because the issues in *U.S.A.* exist primarily in the historical materials, rather than in his reworkings of them: thus *U.S.A.* ratifies the integrity of materials from which modern writers feel alienated. The title of I. Colley's study, *Dos Passos and the Fiction of Despair*[51], suggests his thesis: Dos Passos' affinities with naturalism make him an apostle of despair, failure, and alienation whose synthetic method of presentation makes *Manhattan Transfer* and *U.S.A.* genuinely distinguished works.

[50] *The Wages of Expectation: A Biography of Edward Dahlberg*, by C. De Fanti. New York: New York U.P. pp. xiv + 272. $15.

[51] *Dos Passos and the Fiction of Despair*, by I. Colley. Macmillan. pp. viii + 169. £8.95.

When the tension between antithetical traits, particularly success and failure, dissolves, the technique regresses and crude polemicism comes to the fore. While this is undeniably one kind of description, one may wonder whether it is any kind of explanation.

C. Fanning's *Finley Peter Dunne & Mr. Dooley*[52] makes a well-documented claim for Dunne's recognition as a pioneer social historian and literary realist by setting his work in its ethnic, geographical, and professional context.

T. P. Riggio transcribes an interview with Dreiser held during the San Francisco International Exposition in 1939 and provides a brief analytical introduction (*ALR*). He also examines 'American Gothic: Poe and *An American Tragedy*' (*AL*). Riggio's thesis is that the sixty pages of Clyde Griffiths' disintegration owe more to Poe than to Freudian influences. He notes that Dreiser considered Poe 'our first and greatest literary genius', and proposes that he reworked and adapted Poe's techniques for portraying emotional fragmentation: i.e., Roderick Usher is a type of Clyde Griffiths. Michael Spindler studies 'Youth, Class, and Consumerism in Dreiser's *An American Tragedy*' (*JAmS*). Spindler is interested in Clyde Griffiths as socially representative, and thus in analysing his social framework. Noting that social relationships predominate in the novel, portraying a polarised society, and that Samuel Griffiths is a 'stereotype of late nineteenth-century entrepreneur(s)' and of 'self reliant individualism', and that Clyde relies on kinship when the 'family is becoming a vestigial factor in modern social relations', Spindler concludes that Clyde is 'a mirror for the society in which he lives and dies'. Clyde (poor, dependent, motivationless, passive, malleable) and his fate represent the American capitalistic process, which creates a chimera – an ethic of self-denial, coupled with an ideal of self gratification.

Robert E. Abrams explores 'The Ambiguities of Dreaming in Ellison's *Invisible Man*' (*AL*). Granting that dreams in *The Invisible Man* disrupt the real world's epistemological applecart, Abrams proposes that their ambiguity (that is, their inaccessibility to 'cognitive mastery' even on the level of Freudian interpretation) emphasises the unavailability of the consciousness and identity of the real individual, as well. Dream language, Abrams suggests, is the least deceptive for the American artist, whatever his race or culture, who has no unadulterated symbolic language left to him. V. B. Gray examines *'Invisible Man's' Literary Heritage*[53] and declares it to be *Benito Cerino* and *Moby-Dick*. The basis for the comparison is the concern with democracy. In addition Gray compares the works in terms of their uses of ambiguity concerning appearance and reality, of colour symbolism, and image clusters. The emphasis is on formal comparisons rather than on historical tradition or influence, though Ellison's interest in the earlier period is noted.

A. M. Wald's *James T. Farrell: The Revolutionary Socialist Years*[54] is a

[52] *Finley Peter Dunne & Mr. Dooley*, by C. Fanning. Lexington, Ky.: U. of Kentucky P. pp. x + 286. $14.50.

[53] *'Invisible Man's' Literary Heritage: Benito Cereno and Moby Dick*, by V. B. Gray. Atlantic Highlands, N.J.: Humanities P. pp. 156. $16.75.

[54] *James T. Farrell: The Revolutionary Socialist Years*, by A. Wald. New York: New York U.P. pp. xx + 190. $15.

balanced, scholarly, though somewhat unduly brief account of its subject. Farrell's efforts to reconcile his essentially liberal pragmatism with Marxist radicalism are carefully traced as a seminal background for his fiction, criticism, and intellectual relationships. If it does not materially alter our estimate of Farrell the writer, it nevertheless significantly adds to our understanding of a historical era all too often simplified into pat labels.

The second volume of C. Brooks's *William Faulkner*[55] provides a kind of chronological frame for the first in that it deals with those works that precede the Yoknapatawpha novels and those coming after its major exemplars had appeared. The result is a judicious assessment of the significance as well as weakness of works like *Mosquitoes* and *Pylon*. A concluding chapter addresses Faulner's notions of time and history and Bergson's role in their formulation. Almost a hundred pages of appendixes dealing with such disparate matters as Sutpen, *Absalom, Absalom!*, and Yeats conclude this thoughtful and balanced assessment. A more sharply and perhaps narrowly focused study by A. F. Kinney is *Faulkner's Narrative Poetics*[56]. He begins by placing Faulkner in a philosophical, psychological, and literary context of perceptual and conceptual consciousness: predictably Flaubert, Conrad, James, Joyce, Proust. Faulkner's own stylistic method is then elaborated in terms of structural, narrative, and constitutive modes of consciousness, and this theory applied to individual analyses of some of the major works from *The Sound and the Fury* to *Go Down, Moses*. The same author's 'Form and Function in *Absalom, Absalom!*' (*SoR*) traces some influences on Faulkner in his composition of *Absalom, Absalom!* and finds a place for Faulkner's great-grandfather's literary curio, *The White Rose of Memphis*. Kinney says that Faulkner 'mined' this novel and that the grandfather himself is the very image of Col John Sartoris. Other influences on his writing include Dostoevsky and Conrad. Elizabeth Muhlenfeld claims ' "We have waited long enough": Judith Sutpen and Charles Bon' (*SoR*). Muhlenfeld is calling for another way of reading Faulkner's *Absalom, Absalom!*. It is her belief that a close examination of the triangle between Judith, Bon, and Henry is a key to another way of looking at the structure of the novel. Quoting from Faulkner's remarks about many ways to see the blackbird, she applies this sense of multiple views to an analysis of the 'love' between Judith and Bon and the ability or inability of the other characters to recognise this as 'love'. There is the possibility of Judith and Bon's love 'brightening and strengthening the dark world of *Absalom, Absalom!*' by providing a living alternative.

L. F. Seltzer and J. Viscomi study 'Natural Rhythms and Rebellion: Anse's Role in *As I Lay Dying*' (*MFS*) in order to suggest that Anse, unlike the rest of the characters, does not rebel against natural motion and cycles and so is the novel's model of endurance rather than its fool as most critics think. J. Radomski and Y. Hakutani have collaborated on 'Faulkner's Major Syntactic Features' (*Hiroshima Studies in English Language and Literature*) which concentrates on *Intruder in the Dust* in stressing the use of subordination, nominalisations, relativisations, and adjectives in develop-

[55] *William Faulkner: Towards Yoknapatawpha and Beyond*, by C. Brooks. New Haven, Conn.: Yale U.P. pp. xvi + 445. $20.

[56] *Faulkner's Narrative Poetics*, by A. F. Kinney. Amherst, Mass.: U. of Massachusetts P. pp. xi + 286. $15.

ing Faulkner's recursiveness. In 'Faulkner's *The Unvanquished*: The High Costs of Survival' (*SoR*), M. E. Bradford examines Faulkner's novel carefully and contends that the thematic core of the work is the necessity of preserving community and a particular society as much as saving individuals. The identity of the protagonist is plural and much like Shakespeare's history plays and other Southern literature of the 'plantation' variety there is a 'corporate identity'. *The Unvanquished* is seen as a struggle of a series of protagonists to save themselves and their society. In the final chapter, the success of the efforts of the Sartoris clan in preventing their world and their people from being 'abolished' (from Ringo's reaction to the news that he has been freed: 'I done been abolished') is demonstrated by Bayard's refusal to shoot Redmond. Bradford says, 'contrary to the standard interpretation of this final episode, his decision not to shoot Redmond IS a vindication of all that has been achieved by his predecessors in his place'.

A special Faulkner issue of *MissQ* contains five critical articles, a checklist of Faulkner's film scripts, three brief notes, an unpublished poem and short story by Faulkner, and several reviews. G. M. Morrison examines the quest theme as it appears in *The Sound and the Fury* and three earlier but only recently published works. M. Yonce examines the poem 'The Lilacs' in ' "Shot Down Last Spring": The Wounded Aviators of Faulkner's Wasteland' with a view to relating it to the fiction in terms of both the wounded pilot figure and the notion of the divided psyche. M. J. Dickerson sees 'Faulkner's Golden Steed' as his transformation of his devotion to horses into significant fictional explorations of man's relation to nature, the community, and his own sense of historical event. Instances are found in *Flags in the Dust, The Sound and the Fury, As I Lay Dying*, and *A Fable* among others to evidence the creative–destructive energy he found in the image and the animal. Brief arguments for 'The Comic Structure of *The Sound and the Fury*' are advanced by F. Chappell. H. M. Ruppers suggests that 'The Narrative Structure of *Requiem for a Nun*' is dependent on its being planned as a novel so that the 'play' parts must be taken as dramatic narratives distinguished by narrator almost totally withdrawn from the action. 'Reeling Through Faulkner: Pictures of Motion, Pictures in Motion' (*MFS*) is R. Pearce's analysis of two different kinds of pictorial techniques drawn from the movies by Faulkner, though in practice it seems rather to be a translation of his major narrative strategies into filmic terms.

In 'Toward Underivative Creation: Lawrence Ferlinghetti's *Her* (*Crit*), M. Skau explains how Ferlinghetti explores the dynamics of artistic consciousness and control and uses the 'relationship between author and his creation to image his view of the relationship between God and man' in his complex novel *Her*. 'You Can't Go Home: Jeremiah Johnson and the Wilderness' (*WAL*) by M. McAllister discusses *Mountain Man* by Vardis Fisher, and the movie derivative, remarking that both underscore the message that freedom of the territories and the innocence of the past are both myths.

T. J. Stavola brings a psychoanalytic perspective to bear on *Scott Fitzgerald*[57] whom he feels is peculiarly relevant to modern problems of

[57] *Scott Fitzgerald: Crisis in an American Identity*, by T. Stavola. Vision. pp. 176. £6.50.

individual and American cultural identity. Opening chapters set out Erikson's theory of the life cycle of human development and a psychohistory of Scott and Zelda. They serve as background and context for four chapters focusing on the major male characters of the novels all of whom are beset by an identity crisis resembling that which Stavola finds central to Fitzgerald. *Candles and Carnival Lights* by J. M. Allen[58] is a work with a thesis, namely, that F. Scott Fitzgerald's Roman Catholic experience while growing up contributes significantly to his pre-occupation with the nature and complexity of individual morality and with the recognition of sin's destructiveness for the human condition. She proceeds chronologically dealing in turn with the early formative years and the four novels and related prose. Though the thesis has a number of built-in biographical problems and is perhaps over-developed, it does confirm how the ethical obsession can sustain the transformation of the religious into the secular.

Stephen L. Tanner considers 'Fitzgerald: "What to Make of a Diminished Thing" ' (*ArQ*). Fitzgerald's fiction is uniformly inspired by a combination of two plot elements, the 'Romantic Promise', and the 'Diminished Thing'. His stories exhibit a thematic first part concerned with hope, dream, and enlarging possibilities, which is inevitably followed by a second part whose burden is to confront the aftermath of thwarted dream. This central dualistic plot of promise and disillusionment has biographical connections with Fitzgerald's own obsession with youth and suggests that throughout his work he is attempting to come to terms with a personal pre-occupation with the myth of the Fall.

Christine M. Bird and Thomas L. McHaney explore '*The Great Gatsby* and *The Golden Bough*' (*ArQ*). Examination of the images of vegetation in *Gatsby* suggests that Fitzgerald's hero is intended as a modern counterpart to Frazer's King of the Wood. Although Fitzgerald's first-hand acquaintance with *The Golden Bough* remains unproven, internal evidence of indebtedness to the mythic method of *Ulysses* and *The Waste Land* strongly supports a view of Gatsby as dying god who, in his modern valueless world, cannot be reborn after his ritual death. R. Roulston, takes up 'Tom Buchanan: Patrician in Motley' (*ArQ*). Buchanan is not Fitzgerald's 'embodiment of evil', but rather serves as comic foil to Gatsby. Possessing both malicious and laudable traits, he is regarded as the novel's wise fool whose predictions of a Spenglerian decline of civilisation extend one of the serious themes of the action, while his typical attitudes and actions are treated in such a way as to mark him as the ludicrous figure who stands in counterpoint to Gatsby's tragedy. The same author argues in 'Dick Diver's Plunge into the Roman Void: The Setting of "Tender is the Night" ' (*SAQ*) that the five chapters set in Rome depart from the realistic mode in favour of the use of locale as 'a symbolic embodiment of larger cultural and political forces and simultaneously as a spiritual landscape that reflects the mind of the central character'. As a result these chapters become the narrative and thematic focal point of the novel in that they reveal both the decay of Western civilisation and the waking nightmare that is Dick's psyche.

In ' "Herstory" and Daisy Buchanan' (*AL*), L. S. Person Jr defends

[58] *Candles and Carnival Lights: The Catholic Sensibility of Scott Fitzgerald*, by J. M. Allen. New York: New York U.P. pp. xvi + 164. $15.

Daisy as victim rather than victimiser, seeing her corruption as the result of her treatment by others rather than an inherent malaise: Nick's judgement of her is clouded by his need for a moral vision of the world, and given Gatsby's impossible ideal she couldn't have done anything *but* fail him. He cites her reaction to Gatsby's letter before her marriage to Tom as one indication of interior depths which can never emerge given the novel's construct, which 'doesn't allow her to live'. A. B. Paulson's '*The Great Gatsby*: Oral Aggression and Splitting' (*AL*) relies on three images to discuss *The Great Gatsby*'s doubling of characters and imagery in the Freudian and Ericksonian terms of object splitting, split ego, and oral aggression: the 'fresh, green breast of the new world', both promising and destructive; the 'pap of life' which Paulson sees as the 'original object of Gatsby's quest' and which, along with Gatsby's 'extraordinary gift for hope' leads Paulson to conclude that Gatsby has great oral trust, (an Ericksonian stage of development indicating a basic sense of well-being and trust in the world) is finally Myrtle Wilson s mutilation seen as representative of Fitzgerald's 'terrible infantile hostility'.

S. S. Klemtner describes her concern as ' "For a Very Small Audience": the Fiction of William Gaddis' (*Crit*). By examining Gaddis's novels *The Recognitions* and *JR*, Klemtner hopes to lend credence to her claim that Gaddis is important because of his enduring artistry and powerfully accurate and funny novels and deserves a larger audience than he has as a result of the difficulty of his novels. In 'John Gardner's *Grendel*: Sources and Analogues' (*ConL*), J. Milosh notes that Gardner's plot is obviously based on *Beowulf* but, he claims, Gardner has restructured it in a way which alters the epic material. Among significant alterations by Gardner, Milosh points out the static, predictable character of Grendel in *Beowulf* and the 'humanizing of Grendel' in Gardner's portrayal of the absurdity of war. A related study by Craig J. Stromme, 'The Twelve Chapters of *Grendel*' (*Crit*) examines John Gardner's *Grendel* in terms of Gardner's own comments about the novel (that he wanted to go through the main ideas of Western Civilisation) using the statements of Gardner as clues, not as an 'instant explication', and finds *Grendel* shows a passing of one age to another. Stromme's essay is an attempt to discern the philosophical centre of *Grendel*.

A less well known novelist is taken up by Bruce Bassoff in 'Royalty in A Rainy Country: Two Novels of Paula Fox' (*Crit*). Focusing on deformation as a theme, Bassoff examines Fox's novels *Desperate Characters* and *The Widow's Children*. This is a heavily written essay that argues there is a discrepancy between the inner person and the outer person in these books and that somehow by becoming their own ruler the characters lose what sovereignty they had. They do not follow the advice of Socrates: 'May the outward and inward man be as one'. Instead, they deform.

A special section (roughly half the issue) of *MissQ* (Winter 1978) is devoted to the apprenticeship of Ellen Glasgow. It consists of four articles and an editorial introduction. J. R. Raper examines her library and reading, finding that it does not alter but rather supports her autobiographical account of her intellectual revolution from her family. Her passion for philosophy and science, principally the utilitarians and rationalists like Mill, Spencer, and Lecky, lasted until 1894 when personal tragedy moves her toward stoicism and the works of Marcus Aurelius and Epictetus as well as the *Bhagavad-Gita* and others pre-occupied with the existence of an absolute Being. D. Scura traces her rendering of the Southern woman in the early fiction and shows that it was broader and more subtle than ordinarily thought. D. Kish emphasises the recurring facets of her landscape during the same period and finds these to be a strong sense of place and region in which the attractive and unattractive both figure and cohere with the more symbolic dimensions of character and action. E. MacDonald examines Glasgow's search for a style and shows that it followed a pattern that moves from initial ideas to specific characters and then settings and finally to matters of voice and narration in a protracted but dedicated quest for a language to mirror her convictions.

An additional essay on *Vein of Iron* by L. Payne is a reprint of a 1975 piece. In a gracefully written but rather amorphous piece, C. Hugh Holman looks at Ellen Glasgow's ' "Barren Ground" and the Shape of History' (*SAQ*). His thesis appears to be that because her imagination possessed a powerful historical dimension shaped by the Southern propensity for an Hegelian view, it informed her rendering of an intensely personal, subjective, and psychologically precise character. Susan E. Lorsch writes on 'Gail Godwin's *The Odd Woman*: Literature and the Retreat from Life' (*Crit*). In examining Godwin's *The Odd Woman*, as part of the popular mode of self-conscious fiction, she finds that the novel centres on the relation between literature and life, especially on the effect literature has on those who believe it. This novel reveals ample evidence that Godwin is offering a forceful indictment of literature and the harmful effects it can have on its readers.

Ernest is a handsome combination of Hemingway photographs and a biographical essay by P. Buckley[59]. The latter stresses the perdurable sense of sin developed in Hemingway by his family. M. Bruccoli's *Scott and Ernest*[60] is a scholarly, knowledgeable account of the relationship between Fitzgerald and Hemingway and its impact on their work. It demythologises it while in the process throwing considerable light on the motivations and characters of the two men. The absence of chapter headings and an index complicates the book's ready reference possibilities. A comparative study by B. Stoltzfus brings together *Gide and Hemingway*[61] as writers whose knowledge of the Christian tradition underlies their rebellion against God. This thesis is developed in connection with *The Notebooks of André Walter, Saul*, and *The Old Man and the Sea*. In ' "An Image to Dance Around": Brett and Her Lovers in *The Sun Also Rises*' (*CentR*) S. S. Baskett is seeking to reconcile the different critical readings of what is revealed by the distinctly different experiences of Jake Barnes, Pedro Romero, Robert Cohn, and Bill Gorton in Hemingway's *The Sun Also Rises*. To find the 'moral pattern' of the work, Baskett brings into literary and historical focus the 'counterpointed' experiences of the novel's principal characters. He finds that Lady Brett's lovers fix on her as an uncertain image of great value.

[59] *Ernest*, by P. Buckley. New York: Dial P. pp. 251. $17.50.
[60] *Scott and Ernest: The Fitzgerald Hemingway Friendship*, by M. Bruccoli. The Bodley Head. pp. 168. £6.95.
[61] *Gide and Hemingway: Rebels Against God*, by B. Stoltzfus. Port Washington, N.Y.: Kennikat. pp. ix + 97. $9.95.

N. Joost and A. Brown explore 'T. S. Eliot and Ernest Hemingway: A Literary Relationship' (*PLL*) in an endeavour to show that Eliot taught Hemingway a good deal even though the latter refused to acknowledge it and took a consistently hostile attitude to Eliot. Quotations as contextually illuminating, myths such as that of the Fisher King, the figure of the androgyne, the nature of sexual relationships, and the interest in traditional Christianity are all adduced as instances of Eliot's tutelary role. '*Across the River and Into the Trees* – Hemingway and Psychotherapy' (*IllQ*) by R. Whitlow sees the heroine functioning as a psychotherapist for Cantwell by aiding him to face imminent death although devoid of the usual Hemingway comfort of a mission-oriented existence.

R. Roulston's *James Norman Hall*[62] surveys the literary output of Nordhoff's collaborator in an unpretentious and uncondescending fashion. He finds shared values, notably of peace, brotherhood, and sanity, in Hall's childhood Iowa and adult Polynesia, which are conveyed through his capacity to write never less than entertainingly. *Mark Harris*[63], his fiction and autobiographical prose, are the subject of N. Lavers' study, which seeks to chart a progression from a series of disguises of the self to an absence of self in return for an achievement of pure form. Such an effort scarcely does justice to Harris's gifts of characterisation, humour, and pathos. S. S. Klemtner's ' "A Permanent Game of Excuses": Determinism in Heller's *Something Happened*' (*MFS*) explains the novel's ostensible pessimism as due to critics' misconceiving the credibility of the narrator and the existential nature of his determinism and so failing to recognise that the novel is actually a more subtle exploration of *Catch-22's* themes.

John G. Parks' 'Waiting For the End: Shirley Jackson's *The Sundial*' (*Crit*) examines Jackson's novel in terms of the use of the apocalyptic vision and the nature of belief. He finds Jackson's 'comic apocalyptic' novel one that is conerned with the nature of belief and 'with the way desperate people grasp a belief, make it their truth' and combine it with madness. In a thickly alien style, Krystyna Prendowski examines 'Jerzy Kosinski: A Literature of Contortions' (*JNT*). The argument is that his work bridges post-war European existentialism and American fiction of the 1950s. The achievement of *The Painted Bird* has not been sustained; violence, sadism, amorality, and voyeurism produce a fiction lacking in depth of character, reader identification, and moral significance.

In 'The Knight and the Pioneer: Europe and America in the Fiction of Sinclair Lewis' (*AL*), D. Wagenaar traces Lewis' Europe–America conflict (which he sees as the fictional mirror of Lewis' reality–fantasy psychology) through *Our Mr. Wren, Babbitt, Dodsworth*, and *World So Wide*, emerging with four main proposals: that as Europe's possibilities for realised fantasy faded Lewis substituted an idealised frontier America (the alienated Dodsworth in *World So Wide* advises Hayden Chart to go home); that his exposé of America's impoverishment was engendered by his indignation at the impossibility of that idealisation; that a realistic vision of America emerged as he filled the spaces left by the dream's evaporation with realistic detail; and that in *World So Wide* he approached the idea that a 'sense of self' was more important than country or culture, but was too old and tired to pursue the concept. J. Salzman's study of the social protest

[62] *James Norman Hall*, by R. Roulston. Boston, Mass.: G. K. Hall. pp. 167. $9.95.
[63] *Mark Harris*, by N. Lavers. Boston, Mass.: G. K. Hall. pp. 152. $8.95.

writer *Albert Malz*[64] is an energetic if occasionally strident effort to call attention to his subject's neglected merits and his place among major protest writers of the century. Malz's social and political roles are informatively treated, though there is little of personal biography *per se*. His plays, novels, and short stories are discussed as renderings of the failure of the American Dream and the realities of the Depression.

With 'Mailer's "O'Shaugnessy Chronicle": A Speculative Autopsy' (*Crit*) J. Rother is examining Mailer's plan to write a great series of American novels as all-compassing as Melville's *Moby-Dick*. Rother traces Mailer's struggle with the actual production of the work, the changes in the image of O'Shaugnessy as Mailer moved through differing approaches in working on 'The Man Who Studied Yoga' (the prologue) and *Deer Park*. Rother concludes that Mailer decided for many reasons to give up this chronicle because of changes in society and difficulties in his own life, and sees considerable changes in O'Shaugnessy in *Advertisements for Myself*. It was, however, the publication of Durrell's *The Alexandria Quartet* that forced Mailer completely to rethink his plans and ushered in Mailer's development of a means to put himself into his fiction. Robert Merrill in 'After Armies: Norman Mailer's Recent Nonfiction' (*CentR*) says that Mailer's most recent literary phase 'calls for discreet silence, not critical evaluation'; however, Mailer is too important and interesting to ignore so Merrill takes a look at this 'phase'. He makes three points: (1) *Miami and the Siege of Chicago* and *Of A Fire on The Moon* ultimately fail; (2) *Prisoner of Sex* and Marilyn are better than have been thought; and, (3) Mailer's most distinguished work in this period has been done in literary criticism.

S. Cohen's *Norman Mailer's Novels*[65] advances the thesis – by chronological consideration of the fiction – that its subject can best be seen as a contribution to the genre of the novel of ideas, and particularly as an exploration of the idea of power, whether political, social, intellectual, or psychological. An excess of plot summary, a careless style, and an overly exclusive concentration on theme to the exclusion of stylistic matters make this of limited use. Another study on the same subject by P. H. Bufithis is a more rewarding treatment of *Norman Mailer*[66]. Though no longer, it manages to sketch the main features of the biography, the major development and shifts from *The Naked and the Dead* through to *Genius and Dust*, and some of the central stylistic resources Mailer has exploited throughout his career. Bufithis also finds the controlling theme throughout to be power but power subjoined to will with which it is in conflict. Continuity of theme is offset by a progression in attitude or outlook from mimetic to expressive as first reality and then consciousness become the active agent in the process of existential definition. Another full-length study, which was not available for review, perhaps may be provisionally assessed from its title, *Norman Mailer: The Radical as Hipster*[67]. It is by R Ehrlich.

J. Martin has provided a large biography of Henry Miller[68] that assembles

[64] *Albert Malz*, by J. Salzman. Boston, Mass.: G. K. Hall. pp. 160. $9.95.

[65] *Norman Mailer's Novels*, by S. Cohen. Amsterdam: Rodopi. 1979. pb $13.75.

[66] *Norman Mailer*, by P. H. Bufithis. New York: Ungar. pp. ix + 143. pb $2.95.

[67] *Norman Mailer: The Radical as Hipster*, by R. Ehrlich. Metuchen, N.J.: Scarecrow. $10.

[68] *Always Merry and Bright: The Life of Henry Miller*, by J. Martin. Santa Barbara, Calif.: Capra P. pp. xi + 494. $15.

all the available external evidence into a coherent account of Miller's movements and experiences which at the same time sheds considerable light on the works. Martin is particularly concerned to show how the latter are autobiographical fictions or at least deflections of factual reality. With this in mind, he makes of his study what he aptly calls 'a symbolic rehearsal of the facts of Miller's life'.

Two books with some similarity appear on H. L. Mencken, one by C. A. Fecher and the other by G. H. Douglas[69]. Both are primarily concerned with Mencken's ideas, but they take different approaches. Douglas approaches the subject thematically by attending to Mencken's critique of democratic society, its practice of politics, the peculiarly American manifestations of the psychopathology of everyday life, and his scepticism concerning America's capacity to produce a unified high culture permeating the whole of society. Fecher, on the other hand, attends more to biographical dimensions while also considering his various roles as philosopher, political theorist, critic, and philologian. Roger Dickinson-Brown discusses 'The Art and Importance of N. Scott Momaday' (*SoR*) and acknowledges Momaday's talent but does not feel that the novel for which Momaday (a Kiowa Indian) won the Pulitzer Prize is a successful novel. He calls it 'a memorable failure' and much prefers Momaday's other works such as *Angle of Geese* and *The Way to Rainy Mountain* because they are real poems.

In a long-overdue study G. B. Crump examines *The Novels of Wright Morris*[70] which he finds largely organised around two worlds, one real the other ideal, and which shape his treatment of the hero, time, consciousness, escape, and transcendance. Particular attention is paid to the influences of Bergson, Lawrence, and James.

A. Ensor analyses place names as part of 'The Geography of Mary Noailles Murfree's *In the Tennessee Mountains*' (*MissQ*) and shows that her familiarity with the reaches of the Cumberland Mountain area was quite limited. Lawrence I. Berkove explores 'American "*Midrashim*": Hugh Nissenson's Stories' (*Crit*). He uses Nissenson as an example of the movement, among Jewish authors, toward a renewed commitment to Judaism. He agrees with Ozick that Nissenson's stories are 'midrashim, revelatory commentaries in fiction of religious texts'. The unifying concern in *A Pile of Stones* and *In the Reign of Peace* as well as in Nissenson's other five stories, is the problem of belief. S. Pinsker, turns to 'Joyce Carol Oates's Wonderland: Hungering for Personality' (*Crit*). He analyses Oates's use of hunger and a search for personality, a sort of hunger of the mind, and a hunger of the body, for a stable unified personality. Pinsker is tracing the use of physiology as a vehicle for, or a parallel to, the search for self in Oates's novel. Sister M. K. Grant studies *The Tragic Vision of Joyce Carol Oates*[71], which for her does not appear in all the works, but when it does, it assumes a secular, noncathartic form founded on luck rather than God and dedicated to recognising the existentially paradoxical nature of life and to achieving its transcendence. Her thesis is pursued

[69] *Mencken: A Study of His Thought*, by C. A. Fecher. New York: Knopf. pp. xvi + 391. $15; *H. L. Mencken: Critic of American Life*, by G. H. Douglas. Hamden, Conn.: The Shoe String P. pp. 248. $15.

[70] *The Novels of Wright Morris*, by G. B. Crump. Lincoln, Neb.: U. of Nebraska P. pp. 258. $12.95.

[71] *The Tragic Vision of Joyce Carol Oates*, by M. Grant. Durham, N.C.: Duke U.P. pp. xii + 167. $9.75.

through a detailed consideration of the themes of woman, city, and community and their dependence on a rhetoric and action of violence.

Marion Montgomery faces 'Flannery O'Connor and the Jansenist Problem in Fiction' (*SoR*). He is exploring the difficulty encountered by artists in acknowledging a relationship between the world of art and the world of reality. The artistic representation of free will and grace in O'Connor's works are seen as a 'stylizing' of reality called art. He feels that the charge of being Jansenist which is levelled at O'Connor is really a mistaking of O'Connor's acceptance of the necessity for a dramatic movement to carry the work forward and set the condition for self-determination. 'Flannery O'Connor's Mothers and Daughters' (*TCL*) are the subject of L. Westling's essay which seeks to show that the 'sour deformed daughters and self-righteous mothers' represent a passionate but inadvertent protest against the lot of womankind.

Walker Percy: An American Search is an examination by R. Coles[72] of its subject's philosophical roots in European existentialism, their role in his philosophical, psychological, and theological essays, and, finally, their contribution to the novels. Since Coles knows the novelist personally, the approach is not quite so austere as the foregoing suggests, but is rather a skilful and easy blend of the analytic and the informal.

Two books on Thomas Pynchon have appeared. The one by W. M. Plater, *The Grim Phoenix*, is concerned with the continuities of the fiction from the early stories through to *Gravity's Rainbow*, while the other, M. R. Siegel's *Pynchon: Creative Paranoia in 'Gravity's Rainbow'* has obviously a more limited focus[73]. Plater concentrates on the persistence of duality in the forms of order and disorder, life and death, illusion and reality, and their inter-relationships as they are elaborated in a technological civilisation's increase of entropy, accident, and chance. Particular situations or episodes from the works are examined from several perspectives in order to suggest that each linguistic formulation is necessary as well as arbitrary and so connected as a result of which paranoia becomes the operative condition of reader, author, and text alike. Attention is also given to the shaping role played in the fiction by Henry Adams, Wittgenstein, Clerk-Maxwell and Heisenberg, mystery stories, and films and film techniques. Siegel, on the other hand, though also placing a premium on the notion of paranoia for Pynchon follows a less exclusively thematic or topical approach in that he examines *Gravity's Rainbow* from the standpoint of narrative point of view and structure, characterisation, and macroscopic cultural metaphors. Both works are helpful in dealing with a most complex author, though far from definitive. Plater is the more ambitious but also the more pretentious; Siegel more modest and traditional but perhaps sounder and more trustworthy for this stage of Pynchon studies.

There are several pamphlet-monographs in a series devoted to 'popular' contemporary writers who deal largely in science fiction, fantasy, and terror

[72] *Walker Percy: An American Search*, by R. Coles. Boston, Mass.: Little, Brown. pp. xx + 250. $15.

[73] *The Grim Phoenix: Reconstructing Thomas Pynchon*, by W. Plater. Bloomington, Ind.: Indiana U.P. pp. xiii + 268. $12.50; *Pynchon: Creative Paranoia in 'Gravity's Rainbow'*, by M. Siegel. Port Washington, N.Y.: Kennikat. pp. vii + 136. $11.

tales. They include *The Dream Quest of H. P. Lovecraft* (D. Schweitzer), *The High Crusade of Poul Anderson* (S. Miesel), *The Clockwork Universe of Anthony Burgess* (R. Matthews), and *Conan's World and Robert E. Howard* (D. Schweitzer)[74]. Within their limits they are informed, sophisticated introductions to one aspect of popular culture.

Robert F. Moss takes up 'Suffering, Sinful Catholics' (*AR*). He examines Mario Puzo's *The Godfather*, William Peter Blatty's *The Exorcist*, and George V. Higgins's *The Friends of Eddie Coyle*, all Catholic best-sellers, and concludes that whatever is truly engaging of a 'mature intelligence' in these works comes from their authors' Catholic back-grounds, and that *these* works have some value, whereas their secular companions on the best-seller list have comparatively none. Elements which contribute to literary value are problems of evil, faith, a fallen world, and so on.

S. R. Horton's 'Desire and Depression in Women's Fiction: The Problematics and the Economics of Desire' (*MFS*) polemically argues that the fiction of Glasgow, Wharton, Chopin, and Cather is a more honest and speculatively engaging examination of the price of passion and instinct and the tactics women deploy to avoid paying the price than is to be found in the contemporary instance of Shulman, Jong, and Lessing. Of a related order is J. A. Mintz's 'The Myth of the Jewish Mother in Three Jewish, American Female Writers' (*CentR*). Mintz is concerned with calling our attention to the misuse of the Jewish mother myth as seen in the works of such writers as Roth. She therefore explores how this myth of an over protective, over-concerned and yet symbolic of pure love mother grew and developed into a demeaning 'predictable, impoverished caricature' of the Jewish mother. As examples of authors who are aware of the truth behind the myth and render a more realistic image, Mintz gives us Eva in Tillie Olsen's 'Tell Me A Riddle', Sara in Anzia Yezierska's *Bread Giver*, and Anya in Susan Fromberg Schaeffer's *Anya*. These portrayals show real women struggling for survival. They are women who have 'perceived the discrepancy between the ideal of Mother as love and. . .actual circumstances', but are none the less 'locked into living a lie'.

Max Westbrook considers 'The Authentic Western' (*WAL*). Westbrook resolves authenticity into 'facsimile' and 'denotative'. Denotative authenticity characterises the best of the westerns, going beyond a fidelity to historical fact to the communication of a vision, specifically the 'westering' vision, defined as nature out of human control. This is the vision which allows the western novel universality. C. L. Sonnichsen recoils from 'Sex on the Lone Prairee' (*WAL*). He examines the explicit sex in books like Larry McMurtry's, indicts it, and predicts it will change. John D. Nesbitt explores 'Change of Purpose in the Novels of Louis L'Amour' (*WAL*). L'Amour's novels have changed over the years in terms of their 'moral and historical purpose'. The early phase deals with the individual on the 'borderline of civilization'; the middle phase includes heroes who have a 'continental finish' and an accompanying broader historical context; the

[74] *The Dream Quest of H. P. Lovecraft*, by D. Schweitzer. San Bernardino, Calif.: Borgo P. pp. 63. pb $2.45; *Against Time's Arrow: The High Crusade of Poul Anderson*, by S. Meisel. San Bernardino, Calif.: Borgo P. pp. 64. pb $2.45; *The Clockwork Universe of Anthony Burgees*, by R. Matthews. San Bernardino, Calif.: Borgo P. pp. 65. pb $2.45; *Conan's World and Robert E. Howard*, by D. Schweitzer. San Bernardino, Calif.: Borgo P. pp. 63. pb $2.45.

later phase reveals a diminished autonomy of character, as L'Amour tells the story of the west through a more intricate and structured mechanism, trying for more historical authenticity. P. T. Bryant endeavours to rescue *H. L. Davis*[75] from obscurity and to make a case for him as a novelist to rank with Twain, Steinbeck, and Faulkner. His great achievement, Bryant feels, is to reclaim the American West and the frontier from popular stereotypes and to make it viable for serious imaginative artists through such works as *Winds of the Morning*. G. Topping provides for 'Zane Grey: A Literary Reassessment' (*WAL*). Grey is compared to romantics like Robert Louis Stevenson. Topping alleges that Grey has a moral complexity which elevates his work beyond the stereotypical western. 'Jack Schaefer: The Writer as Ecologist' (*WAL*) is examined by F. Erisman who traces Schaefer's eventual shift to ecological writing in his early fiction. In a related vein, S. K. Winther sketches 'The Emigrant Theme' (*ArQ*). The search for an ideal world, of which the traditional archetype is the Mosaic exodus, is newly incarnated in the emigrant theme of American fiction. Three novelists of Scandinavian origin – Moberg, Rolvaag, and Winther himself – are representative exponents of the theme during the great period of American migration from 1850 to 1925.

A. F. Kinney's *Dorothy Parker*[76] judiciously and fully assesses her achievement in poetry, fiction, and criticism against the backdrop of her most unhappy life. Of a quite different vein is Robert L. Nadeau's 'Physics and Cosmology in the Fiction of Tom Robbins' (*Crit*). Nadeau's essay takes a careful look at Robbin's *Another Roadside Attraction* and *Even Cowgirls Get the Blues* and points out what he thinks lies beneath the comically playful revival of the 1960s. These novels, he contends, reveal 'a very serious effort to evaluate the impact of ideas from contemporary physics upon the moral and intellectual foundations of western values'. B. F. Rodgers Jr examines the fiction of *Philip Roth*[77] chronologically pointing up Roth's pre-eminent concern with the interpenetration of reality and fantasy and his use of various models (James, Kafka, Chekhov, regional humour) in order to register the trends and tensions of contemporary American life. In '"Kinds of Love": Love and Friendship in Novels of May Sarton' (*Crit*), J. S. Bakerman is exploring two 'crucially powerful' patterns in the novels of Sarton. These patterns involve the two central and important themes in Sarton's work: the need of each individual to 'create' himself and reach an understanding that will both liberate and discipline him and also come to understand others: to unite with others, yet remain somewhat aloof. Sarton writes in a cool controlled manner that has left some critics feeling that some energy or force is lacking. Bakerman is concerned with the *central* theme, the difficulty of achieving personal harmony through human relationships. Novels examined include: *As We Are Now, The Birth of a Grandfather, The Small Room, Mrs. Stevens Hears the Mermaids Singing*, and *Kinds of Love*. R. Stinson deals with the career and writings of *Lincoln Steffens*[78] in a brief study that organises

[75] *H. L. Davis*, by P. T. Bryant. Boston, Mass.: G. K. Hall. pp. 173. $9.95.
[76] *Dorothy Parker*, by A. F. Kinney. Boston, Mass.: G. K. Hall. pp. 204. $8.95.
[77] *Philip Roth*, by B. F. Rodgers. Boston, Mass.: G. K. Hall. pp. 192. $8.95.
[78] *Lincoln Steffens*, by R. Stinson. New York: Ungar. pp. vii + 168. $9.95.

itself around its subject's several personae: student and teacher, reporter, muckraker, mediator, and autobiographer.

The entire Spring issue (*TCL*) is devoted to Gertrude Stein. It consists of seven essays and a very brief reprinted item by Thornton Wilder. Among the works dealt with are *The Making of Americans, Tender Buttons, Ida*, 'Composition as Explanation', and her three autobiographical volumes. *Exact Resemblance to Exact Resemblance* by W. Steiner[79] is an examination of Gertrude Stein's literary portraits which sees the genre as possessing an inherent contradiction that is endemic to Stein's whole canon and responsible for her devotion to revision and experiment. The study focuses on the development of Stein's theory and its relation to stream of consciousness, automatic writing, simultaneity, and synesthesia; it then deals with the kinds of portraits: typologising, visually-oriented, and self-contained movement; and finally considers the connections between her techniques and those of cubism as well as her gradual movement toward complete self-reflexiveness. Steiner leans heavily on structural and semiotic views and this lends a certain predictability to her treatment of representation and modernism. Nevertheless, this is a serious and firmly argued work that pushes issues vigorously and makes an undeniable contribution to understanding Stein's work and historical significance.

W. J. Scheik's Discarded Watermelon Rinds: The Rainbow Aesthetic of Styron's *Lie Down in Darkness*' (*MFS*) suggests that it is the author's notion of art that determines several motifs, accounts for certain stylistic features, and even becomes a prominent thematic concern. Styron's idea of beauty, he says, involves perceiving a loveliness intrinsic to human suffering. T. D. Adam's 'Obscuring the Muse: The Mock-Autobiographies of Ronald Sukenick' (*Crit*) is a dense effort to analyse Sukenick's mock-autobiographies as a type of experimental modern literature in which the author uses the pretence of writing about himself 'as a scaffolding for self-creation'. B. A. Schopen examines 'Faith, Morality, and the Novels of Updike' (*TCL*) to find that Updike's conservative Christianity has no room for ethics or morality so that his fictional world renders the latter as ambiguous, relative, and incapable of resolution. When this sharp distinction between faith and morality is not observed, as in *The Poorhouse Fair* and *The Centaur*, the works fail. George W. Hunt S.J. in 'Updike's Omega-Shaped Shelter: Structure and Psyche in *A Month of Sundays*' (*Crit*) calls for a more scholarly scrutiny of Updike's work. Hunt chooses to examine *A Month of Sundays* because it 'capsulizes humorously so much thematic material found in Updike's previous fiction (the what of his vision, so to speak) and more significantly, because its fictive and psychological structure (its how) is somewhat unique in Updike's work'.

R. P. Warren's celebrated novel is the subject of M. R. Winchell's 'O Happy Sin! *Felix Culpa* in *All the King's Men*' (*MissQ*). Taking his cue for American literature from R. W. B. Lewis, he sees Warren working in the tradition of the Party of Irony and the fortunate fall. The purpose of the exercise is to restate the consensus interpretation of the novel 'in a rich and allusive vocabulary'. L. S. Mansfield explores 'History and the Historical

[79] *Exact Resemblance to Exact Resemblance*, by W. Steiner. New Haven, Conn.: Yale U.P. pp. ix + 255. $15.

Process in *All the Kings Men*' (*ContR*). Warren created fictional characters who aided in the exploration of the ramifications of political despotism and his central character incorporated many devices also used by other authors inspired by the life of Huey Long. Warren in fact went further than others (Lewis's *It Can't Happen Here*, Basso's *Sun In Capricorn*, Dos Passos' *Number One*, Langley's *A Lion Is In the Streets*) and embodied in Willie Stark a sense of the indivisibility of past, present, and future, and had Willie use history. He also dramatised the multiple selves of a single personality and depicted the dynamic interaction of these selves to develop character by historical process. This is what made Warren's book a better one, this sense of historical process. Don Kunz's 'Lost in the Distance of Winter: James Welch's *Winter In the Blood*' (*Crit*) examines Welch's use of winter as a timeless and emotionally chilling distancing force, a lost time, for his protagonist in his novel.

A Still Moment is a collection of nine critical essays on various themes and texts from the work of Eudora Welty edited by J. F. Desmond[80]. The result is a series of interesting probes possessing more unity than most such collections and capable of proving a stimulus to more sustained examinations of Welty's canon. Lucinda H. MacKethan tries 'To See Things in Their Time: The Act of Focus in Eudora Welty's Fiction' (*AL*). MacKethan proposes that in Welty's fiction *place*, which holds *time* in check, can yield insight if experienced by a capable perceiver. This insight, though it partakes of memory, must revitalise rather than preserve the past. MacKethan identifies four kinds of perceivers: objects, insiders, outsiders, and seers. Of these the seer is the most focusing, most capable of interior growth, and develops through the fiction with increasing complexity, until we see through his/her eyes. Ultimately, seers 'put place into the context of time. . .past in juxtaposition with the future'. With 'Enlightening Darkness: Theme and Structure in Eudora Welty's *Losing Battles*' (*JNT*) L. J. Reynolds argues that the true strengths of *Losing Battles* 'lie beneath its entertaining surface where the story of an intense struggle for survival is subtly and carefully told'. The key to understanding the novel lies in Julia's death statement about the struggle of the teacher to teach and the pupil to resist learning, for the Renfros and Beechams are a desperate people fighting to survive not only a dry and eroded land but also the truth about themselves. In 'Vinnie Williams' Initiation Theme' (*Crit*) L. York claims that Vinnie Williams has given fresh life to the theme of initiation from adolescence to maturity. Her four novels: *The Fruit Tramp, Walk Egypt, I Resign You, Stallion* and *Greenbones* all are concerned with this theme. York examines this struggle toward maturity in Williams' novels and finds that Williams achieves a new dimension by having her protagonists grow up in the real world, the adult world, rather than the world of the fellow young. *Alexander Woollcott* is the subject of W. Chatteron's[81] competent Twayne study which surveys his career as a raconteur and man of letters.

[80] *A Still Moment: Essays on the Art of Eudora Welty*, ed. by J. Desmond. Metuchen, N.J.: Scarecrow P. pp. vii + 141. $7.

[81] *Alexander Woolcott*, by W. Chatterton. Boston, Mass.: G. K. Hall. pp. 191. $ 8.95.

4. Drama

L. P. Gabbard invokes Bettelheim, Henderson, and Campbell to find in 'Albee's "Seascape": An Adult Fairy Tale' (*MD*) in which symbols 'concretize the evolution of mankind from watery animals, the emergence of the embryo from its watery womb, and the return to consciousness of the repressed self'. More historical concerns are exhibited by C. L. Sutherland in her 'American Women Playwrights as Mediators of the "Woman Problem" ' (*MD*). She focuses on Zona Gale, Zoe Akins, and Susan Glaspell as creators of female characters with a sense of uneasiness over patriarchal attitudes. Their failures at resolving the sensed problems are not instances of artistic incapacity so much as the theatrical encoding of a 'genderlect'.

T. P. Adler surveys the dramatic, film, and functional writing of *Robert Anderson*[82] by grouping the former according to whether they are 'learning', maturation, marriage, or short sketches plays. Adler is sympathetic but judicious, rarely claiming more for his subject than it can sustain. He argues persuasively not only that the loss of innocence, disillusionment, and loneliness are central themes but that the male–female marriage relationship sustains them and provides the basis for their modification over the course of the career. Here *The Footsteps of the Doves*, *Double Solitaire*, and the novel *After* mark an important shift in Anderson's treatment of women.

W. R. Klink's study of the plays of *S. N. Behrman*[83] is an earnest but pedestrian effort that doggedly takes up each of the plays from *The Second Man* to *But For Whom Charlie* and submits them to schematic but simplistic analyses. He concludes that Behrman has a limited range but that he provides 'good entertainment' in which his greatest strength is his characters. H. Cantor approaches *Clifford Odets*[84] from an avowedly formalist point of view in an effort to counterbalance the chronological and historical approaches of his predecessors. Thus the bulk of his study concentrates on matters of theme, structure, and symbol. As dominant themes, he finds them to be: the middle-class family as a social trap and source of affection, the abandonment of moral principle for material rewards, the exploration of love's impact on human relationships. He also emphasises Odets' deployment of symbolic and imagistic clusters such as those of apocalyptic disaster, sleep and death, vegetative and sexual fertility, transcendence, and animality. Whether this study will restore Odets' reputation or not, it deserves credit for trying to look seriously at the strengths as well as the weaknesses of his work.

Eugene O'Neill, edited by V. Floyd[85], offers an international perspective by assembling essays by European and American scholars as well as by performers which deal with various aspects of the career and canon. P. Voelker inquires into 'Eugene O'Neill's Aesthetic of the Drama' (*MD*) and concludes that most of his remarks were informal rather than formal

[82] *Robert Anderson*, by T. P. Adler. Boston, Mass.: G. K. Hall. pp. 166. $8.95.

[83] *S. N. Behrman: The Major Plays*, by W. R. Klink. Atlantic Highlands, N.J.: Humanities P. pp. 272. pb $21.75.

[84] *Clifford Odets: Playwright-Poet*, by H. Cantor. Metuchen, N.J.: Scarecrow P. pp. 212. $10.

[85] *Eugene O'Neill: A World View*, ed. by V. Floyd. New York: Ungar. 1979. pp. 296. $12.95.

and focused on four topics: realism and expressionism, tragedy, affective aspects, and production notes and techniques.

James G. Watson examines 'The Theatre in *The Iceman Cometh*: Some Modernist Implications' (*ArQ*). A part of the modernist tradition of enclosed and autonomous literary structures, *Iceman* is essentially a play about a play. Each of the characters, in nurturing his own pipe dream, is a liar and, therefore, an actor or artist whose preservation of an illusion is also the creation of a 'rival world' of art. Hickey's final madness, Parritt's suicide, and Larry Slade's cynicism represent lesser alternatives to the ordered illusions of the other actor–artists of Harry Hope's theatre. Although aware of the inadequacy of life conducted wholly within the dream of art, O'Neill seems to offer Harry Hope's illusory brand of hope as a form of art and, therefore, as a sustaining faith. Dennis M. Welch considers 'Hickey As Satanic Force in *The Iceman Cometh*' (*ArQ*). Acknowledging earlier readings which recognise O'Neill's Hickey as a 'parody of Christ', Welch argues further that the character is an Antichrist whose panacea of honesty sends the derelicts of Harry Hope's bar hurtling headlong into damnation. By removing their consolatory 'pipe dreams', Hickey removes all hope of life and salvation, thereby serving as the play's false prophet. Textual analysis reveals his association with the Miltonic prince of darkness, and suggests that Hickey's means of converting the barflies, like Satan's method of seducing Adam and Eve, is ultimately one of self-deception projected outward to engulf the innocent characters. The relationship between illusion and reality in six plays by O'Neill is the subject of a book by Günter Ahrends[86]. All the plays are late – *The Iceman Cometh, Hughie, A Moon for the Misbegotten, Long Day's Journey into Night, A Touch of the Poet*, and *More Stately Mansions* -- and they share a disappointed rejection of reality leading to an escape into a variety of dream worlds equally informed by the author's deep pessimism.

E. M. McGovern's *Neil Simon*[87] is another play-by-play examination of a canon. This one's method is so rudimentary that it scarcely deserves the name; plot sketches accompanied by obvious comments make this a useful volume for those who have not read Simon and do not wish to.

Claus Clüver writes on the relationship between Thornton Wilder and André Obey (1897–1975) who adapted Shakespeare's *Rape of Lucrece* as *Le Viol de Lucrèce*, staged in 1931[88]. Wilder was commissioned to translate the successful adaptation and his *Our Town* of 1938 contains striking parallels in scene technique. In turn, Obey read *Our Town* and his next two plays, *Revenue de L'êtoile* and *Maria* reveal several remarkable similarities to Wilder's work. Clüver's book is an illuminating study in parallels and influence, and other areas of concern to the comparatist – thematology, influence, adaptation, translation, and reception. There is a good bibliography on Obey. Finally, *A Portrait of the Artist* is F. Hirsch's[89] rather

[86] *Traumwelt und Wirklichkeit im Spatwek O'Neills*, by G. Ahrends. Heidelberg: Winter (Auglistische Forschungen 123) pp. 286. DM 48.

[87] *Neil Simon: A Critical Study*, by E. M. McGovern. New York: Ungar, 1979. pp. 192. $12.50.

[88] *Thornton Wilder und Andre Obey*, by C. Clüver. Bonn: Bouvier. pp. xii + 374. DM 68.

[89] *A Portrait of the Artist: The Plays of Tennessee Williams*, by F. Hirsch. Port Washington, N.Y.: Kennikat. 1979. pp. 121. $10.

journalistic examination of the plays of Tennessee Williams in terms of his homosexuality, his involvement in the Southern Renaissance, his neurotic struggles with opposing sexual attitudes, and his obsession with the artist's relation to art.

Index I. Critics

Index II. Authors and Subjects Treated